1001
RECIPES

FOR EVERY OCCASION

Good Housekeeping

1001
RECIPES
FOR EVERY OCCASION

Compiled by Barbara Dixon

COLLINS & BROWN

First published in Great Britain in 2005 by
Collins & Brown
The Chrysalis Building
Bramley Road
London W10 6SP

An imprint of **Chrysalis** Books Group plc

Published in association with The National Magazine Company Limited.
Good Housekeeping is a registered trademark of
The National Magazine Company Limited.

1 3 5 7 9 8 6 4 2

British Library Cataloguing-in-Publication Data:
A catalogue record for this book is available from the British Library.

ISBN 1-84340-263-7

Designer: Lotte Oldfield
Layout: Ben Cracknell Studios
Project editors: Nicola Hodgson and Barbara Dixon
Indexer: Michèle Clarke

Reproduction by Anorax Imaging Ltd, UK.
Printed and bound by CT Printing Ltd, China

Picture credits: Marie Louise Avery pages 21, 55, 375, 440, 456, 590, 640; Steve Baxter pages 18 and 32, 61, 137,194, 198, 202 and 233, 252, 272, 290, 331, 534; Martin Brigdale pages 282, 664, 669; Jean Cazals pages 246, 345, 367, 382, 714 ; Laurie Evans pages 81, 106, 155, 426, 532, 624, 637; Ken Field pages 678 and 709; Christine Hanscombe pages 46, 449, 515, 747; Will Heap page 130; Sian Irvine page 85; Daniel Jones pages 248 and 262; John Lawrence Jones pages 165, 242, 328, 335, 342, 351, 358; William Lingwood page 628; Jonathan Lovekin pages 6, 8, 29, 73, 76, 88, 118, 126 and 181, 141, 156, 166, 186, 210, 217, 230, 276, 303, 386, 397, 400, 404, 416, 490, 493 and 495, 498, 499 and 503, 671, 684, 732; David Munns pages 50 and 58, 520, 728, 756; James Murphy pages 125, 287, 310, 463; Mike O'Toole page 390 ; Lis Parsons pages 98 and 114, 215, 370 and 408; Michael Paul pages 62, 102, 269, 395, 414, 418, 468, 471 and 473, 476, 506, 556, 650 and 672; Roger Stowell pages 566, 764, 768; Clive Streeter 94, 135, 528, 598, 725; Lucinda Symons pages 147, 205, 255, 314, 583, 613, 645, 680, 681, 683, 691, 696, 699, 702, 712; Martin Thompson pages 92, 151, 218, 313, 464, 496 and 511, 514, 516 and 553, 538, 560, 606 and 642, 618, 623, 659, 663, 740 ; Tim Winter pages 543 and 575; Phillip Webb page 721; Harry Cory Wright page 751; Elizabeth Zeschin pages 24, 40, 110, 122, 171, 174, 193, 236, 298, 323, 429, 444, 483, 486, 610, 716
Jacket: Peter Cassidy (front), Marie Louise Avery, Elizabeth Zeschin, Clive Streeter, Roger Stowell (back left to right), Laurie Evans (spine)

Contents

Introduction

A recipe book for every occasion – that's the phrase we coined in the
Good Housekeeping offices when we started working on this book. Because,
quite simply, it is just that. Food and the way we cook have changed dramatically
over the past couple of decades. Catching up with friends, once the preserve of
the weekend, can be done over a casual bowl of pasta midweek. A Saturday
night dinner is still special, of course, but more often than not we call it supper.
And where once the host would make everything herself, now a couple of
timesaving ingredients make it easier to create a feast.

This book has everything you need, from quick snacks and simple salads to
basic midweek suppers and easy bakes. Via your queries through the email,
hotline and letters, we know time is precious for many of you, so we've included
lots of recipes that you can whiz up easily. All of them have been triple-tested in
the Good Housekeeping Institute, too, which means they'll work every time you
make them. Plus there's nutritional information for calories, fat and
carbohydrates for each dish and a whole section dedicated to vegetarian
recipes.

Whichever recipe you decide to cook first out of the 1001 recipes, we hope it'll
spur you on to cooking more!

Enjoy,

Emma

Emma Marsden
Good Housekeeping Cookery Editor

Basics

We're all busy, busy, but finding time to make a good stock will really pay off when you use it as the base for your soups and casseroles. You'll know exactly what's gone into it – no additives – and once it's on the heat the stock can be left to simmer away while you get on with life's other pleasures. The four main stocks are light, dark, fish and vegetarian. Once they're made, freeze them in small quantities so you'll always have some available.

Making your own pastry, too, is very satisfying and fun, and some can be made in the food processor, if you don't like getting your hands dirty! Choux must be one of the easiest pastries to make – and just think of all the profiteroles you can produce. Shortcrust is a versatile pastry that can be made plain or with additional ingredients – check out the variations under the recipe, while Sweet Tart Pastry is a richer, sweet version of shortcrust.

There's nothing nicer than homemade – be it a simple chicken soup, a great apple pie, or a crisp salad dressed with your own salad dressing. Try out these recipes and taste the difference.

Fish Stock

900g (2lb) fish bones and trimmings,
   washed and dried
2 carrots, peeled and chopped
1 onion, peeled and chopped
2 celery sticks, sliced

bouquet garni (2 bay leaves, few thyme
   sprigs, small bunch of parsley)
6 white peppercorns
½tsp sea salt

1   Put the fish trimmings into a large pan. Add the vegetables, 900ml (1½ pints) cold water, the bouquet
    garni, peppercorns and salt. Bring slowly to the boil and skim the surface. Cover the pan, reduce the
    heat and simmer for about 30 minutes.
2   Strain the stock through a fine sieve into a bowl and check the seasoning. Cool quickly, cover and
    keep in the fridge for up to two days. Use the stock as required.

Makes 900ml (1½ pints)   preparation: 10 minutes   cooking time: 35 minutes
per 100ml (3½fl oz): 5 cals; trace fat; 1g carbohydrate

Turkey Stock

turkey giblets
1 carrot, peeled and thickly sliced
1 onion, peeled and cut into wedges

1 celery stick, thickly sliced
8 black peppercorns
2 bay leaves

1   Put all the ingredients in a pan with 900ml (1½ pints) cold water. Cover and bring slowly to the boil,
    then reduce the heat and simmer for 2 hours, occasionally skimming any scum from the surface.
2   Strain the stock through a fine sieve into a bowl. Discard the giblets, vegetables and herbs. Cover the
    stock and chill for up to one day. Use the stock as required.

Makes 900ml (1½ pints)   preparation: 5 minutes   cooking time: about 2 hours
per 100ml (3½fl oz): 10 cals; trace fat; 2g carbohydrate

Chicken Stock

225g (8oz) onions, peeled and roughly
  chopped
150g (5oz) trimmed leeks, roughly chopped
225g (8oz) celery sticks, roughly chopped
1.6kg (3½lb) raw chicken bones

bouquet garni (2 bay leaves, few thyme
  sprigs, small bunch of parsley)
1tsp black peppercorns
½tsp sea salt

1 Put all the ingredients in a large pan with 3 litres (5 pints) cold water. Cover the pan, bring slowly to the boil and skim the surface. Partially cover the pan, reduce the heat and simmer gently for 2 hours. Check the seasoning.

2 Strain the stock through a fine sieve into a bowl and cool quickly. Cover and keep in the fridge for up to three days. Remove the fat from the surface and use the stock as required.

Makes 1.2 litres (2 pints)   preparation: 10 minutes   cooking time: about 2 hours
per 100ml (3½fl oz) 10 cals; 1g fat; 1g carbohydrate

Meat Stock

450g (1lb) stewing meat, cut into pieces
  (according to the flavour required, use
  veal, beef, lamb or pork bones)
450g (1lb) meat bones
1 large onion, peeled and sliced
1 large carrot, peeled and sliced

2 celery sticks, sliced
bouquet garni (2 bay leaves, few thyme
  sprigs, small bunch of parsley)
1tsp black peppercorns
½tsp sea salt

1 To impart flavour and colour, first brown the meat and bones. Put them into a roasting tin and roast at 220°C (200°C fan oven) mark 7 for 30–40 minutes until well browned, turning occasionally.

2 Transfer the meat and bones to a large pan, add the remaining ingredients 2 litres (3½ pints) cold water. Cover the pan, bring slowly to the boil and skim the surface. Partially cover the pan, reduce the heat and simmer gently for 4–5 hours. Check the seasoning.

3 Strain the stock through a fine sieve into a bowl and cool quickly. Cover and keep in the fridge for up to three days. Remove the fat layer from the surface and use the stock as required.

Makes 900ml (1½ pints)   preparation: 10 minutes   cooking time: 4–5 hours
per 100ml (3½fl oz): 10 cals; 1g fat; 1g carbohydrate

Vegetable Stock

225g (8oz) onions, peeled and roughly
    chopped
225g (8oz) celery sticks, roughly chopped
225g (8oz) trimmed leeks, roughly chopped
225g (8oz) carrots, peeled and roughly
    chopped

2 bay leaves
few thyme sprigs
small bunch of parsley
10 black peppercorns
½tsp sea salt

1 Put all the ingredients into a large pan with 1.7 litres (3 pints) cold water. Cover the pan, bring slowly to the boil and skim the surface. Partially cover the pan, reduce the heat and simmer for 30 minutes. Check the seasoning.

2 Strain the stock through a fine sieve into a bowl and leave to cool. Cover and keep in the fridge for up to three days. Use the stock as required.

Makes 1.2 litres (2 pints)   preparation: 10 minutes   cooking time: 35 minutes
per 100ml (3½fl oz): 5 cals; trace fat; 1g carbohydrate

Basic Gravy

A rich gravy is traditionally served with roast meat and poultry. If possible, make the gravy in the roasting tin while the joint (or bird) is resting. This will incorporate the meat juices that have escaped during roasting.

1 Carefully pour (or skim) off the fat from a corner of the roasting tin, leaving the sediment behind. Put the tin on the hob over a medium heat and pour in 300–450ml (½–¾ pint) vegetable water, or chicken, vegetable or meat stock as appropriate.

2 Stir thoroughly, scraping up the sediment, and boil steadily until the gravy is a rich brown colour. A little gravy browning can be added to intensify the flavour and colour.

Makes about 300ml (½ pint)   preparation: 2 minutes   cooking time: 2–3 minutes
per 100ml (3½fl oz): 10 cals; 2g fat; 1g carbohydrate

Variations

Thick gravy: Sprinkle 1–2tbsp flour into the roasting tin and cook, stirring, until browned, then gradually stir in the liquid and cook, stirring for 2–3 minutes until smooth and slightly thickened.

Rich wine gravy: Deglaze the roasting tin with about 150ml (¼ pint) red or white wine, or 90ml (3fl oz) fortified wine such as sherry or Madeira, and allow to bubble for a minute or two before adding the stock or water. For a sweeter flavour, add 2tbsp redcurrant jelly with the wine.

Shortcrust Pastry

225g (8oz) plain flour, plus extra to dust
pinch of salt

125g (4oz) butter, or half white vegetable fat
and half butter, cut into pieces

1 Sift the flour and salt into a bowl. Add the fat and mix lightly, then, using your fingertips, rub the fat into the flour until the mixture resembles fine breadcrumbs.
2 Sprinkle 3–4tbsp cold water evenly over the surface and stir with a round-bladed knife until the mixture begins to stick together in large lumps. If the dough seems dry, add a little extra water. With one hand, collect the dough together to form a ball.
3 Knead lightly on a lightly floured surface for a few seconds to form a smooth, firm dough; do not over-work. Wrap the dough in clingfilm and leave to rest in the fridge for 30 minutes before rolling out.

Alternatively, to make the pastry in a food processor, put the flour and salt in the processor bowl with the butter. Whiz until the mixture resembles fine crumbs, then add the water. Process briefly, using the pulse button, until the mixture just comes together in a ball. Continue from step 3. Shortcrust pastry can be stored in the fridge for up to three days, or frozen.

Makes a '225g (8oz) quantity'   preparation: 10 minutes, plus resting
per 25g (1oz): 110 cals; 6g fat; 12g carbohydrate

Variations
Wholemeal pastry: Replace half the white flour with wholemeal flour. A little extra water may be needed to mix the dough.
Nut pastry: Replace 50g (2oz) of the flour with finely chopped or ground walnuts, hazelnuts or almonds, adding them to the rubbed-in mixture just before the cold water.
Cheese pastry: Stir in 3–4tbsp freshly grated Parmesan cheese or 75g (3oz) finely grated Cheddar cheese and a small pinch of mustard powder before adding the water.
Herb pastry: Stir in 3tbsp finely chopped herbs, such as parsley, sage, thyme or rosemary, before adding the water.
Olive pastry: Stir in 4tbsp finely chopped pitted black olives, at stage 2.
Poppy seed pastry: Add 15g ($\frac{1}{2}$oz) poppy seeds before adding the water.

Sweet Tart Pastry

225g (8oz) plain flour
pinch of salt
150g (5oz) butter, cut into pieces

2tbsp golden caster sugar
1 egg yolk

1 Sift the flour and salt into a large bowl and rub in the butter using your fingertips until the mixture resembles breadcrumbs. Stir in the sugar. Alternatively, use a food processor to incorporate the butter into the flour, then add the sugar and pulse to mix. Tip into a bowl and continue.
2 Mix the egg yolk with 3tbsp cold water, then add to the dry ingredients and mix with a round-bladed knife to a dough.
3 Knead gently until just smooth. Wrap the pastry in clingfilm and leave to rest in the fridge for 30 minutes before rolling out. Use as required. Tart pastry can be stored in the fridge for up to three days, or frozen.

Makes a '225g (8oz) quantity' preparation: 10 minutes, plus resting
per 25g (1oz): 110 cals; 7g fat; 11g carbohydrate

Puff Pastry

450g (1lb) strong plain (bread) flour, plus
** extra to dust**
pinch of salt

450g (1lb) butter, chilled
1tbsp lemon juice

1 Sift the flour and salt together into a bowl. Cut off 50g (2oz) butter and flatten the remaining large block with a rolling pin to a slab, about 2cm (¾ inch) thick, and set aside.
2 Cut the 50g (2oz) butter into small pieces and rub into the flour, using your fingertips.
3 Using a round-bladed knife, stir in the lemon juice and enough chilled water to make a soft elastic dough – you will need about 300ml (½ pint).
4 Turn out on to a lightly floured surface and quickly knead the dough until smooth. Cut a cross through half the depth, then open out to form a star.
5 Roll out, keeping the centre four times as thick as the flaps. Put the slab of butter in the centre of the dough. Fold the flaps over the dough, envelope-style.
6 Press gently with a rolling pin and roll out to a rectangle, measuring 40.5 x 20.5cm (16 x 8 inches).
7 Fold the bottom third up and the top third down, keeping the edges straight. Wrap in clingfilm and leave to rest in the fridge for 30 minutes.
8 Put the pastry on a lightly floured surface with the folded edges to the sides. Repeat the rolling, folding, resting and turning sequence five times.
9 Shape the puff pastry as required, then rest it in the fridge for about 30 minutes before baking.

Makes a '450g (1lb) quantity' preparation: 40 minutes, plus resting
per 25g (1oz): 100 cals; 8g fat; 7g carbohydrate

The Shortest-ever Walnut Pastry

50g (2oz) walnuts
175g (6oz) plain flour, sifted, plus extra
   to dust

125g (4oz) chilled unsalted butter, diced

1 Put the walnuts and flour in a food processor and whiz to chop the nuts roughly. Add the butter and continue to process until the mixture resembles fine crumbs. Add 3tbsp cold water and blend to combine.
2 Tip the pastry out on to a floured surface and knead lightly. Shape into a round flat disc, wrap and chill for 1 hour.
3 Roll out the pastry on a lightly floured surface to a 30.5cm (12 inch) circle and use to line a 23 x 4cm (9 x 1½ inch) fluted tin, leaving the edges hanging over the rim of the tin. Prick the base all over, cover with clingfilm and chill for 20 minutes. Preheat the oven to 200°C (180°C fan oven) mark 6.
4 Line the pastry case with greaseproof paper and cover with baking beans. Put on a baking sheet and bake for 20 minutes. Remove the greaseproof paper and beans and continue to cook for a further 15 minutes. Take out of the oven and cool for 5 minutes, then trim the edge with a small sharp knife. Use as required.

Makes 1 x 23 x 4cm (9 x 1½inch) pastry case   preparation: 15 minutes, plus chilling
cooking time: 35 minutes, plus cooling
per 25g (1oz): 110 cals; 8g fat; 9g carbohydrate

Trouble-shooting: if your pastry shrinks

Shrinking is caused when the pastry is overstretched when rolling out or when making it in a processor. If you're doing the latter, once you've added the water you should pulse until the mixture just comes together – no longer – then take it out and knead lightly by hand.

Pastry needs chilling twice to relax it, for 20 minutes each time. First, pop it in the fridge just after you've made it (wrap it in clingfilm to stop it getting too firm, which makes rolling out easier), then chill it again when you've lined the tin.

Lightly dust the work surface with flour to prevent sticking – too much will dry out the pastry and lead to cracking when you're rolling it out.

Lift the pastry into the tin and press down gently. Leave the edges hanging loosely over the rim of the tin and bake.

Suet Crust Pastry

300g (11oz) self-raising flour　　　　**150g (5oz) shredded suet or vegetarian suet**
½tsp salt

1　Sift the flour and salt into a bowl, add the shredded suet and stir to mix.
2　Using a round-bladed knife, mix in enough cold water to make a soft dough – you will need about 175ml (6fl oz). If the dough seems too dry, add a little extra water.
3　Knead very lightly until smooth. Use as required.

Makes a '300g (11oz) quantity'　preparation: 10 minutes
per 25g (1oz): 90 cals; 5g fat; 10g carbohydrate

Choux Pastry

65g (2½oz) plain flour　　　　**50g (2oz) butter**
pinch of salt　　　　**2 eggs, lightly beaten**

1　Sift the flour and salt on to a large sheet of greaseproof paper.
2　Pour 150ml (¼ pint) cold water into a medium pan, add the butter and melt over a low heat. Increase the heat and bring to a rolling boil.
3　Take off the heat, immediately tip in all the flour and beat vigorously, using a wooden spoon. Continue beating until the mixture is smooth and leaves the sides of the pan to form a ball; do not over-beat. Leave for 1–2 minutes to cool slightly.
4　Gradually add the eggs, beating well between each addition, adding just enough to give a smooth dropping consistency. The choux pastry should be smooth and shiny. Use as required. It can be either spooned or piped into shape, usually directly on to a dampened baking sheet.

Makes a '2–egg quantity'　preparation: 10 minutes
per 25g (1oz): 50 cals; 4g fat; 3g carbohydrate

Herb pistou

¾tsp sea salt　　　　**15g (½oz) chopped basil**
6 garlic cloves, peeled and chopped　　　　**12tbsp olive oil**

1　Using a pestle and mortar or a strong bowl and the end of a rolling pin, or a mini processor, pound together the salt and garlic until smooth.
2　Add the basil and pound down to a paste then blend in the olive oil, a little at a time.

Serves 6　preparation: 45 minutes　cooking time: 1 hour　per serving: 291cals; 64g fat; 38g carbohydrate

Two-minute Dressing

2tbsp white wine vinegar
4tbsp olive oil

1½tsp mustard (Dijon or wholegrain)

1   Put all the ingredients into a screw-topped jar, screw the jar shut and shake to emulsify.

Makes 90ml (4fl oz)   preparation: 2 minutes
per 1tbsp serving: 66 cals; 7g fat; 0g carbohydrate

Five-minute Mayonnaise

2 large egg yolks
1tsp English mustard
salt and pepper
200ml (7fl oz) grapeseed or sunflower oil

100ml (3½fl oz) extra-virgin olive oil
1tsp white wine vinegar or lemon juice, plus
   extra to season

1   Put the egg yolks into a 850ml (1½ pint) bowl. Add the mustard and season with 1tsp salt and plenty of pepper, then mix thoroughly with a wooden spoon.
2   Combine the oils in a jug. Sit the bowl on a damp tea-towel to hold it steady. Add about ½tsp oil to the egg mixture and whisk in. Stop whisking as you add each ½tsp oil, then continue whisking until the mixture emulsifies. (The yolks thicken and the mixture starts to look like mayonnaise.) Turn the bowl occasionally to mix everything in. Keep adding the oil, 1tbsp at a time now, until you've added about half of it. If the mayonnaise starts to curdle (called 'splitting') don't worry – add about 1tbsp cold water and stir in with a spoon, then continue with the recipe. If this doesn't work, put another egg yolk in a clean bowl and gradually whisk in the curdled mixture, 1tbsp at a time.
3   Add the vinegar or lemon juice, which will thin the mixture a little. Now begin pouring in the remaining oil in a thin, steady stream, whisking all the time. When all the oil has been added the mayonnaise should be thick and wobbly.
4   Taste the mayonnaise for seasoning and, if necessary, stir in a little more salt and pepper, a splash of vinegar or a squeeze of lemon juice. Cover and keep chilled for up to four days.

Makes 300ml (½ pint)   preparation: 15 minutes
per 1tbsp serving: 110 cals; 12g fat; 0g carbohydrate

Brunch

Brunch can be a fabulous start to the day – especially if shared with friends and family. Everyone can muck in and help – no need for formality – and even if you've only got eggs and bread in the cupboard you can still rustle up some yummy food.

Kick off with a Spicy Tomato Cocktail while you decide what everyone wants – add some vodka to really get things going! Then, how about a pan-fry of Ham and Eggs with Hash Potatoes; Brussels Sprout Bubble and Squeak Cakes; or Simply Sausages – the sound of sausages sizzling in the pan will soon have people sitting at the table. Make big platefuls so that everyone can tuck in.

You can't beat eggs – boiled, poached, scrambled, fried or made into omelettes. Eat them with soldiers, buttery toast or good bread.

Then there's kedgeree, a real brunch favourite, tasty and filling. Try the Kedgeree with Lentils and Salmon, topped with caramelised onions and coriander sprigs.

And to follow? Take your pick from Orange Eggy Bread, indulgent pancakes drizzled with syrup, or naughty French toast.

Next, a delicious, soothing smoothie, to round off a relaxing start to the day ahead.

Scrambled Eggs with Smoked Salmon

6 large eggs	125g pack smoked salmon, torn roughly
salt and pepper	into pieces
25g (1oz) butter	6 slices rye or sourdough bread
100g (3½oz) mascarpone	snipped chives, to garnish

1   Using a sharp knife, carefully crack and tap off the pointed end of each egg. Pour the egg yolks and whites into a bowl. Remove and discard the sac from the bottom of the shells, rinse out the shells, then turn them upside down and leave to dry.
2   Beat the eggs together and season well. Melt the butter in a non-stick pan over a low heat. Add the eggs and stir constantly until the mixture thickens. Add the mascarpone and season well. Cook for 1–2 minutes longer until the mixture becomes just firm, then fold in the smoked salmon.
3   Toast the bread, spread with the butter and cut into soldiers. Spoon the egg mixture back into the eggshells, garnish with chives and serve with the soldiers.

Serves 6   preparation: 15 minutes cooking time: 5 minutes
per serving: 300 cals; 20g fat; 15g carbohydrate

Frittata

50g (2oz) butter	12 eggs, lightly beaten
2tbsp olive oil	salt and pepper
2 large red onions, peeled and finely sliced	2tbsp freshly grated Parmesan cheese
4tbsp chopped flat-leafed parsley	

1   Heat the butter and olive oil gently in a large frying pan. Add the onions and cook over a low heat until they're very soft and lightly caramelised.
2   Add the parsley, then pour in the eggs and season. Cook over a gentle heat, lifting the edges occasionally, until the eggs are nearly cooked through. Sprinkle with the Parmesan, then turn out, cut into wedges and serve with salad.

Serves 8   preparation: 10 minutes   cooking time: 30 minutes
per serving: 410 cals; 45g fat; 0g carbohydrate

Eggs Benedict

2tbsp white wine vinegar, plus extra to
  poach
9 black peppercorns, crushed
2 large or 3 medium egg yolks
250g (9oz) unsalted butter, cut into small
  pieces
2tsp lemon juice

salt and pepper
4 very fresh eggs
4 English muffins
4 slices ham or 150g (5oz) grilled bacon
  rashers
parsley, to garnish

1 Put 2tbsp vinegar in a small pan with 2tbsp water and the black peppercorns. Bring to the boil and simmer until the liquid is reduced by half.

2 Whiz the egg yolks in a food processor for 1 minute. Strain the reduced vinegar, adding it to the yolks while the machine is running.

3 Melt the butter in a small pan, and cook until it begins to brown around the edges. With the food processor running on full speed, add two-thirds of the melted butter. Add the lemon juice, then the remaining butter. Season and put to one side.

4 Take a wide, shallow pan of boiling water and add 1tbsp vinegar to each 600ml (1 pint) water. Carefully break an egg into a saucer, make a whirlpool with a large spoon in the boiling water and lower the egg into the water. Reduce the heat and cook gently for 3 minutes or until the white is just set and the yolk soft. Using a draining spoon, lift the egg out of the pan and put in a shallow dish of warm water. Repeat with the remaining eggs.

5 Meanwhile, split the muffins in half and toast. Warm the ham in the microwave for 1 minute on Medium (based on a 900W oven). Put the ham on the muffin halves, top each with an egg, some Hollandaise sauce and the other muffin half. Garnish with parsley and serve.

Serves 4 preparation: 10 minutes cooking time: 15 minutes
per serving 800 cals; 64g fat; 30g carbohydrate

Creamy Baked Egg Starter

butter, to grease
4 sun-dried tomatoes
salt and pepper

4 eggs
4tbsp double cream

1 Preheat the oven to 180°C (160°C fan oven) mark 4. Grease four ramekins.

2 Put 1 tomato in each ramekin and season. Carefully break an egg on top of each, then drizzle 1tbsp cream over each egg.

3 Bake for 15–18 minutes – the eggs will continue to cook once they have been taken out of the oven.

4 Leave to stand for 2 minutes before serving.

Serves 4 preparation: 5 minutes cooking time: 15–18 minutes
per serving: 170 cals; 14g fat; 3g carbohydrate

Kedgeree with Herb Butter

450g (1lb) smoked haddock or fresh salmon
150ml (¼ pint) full-fat milk
225g (8oz) basmati rice
75g (3oz) cooked cockles, well drained
1tsp coriander seeds, finely crushed
3 hard-boiled eggs, shelled and quartered
2tbsp double cream

3–4tbsp chopped chives
salt and pepper
50g (2oz) butter
1–2tsp lemon juice
2tbsp chopped tarragon
lemon or lime wedges and herbs, to garnish

1 Put the haddock in a shallow pan with the milk. Cover and simmer for 8 minutes or until cooked. Drain, reserving 2–3tbsp of the cooking liquor. Flake the fish, discarding the skin and bones.
2 Cook the rice in boiling salted water for 10 minutes or until just tender. Drain, rinse with boiling water and drain again.
3 Return the rice to the pan and add the haddock, reserved liquor, cockles, coriander seeds, eggs, cream and chives. Season lightly, then heat gently for 2 minutes.
4 Meanwhile, melt the butter, stir in the lemon juice, chopped tarragon and seasoning and pour into a warmed jug.
5 Tip the kedgeree into a serving dish, garnish with the lemon or lime wedges and herbs and serve with the herb butter.

Serves 4   preparation: 10 minutes   cooking time: about 20 minutes
per serving: 540 cals; 22g fat; 47g carbohydrate

Energy-boosting Brunch

2tbsp vegetable oil
1 small onion, peeled and chopped
1 garlic clove, peeled and crushed
1 small chilli, deseeded and finely chopped
1 red, green or yellow pepper, deseeded
   and chopped

400g can chopped tomatoes
salt and pepper
4 eggs
2 flour tortillas

1 Heat 1tbsp oil in a small pan, add the onion and cook gently for 10 minutes. Add the garlic, chilli and chopped pepper and cook for 10 minutes. Add the tomatoes, season and simmer for 10 minutes.
3 Heat the remaining oil in a non-stick pan for 1 minute. Crack 1 egg into a cup, then pour it into the hot fat. Straight away, do the same with the other egg. Cook for a few minutes until the eggs are just set, spooning over the fat from time to time.
4 Toast the tortillas in a dry frying pan over a high heat for 30 seconds on each side. Put on to two plates and top with the sauce, then the eggs and season well. Roll the tortillas up and tuck in the ends. Scrape the rest of the tomato sauce into a sealed container and chill for another use.

Serves 2   preparation: 10 minutes   cooking time: 40 minutes
per serving: 510 cals; 30g fat; 39g carbohydrate

Pan-fried Mushroom and Feta Omelette

50g (2oz) butter
225g (8oz) large mushrooms, thinly sliced
3 garlic cloves, peeled and sliced
50g (2oz) sun-dried tomatoes, chopped

4 large eggs, beaten
black pepper
100g (3½oz) feta cheese, crumbled
thyme sprigs, to garnish

1 Melt the butter in an 18cm (7 inch) non-stick omelette pan and fry the mushrooms with the garlic until they are a deep golden brown and beginning to go crisp around the edges. Add the sun-dried tomatoes and stir over the heat for 1–2 minutes. Preheat the grill.
2 Roughly spread the mushroom mixture over the base of the pan. Beat 2tbsp cold water into the eggs and season with pepper (both feta cheese and the tomatoes can be salty, so no extra salt should be needed). Pour the eggs over the mushrooms, gently swirling the pan to spread the eggs. Leave to set, undisturbed, over a low heat for 1–2 minutes or until the eggs are lightly cooked and the feta is just beginning to melt.
3 Sprinkle the omelette with pepper and scatter with thyme sprigs to garnish. Cut into wedges and serve immediately.

Serves 4   preparation: 5 minutes   cooking time: 15 minutes
per serving: 270 cals; 23g fat; 3g carbohydrate

Brussels Sprout Bubble and Squeak Cakes

5tbsp vegetable oil or dripping
175g (6oz) onions, peeled and finely sliced
175g (6oz) cooked Brussels sprouts,
  roughly chopped
700g (1½lb) leftover mashed potatoes

salt and pepper
nutmeg to taste
Sweet Onion and Mustard Sauce
  to serve
finely chopped chives, to garnish

1 Preheat the oven to 130°C (110°C fan oven) mark ½. Heat the oil or dripping in a non-stick frying pan, add the onions and cook for 10 minutes or until golden. Add the Brussels sprouts and fry for 5 minutes. Tip the sprouts and onions into the mashed potatoes and mix well, then season and add grated nutmeg to taste.
2 Using a 9cm (3½ inch) diameter plain cutter, shape the potato mixture into eight individual cakes. Fry the cakes in a hot, non-stick frying pan for 2–3 minutes on each side. Keep covered in a low oven while you make the Sweet Onion and Mustard Sauce.
3 Serve the bubble and squeak cakes with Sweet Onion and Mustard Sauce, garnished with chopped chives.

Makes 8   preparation: 10 minutes   cooking time: 25 minutes
per serving: 110 cals; 9g fat; 7g carbohydrate

Kedgeree with Lentils and Salmon

50g (2oz) butter
700g (1½lb) onions, peeled and sliced
2tsp garam masala
1 garlic clove, peeled and crushed
75g (3oz) split green lentils, soaked
   in 300ml (½ pint) boiling water for
   15 minutes, then drained

750ml (1¼ pints) vegetable stock
225g (8oz) basmati rice
1 green chilli, deseeded and finely chopped
salt and pepper
350g (12oz) salmon fillet
coriander sprigs, to garnish

1 Melt the butter in a large flameproof casserole. Add the onions and cook for 5 minutes or until soft. Remove one-third from the pan and put to one side. Increase the heat and cook the remaining onions for 10 minutes to caramelise. Remove and put to one side.

2 Return the first batch of onions to the pan, add the garam masala and garlic and cook, stirring, for 1 minute. Add the drained lentils and stock, cover and cook for 15 minutes. Add the rice and chilli, season, then bring to the boil, cover the pan, reduce the heat and simmer for 5 minutes.

3 Put the salmon fillet on top of the rice, cover and cook gently for 15 minutes or until the rice is cooked, the stock is absorbed and the salmon opaque.

4 Lift off the salmon and divide into flakes. Return the salmon to the pan and fork through the rice. Garnish with the reserved caramelised onions and the coriander sprigs and serve.

Serves 4   preparation: 15 minutes, plus soaking   cooking time: 50 minutes
per serving: 540 cals; 21g fat; 62g carbohydrate

Hash Browns with Smoked Salmon and Scrambled Eggs

1.4kg (3lb) unpeeled potatoes, cut into
  2.5cm (1 inch) chunks
salt and pepper
50g (2oz) butter
2tbsp olive oil
1 bunch spring onions, finely sliced on
  the diagonal

50g (2oz) shallots, peeled and chopped
10 large eggs, beaten
4tbsp soured cream
450g (1lb) smoked salmon, sliced
crushed black peppercorns and spring
  onion curls, to garnish

1 To make the hash browns, put the potatoes in a pan of lightly salted, boiling water, bring back to the boil and cook for 3 minutes. Drain well and dry on kitchen paper. Heat 25g (1oz) butter and the olive oil in a large frying pan, add the potatoes and cook for 8 minutes, scraping the crispy bits from the bottom of the pan. Add the spring onions and seasoning and cook for 1–2 minutes or until the potatoes are golden and crisp. Cover with a lid or piece of foil and keep warm.

2 To make the scrambled eggs, heat the remaining butter in a large, non-stick, heavy-based frying pan. Add the shallots and cook for 3 minutes until softened. Put the eggs and soured cream in a bowl with a little seasoning and whisk lightly together. Add the egg mixture to the shallots and cook, stirring with a fork, for about 1 minute, bringing the set eggs in from the side of the pan to the centre. When the eggs are just starting to set, remove the pan from the heat – be careful not to overcook the eggs.

3 Spoon the scrambled eggs over the hash browns and put the smoked salmon on top. Garnish with the peppercorns and spring onion curls and serve.

Serves 6   preparation: 20 minutes   cooking time: 20 minutes
per serving: 550 cals; 29g fat; 37g carbohydrate

Spanish Omelette

225g (8oz) piece salami, chorizo or garlic
sausage, roughly chopped
50g (2oz) stale baguette or garlic bread,
roughly chopped
8 large eggs

2 spring onions, finely chopped
1 small bunch of chives, or any other fresh
herbs you fancy, finely chopped
salt and pepper
1tbsp olive oil

1   Heat a large, 28cm (11 inch), frying pan and fry the salami or chorizo pieces over a gentle heat until the fat begins to run. Increase the heat and cook the meat until golden and crisp. Remove from the pan (leaving the fat in the pan) and set aside. Add the bread to the pan and fry until it's also golden and crisp. Remove the pan from the heat, mix the croûtons with the cooked salami and keep warm until needed.
2   Beat the eggs together with the spring onions and chives, then season well. Heat the olive oil in the pan used for the salami and bread. When very hot, add the egg mixture, allowing the liquid to spread across the base of the pan. Cook for 2 minutes, then, using a spatula, draw the cooked edges into the centre, tilting the pan so the runny mixture runs into the gaps.
3   When the omelette is almost set, reduce the heat and spoon the salami and crouton mixture evenly over the top. Cook for a further 30 seconds, then cut the omelette into four wedges. Serve with a soft, leafy salad and some crusty bread.

Serves 4   preparation: 5 minutes   cooking time: 15 minutes
per serving: 520 cals; 42g fat; 7g carbohydrate

Bacon and Tuna Hash

450g (1lb) new potatoes, cut into small
chunks
salt and pepper
25g (1oz) butter
125g (4oz) streaky bacon rashers or
lardons, cut into 2.5cm (1 inch) strips

1 large onion, peeled and roughly chopped
125g (4oz) pitted green or black olives
200g can tuna in oil, drained and flaked
coriander sprigs, to garnish

1   Put the potatoes in a pan of lightly salted water, bring to the boil, then reduce the heat and simmer, partially covered, for 5–10 minutes or until beginning to soften. Drain and set aside.
2   Melt the butter in a non-stick frying pan, add the bacon and cook on a medium heat until beginning to brown, then add the onion. Cook for 5 minutes or until soft. Add the potatoes and olives, reduce the heat and cook for 10 minutes.
3   Using a spatula, turn the hash over and continue to cook for a further 10 minutes, turning every now and again. Add the tuna and cook for a further 4–5 minutes or until the potatoes are done to the centre and the tuna is hot. Season to taste. Garnish with coriander sprigs and serve.

Serves 4   preparation: 10 minutes   cooking time: 35 minutes
per serving: 430 cals; 31g fat; 22g carbohydrate

Chorizo Hash

700g (1½lb) large floury potatoes, peeled
and cut into large chunks
salt

175g (6oz) chorizo sausage, in one piece
1 large onion, peeled and finely chopped
4 eggs

1 Put the potatoes in a pan of lightly salted water, bring to the boil, then reduce the heat and simmer, partially covered, for 15–20 minutes until just tender. Drain well, then return to the pan and cover with a lid to keep warm and dry off any excess moisture.
2 While the potatoes are cooking, peel and discard the rind from the sausage and cut it into small dice. Fry the diced sausage in a large non-stick ovenproof pan over a high heat until it has turned a deep golden brown and is beginning to go crispy at the edges – about 15 minutes.
3 Remove the sausage from the pan with a slotted spoon and set aside. Add the onion and fry over a medium heat for a good 10 minutes until it turns golden brown (there should be enough oil from the sausage without having to add any extra oil).
4 Preheat the oven to 200°C (180°C fan oven) mark 6. Cut the potatoes into smaller dice. Return the sausage and potatoes to the pan and cook over a medium heat for 5 minutes, without stirring, until a golden crust forms on the bottom of the mixture. Break up the mixture, then cook again until another crust forms. Break up the mixture once more and leave to cook for a further 2–3 minutes.
5 Make four dips in the hash and crack an egg into each one. Bake for about 7 minutes or until the egg whites are set but the yolks are still soft. Season the eggs with salt and serve immediately.

Serves 4   preparation: 10 minutes   cooking time: 35–45 minutes
per serving 340 cals; 16g fat; 32g carbohydrate

Sausage Hash Browns

700g (1½lb) medium potatoes, unpeeled
salt
50g (2oz) butter
1 small onion, peeled and chopped

450g (1lb) pork sausages
2 red onions, peeled and cut into rings
sunflower oil, to brush
450g (1lb) small vine-ripened tomatoes

1 Put the potatoes in a pan of lightly salted water, bring to the boil and par-boil for 10 minutes. Drain, then cut into 2.5cm (1 inch) cubes.
2 Heat the butter in a large heavy-based frying pan. Add the onion and fry for 1 minute. Add the potatoes and fry over a medium heat for 25 minutes or until crisp and brown, turning frequently. Meanwhile, preheat the grill to medium-high.
3 Grill the sausages for about 20 minutes, turning from time to time, until browned and cooked through to the centre. Halfway through cooking, brush the onion rings with oil and add to the grill pan with the tomatoes. Grill until softened and lightly caramelised.
4 Serve the sausages on top of the hash brown potatoes, with the onion rings and tomatoes.

Serves 4   preparation: 15 minutes   cooking time: 35 minutes
per serving: 740 cals; 51g fat; 56g carbohydrate

Ham and Eggs with Hash Potatoes

1.8kg (4lb) potatoes, peeled
salt and pepper
5tbsp olive oil
6 garlic cloves
2 rosemary sprigs or 2tsp dried
6 slices ham off the bone, about 175g (6oz)

6 large eggs
6tbsp double cream
125g (4oz) hard cheese, such as Cheddar,
  grated
rosemary sprigs, to garnish

1 Preheat the oven to 200°C (180°C fan oven) mark 6. Cut the potatoes into small 2cm (¾ inch) cubes and put in a pan of lightly salted water. Bring to the boil and cook for 3 minutes. Drain well.
2 Put the olive oil in a large roasting tin and heat in the oven for 5 minutes. Add the potatoes and whole unpeeled garlic cloves to the hot oil, season well, then return to the oven for 30 minutes. Add the rosemary and return to the oven for a further 20–30 minutes, stirring occasionally.
3 Divide the potatoes among six individual gratin dishes, each about 12.5cm (5 inch) base diameter. When they are cool, arrange a slice of ham on top of each dish of potatoes and make a dip in the centre of each.
4 Crack the eggs carefully one by one on to the ham. Drizzle 1tbsp cream over each egg and season well. Sprinkle the grated cheese on top of the cream.
5 Bake for 20–25 minutes or until the egg white is just set and the yolk still soft. Garnish with rosemary sprigs and serve immediately with a green salad, if wished.

Serves 6   preparation: 35 minutes, plus cooling   cooking time: 1½ hours
per serving: 610 cals; 34g fat; 52g carbohydrate

Simply Sausages

8 thick, good-quality pork sausages
olive oil, if necessary
2 red onions, peeled and finely chopped
2 large red peppers, deseeded and roughly
  chopped

150ml (¼ pint) light stock
1 large glass red wine, about 225ml (8fl oz)
410g can brown or green lentils, drained
  and rinsed
4tbsp chopped flat-leafed parsley

1 Snip the sausage skins to let the fat run, then brown the sausages slowly in a non-stick flameproof casserole for 4–5 minutes. If they begin to stick, add a little olive oil.
2 Add the onions to the pan and fry for about 7 minutes until soft. Stir in the red peppers and fry until they begin to soften.
3 Pour in the stock and red wine, then bring to the boil and let the mixture bubble for 2 minutes. Stir the lentils into the pan, then cover it tightly with a lid or a piece of foil, reduce the heat and simmer gently on the hob for about 15–20 minutes until most of the liquid has been absorbed and the peppers are quite soft. Stir in the chopped parsley, then serve at once.

Serves 4   preparation: 15 minutes;   cooking time: 40 minutes
per serving: 440 cals; 24g fat; 32g carbohydrate

Rösti Potatoes with Fried Eggs

900g (2lb) red potatoes, scrubbed and left
   whole
salt and pepper

40g (1½oz) butter
4 large eggs

1 Put the potatoes in a pan of well salted water, bring to the boil and par-boil for 5–8 minutes. Drain and leave to cool for 15 minutes.
2 Peel the potatoes and coarsely grate them lengthways to give long strands. Divide into eight portions and shape into mounds.
3 Melt half the butter in a large non-stick frying pan. Once it is bubbling and beginning to brown, put four of the potato mounds in the pan, spacing them well apart, and flatten them a little.
4 Preheat the oven to 150°C (130°C fan oven) mark 2. Fry the rosti slowly for about 6–7 minutes until golden brown, then turn them over and brown the other side for 6–7 minutes. Transfer the rösti to a warmed baking tray and keep warm in the oven while you fry the rest.
5 Just before serving, carefully break the eggs into the hot pan and fry for about 2 minutes until the white is set and the yolk is still soft. Season and serve at once, with the rösti.

Serves 4   preparation: 20 minutes, plus cooling   cooking time: 35–40 minutes
per serving: 330 cals; 15g fat; 39g carbohydrate

BLT-topped Bagels with Hollandaise Sauce

3 large bagels, cut in half horizontally
25g (1oz) butter, softened
12 smoked streaky bacon rashers, rind
   removed
2tsp olive oil

3 tomatoes, cut into thick slices
150ml (¼ pint) bought Hollandaise sauce
75g (3oz) mixed lettuce leaves
crushed black pepper, to garnish

1 Preheat the grill to high, then grill the halved bagels until golden. Spread generously with the butter. Cover the bagels with a piece of foil and keep them warm. Grill the bacon for 2–3 minutes or until crisp, then keep warm. Heat the olive oil in a small frying pan until very hot and fry the tomatoes for about 1 minute until lightly charred.
2 Put the Hollandaise sauce in a small pan and heat gently. To assemble, top the warm bagels with a few lettuce leaves, the tomatoes and bacon. Spoon the warm Hollandaise sauce over the bacon and garnish with the pepper. Serve at once.

Serves 6   preparation: 15 minutes   cooking time: 8 minutes
per serving: 500 cals; 40g fat; 22g carbohydrate

Bacon Butty

12 bacon rashers
12 slices crusty white bread

tomato ketchup to taste

1 Heat a griddle pan and fry the bacon over a medium heat until crisp. Remove from the pan and keep warm.

2 Press one side of each bread slice on the griddle to soak up the juices. Put 2 bacon rashers on each of six slices, add ketchup, top with the remaining slices and serve.

Serves 6   preparation: 5 minutes   cooking time: 10 minutes
per serving: 420 cals; 26g fat; 35g carbohydrate

Smoked Haddock and Bacon Bites

350g (12oz) potatoes, peeled
salt and pepper
40g (1½oz) butter
450g (1lb) smoked haddock
4 rashers, about 125g (4oz), smoked streaky
  bacon, rind removed

2tbsp chopped chives
1 large egg, beaten
75g (3oz) fresh white breadcrumbs
oil, for frying
lemon slices and flat-leafed parsley,
  to garnish

1 Put the potatoes in a pan of lightly salted water, cover, bring to the boil, then reduce the heat and simmer for 20 minutes or until soft. Drain, return to the pan and dry over a low heat for a few minutes, then mash them with the butter.

2 Meanwhile, preheat the grill. Put the haddock, skin side up, in a pan with just enough water to cover. Bring to the boil, then reduce the heat and simmer gently for 10 minutes or until just cooked. Remove the fish from the pan and when cool enough to handle skin and flake the flesh. Grill the bacon for 5 minutes or until crisp. Cool and crumble into small pieces.

3 Put the mashed potato, haddock, bacon and chives in a bowl and mix until well combined. Season with pepper. Shape into 20 golf ball-sized pieces. Dip each in the beaten egg, then roll them in breadcrumbs to coat.

4 Heat the oil to 190°C (375°F) or until a cube of bread sizzles when dropped in. Deep-fry the haddock bites until golden and crisp, then drain on kitchen paper. Garnish with the lemon and parsley and serve.

Serves 4   preparation: 30 minutes   cooking time: 35 minutes
per serving: 510 cals; 30g fat; 24g carbohydrate

Smoked Trout Bagels

200g pack cream cheese
3tbsp mayonnaise
1–2tbsp horseradish sauce
salt and pepper

6 bagels, split in half
375g pack cold cure smoked trout
1 lime, cut into six wedges

1   Put the cream cheese, mayonnaise and horseradish sauce in a bowl, beat until smooth and season well.
2   Spread the mixture over the bottom half of each bagel, then arrange some smoked trout on top. Sandwich the bagels together and serve with the lime wedges.

Serves 6   preparation: 10 minutes
per serving: 460 cals; 25g fat; 36g carbohydrate

Smoked Cod Rarebit

450ml (¾ pint) milk
1 bay leaf
2tbsp parsley
1 onion, peeled and sliced
2 slices lemon
2 pieces undyed smoked cod loin, about
    175g (6oz) each, skinned
2 thick slices white crusty bread

125g (4oz) mature Cheddar cheese
1 small egg, beaten
4tbsp double cream
1tsp each Dijon mustard and
    Worcestershire sauce
25g (1oz) butter, softened
black pepper

1   Preheat the grill to high. Heat the milk, bay leaf, parsley, onion and lemon slices together in a small deep-sided frying pan and add the fish. Poach for 6–8 minutes or until the fish is cooked through. Remove the fish from the pan with a fish slice and discard the milk.
2   Toast the bread on both sides until golden, then place in a dish.
3   Mix 75g (3oz) Cheddar with the egg, cream, mustard, Worcestershire sauce, butter and a pinch of pepper in a bowl. Put the fish on the toast, top with the cheese mixture and sprinkle over the remaining Cheddar.
4   Put on the lower shelf of the grill and cook for 5–6 minutes, until the cheese topping is bubbling, golden and set. Serve straight away.

Serves 2   preparation: 15 minutes   cooking time: 15 minutes
per serving: 760 cals; 51g fat; 21g carbohydrate

Cheddar and Stilton Rarebits

1 small thin French stick
50g (2oz) butter, melted
75g (3oz) Stilton cheese
2 large egg yolks
25g (1oz) walnuts, roughly chopped

salt and pepper
75g (3oz) Cheddar cheese, coarsely grated
1tsp English mustard powder
a good pinch of mild chilli seasoning
oregano sprigs, to garnish

1 Preheat the oven to 200°C (180°C fan oven) mark 6. Slice the bread into rounds about 5mm–1cm (¼–½ inch) thick. Brush both sides with the melted butter and bake for 10–12 minutes. Transfer to a wire rack to cool.
2 Using a fork, mash the Stilton with 1 egg yolk and stir in the walnuts. Season and spread over half of the toasts, right to the edges. Mix the Cheddar with the remaining egg yolk, the mustard powder and chilli and spread on the remaining toasts.
3 Preheat the grill to high. Arrange the toasts on a grill pan and grill for a few minutes until bubbling and golden. Cool slightly, then serve warm, garnished with the oregano sprigs.

Makes about 6–8   preparation: 15 minutes   cooking time: 10–15 minutes, plus cooling
per rarebit: 320–240 cals; 21–16g fat; 22–17g carbohydrate

Polenta with Mixed Mushrooms

50g (2oz) butter
1.1kg (2½lb) mixed mushrooms
1 red chilli, deseeded and finely chopped
3 garlic cloves, peeled and sliced
100g (3½oz) sun-dried tomatoes,
   roughly chopped

1tsp chopped thyme, plus thyme sprigs
   to garnish
salt and pepper
1kg pack ready-made polenta
3tbsp olive oil
truffle oil (optional)

1 Melt half the butter in a deep-sided frying pan or wok. Add half the mushrooms and cook over a high heat until all the liquid has evaporated, then put to one side. Repeat with the remaining butter and mushrooms. Fry the chilli and garlic in the pan for 2 minutes, then add to the mushrooms, along with the sun-dried tomatoes and thyme. Mix well and season.
2 Slice the polenta into 16 pieces, about 1cm (½ inch) thick. Heat the olive oil in a non-stick frying pan and fry the polenta in batches, for 3–4 minutes on each side, or until golden.
3 To serve, arrange two slices of polenta per person on a plate, top with the mushroom sauce and drizzle with a little truffle oil, if using. Garnish with thyme sprigs.

Serves 8   preparation: 10 minutes   cooking time: 20 minutes
per serving: 240 cals; 11g fat; 29g carbohydrate

Mini Ham Croissants

oil
225g (8oz) ready-made puff pastry
flour, to dust
3tbsp Dijon mustard

100g (3½oz) sliced ham
1 large egg yolk, beaten
sesame seeds and mustard seeds,
  to sprinkle

1   Preheat the oven to 200°C (180°C fan oven) mark 6. Lightly oil one or two baking sheets. Roll out the pastry on a lightly floured surface until it measures 18 x 23cm (7 x 9 inches). Cut it lengthways to make two equal strips. Spread each strip with mustard and cut diagonally to make 10 triangles. Cut the ham into strips 10cm (4 inches) long and 5mm (¼ inch) wide. Put two strips of ham on the long edge of one triangle and roll it up from that edge. Repeat with each triangle.
2   Put the croissants on the baking sheets, curling the ends to form crescents. Tuck the point of each triangle underneath to stop the croissants unravelling as they bake. Brush the tops with beaten egg and sprinkle the sesame and mustard seeds over. Bake for 10–15 minutes or until crisp and golden. Serve warm. You can freeze the croissants, then heat them in a moderate oven for 5–6 minutes or until crisp.

Makes 20   preparation: 30 minutes   cooking time: 15 minutes
per croissant: 60 cals; 4g fat; 4g carbohydrate

Croque Monsieur

a little softened butter, plus extra to fry
4 slices white bread
a little Dijon mustard

125g (4oz) Gruyère cheese
4 slices ham

1   Butter both sides of each slice of bread. Spread mustard on one side of two slices.
2   Divide the cheese and ham in half and make two sandwiches, with one mustard-spread side facing inwards on each.
3   Heat a griddle pan and fry the sandwiches over a high heat for 2–3 minutes on each side until the bread is golden and crisp and the cheese starts to melt.
4   Slice each sandwich in half and serve.

Serves 2   preparation: 5 minutes   cooking time: 6 minutes
per serving: 720 cals; 49g fat; 39g carbohydrate

French Toast

2 eggs
150ml (¼ pint) semi-skimmed milk
generous pinch of freshly grated nutmeg
　or cinnamon

4 slices white bread, or fruit bread, crusts
　removed and each slice cut into four
　fingers
50g (2oz) butter
vegetable oil
1tbsp golden caster sugar

1　Beat the eggs, milk and nutmeg or cinnamon together in a shallow dish.
2　Dip the pieces of bread into the mixture, coating them well.
3　Heat half the butter with 1tbsp oil in a heavy-based frying pan. When the butter is foaming, fry the egg-coated bread pieces in batches, until golden on both sides, adding more butter and oil as needed. Sprinkle with sugar to serve.

Makes 16 fingers　preparation: 5 minutes　cooking time: 10 minutes
per serving: 70 cals; 5g fat; 5g carbohydrate

Five-minute Do-it-yourself Pain au Chocolat

4 croissants
butter, to spread

100g bar good-quality plain dark chocolate
　(with minimum 50% cocoa solids), broken
　into pieces
icing sugar, to dust

1　Preheat the oven to 200°C (180°C fan oven) mark 6. Split open each croissant, spread with butter and put the chocolate inside.
2　Put them on a baking sheet, cover with foil and bake for 5 minutes or until the chocolate has melted, then dust with icing sugar and serve.

Serves 4　preparation: 5 minutes　cooking time: 5 minutes
per croissant: 379 cals; 25g fat; 42g carbohydrate

Buttermilk Pancakes

125g (4oz) butter
175g (6oz) self-raising flour, sifted with 1tsp
  bicarbonate of soda
½tsp each ground cinnamon and freshly
  grated nutmeg
50g (2oz) golden caster sugar
1 large egg, beaten

284ml carton buttermilk
vegetable oil
700g (1½lb) rindless thin streaky bacon
  rashers
6 apples, cored and cut into eighths
4tbsp maple syrup, plus extra to pour
parsley, to garnish

1 Melt 50g (2oz) butter and leave to cool. Put the flour, cinnamon, nutmeg and sugar in a bowl.
2 Make a well in the centre of the flour and add the melted butter, egg and buttermilk. Mix the liquids together, then stir into the flour until thoroughly combined and smooth.
3 Preheat the oven to 140°C (120°C fan oven) mark 1. Preheat the grill to medium-high. Heat a non-stick frying pan, then brush with a little oil. Pour 1tbsp batter into the pan and cook until the underside is golden brown. Using a palette knife, flip the pancake over and briefly cook the other side. Remove the pancake from the pan and keep it warm in the oven between a folded clean cloth. Repeat with the remaining batter.
4 Grill the bacon until crisp. Drain on kitchen paper.
5 Heat half the remaining butter in a frying pan until foaming, then fry half the apples until golden. Remove the apples from the pan and keep warm. Repeat with the remaining butter and apples. Return the apples to the pan, add the 4tbsp maple syrup, bring to the boil and bubble for 1 minute.
6 Serve the pancakes with apples, bacon and extra maple syrup and garnish with parsley.

Serves 6 preparation: 25 minutes cooking time: 30 minutes
per serving: 820 cals; 56g fat; 53g carbohydrate

Toasted Cheese Sandwich

50g (2oz) mature Cheddar cheese, finely
  grated
2tbsp mayonnaise
pinch of English mustard powder

salt and pepper
2 slices white country-style bread
2tbsp good-quality chutney

1 Preheat the grill to high. Mix the cheese with the mayonnaise and mustard powder and season well.
2 Spread the mixture over one slice of bread and place under the grill for 1–2 minutes until the cheese is bubbling and golden.
3 Spread the chutney over the second slice of bread and sandwich together with the toasted cheese.
4 Grill the sandwich to toast on each side, then cut in half and serve.

Serves 1 preparation: 5 minutes cooking time: 5 minutes
per serving: 700 cals; 43g fat; 60g carbohydrate

Golden Honey Fruits

900g (2lb) selection of tropical fruit, such as
   pineapple, mango, papaya and banana
3tbsp runny honey

Greek-style yogurt, to serve
mixed spice, to sprinkle

1 Preheat the grill to high. Peel the fruit as necessary and cut into wedges.
2 Put the fruit on a foil-lined grill pan, drizzle with the honey and cook under the grill for 5–8 minutes, until caramelised.
3 Serve with the yogurt sprinkled with a little mixed spice.

Serves 4 preparation: 5 minutes   cooking time: 5–8 minutes
per serving: 160 cals; trace fat; 40g carbohydrate

Lemon and Blueberry Pancakes

125g (4oz) plain flour
150g (5oz) caster sugar, plus 3tbsp
1tsp baking powder
1/4tsp bicarbonate of soda
finely grated zest and juice of 1 lemon
125ml (4fl oz) natural yogurt
2tbsp milk

2 eggs
25g (1oz) butter, melted, plus butter
  for frying
sunflower oil, for frying
250g (9oz) blueberries
crème fraîche and lemon zest, to serve

1 Sift the flour into a bowl, add the 3tbsp sugar, the baking powder, bicarbonate of soda and lemon zest. Pour in the yogurt, milk and eggs and whisk together. Add the melted butter.
2 Heat a little sunflower oil and a knob of butter in a frying pan over a medium heat. Add 2tbsp of the mixture to the pan and swirl to spread it out. Drop a few blueberries on to each pancake – use about 100g (31/2oz) in total – and cook for 2 minutes, then flip the pancake and cook for 1–2 minutes. Repeat with the remaining mixture.
3 To make the blueberry syrup, dissolve the remaining sugar in 100ml (3½fl oz) water in a small pan over a low heat. Add the remaining blueberries, bring to the boil and bubble for 1 minute. Add the lemon juice, then put to one side for 2 minutes.
4 To serve, spoon the blueberry syrup over the pancakes and top with the crème fraîche and lemon zest.

Serves 4–8   preparation: 15 minutes   cooking time: 15–20 minutes
per serving: 460–230 cals; 12–6g fat; 83–41g carbohydrate

Orange Pancakes

175g (6oz) plain flour
pinch of salt
2tsp caster sugar
2 large eggs, plus 1 large egg yolk
475ml (16fl oz) milk
150g (5oz) butter

grated zest of 2 small oranges, plus extra
   zest to decorate
75g (3oz) icing sugar
2tbsp Grand Marnier (optional)
475ml (16fl oz) fresh orange juice

1 Sift the flour, salt and caster sugar into a bowl. Beat the eggs and egg yolk together in a separate bowl. Make a well in the centre of the flour mixture and add the eggs. Using a whisk or wooden spoon, and starting in the centre, gradually mix the eggs with the flour, slowly adding the milk as you do. Beat until you have a batter covered with bubbles. Cover and leave to stand in a cold place for at least 30 minutes.

2 Just before cooking the pancakes, melt 50g (2oz) butter and stir into the batter (this improves the flavour and texture of the pancakes and means you don't have to grease the pan after cooking each pancake).

3 Meanwhile, make the orange sauce. Put the remaining butter, the orange zest, icing sugar, Grand Marnier, if using, and orange juice into a pan and cook over a low heat until the butter has melted and the sugar has dissolved.

4 Put a non-stick crêpe pan over a high heat and pour in a small ladleful of batter – enough to form a film on the base. When bubbles appear on the surface, loosen the edges with a palette knife, flip over and cook briefly on the other side. Fold the pancake and slide on to a plate, spoon some of the sauce on top, sprinkle with orange zest and serve. Repeat with the remaining batter.

Makes 14–16 pancakes   preparation: 15 minutes, plus standing   cooking time: 25 minutes
per serving: 200 cals; 11g fat; 22g carbohydrate

Orange Eggy Bread

2 large eggs
150ml (¼pint) milk
finely grated zest and juice of 1 orange
8 slices raisin bread

butter, for frying
1tbsp caster sugar
orange slices, to serve

1 Lightly whisk the eggs with the milk and orange zest, then dip the bread into the mixture.

2 Heat the butter in a frying pan and fry the bread on both sides until golden. Sprinkle with the sugar and serve with orange slices.

Serves 4   preparation: 5 minutes   cooking time: 5 minutes
per serving: 340 cals; 15g fat; 44g carbohydrate

Strawberry and Melon Cup

300g (11oz) ogen melon, quartered, peeled
and deseeded
350g (12oz) strawberries, hulled and sliced
1.3 litres (2¼ pints) chilled lemonade

450ml (¾ pint) Pimms
ice cubes and sprigs of borage or mint,
to serve

1 Put the melon in a food processor or blender and whiz until smooth, then sieve.
2 Pour the melon into a jug, add the strawberries and top up with the lemonade and Pimms. Add plenty
of ice cubes and decorate with sprigs of borage or mint to serve.

Makes 1.7 litres (3 pints)   preparation: 10 minutes
for the whole jug: 590 cals; 0g fat; 253g carbohydrate

Spiked Strawberry Milkshake

450g (1lb) strawberries, hulled, plus extra to
decorate
1.1 litres (2 pints) semi-skimmed milk

8tbsp good-quality strawberry jam
75ml (3fl oz) Grand Marnier
ice cubes, to serve

1 Put the strawberries in a food processor or blender and whiz until smooth. Whisk in the milk and
strawberry jam, then add the Grand Marnier to taste.
2 Pour the milkshake into tall glasses, then top with ice cubes and decorate with extra strawberries to
serve.

Serves 4   preparation: 10 minutes
per serving: 290 cals; 4g fat; 46g carbohydrate

Strawberry and Pineapple Smoothie

225g (8oz) strawberries
200–250ml (7–9fl oz) unsweetened
pineapple juice

150g (5oz) low-fat strawberry yogurt

1 Put all the ingredients in a blender or food processor and whiz for 1 minute or until smooth.
2 Chill well, then pour into glasses and serve.

Serves 2   makes 450ml (¾ pint)   preparation: 5 minutes, plus chilling
per serving: 160 cals; 1g fat; 35g carbohydrate

Berry Smoothie

2 large bananas, about 450g (1lb), peeled
  and chopped
142ml carton natural yogurt

150ml (¼ pint) spring water
500g bag frozen summer fruits

1 Put the bananas, yogurt and spring water in a food processor and whiz until smooth. Add the frozen
   berries and whiz to a purée.
2 Sieve the mixture, using the back of a ladle to press it through. Pour into glasses and serve.

Serves 6 preparation: 10 minutes
per serving: 70 cals; trace fat; 15g carbohydrate

Mango and Passion Fruit Smoothie

4 passion fruit, halved
2 ripe mangoes, peeled and roughly
  chopped

2 bananas, peeled and chopped
600ml (1 pint) orange juice

1 Strain the passion fruit through a sieve into a bowl to get the juice. Discard the seeds and put the juice
   into a food processor or blender.
2 Add the mangoes, bananas and orange juice and whiz until smooth. Pour into glasses and serve.

Serves 6 preparation: 10 minutes
per serving: 100 cals; trace fat; 25g carbohydrate

Cranberry and Mango Smoothie

1 ripe mango, peeled and roughly chopped
200–250ml (7–9fl oz) fresh cranberry juice

150ml (¼ pint) low-fat peach yogurt

1 Put the mango in a blender or food processor with the cranberry juice and whiz for 1 minute or until
   smooth.
2 Add the yogurt, then whiz for 30 seconds or until mixed. Chill well, then pour into glasses and serve.

Serves 2 makes about 400ml (12fl oz) preparation: 5 minutes, plus chilling
per serving: 170 cals; 1g fat; 39g carbohydrate

Passion Fruit, Grape and Banana Smoothie

4 ripe passion fruit
150ml (¼ pint) low-fat bio-yogurt, plus
  1tbsp to decorate
8 ice cubes, crushed

4 ripe bananas, about 550g (1¼lb), peeled
  and roughly chopped
225g (8oz) seedless white grapes

1 Chill four tall glasses in the freezer. Cut the passion fruit in half and remove the pulp. Reserve 1tbsp of pulp to decorate and put the remainder in a blender with the rest of the ingredients and whiz until smooth. (The passion fruit pips will remain whole but are easy to drink.) Pour into the chilled glasses and decorate with the 1tbsp yogurt mixed with the reserved pulp, then serve.

Serves 4   makes 900ml (1½ pints)   preparation: 5 minutes, plus chilling
per serving: 140 cals; 1g fat; 33g carbohydrate

Prune, Apple and Cinnamon Smoothie

125g (4oz) ready-to-eat dried prunes
¼tsp ground cinnamon
300–350ml (10–12fl oz) unsweetened apple
  juice

4tbsp Greek-style yogurt

1 Using a sharp pair of scissors, snip the prunes finely into a bowl. Sprinkle the cinnamon over and pour the apple juice over the top. Cover the bowl and leave to stand overnight.
2 Put the prune mixture in a blender or food processor, add the yogurt and whiz for 1 minute or until smooth. Chill well, then pour into glasses and serve.

Serves 2   makes about 450ml (¾ pint)   preparation: 10 minutes, plus soaking and chilling
per serving: 210 cals; 3g fat; 45g carbohydrate

Raspberry and Kiwi Smoothie

3 kiwi fruit, peeled and roughly chopped
200g (7oz) fresh or frozen raspberries
200–250ml (7–9fl oz) unsweetened orange
  juice

4tbsp Greek-style yogurt
2–3tbsp icing sugar

1 Put the kiwi fruit in a blender or food processor with the raspberries, orange juice and yogurt. Whiz for 1 minute or until smooth, then add icing sugar to taste.
2 Chill well, then pour into glasses and serve.

Serves 2   makes 500–600 ml (1 pint)   preparation: 10 minutes
per serving: 200 cals; 3g fat; 43g carbohydrate

Banana and Mango Smoothie

1 ripe mango, peeled and roughly chopped
1 banana, peeled
200ml (7fl oz) semi-skimmed milk
150–200ml (5–7fl oz) unsweetened orange
   juice

3tbsp Greek-style yogurt
1tbsp icing sugar (optional)

1 Put the mango in a blender or food processor with the remaining ingredients, then whiz for 1 minute or until smooth.
2 Chill well, then pour into glasses and serve.

Serves 2 makes about 600ml (1 pint) preparation: 5 minutes, plus chilling
per serving: 270 cals; 4g fat; 56g carbohydrate

Virgin Strawberry Daiquiri

225g (8oz) strawberries, hulled, plus extra
   to decorate
50ml (2fl oz) lime cordial

3tbsp caster sugar
125g (4oz) ice cubes

1 Put all the ingredients in a blender or food processor, then whiz for 1–2 minutes until smooth.
2 Chill well, then serve the daiquiri in chilled glasses, topped with a fresh strawberry.

Serves 2–3 preparation: 5 minutes, plus chilling
per serving: 150–100 cals; 0g fat; 38–25g carbohydrate

Apricot and Orange Smoothie

400g (14oz) canned apricots in natural juice
150ml (¼ pint) apricot yogurt

200–250ml (7–9fl oz) unsweetened orange
   juice

1 Put all the ingredients in a blender or food processor and whiz for 1 minute or until smooth.
2 Chill well, then pour into glasses and serve.

Serves 2 makes about 450ml (¾ pint) preparation: 5 minutes, plus chilling
per serving: 250 cals; 1g fat; 61g carbohydrate

Spicy Tomato Cocktail

200g (7oz) canned pimientos
juice of 1½ lemons
1 medium onion, peeled and chopped
2tbsp horseradish sauce
1 litre (1¾ pints) tomato juice

2tsp Worcestershire sauce
1tsp Tabasco
pepper
175ml (6fl oz) vodka (optional)
finely chopped spring onions, to garnish

1 Put the pimientos in a blender (better than a food processor as the drink will be smoother), add the lemon juice, onion and horseradish sauce and whiz until blended.
2 Gradually add the tomato juice and stir until smooth. Season with the Worcestershire sauce, Tabasco and pepper. Chill until ready to serve.
3 If using the vodka, put 25ml (1fl oz) into each glass and top up with the tomato mixture. Garnish with the spring onions and serve.

Serves 6   preparation: 10 minutes, plus chilling
per serving: 120 cals (60 cals without vodka); 1g fat; 11g carbohydrate

Citrus Gin Sling

1½ lemons
3tbsp golden caster sugar
150ml (¼ pint) each freshly squeezed lemon
   juice and lime juice

150ml (¼ pint) gin
ice cubes and soda or mineral water, to
   serve

1 Rub half a lemon around the rim of six glasses. Put 1tbsp sugar on a saucer and press the rim of each glass into the sugar.
2 Put the lemon and lime juices in a cocktail shaker or screw-topped jar with the remaining sugar and the gin and shake well.
3 Slice the remaining lemon. Serve the gin sling over ice, topped up with soda or mineral water to taste. Decorate with a slice of lemon.

Serves 6   preparation: 5 minutes
per serving: 90 cals; 0g fat; 9g carbohydrate

Lunch

You want something quick but tasty, filling but light. Soup always fits the bill and there's a soup to suit whatever the weather. Try a bowl of light and refreshing Herb and Lemon Soup for a lazy lunch in the sun, or, when there's a nip in the air, a warming Autumn Vegetable Soup, served with chewy wedges of Welsh rarebit.

Need something a bit more substantial, or perhaps you've got friends coming round? You can't go wrong with fish – light and healthy. Trout with Apple and Watercress Salad is delicious oven-baked fish served with a moreish mixture of baby new potatoes, apples, beetroot and watercress. Or there's Lime and Coriander Crab Cakes, served with a chilli mayo – irresistible. Make and chill them in advance, then all you have to do is whack them in hot oil for a few minutes and hey presto, lunch is served.

And don't forget the lunchtime classics – tortillas and frittatas. How versatile they are, inexpensive, satisfying and nourishing – and a great way to use up vegetables. The Pancetta Tortilla is a meal in itself, stuffed with tender slices of leeks and potatoes and spiced with tasty pancetta. Real feel-good food.

Miso Mushroom and Spinach Soup

1tbsp vegetable oil

1 medium onion, peeled, halved
  and finely sliced

120g pack shiitake mushrooms,
  finely sliced

225g bag baby spinach leaves

4 x 284ml cartons fresh fish stock

4tbsp mugi miso (fermented soya beans)

1 Heat the oil in a large pan and gently sauté the onion for 15 minutes.
2 Add the mushrooms and cook for 5 minutes, then stir in the spinach and stock. Heat for 3 minutes, then stir in the mugi miso – don't boil the soup as miso is a live culture.
3 Spoon into bowls and serve.

Serves 6   preparation: 5 minutes   cooking time: 25 minutes
per serving: 60cals; 3g fat; 6g carbohydrate

Mixed Mushroom Soup

15g (½oz) dried porcini mushrooms

1tbsp oil, plus 50ml (2fl oz) to shallow-fry

1 small onion, peeled and chopped

450g (1lb) chestnut mushrooms, chopped

600ml (1 pint) hot vegetable stock

salt and pepper

2 slices white bread, crusts removed, cut
  into cubes

2 garlic cloves, peeled and finely sliced

chopped flat-leafed parsley, to garnish

1 Put the porcini into a bowl, pour over 75ml (3fl oz) boiling water and soak for 10 minutes. Strain the mushrooms, reserving the liquid, then roughly chop the porcini, keeping 1tbsp to use as a garnish.
2 Heat 1tbsp oil in a pan, add the onion and porcini and cook over a medium heat for 5 minutes. Add the chestnut mushrooms, increase the heat and brown lightly for 5 minutes.
3 Add the porcini liquid and hot stock, season well and bring to the boil. Reduce the heat and simmer for 20 minutes.
4 To make the croûtons, heat the 50ml (2fl oz) oil in a frying pan, add the bread and garlic and stir-fry for 2 minutes until golden. Drain on kitchen paper.
5 Cool the soup slightly, then whiz in a liquidiser until smooth. Pour the soup into a clean pan and reheat gently. Serve in warmed bowls, topped with the croûtons, reserved porcini and a sprinkling of chopped parsley.

Serves 4   preparation: 15 minutes, plus soaking   cooking time: 35 minutes
per serving: 210 cals; 15g fat; 14g carbohydrate

Celery Soup

25g (1oz) butter
1tbsp olive oil
1 medium leek, sliced
6 celery sticks, finely sliced

1tbsp finely chopped sage
600ml (1 pint) hot chicken stock
300ml (½ pint) full-fat milk
salt and pepper

1   Melt the butter in a pan and add the olive oil. Fry the leek for 10–15 minutes until soft.
2   Add the celery and sage to the pan and cook for 5 minutes to soften. Add the hot stock and milk, season, cover the pan and bring to the boil. Reduce the heat and simmer for 10–15 minutes or until the celery is tender. Cool the soup slightly, then whiz in a liquidiser until smooth. Pour the soup into a clean pan, reheat gently and season to taste. Serve in warmed bowls.

Serves 4   preparation: 5 minutes   cooking time: 45 minutes
per serving: 130 cals; 11g fat; 5g carbohydrate

Courgette and Leek Soup

1tbsp olive oil
1 onion, peeled and finely chopped
2 leeks, sliced
900g (2lb) courgettes, grated
1.3 litres (2¼ pints) hot vegetable or
   chicken stock

4 short rosemary sprigs
salt and pepper
1 small baguette
125g (4oz) Gruyère cheese, grated

1   Heat the olive oil in a large pan. Add the onion and leeks and cook for 5–10 minutes. Add the courgettes and cook, stirring, for a further 5 minutes.
2   Add the hot stock and 3 rosemary sprigs, then bring to the boil. Season, reduce the heat and simmer for 20 minutes.
3   Preheat the grill to medium-high. Slice the bread diagonally into eight and grill for 1–2 minutes on one side until golden. Turn the bread over, sprinkle with the cheese and season. Grill for a further 1–2 minutes. Keep the croûtes warm.
4   Cool the soup slightly. Remove the rosemary stalks and whiz the soup in a liquidiser until smooth. Pour the soup into a clean pan and reheat gently. Serve in warmed bowls with the croûtes and sprinkled with the remaining rosemary leaves.

Serves 8   preparation: 15 minutes   cooking time: 35–40 minutes
per serving: 310 cals; 14g fat; 32g carbohydrate

Squash and Sweet Potato Soup

1 tbsp olive oil
1 large onion, peeled and finely chopped
1–2 red chillies, deseeded and chopped
2 tsp coriander seeds, crushed
1 butternut squash, about 750g (1lb 10oz),
   peeled, deseeded and roughly chopped
2 medium sweet potatoes, peeled and
roughly chopped
2 tomatoes, skinned and diced
1.7 litres (3 pints) hot vegetable stock
salt and pepper

1 Heat the olive oil in a large pan, add the onion and fry for about 10 minutes until soft. Add the chillies and coriander seeds to the pan and cook for 1–2 minutes.
2 Add the squash, potatoes and tomatoes and cook for 5 minutes. Add the hot stock, then cover the pan and bring to the boil. Simmer gently for 15 minutes or until the vegetables are soft.
3 Whiz the soup in batches in a blender or food processor until smooth. Adjust the seasoning and reheat to serve.

Serves 8   preparation: 15 minutes   cooking time: 25 minutes
per serving: 100 cals; 2g fat; 19g carbohydrate

Leek and Potato Soup

25g (1oz) butter
1 onion, peeled and finely chopped
1 garlic clove, peeled and crushed
550g (1¼lb) leeks, chopped
200g (7oz) floury potatoes
1.3 litres (2¼ pints) hot vegetable stock
salt and pepper

1 Melt the butter in a pan and cook the onion over a low heat for 10–15 minutes until soft.
2 Add the garlic and cook for 1 minute, then add the leeks and cook for 5–10 minutes until softened. Add the potatoes and toss together with the leeks.
3 Add the hot stock, bring to the boil, then reduce the heat and simmer for 20 minutes until the potatoes are tender.
4 Cool the soup a little, then whiz in a liquidiser until smooth. Pour the soup into a clean pan, reheat gently and season to taste. Serve in warmed bowls.

Serves 6   preparation: 10 minutes   cooking time: 50 minutes
per serving: 90 cals; 4g fat; 11g carbohydrate

Minestrone with Croûtes

1tbsp olive oil
1 onion, peeled and finely sliced
1 garlic clove, peeled and crushed
2 medium courgettes, finely diced
2 red peppers, deseeded and finely diced
1 small aubergine, finely diced
400g can chopped tomatoes
1.3 litres (2¼ pints) hot vegetable stock

50g (2oz) dried soup pasta
400g can cannellini beans, drained
 and rinsed
3tbsp roughly torn basil leaves, plus extra
 sprigs to garnish
4 slices French stick
125g (4oz) grated Cheddar cheese

1 Heat the olive oil in a large pan, add the onion and garlic and cook over a medium heat for 10 minutes until soft.
2 Add the courgettes, peppers and aubergine to the pan and cook for 5 minutes. Stir in the tomatoes, then add the hot stock and simmer, half-covered, for 30 minutes. Stir in the pasta and cannellini beans and simmer for 10 minutes until the pasta is cooked, then stir in the basil.
3 To make the croûtes, grill the French stick slices on one side until golden. Turn them over, sprinkle 25g (1oz) grated Cheddar over each and grill for 1–2 minutes.
4 Pour the soup into warmed bowls, top each with a croûte and serve.

Serves 4 preparation 20 minutes   cooking time: 1 hour
per serving: 340 cals; 10g fat; 51g carbohydrate

Beetroot Soup

750g (1lb 10oz) raw beetroot
1tbsp olive oil
1 onion, peeled and finely chopped
275g (10oz) potatoes, peeled and roughly
 chopped
2 litres (3½ pints) hot vegetable stock

juice of 1 lemon
salt and pepper
125ml (4fl oz) soured cream
25g (1oz) mixed root vegetable crisps
 (optional)
2tbsp snipped chives

1 Peel the beetroot and cut into 1cm (½ inch) cubes. Heat the olive oil in a large pan, add the onion and cook for 5 minutes to soften. Add the beetroot and potatoes and cook for a further 5 minutes.
2 Add the hot stock and lemon juice and bring to the boil. Season, reduce the heat and simmer, half-covered, for 25 minutes. Cool slightly, then whiz in a blender or food processor until smooth.
3 Pour the soup into a clean pan and reheat gently. Divide the soup among warmed bowls. Swirl 1tbsp soured cream on each portion, scatter with a few vegetable crisps, if using, and sprinkle with snipped chives to serve.

Serves 8 preparation: 15 minutes   cooking time: 40–45 minutes
per serving: 290 cals; 25g fat; 15g carbohydrate

Pumpkin and Butternut Squash Soup

900g (2lb) pumpkin, peeled
  and roughly diced
750g (1lb 10oz) butternut squash,
  peeled and roughly diced
125g (4oz) shallots, blanched in boiling
  water, drained, peeled and roughly
  chopped

1 fat garlic clove, peeled and chopped
1tsp coriander seeds, crushed
125g (4oz) butter, melted
salt and pepper
600ml (1 pint) each vegetable
  stock and full-fat milk
basil sprigs and soured cream, to garnish

1 Preheat the oven to 220°C (200°C fan oven) mark 7. Put the pumpkin, squash, shallots, garlic and coriander seeds in a large roasting tin and toss with the melted butter. Season the vegetables well and bake for about 30 minutes until golden and just cooked through.
2 Meanwhile, in separate pans, heat the stock and milk.
3 Transfer the vegetables to a large pan, then pour the hot stock into the roasting tin and stir to loosen the remaining bits in the tin. Add this to the vegetables in the pan, then stir in the milk.
4 Put three-quarters of the soup into a food processor or blender and whiz until smooth. Mash the remaining soup mixture, then stir the two together and reheat gently. Pour into warmed bowls, garnish with basil and swirls of soured cream, then serve with small Yorkshire puddings or crusty bread.

Serves 4 preparation: 20 minutes   cooking time: 40 minutes
per serving: 430 cals; 32g fat; 28g carbohydrate

Hot and Sour Turkey Soup

1tbsp vegetable oil
2 turkey breasts, about 300g (11oz),
  cut into strips
5cm (2 inch) piece fresh root ginger,
  peeled and grated
4 spring onions, finely sliced

1–2tbsp Thai red curry paste
75g (3oz) long-grain wild rice
1.1 litres (2 pints) hot weak chicken or
  vegetable stock or boiling water
200g (7oz) mangetout, sliced
juice of 1 lime

1 Heat the oil in a deep pan. Add the turkey strips and cook over a medium heat for 5 minutes until browned.
2 Add the ginger and spring onions and cook for a further 2–3 minutes. Stir in the curry paste and cook for 1–2 minutes to warm the spices.
3 Add the rice and stir to coat in the curry paste. Pour the hot stock or water into the pan, stir once, then bring to the boil. Reduce the heat, cover the pan and leave to simmer for 20 minutes.
4 Add the mangetout and cook for 5 minutes or until the rice is cooked. Just before serving, squeeze in the lime juice and stir to mix. Ladle into bowls.

Serves 4 preparation: 20 minutes   cooking time: 30–35 minutes
per serving: 210 cals; 6g fat; 18g carbohydrate

Roasted Tomato and Pepper Soup

1.4kg (3lb) full-flavoured tomatoes,
  preferably vine-ripened
2 red peppers, cored, deseeded
  and chopped
4 garlic cloves, peeled and crushed
3 small onions, peeled and thinly sliced

20g (¾oz) thyme sprigs
2 tbsp olive oil
4 tbsp Worcestershire sauce
4 tbsp vodka
Salt and pepper
6 tbsp half-fat crème fraîche

1 Remove any green stalk heads from the tomatoes and discard. Put the tomatoes into a large roasting tin with the peppers, garlic and onions. Scatter 6 thyme sprigs on top, drizzle with the olive oil and roast at 200°C (180°C fan oven) mark 6 for 25 minutes. Turn the vegetables over and roast for a further 30–40 minutes until tender and slightly charred.
2 Put one third of the vegetables into a blender or food processor with 300ml (½ pint) boiled water. Add the Worcestershire sauce and vodka, plus plenty of salt and pepper. Whiz until smooth, then pass through a sieve into a pan.
3 Whiz the remaining vegetables with 450ml (¾ pint) boiled water, then sieve and add to the pan.
4 To serve, warm the soup thoroughly, stirring occasionally. Pour into warmed bowls, add 1 tbsp crème fraîche to each, then drag a cocktail stick through the cream to create a swirl. Scatter a few fresh thyme leaves over the top to finish.

Serves 6   preparation: 15 minutes, plus chilling
per serving: 170 cals; 14g fat; 9g carbohydrate

Herb and Lemon Soup

1.7 litres (3 pints) chicken stock
125g (4oz) dried orzo or other 'soup' pasta
3 eggs
juice of 1 large lemon

2tbsp each finely chopped chives and
    chervil
salt and pepper
very fine lemon slices, to garnish

1   Bring the stock to the boil in a large pan. Add the pasta and cook for 5 minutes or according to the
    time stated on the pack.
2   Beat the eggs in a bowl until frothy, then add the lemon juice and 1tbsp cold water. Slowly stir in two
    ladles of the hot stock. Return the mixture to the pan, then warm through over a very low heat for 2–3
    minutes. Don't boil the soup after adding the eggs – they will curdle.
3   Add the herbs and season. Serve in soup bowls, garnished with lemon slices.

Serves 6   preparation: 10 minutes   cooking time: 15–20 minutes
per serving: 120 cals; 4g fat; 15g carbohydrate

Summer Vegetable Soup with Herb Pistou

3tbsp sunflower oil
1 medium onion, peeled and finely chopped
225g (8oz) waxy potatoes, peeled and
   finely diced
175g (6oz) carrots, peeled and finely diced
1 medium turnip, peeled and finely diced
salt and pepper
4 bay leaves
6 large sage leaves
2 courgettes, about 375g (13oz),
   finely diced

175g (6oz) French beans, trimmed
   and halved
125g (4oz) shelled small peas
225g (8oz) tomatoes, deseeded and
   finely diced
1 small head broccoli, broken into florets
Herb Pistou (see page 16) or ready-made
   pesto, to serve

1   Heat the oil in a large pan, add the onion, potatoes, carrots and turnip and fry over a gentle heat for
    10 minutes. Add 1.7 litres (3 pints) cold water, season well, bring to the boil and add the bay and sage
    leaves. Reduce the heat and simmer for 25 minutes.
2   Add the courgettes, French beans, peas and tomatoes to the pan. Return to the boil, then simmer
    for 10–15 minutes. Add the broccoli 5 minutes before the end of the cooking time.
3   Remove the bay and sage leaves and adjust the seasoning. Pour the soup into bowls, remove 12 French
    beans, add a spoonful of Herb Pistou or pesto and garnish with the reserved French beans.

Serves 4–6   preparation: 45 minutes   cooking time: 1 hour
per serving: 200–130 cals; 11–7g fat ; 20–13g carbohydrate

Spicy Thai Soup

1tbsp vegetable oil
1 medium onion, peeled and finely sliced
1–1½tbsp tom yum soup paste
1.4 litres (2½ pints) hot fish or vegetable
   stock

450g (1lb) raw, shelled prawns
2tbsp chopped coriander, plus sprigs
   to garnish
1 lime, quartered, to serve

1 Heat the oil in a deep pan, add the onion and cook over a medium heat for 10 minutes until softened
   and golden. Stir in the tom yum paste and cook, stirring, for 2 minutes.
2 Pour in the hot stock, bring to the boil, then reduce the heat and simmer for 5 minutes.
3 Add the prawns and cook for a further 3–4 minutes until they're cooked through and have turned bright
   pink. Stir in the chopped coriander, then pour the soup into warmed bowls, garnish each with a
   coriander sprig and serve with a lime wedge to squeeze over.

Serves 4   preparation: 10 minutes   cooking time: 20–25 minutes
per serving:150 cals; 4g fat; 4g carbohydrate

Roasted Tomato Soup with Cod and Pesto

800g (1¾lb) ripe tomatoes, halved
2 garlic cloves, peeled and chopped
1 small red onion, peeled and finely
   chopped
200ml (7fl oz) olive oil
salt and pepper

25g (1oz) each chopped basil and
   flat-leafed parsley
1tbsp lemon juice
450ml (¾ pint) hot vegetable stock
4 x 150g (5oz) thick cod steaks

1 Preheat the oven to 220°C (200°C fan oven) mark 7. Put the tomatoes, 1½ garlic cloves and the
   onion in a roasting tin, drizzle with 50ml (2fl oz) olive oil and season well. Cook in the oven for
   25 minutes, stirring occasionally.
2 Meanwhile, make the pesto: whiz the herbs, the remaining garlic, the lemon juice and 100ml
   (3½fl oz) olive oil in a food processor to form a thick paste; season to taste.
3 Put the tomatoes in a food processor or blender and whiz briefly to form a thick, chunky purée. Pour
   into a pan with the hot stock, stir together and gently heat through.
4 Season the fish. Heat the remaining olive oil in a large non-stick frying pan and fry the fish for about
   2 minutes on each side. Ladle the hot soup into warmed bowls, then put a piece of fish in the middle
   of each. Drizzle with a generous spoonful of pesto and serve.

Serves 4   preparation: 15 minutes   cooking time: 35 minutes
per serving: 498 cals; 0g fat; 0g carbohydrate

Autumn Vegetable Soup

50g (2oz) butter
1 medium onion, peeled and diced
450g (1lb) potatoes, peeled and diced
100g (3½oz) pack diced smoked bacon
1 garlic clove, peeled and chopped
100g (3½oz) white of leek, chopped
2 Cox's Orange Pippins apples, unpeeled,
    cored and chopped

2tsp dried thyme
1tsp dill seeds (optional)
salt and pepper
600ml (1 pint) good-quality dry cider
900ml (1½ pints) hot vegetable stock
125g (4oz) Savoy cabbage leaves, shredded

1   Melt the butter in a large pan, then add the onion, potatoes, bacon, garlic, leek, apple, thyme and dill, if using. Season, stir, then cover and cook gently for 15 minutes.
2   Add the cider and bring to the boil, then reduce the heat and simmer for 5 minutes. Add the hot stock and simmer for about 15 minutes until the potatoes are soft.
3   Pour half the soup into a liquidiser and whiz until smooth, then add to the remaining soup. Reheat gently, add the shredded cabbage and simmer for a further 3 minutes. Ladle into warmed bowls and serve.

Serves 4   preparation: 15 minutes   cooking time: 45 minutes
per serving: 380 cals; 21g fat; 34g carbohydrate

Hot Spicy Gazpacho

75g (3oz) ciabatta, cut into small cubes
4tbsp extra-virgin olive oil
large pinch each sea salt flakes and paprika
900g (2lb) very ripe cherry tomatoes
1 cucumber, peeled, halved lengthways and
    deseeded
1 garlic clove, peeled and chopped
1 red chilli, deseeded and finely chopped

2 spring onions, finely chopped
4tbsp extra-virgin olive oil
1tbsp red wine vinegar
1tbsp golden caster sugar
salt and pepper
extra paprika and a handful of wild rocket,
    to garnish

1   Preheat the oven to 190°C (170°C fan oven) mark 5. To make the croûtons, put the bread in a bowl, add the olive oil and sprinkle with sea salt flakes and paprika. Toss everything together, transfer to a baking tray and bake, turning occasionally, for 10 minutes or until golden brown.
2   To make the soup, put all the remaining ingredients, except the seasoning and garnishes, into a blender or food processor and whiz until smooth. Pour into a pan and heat gently until warm, then season to taste.
3   To serve, spoon the soup into warmed bowls, top each with a few croûtons, sprinkle over a little paprika and garnish with a rocket leaf.

Serves 4   preparation: 20 minutes   cooking time: 15 minutes
per serving: 340 cals; 28g fat; 21g carbohydrate

Smoked Cod and Sweetcorn Chowder

130g pack diced pancetta
50g (2oz) butter
3 leeks, about 450g (1lb), trimmed and
   thinly sliced
25g (1oz) plain flour
568ml carton semi-skimmed or full-fat milk
700g (1½lb) undyed smoked cod loin or
   haddock, skinned and cut into 2cm
   (¾ inch) cubes

326g can sweetcorn in water, drained
450g (1lb) small new potatoes, sliced
142ml carton double cream
½tsp paprika
salt and pepper
2tbsp chopped flat-leafed parsley,
   to garnish

1 Fry the pancetta in a large non-stick pan, until the fat runs out. Add the butter to the pan to melt, then add the leeks and cook until softened.
2 Stir in the flour and cook for a few seconds, then pour in the milk and 300ml (½ pint) water.
3 Add the fish to the pan with the sweetcorn and potatoes. Bring to the boil, then reduce the heat and simmer for 10–15 minutes until the potatoes are cooked.
4 Stir in the cream and paprika, season and cook for 2–3 minutes to warm through. Ladle into wide shallow bowls and sprinkle each with a little chopped parsley.

Serves 6   preparation: 15 minutes   cooking time: 40 minutes
per serving: 530 cals; 30g fat; 36g carbohydrate

Spicy Thai Chicken Soup

1tbsp vegetable oil
1 small onion, peeled and sliced
300g (11oz) stir-fry chicken pieces
1–2tbsp red Thai curry paste
600ml (1 pint) hot chicken stock
400g can chopped tomatoes

100g (3½oz) sugarsnap peas, halved
150g (5oz) baby sweetcorn, halved
4tbsp chopped coriander
grated zest of ½ lime
1 lime, quartered, to serve

1 Heat the oil in a large frying pan or wok. Add the onion and fry for 5 minutes until it begins to soften. Add the chicken and cook for a further 5 minutes until golden brown, then add the curry paste and fry for 1 minute to warm the spices through.
2 Pour in the hot stock and tomatoes, then simmer for 5 minutes. Add the sugarsnap peas and baby sweetcorn and cook for 1 minute until the chicken is cooked through. Pour the soup into warmed bowls, sprinkle with coriander and lime zest, and serve each with a wedge of lime.

Serves 4   preparation: 2–3 minutes   cooking time: 17 minutes
per serving: 180 cals; 8g fat; 8g carbohydrate

Chicken and Bean Soup

1tbsp olive oil
1 onion, peeled and finely chopped
4 celery sticks, chopped
1 red chilli, deseeded and roughly chopped
2 skinless boneless chicken breasts, cut
  into strips
1 litre (1¾ pints) hot chicken or vegetable
  stock

100g (3½oz) bulgur wheat
2 x 400g cans cannellini beans, drained and
  rinsed
400g can chopped tomatoes
25g (1oz) flat-leafed parsley, roughly
  chopped

1 Heat the olive oil in a large heavy-based pan. Add the onion, celery and chilli and cook over a low heat
   for 10 minutes until softened. Add the chicken and stir-fry for 3–4 minutes until golden.
2 Add the hot stock to the pan and bring to a simmer. Stir in the bulgur wheat and simmer for
   15 minutes. Stir in the cannellini beans and tomatoes and return to a simmer. Sprinkle the chopped
   parsley over and ladle into warmed bowls.

Serves 4   preparation: 10 minutes   cooking time: 30 minutes
per serving: 370 cals; 8g fat; 49g carbohydrate

Coconut Broth and Chicken Noodles

1tbsp vegetable oil
2tbsp tom yum (or Thai red curry) soup
  paste
900ml (1½ pints) hot chicken stock
400ml can unsweetened coconut milk
200g (7oz) thread egg noodles

2 x large skinless boneless chicken breasts,
  cut into thin strips
350g (12oz) pack stir-fry vegetables
salt and pepper
coriander leaves, to garnish

1 Heat the oil in a large pan and fry the soup paste for about 10 seconds. Add the hot stock and
   coconut milk, bring to the boil, then reduce the heat and simmer for about 5 minutes.
2 Meanwhile, cook the noodles in plenty of boiling water for the time stated on the packet.
3 Add the chicken strips to the simmering soup and cook for 3 minutes. Add the stir-fry vegetables, mix
   well and season.
4 Divide the egg noodles among four large warmed bowls, pour the soup on top, then garnish with the
   coriander and serve with prawn crackers.

Serves 4   preparation: 5 minutes   cooking time: 15 minutes
per serving: 440 cals; 19g fat; 42g carbohydrate

Easy Pea Soup

1 small loaf of French stick, thinly sliced
2tbsp basil oil, plus extra to drizzle
454g bag frozen peas, defrosted

600ml (1 pint) vegetable stock
salt and pepper

1 Preheat the oven to 220°C (200°C fan oven) mark 7. To make the croûtons, put the bread on a baking sheet, drizzle with 2tbsp basil oil and bake for 10–15 minutes until golden.
2 Meanwhile, put the peas in a food processor, add the stock and season, then whiz for 2–3 minutes.
3 Pour the soup into a pan and bring to the boil, then reduce the heat and simmer for 10 minutes. Spoon into warmed bowls, add the croûtons, drizzle with oil and sprinkle with salt and pepper.

Serves 4 preparation: 2 minutes, plus defrosting   cooking time: 15 minutes
per serving: 260 cals; 10g fat; 35g carbohydrate

Turkey, Ham and Spinach Broth

125g (4oz) green or yellow split peas,
  soaked overnight in double their volume
  of cold water
25g (1oz) butter
225g (8oz) onions, peeled and chopped
1tbsp ground coriander
40g (1½oz) pearl barley
2 litres (3½ pints) ham or turkey stock
1 each bay leaf, celery stick and thyme sprig
225g (8oz) potatoes, peeled and cut into
  chunks

400g (14oz) carrots, peeled and
  cut into chunks
salt and pepper
150g (5oz) each cooked turkey and
ham, cut into chunks
150g (5oz) baby spinach leaves
coriander sprigs and black pepper,
to garnish
50g (2oz) finely grated Parmesan cheese,
to serve (optional)

1 Drain the split peas, put in a pan and cover with cold water. Bring to the boil, reduce the heat and simmer for 10 minutes. Drain the peas and discard the liquid.
2 Meanwhile, melt the butter in a pan, add the onions and cook for 5 minutes or until soft but not coloured. Add the ground coriander and cook for 30 seconds.
3 Add the split peas, pearl barley and stock to the pan. Tie the bay leaf, celery and thyme sprig together and add to the pan. Bring to the boil, reduce the heat and simmer for 40 minutes or until the peas and barley are tender. Add the potatoes and cook for 5 minutes, then add the carrots and cook for 5–10 minutes. Season well.
4 Add the turkey, ham and spinach to the pan and bring back to the boil, then reduce the heat and simmer for 2–3 minutes. Pour into warmed bowls, garnish with coriander sprigs and pepper and serve with grated Parmesan, if using.

Serves 6 preparation: 20 minutes, plus soaking   cooking time: 1¼ hours
per serving: 300 cals; 6g fat; 34g carbohydrate

Grilled Artichoke Salad

400g can artichoke hearts, drained and
    halved
salt and pepper

olive oil
3 little gem lettuces
Vinaigrette Dressing (see below)

1 Preheat the grill. Season the artichoke hearts and brush with the olive oil, then grill until charred.
2 Toss the lettuces in the dressing with the artichokes and serve.

Serves 4   preparation: 2 minutes   cooking time: 5 minutes
per serving without dressing: 40 cals; 4g fat; 2g carbohydrate

Vinaigrette Dressing

200ml (7fl oz) extra-virgin olive oil
200ml (7fl oz) grapeseed oil
125ml (4fl oz) white wine vinegar

pinch each sugar and English
    mustard powder
2 garlic cloves, peeled and crushed
    (optional)

Put the oils, vinegar, sugar, mustard powder and garlic, if using, into a large screw-topped jar. Shake well, season to taste and store in a cool place.

Makes about 600ml (1 pint)   preparation: 5 minutes
per 1tsp: 27 cals; 3g fat; trace carbohydrate

Melon with Cucumber Salad and Bresaola

20 slices Bresaola, about 200g (7oz)
3 Charentais melons, peeled and sliced
½ cucumber, deseeded and finely diced

2tbsp extra-virgin olive oil
salt and pepper
3 ciabatta loaves or country-style bread

1 Preheat the oven to 200°C (180°C fan oven) mark 6. Put the bresaola on two baking sheets and roast for 10–15 minutes or until crisp.
2 Make the salad. Put the melon and cucumber in a large serving bowl, drizzle over the olive oil and season well. Divide between 10 plates and add the crisp bresaola. Serve with the bread.

Serves 10   preparation: 10 minutes   cooking time: 5 minutes
per serving: 300 cals; 9g fat; 45g carbohydrate

Special Green Salad

1 head cos lettuce or Chinese leaves,
  trimmed, shredded and rinsed
200g bag continental salad leaves
1 cucumber, halved lengthways and sliced
3 ripe-and-ready avocados
25g (1oz) pine nuts, toasted

6tbsp olive or walnut oil
4tbsp cider vinegar
2tbsp maple syrup
1tsp English mustard powder
salt and pepper

1 Put the cos lettuce or Chinese leaves into the base of a glass bowl. Top with the salad leaves and cucumber.
2 Quarter the avocados. Peel, remove the stone and slice. Add to the salad with the pine nuts.
3 To make dressing, put the oil into a screw-topped jar with the vinegar, maple syrup and mustard and season. Seal and shake well. Drizzle over the salad just before serving.

Serves 12   preparation: 15 minutes   cooking time: 2–3 minutes
per serving: 170 cals; 16g fat; 3g carbohydrate

Grilled Corn and Sprouting Bean Salad

2 corn on the cob
2.5cm (1 inch) piece fresh root ginger,
  peeled and finely grated
finely grated zest and juice of 1 orange
4tsp soy sauce
salt and pepper

3tbsp olive oil
225g (8oz) beansprouts
2 little gem lettuces
mixed salad leaves, such as baby spinach
  and frisée lettuce

1 Preheat the grill to high. Grill the corn until golden brown on all sides. Cool, then carefully cut the kernels from the cob with a sharp knife.
2 Whisk together the ginger, orange zest, 3tbsp orange juice and the soy sauce and season, then whisk in the olive oil.
3 Toss the corn kernels and beansprouts with the ginger dressing and leave to marinate for 10 minutes.
4 Just before serving, toss the dressing mixture into the salad leaves.

Serves 6–8   preparation: 30 minutes, plus marinating   cooking time: 10 minutes
per serving for 6: 120–90 cals; 7–6g fat; 10–8g carbohydrate

Radicchio and Walnut Salad

1 small radicchio

1 oak leaf lettuce

6tbsp olive oil

1 small red chilli, deseeded and finely

   chopped

2tbsp red wine vinegar

2tsp Dijon mustard

salt and pepper

25g (1oz) walnut pieces

1 red onion, peeled and thinly sliced

1 About 2 hours before serving, separate the leaves from the lettuces and tear large ones in half. Put them in a sink of ice-cold water and swirl around, then dry in a salad spinner or in a colander lined with kitchen paper. Put the leaves on to a clean tea-towel, wrap loosely and put in the salad drawer of the fridge.

2 Preheat the grill to high. Heat 1tbsp olive oil in a pan and fry the chilli for 1–2 minutes. Remove the pan from the heat and stir in the remaining olive oil, the vinegar and the mustard. Cool, season and set aside.

3 Toast the walnuts under the grill for 1 minute then cool, chop and set aside.

4 Just before serving, put the salad leaves into a salad bowl. Add the walnuts, onion and dressing and toss well.

Serves 6   preparation: 15 minutes   cooking time: 5 minutes

per serving: 230 cals; 23g fat; 5g carbohydrate

Asparagus, Spinach and Potato Salad

450g (1lb) small potatoes
125ml (4fl oz) extra-virgin olive oil
salt and pepper
2 shallots, blanched in boiling water,
  drained, peeled and finely chopped

4tbsp white wine vinegar
900g (2lb) asparagus, trimmed and woody
  stems removed
225g (8oz) young spinach leaves, any tough
  stalks removed

1 Preheat the oven to 220°C (200°C fan oven) mark 7. Put the potatoes in a roasting tin, drizzle with
   1tbsp olive oil and season. Roast for 20–30 minutes or until just soft to the centre, then remove from
   the oven and cool.
2 Meanwhile, make the dressing. In a small bowl, whisk together some salt, pepper, the shallots, vinegar
   and the remaining oil. Slice the potatoes thickly, put into a large bowl, pour the dressing over and marinate
   for 10 minutes.
3 Cook the asparagus in boiling salted water for 3–4 minutes – the thick end of the stalks should be
   just tender with some bite. Drain carefully and put into a bowl of ice-cold water to retain the colour
   and stop the spears cooking further. Drain again, then add to the potatoes with the spinach. Toss
   together carefully and serve.

Serves 6   preparation: 5 minutes   cooking time: 20–30 minutes, plus marinating
per serving: 270 cals; 20g fat; 16g carbohydrate

Throw-it-all-together Salad

2–4 chargrilled chicken breasts, torn into
  strips
2 medium carrots, peeled into strips
½ cucumber, cut into ribbons
handful of coriander leaves, roughly
  chopped
½ head Chinese leaves, shredded

4 handfuls of watercress
4 spring onions, shredded
5tbsp peanut butter
2tbsp sweet chilli sauce
juice of 1 lime
salt and pepper

1 Put the chicken, carrot, cucumber, coriander leaves, Chinese leaves, watercress and spring onions
   into a large salad bowl.
2 To make the dressing, put the peanut butter, sweet chilli sauce and lime juice into a small bowl and
   mix well. Season to taste. Add 2–3tbsp cold water, 1tbsp at a time, to thin the dressing if it's too
   thick to pour.
3 Drizzle the dressing over the top of the salad, toss together and serve.

Serves 4   preparation: 10 minutes
per serving with 2 chicken breasts: 220 cals; 13g fat; 7g carbohydrate
per serving with 4 chicken breasts: 300 cals; 16g fat; 7g carbohydrates

Warm Lentil and Poached Egg Salad

1tbsp olive oil
1 onion, peeled and finely chopped
1 carrot, peeled and finely chopped
1 celery stick, finely chopped
2 red peppers, deseeded and roughly
  chopped
200g (7oz) flat mushrooms, sliced

225g (8oz) lentils, rinsed and drained
600ml (1 pint) hot vegetable stock
4 eggs
100g (3½oz) spinach
2tbsp good-quality balsamic vinegar
pepper

1 Heat the olive oil in a large pan. Add the onion, carrot and celery and cook for 5 minutes. Add the red peppers and mushrooms, cover the pan and cook for a further 5 minutes. Stir in the lentils and hot stock. Bring to the boil, then reduce the heat, cover the pan and simmer for 25–30 minutes.
2 Meanwhile, bring a large pan of water to the boil. Carefully break an egg into a saucer, make a whirlpool with a large spoon in the boiling water and lower the egg into the water. Repeat with the remaining eggs. Cook gently for 3–4 minutes, then lift them out with a slotted spoon, drain on kitchen paper and keep warm.
3 A couple of minutes before the end of the lentil cooking time, add the spinach and cook until wilted. Stir in the vinegar. Spoon on to four plates or bowls and top each with a poached egg. Season with pepper and serve.

Serves 4   preparation: 20 minutes   cooking time: 35–40 minutes
per serving 340 cals; 12g fat; 36g carbohydrate

Spring Onion and Potato Salad

900g (2lb) new potatoes
salt and pepper
4 large spring onions, finely sliced

4tbsp each Greek-style yogurt, mayonnaise
  and wholegrain mustard
squeeze of lemon juice

1 Put the potatoes in a pan of lightly salted water, bring to the boil, then reduce the heat and simmer, partially covered, for about 20 minutes until tender. Drain well, then tip into a bowl.
2 Add the remaining ingredients, toss everything together and serve.

Serves 6   preparation: 5 minutes   cooking time: 20 minutes
per serving: 120 cals; 1g fat; 25g carbohydrate

Oriental Duck Salad

225g (8oz) new potatoes
salt and pepper
1tsp Chinese five-spice powder
2 x 150g (5oz) duck breasts, skin removed
2tbsp plum sauce

150g (5oz) cherry tomatoes
1 small mango, peeled and sliced
75g (3oz) watercress
1tbsp rice vinegar

1 Put the potatoes in a pan of lightly salted water, bring to the boil, then reduce the heat and simmer, partially covered, for 15–20 minutes. Drain and set aside. Preheat the oven to 230°C (210°C fan oven) mark 8.

2 Rub the five-spice powder and some salt into the duck. Put the duck in a roasting tin, spoon over the plum sauce and cook in the oven for 10 minutes.

3 Halve the potatoes, add to the roasting tin and cook for 5 minutes. Add the tomatoes and cook for 5 minutes.

4 Remove the tin from the oven, put the duck on a board, cover and leave to rest for 5 minutes. Keep the potatoes and tomatoes warm.

5 Slice the duck and put in a salad bowl with any juices. Add the potatoes, mango, watercress and vinegar to the bowl, then season, toss and top with the roasted tomatoes.

Serves 2   preparation: 15 minutes   cooking time: 35 minutes
per serving: 408 cals; 11g fat; 46g carbohydrate

Chicken and Watercress Salad

4 slices stale bread, cubed
7tbsp olive oil
salt and pepper
50g (2oz) Roquefort cheese, chopped
1tbsp white wine vinegar
2tbsp natural yogurt

100g (3½oz) watercress
2 heads of chicory, leaves separated
4 ready-roasted chicken breasts, sliced
1 large ripe avocado, stoned, peeled and
    sliced

1 Preheat the oven to 200°C (180°C fan oven) mark 6. Put the bread on a baking tray and drizzle with 2tbsp olive oil. Season well, then toss to coat all the cubes in the oil. Bake for 10 minutes until golden brown.

2 To make the salad dressing, put the cheese in a bowl. Add the vinegar, yogurt and remaining olive oil and season to taste. Mix well, then set aside.

3 To assemble the salad, put the watercress in a large bowl and add the chicory leaves, sliced chicken and avocado. Scatter over the croûtons and drizzle over the blue cheese dressing before serving.

Serves 4   preparation: 10 minutes   cooking time: 10 minutes
per serving: 600 cals; 42g fat; 21g carbohydrate

Chicken with Bulgur Wheat Salad

zest and juice of 1 lemon
4 skinless boneless chicken breasts,
    slashed several times
1tbsp ground coriander
2tsp olive oil
225g (8oz) bulgur wheat
6 tomatoes, chopped

½ cucumber, chopped
4 spring onions, chopped
50g (2oz) each dried dates and almonds,
    chopped
3tbsp each chopped flat-leafed parsley and
    mint
salt and pepper

1 Put half the lemon zest and juice into a medium-sized bowl, then add the chicken breasts, coriander and 1tsp olive oil. Toss well to mix and leave to marinate.
2 Meanwhile, cook the bulgur wheat for the time stated on the packet – about 10 minutes. Put the bulgur into a bowl and add the tomatoes, cucumber, spring onions, dates, almonds, parsley and mint and season well. Add the remaining lemon zest, juice and oil and stir well.
3 Preheat the grill to high and cook the chicken for 10 minutes on each side or until cooked through. The juices should run clear when the meat is pierced with a sharp knife. Slice the chicken and serve with the salad.

Serves 4 preparation: 20 minutes   cooking time: 30 minutes, plus marinating
per serving: 530 cals; 18g fat; 55g carbohydrate

Smoked Mackerel Citrus Salad

200g (7oz) green beans
200g (7oz) smoked mackerel fillets
125g (4oz) mixed watercress, spinach and
    rocket
4 spring onions, sliced

1 avocado, halved, stoned, peeled and
    sliced
1tbsp olive oil
1tbsp chopped coriander
zest and juice of 1 orange

1 Preheat the grill to medium. Blanch the green beans in boiling water for 3 minutes until they are just tender, then drain well. Refresh under cold running water and tip into a bowl.
2 Grill the mackerel for 2 minutes until warmed through. Discard the skin and cut the flesh into bite-sized pieces. Add the fish to the bowl with the salad leaves, spring onions and avocado.
3 In a separate bowl, mix the olive oil with the coriander, orange zest and juice. Pour over the salad, toss together well and serve immediately.

Serves 4 preparation: 10 minutes   cooking time: 5 minutes
per serving: 250 cals; 20g fat; 5g carbohydrate

Trout with Apple and Watercress Salad

4 x 150g (5oz) trout fillets
1tbsp olive oil, plus extra to oil
salt and pepper
250g (9oz) cooked baby new potatoes,
  halved
2 apples, cored and cut into chunks

4 cooked beetroot (unpickled), quartered
150g (5oz) watercress
1tbsp extra-virgin olive oil
juice of ½ lemon
2tsp Dijon mustard
1tbsp chopped dill

1   Preheat the oven to 200°C (180°C fan oven) mark 6. Put each piece of fish on a piece of greased foil, brush the top of the fish with olive oil and season. Scrunch the foil around the fish, then roast for 15–20 minutes or until the fish is cooked.
2   Put the potatoes, apples, beetroot and watercress into a large bowl and mix lightly. Mix the oil in a small bowl with the lemon juice, mustard and dill and toss through the salad. Serve with the fish.

Serves 4   preparation: 15 minutes   cooking time: 15–20 minutes
per serving: 370 cals; 16g fat; 20g carbohydrate

Griddled Polenta with Gorgonzola Salad

300ml (½ pint) semi-skimmed milk
10 sage leaves, roughly chopped
salt and pepper
125g (4oz) quick-cook polenta
2 garlic cloves, peeled and crushed
2tbsp olive oil, plus extra to oil

25g (1oz) butter
100g pack salad leaves
150g (5oz) Gorgonzola cheese, cut into
  cubes
125g (4oz) each sunblush tomatoes and
  peppers

1   Put the milk in a pan, add the sage, 1tsp salt and 300ml (½ pint) water and bring to the boil. Add the polenta to the pan in a thin, steady stream, stirring to make a smooth paste.
2   Reduce the heat, add the garlic and cook for about 8 minutes, stirring occasionally. Add the olive oil, then season and stir well. Press the mixture into a lightly oiled 450g (1lb) loaf tin and smooth the top. Cool for 45 minutes. Turn the polenta on to a board and cut into eight slices.
3   Melt the butter in a griddle pan and fry the polenta slices on each side until golden.
4   Divide among four plates. Add the salad leaves, Gorgonzola, sunblush tomatoes and peppers, then season and serve.

Serves 4   preparation: 20 minutes, plus cooling   cooking time: 20 minutes
per serving: 410 cals; 26g fat; 31g carbohydrate

Juicy Prawns

250g (9oz) raw peeled tiger prawns
50g (2oz) butter, plus extra to spread
  on toast
2tbsp capers

20g pack coriander, roughly chopped
2 limes, 1 juiced and 1 cut into wedges,
  to serve
8 slices sourdough bread

1 Prepare the tiger prawns by cutting down the back of each prawn and pulling out the black central vein. Heat the butter in a large frying pan until sizzling, then add the prawns. Fry for 2–3 minutes until they start to turn pink.

2 Add the capers, coriander and lime juice, stirring to coat the prawns, then continue frying until the prawns are cooked through. Serve on toasted and buttered sourdough bread with a wedge of lime, making sure everyone has plenty of buttery juices.

Serves 4   preparation: 5 minutes   cooking time: 5 minutes
per serving: 500 cals; 23g fat; 55g carbohydrate

Prawn Paste with Toast

250g (9oz) peeled cooked prawns
4–6tsp olive oil
pinch of cayenne pepper
½tsp dried basil, warmed in the oven and
  finely crumbled

juice of 1 lime or ½ lemon (lime is much the
  better choice), strained
salt, if needed

1 Mash or pound the prawns to a paste – in a blender or food processor this can be done in a couple of minutes. Very gradually blend in the olive oil. Season with the cayenne pepper and basil. Add the lime or lemon juice.

2 When the prawn mixture is smooth and is seasoned to your satisfaction – salt may or may not be necessary as that depends upon how much has already been cooked with the prawns – pack it into a little jar or terrine. Cover and store in the fridge for up to two days. Serve chilled, with slices of hot thin toast and a little watercress.

Serves 3–4   preparation: 10 minutes
per serving: 150–110 cals; 8–6g fat; 0g carbohydrate

Marinated Tuna with Stir-fried Vegetables

2 thick tuna steaks, each about 175g (6oz)
zest and juice of 1 lime
2cm (¾ inch) piece fresh root ginger, peeled
  and finely chopped
½–1tbsp soy sauce
2tbsp sesame oil
1tbsp sunflower oil
2 garlic cloves, peeled and crushed
½ lemon grass stalk, finely chopped

1 medium red chilli, sliced into rings
  and deseeded
200g (7oz) baby sweetcorn
200g (7oz) baby courgettes, trimmed
  and halved
200g (7oz) baby carrots, halved
200g (7oz) fine green beans, trimmed
2 baby cabbages, pulled into leaves
125g (4oz) baby fennel, cut into strips

1 Preheat the oven to 110°C (90°C fan oven) mark ¼. Put the tuna in a shallow container. Mix the lime zest and juice with half the ginger and the soy sauce and pour over the fish. Leave to marinate while you cook the vegetables.
2 Heat half the sesame oil and all the sunflower oil in a wok, then add the remaining ginger and the garlic, lemon grass and chilli. Cook for 1 minute, then add the sweetcorn, courgettes, carrots, green beans, cabbage and fennel. Stir-fry for 10–15 minutes or until cooked through. Put the vegetables in the oven to keep warm.
3 Heat the remaining sesame oil in a non-stick griddle pan and fry the tuna steaks for 1–2 minutes on each side for rare (depending on thickness) or 3–4 minutes for medium. Serve with the vegetables.

Serves 2 preparation: 25 minutes cooking time: 15–25 minutes
per serving: 400 cals; 13g fat; 20g carbohydrate

Fresh Tuna Niçoise

250g (9oz) small new potatoes, sliced
150g (5oz) French beans
4 eggs
sunflower oil, to oil
4 x 150g (5oz) tuna steaks
4tbsp olive oil

2tbsp white wine vinegar
1tbsp Dijon mustard
salt and pepper
2 little gem lettuces
100g (3½oz) black olives

1   Bring a large pan of water to the boil and add the potatoes. Cook at a gentle boil for 5 minutes, then add the French beans and cook for a further 5 minutes or until the potatoes are tender. Once cooked, drain and refresh the vegetables under cold running water.
2   Meanwhile, bring another, smaller pan of water to the boil and cook the eggs for 6 minutes. Cool under cold running water, then carefully peel off the shells, quarter the eggs and set aside.
3   Brush a non-stick griddle or frying pan with a little sunflower oil and heat until very hot. Cook the tuna steaks for 2–3 minutes on each side.
4   To make the dressing, put the olive oil in a small bowl and add the vinegar, mustard and 1tbsp water, then whisk until emulsified. Season well.
5   To serve the salad, toss the little gem leaves with the olives, potatoes, French beans and hard-boiled eggs. Top with the tuna and drizzle over the dressing.

Serves 4   preparation: 5 minutes   cooking time: 10 minutes
per serving: 490 cals; 29g fat; 12g carbohydrate

Chargrilled Lemon Tuna

3 large lemons
2 garlic cloves, peeled and crushed
100ml (3½fl oz) extra-virgin olive oil
pepper

900g (2lb) fresh tuna in one piece, cut in half
    lengthways, then cut into eight long strips
    about 2cm (¾ inch) thick
flat-leafed parsley

1   Soak eight bamboo skewers in water for 30 minutes to stop them burning when cooking.
2   For the marinade, take two of the lemons, finely grate the zest from one of them and squeeze the juice from them both. Mix with the garlic and olive oil and season well with pepper.
3   Lay the tuna strips in a shallow dish, pour the marinade over them and turn the fish to coat. Cover and leave for at least 30 minutes or overnight.
4   Starting at the thinner end of each strip, roll up the tuna and thread on to a skewer, securing the ends (don't worry if any strips break – roll them up separately and thread on to the same skewer). Cut the remaining lemon into eight wedges and push one on to each skewer. Put in a container, pour over the remaining marinade, sprinkle with the parsley and chill until needed.
5   Put the skewers under a hot grill or on a barbecue and cook for 2–3 minutes on each side, brushing with the marinade. Serve hot.

Serves 8   preparation: 10 minutes, plus soaking and marinating   cooking time: 4–6 minutes
per serving: 250 cals; 15g fat; 0g carbohydrate

Lime and Coriander Crab Cakes with Chilli Mayo

1tbsp sunflower oil
3 spring onions, finely sliced
2 garlic cloves, peeled and crushed
1 red chilli, deseeded and chopped
350g (12oz) crab meat
2tsp tomato ketchup
9tbsp mayonnaise
1tsp Worcestershire sauce
175g (6oz) fresh white breadcrumbs
salt and pepper

50g (2oz) seasoned flour
1 large egg, beaten
2tbsp sweet chilli sauce
1tbsp chopped coriander
grated zest and juice of 1 lime
vegetable oil
spring onion curls, crushed
black pepper and sliced red chilli, to
 garnish

1 Heat the sunflower oil in a pan, add the spring onions and cook, stirring, for 3 minutes. Remove from the heat, stir in the garlic and chilli, transfer to a large bowl and cool.
2 Add the crab meat, ketchup, 4tbsp mayonnaise, the Worcestershire sauce and 50g (2oz) breadcrumbs to the bowl, then stir until well combined and season. Using your hands, shape the mixture into 12 cakes. Put on a baking sheet, cover and chill for at least 1 hour.
3 Dip the cakes into the seasoned flour, then the beaten egg and the remaining breadcrumbs. Return to the baking sheet and chill for 30 minutes.
4 Meanwhile, make the chilli mayonnaise. Put the chilli sauce in a bowl and stir in the coriander, lime zest and juice and the remaining mayonnaise. Season, cover and chill. (This can be made one day in advance.)
5 Heat 2.5cm (1 inch) vegetable oil in a pan. Fry the cakes in batches for 2–3 minutes on each side or until golden. Remove from the pan and drain on kitchen paper. Garnish with the spring onions, black pepper and chilli and serve with the chilli mayonnaise.

Serves 4   preparation: 30 minutes, plus chilling   cooking time: 15 minutes
per serving: 580 cals; 48g fat; 32g carbohydrate

Tapas

8 slices Serrano or Ibérico ham
12 slices Spanish chorizo sausage

190g jar mixed olives
1 slim country loaf, sliced

1 Cut each slice of ham into four pieces and arrange on a platter with the chorizo. Cover with clingfilm and leave at room temperature for 10 minutes to bring out the full flavour of the meat before serving.
2 Arrange the mixed olives in a bowl, put the bread in a basket and serve with the meats.

Serves 4   preparation: 5 minutes
per serving (without the bread): 220 cals; 18g fat; 1g carbohydrate

Quick Fish Cakes with Cucumber Relish

1kg (2¼lb) haddock fillet, skinned
1tsp mixed peppercorns
175g (6oz) large cooked prawns
juice of 1 small lemon
1tbsp capers, roughly chopped
4tbsp chopped chives
2tbsp mayonnaise
400g packet prepared mashed potato

salt and pepper
3tbsp plain flour
½ cucumber, diced
1tsp golden caster sugar
2tbsp extra-virgin olive oil
1tbsp white wine vinegar
sunflower oil
watercress, to garnish

1 Put the haddock in a wide pan, cover with cold salted water and add the peppercorns. Bring to the boil, then reduce the heat and simmer for 5–7 minutes, or until the haddock is opaque and flakes easily. Lift the fish from the pan, put in a bowl and flake it with a fork.

2 Add the prawns, lemon juice, capers, chives, mayonnaise and mashed potato to the flaked fish, season well, then mix thoroughly.

3 Lightly flour a work surface and, using a 7.5cm (3 inch) plain cutter, shape the haddock mixture into 12 cakes. Chill for 1 hour.

4 To make the cucumber relish, put the cucumber in a bowl and mix in the sugar, olive oil and vinegar. Chill until needed.

5 Pour about 2.5cm (1 inch) sunflower oil into a large non-stick frying pan and heat until a cube of bread browns in 50 seconds. Fry the fish cakes in batches, turning once, until golden. Drain on kitchen paper, then garnish with watercress and serve with the cucumber relish.

Serves 6 preparation: 20 minutes, plus chilling   cooking time: 15 minutes
per serving: 360 cals; 12g fat; 17g carbohydrate

Salmon Pâté

250g (9oz) smoked salmon	6tbsp olive oil
3tbsp half-fat fromage frais	1tbsp lemon juice
1½tbsp creamed horseradish	120g bag baby or herb salad
salt and white pepper	6 slices white bread

1 Put the salmon in a blender and whiz to chop roughly. Add the fromage frais and horseradish and pulse briefly to combine. Put in a bowl, season and chill.
2 Pour the olive oil and lemon juice into a screw-topped jar, season well and shake together.
3 To shape the pâté, use two dessertspoons and scrape a spoonful of pâté from one to the other several times to form a smooth oval. Put one on each plate with a pile of salad and drizzle with dressing; serve with melba toast.
4 To make the melba toast, preheat the grill. Toast the bread, remove the crusts and cut through the middle of each slice to make two thin squares. Scrape away and discard any doughy bits. Halve each square diagonally and put on a baking sheet untoasted side up. Grill until golden.

Serves 6   preparation: 15 minutes
per serving: 190 cals; 15g fat; 2g carbohydrate

Smoked Salmon Tortilla

450g (1lb) potatoes, peeled	200g (7oz) broccoli florets, blanched
salt and pepper	75g (3oz) smoked salmon, cut into strips
1tbsp olive oil	4 large eggs, beaten
1 onion, peeled and finely sliced	2tbsp chopped dill

1 Put the potatoes in a pan of lightly salted water, bring to the boil, then reduce the heat and simmer, partially covered, for 12 minutes until just tender. Drain and set aside to cool a little.
2 Meanwhile, heat the olive oil in a 20.5cm (8 inch) non-stick frying pan and fry the onion over a medium heat for 10 minutes until soft and golden.
3 Slice the potatoes into rounds and put into the pan, then add the broccoli and smoked salmon.
4 Preheat the grill to medium-high. Season the beaten eggs, stir in the dill and pour into the pan. Cook over a low heat for 8–10 minutes until set underneath. Run a palette knife around the rim every couple of minutes to prevent the tortilla sticking, and make sure it doesn't catch on the bottom.
5 Put the pan under the grill and cook for 3–4 minutes until the tortilla is completely set and turning golden. Serve with a crisp green salad.

Serves 4   preparation: 10 minutes   cooking time: 35 minutes
per serving: 260 cals; 12g fat; 24g carbohydrate

Frittata

4tbsp vegetable oil
1 onion, peeled and finely sliced
700g (1½lb) potatoes, peeled and sliced
   into rounds

10 eggs
salt and pepper
3tbsp chopped flat-leafed parsley

1 Heat 1tbsp oil in a large non-stick frying pan, add the onion and fry over a medium heat for 5–10 minutes until golden. Remove the onion and set aside. Fry the potatoes, a handful at a time, in the same pan, adding more oil as necessary. Fry each batch until golden on both sides, then set aside with the onions. When all the potatoes are cooked, put them back in the pan with the onions to form an even layer on the bottom of the pan.

2 Preheat the grill to medium-high. Put the eggs in a jug, season well and beat with a whisk or fork until combined. Pour into the pan and cook over a medium heat for 5 minutes until golden and firm underneath.

3 Sprinkle the parsley on top and put under the grill for 2–3 minutes until the top sets.

4 Divide the frittata into wedges and serve immediately.

Serves 4   preparation: 20 minutes   cooking time: 30 minutes
per serving: 440 cals; 26g fat; 29g carbohydrate

Pancetta Tortilla

450g (1lb) potatoes, peeled
salt and pepper
1tbsp olive oil
1 onion, peeled and finely sliced

2 leeks, about 300g (11oz), cut into 5mm
   (¼ inch) rounds
65g pack diced pancetta
4 large eggs, beaten
2tbsp chopped parsley

1 Put the potatoes in a pan of lightly salted water, bring to the boil, then reduce the heat and simmer, partially covered, for 12 minutes until just tender. Drain and set aside to cool a little.

2 Meanwhile, heat the olive oil in a 20.5cm (8 inch) non-stick frying pan and fry the onion over a medium heat for 10 minutes until soft and golden. Add the leeks and pancetta and fry for 10 minutes until the leeks are softened. Remove half the mixture from the pan and set aside.

3 Slice the potatoes into rounds and put into the pan, spooning over the reserved leek and pancetta mixture as you do.

4 Preheat the grill to medium-high. Season the beaten eggs, stir in the parsley and pour into the pan. Cook over a low heat for 8–10 minutes until set underneath. Run a palette knife around the rim every couple of minutes to prevent the tortilla sticking, and make sure it doesn't catch on the bottom.

5 Put the pan under the grill and cook for 3–4 minutes until the tortilla is completely set and turning golden. Serve with a crisp green salad.

Serves 4   preparation: 10 minutes   cooking time: 35 minutes
per serving: 300 cals; 16g fat; 25g carbohydrate

Courgette and Parmesan Frittata

40g (1½oz) butter	salt and pepper
1 small onion, peeled and finely chopped	25g (1oz) freshly grated Parmesan cheese,
225g (8oz) courgettes, finely sliced	plus shavings to garnish
6 eggs	

1 Melt 25g (1oz) butter in an 18cm (7 inch) non-stick frying pan and cook the onion for about 10 minutes until softened. Add the courgettes and fry gently for 5 minutes or until they begin to soften.
2 Meanwhile, beat the eggs in a bowl and season well. Preheat the grill.
3 Add the remaining butter to the pan and heat. Pour in the eggs and cook for 2–3 minutes or until golden underneath and cooked round the edges.
4 Sprinkle the Parmesan over the frittata and grill under a medium-high heat for 1–2 minutes or until just set. Scatter with Parmesan shavings, cut into quarters and serve, with crusty bread.

Serves 4   preparation: 10 minutes   cooking time: 12 minutes
per serving: 260 cals; 20g fat; 4g carbohydrate

Variation
Cherry tomato and rocket frittata: Replace the courgettes with 175g (6oz) vine-ripened cherry tomatoes, frying them for 1 minute only, until they begin to soften. Immediately after pouring in the eggs, scatter 25g (1oz) rocket leaves over the surface. Continue as above.

Mixed Mushroom Frittata

1tbsp olive oil	6 eggs
300g (11oz) mixed mushrooms, sliced	50g (2oz) watercress, chopped
2tbsp chopped thyme	salt and pepper
zest and juice of ½ lemon	

1 Heat the olive oil in a large deep frying pan over a medium heat. Add the mushrooms and thyme and stir-fry for 4–5 minutes until starting to soften and brown. Stir in the lemon zest and juice, then bubble for 1 minute. Reduce the heat.
2 Preheat the grill to medium-high. Break the eggs into a bowl and beat. Add the watercress, season and pour into the pan. Cook on the hob for 7–8 minutes until the sides and base are firm, but the centre is still a little soft.
3 Place under the grill and grill for 4–5 minutes until just set. Cut into quarters to serve.

Serves 4   preparation: 15 minutes   cooking time: 15–20 minutes
per serving: 180 cals; 14g fat; 0g carbohydrate

Moroccan Spiced Chicken Kebabs

2tbsp olive oil
15g (½oz) flat-leafed parsley
1 garlic clove, peeled
½tsp paprika

1tsp ground cumin
zest and juice of 1 lemon
4 skinless chicken, boneless breasts, cut
   into bite-sized chunks

1 Put the olive oil in a blender, add the parsley, garlic, paprika, cumin, lemon zest and juice and whiz
   to a paste.
2 Put the chicken in a medium-sized shallow dish and add the spice paste, then rub in and leave to
   marinate for at least 20 minutes. Preheat the grill to high.
3 Thread the marinated chicken on to skewers and grill for 10–12 minutes, turning occasionally, until
   the meat is cooked through. Serve with a salad.

Serve with 50g (2oz) brown rice per person, cooked according to packet instructions. To make the salad mix a
400g can drained chickpeas, a thinly sliced red onion, 4 roughly chopped tomatoes and 4tbsp chopped parsley in
a bowl with 1tsp olive oil. Serve with a lemon wedge.

Serves 4   preparation: 10 minutes, plus marinating   cooking time: 10–12 minutes
   per serving: 240 cals; 13g fat; 0g carbohydrate

Wild Herb Kebabs

4 long, strong rosemary stalks
2 garlic cloves, peeled and crushed
2tbsp olive oil
350g (12oz) firm white fish, such as cod, cut
   into bite-sized pieces
175g (6oz) large raw prawns, peeled
zest and juice of 1 lemon

salt and pepper
about 350g (12oz) tzatziki (if you can't find
   this ready-made, add chopped cucumber
   and mint to low-fat natural yogurt, or use
   plain yogurt)
1 lemon or lime, cut into wedges, to serve

1 Preheat a grill or barbecue. Strip almost all the leaves from the rosemary, apart from the top 5cm
   (2 inches). Roughly chop the stripped leaves and mix with the garlic and olive oil. Stir in the fish,
   prawns, lemon zest and juice.
2 Cut the bare tip of each rosemary stalk to a sharp point, then use to skewer the fish and prawns. If
   you can't find rosemary, use wooden skewers. (Soak them in cold water for 20 minutes before use
   to prevent them from burning.)
3 Cook the kebabs for about 3 minutes on each side until the fish is opaque. Season and serve with
   tzatziki and lemon or lime wedges with a green salad and couscous or new potatoes.

Serves 4   preparation: 25 minutes   cooking time: 10 minutes
per serving: 350 calories; 19g fat; 7g carbohydrate

Courgette Tortilla

450g (1lb) potatoes, peeled
salt and pepper
1tbsp olive oil
1 onion, peeled and finely sliced
1 large courgette, grated

100g (3½oz) thawed frozen peas
50g (2oz) feta cheese
4 large eggs, beaten
1tbsp chopped mint

1 Put the potatoes in a pan of lightly salted water, bring to the boil, then reduce the heat and simmer, partially covered, for 12 minutes until just tender. Drain and set aside to cool a little.
2 Meanwhile, heat the olive oil in a 20.5cm (8 inch) non-stick frying pan and fry the onion over a medium heat for 10 minutes until soft and golden. Add the courgette to the pan and cook for 5 minutes.
3 Slice the potatoes into rounds and put into the pan, then add the peas and crumble in the feta cheese.
4 Preheat the grill to medium-high. Season the beaten eggs, add the chopped mint and pour into the pan. Cook over a low heat for 8–10 minutes until set underneath. Run a palette knife around the rim every couple of minutes to prevent the tortilla sticking, and make sure it doesn't catch on the bottom.
5 Put the pan under the grill and cook for 3–4 minutes until completely set and turning golden. Serve with a crisp green salad.

Serves 4   preparation: 10 minutes   cooking time: 35 minutes
per serving: 280 cals; 14g fat; 25g carbohydrate

Cherry Tomato Tortilla

450g (1lb) potatoes, peeled
salt and pepper
1tbsp olive oil
1 onion, peeled and finely sliced

250g (9oz) cherry tomatoes
4 large eggs, beaten
2tbsp basil leaves, roughly torn
40g (1½oz) freshly grated Parmesan cheese

1 Put the potatoes in a pan of lightly salted water, bring to the boil, then reduce the heat and simmer, partially covered, for 12 minutes until just tender. Drain and set aside to cool a little.
2 Meanwhile, heat the olive oil in a 20.5cm (8 inch) non-stick frying pan and fry the onion over a medium heat for 10 minutes until soft and golden.
3 Slice the potatoes into rounds and put into the pan, then put the cherry tomatoes on top.
4 Preheat the grill to medium-high. Season the beaten eggs, add the torn basil leaves and pour into the pan. Cook over a low heat for 8–10 minutes until set underneath. Run a palette knife around the rim every couple of minutes to prevent the tortilla sticking, and make sure it doesn't catch on the bottom.
5 Sprinkle the Parmesan over the tortilla, then put the pan under the grill and cook for 3–4 minutes until completely set and turning golden. Garnish with sprigs of basil and serve with a crisp green salad.

Serves 4   preparation: 10 minutes   cooking time: 35 minutes
per serving: 270 cals; 13g fat; 26g carbohydrate

Classic French Omelette

2–3 eggs   1tbsp milk or water

salt and pepper   25g (1oz) unsalted butter

1 Whisk the eggs in a bowl just enough to break them down – over-beating spoils the texture of the omelette. Season and add the milk or water.

2 Heat the butter in an 18cm (7 inch) omelette pan or non-stick frying pan until it is foaming, but not brown.

3 Add the beaten eggs. Stir gently with a fork or wooden spatula, drawing the mixture from the sides to the centre as it sets and letting the liquid egg in the centre run to the sides. When set, stop stirring and cook for a further 30 seconds or until the omelette is golden brown underneath and still creamy on top; don't overcook.

4 If you are making a filled omelette (see below), add the filling at this point.

5 Tilt the pan away from you slightly and use a palette knife to fold over a third of the omelette to the centre, then fold over the opposite third. Slide the omelette out on to a warmed plate, letting it flip over so that the folded sides are underneath. Serve immediately, with a salad and warm bread.

Serves 1   preparation: 5 minutes   cooking time: about 2 minutes
per serving: 300 cals; 28g fat; 0g carbohydrate

Omelette variations and fillings:

Herb: Add 1 tsp each finely chopped chervil, chives and tarragon, or 1tbsp chopped parsley, to the beaten egg mixture before cooking.

Tomato: Fry 2 skinned and chopped tomatoes in a little butter for 5 minutes or until soft and pulpy. Put in the centre of the omelette before folding.

Cheese: Grate 40g (1½oz) Gruyère or Cheddar cheese. Sprinkle half on the omelette before folding. Sprinkle the rest over the finished omelette.

Goat's cheese: Soften about 25g (1oz) mild goat's cheese and blend with a little crème fraîche. Season with salt and pepper and put in the centre of the omelette before folding.

Mushroom: Thickly slice 50g (2oz) mushrooms (preferably wild) and cook in butter until soft. Put in the centre of the omelette before folding.

Smoked salmon: Toss 25g (1oz) chopped smoked salmon with a little chopped dill and 1–2tbsp crème fraîche. Scatter over the omelette before folding.

Mushroom Soufflé Omelette

50g (2oz) small chestnut mushrooms, sliced
3tbsp crème fraîche
2 eggs, separated
salt and pepper

15g (½oz) butter
5 chives, roughly chopped

1   Preheat the grill to medium-high. Heat a small non-stick frying pan for 30 seconds. Add the mushrooms and cook, stirring, for 3 minutes to brown slightly, then stir in the crème fraîche and turn off the heat.
2   Lightly beat the egg yolks in a bowl, add 2tbsp cold water and season.
3   Whisk the egg whites in a clean grease-free bowl until stiff but not dry, then gently fold into the egg yolks. Be careful not to overmix.
4   Heat an 18cm (7 inch) non-stick frying pan and melt the butter in it. Add the egg mixture, tilting the pan in all directions to cover the base. Cook over a medium heat for 3 minutes or until the underside is golden brown.
5   Gently reheat the mushrooms and add the chives. Put the pan under the grill for 1 minute, or until the surface of the omelette is just firm and puffy. Tip the mushroom mixture on top. Run a spatula around and underneath the omelette to loosen it, then carefully fold it and turn on to a plate.

Serves 1   preparation: 5 minutes   cooking time: 7 minutes
per serving: 480 cals; 44g fat; 1g carbohydrate

Spanish Omelette

900g (2lb) potatoes, peeled and left whole
salt and pepper
4tbsp vegetable oil
1 onion, peeled and finely sliced

3tbsp chopped flat-leafed parsley
8 eggs
3 streaky bacon rashers

1 Put the potatoes in a pan of lightly salted water, bring to the boil, then reduce the heat and simmer, partially covered, for 15–20 minutes until just cooked. Drain and set aside to cool a little..
2 Meanwhile, heat 1tbsp oil in an 18cm (7 inch) non-stick frying pan and fry the onion for 5–10 minutes until softened, then remove and set aside.
3 Cut the potatoes into thick slices. Reheat the pan and add the sliced potatoes, onion and 2tbsp parsley in layers, adding more oil as necessary. Preheat the grill to high.
4 Beat the eggs, season well and add to the pan. Cook for 5–10 minutes until firm underneath. Meanwhile, grill the bacon until golden and crisp, then cut into pieces.
5 Grill the omelette in the pan for 2–3 minutes until just set. Scatter the bacon and remaining parsley over the top and cut into wedges. Serve with a green salad.

Serves 4   preparation: 10–15 minutes   cooking time: 30–45 minutes
per serving: 530 cals; 32g fat; 38g carbohydrate

Egg and Bacon Tarts

500g pack shortcrust pastry
6 smoked streaky bacon rashers
6 eggs

3tbsp chopped flat-leafed parsley
salt and pepper

1 Preheat the oven to 200°C (180°C fan oven) mark 6 and put two baking sheets in to heat up. Divide the pastry into six equal pieces, then roll out and use to line individual 10cm (4 inch) fluted flan tins. Prick the bases all over with a fork, line with greaseproof paper, fill with baking beans and chill for 10 minutes.
2 Put the tart tins on to the preheated baking sheets and bake for 10 minutes. Remove the paper and beans and cook for 5 minutes or until the pastry bases are dry. Remove the cases from the oven. Increase the oven temperature to 220°C (200°C fan oven) mark 7.
3 Put a bacon rasher across the base of each tart. One at a time, crack the eggs into a cup and tip one into each tart case. Scatter the chopped parsley over the top, then season and bake for 10 minutes or until the egg white has set.

Serves 6   preparation: 20 minutes, plus chilling   cooking time: 25 minutes
per serving: 500 cals; 35g fat; 33g carbohydrate

Chargrilled Chicken Waldorf

olive oil
2 skinless boneless chicken breasts
salt and pepper
100g bag salad leaves
125g (4oz) black seedless grapes
2 crisp, red apples such as Braeburn, cored
   and thinly sliced

4 celery sticks, sliced into matchsticks
125g (4oz) walnuts, toasted
175g (6oz) Roquefort cheese, thinly sliced
½ quantity of mayonnaise (page 17)
chopped chives, to garnish

1   Brush a griddle or frying pan with a little olive oil and put over a medium heat. Season the chicken and cook for about 8–10 minutes each side. When the chicken is cooked (the juices should run clear when pierced with a skewer) remove and put to one side.
2   In a large bowl, toss together the salad leaves, grapes, apples, celery, walnuts and about two-thirds of the Roquefort. Thickly slice the chicken and arrange on four plates with some salad.
3   Crumble the remaining cheese into the mayonnaise and mix well. Spoon 2tbsp mayonnaise on to each plate and garnish with the chopped chives.

Serves 4   preparation: 10 minutes   cooking time: 16–20 minutes
per serving: 780 cals; 60g fat; 13g carbohydrate

Pasta with Pesto, Potatoes and Beans

350g (12oz) dried pasta shapes,
   such as trofie
salt
175g (6oz) fine green beans, roughly
   chopped

175g (6oz) small salad potatoes, such as
   Anya, thickly sliced
2 x 125g tubs fresh pesto sauce
freshly grated Parmesan cheese, to serve

1   Cook the pasta in a large pan of boiling salted water for 5 minutes.
2   Add the beans and potatoes to the pan and continue to boil for 7–8 minutes or until the potatoes are just tender.
3   Drain the pasta, beans and potatoes in a colander, then tip everything back into the pan and stir in the pesto sauce. Serve scattered with Parmesan.

Serves 4   preparation: 5 minutes   cooking time: 15 minutes
per serving: 710 cals; 35g fat; 74g carbohydrate

Warm Goat's Cheese Salad

1tbsp each walnut oil and sunflower oil
1tsp balsamic or sherry vinegar
salt and pepper
1 quantity pesto (page 670), made with
rocket instead of basil and 1tbsp chopped
parsley added

4 slices goat's cheese log (with rind)
50g (2oz) rocket leaves
1 bunch of watercress, trimmed
40g (1½oz) walnut halves, toasted

1 To make the dressing, whisk the walnut and sunflower oils with the vinger in a bowl, seasoning to taste.
2 Preheat the grill. Lay the goat's cheese slices on a foil-lined baking sheet. Put under the grill, as close to the heat as possible, for 1–2 minutes until browned.
3 Put a slice of goat's cheese on each plate and top with a spoonful of rocket pesto. Toss the rocket and watercress leaves with the dressing and then arrange around the goat's cheese. Scatter the walnuts over the salad and serve immediately.

Serves 4   preparation: 20 minutes   cooking time: 1–2 minutes
per serving: 520 cals; 46g fat; 2g carbohydrate

Variation
Use halved crottins de Chavignol (small hard goat's cheeses) instead of the log chèvre.

Nibbles and snacks

If you want something to nibble on with drinks before a meal, or something to munch on while watching a video, there are plenty here to choose from. Don't just open a packet of nuts – be adventurous and then enjoy the compliments.

Nothing could be easier than Parma Ham Bites – you can't go wrong. Just wrap the ham around stoned prunes and drizzle with luscious extra virgin olive oil – they'll be gobbled up in a flash. Or jazz up mixed olives with chilli, garlic and herbs. Make loads – they'll keep for ages.

Feeling a bit more adventurous? Try Mini Yorkshires with Steak and Horseradish – sounds complicated, but it's easy, and your friends will be amazed.

If you need a quick snack during the day to boost your energy, something with bread usually fits the bill. Check out the toasts, wraps, pittas, crostini, ciabatta, foccaccia and rolls. Feeling hungry yet? These interesting breads will transform the humble sandwich into something to be proud of: Pork Pittas with Salsa; Goat's Cheese and Red Onion Crostini; Marinated Mushrooms in Crusty Rolls – food to enjoy alone or to share.

Nibbles

Roasted Almonds

Preheat the oven to 180°C (160°C fan oven) mark 4. Toss unblanched almonds, a little oil and sea salt in a roasting tin and cook in the oven for 10 minutes. Remove from the oven, cool and store.

Crunchy Breadsticks

Preheat the oven to 180°C (160°C fan oven) mark 4. Wrap pancetta rashers around breadsticks and cook in the oven for 5 minutes. Remove from the oven and serve.

Parma Ham Bites

Wrap half slices of Parma ham firmly around stoned prunes, then drizzle a little extra-virgin olive oil over the top.

Parmesan Crisps

Preheat the oven to 200°C (180°C fan oven) mark 6. Spoon freshly grated Parmesan cheese on to a greaseproof paper-lined baking sheet, season and flatten a little. Cook in the oven for 5 minutes, then remove from the oven and cool a little. Use a spatula to lift the crisps on to a serving dish.

Posh Cheese and Pineapple

Top cubes of hard cheese, such as Spanish Manchego, with pieces of chopped mango and secure each with a cocktail stick.

Chicory Boats

Tear the leaves off a bulb of chicory. Top each leaf with a cube of Shropshire blue or Stilton cheese and a dot of fruity chutney.

Smoked Salmon Rolls

Mix crème fraîche with a little Dijon mustard, spread on strips of smoked salmon and roll up. Dot with black pepper.

Guacamole Crisps

Dollop a little guacamole on to tortilla crisps. Cut a few roasted red peppers into slivers and put on top of the guacamole.

Chorizo Sticks

Wrap a slice of chorizo or salami around a cube of quince paste. Secure with a cocktail stick.

Peppadew Olives

230g jar stuffed green olives, drained
375g jar mild peppadew sweet peppers,
  drained

basil leaves, to garnish

1 Push a cocktail stick through each olive, then push the olives into the peppadew shells.
2 Just before serving, put a basil leaf into each pepper shell to garnish.

Serves 8   preparation: 10 minutes
per serving: 35 cals; 3g fat; 2g carbohydrate

Marinated Mixed Olives

340g jar large green olives, drained,
  reserving jar
340g jar Kalamata or other tasty black
  olives, drained, reserving jar
small pinch of dried oregano
1 thyme sprig
2 bay leaves

3 fat garlic cloves, peeled
1 bird's eye chilli, sliced almost in half but
  keeping the stalk intact
200ml (7fl oz) extra-virgin olive oil
100ml (3½fl oz) red wine vinegar
2tbsp whole black peppercorns

1 Put all the ingredients in a medium-sized plastic container. Cover with a lid and chill for at least one
   day, stirring occasionally.
2 Sterilise the olive jars. Spoon the mixture into the jars and seal.

Makes 2 x 340g jars   preparation: 10 minutes, plus marinating
per serving: 180 cals; 20g fat; 0g carbohydrate

Gravadlax on Rye Bread

4 slices rye bread
2 x 140g packs gravadlax with mustard and
  dill sauce (minimum 4 large slices)

juice of 1 lemon
pepper
dill sprigs, to garnish

1 Spread the bread with the mustard and dill sauce (you may not need it all). Cut each slice lengthways
   into four strips, then widthways in half to make eight pieces.
2 Cut the gravadlax into strips and crumple a strip over each piece of rye bread. Cover with clingfilm.
   Just before serving, squeeze over a little lemon juice, season with pepper and garnish with a dill sprig.

Makes 32   preparation: 15 minutes
per canapé: 20 cals; trace fat; 2g carbohydrate

Roasted Walnuts with Rosemary

200g (7oz) walnut halves
4tbsp extra-virgin olive oil
4 fat garlic cloves, peeled and halved

small handful of rosemary leaves
salt and pepper

1   Put the walnuts, olive oil, garlic and rosemary in a large bowl and mix gently to coat. Cover and leave for 1 hour.
2   Preheat the oven to 180°C (160°C fan oven) mark 4. Spread the mixture out on a foil-lined baking sheet and cook in the oven for about 15 minutes, stirring occasionally. Keep an eye on the nuts – they should be pale golden brown and smell toasted when ready.
3   As soon as the nuts come out of the oven, season them with salt – not too much – and pepper, then pick out and discard the garlic. Leave to cool, then put the nuts into an airtight container and leave to chill until needed.

Makes 1 medium tin   enough for 6 servings   preparation: 10 minutes, plus marinating
cooking time: 20 minutes   per serving: 250 cals; 26g fat; 2g carbohydrate

Spiced Mixed Nuts

400g (14oz) unsalted and unroasted nuts (a
   mixture of Brazil nuts, almonds and
   pecans)
½tsp each cayenne pepper, ground
   cinnamon and sea salt

generous pinch of pepper
2tbsp golden caster sugar
2tbsp olive oil

1   Preheat the oven to 190°C (170°C fan oven) mark 5. Put the nuts in a roasting tin and sprinkle over the cayenne pepper, cinnamon, sea salt, pepper and sugar. Drizzle over the olive oil, stir to mix, then spread out in a single layer.
2   Bake for 15–20 minutes until golden and crisp. Remove from the oven and cool in the tin, then store in an airtight container for up to two weeks.

Serves 8   preparation: 5 minutes   cooking time: 15–20 minutes
per serving: 280 cals; 26g fat; 6g carbohydrate

Hot Stilton Bites

250g (9oz) ready-rolled puff pastry
flour, to dust
125g (4oz) Stilton cheese, crumbled
25g (1oz) freshly grated Parmesan cheese

1tsp each cayenne pepper, poppy seeds
and black mustard seeds

1 Preheat the oven to 220°C (200°C fan oven) mark 7 and put a baking sheet in to heat up. Roll out the pastry on a lightly floured surface to a thickness of 1cm (½ inch) and cut into 5cm (2 inch) squares.
2 Scatter all the remaining ingredients over the pastry. Transfer the squares to the baking sheet and bake for 10 minutes or until golden.
3 Remove from the oven and leave to cool for a few minutes, then transfer to a serving plate.

Serves 6   preparation: 15 minutes   cooking time: 10 minutes
per serving: 260 cals; 19g fat; 15g carbohydrate

Cheese Straws

200g (7oz) self-raising flour, sifted, plus
  extra to dust
pinch of cayenne
125g (4oz) unsalted butter, diced and
  chilled, plus extra to grease
125g (4oz) finely grated Parmesan cheese

2 eggs
1tsp ready-made English mustard
sesame and poppy seeds, to sprinkle

1 Put the flour, cayenne and butter into a food processor and pulse until the mixture resembles breadcrumbs. Add the Parmesan and pulse to mix.
2 Crack 1 egg into a bowl. Separate the other egg, put the white to one side and add the egg yolk to the bowl with the whole egg. Mix in the mustard. Pour into the food processor and whiz to bring the mixture together. Tip on to a board and knead lightly for 30 seconds, then wrap in clingfilm and chill for 30 minutes.
3 Preheat the oven to 180°C (160°C fan oven) mark 4. Grease two baking sheets. Roll out the pastry on a lightly floured surface to a 23 x 30.5cm (9 x 12 inch) rectangle, cut out 24 straws and carefully twist each straw twice. Put on to the baking sheets.
4 Beat the reserved egg white with a fork until frothy and brush over the straws, then sprinkle with the sesame and poppy seeds. Bake for 18–20 minutes or until golden. Remove from the oven and cool for 5 minutes before transferring to a wire rack to cool completely.

Makes 24   Serves 8   preparation: 10 minutes, plus chilling and cooling   cooking time: 18–20 minutes
per serving: 290 cals; 20g fat; 19g carbohydrate

Cheddar Wafers

125g (4oz) Cheddar cheese, finely grated   **pinch of chopped thyme**

1   Preheat the oven to 200°C (180°C fan oven) mark 6. Mix the cheese with the thyme. Put 1tsp of the mixture in a 5cm (2 inch) pastry cutter on a non-stick baking sheet. Repeat with more mixture – about five rounds will fit on the sheet at a time. Cook for 2–3 minutes or until lacy and pale gold (do not overcook them or they'll taste bitter).
2   Remove the sheet from the oven and, using a palette knife, lift each wafer off, curl over a rolling pin to shape, then put to one side to cool. Continue until all the mixture is used. Keep in an airtight container for up to two days.

Makes 28 preparation: 25 minutes   cooking time: 15–20 minutes
per wafer: 20 cals; 2g fat; 0g carbohydrate

Spiced Puff Pastry Nibbles

flour, to dust   **1 egg, beaten**
500g pack puff pastry   **2tbsp Sanchi Furikake Japanese seasoning**

1   Lightly dust a clean work surface and rolling pin with a little flour and roll out the puff pastry along the narrow width until it measures 68.5 x 16cm (27 x 6½ inches). Roll up each long side tightly until the two sides meet in the middle.
2   Cut the pastry into 1–2cm (½–¾ inch) slices, to make 36. Lay each slice on its side, then gently roll out flat to make a heart shape. Put on a baking sheet (you'll need three sheets in total) and chill for 20 minutes. Preheat the oven to 200°C (180°C fan oven) mark 6.
3   Brush each pastry heart with a little beaten egg, then sprinkle over a little of the Furikake seasoning. Bake for 20 minutes until puffed and golden, then remove from the oven and use a palette knife to lift the pastry off the baking sheets and on to a wire rack to cool.

Makes 36   preparation: 15 minutes, plus chilling   cooking time: 20 minutes
per nibble: 50 cals; 3g fat; 5g carbohydrate

Egg Mayo Focaccia

2 sliced focaccia loaves
50g (2oz) butter, melted
6 hard-boiled eggs, peeled
5tbsp mayonnaise
1 bunch of watercress, finely chopped

1tsp Dijon mustard
1tsp anchovy essence
pepper
finely sliced spring onions, to garnish

1 Preheat the oven to 200°C (180°C fan oven) mark 6. Using a 4cm (1½ inch) cutter, stamp out 40 rounds from the focaccia. Brush with melted butter, place on a baking sheet and bake for 15 minutes until golden, turning halfway through.
2 Put the eggs in a bowl with the mayonnaise, watercress, mustard, anchovy essence and pepper and crush with a potato masher until fine.
3 Place 1tsp of the mixture on each toast round, top with the spring onions and dust with pepper.

Makes 40   preparation: 45 minutes   cooking time: 25 minutes
per serving: 80 cals; 5g fat; 7g carbohydrate

Goat's Cheese, Pimiento and Mint Wraps

2 x 150g packs soft goat's cheese, chilled
4tbsp chopped mint
salt and pepper

400g can pimientos, drained
4 large flour tortillas
mint sprigs, to garnish

1 Beat together the goat's cheese and mint, then season and chill.
2 Sandwich the drained pimientos between sheets of kitchen paper. Press down lightly with your hands until they're completely dry, then cut the pimientos into rough pieces.
3 Spread each tortilla with a quarter of the goat's cheese mixture and scatter the chopped pimientos on top. Starting from the nearest end, roll up as tightly as possible.
4 Wrap the filled tortillas in clingfilm and chill for about 15 minutes. To serve, remove the clingfilm and slice each roll into 10 pieces. Serve garnished with mint sprigs.

Makes 40   preparation: 10 minutes, plus chilling
per canapé: 40 cals; 2g fat; 5g carbohydrate

Focaccia Rolls with Goat's Cheese and Almond Pesto

3 x 15g packs basil
1 small shallot, peeled and chopped
1tbsp balsamic vinegar
2tsp Dijon mustard
1 garlic clove, peeled and chopped
150ml (¼ pint) olive oil
50g (2oz) blanched almonds, toasted

juice of 1 lemon, or to taste
salt and pepper
1 olive focaccia loaf, cut into 12 thin slices
100g (3½oz) rindless, soft goat's cheese
3tbsp black olive tapenade
6 slices wafer-thin ham, cut in half
basil leaves, to garnish

1 To make the almond pesto, put the basil, shallot, vinegar, mustard, garlic and olive oil in a food processor and whiz until smooth. Add the almonds and whiz again. Add the lemon juice and season to taste.
2 Preheat the oven to 220°C (200°C fan oven) mark 7. To make the focaccia rolls, use a rolling pin to roll each slice of focaccia to about 3mm (⅛ inch) thick. Spread each slice with a little of the goat's cheese, followed by some tapenade and half a slice of ham. Roll up tightly and secure with cocktail sticks. Place on a baking sheet and bake for 10–15 minutes or until golden.
3 Remove the baking sheet from the oven and pile the rolls on to a serving plate. Garnish with basil leaves and serve with the almond pesto for dipping.

Makes 12   preparation: 30 minutes   cooking time: 15 minutes
per roll: 230 cals; 18g fat; 13g carbohydrate

Tandoori Chicken with Mango on Naan

300g pack ready-to-eat tandoori chicken
   breasts
1 large ripe mango
juice of 1 lemon
300g pack naan bread

2tbsp olive oil
2tbsp coarse sea salt
200g tub tzatziki
coriander leaves, to garnish

1 Cut each chicken breast into thin diagonal slices. Peel and thinly slice the mango and toss it in the lemon juice, then cover with clingfilm.
2 Preheat the oven to 200°C (180°C fan oven) mark 6. Prick the naan bread with a knife, drizzle with olive oil and sprinkle with sea salt. Warm the naan in the oven for the time stated on the packet.
3 Cut the warmed naan bread into 30–36 bite-sized pieces and top each with a slice of chicken and mango. Spoon over a little tzatziki and garnish with a coriander leaf.

Makes 30–36   preparation: 20 minutes   cooking time: 2 minutes
per canapé: 50 cals; 2g fat; 5g carbohydrate

Red Pepper Pesto Croûtons

1 thin French stick, sliced into 24 rounds
olive oil, to brush
190g jar ready-made pesto (or make your
own, page 000)

4 pepper pieces (from a jar of marinated
peppers), each sliced into six strips
24 pine nuts, to garnish

1 Preheat the oven to 200°C (180°C fan oven) mark 6. Brush both sides of the bread with olive oil, put on a baking sheet and bake for 15–20 minutes.
2 Remove the baking sheet from the oven. Spread 1tsp pesto on each croûton and top with a pepper strip and a pine nut.

Makes 24   preparation: 20 minutes, plus cooling   cooking time: 15–20 minutes
per croûton: 80 cals; 4g fat; 9g carbohydrate

Italian Antipasti Platter with Olives and Artichokes

115g pack antipasti containing 4 slices
each Parma ham and Bresaola and 8
slices salami Milano (reserve the Parma
ham for another meal)
2 large green olives

8 large black olives
¼ x 285g jar artichoke antipasto
2 sun-dried tomatoes in oil, drained
basil leaves and ciabatta, to serve

1 Divide the Bresaola and salami between two plates. Top each plate with 1 green and 4 black olives, half the artichoke antipasto and 1 sun-dried tomato.
2 Garnish with basil and serve with ciabatta.

Serves 2   preparation: 5 minutes
per serving: 250 cals; 21g fat; 5g carbohydrate

Melon, Parma Ham and Manchego Cheese

½ ripe Charentais melon, peeled and
deseeded
70g pack Parma ham

30 small basil leaves
75g (3oz) Manchego cheese

1 Cut the melon into 30 bite-sized pieces.
2 Cut the Parma ham into slices and wrap around the melon.
3 Thread the wrapped melon pieces on to cocktail sticks, then spear on a basil leaf and a small chunk of the Manchego.

Makes 30   preparation: 20 minutes
per canapé: 30 cals; 1g fat; 2g carbohydrate

Beef and Parma Ham Bites

olive oil, to brush
350g (12oz) fillet steak, about 2cm (¾ inch)
  thick
salt and pepper

6 slices Parma ham
48 basil leaves
24 sunblush tomatoes

1 Brush a little olive oil over the surface of a griddle pan, then heat until hot. Season the steak on both sides and cook for 3 minutes on each side to seal in all the juices. Leave to rest for 5 minutes. Preheat the oven to 200°C (180°C fan oven) mark 6.
2 Cut each slice of ham lengthways into four strips. Slice the steak into four lengths, then cut each into six pieces. Put a small basil leaf on top of each piece, then wrap a strip of ham around each piece of steak. Place the bites on a lightly oiled baking sheet and roast for 5–7 minutes until just cooked through.
3 Meanwhile, push a basil leaf and one of the sunblush tomatoes on to a cocktail stick and repeat until you have 24 assembled sticks. Remove the baking sheet from the oven and push one of the cocktail sticks halfway into each piece of beef, making sure the sharp end of the stick doesn't protrude. Put on to platters and serve warm.

Makes 24   preparation: 15 minutes, plus resting   cooking time: 11–13 minutes
per bite: 30 cals; 1g fat; trace carbohydrate

Mini Yorkshires with Steak and Horseradish

1tbsp sunflower oil
300g (11oz) rump steak
2 x 120g packs mini Yorkshire puddings
6tbsp crème fraîche

1tbsp horseradish
pepper
sprigs of watercress, to garnish

1 Preheat the oven to 200°C (180°C fan oven) mark 6. Heat the oil in a frying pan, then sear the steak over a medium to high heat to brown on both sides. For rare, remove from the pan immediately and slice into 24 pieces; for medium rare, reduce the heat and cook for a further 3 minutes (5 minutes for well done) before slicing – these timings are a rough guide only.
2 Meanwhile, put the Yorkshires in a roasting tin and heat in the oven for 10 minutes.
3 Mix the crème fraîche with the horseradish. Arrange the steak on the Yorkshires and top with horseradish cream. Season with pepper and garnish each pudding with a watercress sprig.

Makes 24   preparation: 20 minutes   cooking time: 10 minutes
per canapé: 60 cals; 4g fat; 3g carbohydrate

Roquefort and Cranberry Chipolatas

400g pack ready-to-eat cocktail sausages   3tbsp cranberry sauce
75g (3oz) Roquefort cheese, sliced

1 Preheat the grill to medium-high. Cut the sausages lengthways to make a slit, then stuff each with a
   small slice of Roquefort and put on a baking sheet.
2 Cook the sausages under the grill for about 2 minutes or until the cheese starts to melt. Skewer each
   sausage on to a cocktail stick and top with a little cranberry sauce to serve.

Makes 40   preparation: 15 minutes   cooking time: 2 minutes
per canapé: 40 cals; 3g fat; 2g carbohydrate

Sausage and Sage Rolls

6 good-quality pork sausages   1 egg, beaten with a pinch of salt
flour, to dust   24–48 sage leaves
375g pack ready-rolled shortcrust pastry

1 Slit the sausage skins and remove the meat. Put it into a bowl and mix well, using your hands.
2 Lightly dust a clean work surface and rolling pin with flour and open out the pastry. Roll slightly until
   it is about 1cm (½ inch) bigger. Cut in half lengthways to make two long strips, then position one strip
   so that the longest edge is nearest to you.
3 Dust your hands with flour. Take half the sausagemeat and roll it into a long sausage, then lay it down
   the middle of one pastry strip. Brush a little beaten egg along the long edge of the pastry furthest away
   from you. Take the near edge and roll over the sausagemeat to give a neat roll. Trim the long and short
   edges with a sharp knife, then cut the roll into 5cm (2 inch) pieces. Repeat with the rest of the pastry
   and sausagemeat.
4 Brush each roll with beaten egg, put one or two sage leaves on top, then brush again. Put on a baking
   sheet and chill for 15 minutes. Preheat the oven to 200°C (180°C fan oven) mark 6.
5 Bake the sausage rolls for 25 minutes until crispy and golden, then remove from the oven and use a
   palette knife to lift the rolls off the baking sheet and on to a wire rack to cool.

Makes 24   preparation: 20 minutes, plus chilling   cooking time: 25 minutes
per roll: 120 cals; 9g fat; 8g carbohydrate

Anchovy Rolls

14 thin slices white bread
125g (4oz) butter, softened
2tbsp Dijon mustard
4tbsp finely grated Parmesan cheese

50g can anchovies in olive oil, drained
olive oil, to drizzle
black pepper

1   Preheat the oven to 200°C (180°C fan oven) mark 6. Remove the crusts and butter the bread. Spread each slice with mustard, then sprinkle with half the Parmesan and place 1 anchovy fillet on each side of each slice. Roll the bread up tightly and cut in half.
2   Pack the rolls on to a baking sheet, seam side down, drizzle with the olive oil and sprinkle with the remaining cheese and the pepper. Transfer to the oven and cook for 15–20 minutes until golden. Serve warm.

Makes 28   preparation: 15 minutes   cooking time: 15–20 minutes
per roll: 80 cals; 5g fat; 7g carbohydrate

Finger Doughnuts

75g (3oz) unsalted butter, chopped
5tbsp golden caster sugar, plus extra
   to sprinkle
125g (4oz) plain flour

pinch of salt
3 large eggs, beaten
sunflower oil, to deep-fry

1   Put the butter, 1tbsp sugar and 250ml (8fl oz) water into a pan and melt the butter slowly.
2   Bring to the boil, then add the flour and salt. Using a wooden spoon, quickly beat the mixture together until it leaves the sides of the pan. Take off the heat and leave to cool slightly.
3   Add the eggs, a little at a time, and continue to beat the mixture to make a smooth, glossy dough.
4   Heat the oil in a deep-fat fryer to 190°C or until a cube of bread browns in 30 seconds. Spoon the dough into a piping bag fitted with a 2cm ($^3/_4$ inch) star-shaped nozzle. Pipe 10cm (4 inch) lengths of dough straight into the oil and cook for 3–5 minutes until golden, turning the doughnuts halfway through to brown them evenly. Lift out and drain on kitchen paper. Sprinkle heavily with sugar. Serve with hot chocolate .

Serves 6   makes about 24 doughnuts   10–15 minutes   cooking time: 15–20 minutes
per serving: 260 cals; 20g fat; 18g carbohydrate

Snacks

Cheese on Toast

2 slices white or brown bread
2tbsp mayonnaise
Dash of Worcestershire sauce

125g (4oz) Cheddar or Red Leicester
cheese, grated

1 Preheat the grill to high. Toast the bread on one side, then turn over
2 Spread the untoasted side of each slice with mayonnaise and sprinkle a dash of Worcestershire
   sauce onto each. Scatter over the grated cheese, then cook under a hot grill until golden and bubbling.

Serves 1 preparation: 5 minutes   cooking time: 5 minutes
per serving: 910 cals; 67g fat; 40g carbohydrate

Artichoke and Goat's Cheese Toasts

225g jar artichoke antipasto, drained and oil
   reserved
225g (8oz) firm goat's cheese, such as
   Crottin, rind removed and diced
1tbsp chopped thyme
grated zest of 1 lemon
1tbsp lemon juice
½tsp grainy mustard

salt and pepper
4 thick slices flavoured bread, such as olive
   or rosemary, toasted
70g pack cured Serrano or Parma ham
olive oil, to drizzle
thyme sprigs and crushed black pepper, to
   garnish

1 Halve the artichokes and put into a large bowl with the goat's cheese and thyme.
2 Whisk the lemon zest and juice with the mustard, 3tbsp reserved oil and seasoning, then stir into the
   artichoke mixture.
3 Divide the mixture between the slices of toast and arrange the ham on top. Drizzle with olive oil,
   garnish with thyme sprigs and pepper and serve immediately.

Serves 4 preparation: 15 minutes
per serving: 410 cals; 25g fat; 23g carbohydrate

The Ultimate Toasted Sandwich

50g (2oz) mature Cheddar cheese, finely
   grated
2tbsp mayonnaise
pinch of English mustard powder

salt and pepper
2 slices white country-style bread
2tbsp chutney, such as redcurrant and red
   onion chutney

1 Preheat the grill to high. Mix the cheese with the mayonnaise and mustard and season well.
2 Spread the cheese mixture over one slice of bread and place under the grill for 1–2 minutes or until the cheese is bubbling and golden. Remove from the grill.
3 Spread the chutney over the second slice of bread and sandwich together with the toasted cheese.
4 Grill the sandwich on each side to brown, then cut in half and serve.

Serves 1   preparation: 10 minutes   cooking time: 5 minutes
per serving: 700 cals; 43g fat; 60g carbohydrate

The Best Turkey Sandwich

4 slices walnut bread
2–4tbsp mayonnaise
2–4tbsp mango chutney

6 slices cooked cold turkey
2 little gem lettuces, sliced
salt and pepper

1 Spread two slices of bread with 1–2tbsp each of mayonnaise and the other two with 1–2tbsp each of mango chutney. Put 3 slices of turkey on top of the chutney, followed by 2–3 slices of lettuce. Season well, top with the other slice of bread and serve.

Serves 2   preparation: 5 minutes
per serving: 650 cals; 25g fat; 60g carbohydrate

Rustic Bread with Tomato and Ham

4 slices country bread
extra-virgin Spanish olive oil
salt and pepper

2 very ripe tomatoes, cut in half horizontally
4 slices Serrano ham

1 Heat a griddle pan. Brush both sides of the bread with oil and sprinkle with a little salt. Toast the bread on the griddle until golden.
2 Rub the cut side of each tomato over one slice of the bread to spread the flesh all over. Repeat with the remaining tomatoes and bread.
3 Cover each slice of bread with a slice of ham, season well, then drizzle with a little more oil and serve.

Serves 4   preparation: 5 minutes   cooking time: 5–10 minutes
per serving: 170 cals; 5g fat; 24g carbohydrate

Pork Pittas with Salsa

1tbsp olive oil
500g (1lb 2oz) diced pork
4tbsp fajita spicy seasoning
1 ripe avocado
1 red onion, peeled and chopped
4 large tomatoes, roughly chopped

small handful of coriander, roughly chopped
juice of 1 lime
salt and pepper
4 large pitta breads
100g tub Greek-style yogurt

1   Heat the olive oil in a pan and fry the pork over a medium heat for 3–4 minutes. Add the spicy seasoning
    to the pan and stir to coat the pork, then cook for a further 4–5 minutes until cooked through.
2   Meanwhile, make the salsa. Halve the avocado, remove the stone, then peel and chop the flesh. Put
    it in a bowl with the onion, tomatoes, coriander and lime juice. Mix well, season to taste and set aside.
3   Toast the pitta breads until lightly golden, then slit down the side and stuff with the pork, a dollop of
    salsa and a spoonful of yogurt. Serve immediately.

Serves 4   preparation: 10 minutes   cooking time: 10 minutes
per serving: 550 cals; 24g fat; 50g carbohydrate

Pastrami Tortilla Wraps

200g tub guacamole dip
2tbsp canned pimientos, chopped
salt and pepper
4 wheat tortillas
2 x 100g packs pastrami or salt beef

1 small red onion, peeled and very finely
  sliced
endive, mint sprigs and lime wedges, to
  garnish

1   Mix the guacamole with the pimientos and season.
2   Divide the guacamole between the tortillas and arrange the pastrami or salt beef on top. Sprinkle with
    the onion and roll each tortilla up like a sausage. Wrap individually in clingfilm and chill.
3   To serve, unwrap and cut the tortillas in half and garnish with endive, mint sprigs and lime wedges.

Serves 4   preparation: 20 minutes, plus chilling
per serving: 345 cals; 10g fat; 39g carbohydrate

Simple Tomato Salad

8 medium size on-the-vine tomatoes salt
1tbsp extra virgin olive oil black pepper
golden caster sugar

1   Slice and arrange the tomatoes on a plate, sprinkle with a pinch of golden caster and season with salt and freshly ground black pepper.
2   Leave for 20 minutes to allow the seasoning to draw out the juices.
3   Serve with a drizzle of fruity extra virgin olive oil – one made from Italian olives works well – and some toasted bread, rubbed with a garlic clove.

Serves 6   preparation: 15 minutes
  per serving: 60 cals; 4g fat; 5g carbohydrate

Tapenade

3tbsp capers, rinsed and drained 100ml (3½fl oz) olive oil
75g (3oz) pitted black olives 2tbsp brandy
50g can anchovy fillets in oil, drained black pepper

1   Put the capers, olives and anchovies in a blender or food processor and whiz briefly to chop.
2   With the motor running, add the olive oil in a steady stream. Stir in the brandy and season with pepper to taste. Transfer to a serving bowl.
3   Serve the tapenade with raw vegetable sticks and/or grilled vegetables and toasted French bread.

Serves 4–6   preparation: 5 minutes
per serving: 270–180 cals; 26–18g fat; trace carbohydrate

Garlic Bruschetta

3 garlic cloves, peeled and bruised with a
  rolling pin

6 thick slices white country bread
5tbsp olive oil

1 Heat a griddle pan until hot. Meanwhile, rub the garlic cloves on both sides of the bread, then brush both sides with the olive oil.
2 Put the bread on the hot griddle pan and cook until golden brown, pressing down on both sides. Serve with soup.

Serves 6 preparation: 5 minutes cooking time: 5 minutes
per serving: 230 cals; 12g fat; 25g carbohydrate

Cannellini and Chorizo Crostini

70g pack chorizo sausages, thinly sliced
100g can cannellini beans, drained and
  rinsed
2tbsp chopped flat-leafed parsley

2tbsp olive oil
salt and pepper
8 crostini
2tbsp thick mayonnaise

1 Fry the chorizo in a non-stick frying pan until crisp. Remove and drain on kitchen paper.
2 Toss the beans with the parsley and olive oil and season well.
3 Spread each crostini with a little mayonnaise, top with the chorizo and beans and serve.

Makes 8 crostini preparation: 20 minutes cooking time: 5 minutes
per crostini: 150 cals; 9g fat; 13g carbohydrate

Dolcelatte and Prune Crostini

175g (6oz) dolcelatte or Gorgonzola cheese
75g (3oz) pitted ready-to-eat prunes or
  dates, roughly chopped
50g (2oz) walnuts, chopped
1tsp chopped rosemary

pepper
4–8 slices ciabatta
olive oil, to drizzle
rosemary sprigs and coarse sea salt,
  to garnish

1 Preheat the grill to high. Crumble the cheese and mix with the prunes or dates, walnuts, rosemary and pepper.
2 Lightly toast the ciabatta, drizzle with olive oil and spoon the prune mixture on top. Place under the grill until the cheese has melted. Garnish with rosemary sprigs and sea salt, then serve.

Serves 8 preparation: 10 minutes cooking time: 5 minutes
per serving: 450 cals: 27g fat; 38g carbohydrate

Tomato Crostini with Feta and Basil Dressing

1 small garlic clove, peeled and crushed
3tbsp chopped basil
25g (1oz) pine nuts
2tbsp extra-virgin olive oil
grated zest and juice of 1 lime
50g (2oz) feta cheese
salt and pepper

4 large tomatoes, preferably vine-ripened,
   thickly sliced
150g tub fresh tomato salsa
50g (2oz) pitted black olives, roughly
   chopped
4 thick slices country-style bread
basil leaves, to garnish

1   Put the garlic, basil, pine nuts, olive oil, lime zest and juice in a food processor and whiz to a smooth paste. Add the cheese and blend. Thin with 1tbsp water if necessary. Season.
2   Put the tomatoes, salsa and olives in a bowl and toss together. Divide the tomato mixture between the slices of bread and spoon the basil dressing over the top. Garnish with basil leaves and serve.

Serves 2–4   preparation: 20 minutes
per serving: 580–290 cals; 33–16g fat; 57–28g carbohydrate

Chicken and Salsa Verde Crostini

3tbsp each roughly chopped coriander, mint
   and basil
1 garlic clove, peeled and roughly chopped
2tbsp Dijon mustard
3 anchovy fillets
1tbsp capers
50ml (2fl oz) olive oil
juice of ½ lemon
1 loaf walnut bread, cut into 1cm (½ inch)
   slices

2tbsp olive oil
1tbsp sea salt flakes
175g (6oz) cooked chicken breast, cut into
   15 slices
125g (4oz) sun-dried tomatoes in oil,
   drained and sliced into 15 pieces
50g (2oz) walnuts, lightly toasted and finely
   chopped, and flat-leafed parsley,
   to garnish

1   To make the salsa verde, put all the herbs, the garlic, mustard, anchovies, capers, olive oil and lemon juice in a food processor and whiz until smooth. Cover and chill.
2   Preheat the grill to high. To make the crostini, cut the bread slices into 2.5cm (1 inch) pieces. Place on a baking sheet, brush with olive oil and sprinkle with sea salt flakes. Place under the grill for 1 minute on each side or until lightly toasted.
3   To serve, place a slice of chicken on each crostini base, top with a spoonful of salsa verde and a slice of sun-dried tomato, then garnish with a sprinkling of walnuts and flat-leafed parsley.

Makes 15   preparation: 20 minutes, plus chilling   cooking time: 2 minutes
per crostini: 170 cals; 10g fat; 15g carbohydrate

Goat's Cheese and Red Onion Crostini

1 red onion, about 300g (11oz), peeled and
   finely sliced
2tbsp olive oil, plus extra to drizzle
75g (3oz) soft goat's cheese

8 crostini
black pepper
chopped thyme, to garnish

1 Preheat the grill to high. Put the onion on a baking sheet, drizzle with 2tbsp olive oil and grill for 5 minutes or until soft and just beginning to char.
2 Spread the goat's cheese on each crostini, then top with the onion and pepper. Drizzle with oil, garnish with thyme and serve.

Makes 8 crostini   preparation: 20 minutes   cooking time: 5 minutes
per crostini: 130 cals; 7g fat; 14g carbohydrate

Tomato and Garlic Crostini

225g (8oz) cherry tomatoes, halved
2 garlic cloves, peeled and thickly sliced
1tbsp extra-virgin olive oil
pinch of sugar

salt and pepper
1tbsp good-quality pesto
8 crostini
crushed black pepper, to garnish

1 Preheat the grill to medium-high. Put the cherry tomatoes in a roasting tin, scatter over the garlic slices, drizzle with olive oil and grill for 2–3 minutes or until the tomatoes soften. Sprinkle with the sugar and season.
2 Spread the pesto on each crostini, top with the grilled tomatoes and garlic. Garnish with crushed black pepper and serve.

Makes 8 crostini   preparation: 20 minutes   cooking time: 3 minutes
per crostini: 90 cals; 3g fat; 12g carbohydrate

Marinated Mushrooms in Crusty Rolls

1tbsp chopped tarragon

2tbsp red wine vinegar

2tsp wholegrain mustard

4tbsp truffle oil

4tbsp grapeseed oil

salt and pepper

225g (8oz) very fresh button mushrooms,
 halved or quartered

4 crusty bread rolls

tarragon leaves, to garnish

1   For the marinade, put the tarragon, vinegar, mustard and the truffle and grapeseed oils in a small bowl, whisk together and season.

2   Pour the marinade over the mushrooms and marinate for at least 30 minutes.

3   Just before serving, hollow out the crusty rolls and spoon in the mushrooms, then garnish with tarragon leaves.

Serves 4   preparation: 15 minutes, plus marinating

per serving: 360 cals; 27g fat; 25g carbohydrate

Garlic Mushrooms on Ciabatta

3 garlic cloves, peeled and crushed

2tbsp chopped chives

grated zest of 1 lemon

juice of ½ lemon

125g (4oz) unsalted butter, melted

salt and pepper

6 field mushrooms, thinly sliced

6 slices ciabatta bread

chopped parsley, to garnish

1   Preheat the oven to 180°C (160°C fan oven) mark 4. Put the garlic, chives, lemon zest, lemon juice and melted butter in a bowl, mix to combine, then season.

2   Put the mushrooms in an ovenproof dish, pour the butter mixture over, cover with foil and cook in the oven for 40–45 minutes or until the mushrooms are tender.

3   Meanwhile, grill the ciabatta. Remove the mushrooms from the oven and pile on to the ciabatta. Garnish with parsley and serve with salad leaves.

Serves 6   preparation: 5 minutes   cooking time: 45 minutes

per serving: 260 cals; 19g fat; 20g carbohydrate

Supper

Whether it's a tray for one in front of the telly, or a family meal for four, six or eight, supper is generally a time to unwind, relax and eat good food that you've enjoyed making.

A big steaming dish of Cheesy Shepherd's Pie is a real favourite – and it can be made a day or so ahead and reheated, like many stews and braises.

Hate washing up? Try the Foil-baked Haddock – succulent fish and vegetables in their own oven-baked parcel. Just add a big squeeze of lemon to the contents, turn out on to a plate and throw away the foil. Simple!

If you're a bit short of cash, tasty cuts of chicken, fish and meat are an ideal choice – like Sticky Chicken, using chicken thighs; Stuffed Pasta Shells with plump coarse sausages; or Mackerel with Hot Tomato Sauce.

Perhaps you've got a few friends coming round for supper – roasts are popular and can be left to their own devices while you all have a drink and chat. Try Cider Roast Pork cooked with red onions, apples and thyme, or Marinated Lamb with Tapenade Stuffing.

Good food and good company, what could be better?

Roast Chicken with Lemon Couscous

500g (1lb 2oz) couscous
600ml (1 pint) hot chicken stock
zest and juice of 3 lemons
400g can chickpeas, drained and rinsed
10tbsp chopped flat-leafed parsley and
  coriander
75g (3oz) preserved lemons, chopped, plus
  extra to garnish

100g (3½oz) unblanched almonds, roughly
  chopped
8 Medjool dates, halved, stoned and
  quartered
8tbsp extra-virgin olive oil
1 ready-roasted chicken
flat-leafed parsley, to garnish

1   Put the couscous in a large bowl, add the hot stock, lemon zest and juice. Cover and leave to absorb
    for 10 minutes. Fluff up with a fork.
2   Add the chickpeas to the couscous with the herbs, preserved lemons, almonds, dates and olive oil.
    Mix well, then cover and chill.
3   To joint the chicken, use a sharp knife to remove the legs, then slice the breast meat from either side.
    Slice off the wings.
4   Spoon the couscous and chicken on to plates, garnish with extra preserved lemon and flat-leafed parsley
    and serve.

Serves 6   preparation: 25 minutes, plus chilling
per serving: 1050 cals; 49g fat; 100g carbohydrate

Mediterranean Chicken

1tbsp olive oil
1 onion, peeled and finely chopped
2 garlic cloves, peeled and finely chopped
4 x 125g (4oz) skinless chicken breasts
2 courgettes, roughly chopped

400g can chopped tomatoes
100g (3½oz) olives, roughly chopped
2tbsp capers
4tbsp roughly chopped basil

1   Heat the olive oil in a non-stick flameproof casserole. Add the onion and cook gently for 7–8 minutes
    until soft. Add the garlic and cook for 1 minute.
2   Add the chicken to the pan and cook for 5 minutes. Add the courgettes, tomatoes, olives, capers and
    basil, then cover and cook for 30 minutes over a low heat until the chicken is cooked through.

Serves 4   preparation: 15 minutes   cooking time: 45 minutes
per serving: 250 cals; 12g fat; 7g carbohydrate

Spanish Spicy Chicken

½tsp turmeric
1.1 litres (2 pints) hot chicken stock
2tbsp vegetable oil
4 chicken thighs, skinned, boned and
  roughly diced
1 onion, peeled and chopped
1 red pepper, deseeded and sliced

50g (2oz) chorizo sausage, diced
2 garlic cloves, peeled and crushed
300g (11oz) long-grain rice
125g (4oz) frozen peas
salt and pepper
3tbsp chopped flat-leafed parsley

1   Add the turmeric to the hot stock and leave to infuse for at least 5 minutes.
2   Meanwhile, heat the oil in a large (at least 2.8 litres/5 pints capacity) frying pan and fry the chicken
    for 10 minutes or until golden. Remove from the pan and set aside.
3   Add the onion to the pan and cook over a medium heat for 5 minutes until soft. Add the red pepper
    and chorizo and cook for a further 5 minutes, then add the garlic and cook for 1 minute.
4   Return the chicken to the pan, add the rice and mix. Add one-third of the stock and bring to a simmer,
    then stir until all the liquid has been absorbed.
5   Add the remaining stock and the peas and bring to the boil, then reduce the heat to low and cook,
    uncovered, for 15–20 minutes until the rice absorbs all the liquid. Five minutes before the cooking time
    is up, season well and add the parsley. Serve with crusty bread.

Serves 4   preparation: 25 minutes, plus infusing   cooking time: 50 minutes
per serving: 500 cals; 13g fat; 68g carbohydrate

Chicken Cacciatore

2tbsp olive oil
8 skinless boneless chicken thighs
2 garlic cloves, peeled and crushed
1tsp each dried thyme and dried tarragon
150ml (¼ pint) white wine

400g can chopped tomatoes
black pepper
12 pitted black olives
12 capers, rinsed and drained

1   Heat the olive oil in a flameproof casserole over a high heat, add the chicken and brown all over.
    Reduce the heat and add the garlic, thyme, tarragon and wine to the pan. Stir for 1 minute, then add
    the tomatoes and black pepper.
2   Bring to the boil, then reduce the heat, cover the pan and simmer for 20 minutes or until the chicken
    is tender.
3   Lift the chicken out of the pan and put to one side. Bubble the sauce for 5 minutes or until thickened,
    add the olives and capers, stir well and cook for a further 2–3 minutes.
4   Return the chicken to the sauce. Serve with brown rice and broad beans or peas.

Serves 4   preparation: 5 minutes   cooking time: 40 minutes
per serving: 250 cals; 13g fat; 3g carbohydrate

Spicy Chicken with Lentils and Hummus Dressing

1tsp ground cumin

zest of 1 lemon and juice of ½ lemon

4 skinless, boneless chicken breasts

1tbsp olive oil, plus extra to brush

1 onion, peeled and finely chopped

1 carrot, peeled and finely chopped

1 celery stick, finely chopped

200g (7oz) Puy lentils

500ml (17fl oz) hot chicken or
 vegetable stock

225g (8oz) broccoli, chopped into florets

100g (3½oz) hummus

1tsp harissa paste

1   Mix the cumin with 1tsp lemon juice to form a paste. Rub over the chicken and put to one side.
2   Heat the olive oil in a large non-stick pan. Add the onion, carrot and celery and fry over a medium heat
    for 10 minutes. Add the lentils and hot stock and cover the pan, then reduce the heat and simmer
    for 25 minutes. Add the broccoli and cook for a further 7–8 minutes.
3   Meanwhile, brush a griddle or frying pan with a little olive oil. Heat the pan and cook the chicken for
    8–10 minutes on each side.
4   Put the hummus in a bowl, add the lemon zest, remaining lemon juice and the harissa and stir well
    to mix. Serve the chicken and lentils with the hummus dressing.

Serves 4   preparation: 20 minutes   cooking time: 45 minutes
per serving: 430 cals; 15g fat; 32g carbohydrate

Chicken with Peanut Sauce

4 skinless boneless chicken breasts,
  cut into strips

1tbsp ground coriander

2 garlic cloves, peeled and finely chopped

5tbsp vegetable oil

2tbsp runny honey

2tbsp curry paste

2tbsp light muscovado sugar

2tbsp peanut butter

200ml (7fl oz) coconut milk

1   Put the chicken in a bowl and mix in the ground coriander, garlic, 4tbsp oil and the honey. Leave to
    marinate for 15 minutes.
2   To make the peanut sauce, heat the remaining oil in a pan, add the curry paste, sugar and peanut
    butter and fry for 1 minute. Add the coconut milk and bring to the boil, stirring all the time, then reduce
    the heat and simmer for 5 minutes.
3   Meanwhile, preheat a wok and, when hot, stir-fry the chicken in batches for 3–4 minutes or until
    cooked, adding more oil if needed.
4   Serve the chicken on a bed of Thai fragrant rice with chopped coriander, with the peanut sauce
    poured over.

Serves 4   preparation: 5 minutes, plus marinating   cooking time: 20 minutes
per serving: 400 cals ; 24g fat; 13g carbohydrate

Chicken with Spicy Couscous

125g (4oz) couscous
salt and pepper
1 ripe mango, peeled and cut into
  2.5cm (1 inch) chunks
1tbsp lemon or lime juice
125g tub fresh tomato salsa
3tbsp mango chutney

3tbsp orange juice
2tbsp chopped coriander
200g pack chargrilled chicken fillets
4tbsp fromage frais
roughly chopped coriander and lime
  chunks, to garnish

1 Put the couscous into a large bowl, pour over 300ml (½ pint) boiling water, season well and leave to stand for 15 minutes. Put the mango on a plate and sprinkle with the lemon or lime juice.
2 Mix the tomato salsa with the mango chutney, orange juice and coriander.
3 Drain the couscous if necessary. Stir the salsa mixture into the couscous and check the seasoning. Turn on to a large serving dish and arrange the chicken and mango on top. Just before serving, spoon the fromage frais over the chicken and garnish with the coriander and lime chunks.

Serves 4   preparation: 15 minutes, plus soaking
per serving: 290 cals; 4g fat; 44g carbohydrate

Chicken and Leek Pie

5 large potatoes, peeled and
  chopped into chunks
salt and pepper
200g carton half-fat crème fraîche

3 boneless chicken breasts with skin
3 large leeks
about 10 tarragon leaves

1 Preheat the oven to 200°C (180°C fan oven) mark 6. Put the potatoes in a pan of lightly salted water, cover, bring to the boil, then reduce the heat and simmer for 10–12 minutes until soft. Drain, return to the pan, add 1tbsp crème fraîche and seasoning and mash well.
2 Meanwhile, heat a frying pan and add the chicken, skin side down. Fry for 5 minutes until the skin is golden, then turn and fry for 6–8 minutes on the other side. While the chicken is cooking, chop the leeks into chunks and finely chop the tarragon.
3 Transfer the chicken to a board. Tip the leeks into the pan and cook in the chicken juices for 5 minutes to soften.
4 Discard the chicken skin and cut the flesh into bite-sized pieces (don't worry if it's not quite cooked through). Return the chicken to the pan, stir in the remaining crème fraîche and heat for 2–3 minutes until bubbling. Stir in the tarragon, season well, then spoon into a 1.7 litre (3 pint) ovenproof dish. Spread the mash on top.
5 Cook in the oven for 20–25 minutes until golden and cooked through.

Serves 4   preparation: 10 minutes   cooking time: 40–45 minutes
per serving: 470 cals; 14g fat; 54g carbohydrate

Stuffed Chicken with Potatoes and Roasted Tomatoes

3 large potatoes, peeled and sliced
3tbsp olive oil
4 chicken breasts, with skin

125g (4oz) cream cheese with herbs
salt and pepper
300g (11oz) cherry tomatoes on the vine

1   Preheat the oven to 220°C (200°C fan oven) mark 7. Line a roasting tin with baking parchment. Spread the potatoes in the tin, drizzle with 2tbsp olive oil, toss to coat, then roast for 20–25 minutes.
2   Remove the chicken from the oven and, using a sharp knife, ease the skin away from each chicken breast, leaving it attached along one side. Spread the cream cheese across each breast, then smooth the skin back over it. Brush the skin with the remaining oil and season.
3   Heat a non-stick frying pan over a medium heat until hot, then fry the chicken, skin side down, for 5 minutes until browned. Carefully turn the chicken over and fry for 5 minutes on the other side.
4   Reduce the oven temperature to 190°C (170°C fan oven) mark 5. Put the chicken on top of the potatoes, add the tomatoes and roast for 10–12 minutes until the chicken is cooked through, the potatoes are crisp and the tomatoes roasted.

Serves 4   preparation: 10 minutes   cooking time: 30–40 minutes
per serving: 660 cals; 43g fat; 32g carbohydrate

Chicken with Fennel and Tarragon

1tbsp olive oil
4 chicken thighs
1 onion, peeled and finely chopped
1 fennel bulb, sliced

½ lemon
200ml (7fl oz) hot chicken stock
200ml carton crème fraîche
1 small bunch tarragon

1   Preheat the oven to 200°C (180°C fan oven) mark 6. Heat the olive oil in a large flameproof casserole. Add the chicken and fry for 5 minutes until brown, then remove from the pan and put to one side to keep warm.
2   Add the onion to the pan and fry for 5 minutes, then add the fennel and cook for 5–10 minutes until softened.
3   Squeeze the juice from the lemon and pour into the pan, then add the hot stock. Bring to a simmer and cook until the sauce is reduced by half.
4   Stir in the crème fraîche and return the chicken to the pan. Stir once to mix, then cover, transfer to the oven and cook for 25–30 minutes.
5   To serve, roughly chop the tarragon and stir it into the sauce.

Serves 4   preparation: 10 minutes   cooking time: 45–55 minutes
per serving: 280 cals; 22g fat; 6g carbohyydrate

Chicken in a Pot

2tbsp vegetable oil
1 large onion, peeled and cut into wedges
2 rindless streaky bacon rashers, chopped
1.4–1.6kg (3–3½lb) whole chicken
6 medium carrots, peeled
2 small turnips, peeled and cut into wedges
1 garlic clove, peeled and crushed

bouquet garni (2 bay leaves, few thyme
  sprigs, small bunch of parsley)
600ml (1 pint) hot chicken stock
100ml (3½fl oz) dry white wine
salt and pepper
12 button mushrooms
3tbsp chopped flat-leafed parsley

1 Preheat the oven to 200°C (180°C fan oven) mark 6. Heat the oil in a flameproof casserole, then add the onion and bacon and fry for 5 minutes until golden. Remove and set aside.

2 Add the chicken to the casserole and brown all over for 10 minutes, then remove and set aside. Add the carrots, turnips and garlic and fry for 5 minutes.

3 Return the bacon and onion to the pan, then put the chicken back in. Add the bouquet garni, hot stock and wine and season. Bring to the boil, then cover and cook in the oven for 30 minutes.

4 Remove from the oven and add the mushrooms. Baste, then re-cover and cook in the oven for a further 50 minutes.

5 Remove the casserole from the oven and stir in the parsley. Carefully lift the chicken out of the pan – tip any liquid out of it back into the pan. Put the chicken on a board and carve. Serve with the vegetables, cooking liquid and some mashed potatoes.

Serves 6   preparation: 20 minutes   cooking time: 1 hour 40 minutes
per serving: 470 cals; 34g fat; 10g carbohydrate

Spicy Chicken with Tomatoes and Chickpeas

4 chicken breast fillets or skinless boneless
   chicken breasts, about 550g (1¼lb)
salt and pepper
4tsp harissa paste
1tbsp olive oil
3 onions, peeled and sliced
2 garlic cloves, peeled and sliced

2tbsp white wine vinegar
400g can chopped tomatoes
300ml carton fresh chicken stock
400g can chickpeas, drained and rinsed
juice of ½ lemon
coriander leaves, to garnish

1 Season the chicken pieces and rub each with the harissa paste.
2 Heat the olive oil in a frying pan, add the chicken and cook over a high heat for 10 minutes until golden. Remove from the pan and set aside.
3 Reduce the heat to medium, add the onions and garlic to the pan and cook for 10–15 minutes until softened. Add the vinegar, cook for 5 seconds, then add the tomatoes and stock. Return the chicken to the pan, season and bring to the boil, then reduce the heat and simmer for 15 minutes.
4 Add the chickpeas and cook for 5 minutes, then stir in the lemon juice. Serve with coriander leaves sprinkled over.

Serves 4   preparation: 10 minutes   cooking time: 45 minutes
per serving: 316 cals; 10g fat; 20g carbohydrate

Griddled Chicken with Melting Onions and Cheese

8 boned chicken thighs with skin, about
   900g (2lb) in total
3 or 4 rosemary sprigs, roughly chopped
salt and pepper
25g (1oz) ready-made garlic butter

450g (1lb) red onions, peeled and cut into
   thin wedges
125g (4oz) Gruyère or mature Cheddar
   cheese, coarsely grated

1 If using wooden skewers pre-soak four in cold water for 30 minutes.
2 Put the chicken thighs between two sheets of clingfilm and flatten them a little with a rolling pin, then push two on to each skewer. Make two or three slashes in each thigh, then push in some of the rosemary. Season the chicken well.
3 Lightly grease a large griddle pan or non-stick frying pan with a little of the garlic butter. Put the pan over a medium heat, add the chicken, skin side down, and cook for 2–3 minutes until the fat begins to run. Add the onion wedges, increase the heat to high and cook for 12–15 minutes, turning occasionally, until the whole dish is golden and tender and the chicken is cooked through.
4 Mix the remaining garlic butter and rosemary with the cheese, then dot over the chicken. Reduce the heat to low and cook for 2–3 minutes until the butter and cheese mixture has melted over the chicken. Discard the skewers and serve.

Serves 4   preparation: 15 minutes   cooking time: 20–25 minutes
per serving: 620 cals; 42g fat; 9g carbohydrate

Grilled Chicken with Mango and Fennel Salsa

4 skinless chicken breasts
salt and pepper
1 lime, halved
oil-water spray
1 mango, halved and diced

1 small fennel, trimmed and diced
1 fresh chilli, deseeded and finely diced
1tbsp balsamic vinegar
2tbsp chopped flat-leafed parsley
2tbsp chopped mint

1 Preheat the grill to medium. Put the chicken on a grill pan and season generously. Pour over the juice of ½ lime and spray with the oil-water. Grill for 8–10 minutes on each side or until cooked and the juices run clear when pierced with a skewer. Set aside.
2 Combine the remaining ingredients in a bowl with the juice of the remaining lime and season generously. Spoon on top of the chicken and serve with rocket leaves.

Serves 4   preparation: 12 minutes   cooking time: 20 minutes
per serving: 240 cals; 7g fat; 13g carbohydrate

Sticky Chicken

2tbsp sunflower oil
1 large onion, about 225g (8oz),
   peeled and thickly sliced
2tsp turmeric
12 chicken thighs on the bone, with skin

4tbsp runny honey
salt and pepper
2tbsp chopped mint
2tbsp flaked almonds
juice of ½ lemon

1 Heat the oil in a shallow flameproof casserole or gratin dish. Add the onion and cook slowly for 10–15 minutes until soft but not coloured. Add the turmeric and cook for 1 minute.
2 Remove the pan from the heat, then add the chicken, skin side up in a single layer, the honey, seasoning and half the chopped mint. (If your dish isn't suitable for placing under the grill, transfer everything to the grill pan – remove the wire rack and line the pan with foil.)
3 Preheat the grill to its highest setting and put the dish or grill pan about 5cm (2 inches) away from the heat. Cook the chicken for about 30 minutes, basting from time to time. As the chicken begins to brown, reduce the heat to low to medium.
4 Stir the almonds into the pan and continue to cook for 5 minutes until the nuts are golden and the chicken is charred and tender. (To tell whether the chicken thighs are cooked, cut into one to make sure there's no trace of pink flesh.) Just before serving, add the lemon juice to taste and stir in the remaining chopped mint. Serve on a bed of couscous, garnished with mint sprigs.

Serves 4   preparation: 5 minutes   cooking time: 50 minutes
per serving: 530 cals; 34g fat; 16g carbohydrate

Garlic, Orange and Rosemary Roast Turkey

3tbsp olive oil

1 onion, peeled and finely chopped

1 fat garlic clove, peeled and finely chopped

50g (2oz) stale white bread

2tbsp rosemary leaves, plus about 10 extra
   sprigs

3 oranges

1.5kg (3¼lb) boneless rolled turkey breast
   joint

1tbsp paprika

100ml (3½fl oz) Madeira

2 x 300ml cartons fresh chicken stock

salt and pepper

1 Preheat the oven to 200°C (180°C fan oven) mark 6. Heat 2tbsp olive oil in a small pan and sauté the onion over a low heat until soft and transparent. Add the garlic and cook for 1 minute. Cool. Put the bread in a processor with the rosemary leaves and whiz into fine crumbs.

2 Take 1 orange and finely grate half the zest. Peel the orange and discard the skin and pith. Chop the flesh, add to the food processor with the reserved zest and whiz to mix. Add to the onion mixture and season well.

3 Cut the turkey almost in half lengthways. Spoon the orange stuffing on the fleshy half and cover with the other half. Tie securely in several places with string and put in a small roasting tin.

4 Drizzle the remaining oil over the turkey and sprinkle with paprika. Squeeze the juice from the second orange and pour around the turkey. Season well, then roast the turkey for 1 hour, basting every 20 minutes. Take the tin out of the oven, then snip the trussing strings and remove carefully.

5 Slice the third orange thinly and put on top of the turkey, along the centre. Secure with rosemary sprigs. Return the tin to the oven and roast for 30 minutes or until cooked through – the juices should run clear when the meat is pierced in the thickest part with a skewer.

6 Transfer the turkey to a board, cover and leave to rest. Add the Madeira to the roasting tin, put on the hob and bring to the boil, then cook until reduced by half. Add the stock to the tin, bring to the boil and cook for about 15 minutes until reduced by two-thirds. Season to taste and strain into a jug to serve with the turkey.

Serves 8   preparation: 45 minutes   cooking time: 1 hour 35 minutes
per serving: 300 cals; 10g fat; 39g carbohydrate

Chicken in a Pan

2tbsp olive oil

8 small chicken portions, skin left on

1 large Spanish onion, peeled and thinly sliced

1 fat garlic clove, peeled and crushed

few thyme sprigs, roughly chopped

450g (1lb) small new potatoes, scrubbed,
 larger ones cut in half

350ml (12fl oz) chicken stock mixed about half
 and half with any leftover dry white wine

salt and pepper

125g (4oz) fresh peas or broad beans

1 Preheat the oven to 190°C (170°C fan oven) mark 5. Heat the olive oil in a roasting tin or large ovenproof frying pan on the hob. Add the chicken, skin side down, with the onion, garlic and thyme. Fry for 2–3 minutes or until skin is golden. Turn and brown the other side.2 Add the potatoes and cook, stirring, until coated in oil and beginning to turn golden. Add the stock and wine mixture, scraping up the crusty bits from the base of the tin. Season well, bring to the boil, then bubble gently for 5 minutes.

3 Transfer to the oven and roast for about 45 minutes or until the meat and potatoes are tender and golden and the gravy is bubbling.

4 Just before serving, cook the peas or beans in boiling salted water for 3–4 minutes, then drain and stir in with the chicken.

Serves 4   preparation: 15 minutes   cooking time: about 1 hour

per serving: 530 cals; 34g fat; 23g carbohydrate

Chicken Rarebit

4 large chicken breasts, with skin

15g (½oz) butter

1tbsp plain flour

75ml (3fl oz) full-fat milk

175g (6oz) Gruyère cheese, grated

25g (1oz) fresh white breadcrumbs

1tsp English mustard

2 fat garlic cloves, peeled and crushed

1 egg yolk

1 Preheat the oven to 200°C (180°C fan oven) mark 6. Put the chicken in a single layer in a heatproof serving dish and roast for 20 minutes or until cooked through.

2 Meanwhile, melt the butter in a pan over a low heat, then add the flour and stir for 1 minute. Gradually add the milk and stir in to make a smooth sauce.

3 Add the cheese, breadcrumbs, mustard and garlic to the sauce and cook for 1 minute. Cool briefly, then beat in the egg. Preheat the grill to medium-high.

4 Discard the skin from the cooked chicken and beat any pan juices into the cheese mixture. Spread the paste evenly over each chicken breast, then grill for 2–3 minutes or until golden. Serve with boiled new potatoes.

Serves 4   preparation: 5 minutes   cooking time: 25 minutes

per serving: 440 cals; 26g fat; 7g carbohydrate

Guinea Fowl with Apple and Hazelnut Stuffing

3tbsp olive oil
½ onion, peeled and finely chopped, plus
  1 onion cut into quarters
½ small eating apple, cored and chopped,
  plus 1 apple, halved and cored
75g (3oz) stale bread, chopped
25g (1oz) hazelnuts, chopped and toasted
zest of ½ lemon
1 rosemary sprig, leaves picked off and
  chopped

1 egg, beaten
salt and pepper
1kg (2¼lb) guinea fowl
1tbsp plain flour
75ml (3½fl oz) red wine
1tbsp redcurrant jelly
1tbsp balsamic vinegar
bay leaves, to garnish (optional)

1 To make the stuffing, heat 1tbsp olive oil in a pan, add the finely chopped onion and cook over a low heat for 15 minutes until soft. Spoon the onion into a bowl and add the chopped apple, bread, hazelnuts, lemon zest and rosemary. Add the egg to the bowl, season well, then mix well.

2 Preheat the oven to 200°C (180°C fan oven) mark 6. Spoon half the stuffing into the neck end of the guinea fowl and secure with a small metal skewer. Put the remainder into two 150ml (¼ pint) ramekins and set aside. Put two quarters of the second onion into the cavity of the guinea fowl, then tie the legs together with string. Rub the breast with the remaining oil and season well. Put in a roasting tin, add 150ml (¼ pint) water and roast for 20 minutes per 450g (1lb) plus 20 minutes, basting halfway through.

3 Cook the stuffing pots for the last 30 minutes of the roasting time. Add the remaining onion quarters and the halved apple to the roasting tin.

4 Transfer the bird to a warm plate, cover with foil and leave to rest. Keep the onion and apple warm. Add the flour to the roasting tin and cook on the hob for 1 minute, scraping up the goodness from the bottom of the pan. Add the wine, redcurrant jelly and vinegar and season. Bring to the boil and cook, stirring well, for 5 minutes. Pour into a warm jug. Carve the guinea fowl and serve with the gravy, onion and apple. Garnish with bay leaves, if using.

Serves 2 with leftovers   preparation: 20 minutes   cooking time: about 1 hour 25 minutes
per serving: 400 cals; 22g fat; 24g carbohydrate

Duck with Marmalade

4 small duck legs
2 garlic cloves, peeled and crushed
2.5cm (1 inch) piece fresh root ginger,
  peeled and finely grated
pinch of five-spice powder (optional)

2tbsp bitter orange marmalade
grated zest and juice of 1 large orange, plus
  extra wedges to serve
salt and pepper

1 Prick the duck legs all over with a skewer or fork, then put them in a large pan. Cover with cold water, bring to the boil and simmer for 15 minutes.
2 Meanwhile, mix together all the remaining ingredients except the seasoning.
3 Preheat the grill to its highest setting. Drain the duck, then put on a foil-lined grill pan, skin side down, and spoon half the orange mixture evenly over the legs. Grill for 5 minutes, then turn the duck skin side up and spoon over the remaining mixture. Season generously and grill for a further 5 minutes or until the duck skin is charred and crisp. Serve with orange wedges to squeeze over the top of the duck and some couscous.

Serves 4 preparation: 5 minutes cooking time: 25 minutes
per serving: 230 cals; 18g fat; 5g carbohydrate

Chargrilled Lamb with Lemon

about 700g (1½lb) diced leg of lamb (don't
  trim away all the fat)
2 medium onions, peeled and
  cut into thin wedges
2 garlic cloves, peeled and sliced
1tsp cumin seeds or ground cumin
4tbsp olive oil

salt and pepper
few sprigs of thyme, plus extra thyme
  leaves to garnish
1 lemon
170g tub hummus
150g tub Greek-style natural yogurt

1 Put the lamb in a bowl with the onions, garlic, cumin and olive oil. Toss everything together and set aside to marinate for at least 15 minutes, but ideally about 1 hour.
2 Preheat the grill to its highest setting. Spread the lamb mixture in an even layer over the bottom of the grill pan. Season generously and sprinkle with thyme. Roughly chop the lemon and squeeze the juice over the lamb, then add the lemon pieces to the pan.
3 Place the pan under the grill, about 5cm (2 inches) away from the heat. Turn the mixture over with a wooden spoon as it browns. After about 12–15 minutes the lamb should be nicely charred on the outside and just pink in the middle and the flesh in the lemon pieces will be soft and mellow.
4 Put the hummus into a small serving bowl, stir in 2tbsp of the pan juices and the yogurt and serve with the lamb.

Serves 4 preparation: 10 minutes, plus marinating cooking time: 12–15 minutes
per serving: 690 cals; 55g fat; 13g carbohydrate

Greek Lamb and Feta Layer

5tbsp olive oil

1 large onion, peeled and finely chopped

900g (2lb) minced lamb

2 garlic cloves, peeled and crushed

2tbsp tomato purée

2 x 400g cans plum tomatoes in
tomato juice

3tbsp Worcestershire sauce

2tbsp chopped oregano

salt and pepper

3 large potatoes, about 1kg (2¼lb)

2 large aubergines, cut into
5mm (¼ inch) slices

2 x 500g tubs Greek-style yogurt

4 large eggs, beaten

50g (2oz) freshly grated Parmesan cheese

pinch of freshly grated nutmeg

200g pack feta cheese, crumbled

1 Heat 2tbsp olive oil in a large pan, add the onion and cook over a low heat for 10 minutes or until soft. Put the mince in a large non-stick frying pan and cook over a high heat, breaking up the mince with the back of a spoon as it cooks, until the liquid has been driven off and the lamb is brown. This will take 10–15 minutes. Add the garlic and tomato purée to the lamb and cook for a further 2 minutes. Add the lamb to the onion with the tomatoes, Worcestershire sauce and oregano. Bring to the boil and season. Reduce the heat, cover the pan and simmer for 30–40 minutes or until the lamb is tender.

2 Meanwhile, put the potatoes in a pan of lightly salted water, bring to the boil, then reduce the heat and simmer, partially covered, for 20–30 minutes or until tender. Drain and leave to cool, then peel and slice thickly.

3 Brush the aubergine slices with the remaining oil. Preheat two non-stick frying pans and cook the aubergine slices for 2–3 minutes on each side or until soft.

4 Preheat the oven to 180°C (160°C fan oven) mark 4. Mix the yogurt with the eggs and half the Parmesan, season the sauce to taste, then add the nutmeg.

5 Divide the lamb between two 1.4 litre (2½ pint) ovenproof dishes or eight individual ovenproof serving dishes. Layer the potato, feta and aubergine on top of the lamb. Pour the yogurt sauce over the vegetables and sprinkle with the remaining Parmesan.

6 Bake for 35–40 minutes until the top has browned and it's piping hot to the centre. Serve with salad.

Serves 8   preparation: 20 minutes   cooking time: 1 hour 50 minutes
per serving: 650 cals; 41g fat; 28g carbohydrate

Marinated Lamb with Tapenade Stuffing

50g can anchovy fillets, drained and
  chopped
125g (4oz) pitted black olives
2 garlic cloves, peeled
1tbsp each chopped rosemary, thyme and
  flat-leafed parsley
4tbsp olive oil
salt and pepper

1.8kg (4lb) leg of lamb, boned, or 2.7kg (0lb)
  shoulder of lamb, boned
300ml (½ pint) robust red wine
2 sprigs each rosemary and thyme
2 bay leaves
1tsp redcurrant jelly
450ml (¾ pint) lamb stock

1   To make the tapenade, put the anchovies, olives, garlic and chopped herbs in a food processor and whiz until smooth. Gradually add 2tbsp olive oil, then season with pepper.
2   Stuff the bone cavity of the lamb with the mixture and sew up with thread or secure with cocktail sticks. Season again with pepper.
3   Make incisions all over the lamb and put in a large non-metallic bowl with the remaining oil, the wine, rosemary and thyme sprigs and the bay leaves. Marinate for at least 6 hours or overnight.
4   Preheat the oven to 220°C (200°C fan oven) mark 7. Drain the lamb, reserving the marinade, then pat dry. Heat a large frying pan and quickly brown the lamb on all sides over a high heat. Place in a roasting tin and roast for 30 minutes, then reduce the heat to 200°C (180°C fan oven) mark 6 and cook for a further 45 minutes–1 hour, basting from time to time.
5   Remove the tin from the oven, transfer the lamb to a board and keep warm. Skim the fat from the tin and discard. Add the reserved marinating liquor, the redcurrant jelly and stock. Put on the hob, bring to the boil and bubble for 5–10 minutes. Adjust the seasoning and strain.
6   Carve the lamb in thick slices and serve with the pan juices, with ratatouille and sauté potatoes.

Serves 6   preparation: 30 minutes, plus marinating   cooking time: 1 hour 40 minutes
per serving: 480 cals; 29g fat; 1g carbohydrate

Roast Spiced Leg of Lamb

1.6–1.8kg (3½–4lb) leg of lamb
2tbsp each cumin seeds and
  coriander seeds
50g (2oz) blanched or flaked almonds
1 medium onion, peeled and chopped
6 garlic cloves, peeled and roughly chopped
2.5cm (1 inch) piece fresh root ginger,
  peeled and grated
4 hot green chillies, deseeded and
  roughly chopped
500g carton natural yogurt

½tsp cayenne pepper
3½tsp salt
½tsp garam masala
4tbsp vegetable oil
½tsp cloves
16 cardamom pods
1 cinnamon stick
10 black peppercorns
flat-leafed parsley sprigs, to garnish
  (optional)

1   Trim off and discard all the fat and parchment-like skin from the lamb. Put the meat into a large shallow ceramic dish and set aside.

2   Put the cumin and coriander seeds into a pan and cook over a high heat until they begin to release their aromas. Put them into a mortar and grind with the pestle to a fine powder. Set aside.

3   Put the almonds, onion, garlic, ginger, chillies and 3tbsp yogurt into a food processor and whiz to a paste. Put the remaining yogurt into a bowl, stir well and add the paste, the ground cumin and coriander seeds, the cayenne pepper, salt and garam masala. Stir well to combine.

4   Spoon the yogurt mixture over the lamb and use a brush to encourage it into all the nooks and crannies. Turn the lamb over, making sure the leg is well coated, then cover with clingfilm, put into the fridge and leave to marinate for 24 hours.

5   Remove the lamb from the fridge about 45 minutes before you want to cook it, to allow it to come up to room temperature. Preheat the oven to 200°C (180°C fan oven) mark 6. Transfer the lamb and all the marinade to a roasting tin. Heat the oil in a small frying pan, add the cloves, cardamom pods, cinnamon and peppercorns and fry until they begin to release their aromas. Pour over the lamb.

6   Cover the roasting tin with foil and roast for 1½ hours. Remove the foil, put back in the oven and roast for a further 45 minutes, basting occasionally.

7   Transfer the lamb to a serving platter and press the sauce through a fine sieve into a bowl. Garnish the lamb with parsley, if using, and serve the sauce on the side.

Serves 6   preparation: 20 minutes, plus marinating   cooking time: 2¼ hours
per serving: 427 cals; 23g fat; 9g carbohydrate

Lamb and Rosemary Ragu

450g (1lb) minced lamb
225g (8oz) large onion, peeled and
  finely chopped
1 rosemary sprig or 1 large pinch dried
200ml (7fl oz) red wine

350g tub chilled fresh Napoletana sauce
salt and pepper
350g (12oz) dried tagliatelle
Parmesan or feta cheese shavings
rosemary sprigs, to garnish

1 Put the lamb in a non-stick pan over a high heat and brown, stirring to break up any lumps. Allow a good 5–7 minutes to do this, as getting the mince a dark golden brown colour at this stage will add bags of flavour to the finished sauce. Remove the mince and put to one side.

2 Add the onion to the pan with the rosemary (there should be enough fat left from the mince without having to add any extra oil) and fry for about 10 minutes until the onion is soft and golden.

3 Return the mince to the pan, keep over a high heat and stir in the wine. Scrape the bottom of the pan to loosen any crusty bits, then leave to bubble for 1–2 minutes until reduced by half. Stir in the Napoletana sauce, cover the pan, reduce the heat and simmer for 20 minutes. Season to taste.

4 Meanwhile, cook the tagliatelle in a large pan of boiling salted water for about 10 minutes, then drain and pour into a serving dish. Stir the lamb ragu into the pasta, sprinkle the cheese over, garnish with rosemary sprigs and serve.

Serves 4   preparation: 5 minutes   cooking time: 40 minutes
per serving: 640 cals; 19g fat; 76g carbohydrate

Lamb with Butter Beans and Spinach

2tbsp olive oil

1 onion, peeled and finely sliced

1 garlic clove, peeled and crushed

2 x 400g cans butter beans, drained and
   rinsed

200g (7oz) spinach

4 small lamb chops

3tbsp low-fat yogurt

2tbsp tahini

1tsp harissa paste

1 lemon

salt and pepper

1 Heat 1tbsp olive oil in a large pan. Add the onion and fry over a medium heat for 10 minutes until soft
   and golden. Add the garlic, cook for 1 minute, then add the butter beans and spinach and cook for
   1–2 minutes to warm through and wilt the spinach.
2 Meanwhile, brush the lamb chops with a little oil and fry in a separate pan over a medium heat for
   3–4 minutes on each side.
3 To make the dressing, put the remaining oil in a bowl, add the yogurt, tahini, harissa, juice of ½ lemon
   and 2tbsp cold water. Season and mix well.
4 Cut the remaining lemon half into wedges. To serve, divide the butter bean mixture among four
   warmed plates. Top with the lamb chops, add a dollop of dressing and serve with the lemon wedges.

Serves 4   preparation: 5 minutes   cooking time: 12–13 minutes
per serving: 450 cals; 21g fat; 29g carbohydrate

Roasted Tomato Salad with Pan-fried Lamb

6 medium-sized plum tomatoes, halved

1 red onion, peeled and sliced into
   thin wedges

75ml (3fl oz) olive oil

pinch of sugar

leaves from half a 20g pack thyme

salt and pepper

8 small boneless lamb chops

2 garlic cloves, peeled and sliced
   into slivers

2tbsp red wine vinegar

1 Preheat the oven to 200°C (180°C fan oven) mark 6. Pre-soak eight wooden skewers in cold water
   for 30 minutes. Put the tomatoes in a small roasting tin, cut side up. Put the onion wedges into a small
   bowl and stir in the olive oil, sugar and half the thyme leaves. Spoon the mixture over and around the
   tomatoes, then season with salt and plenty of pepper. Roast for 20 minutes or until the tomatoes are
   cooked and about to collapse. The onions should still be quite crisp.
2 Meanwhile, skewer the lamb chops lengthways with wooden skewers. Heat a non-stick frying pan
   over a high heat and fry the chops and garlic for 5–7 minutes on each side or until the lamb is browned
   and just pink in the centre. Remove the skewers.
3 Remove the vegetables from the oven. Sprinkle with the remaining thyme leaves, then pour over the
   vinegar and check the seasoning. Serve warm with the lamb chops.

Serves 4   preparation: 10 minutes   cooking time: 20 minutes
per serving: 180 cals; 17g fat; 6g carbohydrate

Lamb Boulangère with Red Pepper Salsa

100g (3½oz) butter, at room temperature, plus extra to grease
1.8kg (4lb) waxy potatoes, such as King Edward, finely sliced
1 onion, peeled, sliced and blanched in boiling water for 2 minutes
salt and pepper
600ml (1 pint) vegetable stock
3 red peppers

3tbsp extra-virgin olive oil
5 garlic cloves, peeled and crushed
3tbsp finely chopped mint
2tbsp finely chopped rosemary
1 leg of lamb, about 2.3kg (5lb)
1 small red onion, peeled and finely sliced
juice of ½ lemon
1–2tbsp baby capers, rinsed
5 mint leaves, finely chopped

1 Preheat the oven to 200°C (180°C fan oven) mark 6. Grease a 4.5 litre (8 pint) roasting tin and layer the potatoes and blanched onion, seasoning well between each layer. Pour the stock over them and cook in the oven for 30 minutes.

2 Meanwhile, for the salsa, put the red peppers on a roasting tray and drizzle 1tbsp olive oil over them. Roast the peppers for 30–40 minutes or until they are slightly charred. Put them in a bowl, cover with clingfilm and leave to cool.

3 To make the garlic and herb butter, put the butter, garlic, mint and rosemary in a bowl and mix well, then season generously.

4 Put the lamb on a board and trim away any excess fat. Make about six or seven deep cuts all over it and, using a teaspoon, push the garlic and herb butter into the cuts then smear the rest all over the leg. Put the lamb on a roasting rack and place it over the potatoes and onions. Roast it for 1 hour 40 minutes, or 20 minutes per 450g (1lb) – this cooks the meat perfectly for medium.

5 To make the salsa, put the sliced red onion in a bowl, add the lemon juice, season with salt and leave to marinate. Peel the roasted peppers, then slice the flesh and add it to the bowl, along with any juice. Add the capers, the remaining oil and the mint and season well. Stir everything together and set aside.

6 Transfer the lamb to a board, cover it with foil and rest it for 10 minutes, leaving the potatoes in the oven to keep hot. Carve the lamb: with the leg bone to the left, push the carving fork into the meat, about a third of the way up the leg. Using a very sharp carving knife, carve through the meat to the bone. Move the carving knife along by 2–3mm (⅛ inch) and repeat, then angle the knife and carve to remove the slice. Repeat all the way up the leg to remove slices. Serve with the potatoes and onions and the red pepper salsa.

Serves 6   preparation: 40 minutes, plus resting   cooking time: 2 hours 10 minutes
per serving: 680 cals; 33g fat; 48g carbohydrate

Cheesy Shepherd's Pie

450g (1lb) minced lamb

1 large onion, about 225g (8oz), peeled and finely chopped

1 rosemary sprig or 1 large pinch of dried

1 large glass of red wine, about 250ml (8fl oz), or lamb or beef stock

500g tub chilled Napoletana pasta sauce

1kg (2¼lb) large floury potatoes, peeled

salt and pepper

50g (2oz) butter

50g (2oz) coarsely grated Parmesan cheese

1   Put the lamb in a non-stick pan over a high heat and brown, stirring well to break up any lumps. Allow a good 5–7 minutes to do this, as getting the mince a dark golden brown colour at this stage will add bags of flavour to the finished sauce. Remove the lamb and set aside.

2   Add the onion and rosemary to the pan (there should be enough fat left from the mince without having to add any extra oil) and fry for about 10 minutes over a high heat until the onion is soft and golden.

3   Return the lamb to the pan, keep it over a high heat, then stir in the wine or stock, which will bubble immediately. Scrape the bottom of the pan to loosen any crusty bits, then leave the wine to bubble gently until roughly half of it has evaporated. Stir in the pasta sauce, then simmer uncovered for about 20 minutes.

4   Meanwhile, cut the potatoes into large chunks. Put in a pan of lightly salted water, bring to the boil, then reduce the heat and simmer, partially covered, for 10–12 minutes until very tender. Drain the potatoes well and return to the hot pan to dry off any excess moisture. Mash with the butter and half the Parmesan.

5   Preheat the grill to high. Spoon the meat sauce into a medium-sized ovenproof dish. Top with the mash (there's no need to be too neat), then sprinkle with the remaining Parmesan and season with plenty of pepper. Brown under the grill for 2–3 minutes before serving.

Serves 4   preparation: 15 minutes   cooking time: 40–45 minutes
per serving: 640 cals; 31g fat; 52g carbohydrate

Pan-fried Lamb with Orange and Mint

4tbsp olive oil
4 lamb leg steaks, about 700g (1½lb)
185g jar chargrilled sweet red peppers,
   drained and roughly chopped

50g (2oz) black olives
juice of 1 orange and 1 lemon
small bunch of mint, roughly chopped
salt and pepper

1 Heat 2tbsp olive oil in a large non-stick frying pan. Brown the lamb over a high heat, turning occasionally until the meat has formed a deep golden brown crust all over.
2 Reduce the heat and add the red peppers, olives, orange and lemon juice and the remaining oil. Simmer for 5 minutes, stirring to break down the peppers a little.
3 Stir the mint into the pan, then taste for seasoning and serve.

Serves 4   preparation: 10 minutes   cooking time: 20 minutes
per serving: 440 cals; 30g fat; 5g carbohydrate

Braised Lamb Shanks

1tbsp olive oil
6 lamb shanks
salt and pepper
1 onion, peeled and chopped
3 garlic cloves, peeled and crushed
1½ x 400g cans chopped tomatoes

150ml (¼ pint) red wine
2 bay leaves
400g can chickpeas, drained and rinsed
3tbsp chopped parsley
grated zest of 1 lemon

1 Preheat the oven to 170°C (150°C fan oven) mark 3. Heat the olive oil in a large flameproof casserole. Season the lamb, add to the casserole and brown on the hob over a high heat in two batches. Remove and put to one side.
2 Put the onion and 2 crushed garlic cloves into the pan and cook for 4–5 minutes until softened. Add the tomatoes and wine and stir. Return the lamb to the pan, season well and add the bay leaves. Bring to the boil, then cover the pan and cook in the oven for 1½ hours or until the shanks are nearly tender.
3 Remove the pan from the oven, add the chickpeas, cover and return to the oven for a further 30 minutes. Meanwhile, mix the remaining garlic clove with the parsley and lemon zest.
4 Transfer the lamb and sauce to a large serving dish, sprinkle over the parsley mixture and serve with mashed potatoes.

Serves 6   preparation: 15 minutes   cooking time: 2 hours 20–25 minutes
per serving: 600 cals; 41g fat; 14g carbohydrate

Baked Spiced Salmon

2tsp each mild chilli powder, ground cumin,
  ground coriander and ground ginger
1tsp each garlic granules and salt

1 salmon fillet, about 1.4kg (3lb) in weight,
  skinned and small bones removed
sea salt flakes, to garnish

1 Preheat the oven to 200°C (180°C fan oven) mark 6. Line a large roasting tin with a sheet of foil. Mix the spices with the garlic granules and salt. Rub the surface of the salmon with the mixture and cut it into 15 pieces on the diagonal. Place the fish in the roasting tin and bake for 10–15 minutes or until just cooked to the centre. Remove from the oven and leave to cool.
2 To serve, sprinkle the salmon with sea salt flakes and accompany with salad and couscous.

Serves 10 preparation: 10 minutes, plus cooling   cooking time: 15 minutes
per serving: 240 cals; 16g fat; 0g carbohydrate

Salmon with Courgettes and Asparagus

4 salmon fillets with skin, about
  125g (4oz) each
6tbsp extra-virgin olive oil, plus extra
  to drizzle
zest of 1 orange
1 rosemary sprig, roughly chopped
salt and pepper

2 garlic cloves, peeled and crushed
2 large courgettes, cut on the diagonal into
  5mm (¼ inch slices)
1tsp each chopped oregano and mint
1tsp roughly torn basil leaves
8 large asparagus spears, ends peeled
syrupy balsamic vinegar, to drizzle

1 Put the salmon in a large dish. Drizzle over 2tbsp olive oil, then add the orange zest and rosemary and season well. Rub into the salmon and leave to marinate for 30 minutes.
2 Heat the rest of the oil in a large frying pan and cook the garlic for 1 minute over a low heat. Add the courgettes and cook for 3–4 minutes on each side, stirring all the time to cook evenly. Cover the pan and cook over a low heat for a further 5 minutes. Add the remaining herbs, season generously, then stir everything together. Take off the heat and keep covered.
3 Preheat the oven to 200°C (180°C fan oven) mark 6. Heat a griddle or non-stick frying pan until hot, then fry the salmon in batches on either side to sear. Put the fish on a baking sheet, then bake in the oven for 5–10 minutes until opaque all the way through.
4 Bring a large pan of cold salted water to the boil, then cook the asparagus for 3–4 minutes. Drain and refresh in cold water.
5 Drizzle four large dinner plates with a little balsamic vinegar and olive oil. Divide the courgette slices among the plates, then cut the asparagus in half and put the ends on top of the courgettes. Top with the salmon and finish off with a couple of asparagus tips. Carefully spoon over any pan juices and season to taste.

Serves 4 preparation time: 20–25 minutes, plus marinating   cooking time: 20–25 minutes
per serving: 400 cals; 33g fat; 2g carbohydrate

Pan-fried Wild Salmon with Garlic and Dill

4 skinless wild salmon fillets, about 550g
  (1¼lb) in total
2 spring onions, about 50g (2oz), finely
  chopped

20g pack dill, roughly chopped
25g (1oz) ready-made garlic butter
200ml carton crème fraîche

1 Halve each salmon fillet lengthways to give eight 'fingers'. Stir the spring onions and dill together on
   a plate, then press the salmon pieces into the mixture until lightly coated on all sides.
2 Melt the garlic butter in a shallow pan over a medium heat, then carefully lower in the fish. Cook for
   1 minute, then flip over and cook the other side for 1–2 minutes until the flesh has just turned opaque.
3 When the fish is cooked, remove the pan from the heat and spoon in the crème fraîche. Leave it
   melting in the heat of the pan while you put the salmon on to plates and then spoon the sauce over
   to serve.

Serves 4   preparation: 5 minutes   cooking time: 5 minutes
per serving: 490 cals; 42g fat; 2g carbohydrate

Salmon Fillets in Puff Pastry

2 x 375g packs ready-rolled puff pastry
plain flour, to dust
15g (½oz) butter
3 shallots, blanched in boiling water,
  drained, peeled and finely chopped
2tbsp Dijon mustard

1 lemon
salt and pepper
6 x 150g (5oz) skinless salmon fillets
1 egg, beaten
1tbsp poppy seeds

1 Preheat the oven to 200°C (180°C fan oven) mark 6. Roll out the pastry on a lightly floured surface
   until each piece is 40.5cm (16 inches) square. Cut each into six equal pieces, wrap half in clingfilm
   and chill.
2 Put the remaining six pieces of pastry on a large baking sheet, prick all over and cook for 10–15
   minutes or until golden and crisp. Remove from the oven and press the pastry flat with the back of a
   wooden spoon, then cool on a wire rack.
3 Melt the butter in a pan. Add the shallots and fry gently until soft. Put in a bowl and add the mustard.
   Zest the lemon, add to the bowl, season to taste and stir to mix.
4 Put the cooked pastry squares back on to the baking sheet. Put a little shallot mixture in the centre
   of each and top with a salmon fillet. Brush the pastry edges with a little beaten egg, then put the
   remaining raw pastry on top of the fish. Press around the edges to seal. Brush with the remaining beaten
   egg and sprinkle with the poppy seeds.
5 Make a little hole in the top of each parcel with the point of a knife, then cook in the oven for 20 minutes
   or until the pastry is puffed and golden.

Serves 6   preparation: 25 minutes   cooking time: 30–35 minutes
per serving: 600 cals; 38g fat; 58g carbohydrate

Peppered Salmon with Herb Mayonnaise

50g (2oz) baby spinach leaves
25g (1oz) watercress
6tbsp chopped herbs such as parsley, dill
  or tarragon
1tbsp lemon juice

½ quantity of mayonnaise (page 17)
3tbsp coarsely ground black pepper
salt
4 x 175g (6oz) organic salmon fillets
2tbsp olive oil

1 Put the spinach and watercress in a medium pan and stir over a medium heat for 1–2 minutes until it is just starting to wilt. Tip into a colander and refresh briefly under cold water. Squeeze out the excess moisture.
2 Put the spinach, watercress, herbs, lemon juice and mayonnaise in a blender and whiz for 5 seconds. For a smoother sauce, whiz for another 10 seconds. Chill.
3 Put the pepper and a pinch of salt on a plate and press the salmon into it, skin side down.
4 Heat the olive oil in a large frying pan until hot and fry the salmon, skin side down, for 2–3 minutes. Flip the fish and cook for a further 3–4 minutes.
5 Serve each portion with 2tbsp herb mayonnaise and freshly cooked vegetables such as green beans, peas and cherry tomatoes.

Serves 4   preparation: 15 minutes   cooking time: 7–10 minutes
per serving: 680 cals; 52g fat; 0g carbohydrate

Salmon with Roasted Vegetables and Pine Nuts

2 large leeks, cut into chunks
2 large courgettes, sliced
2 fennel bulbs, cut into chunks
125ml (4fl oz) hot vegetable stock

salt and pepper
zest of ½ lemon
4 x 100g (3½oz) salmon fillets
15g (½oz) pine nuts, toasted

1 Preheat the oven to 200°C (180°C fan oven) mark 6. Put the leeks in a roasting tin and add the courgettes and fennel. Pour over the hot stock, season well and roast for 30 minutes or until tender.
2 Meanwhile, sprinkle the lemon zest evenly over the salmon and season to taste . Put on a baking sheet lined with greaseproof paper and cook in the oven with the vegetables for the last 20 minutes of the cooking time.
3 Remove the vegetables and salmon from the oven. Scatter the pine nuts over the roasted vegetables and mix well. Divide the vegetables among four plates and top each with a piece of salmon.

Serves 4   preparation: 20 minutes   cooking time: 30 minutes
per serving: 250 cals; 15g fat; 6g carbohydrate

Baked Plaice with Lemon and Garlic Mayo

50g (2oz) fresh white breadcrumbs

25g (1oz) finely grated hard cheese, such as
Parmesan, mature Cheddar or Crottin
(hard goat's cheese)

50g (2oz) melted butter

4 large plaice fillets, skin on

salt and pepper

175g (6oz) mayonnaise

1tbsp grated lemon zest, plus 1tbsp lemon
juice (reserve the lemon halves)

2 spring onions, finely chopped

1 garlic clove, peeled and crushed

1 Preheat the oven to 220°C (200°C fan oven) mark 7. Mix the breadcrumbs with the grated cheese in a small bowl. Brush a baking sheet with a little melted butter and put the plaice fillets on top, skin side down. Brush the fish with a little more butter, then sprinkle with the breadcrumb and cheese mixture. Season with pepper and a little salt, then drizzle over any remaining butter. Bake for 15–20 minutes or until the breadcrumbs begin to turn golden and crisp.

2 Meanwhile, beat together the remaining ingredients to make a garlicky dip. Check the seasoning, then serve immediately with the fish, the remains of the lemon and some new potatoes.

Serves 4 preparation: 10 minutes cooking time: 15–20 minutes
per serving: 650 cals; 52g fat; 6g carbohydrate

Braised Tuna with Butter Beans

1tbsp olive oil, plus an extra 1tsp

1 garlic clove, peeled and crushed

2tbsp sun-dried tomato paste

4 x 150g (5oz) tuna steaks

8 tomatoes, roughly chopped

1 red onion, peeled and finely sliced

4 celery sticks, finely sliced

300ml (½ pint) hot vegetable stock

2 x 400g cans butter beans,
drained and rinsed

200g (7oz) green beans, blanched

25g (1oz) pack flat-leafed parsley,
roughly chopped

salt and pepper

1 Preheat the oven to 180°C (160°C fan oven) mark 4. Put 1tbsp olive oil into a bowl, add the garlic, tomato paste and tuna and mix well to coat the tuna. Put to one side.

2 Put the tomatoes into a roasting tin and add the onion, celery and hot stock, then top with the tuna and any marinade left behind in the bowl. Roast for 30–40 minutes.

3 Meanwhile, prepare the salad. Put the butter beans in a bowl and add the green beans, parsley and 1tsp olive oil.

4 When the tuna is cooked, put each piece on a warm plate. Add the cooked vegetables and juices to the salad, season and mix well. Serve with the tuna.

Serves 4 preparation: 10 minutes cooking time: 30–40 minutes
per serving: 440 cals; 13g fat; 35g carbohydrate

Lime Peppered Tuna

1tsp olive oil

zest and juice of 1 lime

1tbsp cracked mixed peppercorns

4 x 150g (5oz) tuna steaks

1tbsp extra-virgin olive oil

1tbsp each black and green olives, roughly
  chopped

zest and juice of ½ lemon

2tbsp chopped parsley

1tbsp chopped coriander

1tbsp capers, roughly chopped

salt and pepper

1 Put the olive oil in a large shallow bowl and then add the lime zest and juice and the peppercorns.
  Add the tuna and toss to coat.

2 Heat a non-stick griddle pan until hot. Cook the tuna steaks, two at a time, for 2–3 minutes on
  each side.

3 Put all the remaining ingredients in a bowl, season and mix well, then serve with the tuna.

Serves 4   preparation: 5 minutes   cooking time: 8–12 minutes
per serving: 250 cals; 11g fat; 0g carbohydrate

Foil-baked Haddock

1 small butternut squash, peeled and cut
  into small cubes

½ red onion, peeled and finely sliced

2 garlic cloves, peeled and finely chopped

1tbsp dill, roughly chopped, plus extra to
  garnish

1tbsp olive oil

salt and pepper

4 x 150g (5oz) thick haddock fillets

125g (4oz) spinach

1 Preheat the oven to 220°C (200°C fan oven) mark 7. Cut out four 40.5cm (16 inch) squares of foil.

2 Put the squash in a bowl, add the onion, garlic, dill and olive oil and toss to coat. Season well, then
  divide the vegetable mixture equally among the four squares of foil.

3 Top each pile of vegetables with a piece of fish. Season again, then bring the foil together and crimp
  the edges so the fish and vegetables are completely enclosed. Put the parcels on a baking tray and
  roast for 15 minutes until the fish is cooked through and the squash is just tender.

4 Remove the tray from the oven and carefully open each of the foil parcels and add some spinach to
  each. Close the parcels again, return to the oven and roast for a further 5 minutes until the spinach
  has wilted. Garnish with dill to serve.

Serves 4   preparation: 20 minutes   cooking time: 20 minutes
per serving: 240 cals; 6g fat; 19g carbohydrate

Smoked Haddock and Leek Pie

1tsp olive oil
1 onion, peeled and finely chopped
2 leeks, finely chopped
150g (5oz) spinach
150g (5oz) frozen peas
450g (1lb) undyed smoked haddock fillet

300ml (½ pint) skimmed milk
1tbsp plain flour
40g (1½oz) mature Cheddar cheese
black pepper
3 slices wholemeal bread, whizzed in
    a processor into breadcrumbs

1 Heat the olive oil in a large pan. Add the onion and 2tbsp water and fry for 10 minutes until soft. Add the leeks, spinach and peas, cover and cook for 5 minutes until soft. Take off the heat and set aside.
2 Preheat the oven to 200°C (180°C fan oven) mark 6. Put the fish in another pan, pour the milk over and bring to the boil. Turn off the heat and remove the fish with a slotted spoon, reserving the milk. Put the fish in a 1.4 litre (2½ pint) ovenproof dish and use a spoon to break up the fish, then add the vegetables.
3 Take a small ladleful of reserved milk from the pan, put into a bowl and whisk in the flour. Gradually add to the remaining milk over a low heat, whisking all the time until the sauce simmers and thickens. Stir in half the cheese, season with pepper, then pour over the vegetables.
4 Mix the breadcrumbs and remaining cheese in a bowl and sprinkle over the sauce. Cook the pie in the oven for 25–30 minutes until bubbling. Remove from the oven and serve.

Serves 4   preparation: 25 minutes   cooking time: 45–50 minutes
per serving: 320 cals; 8g fat; 29g carbohydrate

Smoked Haddock and Potato Pie

142ml carton double cream
150ml (¼ pint) fish stock
3 medium baking potatoes, thinly sliced
300g (11oz) skinless smoked haddock
    fillets, roughly chopped

20g pack chives, chopped
1 large onion, peeled and finely chopped
salt and pepper

1 Preheat the oven to 200°C (180°C fan oven) mark 6. Pour the cream into a large bowl, add the fish stock and stir well to combine.
2 Add the potatoes, haddock, chives and onion to the bowl and season. Toss everything together to coat, then spoon the mixture into a 2.3 litre (4 pint) shallow ovenproof dish. Cover the dish with foil, put it on a baking tray and bake for 45 minutes.
3 Remove the foil and cook for a further 30–40 minutes until bubbling and the top is golden. To check the potatoes are cooked, insert a skewer or small knife – it should push in easily.
4 Remove from the oven and, if you like, put the dish under a hot grill to make the top layer really crisp. Cool slightly, then serve with a green salad or green beans, garnished with a slice of lemon.

Serves 4   preparation: 15 minutes   cooking time: 1 hour 15–25 minutes
per serving: 340 cals; 18g fat; 30g carbohydrate

Baked Tatties with Smoked Haddock

4 large baking potatoes – Golden Wonder,
  King Edward or Maris Piper
2tbsp olive oil
salt and pepper
2 medium fillets smoked haddock,
  about 450g (1lb)

50g (2oz) butter
1 small lemon
200ml tub crème fraîche,
  reduced-fat one is fine
1 small bunch of chives or
  spring onions, chopped

Supper

1 Preheat the oven to 200°C (180°C fan oven) mark 6. Scrub the potatoes, dry, then rub with olive oil, salt and pepper. Bake on the rack of the oven for 1¼ hours or a bit longer, depending on the size of potato. The skin should be deep golden and crisp and the flesh soft.

2 While the potatoes are cooking, put the smoked haddock in a bowl, cover with cold water and leave for 10–15 minutes to remove some of its saltiness.

3 When the potatoes have been in the oven for a good 30 minutes, drain the haddock and put it in a buttered shallow ovenproof dish. Squeeze over the juice of ½ lemon, cover with buttered foil, then pop in the oven alongside the potatoes for 10–15 minutes until just cooked. Check after 10 minutes – the fish should be opaque and the flesh moist. When cool, use a fork to pull the fish into large flakes.

4 Remove the potatoes from the oven and split open lengthways. Using a spoon, scoop the flesh out into a bowl and add the remaining butter, the haddock juices and 4tbsp crème fraîche. Mash with a fork until smooth, then stir in the flaked haddock and the chives or spring onions. Don't be too heavy handed or the haddock will break into little pieces. Taste for seasoning and add a little more lemon juice if the haddock is very salty. Chill the remaining crème fraîche.

5 Spoon the mixture back into the potato skins, then put into the oven for 10 minutes until the tops begin to brown. Serve topped with dollops of the remaining crème fraîche and a watercress salad.

Serves 4   preparation: 15 minutes   cooking time: 1 hour 25 minutes
per serving: 510 cals; 25g fat; 45g carbohydrate

Mackerel with Hot Tomato Sauce

2tbsp extra-virgin olive oil
300g punnet cherry tomatoes, halved or,
  if large, quartered
2tbsp creamed horseradish
8 uncooked mackerel fillets

salt and pepper
small handful of rosemary leaves,
  roughly chopped
lemon wedges, to serve

1 Preheat the grill to high. Heat 1tbsp olive oil in a wok or large frying pan and fry the tomatoes for 2–3
   minutes, tossing them occasionally so they cook quickly and evenly until they start to soften at the
   edges. Add the horseradish to the pan and toss together to combine. Reduce the heat to low, cover
   the pan and leave to simmer.

2 Meanwhile, brush the mackerel fillets on both sides with the remaining oil and season well. Grill the
   fish skin side up for 6–7 minutes until the skin starts to blister and turn golden brown. Turn the fillets
   over carefully and grill for a further 1–2 minutes.

3 Stir the rosemary into the tomato sauce and spoon it over the mackerel fillets. Serve with a wedge
   of lemon to squeeze over and some French beans and peas.

Serves 4   preparation: 5 minutes   cooking time: 9–12 minutes
per serving: 540 cals; 40g fat; 4g carbohydrate

Roasted Cod with Fennel

50g (2oz) butter
1tbsp olive oil
2 medium red onions, peeled and
   finely sliced
2 small or 1 large fennel bulb, trimmed
   and finely sliced

2tbsp chopped dill, plus extra to sprinkle
a few glugs of a fruity white wine
4 x 150g (5oz) pieces Icelandic cod
salt and pepper

1 Preheat the oven to 200°C (180°C fan oven) mark 6. Heat the butter and olive oil in a flameproof casserole over a medium heat. When sizzling, add the onions and fennel, then cover and cook, stirring occasionally, for 7 minutes or until soft and translucent.
2 Add the dill and wine and bring quickly to the boil. Sit the fish on top of the fennel mixture, season well, then put the casserole in the oven and cook for 10 minutes, basting the fish occasionally with the juices.
3 Remove from the oven, sprinkle with plenty of extra dill and serve immediately with crusty bread or new potatoes and green beans.

Serves 4   preparation: 3 minutes   cooking time: 17 minutes
per serving: 270 cals; 15g fat; 7g carbohydrate

Oven-roast Cod with Pea Purée

450g (1lb) large potatoes, peeled and cut
   into chips
3tbsp olive oil
2 thick cod fillets, around 200g (7oz) each
salt and pepper

375g (13oz) frozen peas
2tbsp half fat crème fraîcbe
2tbsp chopped mint
sea salt flakes, to sprinkle
lemon wedges, to serve

1 Put a wire rack resting over a roasting tin in the oven and preheat it to 200°C (180°C fan oven) mark 6. Put the chips on the rack and drizzle with 1tbsp olive oil, then roast for 25–30 minutes, turning once, until cooked through and golden.
2 Meanwhile, dry the cod fillets with kitchen paper and season. Heat the remaining oil in a large frying pan and cook the cod, skin side down, until the skin is crisp. Transfer to a baking tray and cook in the oven for 15–20 minutes until the fish is tender and flaking.
3 Cook the peas in boiling salted water for 8–10 minutes until very tender. Drain well and return to the pan, then add the crème fraîche and mint and whiz to a purée with a stick blender until almost smooth.
4 Season the chips with sea salt flakes and divide the pea purée between two plates. Top each with a portion of cod, then serve with a wedge of lemon to squeeze over the fish.

Serves 2   preparation: 15 minutes   cooking time: 25–30 minutes
per serving: 360 cals; 12g fat; 18g carbohydrate

Roast Cod with Herb Crust

4tbsp each chopped parsley and coriander
zest of 1 lemon
2tbsp olive oil
25g (1oz) ground almonds

2 slices wholemeal bread, torn into
 rough chunks
4 x 125g (4oz) cod fillets

1   Preheat the oven to 200°C (180°C fan oven) mark 6. Put all the ingredients except the cod into a food
    processor and whiz to chop finely.
2   Put the cod into a baking dish. Spread the breadcrumb mixture on top of each piece of fish. Roast
    for 15–20 minutes, then serve with boiled new potatoes and green vegetables.

Serves 4   preparation: 5 minutes   cooking time: 15–20 minutes
per serving: 230 cals; 11g fat; 9g carbohydrate

Cod with Sweet Potato Mash

3 large sweet potatoes, peeled and cut
 into cubes
salt and pepper
2tbsp olive oil
4 x 125g (4oz) Icelandic cod fillets
zest and juice of 1 lemon

1tbsp chopped dill, plus 1tbsp extra for
 the sauce
150g tub Greek-style yogurt
1tbsp capers, drained and roughly chopped
3tbsp cornichons, roughly chopped

1   Preheat the oven to 200°C (180°C fan oven) mark 6. Put the potatoes in a pan of lightly salted water,
    bring to the boil, then reduce the heat and simmer, partially covered, for 15 minutes until tender. Drain
    well, return to the pan to dry off and mash. Stir in 1tbsp olive oil and season to taste. Keep warm.
2   Meanwhile, put the cod in a shallow ovenproof dish and drizzle with the remaining oil, the lemon zest
    and juice. Season, cover with foil and bake for 20–25 minutes until cooked through. Remove from
    the oven and sprinkle 1tbsp dill on top.
3   To make the tartare sauce, mix the yogurt, capers and cornichons with the remaining 1tbsp dill in a
    small bowl. Season and stir to mix. Serve the fish with the mash and a dollop of the sauce.

Serves 4   preparation: 20 minutes   cooking time: 20–25 minutes
per serving: 310 cals; 8g fat; 34g carbohydrate

Sun-dried Tomato and Black Olive Lasagne

25g (1oz) butter, plus extra to grease
25g (1oz) plain flour
450ml (¾ pint) full-fat milk
salt and pepper
1 quantity Bolognese sauce (page 177)

4 sun-dried tomato pieces, drained
and chopped
200g (7oz) black olives, drained
6 sheets no-cook lasagne
75g (3oz) mature Cheddar cheese, grated

1　Preheat the oven to 180°C (160°C fan oven) mark 4. Put the butter into a pan and heat gently to melt it. Add the flour and cook, stirring, for 1 minute to make a paste. Gradually stir in the milk, then increase the heat and bring to the boil, whisking constantly. Reduce the heat and simmer, stirring, for 5 minutes to make a smooth sauce. Season well.

2　Meanwhile, put the Bolognese sauce into a pan and heat it through to loosen it. Add the sun-dried tomatoes and olives to the sauce and stir well.

3　Lightly grease a 2 litre (3½ pint) shallow ovenproof dish. Spread half the Bolognese sauce over the base. Cover it with three lasagne sheets, then spoon half the white sauce on top. Repeat the layers, then scatter the Cheddar over the top layer of white sauce. Bake for 30–35 minutes or until golden, then serve the lasagne with a green salad.

Serves 4　preparation: 5 minutes　cooking time: 42–45 minutes
per serving: 540 cals; 29g fat; 29g carbohydrate

Gnocchi and Mozzarella Bake

2 x 500g packs gnocchi
salt and pepper
65g pack diced pancetta
300g tub fresh tomato pasta sauce with
garlic and basil

2tbsp basil leaves, roughly torn
150g bag mozzarella cheese, drained and
roughly cubed
freshly grated Parmesan cheese, to serve

1　Cook the gnocchi in a large pan of boiling salted water for the time stated on the packet.

2　Meanwhile, dry-fry the pancetta cubes in a frying pan for 2–3 minutes – you won't need any oil as the heat will release the fat from the meat. Pour in the pasta sauce and bring to the boil. Stir in the basil, then season.

3　Preheat the grill to high. Drain the gnocchi, add to the tomato sauce, then tip into a 2 litre (3½ pint) ovenproof dish. Dot over the mozzarella, season and grill for 5–6 minutes until golden and bubbling. Sprinkle over a little grated Parmesan to serve.

Serves 4　preparation: 5 minutes　cooking time: 10 minutes
per serving: 620 cals; 19g fat; 91g carbohydrate

Mushroom and Ricotta Cannelloni with Tomato Sauce

15g (½oz) dried mushrooms
15g (½oz) butter, plus a little
  extra for greasing
225g (8oz) brown-cap mushrooms,
  finely chopped
250g (9oz) ricotta cheese
1tsp anchovy essence

salt and pepper
4 sheets fresh lasagne, each measuring
  11.5 x 16.5cm (4½ x 6½ inches)
2 x 300ml tubs fresh tomato sauce
50g (2oz) Parmesan cheese shavings
black pepper and basil sprigs, to garnish

1 Wash the dried mushrooms, then pour 150ml (1/4 pint) boiling water over and leave to stand for 15 minutes. Drain and finely chop. Lightly grease a large, shallow, ovenproof dish with butter.
2 Heat the butter in a large frying pan, add the fresh and soaked dried mushrooms and cook for 10–15 minutes or until they are beginning to brown and any liquid has evaporated. Leave to cool.
3 Put the ricotta cheese in a bowl, add the mushrooms, anchovy essence and the seasoning, then mix until thoroughly combined.
4 Preheat the oven to 200°C (180°C fan oven) mark 6. Cook the lasagne according to the instructions on the packet, then halve widthways. Place about 3tbsp mushroom mixture along one edge of the lasagne, then roll up to enclose the filling. Repeat this process with the remaining lasagne. Arrange the filled pasta, seam side down, in the prepared dish. Pour the tomato sauce over and sprinkle with the Parmesan shavings. Cook in the oven for 35–40 minutes. Garnish with black pepper and basil sprigs to serve.

Serves 4 preparation: 15 minutes cooking time: 50 minutes
per serving: 370 cals; 22g fat; 27g carbohydrate

Pasta with Roasted Squash and Sage

350g (12oz) dried orecchiette pasta
salt
1 butternut squash, peeled and diced
5 sage leaves, chopped

1tbsp olive oil
1tsp chilli flakes
75g (3oz) chopped pancetta
1tbsp each balsamic vinegar and olive oil

1 Preheat the oven to 200°C (180°C fan oven) mark 6. Cook the pasta in a large pan of boiling salted water for the time stated on the packet, then drain.
2 Meanwhile, put the squash in a roasting tin with the sage, olive oil and chilli flakes and toss. Roast in the oven for 20 minutes. Add the pancetta and roast for 20 minutes.
3 Remove the tin from the oven, add the orecchiette and toss through with the balsamic vinegar and olive oil. Serve immediately.

Serves 4 preparation: 10 minutes cooking time: 45 minutes
per serving: 470 cals; 16g fat; 73g carbohydrate

Blue Cheese Lasagne

125g (4oz) fresh or frozen leaf spinach,
  thawed if frozen
2 x 20g packs basil, roughly chopped
250g tub ricotta cheese
5 pieces marinated artichoke, drained and
  chopped

350g carton cheese sauce
175g (6oz) dolcelatte cheese, roughly diced
9 sheets fresh egg lasagne, from the
  chiller cabinet
25g (1oz) pine nuts, toasted

1   Preheat the oven to 180°C (160°C fan oven) mark 4. Chop the spinach finely (if it was frozen, squeeze out excess liquid first) and put in a bowl with the basil, ricotta, artichokes and 6tbsp cheese sauce. Mix well.
2   Beat the dolcelatte into the remaining cheese sauce. Spoon a layer of the ricotta mixture into a 23 x 23cm (9 x 9 inch) ovenproof dish. Cover with a layer of lasagne sheets, then a layer of cheese sauce. Repeat the layers to use up the remainder.
3   Bake the lasagne for 40 minutes. Sprinkle over the pine nuts and return to the oven for a further 10–15 minutes until golden. Serve with a green salad.

Serves 6   preparation: 30 minutes   cooking time: 50–55 minutes
per serving: 390 cals; 25g fat; 24g carbohydrate

Baked Chorizo and Red Onion Pasta

350g (12oz) dried pappardelle noodles or
  tagliatelle
salt
2 chorizo sausages, about 150g (5oz),
  roughly chopped
3 small red onions, peeled and sliced into
  thin wedges

50ml (2fl oz) dry white wine
150g ball mozzarella cheese, diced
350g carton cheese sauce
25g (1oz) freshly grated Parmesan cheese
25g (1oz) ciabatta bread, chopped into
  rough crumbs

1   Preheat the oven to 180°C (160°C fan oven) mark 4. Cook the pasta in a large pan of boiling salted water for the time stated on the packet, then drain.
2   Meanwhile, fry the chorizo in a non-stick pan for 5–10 minutes until browned. Remove with a slotted spoon. Add the onions and cook for 10 minutes or until caramelised.
3   Spoon the pasta, chorizo and onions into a 1.7 litre (3 pint) gratin dish and mix well. Stir the wine and mozzarella into the cheese sauce and spoon over the pasta. Sprinkle with the Parmesan and breadcrumbs. Bake for 30–40 minutes. Serve immediately.

Serves 6   preparation: 20 minutes   cooking time: 45 minutes–1 hour
per serving: 510 cals; 21g fat; 57g carbohydrate

Tagliatelle with Mascarpone and Bacon

150g (5oz) thinly cut streaky bacon rashers
  or pancetta, cut into rough pieces
1tbsp olive oil
125g (4oz) shallots, blanched in boiling
  water, drained, peeled and finely sliced
2 bunches watercress or rocket, about 50g
  (2oz), roughly torn
250g (9oz) mascarpone

4tbsp single cream
1tbsp chopped sage
salt and pepper
125g (4oz) Gorgonzola cheese
225g (8oz) dried pasta, such as tagliatelle
  or pappardelle
deep-fried sage leaves and rocket,
  to garnish

1 Fry the bacon in its own fat in a large frying pan for about 10 minutes until crisp. Remove and put to one side. Add the olive oil and shallots to the pan and fry for 10 minutes until soft and golden. Stir in the watercress or rocket and cook for 2 minutes until just wilted.

2 Add the mascarpone and cream and simmer for 2–3 minutes until hot through. Add the sage, season with pepper and roughly crumble half the Gorgonzola over. Heat through gently for 1–2 minutes.

3 Meanwhile, cook the pasta in boiling salted water for the time stated on the packet. Drain and stir in the sauce. Sprinkle the bacon and remaining cheese over, garnish with deep-fried sage leaves and rocket and serve immediately.

Serves 4 preparation: 15 minutes cooking time: 30 minutes
per serving: 820 cals; 62g fat; 48g carbohydrate

Tomato and Basil Pasta

1tbsp olive oil
1 onion, peeled and finely chopped
1 garlic clove, peeled and crushed
1tbsp tomato purée

400g can chopped tomatoes in rich
  tomato juice
salt and pepper
500g pack fresh penne pasta
2tbsp basil leaves, torn

1 Heat the olive oil in a pan, add the onion and garlic and cook over a medium heat for 10 minutes until soft. Add the tomato purée and cook for 1 minute. Stir in the tomatoes, season well and simmer for 30 minutes.

2 Meanwhile, cook the pasta in boiling salted water for the time stated on the packet. Drain, reserving a little of the water and return to the pan. Add the basil leaves to the tomato sauce, then toss through the cooked pasta, adding a little reserved pasta water if necessary, and serve.

Serves 4 preparation: 5 minutes cooking time: 40 minutes
per serving: 430 cals; 8g fat; 72g carbohydrate

Mozzarella Pasta

1 tbsp olive oil
1 onion, peeled and finely chopped
1 garlic clove, peeled and crushed
1 tbsp tomato purée
400g can chopped tomatoes in
  rich tomato juice

salt and pepper
125g (4oz) low-fat mozzarella cheese,
  roughly chopped
500g pack fresh penne pasta
2 tbsp basil leaves, freshly torn, plus extra
  sprigs to garnish

1 Heat the olive oil in a pan, add the onion and garlic and cook over a medium heat for 10 minutes until soft. Add the tomato purée and cook for 1 minute.
2 Stir in the tomatoes, season well and simmer for 25 minutes. Stir in the mozzarella and cook for a further 5 minutes, stirring, until the cheese has melted.
3 Meanwhile, cook the pasta in boiling salted water for the time stated on the packet. Drain, reserving a little of the water and return to the pan. Add the basil leaves, then toss through the cooked penne, adding a little reserved pasta water if necessary, and garnish with extra basil sprigs to serve.

Serves 4   preparation: 5 minutes   cooking time: 40 minutes
per serving: 560 cals; 11g fat; 100g carbohydrate

Penne with Tomato, Chilli and Basil Sauce

2 tbsp olive oil
1 small onion, peeled and finely chopped
2 garlic cloves, peeled and crushed
2 red chillies, deseeded and finely chopped
200ml (7fl oz) red wine
1kg (2¼lb) ripe plum tomatoes, chopped

salt and pepper
500g (1lb 2oz) dried penne pasta
10 basil leaves, torn
150g (5oz) pecorino or Parmesan cheese,
  freshly shaved, to serve

1 Heat the olive oil in a large pan, add the onion and cook over a low heat for about 10 minutes until soft.
2 Add the garlic and chillies to the pan and cook for 2 minutes. Add the wine, bring to the boil and bubble for 1–2 minutes.
3 Add the tomatoes and bring to the boil, then reduce the heat to a low simmer and cook, stirring occasionally, until the tomatoes have reduced to a thick sauce – this will take about 50 minutes. Season to taste.
4 About 10 minutes before the sauce is ready, cook the pasta in a large pan of boiling salted water for the time stated on the packet. Drain the pasta well, adding a little of the cooking water to the tomato sauce to thin it.
5 Return the pasta to the pan and add the tomato sauce and torn basil. Toss to mix and serve scattered with pecorino or Parmesan shavings.

Serves 6   preparation: 20 minutes   cooking time: about 1 hour
per serving: 460 cals, 10g fat; 69g carbohydrate

Stuffed Pasta Shells

2tbsp olive oil

1 large onion, peeled and finely chopped

a few rosemary or oregano sprigs,
   chopped, plus extra to garnish (optional)

125g (4oz) small flat mushrooms, sliced, or
   1 small aubergine, diced

6 plump coarse sausages, skinned

175ml (6fl oz) red wine

300ml (½ pint) passata

4tbsp sun-dried tomato paste

pinch of sugar

250g (9oz) large dried pasta shells

142ml carton half-fat single cream
   (optional)

1 Heat the olive oil in a deep frying pan. Stir in the onion and rosemary or oregano and cook over a gentle heat for 10 minutes or until the onion is soft and golden.

2 Add the mushrooms and cook over a medium heat until the vegetables are soft and beginning to brown at the edges. Tip the onion mixture into a bowl.

3 Crumble the sausagemeat into the hot pan and stir over a high heat with a wooden spoon, breaking the meat up as you do so, until browned all over.

4 Reduce the heat slightly and pour in the wine. Leave to bubble and reduce down by about half. Return the onion mixture to the pan and add the passata and sun-dried tomato paste. Bubble gently for another 10 minutes. Add a pinch of sugar if the sauce tastes a little sharp.

5 While the sauce is simmering, cook the pasta in a large pan of boiling salted water for 10 minutes or until just tender. Drain well and rinse with cold running water to cool. Meanwhile, preheat the oven to 180°C (160°C fan oven) mark 4.

6 Fill the pasta shells with the sauce and put in a shallow ovenproof dish. Drizzle over any extra sauce and the cream, if using, and bake for 30 minutes or until piping hot. Sprinkle with extra herbs, if using, and serve with a big bowl of salad.

Serves 6   preparation: 15 minutes   cooking time: about 1 hour
per serving: 467 cals; 27g fat; 42g carbohydrate

Spicy Sausages with Pasta

350g (12oz) coarse, spicy pork
  or lamb sausages
1tbsp olive oil
1 small onion, peeled and finely chopped
large pinch of chopped red chilli – no more,
  unless you like a fiery sauce
125ml (4fl oz) dry white wine

150ml (¼ pint) passata with basil
1tbsp sun-dried tomato paste or
  tomato purée
400g (14oz) dried penne pasta
salt
chunk of Parmesan cheese, to serve

1 Split the sausages open, then remove and discard the skin. Heat the olive oil in a deep frying pan. Roughly crumble the sausage meat into the pan and fry over a high heat, stirring all the time to break it up, for about 5 minutes until golden brown. Add the onion and chilli, reduce the heat and cook until the onion is golden and soft – there should be enough fat left in the pan. This will take a good 10 minutes.

3 Pour in the wine and continue to cook, scraping up any bits from the base of the pan as it bubbles. Add the passata and tomato paste or purée. Bring slowly to a gentle simmer and cook for 1–2 minutes.

4 Cook the pasta in a large pan of boiling salted water for the time stated on the packet.

5 Drain the cooked pasta, return it to the pan and add the sauce. Toss well. Divide among four bowls and serve with Parmesan to grate over.

Serves 4   preparation: 10 minutes   cooking time: 30 minutes
per serving: 780 cals; 37g fat; 87g carbohydrate

Steak with Onions and Tagliatelle

250g (9oz) dried tagliatelle pasta
salt and pepper
2 x 200g (7oz) sirloin steaks
2 red onions, peeled and chopped into
  thin wedges

200g carton half-fat crème fraîche
small handful of flat-leafed parsley

1 Cook the pasta in a large pan of boiling salted water for the time stated on the packet.

2 Meanwhile, season the steaks on both sides. Heat a non-stick frying pan until really hot and fry the steaks for 2–3 minutes on each side until golden but still pink inside. Remove from the pan and put to one side.

3 Add the onions to the pan and stir-fry for 8–10 minutes until softened and golden. Add a little water if they're sticking. Season, reduce the heat and stir in the crème fraîche.

4 Cut the fat off the steaks and discard, then cut the meat into thin strips. Add to the pan and heat through for 1–2 minutes, then stir in the tagliatelle. Snip over the parsley, toss again and serve.

Serves 4   preparation: 10 minutes   cooking time: 20 minutes
per serving: 420 cals; 15g fat; 41g carbohydrate

Spaghetti Bolognese

1tbsp vegetable oil
1 onion, peeled and finely chopped
2 garlic cloves, peeled and crushed
450g (1lb) minced beef
1 beef stock cube
2tbsp tomato purée

400g can chopped tomatoes
2tbsp Worcestershire sauce
125g (4oz) button mushrooms, sliced
salt and pepper
500g (1lb 2oz) dried spaghetti
50g (2oz) freshly grated Parmesan cheese

1 Heat the oil in a large pan and fry the onion over a medium heat for 15 minutes until golden. Add the garlic and cook for 1 minute. Add the mince and brown evenly, using a wooden spoon to break up the pieces. Measure 300ml (½ pint) boiling water into a jug, crumble in the stock cube and mix well.
2 Add the tomato purée and hot stock to the browned mince, cover and bring to the boil. Add the tomatoes, Worcestershire sauce and mushrooms, and season. Reduce the heat and simmer, stirring occasionally, for 20 minutes.
3 About 15 minutes before the sauce has finished cooking, cook the pasta in a large pan of boiling salted water for the time stated on the packet. Drain the pasta well, return it to the pan and add the Bolognese sauce. Toss to mix, check the seasoning, then tip into a serving dish. Serve with the Parmesan.

Serves 4   preparation: 15 minutes   cooking time: 40 minutes
per serving: 210 cals; 9g fat; 8g carbohydrate

Linguine with Crab and Crispy Crumbs

4 garlic bread slices (frozen or fresh)
400g (14oz) dried linguine
salt and pepper
6tbsp full-flavoured extra-virgin olive oil
2 fat garlic cloves, peeled and thinly sliced

½ large red chilli, deseeded and
  thinly sliced
4tbsp chopped flat-leafed parsley
170g can white crab meat
juice of 1 lemon

1 Toast the garlic bread under the grill until golden on both sides, then whiz into rough breadcrumbs in a food processor.
2 Cook the pasta in a large pan of boiling salted water for 7–10 minutes until just tender.
3 Meanwhile, heat 2tbsp olive oil in a large frying pan, add the garlic and chilli, then fry over a high heat for 1–2 minutes until the garlic turns golden brown. Stir half the parsley and all the crab meat into the sizzling oil, cook gently for 1–2 minutes, then add the lemon juice.
4 Drain the pasta and toss it with the hot crab mixture, the remaining oil and parsley and the breadcrumbs. Season to taste, then divide among four warmed bowls.

Serves 4   preparation: 10 minutes   cooking time: 10–15 minutes
per serving: 610 cals; 24g fat; 84g carbohydrate

Gammon with Parsley Mash

1.4 kg (3lb) gammon knuckle
1 onion, peeled and quartered
1 carrot, peeled and cut into chunks
1 celery stick, thickly sliced
1tsp black peppercorns
2 bay leaves
700g (1½lb) white potatoes, peeled and cut
into large chunks

salt and pepper
6–8tbsp full-fat milk
40g (1½oz) butter
1tbsp chopped parsley
1 Savoy cabbage, cut into wedges

1 Put the gammon in a deep pan, add the onion, carrot, celery, peppercorns and bay leaves and cover with cold water. Bring very slowly to the boil – this should take 20–30 minutes. Skim off any scum from the surface, then cover the pan, reduce the heat and simmer very gently for 1½ hours or until the meat is cooked through and tender. Leave the gammon to rest in the liquid in the pan for 15 minutes.

2 Meanwhile, put the potatoes in a pan of lightly salted water, bring to the boil and simmer, partially covered, until they're soft to the centre – about 15 minutes. Drain the potatoes and put back in the pan over a low heat to dry off, then take off the heat and mash. Put the pan back over a low heat, push the potatoes to one side of the pan and add the milk and 25g (1oz) butter to warm through. Beat the milk and butter into the mashed potatoes until they're fluffy, adding more milk if necessary. Season and add the chopped parsley.

3 Bring a large pan of salted water to the boil, add the cabbage and return to the boil. Drain and dry on kitchen paper, then melt the remaining butter and brush over the cabbage. Heat a griddle or frying pan, add the cabbage and fry for about 5 minutes until beginning to brown.

4 Lift the gammon from the cooking liquid, then remove and discard the skin. Slice the meat and serve with the mashed potatoes, cabbage and a little liquid from the pan.

Serves 4   preparation: 20 minutes   cooking time: 1 hour 50 minutes, plus resting
per serving: 790 cals; 27g fat; 43g carbohydrate

Spicy Glazed Pork Chops

1tbsp curry paste
1tbsp mango chutney
large pinch of turmeric

1tbsp vegetable oil
4 pork loin chops
salt and pepper

1 Preheat the grill to high. Put the curry paste, mango chutney, turmeric and oil in a bowl and mix well. Put the chops on to a grill rack, season well and brush with half the curry mixture.

2 Grill for 8–10 minutes until golden and slightly charred. Turn the chops over, season again and brush with the remaining curry mixture. Put back under the grill and cook for a further 6–8 minutes until tender and slightly charred. Serve with sautéed potatoes and grilled cherry tomatoes.

Serves 4   preparation: 5 minutes   cooking time: 15–18 minutes
per serving: 260 cals; 15g fat; 2g carbohydrate

Pork with Fruit

1tbsp chilli paste or harissa, or 1 red chilli,
   deseeded and chopped
4tbsp olive oil
zest and juice of 1 large orange
	salt and pepper
	4 pork chops
	2 nectarines or peaches, stoned
	   and chopped

1   Put the chilli paste, harissa or chilli into a small bowl. Add the olive oil, orange zest and juice, then season well. Drizzle the marinade on to the pork and rub all over.
2   Heat a non-stick frying pan and cook the pork over a medium heat for about 3 minutes on each side or until well browned. Add the remaining marinade to the pan with the nectarines or peaches, increase the heat and bring the liquid to the boil. Cook for a further 4–5 minutes until the pork is cooked through. Serve with couscous.

Serves 4   preparation: 10 minutes   cooking time: 10–15 minutes
per serving: 460 cals; 26g fat; 8g carbohydrate

Pork and Mozzarella Parcels

150g (5oz) mozzarella cheese, thinly sliced
4 pork escalopes or shoulder steaks
4 thin slices proscuitto ham or pancetta
4 sage leaves
black pepper
2tbsp olive oil
	1 fat garlic clove, peeled and crushed
	150ml (¼ pint) pure unsweetened apple
	   juice
	25g (1oz) chilled butter
	squeeze of lemon juice or 1tsp
	   sherry vinegar

1   Lay one or two mozzarella slices on each piece of pork. Wrap a slice of ham or pancetta around each one and top with a sage leaf. Carefully secure everything to the pork with a thin wooden skewer, then season with plenty of pepper.
2   Heat the olive oil in a shallow frying pan over a high heat, and fry the garlic for 1 minute until golden. Add the pork parcels, cheese side up, and cook for 7–10 minutes, then turn them over and cook the other side for 2–3 minutes or until golden and the cheese is beginning to melt. Remove the parcels and set aside.
3   Pour the apple juice into the hot pan – it will sizzle immediately. Scrape the bottom to loosen the crusty bits and leave to bubble until reduced by half.
4   Add the butter bit by bit and swirl it around until it melts into the pan juices. Finish with a squeeze of lemon juice or a splash of sherry vinegar. Return the pork parcels to the pan and warm through in the juices for 1–2 minutes. Serve immediately with a tomato salad and crusty bread.

Serves 4   preparation: 5 minutes   cooking time: 10–15 minutes
per serving: 420 cals; 29g fat; 4g carbohydrate

Pork Escalopes with Chutney

4 large, thinly sliced pork escalopes, about
   200g (7oz) each
black pepper
1–2tbsp olive oil
50g (2oz) butter
2 sage leaves (optional)
1½ slices white bread, processed into
   breadcrumbs

50g (2oz) Gruyère cheese, grated
75g (3oz) full-fat soft cheese, or a smooth
   goat's cheese such as Chavroux
4tbsp good-quality fruity chutney
juice of 1 lemon

1   Season the escalopes with plenty of pepper. Drizzle 1tbsp olive oil over the base of a large frying pan and add a small knob of the butter. Heat together and, when the butter starts to foam and sizzle, add the escalopes and sage leaves, if using, and fry briskly for about 1 minute on each side until golden. (Depending on the size of the escalopes, you may have to fry them in batches, adding a little more oil and butter to the pan if it looks dry.) Slide the escalopes on to a baking sheet.

2   Melt the remaining butter in the heat of the frying pan and stir it into the breadcrumbs with the Gruyère.

3   Preheat the grill to high. Spread the soft cheese or goat's cheese roughly over the pork. Dot the chutney on top and sprinkle over the cheese and breadcrumb mixture. Pop the escalopes under the grill, quite close to the heat, for 3–4 minutes until the top turns golden and is just starting to bubble. Squeeze over the lemon juice and serve immediately with a dressed salad.

Serves 4   preparation: 15 minutes   cooking time: 6–7 minutes
per serving: 630 cals; 43g fat; 15g carbohydrate

Pork Chops with Savoy Cabbage Mash

5 large potatoes, peeled and
   chopped into chunks
salt and pepper
½ small Savoy cabbage, sliced

50g (2oz) butter
4 pork chops
300g sachet rich onion gravy

1   Put the potatoes in a pan of lightly salted water, cover, bring to the boil, then reduce the heat and simmer for 10–12 minutes until soft. After the potatoes have been cooking for 5 minutes, add the cabbage to the pan and continue cooking. Drain the potatoes and cabbage, return to the pan and add all but a knob of the butter and season. Mash and keep warm.

2   Meanwhile, heat a griddle pan until hot. Rub the remaining butter into each chop and season. Fry the chops for 4–5 minutes on each side until cooked through. Put on to warm plates (reserve the juices in the pan) and leave to rest for a couple of minutes.

3   Add the gravy to the pan juices and bring to the boil, then reduce the heat and simmer for 1–2 minutes. Spoon the mash on to the plates, top with the pork chops and pour over the gravy.

Serves 4   preparation: 5 minutes   cooking time: 15 minutes
per serving: 640 cals; 26g fat; 62g carbohydrate

Pork Chops with Parsnips, Apples and Leeks

4 pork loin chops
3tbsp olive oil
1tbsp fennel seeds or 5cm (2 inch) piece
  fresh root ginger, peeled and grated
450g (1lb) small parsnips, peeled and
  halved lengthways
200g (7oz) small leeks, trimmed and roughly
  sliced

4 Granny Smith apples, peeled,
  halved and cored
300ml (½ pint) apple juice
1 bay leaf
25g (1oz) butter
142ml carton single cream (optional)
salt and pepper

1 Preheat the oven to 220°C (200°C fan oven) mark 7. Rub the pork all over with 1tbsp olive oil and the fennel seeds or ginger. Heat the remaining oil in a large roasting tin on the hob, add the chops and brown them on all sides over a medium heat. Turn the chops and press the fat into the pan to brown that, too. Remove the chops, add the parsnips and stir over the heat until these are golden brown.
2 Add the leeks and apple to the tin, then sit the chops on top. Pour in half the apple juice, add the bay leaf and bake for about 30 minutes depending on the thickness of the chops. Turn everything occasionally during cooking so it colours evenly.
3 Transfer the chops, parsnips, leeks and apple to a serving dish, then cover and keep warm. Put the tin back on the hob over a high heat and stir the remaining apple juice into the caramelised juices. Let it bubble, stirring in any stuck bits with a wooden spoon. Add the butter and cream, if using, and leave to bubble until it reduces to a syrupy liquid. Taste for seasoning, then spoon over the chops to serve.

Serves 4   preparation: 15 minutes   cooking time: about 1 hour
per serving: 650 cals; 32g fat; 40g carbohydrate

Cider Roast Pork

1.1kg (2½lb) boned, rolled loin of
  pork, fat removed
1tbsp olive oil
2 onions, peeled and quartered

2 apples, quartered and cored
handful of thyme sprigs
440ml can dry cider
salt and pepper

1 Put the pork in a large bowl with the olive oil, onions, apples and thyme. Pour the cider over and marinate in the fridge for 4 hours or overnight.
2 When ready to cook the pork, remove from the fridge 20 minutes before putting in the oven. Preheat the oven to 200°C (180°C fan oven) mark 6. Put the joint in a roasting tin with the marinade ingredients and season, then roast for 25 minutes per 450g (1lb) plus 25 minutes.
3 Remove the tin from the oven and transfer the pork to a board. Drain the roasting juices into a pan, bring to the boil and bubble for 5 minutes until reduced. Slice the pork and serve with the pan juices and some new potatoes and green beans.

Serves 4   preparation: 5 minutes, plus marinating   cooking time: 1 hour 20 minutes
per serving: 280 cals; 10g fat; 1g carbohydrate

Fennel Pork with Cabbage and Apple

2tbsp olive oil
½tbsp fennel seeds, crushed
1tbsp chopped sage
salt and pepper
4 x 125g (4oz) lean pork medallions

½ small red cabbage, shredded
450g (1lb) purple sprouting broccoli, tough
  ends removed
1 apple, cored and sliced into rings

1   Put 1tbsp olive oil in a large shallow bowl. Add the fennel seeds and sage, season and mix well. Add
    the pork and rub the mixture into the meat.
2   Heat the remaining oil in a wok. Stir-fry the cabbage and broccoli for 6–8 minutes until starting to char.
3   Meanwhile, heat a non-stick griddle pan until hot and fry the pork for 2–3 minutes on each side or
    until cooked through. Remove and put to one side. Add the apple rings to the pan and griddle for 1–2
    minutes on each side until starting to char and caramelise. Serve with the pork and vegetables.

Serves 4   preparation: 15 minutes   cooking time: 12–15 minutes
per serving: 300 cals; 17g fat; 7g carbohydrate

Pork Chops with Fresh Ginger and Apple

4 chunky pork loin chops, about 700g
  (1½lb) in total
salt and pepper
3 red apples, about 350g (12oz), cored and
  roughly diced

5cm (2 inch) piece fresh root ginger, peeled
  and grated
300ml (½ pint) pure unsweetened
  apple juice
25g (1oz) chilled unsalted butter, diced

1   Using a sharp knife, make several deep cuts through the rind and fat of the chops – this will stop them
    curling up in the pan. Rub the chops all over – particularly the fat – with plenty of seasoning. Put the
    apples in a small bowl and stir in the ginger.
2   Heat a non-stick frying pan over a medium heat, then add the chops. Leave them undisturbed for 3–4
    minutes, by which time some of the fat will have been released and the underside of the meat should
    be a deep golden brown. Press the fat down into the pan occasionally with the back of a wooden spoon
    while the chops are cooking – this will help them brown and improves the flavour of the finished
    sauce. Turn the chops over.
3   After 1–2 minutes add the apples and ginger to the pan and cook for a further 2–3 minutes until the
    pork is cooked through. Remove the chops (leaving the apples in the pan) and keep them warm.
4   Increase the heat to high and pour the apple juice into the pan – it should bubble immediately. Scrape
    the pan with a wooden spoon to loosen any crispy brown bits from the bottom, then let the juices bubble
    for about 5 minutes until reduced by half.
5   Swirl the butter into the pan juices to make a glossy sauce to spoon over the pork. Taste for seasoning,
    then serve with new potatoes and spring greens.

Serves 4   preparation: 10 minutes   cooking time: 15 minutes
per serving: 360 cals; 17g fat; 18g carbohydrate

Italian Sausage Stew

25g (1oz) dried porcini mushrooms
300g (11oz) whole rustic Italian salami
  sausages, such as salami Milano
2tbsp olive oil
1 onion, peeled and sliced
2 garlic cloves, peeled and chopped
1 small chilli, chopped
1 tender rosemary stem, plus sprigs
  to garnish

400g can chopped tomatoes
200ml (7fl oz) red wine
salt and pepper
175g (6oz) instant polenta
50g (2oz) butter
50g (2oz) freshly grated Parmesan cheese,
  plus shavings to serve (optional)
75g (3oz) fontina cheese, cubed

1 Put the dried mushrooms into a small bowl, pour on 100ml (3½fl oz) boiling water and leave to soak for 20 minutes (or soften in the microwave on High for 3½ minutes and leave to cool). Cut the salami into 1cm (½ inch) slices and put to one side.

2 Heat the olive oil in a pan, add the onion, garlic and chilli and fry gently for 5 minutes. Meanwhile, strip the leaves from the rosemary stem and add them to the pan, stirring.

3 Add the salami and fry for 2 minutes on each side or until browned. Drain and chop the mushrooms and add them to the pan. Stir in the tomatoes and wine, season with pepper and simmer uncovered for 5 minutes.

4 Meanwhile, make the polenta. Put 750ml (1¼ pints) boiling water and 1tsp salt into a heavy-based pan. Return to the boil, sprinkle in the polenta, stirring, and cook according to the instructions on the packet. Add the butter, Parmesan and fontina and mix well.

5 Serve the sausage stew accompanied by the polenta, topped with Parmesan shavings, is you like, and garnished with rosemary sprigs.

Serves 4   preparation: 10 minutes, plus soaking   cooking time: 15 minutes
per serving: 780 cals; 48g fat; 47g carbohydrate

Sausages with Mustard Mash and Red Onion Gravy

900g (2lb) floury potatoes, such as Maris
  Piper, peeled and cut into even chunks
25g (1oz) butter
1 red onion, peeled and sliced
2tbsp plain flour
450ml (¾ pint) hot beef stock
1tsp tomato purée

2tbsp chopped flat-leafed parsley
salt and pepper
2tbsp milk
2tbsp wholegrain mustard
1tsp vegetable oil
8 thick pork sausages

1 Put the potatoes in a pan of lightly salted water, bring to the boil, then reduce the heat and simmer, partially covered, for 15–20 minutes until tender.
2 Melt half the butter in a small pan and fry the onion over a medium heat for 10 minutes until soft and translucent. Stir in the flour and cook for 1 minute. Add the hot stock gradually, stirring the gravy until smooth. Stir in the tomato purée and simmer for 5 minutes until thickened. Stir in the parsley and season.
3 Drain the potatoes well and return to the hot pan to dry, then mash. Put the pan back on the hob over a low heat, push the potatoes to one side of the pan and add the milk and remaining butter to warm through. Beat the milk and butter into the potatoes, then season, stir in the mustard and keep warm.
4 Heat the oil in a frying pan and fry the sausages over a medium heat for 10–12 minutes, turning occasionally, until golden and cooked through. Serve with the mash, drizzled with the gravy.

Serves 4   preparation: 15 minutes   cooking time: 30–35 minutes
per serving: 620 cals; 35g fat; 61g carbohydrate

Winter Roasted Vegetables with Chipolatas

900g (2lb) chipolatas, twisted and
  separated, or cocktail sausages
1 small red apple, quartered and cored
2 raw baby beetroot, about 175g (6oz),
  peeled and thickly sliced
4 baby aubergines, about 225g (8oz), cut
  into chunks

2 garlic cloves, peeled and crushed
juice of ½ lemon
1tbsp chopped thyme
2tbsp olive oil
salt and pepper
225g (8oz) chestnut mushrooms, halved
150g (5oz) cooked chestnuts

1 Preheat the oven to 200°C (180°C fan oven) mark 6. Put the sausages into a small roasting tin and roast for 40 minutes until golden brown. Cut the apples into chunky wedges.
2 Meanwhile, put the beetroot, aubergines, apple and garlic into another roasting tin. Squeeze over the lemon juice, scatter over the thyme and drizzle with olive oil. Season, stir and roast for 20 minutes, then add the mushrooms and chestnuts and roast for 20 minutes until the vegetables are tender.
3 Remove the vegetables and sausages from the oven and tip the vegetables into a serving dish. Top with the sausages and serve.

Serves 8   preparation: 20 minutes   cooking time: 30 minutes
per serving: 390 cals; 27g fat; 24g carbohydrate

Spicy Pork and Bean Stew

3tbsp olive oil
400g (14oz) pork escalopes, cubed
1 red onion, peeled and sliced
2 leeks, cut into chunks
2 celery sticks, cut into chunks
1tbsp harissa paste
1tbsp tomato purée
400g can cherry tomatoes
300ml (½ pint) hot vegetable or
   chicken stock

salt and pepper
400g can cannellini beans,
   drained and rinsed
1 marinated red pepper, sliced
1tbsp chopped parsley
1 lemon, quartered, to serve
150g tub Greek-style yogurt, to serve

1 Preheat the oven to 180°C (160°C fan oven) mark 4. Heat 2tbsp olive oil in a flameproof casserole and fry the pork in batches until golden. Remove the pork from the pan and set aside.
2 Heat the remaining oil in the pan and fry the onion for 5–10 minutes until softened. Add the leek and celery and cook for 5 minutes. Return the pork to the pan and add the harissa and tomato purée. Cook for 1–2 minutes, stirring all the time. Add the tomatoes and stock and season well. Bring to the boil, then transfer the pan to the oven and cook for 25 minutes.
3 Remove the pan from the oven, add the drained beans and red pepper to the mixture and return to the oven for 5 minutes to warm through.
4 Take out of the oven, stir in the parsley and serve with lemon wedges and yogurt.

Serves 4 preparation: 15 minutes   cooking time: 50–55 minutes
per serving: 370 cals; 20g fat; 21g carbohydrate

Cheat's Sausage and Goat's Cheese Pizza

2 x 20.5cm (8 inch) pizza bases
4tsp Dijon mustard
1 large red onion, peeled and
   very thinly sliced
225g (8oz) courgettes, very thinly sliced

salt and pepper
2 spicy sausages
2 x 100g packs soft goat's cheese
thyme sprigs
olive oil, to drizzle

1 Preheat the oven to 200°C (180°C fan oven) mark 6. Preheat two baking sheets for a crispy pizza base. Put the pizza bases on the baking sheets and spread them with the mustard, sprinkle over the onion and courgette slices and season.
2 Remove the sausages from their casing and crumble on top of each pizza with the goat's cheese. Sprinkle the thyme over and drizzle with olive oil. ·
3 Bake for 45 minutes or until the crust and sausage is brown and the vegetables are cooked. Swap the pizzas around in the oven halfway so they cook evenly.

Serves 4 preparation: 15 minutes   cooking time: 45 minutes
per serving: 400 cals; 16g fat; 50g carbohydrate

Beef and Venison Stew

50g (2oz) butter

550g (1¼lb) each braising beef and venison, cut into 4cm (1½ inch) cubes

1 Spanish onion, peeled and finely chopped

1 garlic clove, peeled and crushed

1tbsp plain flour

1tsp chopped thyme

6 juniper berries, crushed

150ml (¼ pint) red wine

300ml (½ pint) beef stock

salt and pepper

350g (12oz) each parsnips and carrots, peeled and cut into rough chunks

1tbsp golden caster sugar

225g (8oz) leeks, cut into rough chunks

2 large celery sticks, cut into rough chunks

small thyme sprigs, to garnish

1   Preheat the oven to 170°C (150°C fan oven) mark 3. Heat half the butter in a large non-stick casserole until foaming and brown the beef and venison in batches. Remove from the pan and put to one side.

2   Reduce the heat, add the onion and garlic and cook for 5 minutes or until soft. Stir in the flour, thyme and juniper berries and cook for 1 minute. Pour in the wine, bring to the boil and bubble for 2–3 minutes or until reduced by half. Add the stock and season. Return the beef and venison to the pan, bring to the boil, cover and cook for 5 minutes.

3   Heat the remaining butter and fry the parsnips and carrots. Sprinkle the sugar over, fry until caramelised, then put on top of the meat. Fry the leeks and celery until golden and put to one side.

4   Cover the casserole, transfer to the oven and cook for 1¼ hours, then add the leek and celery and return to the oven for 15 minutes or until all the ingredients are tender. Garnish with thyme sprigs to serve.

Serves 6   preparation: 30 minutes   cooking time: 1 hour 20 minutes
per serving: 440 cals; 17g fat; 20g carbohydrate

Beefburgers

600g (1¼lb) minced beef
¼ onion, peeled and grated
1tsp Worcestershire sauce

salt and pepper
1–2tsp vegetable oil

1 Mix the mince with the onion and Worcestershire sauce and season well. Shape into four rounds.
2 Heat the oil in a frying pan and cook the burgers two at a time if necessary for 5–6 minutes on
   each side.

Makes 4 preparation: 5 minutes   cooking time: 12–24 minutes
per serving: 250 cals; 13g fat; 2g carbohydrate

Braised Beef with Mustard and Capers

50g can anchovy fillets in oil, drained,
  chopped and oil reserved
olive oil
700g (1½lb) braising steak, cut into
  small strips
2 large Spanish onions, peeled and
  thinly sliced

2tbsp capers
1tsp English mustard
6 thyme sprigs
20g pack flat-leafed parsley,
  roughly chopped
salt and pepper

1 Preheat the oven to 170°C (150°C fan oven) mark 3. Measure the anchovy oil into a deep flameproof
   casserole, then make up to 3tbsp with the olive oil. Heat the oil on the hob over a high heat and
   brown the meat well, a few pieces at a time. When all the meat has been browned, pour 4tbsp cold
   water into the empty casserole and stir to loosen any bits on the bottom.
2 Return the meat to the pan and add the onions, anchovies, capers, mustard, half the thyme and all
   but 1tbsp of the parsley. Stir until thoroughly mixed.
3 Tear off a sheet of greaseproof paper big enough to cover the pan. Crumple it up and wet it under
   the cold tap. Squeeze out most of the water, open it out and press down the surface of the meat.
4 Cover with a tightly fitting lid, and cook in the oven for 2 hours or until the beef is meltingly tender. Check
   the casserole after 1 hour to make sure it's still moist – if it looks dry, add a little hot water.
5 Check for seasoning, then stir in the remaining thyme and parsley. Serve with a green salad and
   crusty bread or mashed potato.

Serves 4 preparation: 15 minutes   cooking time: 2 hours 20 minutes
per serving: 330 cals; 16g fat; 8g carbohydrate

Beef with Beer and Mushrooms

700g (1½lb) braising steak, cut into large
   chunks about 5cm (2 inches) across
2tsp plain flour
2tbsp oil
25g (1oz) butter
2 large onions, peeled and finely sliced
225g (8oz) carrots, peeled and cut into large
   sticks
200ml (7fl oz) Guinness
300ml (½ pint) vegetable stock
2tsp tomato purée
2tsp English mustard
2tsp light muscovado sugar
salt and pepper
225g (8oz) large field or portabellini
   mushrooms

1 Preheat the oven to 150°C (130°C fan oven) mark 2. Toss the meat in the flour. Heat the oil and butter in a large casserole over a medium heat and brown the meat a few pieces at a time, removing it with a slotted spoon. The flavour and colour of the finished casserole depend on the meat taking on a good deep colour now. Stir the onions into the pan and cook for about 10 minutes until golden brown and beginning to soften and caramelise.

2 Return all the meat to the pan, then add the carrots and stir in the Guinness, stock, tomato purée, mustard, sugar and plenty of seasoning. Bring to the boil, stir well, then cover tightly with foil or a lid, and simmer gently in the oven for 1½ hours.

3 Remove the pan from the oven, stir in the whole mushrooms and return to the oven for a further 45 minutes–1 hour until the meat is meltingly tender. Serve with plenty of buttery mashed potatoes.

Serves 4   preparation: 15 minutes   cooking time: 2¾–3 hours
per serving: 420 cals; 20g fat; 19g carbohydrate

Chilli Steak and Corn on the Cob

50g (2oz) butter, softened
1 large red chilli, deseeded and
   finely chopped
1 garlic clove, peeled and crushed
25g (1oz) freshly grated Parmesan cheese
1tbsp finely chopped basil
4 corn on the cob, each cut into three
1tbsp olive oil
4 x 150g (5oz) sirloin steaks

1 Put the butter in a bowl and beat with a wooden spoon. Mix in the chilli, garlic, Parmesan and basil. Cover and chill to firm up.

2 Meanwhile, bring a large pan of water to the boil. Add the corn, cover to bring back up to the boil, then simmer half-covered for about 10 minutes or until tender. Drain well.

3 Heat a little olive oil in a large frying pan or griddle and cook the steaks on a high heat for 2–3 minutes on each side for medium-rare or 4–5 minutes for medium, 6–7 minutes for well done. Divide the corn and steaks among four warmed plates and top with the butter. Serve with a mixed green salad.

Serves 4   preparation: 5 minutes   cooking time: 15 minutes
per serving: 390 cals; 23g fat; 10g carbohydrate

Cottage Pie

1tbsp olive oil
2 onions, peeled and chopped
1 garlic clove, peeled and crushed
500g (1lb 2oz) extra-lean minced beef
2tbsp tomato purée
2tbsp plain flour

1tbsp Worcestershire sauce
450ml (¾ pint) hot beef stock
2 bay leaves
salt and pepper
900g (2lb) potatoes, cut into large chunks
75ml (3fl oz) skimmed milk

1   Heat the olive oil in a pan and fry the onions and garlic gently for 10 minutes. Add the mince and cook on a higher heat, stirring constantly with a wooden spoon, until the mince is broken up and well browned.
2   Stir in the tomato purée and flour and cook for 1 minute. Add the Worcestershire sauce, hot stock and bay leaves. Cover, bring to the boil and season generously, then reduce the heat and simmer for 30–40 minutes until the meat is tender. Remove the bay leaves and discard, then spoon the mixture into a 1.8 litre (3¼ pint) ovenproof dish.
3   Meanwhile, put the potatoes in a pan of lightly salted water, cover, bring to the boil, then reduce the heat and simmer for about 15 minutes until soft. Drain well, tip the potatoes back into the pan and heat for 1 minute to dry off. Add the milk, season and mash well. Preheat the oven to 200°C (180°C fan oven) mark 6. Spoon the mash on top of the mince, spread over evenly and rough up the surface with a fork. Put the dish on a baking sheet to catch any spillages, transfer to the oven and cook for 20–25 minutes until golden and bubbling.

Serves 4   preparation: 15 minutes   cooking time: 1–1¼ hours
per serving: 420 cals; 10g fat; 53g carbohydrate

Chilli Bolognese

1tbsp olive oil
1 large onion, peeled and finely chopped
½ large red chilli, deseeded and
   thinly sliced
450g (1lb) minced beef or lamb
125g (4oz) smoked bacon lardons
3 roasted red peppers, drained and finely
   chopped

400g can chopped tomatoes
125ml (4fl oz) red wine
salt and pepper
300g (11oz) dried spaghetti
25g (1oz) grated Cheddar or
   Gruyère cheese
2tbsp chopped flat-leafed parsley (optional)

1 Heat the olive oil in a large pan over a medium heat. Add the onion and chilli and fry for 5–10 minutes until soft and golden. Add the beef and lardons and stir over the heat for 5–7 minutes or until well browned.
2 Stir in the red peppers, tomatoes and wine. Season, bring to the boil, then reduce the heat and simmer for 15–20 minutes.
3 Cook the pasta in a large pan of boiling salted water for the time stated on the packet, then drain.
4 Just before serving, stir the grated cheese, parsley, if using, and the sauce into the spaghetti.

Serves 4   preparation: 15 minutes   cooking time: 26–38 minutes
per serving: 400 cals; 23g fat; 12g carbohydrate

Steak au Poivre

2tbsp black or green peppercorns
4 rump or sirloin steaks, 200g (7oz) each
25g (1oz) butter
1tbsp oil

salt
2tbsp brandy
150ml (¼ pint) double cream or
   crème fraîche

1 Crush the peppercorns coarsely using a pestle and mortar, or rolling pin. Scatter the peppercorns on a board, lay the steaks on top and press hard to encrust the surface of the meat; repeat with the other side.
2 Heat the butter and oil in a frying pan and quickly sear the steaks over a high heat. Reduce the heat to medium and cook for 2–3 minutes on each side for medium-rare or 4–5 minutes for medium, according to taste, turning every 2 minutes. Season with salt.
3 Remove the steaks from the pan and keep warm. Add the brandy to the pan, take off the heat and set alight. When the flame dies, stir in the cream or crème fraîche, season and reheat gently. Pour the sauce over the steaks to serve.

Serves 4   preparation: 10 minutes   cooking time: 4–12 minutes
per serving: 480 cals; 35g fat; 1g carbohydrate

Lemon Peppered Steak

½tsp coarsely ground black pepper
40g (1½oz) butter, at room temperature
grated zest of ½ lemon
2tsp chopped thyme

4 x 175g (6oz) rump or sirloin steaks, each
  about 2cm (¾ inch) thick
salt

1 Put the pepper, butter, lemon zest and thyme in a bowl and mix to combine. Put the mixture on a sheet of greaseproof paper, roughly shape into a roll and chill until hard, or freeze for 10 minutes if you're short of time.
2 Preheat a griddle pan until hot. Season the steaks well with salt and griddle for 2 minutes on each side for rare, 4–5 minutes for medium and 6–7 minutes for well done.
3 Meanwhile, slice the chilled butter into four rounds. As soon as the steak is cooked on one side, flip it over and top with the butter, allowing it to melt slowly as the other side cooks. Serve at once.

Serves 4   preparation: 10 minutes, plus chilling   cooking time: 5–15 minutes
per serving: 290 cals; 16g fat; 0g carbohydrate

Chilli con Carne

2tbsp sunflower oil
1 onion, peeled and roughly chopped
2 garlic cloves, peeled and crushed
1 red pepper, cored, deseeded and chopped
450g (1lb) beef mince
1tsp each chilli powder and chilli flakes, or
  to taste
1tsp each ground cumin and ground
  coriander

300ml (½ pint) red wine
1tbsp Worcestershire sauce
400g can chopped tomatoes
salt and pepper
400g can kidney beans, drained and rinsed
grated cheese, to sprinkle
guacamole or soured cream, to serve

1 Heat the oil in a large frying pan, add the onion, garlic and red pepper and cook gently for 5 minutes.
2 Add the beef mince to the pan, stirring to break it up, and cook over a high heat for 5 minutes or until well browned.
3 Stir in the chilli powder and flakes, cumin and coriander, then cook for 2 minutes. Add the wine and simmer for 2 minutes.
4 Stir in the Worcestershire sauce and tomatoes and season, then cook for 30 minutes. Add the kidney beans to the mixture and cook for a further 20 minutes.
5 Serve the chilli with rice, or piled on top of baked potatoes. Sprinkle with the grated cheese and serve with guacamole or soured cream.

Serves 6   preparation: 10 minutes   cooking time: about 1 hour
per serving (without guacamole): 270 cals; 12g fat; 13g carbohydrate

Italian Meatballs in Tomato Sauce

2tbsp olive oil
350g (12oz) onions, peeled and chopped
3 garlic cloves, peeled and crushed
2 x 400g cans chopped tomatoes
1tsp salt
1tbsp cider vinegar
½tsp ground cinnamon
450g (1lb) lean beef mince
2tbsp chopped basil

1tsp dried oregano
75g (3oz) fresh breadcrumbs
1 egg, plus 1 egg yolk, beaten
2tbsp chopped parsley, plus
   extra to garnish
3tbsp freshly grated Parmesan cheese
salt and pepper
12 thin smoked streaky bacon rashers,
   about 200g (7oz)

1   Heat the olive oil in a shallow flameproof casserole, add the onions with two-thirds of the garlic and
    fry gently for 5–7 minutes until beginning to soften. Add the tomatoes, salt, vinegar and cinnamon.
    Bring to the boil, then cover the pan, reduce the heat and simmer for 20 minutes.
2   Preheat the oven to 180°C (160°C fan oven) mark 4. Put the beef mince in a bowl with the basil,
    oregano, breadcrumbs, remaining garlic, the egg, egg yolk, parsley and 1tbsp Parmesan and season.
    Work the ingredients together with your hands until evenly mixed.
3   With dampened hands, shape the mixture into 12 even-sized balls, then wrap a bacon rasher around
    each one. Put the meatballs in the casserole on top of the tomato sauce. Cover the pan and cook in
    the oven for about 45 minutes or until piping hot and cooked through.
4   Scatter with the remaining Parmesan and plenty of chopped parsley. Serve with rice.

Serves 4   preparation: 20 minutes   cooking time: 1¼ hours
per serving: 580 cals; 37g fat; 22g carbohydrate

Supper

Risotto with Pancetta and Broad Beans

225g (8oz) fresh broad beans
salt and pepper
50g (2oz) unsalted butter, plus a drop
  of olive oil
125g (4oz) pancetta, cut into small strips
1 medium onion, peeled and very
  finely chopped
225g (8oz) arborio or carnaroli rice

150ml (¼ pint) dry white wine
about 1 litre (1¾ pints) fresh hot vegetable
  stock or vegetable bouillon
2tbsp chopped flat-leafed parsley
1tbsp chopped tarragon
freshly grated Parmesan cheese, to sprinkle

1 Cook the beans in boiling, lightly salted water for about 4 minutes. Drain under cold running water then carefully break the skin at one end between your finger and thumb and pop the beans out. Put on one side.
2 Melt half the butter with the olive oil in a large saucepan, add the pancetta and cook until golden. Add the onion and continue to cook gently for about 5 minutes, stirring from time to time.
3 When the onion is soft and translucent, add the rice and stir well to ensure each grain is coated in butter. Pour in the wine and continue to stir over a lowish heat until it has almost evaporated.
4 Add the hot stock, a ladleful at a time, stirring as you do so and waiting for the liquid to be absorbed before adding more. This will probably take about 20 minutes but start tasting after 18 minutes. The consistency of the risotto should be dense and creamy but the individual grains of rice distinct and firm.
5 Remove from the heat and gently stir in the beans and the remaining butter. Season to taste (pancetta and bouillon are salty so you may not need any extra), then stir in the parsley and tarragon. Serve straight away, sprinkled with plenty of Parmesan.

Serves 2 generously   preparation: 15 minutes   cooking time: 35 minutes
per serving: 1020 cals; 50g fat; 104g carbohydrate

One pot

What better than to assemble all the ingredients you need for a great meal, cook it and then tuck in, knowing you've only got one pan to wash up? Casseroles, roasts, stews and braises are not only delicious, they can have all kinds of amazing vegetables, beans and pasta added to make complete meals in just one pot, giving you time to finish off that good book, watch your favourite soap, or just relax.

There are classics such as Seafood Paella, with the wonderful colour, flavour and aroma of saffron. Make it in a lovely big paella or frying pan and take to the table so that everyone can dig in.

Then the slow-cooked dishes – Braised Oxtail, full of flavour, sticky and warming; Chicken in a Pot, cooked in wine with bacon, carrots, parsnips and celery; or Beef Casserole with Black Olives – chunks of beef simmered with bacon, mushrooms, onions and olives in a gravy enriched with brandy and red wine.

And the exotics: bring back memories of holidays in the sun with Caribbean Chicken – a hint of chilli, a dash of rum, some black-eyed beans, and lashings of cool beer to enjoy it with.

One pot – many flavours.

Mussels with Cider and Red Onions

75g (3oz) butter
450g (1lb) red onions, peeled and
  finely chopped
3 garlic cloves, peeled
300ml (½ pint) cider

2kg (4½lb) very fresh mussels, washed,
  debearded, tapped and any open or
  damaged ones discarded
284ml carton double cream
salt and pepper
parsley sprigs, to garnish

1 Melt the butter in a large heavy-based pan. Add the onions and cook, stirring, for 10 minutes or until soft, then add the garlic and cook for 2 minutes. Stir in the cider and bring to the boil, then add the mussels. Cover, reduce the heat and simmer for 4–5 minutes or until the mussels have opened.
2 Remove the mussels with a large draining spoon and put them into their serving bowls, discarding any mussels that haven't opened. Add the cream to the liquor and bring to the boil, then bubble for 10 minutes or until reduced and lightly syrupy.
3 Pour the sauce over the mussels and season to taste. Serve immediately, garnished with parsley.

Serves 4 preparation: 20 minutes cooking time: 30 minutes
per serving: 650 cals; 53g fat; 13g carbohydrate

Thai Fish Stew

1 large red chilli, halved, deseeded and
  roughly chopped
grated zest and juice of 1 lime
2 lemon grass stalks, roughly chopped
5cm (2 inch) piece fresh root ginger,
  peeled and roughly chopped
2 fat garlic cloves, peeled and
  roughly chopped
1tbsp light muscovado sugar
3tbsp Thai fish sauce

2tbsp olive oil
2 shallots, blanched in boiling water,
  drained, peeled and thinly sliced
2 small pak choi, roughly chopped
2 x 400g cans coconut milk
125g (4oz) straight-to-wok noodles
700g (1½lb) cod or haddock, skinned
  and cut into large chunks
4tbsp chopped coriander
small bunch of basil, roughly chopped

1 To make the spice paste, put the first seven ingredients into a food processor and whiz to a rough paste.
2 Heat half the olive oil in a deep pan and add the shallots. Cook, stirring, until dark golden and crisp, then remove from the pan and put to one side. Add the remaining oil and stir-fry the pak choi for 1–2 minutes, then add the spice paste and cook for 1 minute. Add the coconut milk, noodles and fish, then simmer for 2–3 minutes. Stir in the coriander, basil and some of the crispy shallots. Sprinkle the rest of the shallots over the top, then serve.

Serves 4 preparation: 15 minutes cooking time: 10–15 minutes
per serving: 650 cals; 40g fat; 36g carbohydrate

Seafood Paella

3tbsp olive oil
2 garlic cloves, peeled and crushed
1 onion, peeled and finely chopped
2tsp paprika
1 green pepper, deseeded and cut
  into strips
1tsp saffron strands
200ml (7fl oz) passata
300g (11oz) arborio or paella rice

1 litre (1¾ pints) hot fish stock
225g (8oz) large prepared squid, sliced
  into rings
450g (1lb) fresh mussels, washed,
  debearded, tapped and any open or
  damaged ones discarded
225g (8oz) raw tiger prawns, with shells on
1 lemon, cut into wedges

1 Heat the olive oil in a large frying pan. Fry the garlic and onion for 5 minutes, add the paprika and green pepper and cook for 2 minutes.
2 Stir in the saffron and passata and cook for 2 minutes, then add the rice and stir until translucent. Pour in one-third of the hot stock, bring to a simmer and cook for 5 minutes until most of the liquid is absorbed. Add half the remaining stock and cook, stirring, for 5 minutes.
3 Add the squid, mussels and prawns to the pan and stir. Pour in the remaining stock and cook for 10 minutes, stirring occasionally, until almost all the liquid has been absorbed.
4 Serve garnished with lemon wedges.

Serves 4 preparation: 20 minutes cooking time: 27–30 minutes
per serving: 480 cals; 12g fat; 66g carbohydrate

Spicy Monkfish Stew

1tbsp olive oil
1 onion, peeled and finely sliced
1tbsp tom yum soup paste
450g (1lb) potatoes, peeled and cut into
  2cm (¾ inch) chunks
400g can chopped tomatoes in rich
  tomato juice

600ml (1 pint) hot fish stock
salt and pepper
450g (1lb) monkfish, cut into
  2cm (¾ inch) chunks
200g bag baby spinach leaves

1 Heat the olive oil in a pan and fry the onion over a medium heat for 5 minutes until golden.
2 Add the soup paste and potatoes and stir-fry for 1 minute. Add the tomatoes and hot stock, season well and cover the pan. Bring to the boil, then reduce the heat and simmer, partially covered, for 15 minutes or until the potatoes are just tender.
3 Add the monkfish to the pan and continue to simmer for 5–10 minutes or until the fish is cooked. Add the spinach and stir through until wilted.
4 Spoon the fish stew into warmed bowls and serve immediately with crusty bread.

Serves 6 preparation: 10 minutes cooking time: 35 minutes
per serving: 160 cals; 3g fat; 18g carbohydrate

Navarin of Cod

175g (6oz) podded broad beans
25g (1oz) butter
2tbsp sunflower oil
1 onion, peeled and sliced
225g (8oz) baby carrots, scrubbed
　and trimmed
225g (8oz) courgettes, trimmed and cut
　into 2cm (¾ inch) chunks
1 garlic clove, peeled and crushed

1.1kg (2½lb) thick chunky cod fillet, skinned
salt and pepper
4tbsp plain flour
150ml (¼ pint) dry white wine
300ml (½ pint) fish stock
1tbsp lemon juice
3tbsp double cream
2tbsp chopped flat-leafed parsley

1　If the beans are large, blanch them in boiling water for 1–2 minutes, then drain and refresh in cold water.
2　Heat half the butter and half the oil in a large sauté pan. Add the onion, carrots, courgettes and garlic and cook gently until softened and just beginning to brown. Remove from the pan and put to one side.
3　Season the fish, then dust lightly with the flour. Heat the remaining butter and oil in the pan, add the fish and brown on all sides. Remove from the pan and put to one side.
4　Add the wine to the pan, scraping up any sediment from the bottom. Simmer for 1–2 minutes, then return the carrots, courgettes, onion, garlic and fish to the pan, with the beans and stock. Bring to a simmer, cover and simmer gently for about 10 minutes or until the fish is opaque and flakes easily.
5　Stir in the lemon juice, cream and parsley. Divide among six bowls, grind over some coarse black pepper and serve with buttered baby new potatoes.

Serves 6　preparation: 15 minutes　cooking time: 25 minutes
per serving: 340 cals; 13g fat; 16g carbohydrate

Mussel and Potato Stew

25g (1oz) butter
200g pack rindless back bacon rashers,
　cut into strips
700g (1½lb) white potatoes, peeled and cut
　into large chunks
salt and pepper

198g can sweetcorn kernels, drained
1kg (2¼lb) fresh mussels, washed,
　debearded, tapped and any open or
　damaged ones discarded
142ml carton single cream
1tbsp chopped parsley

1　Melt the butter in a large pan, add the bacon and cook, stirring, until the strips separate.
2　Add the potatoes and 150ml (¼ pint) cold water to the pan and season lightly. Cover with a tight-fitting lid and cook for 10 minutes or until the potatoes are almost tender.
3　Add the sweetcorn and mussels to the pan. Cover the pan and bring to the boil, then reduce the heat and simmer for 2–3 minutes or until the mussels open. Discard any mussels that don't open. Add the cream and the parsley and serve in warmed bowls.

Serves 4　preparation: 15 minutes　cooking time: 20 minutes
per serving: 590 cals; 35g fat; 45g carbohydrate

Seafood Gumbo

125g (4oz) butter
50g (2oz) plain flour
1–2tbsp Cajun spice
1 onion, peeled and chopped
1 green pepper, cored, deseeded
and chopped
5 spring onions, sliced
1tbsp chopped flat-leafed parsley
1 garlic clove, peeled and crushed
1 beef tomato, chopped
125g (4oz) garlic sausage, finely sliced
75g (3oz) American easy-cook rice

1.1 litres (2 pints) vegetable stock
450g (1lb) okra, sliced
1 each bay leaf and thyme sprig
2tsp salt
¼tsp cayenne pepper
juice of ½ lemon
4 cloves
black pepper
500g (1¼lb) frozen mixed seafood –
containing mussels, squid and prawns –
thawed and drained

1   Heat the butter in a 2.5 litre (4¼–4½ pint) heavy-based pan over a medium heat. Add the flour and
    Cajun spice and cook for 1–2 minutes or until golden brown. Add the onion, green pepper, spring onions,
    parsley and garlic and cook for 5 minutes.
2   Add the tomato, garlic sausage and rice to the pan and stir well to coat. Add the stock, okra, bay leaf,
    thyme, salt, cayenne pepper, lemon juice and cloves and season with pepper. Bring to the boil, then
    cover the pan, reduce the heat and simmer for 12 minutes or until the rice is tender.
3   Add the seafood and cook for 2 minutes to heat through. Serve the gumbo in deep bowls.

Serves 4   preparation time: 10 minutes   cooking time: 30 minutes
per serving: 570 cals; 34g fat; 33g carbohydrate

Prawn and Spinach Pancakes

100g (3½oz) frozen leaf spinach, thawed
salt and pepper
1tbsp olive oil
200g pack (containing six) pancakes
3tbsp light mayonnaise
200g (7oz) low-fat mature Cheddar
  cheese, grated

25g (1oz) freshly grated Parmesan cheese
3 spring onions, finely chopped
300g (11oz) large cooked peeled prawns
142ml carton double cream

1 Preheat the oven to 200°C (180°C fan oven) mark 6. Squeeze the thawed spinach in your hands to remove as much excess liquid as possible, then roughly chop and season with just a little salt but plenty of pepper.

2 Lightly oil a medium-sized ovenproof dish, about 20.5cm (8 inches) square. Open each pancake out and spread a little mayonnaise over the centre of each one, leaving a 2.5cm (1 inch) clear edge. Sprinkle a little of the Cheddar and Parmesan into each pancake, then top with spring onion, spinach and prawns. Gather the edges of the pancakes loosely together and tuck side by side in the dish, leaving the filling exposed. There should be just enough space in the dish to hold all the pancakes in a single layer.

3 Spoon the cream over the pancakes and sprinkle with the remaining cheese. Bake for 20 minutes or until the tops are crisp and golden and everything is heated through. Serve immediately with a green salad.

Serves 6   preparation: 10 minutes   cooking time: 20 minutes
per serving: 390 cals; 25g fat; 17g carbohydrate

Caribbean Chicken

10 chicken pieces, about 1.4kg (3lb), such
  as thighs, drumsticks, wings or breasts
1tsp salt
black pepper
1tbsp ground coriander
2tsp ground cumin
1tbsp paprika
pinch of freshly grated nutmeg
1 Scotch bonnet chilli, deseeded
  and chopped
1 onion, peeled and chopped
leaves of 5 thyme sprigs, plus thyme sprigs
  to garnish

4 garlic cloves, peeled and crushed
2tbsp dark soy sauce
juice of 1 lemon
2tbsp vegetable oil
2tbsp light muscovado sugar
350g (12oz) – or pour into a measuring jug
  up to 450ml (¾ pint) – American easy-
  cook rice
3tbsp dark rum (optional)
25g (1oz) butter
2 x 300g cans black-eyed beans,
  drained and rinsed

1 Remove the skin from the chicken pieces and discard. Pierce the meat with a knife, put in a container and sprinkle with ½tsp salt, some black pepper, the coriander, cumin, paprika and nutmeg. Add the chopped chilli, onion, thyme and garlic, then pour the soy sauce and lemon juice over and stir to combine. Cover and chill for at least 4 hours.

2 Heat a 3.4 litre (6 pint) heavy-based pan over a medium heat for 2 minutes. Add the oil and sugar, then cook over a medium heat for 3 minutes or until it turns a rich golden caramel colour. (Be careful not to overcook it as the mixture will blacken and taste burnt – so watch it very carefully.)

3 Remove the chicken pieces from the marinade and add to the sugar and oil mixture in the hot pan. Cover and cook over a medium heat for 5 minutes, then turn the chicken and cook, covered, for another 5 minutes until evenly browned. Add the onion and any remaining juices from the marinade. Turn again, then cover and cook for 10 minutes.

4 Add the rice, stir to combine with the chicken, then pour in 900ml (1½ pints) cold water. Add the rum, if using, the butter and ½tsp salt. Cover the pan and bring to the boil, then reduce the heat and simmer over a gentle heat, without lifting the lid, for 20 minutes or until the rice is tender and most of the liquid has been absorbed.

5 Add the black-eyed beans to the pan and mix well. Cover and cook for 3–5 minutes until the beans are just warmed through and all the liquid has been absorbed, taking care the rice doesn't stick to the base of the pan. Garnish with thyme sprigs and serve.

Serves 5   preparation: 40 minutes, plus marinating   cooking time: 45–50 minutes
per serving: 660 cals; 19g fat; 85g carbohydrate

Spanish Chicken

1½tsp ground turmeric
1.1 litres (2 pints) hot chicken stock
2tbsp vegetable oil
4 chicken thighs, skinned, boned and
  roughly diced
1 onion, peeled and chopped
1 red pepper, deseeded and sliced

50g (2oz) chorizo sausage, diced
2 garlic cloves, peeled and crushed
300g (11oz) long-grain rice
125g (4oz) frozen peas
salt and pepper
3tbsp chopped flat-leafed parsley

1   Add the turmeric to the hot stock and leave to infuse for at least 5 minutes. Meanwhile, heat the oil in a large (at least 2.8 litres/5 pints capacity) frying pan and fry the chicken for 10 minutes or until golden. Remove from the pan and put to one side.
2   Add the onion to the pan and cook over a medium heat for 5 minutes until soft. Add the red pepper and chorizo and cook for a further 5 minutes, then add the garlic and cook for 1 minute.
3   Return the chicken to the pan, add the rice and mix. Add one-third of the stock and bring to a simmer, then stir until all the liquid has been absorbed.
4   Add the remaining stock and the peas and bring to the boil, then reduce the heat to low and continue to cook, uncovered, for 15–20 minutes until the rice absorbs all the liquid. Five minutes before the cooking time is up, season well and add the parsley. Serve with crusty bread.

Serves 4   preparation: 25 minutes, plus infusing   cooking time: 50 minutes
per serving: 500 cals; 13g fat; 68g carbohydrate

Coconut and Coriander Chicken

2tbsp roughly chopped coriander
4 skinless boneless chicken breasts
3tbsp vegetable oil
1 large onion, about 225g (8oz), peeled and
  finely chopped
350g (12oz) sweet potato, peeled and chopped

2tbsp mild curry paste
400ml can coconut milk
400g can chopped tomatoes
salt and pepper
coriander leaves and lime halves,
  to garnish

1   Tuck a little coriander in the centre of each piece of chicken, then roll up and secure with a wooden cocktail stick. (Or, to save time, simply add the coriander to the sauce in step 3.)
2   Heat the oil in a deep frying pan or a shallow heatproof casserole, then fry the onion and the sweet potato for about 10 minutes until the onion is soft (this brings out the natural sweetness of the onion and adds to the flavour of the finished dish). Add the curry paste and cook, stirring, for 3–4 minutes.
3   Add the coconut milk, tomatoes and the chicken, then cover and simmer very gently for about 30 minutes or until the chicken is tender. If the pieces aren't completely covered in sauce, turn the chicken over halfway through cooking. Adjust the seasoning and serve garnished with coriander and lime halves.

Serves 4   preparation: 10 minutes   cooking time: 45 minutes
per serving: 560 cals; 34g fat; 29g carbohydrate

Tarragon Chicken

1tbsp olive oil

salt and pepper

1kg (2¼lb) chicken pieces (eight in total), such as thighs and drumsticks

1 onion, peeled and finely sliced

2 garlic cloves, peeled and crushed

2 celery sticks, thickly sliced

2 carrots, peeled and cut into 2cm (¾ inch) chunks

2 leeks, cut into 2cm (¾ inch) chunks

600g (1lb 6oz) potatoes, peeled and cut into large chunks

6 streaky bacon rashers, chopped

2tbsp Dijon mustard

1tbsp plain flour

250g (9oz) sliced chestnut mushrooms

600ml (1 pint) hot chicken stock

3tbsp chopped tarragon

½ lemon

200g carton half-fat crème fraîche

1 Heat the olive oil in a large, flameproof casserole. Season the chicken pieces and brown all over for 10 minutes. Remove from the pan and put to one side. Drain the fat from the pan – there should be about 75ml (3fl oz). Pour just 1tbsp oil back into the pan and discard the rest. Preheat the oven to 200°C (180°C fan oven) mark 6.

2 Add the onion, garlic, celery, carrots, leeks and potatoes to the pan, and cook, stirring, for 5–10 minutes, then add the bacon while the vegetables are sautéing. Add the mustard with the flour, cook for 2 minutes, then add the mushrooms and pour in the hot stock. Season well, then return the browned chicken to the pan. Add the tarragon, squeeze over the juice from the lemon half and pop the squeezed lemon half into the pan. Cover and bring the casserole to the boil.

3 Transfer the casserole to the oven and cook for 25–30 minutes until the chicken is cooked through and the sauce is piping hot and thickened. Once cooked, stir in the crème fraîche to serve.

Serves 4   preparation: 15 minutes   cooking time: 45–50 minutes
per serving: 640 cals; 36g fat; 33g carbohydrate

Spicy Chicken

1kg (2¼lb) skinless chicken drumsticks
and thighs
1 onion, peeled and sliced
1 garlic clove, peeled and sliced
2tbsp each chicken seasoning, ground
coriander and ground cumin
1tbsp paprika
1 hot red chilli, deseeded and chopped
juice of ½ lemon

2tbsp soy sauce
8 thyme sprigs, plus extra to garnish
2tbsp sunflower oil
2tbsp light muscovado sugar or
granulated sugar
500g (1lb 2oz) potatoes, peeled and cut
into 5cm (2 inch) pieces
600ml (1 pint) hot chicken stock

1 Put the chicken in a shallow, sealable container and pierce each piece several times. Sprinkle over the onion, garlic, chicken seasoning, spices, chilli, lemon juice, soy sauce and thyme. Stir well to combine, then cover and chill for 30 minutes or overnight.
2 Heat the oil and sugar in a large heavy-based casserole over a medium heat until the sugar dissolves and turns a dark, golden brown. Add the chicken immediately, reserving the onion and marinade, and brown for 5 minutes, turning as needed.
3 Add the potatoes, marinade and onion and cook for 10 minutes over a gentle heat, turning as needed. Pour in the hot stock, cover and simmer for 25 minutes. Uncover and cook for 10 minutes until the chicken and potatoes are tender and the gravy has reduced slightly. Garnish with thyme sprigs and serve.

Serves 4   preparation: 20 minutes, plus marinating   cooking time: 50 minutes
per serving: 400 cals; 14g fat; 31g carbohydrate

Moroccan Chicken

12 chicken pieces, to include thighs,
drumsticks and breast
25g (1oz) butter
1 large onion, peeled and sliced
2 garlic cloves, peeled and crushed
2tbsp harissa paste
generous pinch of saffron strands

1tsp salt
1 cinnamon stick
black pepper
600ml (1 pint) chicken stock
75g (3oz) raisins
2 x 400g cans chickpeas, drained
and rinsed

1 Heat a large, wide non-stick pan. Add the chicken pieces and fry over a high heat until well browned all over. Add the butter and when melted, add the onion and garlic and stir together for 5 minutes.
2 Add the harissa, saffron, salt and cinnamon stick and season well with pepper. Pour over the stock and bring to the boil, then reduce the heat, cover the pan and simmer gently for 25–30 minutes.
3 Add the raisins and chickpeas to the pan and bring to the boil. Reduce the heat and simmer, uncovered, for 5–10 minutes, then serve with warm flat bread such as plain naan or pitta.

Serves 6   preparation: 10 minutes   cooking time: 50 minutes
per serving: 350 cals; 15g fat; 18g carbohydrate

Chicken Casserole

1tbsp olive oil

salt and pepper

1kg (2¼lb) chicken pieces, such as thighs and drumsticks

1 onion, peeled and finely sliced

2 garlic cloves, peeled and crushed

2 celery sticks, thickly sliced

2 carrots, peeled and cut into 2cm (¾ inch) chunks

2 leeks, trimmed and cut into 2cm (¾ inch) chunks

600g (1¼lb) potatoes, peeled and cut into large chunks

1tbsp plain flour

600ml (1 pint) hot chicken stock

2 rosemary sprigs

½ lemon

1 Preheat the oven to 180°C (160°C fan oven) mark 4. Heat the olive oil in a large flameproof casserole. Season the chicken pieces and add to the casserole. Cook over a medium heat for 10 minutes until browned all over, stirring occasionally. Remove with a slotted spoon and put to one side. Drain off all but 1tbsp of the fat from the casserole.

2 Add the onion, garlic, celery, carrots, leeks and potatoes to the casserole and cook, stirring, for 5–10 minutes. Stir in the flour and cook for 2 minutes.

3 Pour in the hot stock, return the chicken to the casserole and season well. Add the rosemary sprigs, squeeze over the juice from the lemon and add the spent lemon half to the casserole. Cover and bring to a simmer.

4 Transfer to the oven and cook for 25–30 minutes until the chicken is cooked through and the sauce is thickened. Serve at once.

Serves 4   preparation: 25 minutes   cooking time: 45–50 minutes

per serving: 380 cals; 14g fat; 31g carbohydrate

Chicken in a Pot

3tbsp olive oil
1.4kg (3lb) chicken
225g (8oz) streaky bacon rashers, chopped
1 large onion, peeled and roughly chopped
5 carrots, peeled and halved
  lengthways if large
4 small parsnips, peeled and
  halved lengthways

2 large celery stalks, cut into large slices,
  leaves reserved
300ml (½ pint) dry white wine
25g (1oz) butter
salt and pepper

1 Preheat the oven to 200°C (180°C fan oven) mark 6. Heat the olive oil in a large 6.3 litre (11 pint) casserole and brown the chicken all over. Transfer the chicken to a plate and add the bacon, onion, carrots, parsnips and celery to the pan. Fry, stirring, over a moderate heat until the onion is soft and all the vegetables are golden.
2 Put the chicken back in the pan, breast side down, on top of the vegetables. Pour in the wine and 450ml (¾ pint) water and bring to the boil. Cover with a well-fitting lid, then transfer to the oven and cook for 30 minutes.
3 Turn the chicken breast side up and put back in the oven, uncovered, for 30 minutes or until the chicken is cooked – the juices should run clear when a skewer is inserted into the thigh. Remove from the oven and put the cooked chicken and the vegetables into a serving dish, leaving the liquid in the pan, and cover loosely with foil.
4 To make the gravy, put the casserole on the hob and bring the liquid to the boil. Add the butter and leave it to bubble until the liquid has reduced down and thickened slightly. Taste and season with a little salt and plenty of pepper.
5 Carve the chicken, arrange on warmed plates with the vegetables and pour over some of the gravy. Roughly chop the reserved celery leaves, sprinkle on top and serve.

Serves 6   preparation: 15 minutes   cooking time: 1½ hours
per serving: 590 cals; 42g fat; 16g carbohydrate

One-pot Chicken Thigh Roast

8 chicken thighs, skin removed
salt and pepper
2tbsp chicken seasoning
1 onion, peeled and chopped
1 garlic clove, peeled and crushed
2tbsp vegetable oil
2tbsp light muscovado sugar

900g (2lb) potatoes, peeled and cut into
   small chunks
450g (1lb) carrots, peeled and cut into
   small chunks
1 chicken stock cube
400g can chopped tomatoes
400g can chickpeas, drained and rinsed

1   Put the chicken into a large dish and season generously. Sprinkle over the chicken seasoning, turning the chicken to coat evenly, then stir in the onion and garlic. You can cook the chicken straight away or cover and chill it for several hours until needed. This will improve the flavour.

2   Take a large heavy-based pan and add the oil and sugar. Cook on a medium heat for 3 minutes until it turns a rich golden caramel colour, making sure it doesn't burn.

3   Without wasting a second, add the seasoned chicken – stand back, as the fat may splatter. Cook, without stirring, for 5 minutes, then turn the chicken over and cook for a further 5 minutes until it is evenly browned.

4   Add the potatoes and carrots to the pan, stir together well and cook for 5 minutes. Pour 600ml (1 pint) boiling water into a measuring jug and crumble in the stock cube. Stir to mix, then add to the chicken with the tomatoes. Cover and simmer gently for 20 minutes, then add the chickpeas and cook for 5 minutes.

Serves 4   preparation: 20 minutes   cooking time: 45 minutes
per serving: 630 cals; 28g fat; 60g carbohydrate

Herby Chicken

450g (1lb) shallots, blanched in
   boiling water, drained and peeled,
   or 3 large onions, peeled and cut
   into medium wedges
500g (1lb 2oz) small salad potatoes
700g (1½lb) free-range chicken pieces,
   skin on

6–8 garlic cloves, unpeeled
small handful of rosemary sprigs
50ml (2fl oz) olive oil
pared zest of 1 large orange and
   the juice of 2
salt and pepper

1 Preheat the oven to 220°C (200°C fan oven) mark 7. Put all the ingredients, except the orange juice, into a large roasting tin. Season generously, then toss in one of the orange halves and mix well to coat everything with the oil.
2 Roast for about 20 minutes, then turn the chicken and vegetables. Continue to cook for 40 minutes until the chicken and potatoes are golden and the onions and garlic are caramelised.
3 Add the orange juice to the roasting tin, scraping away at any stuck bits in the pan to make a thin liquor to spoon over the chicken. Return to the oven for 10 minutes to heat through, then serve.

Serves 4   preparation: 10 minutes   cooking time: 1 hour 10 minutes
per serving: 640 cals; 42g fat; 34g carbohydrate

Chicken with Chickpeas

2tbsp sunflower oil
1 onion, peeled and finely chopped
1tsp ground turmeric
4 large skinless chicken breasts
juice of 1 lemon, or to taste

3 large garlic cloves, peeled and crushed
salt and pepper
400g can chickpeas, drained and rinsed
pinch of cayenne pepper
chopped flat-leafed parsley, to garnish

1 Heat the oil in a large frying pan, add the onion and fry over a low heat for 5–6 minutes until translucent and softened. Stir in the turmeric.
2 Add the chicken and turn in the turmeric mixture until yellow all over. Add the lemon juice, garlic, 300ml (½ pint) cold water and season.
3 Bring to the boil, reduce the heat, cover the pan and simmer for about 20 minutes, then add the chickpeas and simmer for 5–10 minutes until the chicken is cooked.
4 Remove the chicken with a slotted spoon and keep covered. Bring the remaining liquid and chickpeas to the boil and bubble for 4–5 minutes until the liquid has reduced and thickened. Return the chicken to the pan for 1–2 minutes to heat through, then sprinkle with cayenne pepper. Garnish with the parsley and serve.

Serves 4   preparation: 10 minutes   cooking time: 45 minutes
per serving: 330 cals; 15g fat; 14g carbohydrate

Glazed Duck with Rosemary and Garlic

4 duck breasts, about 175–200g
  (6–7oz) each
finely grated zest and juice of 1 lemon
1 garlic clove, peeled and crushed
salt and pepper
450g (1lb) new potatoes, scrubbed
  and halved
125g (4oz) shallots, blanched in boiling
  water, drained, peeled and halved if large

225g (8oz) baby leeks, trimmed, or regular
  leeks cut into 7.5cm (3 inch) pieces
225g (8oz) small carrots, peeled and
  halved lengthways
2tbsp olive oil
sea salt, to sprinkle
2tbsp chopped rosemary, plus rosemary
  sprigs to garnish
4tsp runny honey

1 Score the skin of the duck breasts with a sharp knife and put them back on the plastic trays they were bought in. Sprinkle over the lemon zest and juice and garlic and season. Turn several times to coat in the juice mix, cover and leave for 1 hour for the flavours to mingle.
2 Preheat the oven to 220°C (200°C fan oven) mark 7. Put the potatoes, shallots, leeks and carrots into a large roasting tin. Add the olive oil and toss together, then sprinkle with sea salt and chopped rosemary. Roast for 30 minutes.
3 Put the duck breasts on a metal rack, smear the skin with the honey and sprinkle generously with sea salt. Remove the tray of vegetables from the oven and turn them, draining off any oil. Position the duck on the rack over the vegetables. Roast for 25–30 minutes, or until the duck is brown and tender and the vegetables tender and a little charred.
4 Transfer the duck to a serving dish, surround with the vegetables, garnish with the rosemary sprigs and serve.

Serves 4   preparation: 20 minutes, plus marinating   cooking time: 1 hour
per serving: 660 cals; 47g fat; 29g carbohydrate

Turkey, Pepper and Haricot Bean Casserole

350g (12oz) dried haricot beans, soaked in
  cold water overnight
2 large onions, peeled
2 small carrots, peeled and cut into chunks
bouquet garni (2 bay leaves, few thyme
  sprigs, small bunch of parsley)
1tbsp olive oil
2 red chillies, deseeded and chopped
2 garlic cloves, peeled and crushed

350g (12oz) lean turkey meat, cut into bite-
  sized pieces
1 large red pepper and 1 large orange
  pepper, both deseeded and finely diced
2 courgettes, trimmed and finely diced
salt and pepper
400g can chopped tomatoes
1tbsp sun-dried tomato paste
large handful of basil leaves

1 Drain the soaked haricot beans, put them into a large flameproof casserole and cover with fresh water. Quarter 1 onion and add to the casserole with the carrots and bouquet garni. Bring to the boil, then cover, reduce the heat and simmer for 45 minutes or until the beans are tender. Drain the beans, reserving 150ml (¼ pint) of the cooking liquid; discard the flavouring vegetables. Spoon the beans into a bowl and put to one side. Wipe out the casserole.
2 Finely slice the remaining onion. Heat the olive oil in the casserole, add the onion and cook gently for 5 minutes. Add the chillies and garlic and cook for 1 minute until softened.
3 Add the turkey to the pan and stir-fry for 5 minutes, then add the diced peppers and courgettes and season well. Cover the casserole and cook for 5 minutes until the vegetables are slightly softened.
4 Add the tomatoes and sun-dried tomato paste, cover and bring to the boil. Add the haricot beans and reserved cooking liquid. Stir and season well, then cover, reduce the heat and simmer for 15 minutes. Stir in the basil leaves just before serving.

Serves 6   preparation: 20 minutes, plus soaking   cooking time: 1 hour 20 minutes
per serving: 310 cals; 5g fat; 41g carbohydrate

Pot-roasted Pheasant with Red Cabbage

25g (1oz) butter
1tbsp oil
2 oven-ready young pheasants, halved
2 onions, peeled and sliced
450g (1lb) red cabbage, cored and
   finely shredded
1tsp cornflour

250ml (8fl oz) red wine
2tbsp redcurrant jelly
1tbsp balsamic vinegar
salt and pepper
4 rindless smoked streaky
   bacon rashers, halved

1 Preheat the oven to 200°C (180°C fan oven) mark 6. Melt the butter with the oil in a large flameproof casserole. Add the pheasant halves and brown on all sides, then remove and put to one side. Add the onions and cabbage to the casserole and fry for 5 minutes, stirring frequently, until softened.

2 Blend the cornflour with a little water. Add to the casserole with the wine, redcurrant jelly, vinegar and seasoning. Bring to the boil, stirring.

3 Arrange the pheasant halves, skin side up, on the cabbage. Lay the bacon on top. Cover the casserole and cook for 30 minutes or until tender (older pheasants will take an extra 10–20 minutes).

4 Serve the pheasant and cabbage with the cooking juices spooned over.

Serves 4   preparation: 20 minutes   cooking time: 40 minutes
per serving: 570 cals; 31g fat; 15g carbohydrate

Pheasant Casserole with Cider and Apples

2 large oven-ready pheasants
salt and pepper
2tbsp plain flour, plus extra to dust
4 crisp eating apples, such as
  Granny Smiths
1tbsp lemon juice
50g (2oz) butter
4 rindless streaky bacon rashers, halved

2 onions, peeled and chopped
2 celery sticks, chopped
1tbsp dried juniper berries, lightly crushed
2.5cm (1 inch) piece fresh root ginger,
  peeled and finely chopped
300ml (½ pint) pheasant or chicken stock
750–900ml (1¼–1½ pints) dry cider
150ml (¼ pint) double cream

1 Cut each pheasant into 4 portions, season and dust with flour. Quarter, core and cut the apples into wedges, then toss in the lemon juice.
2 Melt the butter in a large flameproof casserole and brown the pheasant portions, in batches, over a high heat until deep golden brown on all sides. Remove with a slotted spoon and put to one side.
3 Preheat the oven to 170°C (150°C fan oven) mark 3. Add the bacon to the casserole and fry for 2–3 minutes until golden. Add the onions, celery, apples, juniper and ginger and cook for 8–10 minutes. Stir in the flour and cook, stirring, for 2 minutes, then add the stock and cider and bring to the boil, stirring.
4 Return the pheasant to the casserole and bring to a simmer. Cover and cook for 45 minutes to 1 hour, or until the pheasant is tender (older pheasants will take a little longer).
5 Transfer the pheasant to a warmed dish and keep warm. Strain the sauce through a sieve and return to the casserole. Stir in the cream, bring to the boil and let bubble for 10 minutes or until syrupy. Return the pheasant to the sauce and check the seasoning before serving.

Serves 6–8   preparation: 50 minutes   cooking time: 1¾ hours
per serving: 670–500 cals; 40–31g fat; 20–15g carbohydrate

Peppered Winter Stew

25g (1oz) plain flour
salt and pepper
900g (2lb) stewing venison, beef or lamb,
   cut into 4cm (1½ inch) cubes
5tbsp oil
225g (8oz) button onions or shallots,
   blanched in boiling water, drained and
   peeled with root end intact
225g (8oz) onion, peeled and finely chopped
4 garlic cloves, peeled and crushed
2tbsp tomato paste
125ml (4fl oz) red wine vinegar

75cl bottle red wine
2tbsp redcurrant jelly
1 small bunch of thyme
4 bay leaves
1tbsp coarsely ground black pepper
6 cloves
600–900ml (1–1½ pints) beef stock
900g (2lb) mixed root vegetables, such as
   carrots, parsnips, turnips and celeriac,
   peeled and cut into 4cm (1½ inch) chunks,
   carrots cut a little smaller
thyme sprigs, to garnish

1   Put the flour into a plastic bag and season, then toss the meat in it.
2   Heat 3tbsp oil in a large deep flameproof casserole and brown the meat well in small batches. Remove and put to one side.
3   Heat the remaining oil and fry the button onions or shallots for 5 minutes or until golden. Fry the mixed root vegetables. Add the chopped onion and the garlic and cook, stirring, until soft and golden. Add the tomato paste and cook for a further 2 minutes, then add the vinegar and wine and bring to the boil. Bubble for 10 minutes. Meanwhile, preheat the oven to 180°C (160°C fan oven) mark 4.
4   Add the redcurrant jelly, thyme, bay leaves, pepper, cloves and meat to the pan and enough stock to barely cover the meat. Bring to the boil and cover, then transfer to the oven and cook for 1³/₄–2¹/₄ hours or until the meat is very tender.
5   Serve the stew from the casserole, garnished with the thyme sprigs.

Serves 6   preparation: 20 minutes   cooking time: 2 hours 25 minutes
per serving: 480 cals; 18g fat; 25g carbohydrate

Rabbit Casserole with Red Wine and Sherry

1.4kg (3lb) rabbit joints
4 garlic cloves, peeled and crushed
2 thyme sprigs
2 bay leaves
600ml (1 pint) red wine
salt and pepper
2tbsp plain flour, plus extra to dust
4tbsp olive oil
75g (3oz) rindless streaky bacon rashers,
  diced

350g (12oz) onions, peeled and r
  oughly chopped
350g (12oz) carrots, peeled and chopped
350g (12oz) fennel, roughly chopped
2 celery sticks, roughly chopped
150ml (¼ pint) medium dry sherry
600ml (1 pint) chicken stock
1tbsp redcurrant jelly

1   Put the rabbit into a large bowl with the garlic, thyme, bay leaves and red wine. Cover and leave to marinate in the fridge for at least 6 hours, preferably overnight.
2   Drain the rabbit, reserving the marinade. Pat dry, season and dust lightly with flour. Heat the olive oil in a large flameproof casserole. Brown the rabbit joints, in batches on all sides, over a high heat. Remove and set aside.
3   Preheat the oven to 170°C (150°C fan oven) mark 3. Add the bacon and fry for 2–3 minutes. Add the vegetables and cook gently for 10 minutes or until softened and beginning to colour. Stir in the flour and cook for 2 minutes.
4   Return the rabbit to the casserole, and add the reserved marinade, sherry and stock. Bring to the boil, cover and cook for 1–1½ hours until the rabbit is tender.
5   Transfer the rabbit to a warmed dish, using a slotted spoon, and keep warm. Strain the sauce through a sieve, pressing as much of the vegetable mixture through as possible, and pour back into the casserole. Add the redcurrant jelly and bubble for 5–10 minutes until syrupy; adjust the seasoning.
6   Return the rabbit to the casserole and simmer for 5 minutes before serving.

Serves 6   preparation: 40 minutes, plus marinating   cooking time: 1½–2 hours
per serving: 460 cals; 23g fat; 14g carbohydrate

Beef Jambalaya

275g (10oz) fillet steak, cut into thin strips
4tsp mild chilli powder
black pepper
4tbsp oil
140g (4½oz) pack chorizo sausage, sliced
   and cut into strips, or 125g (4oz) cubed
2 celery sticks, cut into 5cm (2 inch) strips
2 red peppers, deseeded and cut into 5cm
   (2 inch) strips
150g (5oz) onion, peeled and roughly
   chopped

2 garlic cloves, peeled and crushed
275g (10oz) long-grain white rice
1tbsp tomato paste
1tbsp ground ginger
2tsp Cajun seasoning
900ml (1½ pints) beef stock
salt
8 large cooked prawns, peeled
Tabasco sauce (optional)
soured cream, to serve (optional)

1 Put the steak into a plastic bag with 1tsp each mild chilli powder and pepper, seal and shake to mix.
2 Heat 1tbsp oil in a large frying pan and cook the chorizo until golden. Add the celery and red peppers to the pan and cook for 3–4 minutes or until just beginning to soften and brown. Remove from the pan and put to one side. Add 2tbsp oil to the pan and fry the steak in batches; put to one side and keep warm.
3 Add a little more oil to the pan if necessary and cook the onion until transparent. Add the garlic, rice, tomato paste, remaining chilli powder, the ground ginger and Cajun seasoning, then cook for 2 minutes until the rice turns translucent. Stir in the stock, season with salt and bring to the boil. Cover the pan, reduce the heat and simmer for about 20 minutes, stirring occasionally, until the rice is tender and most of the liquid has been absorbed (add a little more water during cooking if necessary).
4 Add the reserved steak, chorizo, peppers, celery, prawns and Tabasco, if using. Heat gently, stirring, until piping hot. Adjust the seasoning and serve with soured cream, if you like, and a green salad.

Serves 4   preparation: 10 minutes   cooking time: 40 minutes
per serving: 600 cals; 25g fat; 63g carbohydrate

Braised Oxtail

2 oxtails, about 1.6kg (3½lb) in total, trimmed
2tbsp plain flour
salt and pepper
4tbsp oil
2 large onions, peeled and sliced
900ml (1½ pints) beef stock
150ml (¼ pint) red wine
1tbsp tomato purée
finely grated zest of ½ lemon
2 bay leaves
2 medium carrots, peeled and chopped
450g (1lb) parsnips, peeled and chopped
chopped flat-leafed parsley, to garnish

1 Cut the oxtails into large pieces. Season the flour and use to coat the pieces. Heat the oil in a large flameproof casserole and brown the oxtail pieces, a few at a time. Remove from the casserole with a slotted spoon and put to one side.
2 Add the onions to the casserole and fry over a medium heat for about 10 minutes until softened and lightly browned. Stir in any remaining flour.
3 Stir in the stock, wine, tomato purée, lemon zest and bay leaves and season to taste. Bring to the boil, then return the oxtail and reduce the heat. Cover and simmer very gently for 2 hours.
4 Skim off the fat from the surface, then stir in the carrots and parsnips. Re-cover the casserole and simmer very gently for a further 2 hours until the oxtail is very tender.
5 Skim off all fat from the surface, then check the seasoning. Serve scattered with chopped parsley.

Serves 6   preparation: 20 minutes   cooking time: about 4 hours
per serving: 580 cals; 33g fat; 20g carbohydrate

One-pot Spicy Beef

2tsp sunflower oil
1 large onion, peeled and roughly chopped
1 garlic clove, peeled and finely chopped
1 small red chilli, finely chopped
2 red peppers, deseeded and roughly
  chopped

2 celery sticks, diced
400g (14oz) lean beef mince
400g can chopped tomatoes
2 x 400g cans mixed beans, drained
  and rinsed
1–2tsp Tabasco

1   Heat the oil in a large frying pan. Add the onion to the pan with 2tbsp water and cook for 10 minutes
    until softened. Add the garlic and chilli and cook for 1–2 minutes until golden, then add the red
    peppers and celery and cook for 5 minutes.
2   Add the beef to the pan and brown all over. Add the tomatoes, beans and Tabasco, then simmer for
    20 minutes. Serve with Quick Salsa (page 673).

Serves 4   preparation: 15 minutes   cooking time: about 40 minutes
per serving: 380 cals; 13g fat; 36g carbohydrate

Beef Casserole with Black Olives

6tbsp oil

1.1kg (2½lb) stewing steak, preferably in
one piece, cut into 4cm (1½ inch) cubes

350g (12oz) streaky bacon rashers,
preferably unsmoked, rind removed
and sliced into thin strips, or pre-cut
bacon lardons

450g (1lb) onions, peeled and roughly
chopped

3 plump garlic cloves, peeled and crushed

2tbsp tomato paste

125ml (4fl oz) brandy

1tbsp plain flour

150ml (¼ pint) red wine

300ml (½ pint) beef stock

bouquet garni (2 bay leaves, few thyme
sprigs, small bunch of parsley)

225g (8oz) flat mushrooms, quartered
if large

125g (4oz) black olives

flat-leafed parsley sprigs, to garnish

1 Heat half the oil in a large flameproof casserole. Brown the stewing steak over a high heat in batches until it's a dark chestnut brown, then remove and keep warm. Add the bacon to the casserole and fry until golden brown, then add to the beef. Add the remaining oil and cook the onions over a medium heat for 10–15 minutes or until golden brown. Add the garlic, fry for 30 seconds, then mix in the tomato paste. Cook, stirring, for 1–2 minutes, then pour in the brandy.

2 Preheat the oven to 170°C (150°C fan oven) mark 3. Bring the casserole to the boil and bubble to reduce by half, then add the flour and mix until smooth. Pour in the wine, bring back to the boil and bubble for 1 minute. Return the stewing steak and bacon to the casserole and add enough stock to barely cover the meat. Add the bouquet garni. Bring to the boil, then cover, transfer to the oven and cook for 1¼–1½ hours or until the stewing steak is tender. Add the mushrooms and cook for a further 4–5 minutes.

3 Just before serving, remove the bouquet garni from the beef casserole, stir in the olives and garnish with the parsley sprigs. This casserole improves if it's eaten the day after it's cooked. Complete the recipe to the end of step 2, cool quickly, then cover and chill for up to two days. To use, bring the casserole slowly to the boil and cook at 180°C (160°C fan oven) mark 4 for 15–20 minutes or until heated through, then complete as step 3.

Serves 6   preparation: 40 minutes   cooking time: 2 hours 10 minutes
per serving: 900 cals; 60g fat; 34g carbohydrate

Pan-fried Pork Chops with Lentils

2tbsp olive oil

4 pork loin chops, about 175g (6oz) each, with bone

125g (4oz) lardons or bacon pieces

1 medium onion, peeled and chopped

2 garlic cloves, peeled and finely chopped

250g (9oz) small green lentils, such as Puy lentils, rinsed

200g (7oz) can chopped tomatoes

900ml (1½ pints) stock

salt and pepper

2tbsp chopped flat-leafed parsley

1 Heat the olive oil in a large frying or sauté pan. Add the pork chops and brown well on both sides, then remove from the pan. Add the lardons or bacon and cook until the fat runs, then drain away the fat, leaving about 1tbsp.

2 Add the onion and garlic and cook until softened. Add the lentils and tomatoes and stir well, then pour in the stock, bring to the boil and cook for 10 minutes, then reduce to a simmer. Put the pork chops on top, cover and cook for 35 minutes, adding more stock if necessary during cooking.

3 Season to taste. Transfer the pork chops to warmed plates, stir the parsley into the cooked lentils and serve with the pork.

Serves 4   preparation: 10 minutes   cooking time: 55 minutes
per serving: 640 cals; 31g fat; 40g carbohydrate

Pork Tenderloin with Creamy Mustard Sauce

1tbsp groundnut oil

500g (1lb 2oz) pork tenderloin, cut into 2cm (¾ inch) slices

7g (¼oz) butter

1 onion, peeled and finely chopped

1 small, red-skinned eating apple, cored and cut into eight wedges, then tossed in the juice of ½ lemon

1tsp light muscovado sugar

100ml (3½fl oz) each dry cider and chicken stock

100ml (3½fl oz) half-fat crème fraîche

1tsp wholegrain Dijon mustard

1tbsp chopped tarragon

salt and pepper

1 Heat the oil in a non-stick frying pan and cook the pork in two batches over a high heat for 5 minutes or until golden all over. Put to one side.

2 Heat the butter in the pan, then add the onion and cook for 1–2 minutes. Add the apple with any lemon juice and sauté over a medium heat for 5 minutes. Increase the heat, add the sugar and stir-fry for about 3 minutes, until everything is just golden.

3 Add the cider and bring to the boil, then pour in the stock and return the meat to the pan. Reduce the heat and simmer, uncovered, for 1–2 minutes. Add the crème fraîche, mustard and tarragon, season and cook for 1–2 minutes until the sauce is heated through, then serve.

Serves 4   preparation: 10 minutes   cooking time: 30 minutes
per serving: 290 cals; 12.8g fat; 10.2g carbohydrate

Pumpkin Mash and Sausages

500g (1lb 2oz) whole pumpkin (or
  a wedge, see below), or kabocha
  or harlequin squash
10 pork chipolata sausages

salt and pepper
25g (1oz) butter
½tsp freshly grated nutmeg

1 Preheat the oven to 200°C (180°C fan oven) mark 6. Put the pumpkin or squash in a roasting tin and put in the oven to roast. If using a wedge, scoop out the seeds and wrap entirely in aluminium foil before putting in the oven.
2 After the pumpkin has been in the oven for 15 minutes, cut between each sausage to separate them and add to the roasting tin. Cook for 15 minutes, then turn the sausages over so they brown evenly. Turn over the pumpkin, too, and return the tin to the oven for 30 minutes, or until the sausages are cooked and the pumpkin is tender (the skin should give slightly when touched).
3 Remove from the oven and halve the pumpkin, then use a spoon to scoop out all the seeds and discard them. Season the roasted pumpkin flesh, put a large knob of butter in each half and sprinkle over the nutmeg.
4 To serve, use a large spoon to scoop out the pumpkin flesh and divide among the plates, putting two-and-a-half pork sausages on each.

Serves 4 preparation: 10 minutes cooking time: 40 minutes
per serving: 260 cals; 21g fat; 10g carbohydrate

One-pot Gammon Stew

1tbsp olive oil
1.1kg (2½lb) smoked gammon joint
8 shallots, blanched in boiling water,
  drained, peeled and chopped into chunks
3 carrots, peeled and chopped into chunks
3 celery sticks, chopped into chunks

4 large Desirée potatoes, unpeeled
450ml (¾ pint) each apple juice and hot
  vegetable stock
½ small Savoy cabbage
25g (1oz) butter

1 Preheat the oven to 190°C (170°C fan oven) mark 5. Heat the olive oil in a large flameproof casserole. Add the gammon and cook for 5 minutes until brown all over. Remove from the pan.
2 Add the shallots, carrots and celery to the pan and fry for 3–4 minutes until starting to soften.
3 Return the gammon to the pan. Chop the potatoes into quarters and add to the pan with the apple juice and hot stock. Cover and bring to the boil, then transfer to the oven and cook for 50 minutes until the meat is cooked through and the vegetables are tender.
4 Remove from the oven and put the dish back on the hob over a low heat. Shred the cabbage and stir into the pan. Simmer for 2–3 minutes, then stir in the butter and serve.

Serves 4 preparation: 15 minutes cooking time: 1 hour 10 minutes
per serving: 680 cals; 23g fat; 41g carbohydrate

Chorizo Sausage and Potato Pan-fry

2tbsp olive oil

450g (1lb) potatoes, cut into
  2.5cm (1 inch) cubes

2 red onions, peeled and sliced

1 red pepper, deseeded and diced

1tsp paprika

300g (11oz) piece chorizo sausage, skinned
  and cut into chunky slices

250g pack cherry tomatoes

100ml (3½fl oz) dry sherry

2tbsp chopped flat-leafed parsley

1 Heat the olive oil in a large heavy-based frying pan. Add the potatoes and fry for 7–10 minutes until lightly browned, turning regularly.

2 Reduce the heat, add the onions and red pepper and cook for 10 minutes, stirring from time to time until they have softened but not browned.

3 Add the paprika and chorizo sausage to the pan and cook for 5 minutes, stirring from time to time.

4 Add the tomatoes and pour in the sherry. Stir everything together and cook for 5 minutes, until the sherry has reduced down and the tomatoes have softened and warmed through.

5 Sprinkle the chopped parsley over the top and serve.

Serves 4 preparation: 10 minutes cooking time: 30 minutes
per serving: 430cals; 24g fat; 30g carbohydrate

Sausages with Roasted Potato and Onion Wedges

900g (2lb) Desirée potatoes,
  cut into wedges

4tbsp olive oil

salt and pepper

3–4 rosemary sprigs (optional)

2 red onions, peeled and each cut into
  eight wedges

8 sausages

1 Preheat the oven to 220°C (200°C fan oven) mark 7. Put the potatoes in a roasting tin in one layer. Drizzle over the olive oil and season. Toss well to coat the potatoes in oil, then put the rosemary on top, if using, and roast for 20 minutes.

2 Remove the roasting tin from the oven and add the onion wedges. Toss again to coat the onions and turn the potatoes. Put the sausages in between the potatoes and onions. Return the tin to the oven for 50 minutes–1 hour.

3 Divide among four plates and serve immediately with some tomato chutney.

Serves 4 preparation time: 10 minutes cooking time: 1 hour 20 minutes
per serving: 490cals; 26g fat; 53g carbohydrate

Spicy Bean and Chorizo Casserole

6 chorizo sausages, about 50g (2oz) each
1 onion, peeled and chopped
2 garlic cloves, peeled and crushed
1 red pepper, deseeded and cut into strips
1tsp smoked paprika
1tsp red wine vinegar
400g can chopped tomatoes
4 sun-dried tomatoes, drained from oil and
   chopped

1tbsp each tomato purée, treacle, dark
   muscovado sugar
1 bay leaf
salt and pepper
435g can pinto beans, drained and rinsed
4tbsp breadcrumbs
2tbsp chopped flat-leafed parsley

1 Heat a 2.5 litre (4¼–4½pint) flameproof casserole for 2–3 minutes, add the chorizo sausages and cook until lightly browned. Add the onion, garlic and red pepper, then fry until softened and golden. Add the paprika and vinegar, then stir well and cook for 30 seconds.
2 Add the tomatoes, sun-dried tomatoes, tomato purée, treacle, sugar and bay leaf and season. Bring to the boil, cover the pan, reduce the heat and simmer gently for 20 minutes.
3 Add the beans, cover and cook for 10 minutes, then remove from the oven. Preheat the grill. Uncover the casserole, sprinkle the breadcrumbs and parsley over and grill for 2–3 minutes until the breadcrumbs are crisp and golden, then serve.

Serves 4   preparation: 10 minutes   cooking time: 40 minutes
per serving: 400 cals; 18g fat; 38g carbohydrate

Ribs and Beans in a Sticky Barbecue Sauce

8 meaty pork spare ribs

salt and pepper

1 large onion, peeled and chopped

2 large garlic cloves, peeled and chopped

4tbsp light muscovado sugar

1tbsp French mustard

4tbsp sun-dried tomato paste

150g (5oz) passata

4tbsp malt vinegar

4tbsp tomato ketchup

2tbsp Worcestershire sauce

568ml can dry cider

2 x 410g cans black-eyed beans, drained
  and rinsed

4tbsp chopped flat-leafed parsley

1 Preheat the oven to 210°C (190°C fan oven) mark 6½. Trim the spare ribs of excess fat if necessary and season.
2 Put the onion, garlic, sugar, mustard, tomato paste, passata, vinegar, ketchup and Worcestershire sauce in a large roasting tin and stir well. Add the spare ribs and stir to coat in the sauce. Cook in the oven for 30 minutes, then turn the ribs over and cook for 30 minutes until they are crisp and brown.
4 Add the cider and stir to mix well with the sauce, scraping up the sediment from the bottom of the pan. Add the beans, stir and return to the oven for a further 15 minutes. Scatter with the chopped parsley to serve.

Serves 4   preparation: 10 minutes   cooking time: 1¼ hours
per serving: 620 cals; 25g fat; 53g carbohydrate

Turkish Lamb Stew

2tbsp olive oil

400g (14oz) lean lamb fillet, cubed

1 red onion, peeled and sliced

1 garlic clove, peeled and crushed

1 potato, cubed

400g can chopped plum tomatoes

1 red pepper, deseeded and sliced

200g (7oz) canned chickpeas, drained
  and rinsed

1 aubergine, cut into chunks

200ml (7fl oz) lamb stock

1tbsp red wine vinegar

1tsp each chopped thyme, rosemary
  and oregano

salt and pepper

8 black olives, halved and pitted

1 Heat 1tbsp olive oil in a flameproof casserole and brown the lamb over a high heat. Reduce the heat and add the remaining oil, the onion and garlic, then cook until soft.
2 Preheat the oven to 170°C (150°C fan oven) mark 3. Add the potato, tomatoes, red pepper, chickpeas, aubergine, stock, vinegar and herbs to the pan. Season, stir and bring to the boil. Cover the pan, transfer to the oven and cook for 1–1½ hours or until the lamb is tender.
3 About 15 minutes before the end of cooking time, add the olives.

Serves 4   preparation time: 10 minutes   cooking time: 1½–2 hours
per serving: 360 cals; 18g fat; 24g carbohydrate

One-pot Roast Lamb with Smoky Bacon Pasta

1 mini boneless leg of lamb roasting joint,
about 450g (1lb) total weight

125g (4oz) smoked bacon lardons

150ml (¼ pint) red wine

300–350g carton or jar tomato pasta
sauce with chilli

300ml (½ pint) hot chicken stock

75g (3oz) dried pasta shapes, such
as penne

4 sun-dried tomatoes, drained of oil and cut
into strips

1tbsp capers, rinsed

1tsp golden caster sugar (optional)

150g (5oz) chargrilled artichokes
in oil, drained

flat-leafed parsley, to garnish

1 Preheat the oven to 200°C (180°C fan oven) mark 6. Put the lamb and lardons in a small deep roasting tin just large enough to hold the lamb. Fry on the hob over a high heat for 5 minutes or until the lamb is brown all over and the lardons are beginning to crisp.

2 Remove the lamb and put to one side. Stir the wine into the tin (it should bubble immediately). Scrape the tin to loosen any crusty bits, then bubble the wine until half has evaporated. Stir in all the remaining ingredients except the artichokes.

3 Put the lamb on a rack over the roasting tin so the meat juices drip into the pasta. Transfer to the oven, uncovered, and cook for about 50 minutes. The high temperature keeps the liquid bubbling and cooks the pasta. If the sauce reduces too much, stir in a little extra stock or water. Stir in the drained artichokes 5 minutes before the end of the cooking time.

4 Transfer the lamb to a board. Slice the lamb and serve on top of the pasta, garnished with the parsley.

Serves 4   preparation time: 5 minutes   cooking time: 1 hour
per serving: 500cals; 30g fat; 22g carbohydrate

Lamb and Pumpkin Curry

800g (1¾lb) boneless lamb
450g (1lb) pumpkin, peeled and deseeded
1 medium aubergine
5tbsp olive oil
3 large red onions, peeled and sliced
2 garlic cloves, peeled and crushed
2.5cm (1 inch) piece fresh root ginger,
  peeled and grated
1 red chilli, sliced into rounds

4tbsp red balti curry paste
400ml can coconut milk
450ml (¾ pint) hot lamb stock
salt and pepper
1 onion, peeled and sliced
juice of 1 lime
4tbsp chopped coriander, plus sprigs
  to garnish

1 Cut the lamb into 2.5cm (1 inch) cubes. Cut the pumpkin and aubergine into 2.5cm (1 inch) pieces and put to one side.
2 Heat 2tbsp olive oil in a large pan and fry the red onions over a medium heat for 5–10 minutes until lightly coloured. Add the garlic and ginger and cook for 1 minute. Remove with a slotted spoon and put to one side.
3 Heat the remaining oil in the pan and brown the lamb in batches over a high heat, on all sides. Add the pumpkin and aubergine and cook for 5 minutes. Return the onions to the pan and stir well.
4 Add the red chilli and curry paste and cook, stirring, for 1 minute, then pour in the coconut milk and hot stock and season. Cover, bring to the boil, then reduce the heat and cook gently on the hob for 1 hour or until the lamb is tender.
5 Meanwhile, put the sliced onion, lime juice and coriander in a bowl, add a pinch of salt and toss well; chill until needed.
6 Spoon the curry into warmed dishes, garnish with coriander sprigs and serve with the salsa.

Serves 4–6   preparation: 30 minutes   cooking time: 1¼ hours
per serving: 740–490 cals; 54–36g fat; 17–12g carbohydrate

Luxury Lamb and Leek Hot Pot

50g (2oz) butter
400g (14oz) leeks, trimmed and sliced
1 medium onion, peeled and chopped
1tbsp olive oil
800g (1¾lb) casserole lamb, cubed and
 tossed with 1tbsp plain flour
2 garlic cloves, peeled and crushed
salt and pepper

800g (1¾lb) waxy potatoes, such as
 Desirée, peeled and sliced
3tbsp chopped flat-leafed parsley
1tsp chopped thyme
300ml (½ pint) lamb stock
142ml carton double cream

1 Melt half the butter in a 3.5 litre (6¼ pint) flameproof casserole. Add the leeks and onion, stir to coat, then cover and cook over a low heat for 10 minutes.
2 Transfer the leeks and onion on to a large sheet of greaseproof paper. Add the olive oil to the casserole and heat, then brown the meat in batches with the garlic and plenty of seasoning. Remove and put to one side on another large sheet of greaseproof paper.
3 Preheat the oven to 170°C (150°C fan oven) mark 3. Put half the potatoes in a layer over the bottom of the casserole and season. Add the meat, then spoon the leek mixture on top. Arrange a layer of overlapping potatoes on top of that, sprinkle with herbs, then pour in the stock.
4 Bring the casserole to the boil, cover, then transfer to a low shelf in the oven and cook for about 1 hour 50 minutes. Remove from the oven, dot with the remaining butter and add the cream. Return to the oven and cook, uncovered, for 30–40 minutes until the potatoes are golden brown.

Serves 6   preparation time: 20 minutes   cooking time: 2 hours 50 minutes
per serving: 530cals; 33g fat; 27g carbohydrate

Lean Lamb and Tomato Gratin

450g (1lb) vine-grown tomatoes
900g (2lb) lean casserole lamb
salt and pepper
1tbsp olive oil
1 large onion, peeled and finely chopped

2 garlic cloves, peeled and crushed
4tbsp chopped flat-leafed parsley
2 bay leaves
125g (4oz) fresh white breadcrumbs

1   Preheat the oven to 180°C (160°C fan oven) mark 4. Score the tomatoes and plunge into a bowl of boiling water for about 30 seconds. Drain the water and peel off the tomato skins. Cut the tomatoes in half and scoop the seeds into a sieve resting over a bowl to catch any juice. Chop the flesh and add to the juice, then put to one side. Discard the seeds.

2   Trim any fat off the lamb and season well. Heat the olive oil in a large casserole and brown the lamb in batches, then spoon each batch into a colander resting over a bowl to drain off all the fat.

3   Add the onion and garlic to the casserole and cook for 5 minutes, stirring occasionally until softened. Return the lamb to the pan, scatter over half the parsley and stir well. Spoon the tomatoes and juice evenly over the top and season. Push in the bay leaves. Cover and transfer to the oven and bake for 1½ hours or until the lamb is tender. Preheat the grill to high.

4   Take the casserole out of the oven and remove the bay leaves. Mix the breadcrumbs with the remaining parsley and season well. Sprinkle over the lamb and grill, uncovered, for 3–5 minutes or until golden. Serve at once.

Serves 4   preparation: 20 minutes   cooking time: 1 hour 40 minutes
per serving: 490 cals; 24g fat; 19g carbohydrate

Tagine of Lamb with Apricots

2tbsp vegetable oil
2 large onions, peeled and chopped
1½tsp ground cinnamon
½tsp each ground cumin and ground ginger
good pinch of ground chilli pepper, to taste
900g (2lb) shoulder of lamb, trimmed of
    some fat and cut into 2.5cm (1 inch) cubes
3 garlic cloves, peeled and crushed

225g (8oz) chickpeas, soaked for at least 4
    hours, then drained, or 2 x 410g cans,
    drained and rinsed
salt and pepper
450g (1lb) organic dried apricots
2tbsp runny honey
50g (2oz) blanched almonds, thinly sliced
    and toasted, or toasted flaked almonds, to
    garnish

1 Heat the oil in a large lidded pan and fry the onions gently for about 10 minutes until soft.
2 Add the cinnamon, cumin, ginger and chilli, then mix with the onion. Add the lamb and stir to coat in
the spices, then add the garlic and about 900ml (1½ pints) water, plus the soaked dried chickpeas,
if using.
3 Cover the pan and bring the liquid to simmering point, then cook, partly covered, for 1½ hours,
stirring from time to time and adding more water if necessary. Season after 45 minutes.
4 Add the apricots and honey and canned chickpeas, if using, then cook for a further 30 minutes until
little liquid remains.
5 Transfer the stew to a warmed serving dish, sprinkle the almonds on top and serve.

Serves 8 preparation: 20 minutes, plus soaking (optional)   cooking time: 2 hours 10 minutes
per serving: 560 cals; 29g fat; 45g carbohydrate

Pumpkin and Cheese Bake

450g (1lb) new potatoes, halved
450g (1lb) pumpkin, peeled and thinly sliced
1 large onion, about 175g (6oz), peeled and
    finely sliced

salt and pepper
225g (8oz) buttery cheese, e.g. Taleggio,
    Gruyère or Fontina, thinly sliced
300ml (½ pint) crème fraîche

1 Preheat the oven to 220°C (200°C fan oven) mark 7. Boil the potatoes, pumpkin and onion together
in salted water in a shallow flameproof casserole for 3–4 minutes. Drain off all the liquid and roughly
mix in the cheese.
2 Beat a little cold water into the crème fraîche to give a thick pouring consistency. Season with pepper,
then pour over the vegetables. Put the casserole on the hob and bring to the boil.
3 Transfer to the oven and cook, uncovered, for 40 minutes or until bubbling and golden. Two or three
times during the cooking time, stir the crust that forms on top into the dish to add to the flavour. To
check the dish is cooked, press the tip of a knife into the centre of a potato, which should be tender.
Serve with a baguette and green salad.

Serves 4 preparation time: 15 minutes   cooking time: 50 minutes
per serving: 660 cals; 51g fat; 27g carbohydrate

Roasted Mediterranean Vegetables

8 large plum tomatoes, halved

2 large red peppers, deseeded and each cut
into eight

2 fat garlic cloves, peeled and crushed

50g can anchovy fillets in oil, drained and
the oil reserved, roughly chopped

50g (2oz) pine nuts

black pepper

1tbsp balsamic vinegar

2tbsp capers

handful of thyme leaves

1   Preheat the oven to 220°C (200°C fan oven) mark 7. Put the tomatoes in a roasting tin with the red
peppers, garlic, anchovies and pine nuts. Drizzle over the oil from the can of anchovies and toss so
that all the vegetables are coated. Season with pepper and roast for 15 minutes.

2   Add the vinegar, capers and thyme to the roasting tin. Mix gently to combine and serve with plenty
of crusty bread to mop up the juices.

Serves 4   preparation: 5 minutes   cooking time: 15 minutes
per serving: 160 cals; 12g fat; 8g carbohydrate

Cornish Pasties

450g (1lb) stewing steak, trimmed

175g (6oz) potato, peeled and diced

175g (6oz) swede, peeled and diced

1 onion, peeled and chopped

1tbsp each chopped thyme and parsley

1tbsp Worcestershire sauce

salt and pepper

shortcrust pastry (page 13), made with 500g
(1lb 2oz) plain flour, plus flour to dust

25g (1oz) butter

1 egg, beaten, to glaze

1   Preheat the oven to 220°C (200°C fan oven) mark 7. To make the filling, cut the meat into very small
pieces and put into a bowl with the potato, swede and onion. Add the herbs, Worcestershire sauce
and seasoning, then mix well.

2   Divide the pastry into six and roll out each piece thinly on a lightly floured surface to a 20.5cm (8 inch)
round. Spoon the filling on to one half of each round and top with a small knob of butter.

3   Brush the edges of the pastry with water, then fold the uncovered side over to make pasties. Press
the edges firmly together to seal and crimp them. Make a slit in the top of each pasty. Put on a
baking sheet.

4   Brush the pastry with beaten egg to glaze and bake the pasties for 15 minutes. Reduce the oven
temperature to 170°C (150°C fan oven) mark 3 and bake for a further 1 hour to cook the filling. Serve
the pasties warm or cold.

Serves 6   preparation: 30 minutes   cooking time: 1¼ hours
per serving: 640 cals; 36g fat; 59g carbohydrate

Roasted Ratatouille

400g (14oz) red peppers, deseeded and
   roughly chopped
700g (1½ lb) aubergines, cut into chunks
450g (1lb) onions, peeled and cut into petals
4–5 garlic cloves, peeled

150ml (¼ pint) olive oil
1tsp fennel seeds
sea salt and pepper
200ml (7fl oz) passata
thyme sprigs, to garnish

1 Preheat the oven to 240°C (220°C fan oven) mark 9. Put the red peppers, aubergines, onions, garlic, olive oil and fennel seeds in a roasting tin, then season and toss together.
2 Transfer to the oven and cook for 30 minutes, tossing frequently during cooking, or until the vegetables are charred and beginning to soften.
3 Stir the passata through the vegetables and return the roasting tin to the oven for 50–60 minutes, stirring occasionally. Garnish with the thyme sprigs and serve hot or cold.

Serves 6   preparation: 15 minutes   cooking time: 1½ hours
per serving: 270 cals; 23g fat; 14g carbohydrate

Chilli Vegetable and Coconut Stir-fry

2tbsp sesame oil
2 green chillies, deseeded and
   finely chopped
2.5cm (1 inch) piece fresh root ginger,
   peeled and finely grated
2 garlic cloves, peeled and crushed
1tbsp Thai green curry paste
125g (4oz) each carrot and mooli, cut into
   fine matchsticks
125g (4oz) baby sweetcorn, halved
125g (4oz) mangetout, halved on
   the diagonal

2 large red peppers, deseeded and
   finely sliced
2 small pak choi, quartered
4 spring onions, finely chopped
300ml (½ pint) coconut milk
2tbsp each peanut satay sauce and
   soy sauce
1tsp light muscovado sugar
black pepper
4tbsp chopped coriander
whole roasted peanuts and fresh coriander
   sprigs, to garnish

1 Heat the oil in a wok or large non-stick frying pan and stir-fry the chillies, ginger and garlic for 1 minute. Add the curry paste and fry for 30 seconds.
2 Add the carrot, mooli, baby sweetcorn, mangetout and red peppers. Stir-fry over a fierce heat for 3–4 minutes, then add the pak choi and spring onions. Cook, stirring, for 1–2 minutes.
3 Pour in the coconut milk, satay sauce, soy sauce and sugar. Season with pepper, bring to the boil and cook for 1–2 minutes, then add the coriander. Garnish with the peanuts and coriander sprigs and serve with prawn crackers.

Serves 4–6   preparation: 25 minutes   cooking time: about 10 minutes
per serving: 290–200 cals; 22–15g fat; 17–11g carbohydrate

Mauritian Vegetable Curry

3tbsp vegetable oil
1 onion, peeled and finely sliced
4 garlic cloves, peeled and crushed
2.5cm (1 inch) piece fresh root ginger,
   peeled and grated
3tbsp medium curry powder
6 fresh curry leaves
150g (5oz) potato, peeled and cut into 1cm
   (½ inch) cubes
125g (4oz) aubergine, cut into 2cm (1 inch)
   long sticks, 5mm (¼ inch) wide

150g (5oz) carrots, peeled and cut into 5mm
   (¼ inch) dice
900ml (1½ pints) vegetable stock
pinch of saffron
1tsp salt
black pepper
150g (5oz) green beans, trimmed
75g (3oz) frozen peas
3tbsp chopped coriander

1   Heat the oil in a large heavy-based pan. Add the onion and fry over a gentle heat for 5–10 minutes until golden. Add the garlic, ginger, curry powder and curry leaves and fry for 1 minute.
2   Add the potato and aubergine to the pan and fry, stirring, for 2 minutes. Add the carrots, stock, saffron, the salt and plenty of pepper. Cover and cook for 10 minutes until the vegetables are almost tender.
3   Add the beans and peas to the pan and cook for 4 minutes. Transfer to a serving dish, sprinkle with the chopped coriander and serve with some Indian bread such as naan, chapati or roti.

Serves 4   preparation: 20 minutes   cooking time: 30 minutes
per serving: 190 cals; 11g fat; 19g carbohydrate

Chickpea Stew

1 red, 1 green and 1 yellow pepper, each
   halved and deseeded
2tbsp olive oil
1 onion, peeled and finely sliced
2 garlic cloves, peeled and crushed
1tbsp harissa paste
2tbsp tomato paste
½tsp ground cumin
1 aubergine, diced
400g can chickpeas, drained and rinsed
450ml (¾ pint) vegetable stock
salt and pepper
4tbsp roughly chopped flat-leafed parsley

1 Preheat the grill and lay the peppers skin-side up on a baking sheet. Grill for about 5 minutes or until the skin begins to blister and char. Put the peppers in a plastic bag, seal and put to one side for a few minutes. When cooled a little, peel the skins and discard, then slice the peppers and put to one side.
2 Heat the olive oil in a large frying pan, add the onion and cook for 5–10 minutes or until softened. Add the garlic, harissa, tomato paste and cumin and cook for 2 minutes.
3 Add the sliced peppers to the pan with the aubergine. Stir everything to coat evenly with the spices and cook for 2 minutes. Add the chickpeas and stock, season well and bring to the boil. Reduce the heat and simmer for 20 minutes.
4 Stir the parsley through the chickpea stew and serve.

Serves 4 preparation: 10 minutes cooking time: 40 minutes
per serving: 210 cals; 10g fat; 24g carbohydrate

Spiced Bean and Vegetable Stew

3tbsp olive oil
2 small onions, peeled and sliced
2 garlic cloves, peeled and crushed
1tbsp sweet paprika
1 small dried red chilli, deseeded and
   finely chopped
700g (1½lb) sweet potatoes, peeled
   and cubed
700g (1½ lb) pumpkin, peeled and cut
   into chunks
125g (4oz) okra, trimmed
500g jar passata
salt and pepper
400g can haricot or cannellini beans,
   drained and rinsed

1 Heat the olive oil in a large heavy-based pan, add the onions and garlic and cook over a very gentle heat for 5 minutes.
2 Stir in the paprika and chilli and cook for 2 minutes, then add the sweet potatoes, pumpkin, okra, passata and 900ml (1½ pints) cold water. Season generously.
3 Cover the pan and bring to the boil, then reduce the heat and simmer for 20 minutes until the vegetables are tender. Add the beans, cook for 3 minutes to warm them through, then serve.

Serves 6 preparation: 20 minutes cooking time: 35 minutes
per serving: 250 cals; 8g fat; 42g carbohydrate

Vegetarian

Cooking vegetarian food is a great chance to be creative and inventive. There are loads of lovely spices, herbs, pulses and grains just waiting for a chance to get together with luscious vegetables in tarts, pies, bakes and stews.

Take some creamy, cheesy polenta, top with vivid broad beans, tender asparagus and baby carrots and sit back and wait for the compliments – that's Parmesan Polenta with Minted Summer Vegetables.

Or, for a real winter treat, roasted vegetables must be up there with the best. Winter Roasted Vegetable Tart gives you a chance to show off your pastry-making skills (or buy ready-made to save time) and then fill the tart with vegetables, mushrooms and chestnuts – great comfort food.

Then for anyone who sneers at nut roast, give them a slice of Nut and Cranberry Terrine, with its filling of walnuts, leeks, rice and dolcelatte cheese and the topping of cranberries in redcurrant jelly.

And who can resist risottos? Try the moreish Garlic and Parmesan Risotto, or the Risotto Galette with melted Taleggio – a risotto 'sandwich' oozing with melted cheese. Spectacular.

Jerusalem Artichoke Soup

125g (4oz) butter
175g (6oz) onions, peeled and chopped
1 garlic clove, peeled and crushed
50g (2oz) celery, chopped
900g (2lb) Jerusalem artichokes, peeled
and chopped

125g (4oz) carrots, peeled and chopped
300ml (½ pint) dry white wine
1 sachet bouquet garni
salt and pepper
142ml carton double cream

1 Melt the butter in a large pan, add the onions and garlic and cook for 2 minutes. Add the remaining vegetables and cook for 5 minutes.
2 Add the wine, bring to the boil and simmer until reduced by half. Add 1.1 litres (2 pints) water and the bouquet garni. Bring back to the boil, then reduce the heat and simmer until the vegetables are tender.
3 Cool slightly, remove the bouquet garni, then blend in a liquidiser until smooth.
4 Pour the soup into a clean pan and gently reheat, season and add half the cream. Spoon into bowls, drizzle with the remaining cream and serve.

Serves 6 preparation: 10 minutes cooking time: 45 minutes
per serving: 350 cals; 29g fat; 19g carbohydrate

Stuffed Acorn Squash

1 small acorn squash
salt and pepper
1tbsp olive oil

2tbsp stuffing mix without sausage
meat, thawed
thyme sprigs, to garnish (optional)

1 Preheat the oven to 200°C (180°C fan oven) mark 6. Cut the stalk off the squash, then scoop out and discard the seeds.
2 Season the squash, drizzle with olive oil and spoon in the stuffing. Cover with foil, then roast for 1 hour or until tender. Remove from the oven, garnish with thyme, if using, and serve.

Serves 1 preparation: 10 minutes cooking time: 1 hour
per serving: 280 cals; 15g fat; 32g carbohydrate

Creamed Celeriac and Fresh Parmesan Soup

2tbsp oil
175g (6oz) onions, peeled and
  roughly chopped
1 garlic clove, peeled and crushed
450g (1lb) each celeriac and potatoes,
  peeled and roughly chopped
1.1 litres (2 pints) vegetable stock
1 sachet bouquet garni

600ml (1 pint) full-fat milk
284ml carton double cream
1tbsp lemon juice
salt and pepper
8tbsp grated Parmesan cheese
Toasted Parmesan cheese, to garnish
  (see below)

1 Heat the oil in a large pan, then add the onions and garlic. Cook slowly for 4–5 minutes or until golden brown.
2 Add the celeriac, potatoes, stock and bouquet garni, bring to the boil, then reduce the heat and simmer for 20–25 minutes or until the celeriac and potatoes are tender.
3 Remove the pan from the heat, cool slightly and discard the bouquet garni. Blend the soup in a liquidiser in batches until smooth. Pour into a clean pan, add the milk, cream and lemon juice and season. Simmer for a further 10 minutes.
4 To serve, put 1tbsp grated Parmesan in the bottom of each serving bowl. Ladle in the soup, grind over some black pepper and garnish with the toasted Parmesan.

Serves 8 preparation: 10 minutes   cooking time: 35 minutes
per serving: 385 cals; 29g fat; 18g carbohydrate

Toasted Parmesan

To make the toasted Parmesan, sprinkle 25g (1oz) finely grated Parmesan cheese on a baking sheet. Put under a hot grill until melted and golden. Cool, then crumble and store in an airtight container for up to one week.

Serves 8 preparation: 25 minutes   cooking time: 35 minutes
per serving: 310 cals; 24g fat; 16g carbohydrate

Glamorgan Sausages

150g (5oz) Caerphilly cheese, grated
200g (7oz) fresh white breadcrumbs
3 spring onions, finely chopped
1tbsp chopped flat-leafed parsley

leaves of 4 thyme sprigs
salt and pepper
3 large eggs, 1 separated
vegetable oil

1 Preheat the oven to 140°C (120°C fan oven) mark 1. Mix the cheese with 150g (5oz) breadcrumbs, the spring onions and herbs in a large bowl. Season well.
2 Add the whole eggs plus the extra yolk and mix well to combine. Cover and chill for 5 minutes.
3 Lightly beat the egg white in a shallow bowl. Tip the rest of the breadcrumbs on to a large plate.
4 Take 2tbsp of the mixture and shape into a small sausage, about 4cm (1½ inches) long. Roll first in the egg white, then in the breadcrumbs to coat. Repeat to make 12 sausages in total.
5 Heat 2tsp oil in a large heavy-based pan until hot and fry the sausages in two batches for 6–8 minutes, turning until golden all over. Keep warm in the oven while cooking the rest. Serve with a chutney.

Serves 4 preparation: 25 minutes   cooking time: 15 minutes
per serving: 380 cals; 24g fat; 25g carbohydrate

Halloumi with Spicy Couscous

300g (11oz) couscous
600ml (1 pint) hot vegetable stock
270g jar roasted red peppers, drained and
  oil reserved
1tsp chilli flakes

grated zest and juice of 1 lemon
2 x 250g blocks halloumi cheese, cut into
  thick slices
2tbsp chopped mint

1 Put the couscous in a bowl and pour over the hot stock. Cover and leave to stand for 5–10 minutes.
2 Meanwhile, put 6tbsp oil reserved from the peppers into a bowl and add the chilli flakes, lemon zest and juice. Add the halloumi and mix together to coat, then put to one side.
3 Heat a large frying pan over a medium heat. Fry the cheese slices in batches, spaced well apart, for 2 minutes on each side until golden. Cover and keep warm.
4 Use a fork to fluff up the couscous, then add the peppers, mint and any remaining oil from the halloumi marinade. Toss well and serve with the cheese.

Serves 4 preparation: 5 minutes   cooking time: 8–12 minutes
per serving: 860 cals; 50g fat; 58g carbohydrate

Mozzarella and Tomato Pizza

350g (12oz) strong white bread flour, plus
  extra to dust
1tsp salt
7g sachet fast-action dried yeast
1tbsp olive oil
½ x 400g can chopped tomatoes

125g (4oz) mozzarella, sliced
50g (2oz) piece Parmesan cheese
8 black olives, halved
salt and pepper
handful of roughly chopped basil leaves
  (optional)

1 Tip the flour and salt into the bowl of a freestanding mixer and stir in the yeast. Add the olive oil and pour in 200ml (7fl oz) hand-hot water. Mix with a dough hook until soft and sticky. Alternatively, put in a processor and mix with a plastic blade. Cover and leave in a warm place for 30 minutes until doubled in size.

2 Preheat the oven to 230°C (210°C fan oven) mark 8. Put a lightly floured pizza stone or a baking sheet in the oven to preheat.

3 Put the dough on a lightly floured surface and punch to knock out the air. Roll into a large rectangle and put on the hot pizza stone or baking sheet. Spoon over the tomatoes, top with mozzarella and grate over the Parmesan. Add the olives and season.

4 Bake for 25 minutes or until the pizza is golden and the cheeses have melted. Remove from the oven and leave to stand for 5 minutes. Scatter with the basil leaves, if using, cut the pizza into quarters and serve.

Serves 4 preparation: 20 minutes, plus resting   cooking time: 25 minutes, plus standing
per serving: 520 cals; 19g fat; 67g carbohydrate

Family-size Tomato, Basil and Mozzarella Sandwich

1 loaf of bread, such as cholla
4 ripe plum tomatoes
2tbsp extra-virgin olive oil
salt and pepper

1–2 fresh mozzarella, about 150g (5oz),
  drained, sliced and seasoned
12–15 basil leaves

1 Put the bread on a board. Make two deep parallel cuts along the length of the loaf, but don't go all the way through.

2 Cut the tops off 2 tomatoes and use a teaspoon to scoop the juice and seeds into a bowl. Add the olive oil and season well.

3 Slice the 2 hollow and the 2 whole tomatoes finely and season well.

4 Divide the tomato juice between the open sections in the bread, then do the same with the sliced tomatoes, followed by the mozzarella and basil. Slice the loaf horizontally to serve.

Serves 4 preparation: 10 minutes
per serving: 360 cals; 17g fat; 37g carbohydrate

Deli Pizza

6tbsp tomato pizza sauce
2 pizzeria-style pizza bases
100g (3½oz) soft goat's cheese
1 red onion, peeled and finely sliced

100g (3½oz) sunblush tomatoes
100g (3½oz) olives
handful of basil, roughly torn

1 Put a large baking sheet on the top shelf of the oven and preheat to 220°C (200°C fan oven) mark 7.
2 To make the pizza topping, spread a thin layer of the tomato sauce over the pizza bases. Top with dollops of goat's cheese, then scatter over the onion, tomatoes and olives.
3 Bake on the preheated baking sheet for 15 minutes or until golden and crispy. Remove from the oven, scatter over the torn basil and serve immediately with a crisp green salad.

Serves 4 preparation: 5 minutes   cooking time: 15 minutes
per serving: 370 calories; 10g fat; 57g carbohydrate

Parmesan Polenta with Minted Summer Vegetables

900ml (1½ pints) vegetable stock
125g (4oz) polenta
3tbsp double cream
125g (4oz) Parmesan cheese, finely grated
4tbsp chopped mint, plus mint sprigs
  to garnish
salt and pepper
50g (2oz) butter
50g (2oz) shallots, blanched in boiling
  water, drained, peeled and finely chopped

2 garlic cloves, peeled and thinly sliced
125g (4oz) fresh broad beans, skinned, or
  fresh peas, shelled
125g (4oz) asparagus tips or French beans,
  cut on the diagonal
125g (4oz) baby carrots
1tbsp golden caster sugar
2tsp grainy mustard
1tbsp white wine vinegar

1 To make the Parmesan polenta, bring 600ml (1 pint) stock to the boil in a large pan, then reduce to a simmer. Add the polenta in a slow, steady stream, stirring all the time for about 5 minutes until thick. Stir in the remaining stock and the cream, then cook for a further 10 minutes, stirring all the time, until the polenta resembles mashed potato. Add the Parmesan and 2tbsp mint, then season well. Remove from the heat and keep warm.
2 To make the minted vegetables, melt the butter in a large pan and add the shallots and garlic. Cook for 5 minutes, then add the vegetables, sugar and 50ml (2fl oz) water. Bring to the boil, cover and cook for about 5 minutes or until the vegetables are tender and the liquid becomes syrupy.
3 Toss the hot vegetables with the remaining mint, the mustard and vinegar and season well. Serve immediately with the polenta and garnish with mint sprigs.

Serves 4 preparation: 10 minutes   cooking time: 15 minutes
per serving: 450 cals; 27g fat; 35g carbohydrate

Summer Vegetable and Pasta Bake

125g (4oz) dried pasta shapes
salt and pepper
75g (3oz) each baby carrots, washed and
 trimmed, and asparagus, trimmed and cut
 into 7.5cm (3 Inch) pieces
175g (6oz) broccoli, cut into small florets

200g can artichoke hearts in water, drained
 and roughly chopped
350g carton cheese sauce
1tbsp olive oil
25g (1oz) Gruyère cheese, grated
15g (½oz) sunflower seeds, toasted
50g (2oz) fresh breadcrumbs

1 Preheat the oven to 200°C (180°C fan oven) mark 6. Cook the pasta in a large pan of boiling salted water for the time stated on the packet. Drain and transfer to an ovenproof dish.
2 Put the carrots in a pan of boiling water and cook for 3 minutes. Add the asparagus and broccoli and cook until just tender. Drain well.
3 Stir the cooked vegetables, artichoke hearts and cheese sauce into the pasta and season. Mix the olive oil, cheese and sunflower seeds into the breadcrumbs, then sprinkle over the vegetables.
4 Bake for 20 minutes. Serve immediately.

Serves 4   preparation: 10 minutes   cooking time: 30 minutes
per serving: 400 cals; 20g fat; 41g carbohydrate

07

Vegetarian

Dinner-for-two Dolcelatte Gnocchi

500g pack gnocchi
200ml carton crème fraîche
125g (4oz) dolcelatte, roughly chopped

1tbsp chopped sage, plus extra to garnish
salt and pepper

1 Preheat the oven to 200°C (180°C fan oven) mark 6. Bring a large pan of water to the boil and cook the gnocchi for the time stated on the pack. Drain well and return to the pan. Add the crème fraîche, dolcelatte and sage and season well.
2 Pour the mixture into a gratin dish on top of a baking sheet and bake for 25 minutes until bubbling and golden. Remove from the oven, garnish with the remaining sage leaves and serve.

Serves 2   preparation: 50 minutes   cooking time: 40 minutes
per serving: 760 cals; 33g fat; 90g carbohydrate

Artichoke and Mushroom Lasagne

3tbsp olive oil
225g (8oz) onions, peeled and
  roughly chopped
3 garlic cloves, peeled and crushed
25g (1oz) walnuts
1.1kg (2½lb) mixed mushrooms, such as
  brown-cap and button, roughly chopped
125g (4oz) cherry tomatoes
50g (2oz) butter, plus extra for greasing
50g (2oz) plain flour

1.1 litres (2 pints) full-fat milk
2 bay leaves
2tbsp lemon juice
salt and pepper
200g fresh lasagne
397g can artichoke hearts in water, drained
  and halved
75g (3oz) freshly grated Parmesan cheese
oregano sprigs, to garnish

1 Heat the olive oil in a large pan and fry the onions gently for 10 minutes until soft. Add the garlic and walnuts and fry for 3–4 minutes. Stir in the mushrooms and cook for 10 minutes. Bubble briskly for a further 10 minutes or until no liquid is left. Add the tomatoes and put to one side.
2 To make the sauce, melt the butter in a pan, add the flour and stir over a gentle heat for 1 minute. Slowly whisk in the milk until you have a smooth mixture. Bring to the boil, add the bay leaves and stir over a gentle heat for 10 minutes. Add the lemon juice and season. Discard the bay leaves.
3 Preheat the oven to 200°C (180°C fan oven) mark 6. Grease a shallow ovenproof dish and layer the lasagne over the base. Spoon half the mushroom mixture over, then half the artichokes. Cover with a layer of lasagne and half the sauce. Spoon the remaining mushroom mixture over, then the remaining artichokes. Top with the remaining lasagne. Stir the Parmesan into the remaining sauce and spoon evenly over the top.
4 Bake for 40–50 minutes until golden and bubbling, then remove from the oven, garnish with oregano sprigs and serve.

Serves 4   preparation: 20 minutes   cooking time: 1 hour 40 minutes
per serving 740 cals; 44g fat; 57g carbohydrate

Mixed Mushroom Cannelloni

6 sheets fresh lasagne
3tbsp olive oil
1 small onion, peeled and finely chopped
3 garlic cloves, peeled and sliced
20g pack thyme, finely chopped
225g (8oz) chestnut or brown cap
  mushrooms, roughly chopped

125g (4oz) flat cap mushrooms,
  roughly chopped
salt and pepper
2 x 125g goat's cheese logs, with rind
350g carton cheese sauce

1 Cook the lasagne sheets in boiling water until just tender. Drain well, then run them under cold water to cool. Keep covered with cold water until ready to use.

2 Heat the olive oil in a large pan and add the onion. Cook over a medium heat for 7–10 minutes until the onion is soft. Add the garlic and fry for 1–2 minutes, then reserve a few slices of garlic.

3 Preheat the oven to 180°C (160°C fan oven) mark 4. Reserve a little thyme for sprinkling over later, then add the rest to the pan with all the mushrooms. Cook for 5 minutes until the mushrooms are golden brown and there is no excess liquid in the pan. Season, remove from the heat and put to one side to cool.

4 Crumble one of the goat's cheese logs into the cooled mushroom mixture and stir together. Drain the lasagne sheets and pat dry with kitchen paper. Spoon 2–3tbsp of the mushroom mixture along the long edge of each lasagne sheet, leaving a 1cm (½ inch) border. Roll up the pasta sheets and cut each roll in half.

5 Put the pasta in a shallow ovenproof dish and spoon over the cheese sauce. Slice the remaining goat's cheese into thick rounds and arrange across the middle of the pasta rolls. Sprinkle the reserved garlic and thyme on top. Bake for 30–35 minutes or until golden and bubbling. Serve at once.

Serves 4   preparation: 15 minutes   cooking time: 46–55 minutes
per serving: 470 cals; 32g fat; 29g carbohydrate

Vegetable Lasagne

2tbsp olive oil

1 onion, peeled and finely sliced

1 garlic clove, peeled and crushed

2 medium courgettes, roughly chopped

2 red peppers, deseeded and sliced

1 small aubergine, diced

400g can chopped tomatoes

salt and pepper

4 sheets fresh lasagne

25g (1oz) butter

40g (1½oz) plain flour

450ml (¾ pint) skimmed milk

nutmeg, to taste

25g (1oz) freshly grated Parmesan cheese

1 Heat the olive oil in a large pan, add the onion and garlic and cook over a medium heat for 10 minutes until soft. Add the courgettes, red peppers and aubergine, then the tomatoes. Rinse the can with 200ml (7fl oz) water and add to the pan. Season well. Cover the pan and bring to the boil, then reduce the heat and simmer for 25 minutes until the vegetables are nearly tender.

2 Meanwhile, soak the lasagne in boiling water for 5 minutes, then drain. Preheat the oven to 200°C (180°C fan oven) mark 6.

3 To make the sauce, melt the butter in a pan, stir in the flour and cook for 1 minute, stirring. Remove from the heat and slowly whisk in the milk. Season and add a little nutmeg. Cook over a medium heat, stirring, until thick and smooth.

4 Layer the vegetable ragout, pasta and sauce in a 1.6 litre (2¾ pint) dish, then sprinkle over the Parmesan and bake for 45–50 minutes.

Serves 4 preparation: 10 minutes cooking time: 1½ hours
per serving: 330 cals; 15g fat; 33g carbohydrate

Mushroom Stroganoff with Fettuccine

200g (7oz) dried fettuccine pasta

1tbsp olive oil

salt and pepper

6 spring onions, finely sliced

450g (1lb) mixed mushrooms, roughly chopped

100ml (3½fl oz) dry white wine

400ml (14fl oz) hot vegetable stock

small handful of flat-leafed parsley, finely chopped

100g (3½oz) rocket or watercress

50g (2oz) freshly grated Parmesan cheese

1 Cook the fettuccine in a large pan of boiling salted water for the time stated on the packet.

2 Heat the olive oil in a large deep frying pan and cook the onions for 5 minutes or until starting to soften. Increase the heat and add the mushrooms, frying quickly for 5 minutes until browned. Season.

3 Pour in the wine, bubble until reduced by half, then add the hot stock. Bring to the boil, then reduce the heat and simmer for 5 minutes.

4 Take the pan off the heat and stir in the fettuccine, parsley, rocket or watercress and the Parmesan and serve immediately.

Serves 4 preparation: 10 minutes cooking time: 25 minutes
per serving: 300 cals; 9g fat; 42g carbohydrate

Tagliatelle with Summer Vegetables and Herb Sauce

25g (1oz) mixed herbs, such as basil,
  chervil, chives, dill and parsley, roughly
  chopped
1tbsp chopped oregano or 1tsp dried
125ml (4fl oz) extra-virgin olive oil
700g (1½lb) mixed summer vegetables:
  cherry tomatoes (optional), courgettes,
  thinly sliced, asparagus spears, trimmed,
  shelled broad beans and/or peas, baby
  carrots, peeled

salt
2 shallots, blanched in boiling water,
  drained, peeled and finely chopped
1 garlic clove, peeled and crushed
400g (14oz) dried tagliatelle
6tbsp single cream
Parmesan cheese, freshly shaved, to serve
  (optional)

Vegetarian

1 Put the herbs and oregano in a bowl. Add all but 2tbsp olive oil. Stir well, then put to one side for a few hours, if possible.
2 Blanch all the vegetables, except the tomatoes, separately, in a large pan of boiling, lightly salted water for 1–3 minutes, depending on the size and the vegetable. Drain, refresh under cold water and pat dry.
3 Heat the remaining oil in a large frying pan, add the shallots and garlic and sauté for 5 minutes. Add the vegetables and tomatoes and stir-fry over a gentle heat then add the herb mixture.
4 Meanwhile, cook the pasta in a large pan of boiling, lightly salted water for the time stated on the packet.
5 Drain the pasta, reserving 4tbsp of the cooking water, and add the pasta and water to the frying pan. Toss with the vegetables and herb sauce, stir in the cream and heat through briefly. Serve at once, seasoned and scattered with Parmesan shavings, if using.

Serves 4–6   preparation: 20 minutes, plus infusing   cooking time: 15 minutes
per serving: 680–450 cals; 34–23g fat; 83–55g carbohydrate

Very Easy Four-cheese Gnocchi

2tsp salt
2 x 350g packs fresh gnocchi
500g tub fresh four-cheese sauce
2 x 240g packs sunblush tomatoes

salt and pepper
4tbsp torn basil leaves
2tbsp freshly grated Parmesan cheese
25g (1 oz) butter, chopped

1 Bring two large pans of water to the boil, add 1tsp salt and 1 pack gnocchi to each and cook for the time stated on the pack or until all the pieces have floated to the surface. Drain well and put back into one pan.
2 Preheat the grill. Pour the cheese sauce and tomatoes over the gnocchi and heat gently, stirring, for 2 minutes. Season, then add the basil and stir again. Put into individual heatproof bowls, sprinkle over the Parmesan and dot with the butter. Grill for 3–5 minutes or until golden and bubbling, then serve.

Serves 4   preparation: 2 minutes   cooking time: 20 minutes
per serving: 580 cals; 24g fat; 75g carbohydrate

Butternut Squash and Spinach Lasagne

2tbsp olive oil
1 butternut squash, peeled, deseeded
  and cubed
1 medium onion, peeled and sliced
salt and pepper
25g (1oz) butter
25g (1oz) plain flour
600ml (1 pint) semi-skimmed milk

225g bag baby spinach leaves
250g tub ricotta
1tsp freshly grated nutmeg
6 sheets pre-cooked lasagne, about 100g
  (3½oz)
50g (2oz) freshly grated pecorino or
  Parmesan cheese

1 Preheat the oven to 200°C (180°C fan oven) mark 6. Put the olive oil in a large roasting tin and add the squash, onion and 1tbsp water. Toss everything together and season well. Roast for 25 minutes, tossing halfway through.
2 To make the white sauce, put the butter, flour and milk in a small pan and bring slowly to the boil, whisking constantly. Reduce the heat to a simmer and cook for 5 minutes or until the white sauce has thickened slightly and coats the back of a wooden spoon generously.
3 Put 1tbsp water in the bottom of a pan and heat. Add the spinach, cover and cook until the leaves are just wilted. (Alternatively, pierce the bag and heat in the microwave for 1–2 minutes.)
4 Add the ricotta and nutmeg to the white sauce, season well to taste and mix thoroughly.
5 Layer the lasagne in a 1.7 litre (3 pint) dish, starting with the squash and onion mixture, then the spinach, lasagne sheets and the cheese sauce, seasoning each layer. Sprinkle the grated cheese on top.
6 Bake at the same temperature for 30–35 minutes or until the cheese is golden on top and the pasta is cooked.

Serves 6   preparation: 40 minutes   cooking time: 1 hour–1 hour 5 minutes
per serving: 320 cals; 17g fat; 30g carbohydrate

Easy Leek Pie

275g (10oz) plain flour, plus extra to dust
1tsp English mustard powder
175g (6oz) cold butter, cut into cubes
salt and pepper
50g (2oz) mature Cheddar cheese, grated
2 egg yolks, lightly beaten

900g (2lb) leeks, trimmed
2 medium red onions, peeled
juice of ½ lemon
leaves of 5 thyme sprigs
4tbsp olive oil
1 small egg, lightly beaten

1 To make the pastry, put the flour, mustard powder, butter and ½tsp salt into a food processor. Pulse until the mixture forms crumbs, then add the cheese, egg yolks and 2–3tbsp cold water. Whiz briefly until the mixture comes together, then form into a ball, wrap in clingfilm and put in the freezer for 10 minutes.

2 Preheat the oven to 200°C (180°C fan oven) mark 6. Cut the leeks into 1cm (½ inch) slices, then wash and drain. Put the leeks into a microwave-proof bowl, add 3tbsp water, cover with clingfilm, pierce the top and microwave on High for 8 minutes (based on a 900W oven). (Alternatively, cook the leeks with the water in a small covered pan over a low heat until softened.) Drain in a colander, then set aside.

3 Cut each onion into 8 wedges, put into the bowl and toss in the lemon juice. Cover, pierce as before and microwave on High for 5 minutes. (Alternatively, gently cook the onions with the lemon juice in a small covered pan until softened.)

4 Roll out the pastry on a lightly floured large sheet of baking parchment to a 38cm (15 inch) round. Lift the paper and pastry on to a large baking sheet.

5 Put the onions and leeks in the centre of the pastry, leaving a 7.5cm (3 inch) border all round. Sprinkle the thyme leaves over the vegetables, season and drizzle with the olive oil.

6 Lift the pastry edges up and fold them over the vegetables at the edge. Brush the pastry rim with beaten egg and bake for 50 minutes or until the pastry is golden and the vegetables are tender.

Serves 6 preparation: 15 minutes cooking time: 1 hour
per serving: 540 cals; 38g fat; 42g carbohydrate

Leek, Mushroom and Artichoke Croûte

3tbsp olive oil, plus extra to serve
2 garlic cloves, peeled and crushed
125g (4oz) shiitake mushrooms, sliced
1tbsp balsamic vinegar
50g (2oz) whole cooked chestnuts,
   roughly chopped
thyme sprigs
400g can artichoke hearts, drained
   and quartered

350g (12oz) leeks, sliced
375g sheet ready-rolled puff pastry
flour, to dust
salt and pepper
1 egg, lightly beaten, to glaze
cranberry sauce, to serve

1 Heat 2tbsp olive oil in a large pan and fry the garlic for 1 minute. Add the mushrooms and cook over a low heat for 3 minutes to soften. Add the vinegar, chestnuts, ½tsp thyme leaves stripped off the sprigs and the artichokes, then cook for 1 minute.
2 Heat the remaining oil in a large clean pan, add the leeks and cook for 4 minutes to soften slightly. Turn into a bowl and cool for 5 minutes.
3 Unroll the pastry on to a lightly floured surface and sprinkle the surface with the remaining thyme sprigs. Roll the leaves slightly into the pastry. Flip the pastry over so that the herbs are on the underside and roll the pastry out lightly to a 38 x 25.5cm (15 x 10 inch) rectangle. Using a sharp knife, cut the pastry in half vertically to create two long thin rectangles.
4 Spoon half the mushroom mixture down the centre of each piece of pastry, top with the leeks and season. Brush the pastry edges with water and fold each side of the pastry up over the filling to seal.
5 Cut both rolls in half and put on to a greased baking sheet. Cover and chill overnight.
6 Preheat the oven to 200°C (180°C fan oven) mark 6. Brush the pastry with egg to glaze, then bake for 20 minutes until the pastry is golden.
7 Remove from the oven and slice each croûte into six and serve three slices per person, topped with a dollop of cranberry sauce and a light drizzle of olive oil.

Serves 8   preparation: 30 minutes, plus cooling and chilling   cooking time: 30–35 minutes
per serving: 270 cals, 19g fat; 22g carbohydrate

Spicy Vegetable Stew

4tbsp sunflower oil
2.5cm (1 inch) piece fresh root ginger,
  peeled and grated
1tsp ground cinnamon
2tsp each ground coriander, ground cumin
  and ground turmeric
1kg (2¼lb) plum tomatoes, peeled,
  deseeded and flesh roughly chopped
2 bay leaves
8 cloves, crushed
750ml (1¼ pints) vegetable stock

175g (6oz) ground almonds
salt and pepper
350g (12oz) carrots, peeled and cut into
  2.5cm (1 inch) pieces
1 cauliflower, about 1kg (2¼lb), broken into
  small florets
350g (12oz) green beans, topped and halved
350g (12oz) young courgettes, cut into 5cm
  (2 inch) lengths and sliced into quarters
142ml carton double cream
coriander sprigs, to garnish

1 Heat the oil in a large casserole, add the ginger and all the spices and fry for 1–2 minutes or until the spices release their aroma.
2 Add the tomatoes and cook over a high heat until the tomatoes are soft and pulpy – about 10 minutes. Add the bay leaves, cloves, stock and ground almonds to the pan, then season well. Bring to the boil, add the carrots and cook for 5 minutes. Add the cauliflower and cook for 5–7 minutes.
3 Meanwhile, bring a large pan of cold water to the boil. Add the green beans, bring back to the boil, then add the courgettes. Bring back to the boil again, then drain thoroughly.
4 Add the beans, courgettes and cream to the pan. Bring to the boil, then reduce the heat and simmer for 5 minutes to heat through. Spoon into a warmed dish and garnish with coriander to serve.

Serves 10 preparation: 40 minutes cooking time: 35 minutes
per serving: 290 cals; 23g fat; 11g carbohydrate

Sweet Pepper Stew

100ml (3½fl oz) olive oil
2 garlic cloves, peeled and crushed
4 red peppers, halved, sliced and deseeded
3 orange peppers, halved, sliced and
  deseeded

1 green pepper, halved, sliced
  and deseeded
salt and pepper
2tbsp capers in brine, rinsed
18 black olives
1tbsp chopped flat-leafed parsley

1 Heat the olive oil in a very large pan, add the garlic and stir-fry over a medium heat for 1 minute. Add the sliced peppers, season well and stir to toss in the oil. Cover the pan with a lid and cook over a low heat for 40 minutes.
3 Add the capers, olives and parsley and stir. Serve immediately or cool, chill and enjoy a couple of days later with crusty bread.

Serves 6–8 preparation: 15 minutes cooking time: 40 minutes
per serving: 180–130 cals; 16–12g fat; 7–6g carbohydrate

Easy Basmati Pilaf

50g (2oz) butter
1 onion, peeled and finely chopped
1 garlic clove, peeled and crushed
225g (8oz) basmati rice

750ml (1¼ pints) hot stock
salt and pepper
1tbsp chopped flat-leafed parsley

1   Preheat the oven to 170°C (150°C fan oven) mark 3. Melt the butter in a heavy-based casserole, add
     the onion and cook over a low heat for 10–12 minutes or until soft. Add the garlic and rice and stir
     over a low heat for 1–2 minutes. Add the hot stock and season lightly.
2   Bring to the boil, cover with a tight-fitting lid and cook in the oven for 20–25 minutes. Stir with a fork
     halfway through the cooking time. The rice is cooked when it's just soft to the centre and all the liquid
     is absorbed. Remove from the oven and add the parsley just before serving.

Serves 4   preparation: 15 minutes   cooking time: 40 minutes
per serving: 310 cals; 11g fat; 48g carbohydrate

Courgette Puff Pie

450g (1lb) courgettes, trimmed and sliced
3tbsp olive oil
375g pack ready-rolled puff pastry
flour, to dust
2 eggs
2tbsp crème fraîche

75g (3oz) Gruyère cheese, grated
2 garlic cloves, peeled and crushed
4tbsp chopped flat-leafed parsley
salt and pepper
50g (2oz) fresh white breadcrumbs

1   Preheat the oven to 200°C (180°C fan oven) mark 6. Put the courgettes on a large baking sheet and
     drizzle with the olive oil. Roast for 8 minutes, then transfer the courgettes to a sheet of grease-
     proof paper.
2   Roll out the pastry on a floured surface to a 30.5cm (12 inch) square. Lift on to the baking sheet.
3   Crack 1 egg into a bowl, add the crème fraîche and whisk lightly. Add 50g (2oz) of the cheese, along
     with the garlic and parsley. Season and mix until well combined.
4   Arrange the courgettes on top of the pastry, leaving a clear margin around the edge, and pour the
     egg and crème fraîche mixture over them. Scatter the breadcrumbs and remaining cheese over
     the filling.
5   Lift the pastry sides up and over the edge of the filling to create a thick pastry rim. Chill for 10 minutes.
     Beat the remaining egg and brush over the pastry. Bake for 30 minutes or until the pastry is crisp and
     golden brown.

Serves 4   preparation: 25 minutes, plus resting   cooking time: 40 minutes
per serving: 650 cals; 47g fat; 43g carbohydrate

Winter Roasted Vegetable Tart

250g ready-rolled shortcrust pastry, removed
   from the fridge 5 minutes before using
1 small red onion, peeled and cut into
   six wedges
1 raw baby beetroot, peeled and
   thickly sliced
1 baby aubergine, quartered
1 small red apple, quartered, cored and
   cut into chunky slices
1 garlic clove, peeled and crushed

juice of ½ lemon
1tsp chopped thyme
1tbsp olive oil
125g (4oz) Cranberry and Red Onion
   Marmalade (page 665)
25g (1oz) chestnut mushrooms, halved
50g (2oz) chestnuts, cooked, peeled
   and chopped
salt and pepper
1tbsp redcurrant jelly, warmed

1   Preheat the oven to 200°C (180°C fan oven) mark 6. Sit an 11.5 x 20.5cm (4½ x 8 inch) loose-bottomed tart tin on a baking sheet. Unroll the shortcrust pastry and use it to line the tin, trimming off any excess. Prick the base several times with a fork, then line the pastry with baking parchment and weigh down with pieces of leftover pastry or fill with baking beans.

2   Bake the pastry case for 15 minutes, then remove the weighted paper and cook for a further 5 minutes until golden. Remove from the oven and leave to cool, then remove from the tin and put to one side.

3   Put the onion, beetroot, aubergine, apple and garlic into a roasting tin. Squeeze over the lemon juice, scatter over the thyme and drizzle with olive oil, then roast for 20 minutes.

4   Put the pastry case on to a baking sheet and spoon the onion marmalade over the base. Arrange the roasted vegetables and the mushrooms on top and sprinkle with the chestnuts, then season. Brush the redcurrant jelly over the vegetables to glaze. Cook in the oven for 20 minutes.

Serves 3   preparation: 20 minutes   cooking time: 40 minutes
per serving: 570 cals; 26g fat; 83g carbohydrate

Tomato and Butter Bean Stew

2tbsp olive oil
1 onion, peeled and finely sliced
2 garlic cloves, peeled and finely chopped
2 large leeks, sliced
2 x 400g cans cherry tomatoes

2 x 400g cans butter beans, drained
   and rinsed
150ml (¼ pint) hot vegetable stock
salt and pepper
1–2tbsp balsamic vinegar

1   Preheat the oven to 180°C (160°C fan oven) mark 4. Heat the olive oil in a flameproof casserole on the hob over a medium heat. Add the onion and garlic and cook for 10 minutes until golden and softened. Add the leeks and cook, covered, for 5 minutes. Add the tomatoes, beans and hot stock and season well. Bring to the boil, then cover and cook in the oven for 35–40 minutes until the sauce has thickened. Remove from the oven, stir in the vinegar and spoon into warmed bowls.

Serves 4   preparation: 10 minutes   cooking time: 50–55 minutes
per serving: 280 cals; 8g fat; 39g carbohydrate

Roasted Vegetable and Rocket Tartlets

375g pack ready-rolled puff pastry
plain flour, to dust
1 egg, beaten
2tbsp coarse sea salt
300g (11oz) vegetable antipasti in olive oil
(mixed roasted peppers, artichokes,
onions etc.)

a little olive oil, if needed
2tbsp balsamic vinegar
salt and pepper
190g tub red pepper hummus
50g bag wild rocket

1 Preheat the oven to 220°C (200°C fan oven) mark 7. Unroll the puff pastry on a lightly floured surface and cut it into six equal-sized squares.
2 Put the pastry squares on a large baking sheet and prick each one all over with a fork. Brush all over with beaten egg and sprinkle the edges with sea salt. Bake for 5–7 minutes or until the pastry is golden brown and cooked through.
3 To make the dressing, pour off 4tbsp olive oil from the antipasti (you may need to add a little extra olive oil) into a bowl. Add the vinegar, season well, then put to one side.
4 To serve, divide the hummus among the pastry bases, spreading it over each. Put a tartlet on each plate and spoon over the antipasti – there's no need to be neat.
5 Whisk the dressing again. Add the rocket and toss to coat, then pile a small handful of leaves on top of each tartlet. Serve immediately.

Serves 6   preparation: 10 minutes   cooking time: 5–7 minutes
per serving: 340 cals; 23g fat; 27g carbohydrate

Spinach-baked Eggs with Mushrooms

3tbsp olive oil
125g (4oz) closed-cup chestnut
mushrooms, quartered
225g bag baby spinach leaves

salt and pepper
2 large eggs
4tbsp double cream

1 Preheat the oven to 200°C (180°C fan oven) mark 6. Heat the olive oil in a large frying pan, add the mushrooms and stir-fry for 30 seconds, then add the spinach and stir-fry until wilted. Season well and divide between two 600ml (1 pint) ovenproof dishes.
2 Carefully break an egg into the centre of each dish and spoon the double cream over the top. Season well.
3 Cook for about 12 minutes, or until the eggs are just set. (Remember that they will continue to cook a little once they're out of the oven.) Serve immediately.

Serves 2   preparation time: 5 minutes   cooking time: 13 minutes
per serving: 440cals; 42g fat; 35g carbohydrate

Soured Cream and Onion Tarts

700g (1½lb) tomatoes, halved
salt and pepper
1tbsp chopped thyme or ½tsp dried
2tbsp olive oil
200g (7oz) chilled butter

175g (6oz) plain flour, plus extra to dust
6–7tbsp soured cream
900g (2lb) onions, peeled and finely sliced
125g (4oz) Roquefort cheese
thyme sprigs, to garnish

1   Preheat the oven to 170°C (150°C fan oven) mark 3. Put the tomatoes on a baking sheet, season, sprinkle with the thyme, drizzle with the olive oil and cook, uncovered, in the oven for 40 minutes until slightly shrivelled.
2   Meanwhile, cut 150g (5oz) butter into small dice and put in a food processor with the flour. Pulse until the butter is roughly cut up through the flour (you should still be able to see pieces of butter), then add the soured cream and pulse again for 2–3 seconds until just mixed.
3   Turn the dough out on to a lightly floured surface, cut into six and roll each piece thinly into a 12.5cm (5 inch) round. Put on two baking sheets, cover and chill for 30 minutes.
4   Melt the remaining butter in a pan, add the onions and cook slowly for about 15 minutes until very soft. Increase the heat and fry the onions for 3–4 minutes or until well browned and caramelised. Take off the heat and cool.
5   Spoon the onions into the centre of the pastries, leaving a 1cm (½ inch) edge. Crumble the cheese on top and add the tomatoes. Season, then roughly fold up the pastry edge.
6   Increase the oven temperature to 200°C (180°C fan oven) mark 6, and cook the tarts for 30 minutes until golden. Garnish with thyme sprigs and serve immediately.

Serves 6   preparation: 20 minutes, plus chilling   cooking time: about 1 hour
per serving: 570cals; 42g fat; 39g carbohydrate

Artichokes with Broad Beans

2 x 400g (14oz) packs artichoke bottoms,
   defrosted and cut in half, or 4 x 390g cans
   artichoke bottoms, drained and cut in half
400g (14oz) fresh or defrosted broad beans
6tbsp mild extra-virgin olive oil
4 garlic cloves, peeled and crushed

juice of 1 lemon
2tsp golden caster sugar
salt and pepper
4 sprigs of mint or dill, chopped, plus extra
   sprigs to garnish

1   Put all the ingredients except the herbs into a pan and just cover with water. Season well. Bring to the boil, then reduce the heat and simmer for 10–15 minutes. Drain, reserving the liquid.
2   Return the liquid to the pan and boil for 20 minutes, or until reduced to 150ml (¼ pint). Add the vegetables and herbs and heat through for 1 minute. Serve hot or cold, garnished with the mint or dill sprigs.

Serves 8   preparation: 10 minutes   cooking time: 30–40 minutes
per serving: 130 cals; 10g fat; 7g carbohydrate

Aubergine and Pepper Balti with Carrot Relish

1tbsp each fennel seeds and
  ground allspice
2–3 garlic cloves, peeled and
  roughly chopped
1cm (½ inch) piece fresh root ginger,
  peeled and roughly chopped
50g (2oz) garam masala
25g (1oz) curry powder
salt and pepper
4tbsp groundnut oil, plus 1tsp for the relish
1 onion, peeled and finely sliced
1 aubergine, cut into 2cm (¾ inch) dice
1 red and 1 green chilli, deseeded and

roughly chopped
1 red and 1 green pepper, deseeded
  and sliced
4 tomatoes, about 300g (11oz), quartered
600ml (1 pint) vegetable stock
salt and pepper
2tsp black mustard seeds
450g (1lb) carrots, peeled and grated
2tbsp tamarind paste
2tbsp dark muscovado sugar
1tbsp white wine vinegar
50g (2oz) baby spinach leaves

1   To make the balti paste, put the fennel seeds, allspice, garlic, ginger, garam masala and curry powder
    into a mini processor with 1tsp salt and 8tbsp water, and whiz. Divide it into three equal portions. Freeze
    two in separate bags to use within 3 months, and put to one side the remaining portion.
2   To make the curry, heat 4tbsp oil in a large flameproof casserole and fry the onion over a high heat
    for 10–15 minutes until golden. Add the aubergine and cook for another 5 minutes.
3   Add the reserved balti paste and the chillies to the casserole, stir well to mix and cook for 1–2 minutes.
    Add the sliced peppers and tomatoes and cook for 5 minutes, then add the stock and season well.
    Cover and bring to the boil, then reduce the heat and simmer the balti for 15 minutes or until the
    vegetables are tender.
4   Meanwhile, make the relish. Heat the 1tsp oil in a pan and add the mustard seeds. Cover with a lid
    and cook until they start to pop – you'll hear them jumping against the lid. Add the carrots, tamarind
    paste, sugar and vinegar to the pan, and cook for 1–2 minutes. Stir the curry well.
5   Stir the spinach into the curry and serve with the carrot relish and pilau rice to soak up the sauce.

Serves 4   preparation time: 30 minutes   cooking time: 45 minutes
per serving: 240 calories; 14g fat; 25g carbohydrate

Aubergine and Pepper Parmigiana

4 large red peppers, quartered, cored
  and deseeded
oil, to brush
3 aubergines

1 quantity Rich Tomato Sauce (page 655)
225g (8oz) grated Cheddar cheese
50g (2oz) freshly grated Parmesan cheese
black pepper

1 Preheat the oven to 200°C (180°C fan oven) mark 6. Preheat the grill to high. Put the peppers, skin side up, on the grill rack, brush with a little oil and grill for 5–6 minutes each side until charred and tender. Transfer to a bowl, cover tightly and leave until cool; peel away the skin from the cooled peppers.

2 Cut the aubergines lengthways into thick slices, place on the grill rack and brush with oil. Grill for 6–8 minutes on each side, then leave to cool. Grease a large baking dish.

3 Spoon a little tomato sauce over the base of the baking dish and cover with a layer of aubergines and peppers. Sprinkle with a little of the Cheddar. Repeat layering the sauce, vegetables and cheese until all these ingredients are used, finishing with a layer of cheese. Sprinkle with the Parmesan and pepper to taste.

4 Bake for 30–40 minutes until golden. Serve immediately.

Serves 6   preparation: 15 minutes   cooking time: 1¼ hours
per serving: 300 cals; 21g fat; 12g carbohydrate

Lentils with Red Pepper

1tbsp olive oil
1 very small onion, peeled and finely
  chopped
1 celery stick, diced
1 carrot, peeled and diced
2 bay leaves, torn
150g (5oz) Puy lentils

600ml (1 pint) hot vegetable stock
1 marinated red pepper, drained
  and chopped
2tbsp chopped flat-leafed parsley, plus
  extra to garnish
black pepper

1 Heat the olive oil in a pan, add the onion and cook over a low heat for 15 minutes until soft. Add the celery, carrot and bay leaves and cook for 2 minutes.

2 Add the lentils with the hot stock and stir everything together. Half cover the pan with a lid and simmer over a low heat for 25–30 minutes.

3 Add the red pepper and parsley and season with pepper. Stir everything together well, spoon into a warmed serving dish, garnish with extra parsley and serve as an accompaniment.

Serves 2   preparation: 10 minutes   cooking time: 32 minutes
per serving: 260 cals; 2g fat; 45g carbohydrate

Autumn Pumpkin and Mushroom Bake

50g (2oz) butter, plus extra if needed
1 small onion, peeled and finely diced
2 garlic cloves, peeled and crushed
½tsp chopped thyme, plus extra to garnish
800g (1¾lb) pumpkin or butternut squash,
  peeled and chopped

400g (14oz) field mushrooms, broken into
  even pieces
salt and pepper
284ml carton double cream
100g (3½oz) freshly grated Parmesan
  cheese

1 Preheat the oven to 200°C (180°C fan oven) mark 6. Warm 50g (2oz) butter in a frying pan until foaming, then add the onion, garlic and thyme and stir-fry over a medium heat until the onion becomes soft but not coloured.
2 Add the pumpkin or squash and cook, tossing gently, for 3–4 minutes, until it starts to soften. Increase the heat, add the mushrooms, then season and cook until the mushroom juices start to flow (add extra butter if it looks dry). Add the cream, bring to the boil, and cook for 5–10 minutes or until the sauce looks syrupy.
3 Spoon into a large flameproof dish, sprinkle with the Parmesan and bake for 10 minutes. Garnish with thyme and serve.

Serves 4–6   preparation: 5 minutes   cooking time: 20–25 minutes
per serving 570–380 calories; 53–36g fat; 9–6g carbohydrate

Fennel Bake

2tbsp olive oil
3 fennel bulbs, finely sliced
1 broccoli head, broken into florets
1 onion, peeled and finely chopped
2 garlic cloves, peeled and crushed
2 red peppers, halved, deseeded and finely
  sliced

2 x 400g cans chopped tomatoes
small handful of basil leaves, roughly torn
salt and pepper
150g (5oz) porridge oats
50g (2oz) freshly grated Parmesan cheese

1 Preheat the oven to 180°C (160°C fan oven) mark 4. Heat 1tbsp olive oil in a pan. Add the fennel and fry for 5 minutes. Remove with a slotted spoon and put into an ovenproof dish. Add the broccoli to the dish.
2 Add the onion to the pan and fry for 10 minutes until softened. Add the garlic and red peppers and fry for 1 minute. Add the tomatoes and basil, then season. Reduce the heat and simmer for 15 minutes, stirring occasionally. Pour the tomato mix over the fennel.
3 Put the oats into a large bowl. Add the remaining oil and the Parmesan and mix well, then sprinkle over the fennel in a thick layer. Bake for about 30 minutes until the topping is golden, then serve.

Serves 4   preparation: 15 minutes   cooking time: about 1 hour
per serving: 360 cals; 15g fat; 44g carbohydrate

Stuffed Peppers

4 large red peppers, halved and deseeded	2 courgettes, finely chopped
2tbsp olive oil	200g (7oz) chestnut mushrooms,
100g (3½oz) bulgur wheat	finely chopped
1 red onion, peeled and finely chopped	25g (1oz) pine nuts
1tsp ground coriander	100g (3½oz) goat's cheese, roughly chopped
2 celery sticks, finely chopped	salt and pepper

1   Preheat the oven to 200°C (180°C fan oven) mark 6. Put the red peppers in a roasting tin, brush with 1tbsp olive oil and roast for 20 minutes. Cook the bulgur wheat according to the packet instructions.
2   Heat the remaining oil in a frying pan. Fry the onion for 5–7 minutes until soft. Add the coriander and fry for 1 minute. Add the celery, courgettes and mushrooms and cook for 10 minutes. Tip into a bowl.
3   Add the cooked bulgur wheat, the pine nuts and goat's cheese to the onion mixture, season well and mix thoroughly. Spoon the mixture into the pepper halves and return to the oven to heat through.

Serves 4   preparation: 20 minutes   cooking time: 35–45 minutes
per serving: 350 cals; 20g fat; 31g carbohydrate

Aubergine and Red Pepper Moussaka

450g (1lb) potatoes, peeled	225g (8oz) tomatoes, thickly sliced
salt and pepper	2 garlic cloves, peeled and sliced
1 aubergine, sliced into rounds	250g carton passata
1 large red onion, peeled and cut	2 x 125g packs soft goat's cheese
into wedges	2 x 150ml cartons natural yogurt
2 red peppers, cored, deseeded and sliced	3 eggs
4tbsp olive oil	25g (1oz) Parmesan cheese, freshly grated
2tbsp chopped thyme	

1   Preheat the oven to 230°C (210°C fan oven) mark 8. Cut the potatoes lengthways into 5mm (¼ inch) slices. Put in a pan of lightly salted water, bring to the boil and par-boil for 5 minutes. Drain well.
2   Put the potatoes in a large roasting tin with the aubergine, onion and red peppers. Drizzle with the olive oil, add the thyme and toss to mix. Season generously and roast for 30 minutes, stirring occasionally.
3   Add the tomatoes and garlic to the tin and roast for a further 15 minutes. Remove the tin from the oven and reduce the heat to 200°C (180°C fan oven) mark 6.
4   Spread half the vegetables in a 1.7 litre (3 pint) ovenproof dish, then cover with half the passata. Spoon the goat's cheese evenly on top. Layer the rest of the roasted vegetables over the cheese and cover with the remaining passata.
5   Lightly whisk the yogurt, eggs and Parmesan together in a bowl and season generously. Pour on top of the moussaka, then bake for 45 minutes until golden and bubbling.

Serves 6   preparation: 45 minutes   cooking time: 1½ hours
per serving: 340 cals; 21g fat; 23g carbohydrate

Mediterranean Stew

2tbsp olive oil
1 onion, peeled and finely sliced
1 garlic clove, peeled and crushed
pinch of crushed chilli flakes
2tbsp tomato purée
2 medium courgettes, roughly chopped
2 red peppers, deseeded and sliced

1 small aubergine, diced
400g can chopped tomatoes, can reserved
salt and pepper
500g pack dried pappardelle pasta
3tbsp roughly torn basil leaves, plus extra
    sprigs to garnish

1 Heat the olive oil in a large pan, add the onion and garlic and cook over a medium heat for 10 minutes until soft. Add the chilli flakes with the tomato purée and cook for 1–2 minutes. Add the courgettes, red peppers and aubergine, then the tomatoes. Rinse the can with 200ml (7fl oz) water and add to the pan. Season well. Cover the pan and bring to the boil, then reduce the heat and simmer for 30 minutes.
2 Meanwhile, cook the pasta in a large pan of boiling salted water for the time stated on the packet. Drain well. Just before serving, stir through the basil leaves. Serve the stew, garnished with basil sprigs, if using, with the pasta.

Serves 4   preparation: 15 minutes   cooking time: 50–55 minutes
per serving: 560 cals; 10g fat; 106g carbohydrate

Greek Spinach and Feta Pie

2tbsp olive oil, plus extra to brush the
    filo pastry
2 small onions, peeled and chopped
500g (1lb 2oz) spinach
2 large eggs, plus extra beaten egg to glaze

200g (7oz) feta cheese, crumbled
2tsp dill seeds
black pepper
270g pack filo pastry

1 Preheat the oven to 200°C (180°C fan oven) mark 6. Heat the olive oil in a pan and cook the onions for 5–10 minutes or until transparent. Add the spinach and cook for 3 minutes or until wilted. Take off the heat and leave to cool.
2 In a separate bowl, combine the two eggs with the feta cheese and half the dill seeds, then season with pepper. Add the spinach and onion to the feta cheese mixture and stir until well combined.
3 Cut the pastry into 30.5 x 15cm (12 x 6 inch) sheets. Layer four sheets on a large baking sheet, brushing each piece with olive oil.
4 Spoon the spinach and feta mixture over the pastry and spread with a palette knife. Cover with six more layers of pastry, brushing each sheet with olive oil.
5 Glaze the pie with beaten egg and sprinkle the remaining dill seeds on top. Bake for 30–40 minutes or until golden.

Serves 6   preparation: 15 minutes   cooking time: 50 minutes
per serving: 320 cals; 16g fat; 31g carbohydrate

Spring Vegetable Stew

225g (8oz) new potatoes, scrubbed
salt and pepper
75g (3oz) unsalted butter
4 shallots, blanched in boiling water,
  drained, peeled and thinly sliced
1 garlic clove, peeled and crushed
2tsp chopped thyme
1tsp grated lime zest

6 baby leeks, trimmed and sliced into 5cm
  (2 inch) lengths
125g (4oz) baby carrots, scrubbed
125g (4oz) each podded peas and podded
  broad beans
300ml (½ pint) vegetable stock
1 little gem lettuce, shredded
4tbsp chopped herbs, such as chervil,
  chives, mint and parsley

1 Put the potatoes in a pan of lightly salted water, bring to the boil, cover and par-boil for 5 minutes.
   Drain and refresh under cold water.
2 Meanwhile, melt half the butter in a large sauté pan, add the shallots, garlic, thyme and lime zest, and
   fry gently for 5 minutes until softened and lightly golden. Add the leeks and carrots and sauté for a
   further 5 minutes. Stir in the potatoes, peas and broad beans, then pour in the stock and bring to the
   boil. Cover the pan, reduce the heat and simmer gently for 10 minutes. Remove the lid and cook,
   uncovered, for a further 5–8 minutes until all the vegetables are tender.
3 Add the shredded lettuce to the stew with the chopped herbs and remaining butter. Heat through until
   the butter is melted. Check the seasoning and serve at once.

Serves 4   preparation: 30 minutes   cooking time: 25–30 minutes
per serving: 270 cals; 17g fat; 23g carbohydrate

Smoked Sesame Tofu

2tbsp toasted sesame seeds
2tbsp reduced salt soy sauce
1tsp light muscovado sugar
1tsp rice wine vinegar
1tbsp sesame oil
220g pack smoked tofu, cubed

½ small white or green cabbage, shredded
2 carrots, peeled and cut into strips
200g pack beansprouts
4 marinated roasted red peppers,
  roughly chopped
2 spring onions, shredded

1 Put the sesame seeds in a bowl, add the soy sauce, sugar and vinegar and ½tbsp sesame oil and
   mix. Add the smoked tofu, stir to coat, then put to one side to marinate for 10 minutes.
2 Heat a large wok or non-stick frying pan. Add the marinated tofu, reserving the marinade, and fry for
   5 minutes until golden all over. Remove from the wok with a slotted spoon and put to one side.
3 Heat the remaining oil in the wok. Add the cabbage and carrots and stir-fry for 5 minutes. Stir in the
   beansprouts, red peppers, spring onions, cooked tofu and reserved marinade and cook for a further
   2 minutes. Serve immediately with brown rice.

Serves 4   preparation: 20 minutes   cooking time: 12 minutes, plus marinating
per serving: 210 cals; 11g fat; 18g carbohydrate

Spiced Ratatouille with Sweet Potatoes

3 courgettes and 1 medium aubergine, each
  cut into 1cm (½ inch) cubes
1 red onion, peeled and sliced
3 garlic cloves, peeled and sliced
1 red pepper, halved, deseeded and sliced
3 medium carrots, about 225g (8oz), peeled
  and cut into 1cm (½ inch) cubes

2 sweet potatoes, about 450g (1lb), peeled
  and cut into 1cm (½ inch) cubes
3tbsp olive oil
½tsp ground allspice
2tsp coriander seeds
500ml carton or bottle passata
salt and pepper

1 Preheat the oven to 200°C (180°C fan oven) mark 6. Take two large roasting tins and put the courgettes, aubergine, onion, garlic and red pepper into one and the carrots and sweet potatoes into the other. Drizzle both lots of vegetables with olive oil and sprinkle with allspice and coriander seeds. Toss well.

2 Roast the vegetables for 20 minutes, then turn and continue to roast for 20 minutes until tender and slightly charred.

3 To serve, add the passata to the vegetables and toss well. Season generously and cook for 20 minutes.

4 To serve in a neat shape, put a 7.5cm (3 inch) plain cutter on a serving plate, spoon in the ratatouille and lift up the cutter.

Serves 6 preparation: 25 minutes cooking time: 1 hour
per serving: 170 cals; 8g fat; 24g carbohydrate

Red Rice, Spinach and Bean Pilaf

2tbsp vegetable oil
225g (8oz) onions, peeled and chopped
2 garlic cloves, peeled and crushed
75g (3oz) each red rice and long-grain rice
450ml (¾ pint) vegetable stock

salt and pepper
400g can beans, such as pinto, chickpeas,
  kidney beans or mixed pulses, drained
  and rinsed
225g (8oz) spinach, roughly chopped

1 Preheat the oven to 200°C (180°C fan oven) mark 6. Heat the oil in a large flameproof casserole, add the onions and cook, stirring, for 10 minutes or until they are golden and soft.

2 Add the garlic and red rice to the onions and cook, stirring, for 1 minute. Add the stock, bring to the boil and season, then cover the pan, reduce the heat and simmer for 10 minutes.

3 Transfer to the oven and cook for 30 minutes. Remove from the oven and add the long-grain rice to the casserole and bring back to the boil on the hob. Put back in the oven and cook for 25 minutes or until the rice is just tender.

4 Stir in the beans and put back in the oven for 5 minutes. Just before serving, stir the spinach through the pilaff until wilted. Season and serve.

Serves 4 preparation: 15 minutes cooking time: 1½ hours
per serving: 230 cals; 6g fat; 36g carbohydrate

Mushroom and Spinach Pancakes

50g (2oz) plain white flour
50g (2oz) plain wholemeal flour
1 egg
350ml (12fl oz) skimmed milk
salt and pepper
300ml (½ pint) vegetable stock
25g (1oz) dried mushrooms
1tbsp vegetable oil, plus extra to oil

450g (1lb) fresh spinach, or 350g (12oz)
  frozen-leaf spinach, thawed
225g (8oz) reduced-fat soft cheese
450g (1lb) brown-cap mushrooms, roughly
  chopped
1 bunch of spring onions, roughly chopped
flat-leafed parsley, to garnish

1 Whiz together the flours, egg, milk and a pinch of salt in a food processor to make a batter. Cover and leave for 30 minutes. Pour the stock over the dried mushrooms and leave to soak for 30 minutes.
2 Lightly oil a small non-stick crêpe pan. When hot, add enough batter to coat the base of the pan thinly. Cook the pancake for 1–2 minutes until golden brown, then flip over and cook for a further 30 seconds. Transfer to a plate. Continue with remaining batter to make 10–12 pancakes.
3 Cook the spinach in a pan for 2–3 minutes until just wilted. Cool, squeeze and chop. Mix with the soft cheese and season to taste.
4 Heat 1tsp oil in a pan, add the mushrooms and spring onions and cook for about 10 minutes or until lightly browned. Add the soaked dried mushrooms and stock, bring to the boil, then reduce the heat and simmer for 15–20 minutes or until syrupy. Season. Blend half the mushroom mixture in a food processor until smooth. Return to the pan and combine with the remaining mushrooms.
5 Preheat the oven to 200°C (180°C fan oven) mark 6. Put half the spinach mixture in a lightly oiled, 1.1 litre (2 pint) shallow, ovenproof dish. Using about six pancakes, layer them with the mushroom mixture and remaining spinach mixture, finishing with a mushroom layer.
6 Bake for 30 minutes or until well browned and hot. Serve garnished with the parsley.

Serves 4   preparation: 1 hour, plus standing and soaking   cooking time: 1½ hours
per serving: 320 cals; 14g fat; 30g carbohydrate

Mixed Vegetable Tempura

1.8 litres (3¼ pints) vegetable oil
150g pack tempura mix
330ml bottle Japanese lager
  (or a substitute lager)
40g (1½oz) sesame seeds
1tsp salt
150g (5oz) sweet potato, peeled and cut
  into fine matchsticks

1 onion, peeled and cut into wedges
150g (5oz) baby leeks, cut into 5cm
  (2 inch) pieces
1 red pepper, deseeded and cut
  into 12 wedges
200g (7oz) fine green beans, trimmed
Thai sweet chilli dipping sauce, to serve

1 Preheat the oven to 110°C (90°C fan oven) mark ¼. Heat the oil in a deep-fat fryer on the chip setting or until 190°C. Put the tempura mix into a bowl and gradually whisk in the lager to make a smooth batter. Add the sesame seeds and salt.
2 Drop six pieces of vegetable into the tempura batter to coat, then, using a draining spoon, lower into the hot oil. Cook for 3 minutes until golden and puffy, drain on kitchen paper, then keep warm in the oven. Repeat with the remaining vegetables. Serve with a bowl of chilli dipping sauce.

Serves 6   preparation: 10 minutes   cooking time: 15 minutes
per serving: 240 cals; 9g fat; 33g carbohydrate

Cheap and Cheerful Vegetable Curry

3tbsp vegetable oil
1 onion, peeled and finely sliced
2 garlic cloves, peeled and crushed
2tbsp Balti curry paste
2 medium potatoes, about 225g (8oz),
  peeled and cut into small cubes
1 small cauliflower, cut into large florets,
  smaller leaves roughly torn and reserved

2 medium carrots, about 175g (6oz),
  peeled and cut into small cubes
1 vegetable stock cube
400g can chopped tomatoes (optional)
salt and pepper
75g (3oz) frozen peas (optional)

1 Heat the oil in a large heavy-based pan and add the onion. Fry over a medium heat for 10–15 minutes until golden. Add the garlic, cook for 30 seconds, then add the curry paste and cook for 1 minute, stirring regularly.
2 Add the potatoes and cauliflower florets and fry, stirring to coat in the oil, for 2 minutes. Add the carrots and cook for 1 minute. Pour 600ml (1 pint) boiling water into a jug and crumble in the stock cube. Add the stock to the vegetables with the tomatoes, if using. Season well.
3 Cover and simmer for 10 minutes until the vegetables are almost tender. Add the peas, if using, and cook for 2 minutes. Add the cauliflower leaves and cook for 30 seconds. Serve with bread, rice or on its own.

Serves 4   preparation: 20 minutes   cooking time: 35 minutes
per serving: 230 cals; 12g fat; 24g carbohydrate

Spicy Bean and Tomato Fajitas

2tbsp sunflower oil

1 medium onion, peeled and sliced

2 garlic cloves, peeled and crushed

½tsp hot chilli powder

1tsp each ground coriander and
  ground cumin

1tbsp tomato purée

400g can chopped tomatoes

220g can red kidney beans, drained
  and rinsed

300g can borlotti beans, drained and rinsed

300g can flageolet beans, drained
  and rinsed

150ml (¼ pint) hot vegetable stock

salt and pepper

2 ripe avocados

juice of ½ lime

1tbsp chopped coriander, plus sprigs
  to garnish

pack containing 8 ready-made flour tortillas

142ml carton soured cream

lime wedges, to serve

1 Heat the oil in a large pan, add the onion and cook gently for 5 minutes. Add the garlic and spices and cook for 2 minutes.

2 Add the tomato purée and cook for 1 minute, then add the tomatoes, all the beans and the hot stock. Season well, bring to the boil, then reduce the heat and simmer for 15 minutes, stirring occasionally.

3 Meanwhile, quarter, peel and chop the avocado and put into a bowl with the lime juice and the chopped coriander and mash together. Season well.

4 Warm the tortillas: either wrap them in foil and heat in the oven at 180°C (160°C fan oven) mark 4 for 10 minutes or put on a plate and microwave on High for 45 seconds (based on a 900W oven).

5 Spoon the bean mixture down the centre of each tortilla. Fold up one edge to keep the filling inside, then wrap the two sides in so they overlap. Dollop on the avocado and top with soured cream. Garnish with coriander sprigs and serve with lime wedges.

Serves 4   preparation: 15 minutes   cooking time: 23 minutes
per serving: 620 cals; 28g fat; 74g carbohydrate

Saffron Pilaf with Chickpeas and Raisins

1tbsp olive oil
1 large onion, peeled and finely chopped
1 garlic clove, peeled and crushed
½tsp each ground cumin and
   ground cinnamon
a pinch of saffron strands
125g (4oz) brown rice, washed and dried

600ml (1 pint) vegetable stock
25g (1oz) raisins
400g can chickpeas, drained and rinsed
salt and pepper
toasted almonds or cashew nuts,
   to garnish (optional)

1 Heat the olive oil in a heavy-based pan, then add the onion, garlic, cumin, cinnamon and saffron. Cover and cook over a low heat for 4–5 minutes until the onions are soft.
2 Add the rice to the onions, then cover with the stock, add the raisins and chickpeas and season well. Bring to the boil, then reduce the heat, cover the pan and simmer gently for 40–45 minutes, stirring frequently to prevent the rice catching on the bottom of the pan. If you like, sprinkle a few toasted almonds or cashew nuts over the pilaf. Serve with a salad of raw spinach leaves, rocket and lettuce.

Serves 2   preparation: 5 minutes   cooking time: 55 minutes
per serving (without nuts): 500 cals; 12g fat; 89g carbohydrate

Mushroom and Madeira Risotto

25g (1oz) dried porcini mushrooms
75g (3oz) butter
1 medium onion, peeled and finely chopped
1 medium leek, finely chopped
2tbsp chopped tarragon or a pinch of dried
450g (1lb) chestnut mushrooms, roughly
   chopped

350g (12oz) risotto rice, such as arborio
300ml (½ pint) Madeira
salt and pepper
75g (3oz) freshly grated Parmesan cheese
4tbsp chopped flat-leafed parsley

1 Put the dried mushrooms in a large heatproof bowl and pour over 1 litre (1¾ pints) boiling water. Soak for 30 minutes.
2 Melt the butter in a 3 litre (5¼ pint) shallow flameproof dish and fry the onion, leek and tarragon for 10 minutes. Add the fresh mushrooms and cook over a medium heat for 5 minutes.
3 Strain the porcini, reserving the soaking liquid. Set this aside. Finely chop the softened mushrooms. Add to the dish and cook, stirring, for a further 10 minutes.
4 Preheat the oven to 150°C (130°C fan oven) mark 2. Add the rice to the mushroom mixture and stir over a gentle heat for 2–3 minutes. Add the Madeira and reserved soaking liquid, and season. Bring to the boil, then transfer to the oven and cook, uncovered, for 25 minutes.
5 Stir one-third of the Parmesan into the risotto and return to the oven for 15 minutes. Stir in the parsley and season to taste. Put the remaining cheese into a bowl and serve separately with the risotto.

Serves 6   preparation: 15 minutes, plus soaking   cooking time: 1¼ hours
per serving: 470 cals; 15g fat; 56g carbohydrate

Risotto with Saffron, Lemon and Basil

50g (2oz) unsalted butter, plus a splash
  of olive oil
1 medium onion, peeled and very
  finely chopped
225g (8oz) arborio or carnaroli rice
150ml (¼ pint) dry white wine
about 1 litre (1¾ pints) fresh hot stock

2 large pinches of saffron strands
grated zest of ½ lemon and lemon
  juice to taste
decent handful of basil leaves,
  roughly chopped
salt and pepper
50g (2oz) freshly grated Parmesan cheese

1 Melt half the butter with the olive oil in a large pan, then add the onion and cook gently for a few minutes. When the onion is soft and translucent, add the rice and stir well to ensure each grain is coated in butter. Pour in the wine and continue to stir over a lowish heat until it has almost evaporated.
2 Begin to add the hot stock, a ladleful at a time, stirring as you do so and waiting for the liquid to be absorbed before adding more. The rice will absorb the liquid as it cooks, so keep stirring to keep it moving. After about 15 minutes, add the saffron strands and continue cooking and stirring.
3 After 18–20 minutes when the rice is almost cooked, add the lemon zest and juice and the basil leaves. Stir well. The consistency of the risotto should be dense and creamy but the individual grains of rice distinct and firm. When you're happy with the consistency – not too dry nor too sloppy – turn off the heat. Check for seasoning (it may need a little extra salt), then add the remaining butter and the Parmesan. Stir again and serve straight away.

Serves 2 generously preparation: 15 minutes cooking time: 25 minutes
per serving: 800 cals; 30g fat; 97g carbohydrate

Vegetable and Saffron Risotto

1 large courgette, chopped
1 yellow and 1 red pepper, each deseeded
  and chopped
600ml (1 pint) vegetable stock
175g (6oz) flat mushrooms, chopped
generous pinch of saffron strands

250g (9oz) risotto rice
1 bunch of spring onions, finely sliced
2 tomatoes, deseeded and chopped
salt and pepper
Parmesan cheese shavings, shredded basil
  and basil leaves, to garnish

1 Put the courgette and chopped peppers in a large pan, add the stock and bring to the boil. Reduce the heat and simmer for 5 minutes, then add the mushrooms and simmer for a further 5 minutes. Drain and reserve the stock. Add the saffron to the stock.
2 Cook the risotto rice, according to the instructions on the packet, in the reserved stock.
3 When the rice is tender – about 18–20 minutes – stir in the cooked vegetables, the spring onions and tomatoes. Season generously and garnish with the Parmesan shavings and basil to serve.

Serves 4 preparation: 8 minutes cooking time: 30 minutes
per serving 280 cals; 2g fat; 56g carbohydrate

Broad Bean and Lemon Risotto

350g (12oz) frozen broad beans
salt and pepper
25g (1oz) butter
1 medium onion, peeled and finely chopped
200g (7oz) arborio rice

1 litre (1¾ pints) hot vegetable stock
grated zest and juice of 1 lemon, plus extra
   zest to garnish
75g (3oz) freshly grated Parmesan cheese,
   plus extra to garnish

1 Cook the broad beans in a large pan of boiling salted water for 3–5 minutes or until just tender. Plunge into icy cold water to cool. Drain, peel off the outer skins (optional) and put to one side.
2 Melt the butter in a large pan, add the onion and cook over a medium heat for 5 minutes or until beginning to soften. Add the rice and continue to cook, stirring, for 1–2 minutes.
3 Begin to add the hot stock, a ladleful at a time, stirring as you do so and waiting for the liquid to be absorbed before adding more. The rice will absorb the liquid as it cooks, so keep stirring to keep it moving. Cook for about 15–20 minutes until the consistency of the risotto is dense and creamy but the individual grains of rice are distinct and firm.
4 Add the broad beans, lemon zest and juice and warm through. Stir in the Parmesan and season to taste. Serve the risotto immediately, garnished with grated Parmesan and lemon zest.

Serves 4   preparation: 25 minutes   cooking time: 35 minutes
per serving: 380 cals; 12g fat; 50g carbohydrate

Garlic and Parmesan Risotto

50g (2oz) butter
175g (6oz) onion, peeled and finely chopped
3 garlic cloves, peeled and crushed
225g (8oz) risotto rice
750–900ml (1¼–1½ pints) hot light
   vegetable stock with a splash of white
   wine (optional)

50g (2oz) freshly grated Parmesan cheese
salt and pepper
4–5tbsp chopped flat-leafed parsley

1 Melt half the butter in a large heavy-based pan and stir in the onion. Cook for 8–10 minutes until very soft but not too coloured, then stir in the garlic and rice. Stir thoroughly over the heat to fry the rice lightly in the butter for 2–3 minutes.
2 Pour in a ladleful of the hot stock and let it simmer gently, stirring frequently until the rice has absorbed most of it. Keep adding the stock in this way until the rice is tender but still has a little bite to it; this will take 20–25 minutes and the end result should look creamy and soft.
3 Stir in the remaining butter, the Parmesan, seasoning and parsley and serve.

Serves 4   preparation: 5 minutes   cooking time: 35 minutes
per serving: 370 cals; 15g fat; 48g carbohydrate

Vegetarian

Vegetable Risotto

225g (8oz) broccoli florets
175g (6oz) French beans
salt and pepper
2tbsp olive oil
1 medium onion, peeled and finely chopped
350g (12oz) long-grain or arborio rice

pinch of saffron strands (optional)
4tbsp dry white wine
pared zest and juice of 1 lemon
750ml (1½ pints) hot vegetable stock
175g (6oz) flat mushrooms, sliced
Parmesan cheese, freshly shaved, to serve

1 Blanch the broccoli and beans together in boiling salted water for 3–4 minutes; drain and refresh under cold running water.
2 Heat the olive oil in a heavy-based pan and cook the onion gently for about 2–3 minutes until beginning to soften. Stir in the rice and saffron. Season well and pour in the wine. Add the lemon zest, 2tbsp lemon juice and the hot stock and bring to the boil, stirring.
3 Reduce the heat, cover the pan and simmer for 5 minutes. Stir in all the vegetables, re-cover the pan and simmer for 5 minutes or until the rice is tender and most of the liquid is absorbed.
4 Discard the lemon zest. Serve the risotto topped with Parmesan shavings.

Serves 4   preparation: 15 minutes   cooking time: 20 minutes
per serving: 450 cals; 9g fat; 76g carbohydrate

Lentil Chilli

oil-water spray
2 red onions, peeled and chopped
1½tsp each ground coriander and
   ground cumin
½tsp ground paprika
2 garlic cloves, peeled and crushed
2 sun-dried tomatoes, chopped
¼tsp crushed dried chilli flakes
125ml (4fl oz) red wine

300ml (½ pint) stock
2 x 410g cans brown or green lentils,
   drained and rinsed
2 x 400g cans chopped tomatoes
salt and pepper
sugar, to taste
natural low-fat yogurt and chopped
   coriander or flat-leafed parsley, to garnish

1 Spray a pan with the oil-water spray and cook the onions for 5 minutes. Add the coriander, cumin and paprika. Combine the garlic, sun-dried tomatoes, chilli, wine and stock and add to the pan. Cover and simmer for 5–7 minutes. Uncover and simmer until the onions are very tender and the liquid is almost gone.
2 Stir in the lentils and tomatoes and season to taste. Simmer, uncovered, for 15 minutes until thick and savoury. Stir in the sugar and remove from the heat.
3 Ladle out a quarter of the mixture and whiz in a processor or liquidiser. Combine the puréed and unpuréed portions. Garnish with yogurt and coriander or parsley and serve with rice.

Serves 6   preparation: 10 minutes   cooking time: 30 minutes
per serving: 160 cals; 1g fat; 24g carbohydrate

Stuffed Mushrooms with Wine Risotto

6 large flat mushrooms or 12 small
  flat mushrooms
salt and pepper
4tbsp olive oil
2 shallots, blanched in boiling water,
  drained, peeled and finely chopped
50g (2oz) pitted Kalamata olives, roughly
  chopped
1 garlic clove, peeled and crushed
75g (3oz) fresh breadcrumbs

1tbsp chopped flat-leafed parsley
1tbsp chopped lemon thyme, plus extra
  sprigs to garnish
300ml (½ pint) red wine, plus 2tbsp
75g (3oz) freshly grated Parmesan cheese
125g (4oz) butter
1 onion, peeled and finely chopped
1 stick celery, finely chopped
450g (1lb) risotto rice
1.4 litres (2½ pints) hot vegetable stock

1 Preheat the oven to 180°C (160°C fan oven) mark 4. To make the stuffed mushrooms, cut the stems out of the mushrooms, then chop the stems and put to one side. Lay the mushrooms, stalk side up, in a single layer in a shallow ovenproof dish and season.

2 Heat half the olive oil in a pan, add the shallots and cook until soft. Add the mushroom stalks and olives and cook, stirring, until the shallots are golden. Add the garlic, cook for 1 minute, then remove from the heat. Stir in the breadcrumbs, herbs and the 2tbsp wine and season.

3 Pile the stuffing into the mushrooms, pressing down lightly. Sprinkle with 2tbsp Parmesan and drizzle with the remaining oil. Roast for 25–30 minutes until the mushrooms are tender and the stuffing is golden brown.

4 Meanwhile, make the risotto. Melt half the butter in a large pan, add the onion and celery and cook gently for 10 minutes until soft. Add the remaining wine, bring to the boil, then bubble to reduce to half the original volume.

5 Add the rice and stir to coat with the liquid. Begin to add the hot stock, a ladleful at a time, stirring as you do so and waiting for the liquid to be absorbed before adding more. The rice will absorb the liquid as it cooks, so keep stirring to keep it moving. Cook for 18–20 minutes until the consistency of the risotto is dense and creamy but the individual grains of rice are distinct and firm. Season and stir in the remaining butter and Parmesan. Cover the pan and leave to stand for 5 minutes.

6 Serve the risotto in bowls, topped with the mushrooms and thyme sprigs.

Serves 6   preparation: 25 minutes, plus resting   cooking time: 25–30 minutes
per serving: 660 cals; 32g fat; 70g carbohydrate

Risotto Galette with Melted Taleggio

large pinch of saffron strands
900ml (2 pints) hot vegetable stock
50g (2oz) butter
1 onion, peeled and finely chopped
3 garlic cloves, peeled and crushed
350g (12oz) arborio rice
125ml (4fl oz) dry white wine
4tbsp chopped mixed herbs, such as basil,
  chives, parsley and tarragon

25g (1oz) Parmesan or Cheddar
  cheese, grated
2 large eggs, beaten
salt and pepper
oil, to shallow-fry
225g (8oz) Taleggio cheese, diced

1   Infuse the saffron strands in the hot stock for 10 minutes, then transfer to a pan.
2   Melt the butter in a large heavy-based frying pan over a medium heat, add the onion and garlic and fry for 10 minutes until soft and golden.
3   Add the rice to the onion and stir over the heat for 1 minute until the grains are glossy. Add the wine and boil rapidly until almost all the liquid has evaporated. Heat the saffron-infused stock and keep at a very low simmer.
4   Pour in a ladleful of the hot saffron stock and let it simmer gently, stirring frequently until the rice has absorbed most of it. Keep adding the stock in this way until the rice is tender but still has a little bite to it; this will take 20–25 minutes and the end result should look creamy and soft.
5   Take the pan off the heat, stir in the herbs and grated cheese. Cover with greaseproof paper, press down firmly and put to one side to cool.
6   Stir the eggs into the risotto and season, then divide the mixture in half. Pour a little oil into a 23cm (9 inch) non-stick grill-proof frying pan and heat gently.
7   Spoon half the risotto into the pan and spread evenly to the edges with a palette knife. Sprinkle the Taleggio over and carefully spread the remaining risotto on top. Cook over a low heat for 20 minutes until golden underneath. Preheat the grill to medium-high.
8   Position the frying pan under the grill and cook for 10 minutes until the top is golden. Turn out on to a large plate and allow to cool slightly for 10–15 minutes. Serve warm, cut into wedges.

Serves 4–6   preparation: 15 minutes, plus cooling   cooking time: 1 hour
per serving: 720–480 cals; 34–23g fat; 73–49g carbohydrate

Roasted Vegetable Couscous with Feta

2 peeled red onions, 2 courgettes and 1
   aubergine, all roughly chopped
2 red peppers, halved, deseeded and
   roughly chopped
2 garlic cloves, peeled and sliced
4tbsp olive oil
salt and pepper

350g (12oz) tomatoes, halved
300ml (½ pint) couscous
300ml (½ pint) hot vegetable stock
4tbsp roughly chopped flat-leafed parsley
   (optional)
2tbsp balsamic vinegar
200g (7oz) feta cheese, cubed

1 Preheat the oven to 200°C (180°C fan oven) mark 6. Put the onions, courgettes, aubergine, red peppers and garlic in a roasting tin and drizzle with olive oil. Season, then toss together and roast for 30 minutes.
2 Add the tomatoes to the tin. Toss together and roast for another 30 minutes.
3 Meanwhile, put the couscous in the large bowl. Pour in the hot stock, stir, cover the bowl and soak for 10 minutes.
4 Fluff up the couscous with a fork, then add the parsley, if using, the vinegar and roasted vegetables. Toss together, then spoon into four warmed bowls, sprinkle with the feta cheese and serve.

Serves 4   preparation: 20 minutes, plus soaking   cooking time: 1 hour
per serving: 580 cals; 25g fat; 73g carbohydrate

Roasted Vegetable Salad with Mustard Mayonnaise

900g (2lb) mixed vegetables, such as fennel,
   courgettes, leeks, aubergines, baby
   turnips, new potatoes and red onions
2 garlic cloves, unpeeled
4–5 marjoram or rosemary sprigs
5tbsp olive oil
1tsp flaked sea salt

mixed crushed peppercorns, to taste
4tsp balsamic vinegar
150ml (¼ pint) mayonnaise
2tbsp Dijon mustard
salt and pepper
marjoram sprigs and green olives,
   to garnish

1 Preheat the oven to 220°C (200°C fan oven) mark 7. Quarter the fennel, chop the courgettes, potatoes, leeks and aubergines, trim the turnips and peel the onions and cut into petals. Place the vegetables, garlic, marjoram or rosemary, olive oil, salt and peppercorns in a roasting tin and toss well.
2 Roast for 30–35 minutes, tossing frequently, or until the vegetables are golden. Sprinkle over the vinegar and return to the oven for a further 5 minutes.
3 Mix the mayonnaise with the mustard, then season and put to one side.
4 Arrange the roasted vegetable salad on a plate and garnish with the marjoram sprigs and olives. Serve with the mustard mayonnaise and crusty bread.

Serves 4–6   preparation: 10 minutes   cooking time: 40 minutes
per serving: 490–320 cals; 47–31g fat; 13–8g carbohydrate

Lentil and Ginger Stew

1tbsp olive oil
1 leek, diced
2 carrots, peeled and diced
250g (9oz) Puy lentils
1.4 litres (2½ pints) hot vegetable stock
salt and pepper

200g (7oz) cherry tomatoes on the vine
2 oranges
2.5cm (1 inch) piece fresh root ginger,
   peeled and grated
25g (1oz) almonds, roughly chopped
100g (3½oz) spinach leaves

1 Preheat the oven to 200°C (180°C fan oven) mark 6. Heat 2tsp olive oil in an ovenproof pan. Add the leek and carrots and fry for 6–8 minutes. Stir in the lentils, coating them with the mixture, then pour in the hot stock. Season, cover and bring to the boil, then reduce the heat and cook for a few minutes. Transfer to the oven for 20 minutes or until the lentils are just tender with a slight bite.
2 After the lentils have been cooking for 10 minutes, put the tomatoes in a roasting tin, drizzle with the remaining oil and roast for 8–10 minutes.
3 Meanwhile, remove the skin from the oranges with a sharp knife and cut the flesh into slices, reserving the juice. When the lentils are cooked, remove from the oven and add the orange slices, juice and remaining ingredients. Spoon into bowls with the tomatoes and serve.

Serves 4   preparation: 15 minutes   cooking time: 26–28 minutes
per serving: 310 cals; 9g fat; 42g carbohydrate

Aubergine, Tomato and Lentil Curry

3tbsp olive oil
2 aubergines, cut into 2.5cm (1 inch) chunks
1 onion, peeled and chopped
2tbsp mild curry paste
3 x 400g cans chopped tomatoes

200ml (7fl oz) hot vegetable stock
150g (5oz) red lentils
100g (3½oz) spinach leaves
25g (1oz) coriander, roughly chopped
2tbsp Greek-style 0% fat yogurt

1 Heat 2tbsp olive oil in a large pan and fry the aubergines until golden. Remove from the pan and put to one side.
2 Heat the remaining oil and fry the onion for 8–10 minutes until soft. Add the curry paste and stir-fry for 2 minutes to warm through.
3 Add the tomatoes, hot stock, lentils and reserved aubergine to the pan. Bring to the boil, then reduce the heat to a low simmer, half cover with a lid and simmer for 25 minutes or according to the time stated on the packet.
4 At the end of cooking, stir through the spinach, coriander and yogurt and serve.

Serves 4   preparation: 10 minutes   cooking time: 40–45 minutes
per serving: 310 cals; 13g fat; 37g carbohydrate

Chickpea Curry

2tbsp vegetable oil
2 onions, peeled and finely sliced
2 garlic cloves, peeled and crushed
1tbsp ground coriander
1tsp mild chilli powder
1tbsp black mustard seeds
2tbsp each tamarind paste and sun-dried
   tomato paste

750g (1lb 11oz) new potatoes, quartered
400g can chopped tomatoes
1 litre (1¾ pints) hot vegetable stock
salt and pepper
250g (9oz) green beans, trimmed
2 x 400g cans chickpeas, drained
   and rinsed
2tsp garam masala

1 Heat the oil in a pan and fry the onions for 10–15 minutes until golden – when they've got a good colour they will add depth of flavour. Add the garlic, coriander, chilli, mustard seeds, tamarind paste and sun-dried tomato paste. Cook for 1–2 minutes until the spices release their aroma.
2 Add the potatoes and toss in the spices for 1–2 minutes. Add the tomatoes and hot stock and season. Cover and bring to the boil, then reduce the heat and simmer, half covered, for 20 minutes until the potatoes are just cooked. Add the beans and chickpeas and cook for 5 minutes until the beans are tender and the chickpeas are warmed through. Stir in the garam masala and serve.

Serves 6   preparation: 20 minutes   cooking time: 40–45 minutes
per serving: 220 cals; 7g fat; 35g carbohydrate

Tofu Laksa Curry

2tbsp light soy sauce
½ chopped red chilli
5cm (2 inch) piece fresh root ginger,
   peeled and grated
250g pack organic fresh tofu
1tbsp olive oil
1 onion, peeled and finely sliced
3tbsp laksa paste
200ml (7fl oz) coconut milk

900ml (1½ pints) hot vegetable stock
200g (7oz) baby sweetcorn, halved
   lengthways
salt and pepper
200g (7oz) fine green beans
250g pack medium rice noodles
2 spring onions, sliced diagonally
2tbsp chopped coriander
1 lime, cut into four wedges

1 Put the soy sauce, chilli and ginger in a bowl, add the tofu and leave to marinate.
2 Heat the olive oil in a large pan. Add the onion and fry over a medium heat for 10 minutes, stirring, until golden. Add the laksa paste and cook for 2 minutes. Add the tofu, coconut milk, hot stock and sweetcorn and season. Bring to the boil, add the green beans, reduce the heat and simmer for 8–10 minutes.
4 Meanwhile, put the noodles in a large bowl, pour boiling water over and soak for 30 seconds. Drain, then stir into the curry. Pour into bowls and garnish with the spring onions, coriander and lime. Serve immediately.

Serves 4   preparation: 15 minutes   cooking time: 22 minutes
per serving: 450 cals; 18g fat; 59g carbohydrate

Roasted Vegetables with Mozzarella

2 red onions, peeled, halved and sliced
juice of 1 lemon
2 aubergines, about 600g (1¼lb), halved
   lengthways and sliced
2 yellow and 2 red peppers, each quartered
   and deseeded
2 x 300g packs cherry vine tomatoes
3tbsp olive oil

salt and pepper
4 garlic cloves, unpeeled
2tbsp balsamic vinegar
pinch of sugar
16 basil leaves
125g pack buffalo mozzarella,
   drained and sliced

1   Preheat the oven to 220°C (200°C fan oven) mark 7. Toss the onions together with the lemon juice.
2   Divide the onions, vegetables, tomatoes and olive oil between two roasting tins, season and toss well. Tuck in the garlic and roast for 30–35 minutes or until the tomato skins split. Remove the tomatoes and garlic and put to one side. Roast the remaining vegetables, turning occasionally, for 20–30 minutes.
3   To make the dressing, put half the tomatoes into a food processor. Squeeze the garlic pulp out of the skins and add with the vinegar and sugar and whiz to a purée, then season.
4   Stir the remaining tomatoes into the roasted vegetables and drizzle over the dressing. Scatter with the basil and serve with the mozzarella.

Serves 4   preparation: 30 minutes   cooking time: 50 minutes–1 hour 5 minutes
per serving: 300 cals; 19g fat; 20g carbohydrate

Roasted Vegetable Bake

12 shallots, blanched in boiling water,
   drained, peeled and halved
1 small squash, about 450g (1lb), halved,
   deseeded and cut into large chunks
2 medium sweet potatoes, about 350g
   (12oz), peeled and cut into large chunks
3tbsp olive oil

1 small red chilli, deseeded and
   finely chopped
1 marinated red pepper, drained
100ml (3½fl oz) vinaigrette dressing
125g (4oz), about 5 slices, chilled
   garlic bread
small handful of flat-leafed parsley

1   Preheat the oven to 220°C (200°C fan oven) mark 7. Put the shallots, squash and sweet potatoes in a roasting tin with the olive oil and the chilli, then toss well. Roast for about 40 minutes until the vegetables are golden and tender.
2   Meanwhile, put the red pepper and vinaigrette in a blender or food processor and whiz together. Gently stir this pepper dressing into the hot roasted vegetables. Put the garlic bread and parsley in the processor or blender (no need to rinse it), and whiz to make rough breadcrumbs. Sprinkle over the roasted vegetables and return to the oven for 10–15 minutes until crisp and golden.

Serves 4   preparation: 15 minutes   cooking time: 50–55 minutes
per serving: 470 cals; 26g fat; 54g carbohydrate

Nut and Cranberry Terrine

125g (4oz) long-grain rice
salt and pepper
4tbsp olive oil
1 onion, peeled and finely chopped
1 leek, thinly sliced
4 celery sticks, thinly sliced
4tbsp chopped mixed herbs, such as sage,
   parsley and thyme
40g (1½oz) walnuts, toasted and
   roughly ground
125g (4oz) dolcelatte cheese, crumbled
1 large egg, lightly beaten

40g (1½oz) fresh white breadcrumbs
125ml (4fl oz) fromage frais or
   crème fraîche
225g (8oz) plain flour, plus extra to dust
45g (1½oz) white vegetable fat
15g (1oz) butter
125g (4oz) redcurrant jelly
1tsp lemon juice
125g (4oz) cranberries or redcurrants,
   thawed if frozen
bay leaves, to garnish

1   Cook the rice in boiling salted water for the time stated on the packet, until just tender. Refresh under cold running water, drain thoroughly and put to one side.

2   Heat the olive oil in a frying pan, add the onion, leek, celery and herbs and fry gently for 10 minutes until softened; transfer to a bowl. Add the walnuts, cheese and beaten egg to the fried mixture with the rice, breadcrumbs and fromage frais or crème fraîche. Season generously and stir until evenly combined.

3   Preheat the oven to 220°C (200°C fan oven) mark 7. For the pastry, sift the flour with a pinch of salt into a bowl and make a well in the middle. Heat 100ml (3½fl oz) water with the fat and butter in a pan until the liquid comes to the boil. Pour into the flour and gradually work together, using a wooden spoon.

4   When cool enough to handle, bring the dough together and knead lightly until smooth. Roll out on a lightly floured surface to a 25.5 x 20.5cm (10 x 8 inch) rectangle and use to line a 900g (2lb) loaf tin, pressing the dough into the corners; trim the overhanging pastry and reserve.

5   Spoon the filling into the pastry case and smooth the surface. Divide the pastry trimmings in half, roll each piece into a long thin rope and plait together.

6   Dampen the pastry edges and top with the pastry plait, pressing down gently. Bake for 45–50 minutes until golden and a skewer inserted into the centre comes out hot. Remove from the oven and leave to cool.

7   For the topping, heat the redcurrant jelly in a small pan with the lemon juice and 1tbsp water until melted, then simmer for 3 minutes. Remove from the heat and stir in the fruit.

8   To unmould the pie, upturn and tap gently, then set on a board. Spoon the topping over and leave to set. When cold, garnish with bay leaves. Cut into generous slices to serve.

Serves 8–10   preparation: 45 minutes, plus cooling   cooking time: 45–50 minutes
per serving: 450–360 cals; 23–18g fat; 52–41g carbohydrate

No cook

Sometimes you just can't be bothered to cook. It's too hot, you're tired, short of time, or just want something light.

Crunchy, refreshing salads are the obvious answer, whether fruit-, fish-, meat- or cheese-based; with vegetables; or just green leaves – such as Crisp Green Salad with Blue Cheese Dressing, pairing crisp salad leaves with a Roquefort dressing and croûtons.

Fennel is great either cooked or raw – in Fennel Salad its lovely aniseed flavour works brilliantly with just a simple walnut oil and mustard dressing. Peppery watercress is another healthy salad choice – low in calories and rich in vitamins. Combined with pears and blue cheese it makes a salad bursting with flavour.

For something more substantial, grains, pulses and beans go really well with onions, herbs and a good dressing and are very quick to put together. Try a robust Bean, Celery and Chorizo Salad, or a Chickpea Salad with Lemon and Parsley. Dare to be different? Japanese Crab Salad looks fantastic and has a taste to match, while Thai Prawn Salad combines tiger prawns with chilli, ginger and sesame oil.

Classic Little Gem Salad

4 little gem lettuce
6tbsp extra-virgin olive oil

juice of 1 lemon
salt and pepper

1 Pull off the leaves separately from each lettuce – the further into the heart you go, the sweeter and crisper the leaves become – then arrange in individual bowls.
2 To make the salad dressing, put the olive oil and lemon juice in a screw-topped jar. Season and shake well to combine. Drizzle over the lettuces and serve as a side salad.

Serves 4 preparation: 10 minutes
per serving: 180 cals; 20g fat; 1g carbohydrate

Fennel Salad

2 fennel bulbs
2tbsp white wine vinegar
6tbsp walnut oil

2tsp Dijon mustard
salt and pepper

1 Trim the ends from the fennel and reserve any fronds to garnish. Use a mandolin or very sharp knife to slice the bulbs really finely lengthways. Put in a bowl and sprinkle over half the vinegar.
2 In another bowl, mix the walnut oil with the remaining vinegar and mustard, then season well. Drizzle over the fennel and toss well, then garnish with the fennel fronds and serve.

Serves 6 preparation: 10 minutes
per serving: 110 cals; 11g fat; 1g carbohydrate

Antipasti Salad

juice of 1 lime
black pepper
4 ripe peaches or nectarines, halved,
  stoned and sliced
50g (2oz) rocket leaves
4–5 small firm round goat's cheeses,
  thickly sliced

4 grilled red peppers, sliced, or a 285g
  jar pimientos, drained
2 small red onions, peeled and sliced
  into petals
handful of black olives
olive oil, to drizzle

1 Squeeze the lime juice over the fruit and add a sprinkling of pepper.
2 Starting in the centre with the rocket, arrange all the ingredients in lines on a large serving plate. Cover with clingfilm and keep in a cool place. Use within 2 hours. Drizzle with oil just before serving.

Serves 6 preparation: 20 minutes
per serving: 150 cals; 9g fat; 13g carbohydrate

Rocket and Onion Salad

salt and pepper
2tbsp lemon juice
4tbsp olive oil

1 small white onion, peeled and finely sliced
225g (8oz) rocket
lemon zest, to garnish

1 To make the dressing, put the seasoning in a small bowl and whisk in the lemon juice and olive oil.
2 To make the salad, put the onion in a large bowl with the rocket. Pour over the dressing and toss, then garnish with lemon zest. Serve either in a large salad bowl or on individual plates.

Serves 2   preparation: 10 minutes
per serving: 270 cals; 26g fat; 7g carbohydrate

Sweet Cucumber Salad

1tbsp white wine vinegar
2tbsp golden caster sugar
½tsp salt

pepper
½ cucumber, sliced into thin strips
basil leaves, to garnish

1 Mix the vinegar with the sugar, 2tbsp boiling water and the salt. Season with pepper and leave to cool.
2 Mix the cucumber and dressing together, cover and chill for up to 1 hour. Garnish with basil leaves and serve.

Serves 2   preparation: 5 minutes, plus chilling
per serving: 70 cals; trace fat; 17g carbohydrate

Three-pepper Salad

3tbsp olive oil
2 tsp balsamic vinegar
½tsp golden caster sugar
1tsp Dijon mustard
2tsp pink peppercorns

175g (6oz) frisée lettuce
25g (1oz) rocket leaves
125g (4oz) radishes, leaves and
   roots removed

1 To make the dressing, combine the olive oil, vinegar, sugar, mustard and peppercorns in a bowl, then whisk thoroughly.
2 Put the lettuce and rocket in a large bowl. Thinly slice the radishes into sticks, and toss with the frisée and rocket. Cover and chill.
3 Just before serving, stir the dressing and pour over the leaves. Toss well until evenly mixed, then serve immediately.

Serves 4–6   preparation: 15 minutes
per serving: 100–70 cals; 10–7g fat; 2–1g carbohydrate

Avocado Salad

2 large ripe avocados, halved, stoned,
  peeled and cut into eight lengthways
300g (11oz) small tomatoes on the
  vine, halved
1 fennel bulb, thinly sliced
1 small red onion, peeled and sliced
100g (3½oz) feta cheese, diced

50g (2oz) small pepperoni sausage – or
  any other spicy sausage – thinly sliced
plenty of cress or 1 bunch of watercress
75ml (3fl oz) salad dressing – either our
  easy Two-minute Dressing (page 17),
  or a good-quality ready-made one

1 Put the avocados into a large salad bowl. Add the tomatoes, fennel, onion, feta, pepperoni and cress or watercress.
2 Drizzle over the dressing, then toss carefully and serve.

Serves 4 preparation: 15 minutes
per serving: 380 cals; 35g fat; 5g carbohydrate

Spinach and Beetroot Salad

2–3tbsp extra-virgin olive oil
1tbsp balsamic vinegar
salt and pepper
100g (3½oz) fresh spinach

2 cooked beetroot, halved and sliced
leaves from 2 mint sprigs, roughly torn
100g (3½oz) feta cheese, roughly crumbled

1 Put the olive oil in a large bowl. Add the balsamic vinegar, season well and use a balloon whisk to mix. Add the spinach, beetroot and mint and toss in the dressing.
2 Divide the salad between two plates, sprinkle with the feta cheese, season with pepper and serve.

Serves 2 preparation: 10 minutes
per serving: 280 cals; 24g fat; 6g carbohydrate

Tomato and Oregano Salad

700g (1½lb) beef tomatoes, sliced
1 bunch of spring onions, sliced
6 oregano sprigs

salt and pepper
pinch of golden caster sugar
3tbsp olive oil, to drizzle

1 Arrange a layer of tomatoes on a plate, then scatter on a few spring onions, some oregano, seasoning, sugar and olive oil.
2 Layer the remaining ingredients; cover and chill for 1–2 hours.

Serves 6 preparation: 10 minutes, plus chilling
per serving: 80 cals; 7g fat; 5g carbohydrate

Summer Crunch Salad

2tbsp lemon juice
125ml (4fl oz) olive oil
salt and pepper
150g (5oz) French beans, halved
150g (5oz) courgettes, cut into thin
  matchsticks
150g (5oz) fennel, cut into thin matchsticks

200g (7oz) cherry tomatoes, halved if large
25g (1oz) roughly chopped basil
4 slices Parma ham
1tbsp light muscovado sugar
25g (1oz) flaked almonds, lightly toasted
Parmesan cheese, freshly shaved and basil
  sprigs, to garnish

1 To make the dressing, put the lemon juice, olive oil and seasoning in a small bowl, whisk to combine, then cover and set aside.
2 For the salad, blanch the French beans in boiling salted water for 1 minute, drain, refresh in cold water and drain again. Mix all the vegetables together in a large bowl, toss the chopped basil through and season.
3 Preheat the grill to hot. Put the Parma ham on a baking sheet, sprinkle with the sugar and put under the grill for 2–3 minutes or until golden.
4 Mix the dressing and almonds into the salad and serve with the Parma ham, garnished with Parmesan shavings and basil sprigs.

Serves 4   preparation: 15 minutes
per serving: 370 cals; 34g fat; 8g carbohydrate

08

No cook

Panzanella Salad

2–3 thick slices from a day-old country loaf,
  about 100g (3½oz), crusts removed, cubed
450g (1lb) ripe tomatoes, roughly chopped
2tbsp capers
1tsp chopped thyme
1 small red onion, peeled and thinly sliced
2 garlic cloves, peeled and crushed
2 small red chillies, deseeded and
  finely chopped
4tbsp extra-virgin olive oil

125g (4oz) pitted black olives
50g (2oz) sun-dried tomatoes,
  roughly chopped
salt and pepper
8 basil leaves
25g (1oz) Parmesan cheese, freshly shaved
thyme sprigs and crushed black pepper,
  to garnish

1 Put the bread in a large bowl with the tomatoes, capers, thyme, onion, garlic, chillies, olive oil, black olives and sun-dried tomatoes. Season well, then toss together and leave in a cool place for 30 minutes.
2 Toss the salad thoroughly again and scatter the torn basil leaves and Parmesan shavings over. Garnish with thyme sprigs and crushed black pepper, then serve.

Serves 4   preparation: 20 minutes, plus 30 minutes chilling
per serving: 300 cals; 19g fat; 23g carbohydrate

Carrot and Celeriac Salad

2tsp hoisin sauce
4tsp rice wine vinegar
2tsp soy sauce
1tbsp peanut oil
1tsp sesame oil

2tsp runny honey
225g (8oz) each carrot and celeriac or mooli
75g (3oz) roasted, salted peanuts,
  finely chopped
50g (2oz) alfalfa or 125g (4oz) beansprouts

1 Whisk the first six ingredients together in a small bowl.
2 Peel and coarsely grate or shred the carrot and celeriac. Put in a large bowl with the peanuts, pour the dressing over and mix well. Stir in the alfalfa or beansprouts and serve immediately.

Serves 4 preparation: 20 minutes
per serving: 200 cals; 14g fat; 11g carbohydrate

Vegetable Crudités

2 small carrots, peeled and chopped
  into batons
2 celery sticks, chopped into batons
½ cucumber, chopped into batons

1 bunch of radishes, leaves
  and roots removed
handful of cherry tomatoes
1 loaf of French bread
garlic mayonnaise, to serve

1 Arrange all the vegetables on a plate.
2 Slice the French bread into chunks and serve with the crudités and garlic mayonnaise for dipping.

Serves 4 preparation: 10 minutes
per serving: 350 cals; 4g fat; 71g carbohydrate

Crisp Green Salad with Blue Cheese Dressing

100g (3½oz) Roquefort cheese
2tbsp low-fat natural yogurt
1tbsp white wine vinegar
5tbsp extra-virgin olive oil

salt and pepper
2 baby cos or 2 hearts of romaine lettuce
50g (2oz) croûtons

1 To make the dressing, put half the Roquefort into a food processor, add the yogurt, vinegar and olive oil and whiz for 1 minute until combined. Season. Separate the lettuce leaves, wash in cold water and dry in a salad spinner or on kitchen paper. Arrange in a shallow dish, tearing any large leaves in two, and scatter the croûtons over. Pour over the dressing and crumble over the remaining Roquefort.

Serves 4 preparation: 15 minutes
per serving: 310 cals; 29g fat; 7g carbohydrate

Mexican Gazpacho with Tortilla Chips

900g (2 lb) ripe tomatoes
4 garlic cloves, peeled
50g (2oz) fresh white breadcrumbs
6tbsp extra-virgin olive oil
juice of 1½ small limes
1 red chilli, deseeded and chopped
2 cucumbers, deseeded and chopped
2 bunches of spring onions, chopped
1 red pepper, deseeded and chopped

600ml (1 pint) tomato juice
6tbsp chopped coriander leaves, plus
    coriander sprigs to garnish
salt and pepper
1 large avocado
juice of ½ small lime
142ml carton soured cream (optional)
175g bag tortilla chips, to serve

1   Score a cross in the skin at the base of each tomato, then put into a bowl. Pour over enough boiling
    water to cover, leave for 30 seconds, then transfer to a bowl of cold water. Peel, discarding the skins,
    then cut into quarters. Discard the seeds.
2   Put the tomatoes, garlic, breadcrumbs, olive oil, lime juice, chilli, cucumbers, spring onions, red
    pepper, tomato juice and coriander into a large bowl and mix well, then whiz together in batches in
    a food processor until smooth. Transfer to a bowl, season and stir. Cover and chill for at least 2 hours.
3   Just before serving, halve, stone, peel and roughly dice the avocado, then toss in lime juice to coat.
    Serve the soup garnished with soured cream, if using, the avocado, a sprinkling of black pepper and
    coriander. Serve the tortilla chips separately.

Serves 8   preparation: 25–30 minutes, plus chilling
per serving: 330 cals; 22g fat; 28g carbohydrate

Chilli Beef Noodle Salad

150g (5oz) dried rice noodles
juice of 1 lime
1 lemon grass stalk, outside leaves
    discarded, and finely chopped
1 red chilli, deseeded and chopped
2tsp finely chopped fresh root ginger
2tsp golden caster sugar

2 garlic cloves, peeled and crushed
1tbsp Thai fish sauce
3tbsp extra-virgin olive oil
salt and pepper
50g (2oz) rocket, preferably wild
125g (4oz) sliced cold roast beef
125g (4oz) sunblush tomatoes, chopped

1   Put the noodles in a large bowl and pour over boiling water to cover. Put to one side for 15 minutes.
2   Meanwhile, in a small bowl, whisk together the lime juice, lemon grass, chilli, ginger, sugar, garlic, fish
    sauce and olive oil. Season to taste.
3   While the noodles are still warm, drain well, then put them in a large bowl and toss with the dressing.
    Leave to cool.
4   Just before serving, toss the rocket leaves, sliced beef and sunblush tomatoes through the noodles.

Serves 4   preparation: 15 minutes, plus soaking
per serving: 310 cals; 13g fat; 36g carbohydrate

Spinach, Dolcelatte Cheese and Walnut Salad

1 ciabatta or small baguette
9tbsp walnut oil
200g (7oz) baby leaf spinach
250g (9oz) dolcelatte cheese, sliced
1 fennel bulb, sliced

50g (2oz) walnut pieces
2 oranges, peeled, pith removed,
   segmented and juice put to one side
salt and pepper
1tbsp Dijon mustard

1   Preheat the oven to 200°C (180°C fan oven) mark 6. Cut the loaf into three slices lengthways, then cut each slice into two. Put on to a baking sheet and drizzle with 3tbsp oil. Bake for 15–20 minutes or until crisp and light brown.
2   Arrange the spinach, cheese and fennel in six salad bowls, scatter over the walnut pieces and orange segments and season generously.
3   Whisk together the orange juice, remaining oil and the mustard. Drizzle over the salad and serve.

Serves 6   preparation: 5 minutes   cooking time: 15–20 minutes
per serving: 470 cals; 36g fat; 23g carbohydrate

Goat's Cheese and Walnut Salad

1 large radicchio
2 bunches of watercress, trimmed
1 red onion, peeled and finely sliced
2tbsp red wine vinegar
8tbsp olive oil

large pinch of golden caster sugar
salt and pepper
2 x 100g packs mild goat's cheese
150g (5oz) walnut pieces

1   Tear the radicchio leaves into bite-sized pieces and put into a large salad bowl with the watercress and red onion.
2   To make the dressing, put the wine vinegar, olive oil and sugar in a screw-topped jar and season, then shake well to combine.
3   Pour the dressing over the salad and toss. Crumble the goat's cheese on top and sprinkle with the walnuts. Serve with French bread as a starter, or light lunch.

Serves 6   preparation: 10 minutes
per serving: 370 cals, 36g fat; 4g carbohydrate

Pear, Grape and Parmesan Salad

1tbsp white wine vinegar
½tsp Dijon mustard
3tbsp walnut oil
1tbsp sunflower oil
salt and pepper
125g (4oz) white seedless grapes, halved

2 large ripe pears, peeled, cored
 and thickly sliced
2 x 70g bags rocket
175g (6oz) Parmesan cheese, freshly
 shaved
50g (2oz) walnut pieces

1 Put the vinegar, mustard and oils into a small bowl. Season, then whisk together until thoroughly emulsified.
2 Put the grapes and pears into a bowl, pour the dressing over and toss together. Leave to marinate for 15 minutes.
3 At the last minute, tear the rocket into smallish pieces, put in a large bowl, add the grape mixture and toss together. Serve the salad topped with the Parmesan shavings and the walnuts.

Serves 4   preparation: 15 minutes, plus marinating
per serving: 460 cals; 34g fat; 20g carbohydrate

Tomato, Rocket and Parmesan Salad

150g bag gourmet salad leaves
50g bag rocket
250g punnet baby plum tomatoes, cut in
 half lengthways
50g (2oz) pine nuts, toasted

3tbsp extra-virgin olive oil
1tbsp balsamic vinegar
salt and pepper
75g (3oz) Parmesan cheese, freshly shaved

1 Put the salad leaves and rocket in a bowl of ice-cold water. Leave for a few minutes to crisp up, then drain through a colander and shake to remove excess water. Put in a serving dish, add the tomatoes and pine nuts and toss well.
2 Mix the olive oil with the vinegar in a separate bowl and season. Pour over the salad, toss well, then scatter the Parmesan shavings on top and serve.

Serves 6   preparation: 10–15 minutes
per serving: 190 cals; 17g fat; 2g carbohydrate

Roquefort and Redcurrant Salad

1½tbsp redcurrant jelly
1tbsp white wine vinegar
pinch of English mustard powder
4tbsp extra-virgin olive oil
salt and pepper
a selection of bitter leaves such as curly
  endive, radicchio and chicory

225g (8oz) Roquefort cheese, crumbled
125g (4oz) punnet fresh redcurrants –
  reserve four sprays to garnish and
  destalk the rest

1 In a small bowl, whisk together the redcurrant jelly, 1tsp boiling water, the vinegar, mustard powder and olive oil, then season to taste.
2 Arrange the mixed salad leaves and Roquefort on a large plate. Spoon the dressing over the top and sprinkle with the redcurrants. Garnish with redcurrant sprays and serve immediately.

Serves 4 preparation: 10 minutes
per serving: 360 cals; 32g fat; 6g carbohydrate

Watercress, Pear and Blue Cheese Salad

2tbsp balsamic vinegar
2tbsp walnut or hazelnut oil
3tbsp olive oil
1 garlic clove, peeled
½tsp sea salt
1tsp English mustard powder
pepper

2 large pears
1 bunch of watercress, about 175g (6oz), or
  mixed green salad leaves such as rocket,
  endive and frisée
150g (5oz) sprouted beans
125g (4oz) blue cheese, e.g. Roquefort,
  Gorgonzola or Stilton, roughly crumbled

1 Combine the vinegar and oils in a bowl. Using a pestle and mortar or with the back of a strong knife on a chopping board, crush the garlic with the salt until it's creamy. Add the mustard and work that into the paste. Whisk into the vinegar and oils and season to taste with pepper.
2 Quarter or halve the pears (peel, if wished) and brush with a little of the dressing to prevent discolouration.
3 Mix the watercress, sprouted beans and pears in a large bowl and drizzle with 3tbsp dressing. Add the cheese and toss the salad. Serve immediately.

Serves 4 preparation: 20 minutes
per serving: 350 cals; 28g fat; 15g carbohydrate

Tomato, Mozzarella and Red Pesto Salad

225g (8oz) baby plum tomatoes, halved
225g (8oz) baby mozzarella, drained
100g jar red pepper pesto
185g jar pitted black olives, drained

salt and pepper
100g bag mixed salad leaves
basil sprigs, to garnish

1 Put the tomatoes, mozzarella, pesto and olives in a large bowl. Season with pepper, but check the seasoning before adding any salt, as the olives are already salty. Cover the bowl and put to one side.
2 Just before serving, toss the mixed leaves with the tomato mixture and garnish with fresh basil sprigs.

Serves 4   preparation: 10 minutes
per serving: 350 cals; 28g fat; 3g carbohydrate

Tomato, Mozzarella and Basil Salad with Balsamic Dressing

2tbsp balsamic vinegar
4tbsp extra-virgin olive oil
salt and pepper
25g (1oz) pine nuts

3 ripe beef tomatoes, sliced
125g pack buffalo mozzarella, drained and
  torn into bite-sized pieces
15 small basil leaves

1 To make the dressing, put the balsamic vinegar and olive oil into a small bowl, whisk together and season generously.
2 Put the pine nuts into a dry frying pan and toast, stirring, for 3 minutes. Set aside to cool.
3 Arrange the tomatoes and mozzarella on a large plate or shallow dish, season and drizzle with the dressing. Scatter the pine nuts and basil on top and serve.

Serves 4   preparation: 15 minutes
per serving: 260 cals; 24g fat; 2g carbohydrate

Tomato, Basil and Olive Salad

700g (1½lb) on-the-vine tomatoes, sliced
2 x 200g tub Pomodorino (baby plum)
  tomatoes, halved lengthways
20 basil leaves, roughly torn

340g jar queen green olives in brine, drained
salt and pepper
3tbsp balsamic vinegar
3tbsp extra-virgin olive oil

1 Layer all the tomatoes in a glass bowl with the basil and olives, seasoning as you go.
2 To make the dressing, put the balsamic vinegar and olive oil in a screw-topped jar. Seal and shake well, then pour over the salad. Chill for up to 4 hours until needed.

Serves 12   preparation: 15 minutes
per serving: 70 cals; 6g fat; 3g carbohydrate

Tomato and Red Onion Salad

100ml (3½fl oz) extra-virgin olive oil
50ml (2fl oz) balsamic vinegar
pinch of golden caster sugar
salt and pepper
500g (1lb 2oz) baby plum tomatoes, halved
bunch of spring onions, sliced
500g (1lb 2oz) plum tomatoes, sliced
  lengthways

15g pack basil leaves, roughly torn, and
  large sprigs reserved to garnish
2 beef tomatoes, about 600g (1¼lb), sliced
100g (3½oz) pine nuts, toasted
250g (9oz) medium tomatoes, cut
  into wedges

1 Put the olive oil in a bowl, mix in the balsamic vinegar and sugar, then season well.
2 Layer the baby plum tomatoes, spring onions, plum tomatoes, basil, beef tomatoes, pine nuts and finally the medium tomatoes in a deep bowl or vase, seasoning between each layer.
3 Drizzle the dressing over to finish and set aside for 1 hour. Garnish with the basil sprigs before serving.

Serves 8   preparation: 25 minutes, plus standing
per serving: 230 cals; 25g fat; 6g carbohydrate

Mixed Bean Salad with Lemon Vinaigrette

400g can mixed beans, drained and rinsed
400g can chickpeas, drained and rinsed
2 shallots, peeled and chopped
2tbsp lemon juice
salt and pepper

2tsp runny honey
8tbsp extra-virgin olive oil
3tbsp chopped fresh mint
4tbsp roughly chopped flat-leafed parsley
mint sprigs and lemon zest, to garnish

1 Put the beans, chickpeas and shallots in a bowl.
2 To make the vinaigrette, whisk together the lemon juice, seasoning and honey. Gradually whisk in the olive oil and stir in the chopped herbs.
3 Toss the bean mixture in the dressing, then garnish with the mint and lemon zest and serve.

Serves 6   preparation: 15 minutes
per serving: 260 cals; 19g fat; 18g carbohydrate

Herbed Bulgur Wheat Salad

175g (6oz) bulgur or cracked wheat
2 tomatoes, deseeded and diced
½ cucumber, deseeded and diced
2 shallots, peeled and chopped
4tbsp chopped mint, plus leaves to garnish

4tbsp chopped flat-leafed parsley
salt and pepper
3tbsp olive oil
juice of 1 lemon

1 Put the bulgur wheat in a bowl, pour on 300ml (½ pint) boiling water and cover. Leave to soak for 5–10 minutes until all the water is absorbed. Fork through, then set aside to cool.
2 Add the tomatoes, cucumber, shallots and chopped herbs to the bulgur. Mix well and season to taste.
3 Add the olive oil and lemon juice and toss to mix. Leave to stand for a few hours if time, to allow the flavours to infuse. Garnish with mint leaves to serve.

Serves 8   preparation: 10 minutes plus standing
per serving: 130 cals, 5g fat; 18g carbohydrate

Bean, Celery and Chorizo Salad

410g can borlotti beans, drained and rinsed
4 large sticks celery, finely sliced
75g pack chorizo sausage, diced
2 shallots, peeled and finely chopped

2tbsp roughly chopped flat-leafed parsley
grated zest of ½ lemon and 1tbsp lemon juice
4tbsp extra-virgin olive oil
salt and pepper

1 Put the borlotti beans in a large bowl, add the celery, chorizo, shallot and parsley.
2 Put the lemon zest, lemon juice and olive oil into a small bowl and season, then whisk to combine.
3 Pour the dressing over the bean mixture, toss and serve.

Serves 4   preparation: 20 minutes
per serving: 250 cals; 18g fat; 15g carbohydrate

Bean and Avocado

4tbsp lemon juice
4tbsp olive oil
400g can mixed beans, drained and rinsed
1 red onion, peeled and chopped

4 celery sticks, diced
2 avocados, halved, stoned,
   peeled and diced
chopped coriander, to garnish

Put the lemon juice in a serving bowl and mix in the olive oil. Put the beans, onion, celery and avocado in the bowl and toss in the dressing. Add the coriander and serve.

Serves 4   preparation: 10 minutes
per serving: 370 cals; 30g fat; 17g carbohydrate

Bulgur and Carrot Salad

250g (9oz) bulgur wheat
1 cucumber, halved, deseeded and diced
15g pack each flat-leafed parsley, mint and
   coriander, roughly chopped
juice of 1 lemon
100ml (3½fl oz) olive oil

salt and pepper
2 large carrots, peeled and grated
50g (2oz) sunflower seeds
juice of 1 small orange
125g (4oz) alfalfa sprouts (from healthfood
   stores) or beansprouts

1 Put the bulgur wheat into a large bowl and cover with 300ml (½ pint) boiling water. Cover and set aside
   for 15 minutes to absorb the water and soften, yet still retain a slight bite.
2 Add the cucumber, herbs, lemon juice and olive oil to the bowl, season well and stir together. Spoon
   the bulgur into the bottom of a deep serving dish.
3 Mix the grated carrot with the sunflower seeds and orange juice, season, then spoon on top of the
   bulgur. Top with alfalfa or beansprouts and serve.

Serves 8   preparation: 20 minutes, plus standing
per serving: 260 cals; 14g fat; 28g carbohydrate

Chickpea Salad with Lemon and Parsley

juice of ½ lemon
6tbsp extra-virgin olive oil
salt and pepper
2 x 400g cans chickpeas, drained
   and rinsed

1 small red onion, peeled and finely sliced
4tbsp chopped flat-leafed parsley, plus
   extra sprigs to garnish

1 First make the dressing. Put the lemon juice and olive oil into a bowl and whisk together. Season
   generously.
2 Tip the chickpeas into a large salad bowl, add the onion and chopped parsley, then drizzle over the
   dressing. Mix well and check the seasoning. Set aside for 5 minutes to allow the onion to soften
   slightly in the dressing.
3 Serve the salad garnished with parsley sprigs.

Serves 4   preparation: 15 minutes, plus standing
per serving: 350 cals; 23g fat; 25g carbohydrate

Japanese Crab Salad

300g (11oz) courgettes
300g (11oz) carrots
1tbsp rice wine vinegar
3tbsp mirin (a Japanese seasoning,
  available from supermarkets) or
  sweet sherry

salt and pepper
2 dressed crab, 175g (6oz) each
1–2tsp Japanese pickled ginger,
  sliced or chopped
1/8tsp wasabi paste, plus a little to garnish
pickled ginger, to garnish

1 Using a wide vegetable peeler, cut the courgettes and carrots into thin ribbons, put into a bowl of iced water and chill for 15 minutes.
2 Drain and dry the ribbons very well, then put them into a large bowl, add the vinegar and 2tbsp mirin and season. Divide between four plates.
3 Pick over the crab meat and remove any remnants of shell, then put the crab meat into a bowl. Add the pickled ginger, wasabi paste and remaining mirin and season.
4 Spoon the crab meat on top of the vegetable ribbons, garnish with the pickled ginger and a little – make sure it's a little! – wasabi. Serve chilled.

Serves 4 preparation: 20 minutes, plus chilling
per serving: 160 cals; 5g fat; 7g carbohydrate

Crab, Melon and Cucumber Salad

2tbsp white wine vinegar
150ml (1/4 pint) olive oil
salt and pepper
2tbsp pickled ginger, chopped
2.5cm (1 inch) piece fresh root ginger,
  peeled and grated
225g (8oz) fresh white crab meat, flaked,
  with claws if available

1 large head chicory, trimmed and leaves
  separated
1/2 cucumber, about 275g (10oz), pared into
  ribbons with a peeler
1 charentais melon, peeled and cut into
  quarters, each about 175g (6oz)
pickled ginger and chives, to garnish

1 To make the dressing, whisk the vinegar and olive oil together and season. Put the pickled ginger and root ginger in a bowl. Toss the crab meat in half the dressing.
2 Arrange a few chicory leaves, cucumber ribbons and a melon quarter on each plate. Spoon over the crab meat and remaining dressing and garnish with pickled ginger and chives to serve.

Serves 4 preparation: 20 minutes
per serving: 360 cals; 33g fat; 4g carbohydrate

Gravadlax with Cucumber Salad

1 small cucumber, halved,
   deseeded and thinly sliced
3tbsp white wine vinegar
1tbsp golden caster sugar
3tbsp chopped dill
salt and pepper

2 x 125g packs gravadlax with dill and
   mustard sauce
4tbsp crème fraîche
12 mini blinis
dill sprigs, to garnish

1 Arrange the cucumber slices on a large plate. Mix the white wine vinegar with the sugar and dill, then season to taste. Pour the dressing over the cucumber and marinate for 15 minutes.
2 Mix the dill and mustard sauce into the crème fraîche and season to taste.
3 Lightly toast the mini blinis. Arrange the marinated cucumber on four serving plates with the slices of gravadlax, the crème fraîche sauce and the blinis. Garnish with dill sprigs to serve.

Serves 4   preparation: 15 minutes, plus marinating
per serving: 340 cals; 10g fat; 42g carbohydrate

Thai Prawn Salad

1 red pepper, halved, deseeded and sliced
50g (2oz) beansprouts
2 celery sticks, sliced finely
1 carrot, cut into ribbons
   with a vegetable peeler
125g (4oz) cucumber, cut into fine strips
50g (2oz) cashews, chopped and toasted
125g (4oz) cooked tiger prawns
1 small red chilli, halved, deseeded
   and diced

2.5cm (1 inch) fresh root ginger,
   peeled and diced
½ lemon grass stalk, diced
4tbsp seasoned rice wine vinegar,
   such as Mitsukan
2tsp sesame oil
salt and pepper
4tbsp roughly chopped coriander leaves

1 Put the red pepper, beansprouts, celery, carrot, cucumber, cashew nuts and prawns in a large bowl.
2 To make the dressing, mix the chilli, ginger, lemon grass, vinegar and sesame oil and season well.
3 Pour the dressing over the salad and toss together. Add the chopped coriander leaves and serve immediately.

Serves 2   preparation: 10 minutes
per serving: 292 cals; 19g fat; 12g carbohydrate

Trout, Tomato and Lemon Salad

4 ripe tomatoes, preferably
   vine-ripened, sliced
golden caster sugar, to sprinkle
salt and pepper
1½ thin-skinned lemons
5tbsp crème fraîche

2tbsp horseradish cream
2tbsp dill and mustard sauce
2tbsp lemon juice
2 x 135g packs smoked trout fillets, flaked
4 thick slices country-style bread, toasted
1 little gem lettuce, broken into small leaves

1   Put the tomatoes on a plate, sprinkle on a little sugar and season. Cover and put to one side.
2   Finely grate the zest from ½ lemon and put in a bowl with the crème fraîche, horseradish cream, dill and mustard sauce and lemon juice, then whisk together and season.
3   Add the smoked trout to the crème fraîche mixture and toss together. Arrange the tomatoes on the toast and spoon any tomato juice over. Arrange the lettuce leaves and trout mixture on top of the tomatoes. Peel and very thinly slice the remaining lemon. Garnish the trout with the lemon slices and serve.

Serves 4   preparation: 20 minutes
per serving: 330 cals; 13g fat; 33g carbohydrate

Smoked Mackerel Salad

450g (1lb) new potatoes, halved lengthways
4tbsp extra-virgin olive oil
salt and pepper
3 smoked mackerel fillets, skinned and
   broken into strips

250g (9oz) cherry tomatoes, halved
½ cucumber, diced
85g bag watercress
2tsp creamed horseradish
2tbsp white wine vinegar

1   Put the potatoes in a pan of lightly salted water, bring to the boil, then reduce the heat and simmer for 10 minutes or until tender.
2   Drain the potatoes well, tip back into the pan and add 1tbsp olive oil. Season well. Cover the pan and shake to mix everything together.
3   Spoon the potatoes into a large bowl. Add the fish, tomatoes and cucumber, top with the watercress and season.
4   Put the horseradish, remaining oil and the wine vinegar in a bowl, season well and stir to mix. Pour over the salad, toss and serve.

Serves 6   preparation: 20 minutes   cooking time: 10 minutes
per serving: 250 cals; 19g fat; 14g carbohydrate

Salade Niçoise

2 small red peppers, halved and deseeded	2 large basil sprigs, leaves only
2 large eggs	350g (12oz) vine-ripened tomatoes,
250g (9oz) podded broad beans	skinned and thickly sliced
2tbsp lemon juice	½ cucumber, deseeded and cut into chunks
1tsp Dijon mustard	50g (2oz) small black olives
6tbsp extra-virgin olive oil	6 spring onions, chopped
salt and pepper	50g can anchovy fillets,
2 x 200g cans tuna steak in olive oil,	drained and chopped
well drained	50g (2oz) rocket or other salad leaves

1 Preheat the grill to high. Grill the peppers, skin-side up, until charred. Put in a bowl, cover with clingfilm and leave until cool. Skin the peppers, cut into thick strips and put to one side.

2 Bring a small pan of water to the boil, add the eggs (making sure they're covered with water) and simmer for 8 minutes. Cool under cold running water, shell and quarter. Add the broad beans to a pan of boiling water and cook for 2–3 minutes. Drain and refresh in cold water, then slip off the skins.

3 For the dressing, put the lemon juice, mustard and olive oil in a screw-topped jar, season and shake well until combined.

4 Break the tuna into large flakes. Pound the basil leaves with 1tsp salt in a wide salad bowl to release their flavour. Add the peppers, tomatoes, eggs, cucumber, olives, spring onions, anchovies and broad beans. Add just enough dressing to moisten the salad and toss gently. Check the seasoning.

5 Serve on a bed of rocket or other leaves as a main course. Hand the rest of the dressing separately.

Serves 4–6   preparation: 40 minutes, plus marinating   cooking time: 30 minutes
per serving: 570–380 cals; 41–27g fat; 11–7g carbohydrate

Tuna Bean Salad

2tbsp balsamic vinegar
3tbsp orange juice
juice of 2 limes
several dashes of Tabasco sauce
2 garlic cloves, peeled and crushed
1tbsp golden caster sugar
200g can tuna in brine, drained

4 spring onions, sliced
2 inner stalks of celery, chopped
400g can cannellini beans, drained
 and rinsed
1tbsp drained capers
2tbsp freshly chopped flat-leafed parsley

1 To make the vinaigrette, put the first six ingredients in a screw-topped jar and shake well to combine.
2 To make the salad, put the tuna in a bowl and flake it with a fork. Toss in the spring onions and celery, then stir in the beans and capers.
3 Pour over the vinaigrette, add the parsley and toss to distribute evenly. Cover and chill until needed.

Serves 4   preparation: 12 minutes
per serving: 130 cals; 1g fat; 17g carbohydrate

08

No cook

Marinated Herring, Potato and Dill Salad

1kg (2¼lb) new potatoes
2tbsp soured cream
6tbsp mayonnaise
2tbsp freshly chopped dill

salt and pepper
8 pickled gherkins, thinly sliced
550g (1¼lb) sweet cured herrings, drained,
    sliced into 2cm (¾ inch) strips

1   Put the potatoes in a pan of lightly salted water, bring to the boil, then reduce the heat and simmer for 15–20 minutes or until tender. Drain, then cut into wedges.
2   Meanwhile, make the dressing. Mix the soured cream, mayonnaise and dill in a large bowl and season well.
3   To assemble the salad, put the potatoes, gherkins and herrings in a bowl with the dressing and toss together. Check the seasoning and serve.

Serves 4   preparation: 5 minutes   cooking time: 20–25 minutes
per serving: 640 cals; 42g fat; 41g carbohydrate

Apple, Chicory, Ham and Pecan Salad

1tsp runny honey
2tsp German or Dijon mustard
3tbsp cider vinegar
salt and pepper
9tbsp vegetable oil
2tsp poppy seeds
2 large Braeburn or Cox apples, about 450g
    (1lb), quartered, cored and sliced

450g (1lb) fennel, halved, centre core
    removed, and thinly sliced lengthways
75g (3oz) shelled pecan nuts
300g (11oz) cooked ham, cut into
    wide strips
1 head chicory, divided into leaves
flat-leafed parsley sprigs, to garnish

1   To make the dressing, put the honey, mustard, vinegar and seasoning in a small bowl and whisk. Whisk in the oil, then the poppy seeds and set aside.
2   Put all the remaining ingredients in a large bowl, toss with the dressing and correct the seasoning, if necessary. Garnish with parsley sprigs and serve.

Serves 6   preparation: 30 minutes
per serving: 360 cals; 32g fat; 10g carbohydrate

Chicory, Fennel and Orange Salad

300g (11oz) fennel bulb, with fronds
250g (9oz) heads of chicory, sliced
2 oranges
25g (1oz) hazelnuts, chopped and toasted

juice of ½ orange
2tbsp hazelnut oil (preferably toasted)
salt and pepper

1 Trim the fronds from the fennel, chop them roughly and put to one side.
2 Finely slice the fennel bulb lengthways and put into a bowl with the chicory.
3 Peel the oranges, removing all white pith and pips, then slice into rounds and add to the salad with the toasted hazelnuts.
4 For the dressing, put the orange juice and hazelnut oil into a small bowl, season well and whisk to combine.
5 Pour the dressing over the salad, add the reserved fennel fronds and toss well. Serve at once.

Serves 4–6 preparation: 10 minutes
per serving: 125–85 cals; 9–6g fat; 10–7g carbohydrate

Avocado and Papaya Salad

2 romaine lettuces, leaves separated,
 washed and dried
1 papaya, peeled, deseeded and sliced
1 large ripe avocado, quartered, stoned,
 peeled and sliced
1 green pepper, deseeded and thinly sliced
1 large white onion, peeled and sliced into
 rings

2tbsp extra-virgin olive oil
2tbsp lemon juice
1tbsp sweet chilli sauce
salt and pepper
20 chives
2tbsp finely chopped flat-leafed parsley,
 to serve
1tsp paprika, to serve

1 Take 2 lettuce leaves, put one on top of the other, then scatter a couple of slices each of papaya, avocado and pepper over them. Top with 2 more lettuce leaves. Hold the leaves together firmly and ease 3 onion rings up and over the stalks to secure the bundles. Make up three more lettuce bundles. Stand each on a serving plate and arrange the remaining papaya, avocado and pepper around the lettuce.
2 To make the dressing, mix the olive oil with the lemon juice and sweet chilli sauce and season. Drizzle the dressing over the lettuce parcel, garnish with chives and sprinkle the edge of the plate with a little parsley and paprika to serve.

Serves 4 preparation: 15 minutes
per serving: 190 cals; 15g fat; 10g carbohydrate

Sprouted Bean and Mango Salad

3tbsp mango chutney
juice and grated zest of 1 lime
2tbsp olive oil
salt and pepper
1 red pepper, deseeded and finely diced
1 yellow pepper, deseeded and finely diced
1 mango, halved, peeled and finely diced

1 small red onion, peeled and
  finely chopped
4 plum tomatoes, quartered,
  deseeded and diced
4tbsp chopped coriander
150g (5oz) sprouted beans

1 Put the mango chutney in a small bowl and add the lime zest and juice. Whisk in the olive oil and season.
2 Put the peppers and mango in a large bowl and add the onion, tomatoes, coriander and sprouted beans. Pour the dressing over and mix well. Serve the salad immediately.

Serves 6 preparation: 15 minutes
per serving: 120 cals; 5g fat; 19g carbohydrate

Basil and Lemon Marinated Chicken

grated zest of 1 lemon
4tbsp lemon juice
1tsp golden caster sugar
1tsp Dijon mustard
175ml (6fl oz) lemon-flavoured oil
salt and pepper

4tbsp chopped basil
2 x 210g packs roast chicken
2 x 120g bags baby leaf spinach
55g pack crisp bacon, broken into
  small pieces

1 Put the lemon zest, lemon juice, sugar, Dijon mustard and oil into a small bowl and season. Whisk thoroughly together and add the basil.
2 Remove any bones from the roast chicken, leave the skin attached and slice into five or six pieces. Arrange the sliced chicken in a dish and pour the dressing over, then cover and leave to marinate for at least 15 minutes.
3 Just before serving, lift the chicken from the dressing and put to one side.
4 Put the spinach in a large bowl, pour the dressing over and toss together. Arrange the chicken on top of the spinach and sprinkle with the bacon. Serve immediately.

Serves 4 preparation: 15 minutes, plus marinating
per serving: 660 cals; 59g fat; 3g carbohydrate

Parma Ham, Marinated Onion and Rocket

150g (5oz) small marinated onions, drained,
reserving 1tbsp of the marinade
4tbsp olive oil
salt and pepper

200g (7oz) rocket
8 slices Parma ham, about 100g (3½oz)
75g (3oz) Parmesan cheese, freshly shaved

1   To make the dressing, put the reserved marinade and the olive oil in a bowl, add seasoning and whisk until combined.
2   Halve the onions and put in a large bowl with the rocket, Parma ham, Parmesan shavings and the dressing. Toss together and serve at once.

Serves 4   preparation: 10 minutes
per serving: 300 cals; 25g fat; 4g carbohydrate

Spiced Salad

4tbsp olive oil
4tsp lime juice
large pinch of golden caster sugar
salt and crushed black peppercorns
50g (2oz) chorizo sausage, thinly shredded

2 mild red chillies, chopped
2 red peppers, deseeded and sliced
2 shallots, peeled and chopped
4 tomatoes, chopped
large bag mixed crisp lettuce leaves

1   Put the olive oil, lime juice, sugar, some salt and crushed black peppercorns into a bowl and stir to combine. Add the chorizo sausage, chillies, red peppers, shallots, tomatoes and lettuce leaves and turn in the dressing. Serve with wholemeal rolls or slices of rye bread.

Serves 4   preparation: 5 minutes
per serving: 200 cals; 17g fat; 9g carbohydrate

Waldorf Salad

2 large eating apples, cored and sliced
juice of ½ lemon
100g bag rocket
½ celery head, trimmed and finely chopped

50g (2oz) chopped walnuts.
100ml (3½fl oz) olive oil
1tsp Dijon mustard
1tbsp white wine vinegar

1   Put the apples in a bowl, then toss with the lemon juice. Add the rocket, celery and walnuts.
2   Mix the olive oil with the Dijon mustard and white wine vinegar, pour over the salad and serve.

Serves 3–4   preparation: 10 minutes
per serving: 400–300 cals; 38–28g fat; 14–10g carbohydrate

Chicken, Avocado and Peanut Salad

2tbsp cider vinegar
1tsp English mustard
5tbsp groundnut oil
salt and pepper
1 large ripe avocado, halved, stoned,
    peeled and thickly sliced

2 roasted chicken breasts, about 250g
    (9oz) total weight, skin discarded and
    meat sliced
70g bag watercress
50g (2oz) roasted salted peanuts,
    roughly chopped

1   To make the dressing, put the vinegar, mustard and oil in a bowl, season and whisk until well emulsified.
    Add the avocado and gently toss in the dressing, making sure each slice of avocado is well covered.
2   Arrange the chicken on top of the watercress, cover with clingfilm and chill.
3   Just before serving, spoon the avocado and dressing over the chicken and watercress. Sprinkle with
    the chopped peanuts and serve immediately.

Serves 4   preparation: 15 minutes, plus chilling
per serving: 400 cals; 34g fat; 2g carbohydrate

Guacamole Salad

3 beef tomatoes, each cut
    horizontally into six
1 small onion, peeled and finely sliced
1 garlic clove, peeled and crushed
1tbsp chopped coriander, plus extra to
    garnish

4 'ripe and ready' avocados
juice of 1 lime
200g (7oz) feta cheese, cut into cubes
100g (3½oz) sunblush tomatoes in oil
salt and pepper
1 small seeded wholemeal loaf, to serve

1   Divide the tomato slices among six serving plates, then scatter over the onion, garlic and coriander.
2   Cut each avocado into quarters as far as the stone. Keeping the avocado whole, start at the pointed
    end and peel away the skin. Separate each quarter, remove the stone, then slice each quarter
    lengthways. Squeeze the lime juice over to stop the avocados from browning and arrange on the plates.
3   Top with the feta cheese, sunblush tomatoes and a sprig of coriander. Finish each salad with a drizzling
    of oil reserved from the tomatoes and season well. Serve with wholemeal bread.

Serve 6   preparation: 20 minutes
per serving (without bread). 290 cals; 26g fat; 5g carbohydrate

Fast food

You're hungry, you want food – and you want it now. Well, here are some solutions.

Stir-fries: yes, there's a bit of chopping involved, but buy a ready-prepared pack of vegetables and you're halfway there. The key to success is heat – whack up the heat under your wok or pan and keep the ingredients moving. Stir-fries can be as simple or as substantial as you feel like making them, from Chicken Stir-fry with Noodles – just eight ingredients, to Turkey and Broccoli Stir-fry, where beansprouts, mushrooms, spring onions and ginger are added to the main ingredients for a tasty quick meal.

Then there's nothing more satisfying than a plate of steaming hot pasta. Serve with a rich tomato sauce, such as Quick Tomato Sauce with Bacon, or indulge yourself with a bowl of penne and Smoked Salmon, Dill and Cream sauce. For something cheesy, try Walnut and Creamy Blue Cheese Tagliatelle – very moreish!

Or how about a Warm Spicy Chorizo Sausage and Chickpea Salad – warm salads are delicious. Try Chèvre en Croute; Egg and Pepper Pizza; or Flash-in-the-Pan Pork – pork escalopes, new potatoes and runner beans cooked in a creamy mustard and tarragon sauce and ready in 15 minutes.

Prawn and Pak Choi Stir-fry

2tsp sesame oil

1tbsp vegetable oil

1 medium onion, peeled and finely chopped

2 garlic cloves, peeled and finely chopped

2.5cm (1 inch) piece fresh root ginger,
  peeled and grated

1 small red chilli, deseeded
  and finely chopped

450g (1lb) peeled raw king
  prawns, deveined

200g (7oz) pak choi, roughly chopped

1–2tbsp teriyaki sauce

1   Heat both oils in a wok or large frying pan over a high heat. Add the onion, garlic, ginger and chilli and stir-fry for 3–4 minutes.

2   Add the prawns and cook for 2–3 minutes, stirring constantly, until they're cooked through and pink. Add the pak choi and teriyaki sauce, stir-fry for a further 2 minutes, then serve.

Serves 4   preparation: 10 minutes   cooking time: 7–9 minutes

per serving: 170 cals; 7g fat; 6g carbohydrate

Stir-fry with Tofu

200g pack fresh tofu, cubed

4tbsp sweet chilli sauce

2tbsp light soy sauce

1tbsp sesame seeds

2tbsp toasted sesame oil

2 x 300g packs stir-fry vegetables

1   Put the tofu in a shallow container, pour over 1tbsp each sweet chilli sauce and light soy sauce, cover and marinate for 10 minutes.

2   Meanwhile, dry-fry the sesame seeds in a hot wok until golden. Remove and put to one side.

3   Add 1tbsp oil to the wok, add the marinated tofu and stir-fry for 5 minutes until golden. Remove and put to one side.

4   Heat the remaining oil in the wok, add the vegetables and stir-fry for 3–4 minutes. Stir in the cooked tofu.

5   Pour the remaining sweet chilli sauce and soy sauce over, then toss together and cook for 1 minute to heat through. Sprinkle with the sesame seeds and serve.

Serves 4   preparation: 5 minutes, plus marinating   cooking time: 12 minutes

per serving: 170 cals; 11g fat; 10g carbohydrate

Stir-fried Prawns with Cabbage and Mangetout

225g (8oz) pak choi or Chinese
  mustard cabbage
2tbsp vegetable oil
2 garlic cloves, peeled and thinly sliced
1 lemon grass stalk, cut in half and bruised
2 kaffir lime leaves, torn into small pieces
1 small red onion, peeled and thinly sliced
1 hot red chilli, deseeded and thinly sliced
4cm (1½ inch) piece fresh root ginger,
  peeled and cut into long thin shreds

1tbsp coriander seeds, lightly crushed
450g (1lb) large peeled raw prawns,
  deveined
175g (6oz) mangetout, halved diagonally
2tbsp Thai fish sauce (*nam pla*)
juice of 1 lime, or to taste
fried sliced red chilli, deseeded, to garnish

1 Trim the pak choi or cabbage, discarding any damaged or discoloured leaves. Tear the leaves into manageable-sized pieces.

2 Heat the oil in a wok or large frying pan. Add the garlic, lemon grass, lime leaves, onion, chilli, ginger and coriander seeds and stir-fry for 2 minutes. Add the prawns, mangetout and pak choi or cabbage and stir-fry until the vegetables are cooked but still crisp and the prawns are pink and opaque, about 2–3 minutes.

3 Add the fish sauce and lime juice and heat through for 1 minute. Discard the lemon grass. Garnish with sliced red chilli and serve immediately while the vegetables are crisp.

Serves 4   preparation: 30 minutes   cooking time: 6 minutes
per serving: 200 cals; 8g fat; 9g carbohydrate

Sweet Chilli Prawn Stir-Fry

1tbsp sesame oil
175g (6oz) peeled raw tiger prawns,
  deveined
220g pack green vegetable stir-fry,
  containing Swiss chard, courgettes,

broccoli, green beans
60ml pack sweet chilli and ginger sauce

1 Heat the oil in a large wok, add the prawns and stir-fry for 2 minutes.

2 Add the courgettes, broccoli and green beans from the vegetable pack and stir-fry for 2–3 minutes.

3 Add the Swiss chard and the chilli and ginger sauce and cook for 1–2 minutes to heat through, then serve immediately.

Serves 2   preparation: 2 minutes   cooking time: 7 minutes
per serving: 170 cals; 8g fat; 4g carbohydrate

Turkey and Broccoli Stir-fry

2tbsp vegetable or sunflower oil
500g (1lb 2oz) turkey fillet, cut in strips
2 garlic cloves, peeled and crushed
2.5cm (1 inch) piece fresh root ginger,
  peeled and grated
1 broccoli head, chopped into florets
8 spring onions, finely chopped

125g (4oz) button mushrooms, halved
100g (3½oz) beansprouts
3tbsp oyster sauce
1tbsp light soy sauce
125ml (4fl oz) hot chicken stock
juice of ½ lemon

1 Heat 1tbsp oil in a large non-stick frying pan or wok and stir-fry the turkey strips over a medium-high heat for 4–5 minutes until golden and cooked through. Remove from the pan and put to one side.
2 Heat the remaining oil in the same pan over a medium heat, then cook the garlic and ginger for 30 seconds, stirring all the time so they don't burn. Add the broccoli, spring onions and mushrooms, increase the heat and cook for 2–3 minutes until the vegetables start to brown but are still crisp.
3 Return the turkey to the pan and add the beansprouts, sauces, hot stock and lemon juice. Cook for 1–2 minutes, tossing well to heat everything through, then serve.

Serves 4   preparation: 15 minutes   cooking time: 7–11 minutes
per serving: 240 cals; 9g fat; 5g carbohydrate

Pork and Noodle Stir-fry

1tbsp sesame oil
5cm (2 inch) piece fresh root ginger,
  peeled and grated
2tbsp soy sauce
1tbsp fish sauce
½ red chilli, finely chopped
450g (1lb) stir-fry pork strips

2 red peppers, halved, deseeded
  and roughly chopped
250g (9oz) baby sweetcorn, halved
  lengthways
200g (7oz) sugarsnap peas, halved
300g (11oz) beansprouts
250g pack rice noodles

1 Put the oil into a large bowl. Add the ginger, soy sauce, fish sauce, chilli and pork strips. Mix well and leave to marinate for 10 minutes.
2 Heat a large wok until hot. Lift the pork out of the marinade with a slotted spoon, add to the pan and stir-fry over a high heat for 5 minutes. Add the red peppers, sweetcorn, sugarsnap peas, beansprouts and remaining marinade and stir-fry for a further 2–3 minutes until the pork is cooked.
3 Meanwhile, cook the noodles in a large pan of boiling water for the time stated on the pack. Drain the noodles, tip into the wok and toss together, then serve immediately.

Serves 4   preparation: 10 minutes, plus marinating   cooking time: 7–8 minutes
per serving: 500 cals; 12g fat; 62g carbohydrate

Turkey and Sesame Stir-fry with Noodles

300g pack stir-fry turkey strips
3tbsp teriyaki marinade
3tbsp runny honey
500g pack egg noodles

1tbsp sesame oil, plus extra for the noodles
2tbsp sesame seeds
300g pack stir-fry vegetables

1   Put the turkey strips in a large glass bowl with the teriyaki marinade and honey and stir to coat. Cover and leave for 5 minutes to allow the flavours to soak in.
2   Cook the noodles in a large pan of boiling water according to the time stated on the packet. Drain well, then toss in a little oil.
3   Meanwhile, toast the sesame seeds in a dry wok over a medium heat, stirring until they turn golden. Tip on to a plate.
4   Heat 1tbsp oil in the same wok and add the turkey, reserving the marinade. Stir-fry on a very high heat for 2–3 minutes until cooked through and beginning to brown.
5   Add a drop more oil, if needed, then add the vegetables and leftover marinade. Continue to cook over a high heat, stirring, until the vegetables have started to soften and the sauce is warmed through.
6   Scatter with the sesame seeds and serve immediately with the drained egg noodles.

Serves 4   preparation: 5 minutes   cooking time: 10 minutes
per serving: 660 cals; 15g fat; 100g carbohydrate

Chicken Stir-fry with Noodles

250g pack thick egg noodles
2tbsp vegetable oil
2 garlic cloves, peeled and crushed
4 skinless boneless chicken breasts, each
  sliced into 10 pieces

3 medium carrots, about 450g (1lb), cut into
  thin strips, about 5cm (2 inches) long
1 bunch of spring onions, sliced
200g (7oz) mangetout, ends trimmed
155g jar sweet chilli and lemon grass sauce

1   Cook the noodles in plenty of boiling water for the time stated on the packet.
2   Meanwhile, heat the oil in a wok or frying pan, then add the garlic and stir-fry for 1–2 minutes. Add the chicken pieces and stir-fry for 5 minutes, then add the carrot strips and stir-fry for a further 5 minutes. Add the spring onions, mangetout and sauce to the wok and stir-fry for 5 minutes.
3   Drain the cooked noodles well and add to the wok. Toss everything together and serve.

Serves 4   preparation: 20 minutes   cooking time: 20 minutes
per serving: 540 cals; 14g fat; 70g carbohydrate

Stir-fried Pork with Chinese Greens

350g (12oz) stir-fry pork strips
4tbsp rice wine or dry sherry
2tbsp soy sauce
3tbsp stir-fry oil

450g (1lb) Chinese greens
2 x 300g packs stir-fry vegetables
about 1tbsp Chinese five-spice paste

1 Toss the pork with the rice wine or sherry, the soy sauce and 1tbsp oil (if you have time, leave the pork to marinate for 1 hour at this stage). Shred the Chinese greens and, together with the stir-fry vegetables, rinse in cold water.

2 Using a slotted spoon, lift the pork from the marinade; reserve the marinade. Heat a wok or large deep frying pan until very hot. Add 1tbsp oil to the wok, add half the pork – cook it in batches to ensure it fries and seals quickly – and stir-fry for about 1 minute or until beginning to brown at the edges. Put to one side and stir-fry the remaining pork.

3 Wipe out the wok, add the remaining oil and heat. Add the five-spice paste and all the vegetables and fry for a further 3–4 minutes. Return the pork and reserved marinade to the wok, bring to the boil and bubble for 1–2 minutes. Serve immediately.

Serves 6   preparation: 5 minutes   cooking time: 10 minutes
per serving: 200 cals; 11g fat; 7g carbohydrate

Sweet Chilli Beef Stir-fry

1tsp chilli oil
1tbsp each soy sauce and runny honey
1 garlic clove, peeled and crushed
1 large red chilli, halved, deseeded
  and chopped
400g (14oz) lean beef, cut into strips

1tsp sunflower oil
1 broccoli head, shredded
200g (7oz) mangetout, halved
1 red pepper, halved, deseeded and
  cut into strips

1 Put the chilli oil in a medium-sized shallow bowl. Add the soy sauce, honey, garlic and chilli and stir well. Add the beef strips and toss in the marinade.

2 Heat the sunflower oil in a wok over a high heat until very hot. Cook the beef strips in two batches, then remove them from the pan and put to one side. Wipe the pan with kitchen paper to remove any residue.

3 Add the broccoli, mangetout, red pepper and 2tbsp water to the pan. Stir-fry for 5–6 minutes until starting to soften. Return the beef to the pan to heat through, then serve.

Serves 4   preparation: 10 minutes   cooking time: 10–11 minutes
per serving: 200 cals; 7g fat; 8g carbohydrate

Quick Sauces for Pasta

How much pasta do I need?

Allow 75g (3oz) dried pasta shapes or noodles or 125g (4oz) fresh or filled pasta shapes per person. Cook the pasta until al dente – the pasta should have a slight bite. Follow the timings on the packet and start testing 1 minute before the recommended time. The pasta will continue to cook a little after draining.

Quick Tomato Sauce

1tbsp vegetable oil
1 small onion, peeled and finely chopped
1 garlic clove, peeled and chopped

400g can chopped tomatoes, can reserved
salt and pepper

1   Heat the oil in a medium pan for 30 seconds, then add the onion and cook over a very gentle heat for 15 minutes, stirring regularly until the onion is softened and translucent, but not browned. Add the garlic and continue to cook gently for 1 minute.
2   Add the tomatoes and stir well. Fill the empty tomato can up to about halfway with cold water and give it a swirl to catch any tomato juice, then add to the pan. Season the tomato sauce generously, then increase the heat to medium and leave the sauce to simmer for about 15 minutes until slightly thickened.

Serves 4   preparation: 10 minutes   cooking time: 35 minutes
per serving: 60 cals; 3g fat; 6g carbohydrate

Variations on Quick Tomato Sauce

Quick Tomato Sauce with Bacon: Chop 2 rindless streaky bacon rashers and add to the pan when frying the onion at step 1. Cook for 10–15 minutes until the bacon is browned, then add the tomatoes and complete the recipe.

Serves 4   preparation: 10 minutes   cooking time: 35 minutes
per serving: 110 cals; 8g fat; 6g carbohydrate

Quick Tomato Sauce with Red Pepper and Olives: Add 1 deseeded and sliced red pepper to the pan when frying the onion at step 1. At the end of step 2, when the tomato sauce has thickened and finished simmering, add 6 pitted, chopped olives and cook for 1–2 minutes to heat through.

Serves 4   preparation: 15 minutes   cooking time: 37 minutes
per serving: 70 cals; 4g fat; 8g carbohydrate

Quick Tomato Sauce with Tuna: Drain an 80g can of tuna in oil or brine (you can use some of the oil to cook the onion in step 1). At the end of step 2, when the tomato sauce has thickened and finished simmering, stir in the tuna and cook for 2–3 minutes to warm through. Toss with the pasta.

Serves 4   preparation: 10 minutes   cooking time: 38 minutes
per serving: 80 cals; 4g fat; 6g carbohydrate

Tomato, Prawn and Garlic sauce

350g (12oz) cooked peeled prawns	4 large tomatoes, about 400g
4tbsp sun-dried tomato paste	(14oz), chopped
1tbsp olive oil	125ml (4fl oz) white wine
15g (½oz) butter	20g pack flat-leafed parsley,
3 garlic cloves, peeled and sliced	roughly chopped

1   Put the prawns in a bowl with the tomato paste and stir well.
2   Heat the olive oil and butter in a frying pan and gently cook the garlic until golden. Add the tomatoes and wine. Leave the sauce to bubble for about 5 minutes, then stir in the prawns and parsley. Stir through drained, cooked tagliatelle.

Serves 4   preparation: 10 minutes   cooking time: 10 minutes
per serving (sauce only): 190 cals; 8g fat; 5g carbohydrate

Cherry Tomato Vinaigrette

1tbsp olive oil

2 x 250g packs cherry tomatoes

salt and pepper

1tbsp balsamic vinegar

pinch of sugar

20g pack basil, roughly chopped

1 Heat the olive oil in a large frying pan and add the tomatoes. Season generously and leave to simmer gently for 5 minutes.
2 Add the vinegar, a pinch of sugar and the basil and cook for 1–2 minutes, then stir through drained, cooked penne.

Serves 4 preparation: 5 minutes   cooking time: 7 minutes
per serving (sauce only): 60 cals; 4g fat; 5g carbohydrate

Lemon and Parmesan

salt and pepper

125g (4oz) frozen petit pois

zest and juice of ½ lemon

75g (3oz) freshly grated Parmesan cheese

1 Cook conchiglione pasta in a large pan of boiling salted water for the time stated on the packet. Add the petit pois to the pasta water for the last 5 minutes of the cooking time.
2 Drain the pasta and peas, put back in the pan and add the lemon zest and juice and Parmesan. Season with plenty of pepper, toss and serve immediately.

Serves 4 preparation: 5 minutes   cooking time: 12 minutes
per serving (sauce only): 100 cals; 6g fat; 3g carbohydrate

Fast food

Wine and Mushroom

1tbsp olive oil

1 onion, peeled and finely chopped

300g (11oz) mushrooms, sliced

125ml (4fl oz) white wine

500ml carton low-fat crème fraîche

2tbsp chopped tarragon

1 Put the olive oil in a large pan and fry the onion for 7–10 minutes until soft. Add the mushrooms and cook for 3–4 minutes.
2 Pour in the wine and bubble for 1 minute, then stir in the crème fraîche. Heat until bubbling, then stir in the tarragon and stir through drained, cooked pappardelle.

Serves 4 preparation: 5 minutes   cooking time: 12–16 minutes
per serving (sauce only): 310 cals; 22g fat; 10g carbohydrate

Courgette and Anchovy

50g can anchovies
1 garlic clove, peeled and crushed
pinch of dried chilli

400ml (14fl oz) passata
2 courgettes, diced

1 Gently heat the oil from the anchovies in a frying pan. Add the garlic and chilli and cook for 1 minute.
2 Add the passata, courgettes and anchovies. Bring to the boil, then reduce the heat and simmer for about 10 minutes, stirring well, until the anchovies have melted. Stir through drained, cooked penne.

Serves 4   preparation: 5 minutes   cooking time: 15 minutes
per serving (sauce only): 60 cals; 3g fat; 4g carbohydrate

Smoked Salmon, Dill and Cream

200ml carton half-fat crème fraîche
140g pack smoked salmon,
  roughly chopped

20g pack dill, finely chopped
salt and pepper
lemon wedges, to serve

1 Put the crème fraîche into a large bowl and add the smoked salmon and dill. Season well and mix, then gently stir through drained, cooked penne and serve immediately with lemon wedges to squeeze over.

Serves 4   preparation: 5 minutes
per serving (sauce only): 140 cals; 9g fat; 2g carbohydrate

Tuna, Capers, Chilli and Olive

2tbsp olive oil
2 garlic cloves, peeled and sliced
1 red chilli, deseeded and chopped
2 x 200g cans tuna, drained
50g (2oz) pitted black olives, chopped

2tbsp capers
juice of ½ lemon
salt and pepper
4tbsp chopped flat-leafed parsley

1 Heat the olive oil in a pan. Add the garlic and chilli and cook gently for 2 minutes, then add the tuna, olives, capers and lemon juice.
2 Season and heat through, then stir into drained, cooked linguine and scatter with the parsley.

Serves 4   preparation: 5 minutes   cooking time: 5 minutes
per serving (sauce only): 150 cals; 8g fat; Tr carbohydrate

Salmon and Broccoli

225g (8oz) salmon fillets
2tsp sesame oil
200g (7oz) cooked peeled king prawns
150g (5oz) mangetout

150g (5oz) purple sprouting
   broccoli, shredded
2tbsp teriyaki marinade
small handful of roughly chopped coriander

1 Preheat the grill to medium-high. Put the salmon on a baking sheet and grill for 4 minutes on each side.
2 Heat the oil in a large wok and stir-fry the prawns, mangetout and broccoli for 3–4 minutes or until just tender.
3 Flake the salmon into the wok and add the teriyaki marinade. Warm through, then stir into cooked pappardelle and serve scattered with coriander, if you like.

Serves 4   preparation: 5 minutes   cooking time: 10 minutes
per serving (sauce only): 230 cals; 13g fat; 3g carbohydrate

Quick and Easy Carbonara

150g (5oz) smoked bacon rashers, chopped
1tbsp olive oil
2 large egg yolks

142ml carton double cream
50g (2oz) freshly grated Parmesan cheese
chopped flat-leafed parsley

1 Fry the bacon in the olive oil for 4–5 minutes. Add to drained, cooked pasta, such as tagliatelle and keep hot.
2 Put the egg yolks in a bowl, add the cream and whisk together. Add to the pasta with the Parmesan and some parsley and toss well.

Serves 4   preparation: 5 minutes   cooking time: 5 minutes
per serving (sauce only): 440 cals; 42g fat; 1g carbohydrate

Simple Salmon Pasta

500 pack dried linguine pasta
salt and pepper
a little olive oil
1 fat garlic clove, peeled and crushed

200ml carton half-fat crème fraîche
225g (8oz) hot-smoked salmon, flaked
200g (7oz) peas
two handfuls of basil, roughly torn

1 Cook the pasta in a large pan of boiling salted water for the time stated on the packet, then drain, reserving a couple of tablespoons of the cooking water.
2 Meanwhile, heat the olive oil in a large pan, add the garlic and fry gently until golden. Add the crème fraîche, the flaked salmon and peas and stir in. Cook for 1–2 minutes until warmed through, then add the reserved water from the pasta – this stops the pasta absorbing too much of the crème fraîche.
3 Toss the pasta into the sauce, season well and serve garnished with the torn basil.

Serves 4   preparation: 2 minutes   cooking time: 8 minutes
per serving: 680 cals; 19g fat; 100g carbohydrate

Spaghetti with Lemon and Nut Butter

50g (2oz) butter
75g (3oz) toasted hazelnuts,
  roughly chopped
6 garlic cloves, peeled and thinly sliced
grated zest and juice of 2 lemons
450g (1lb) fresh spaghetti or
  225g (8oz) dried

salt and pepper
4tbsp each chopped basil and
  flat-leafed parsley
2tbsp single cream (optional)

1 Melt the butter in a medium-sized pan until it turns a pale golden brown. Add the hazelnuts and garlic and fry for about 30 seconds. Add the lemon zest and put to one side.
2 Cook the pasta in a large pan of boiling salted water for the time stated on the packet. Drain well, add to the butter mixture and stir over a low heat for 2–3 minutes. Stir in the herbs, 4tbsp lemon juice and the cream, if using. Season generously and serve immediately.

Serves 4   preparation: 10 minutes   cooking time: 15 minutes
per serving (fresh pasta): 500 cals; 23g fat; 60g carbohydrate
per serving (dried pasta): 370 cals; 19g fat; 44g carbohydrate

Clam Spaghetti

450g (1lb) dried spaghetti or linguine pasta
salt and pepper
150ml (¼ pint) olive oil
3 garlic cloves, peeled and crushed
150ml (¼ pint) dry white wine

2 x 400g cans chopped tomatoes
squeeze of lemon juice
1.1kg (2½lb) clams, cleaned
chives, parsley and lemon wedges,
   to garnish

1 Cook the pasta in a pan of boiling salted water for the time stated on the packet. Drain and return to the pan with a little of the cooking liquid.
2 Meanwhile, heat the olive oil in a large heavy-based pan. Add the garlic and cook for 30 seconds. Add the wine and leave to bubble for 1 minute, then add the tomatoes and bubble for a further 2 minutes. Add the lemon juice and season.
3 Add the clams to the tomato sauce, cover and simmer for 1 minute or until the clams have opened up. Discard any clams that do not open. Toss the cooked pasta with the sauce and add a good grinding of black pepper. Garnish with chives, parsley and lemon wedges and serve.

Serves 4   preparation: 10 minutes   cooking time: 15 minutes
per serving: 800 cals; 36g fat; 90g carbohydrate

Fast food

Courgette and Lemon Spaghetti

350g (12oz) dried spaghetti
salt and pepper
4tbsp olive oil
1–2 garlic cloves, peeled and sliced
1 rosemary sprig
700g (1½lb) courgettes, pared into ribbons

grated zest and juice of 1 large lemon
5tbsp double cream
50g (2oz) pine nuts, toasted
zest of 1 lemon and crushed black pepper,
  to garnish

1   Cook the pasta in a large pan of boiling salted water for the time stated on the packet, then drain.
2   Meanwhile, heat the olive oil in a large frying pan, add the garlic and rosemary and cook for 1–2 minutes. Remove from the heat and leave the oil to infuse for 5 minutes. Strain and reserve the oil and garlic, then discard the rosemary sprig.
3   Pour half the oil back into the pan, add half the courgettes and cook over a high heat for 1–2 minutes or until golden, then put to one side. Repeat with the remaining oil and courgettes. Wipe out the pan. Return the courgettes to the pan with the reserved garlic, the lemon zest, juice and cream and bring to the boil, then bubble for 1–2 minutes or until the sauce has thickened slightly. Season well.
4   Add the spaghetti to the courgette mixture, toss well together and heat through. Divide between bowls, sprinkle the pine nuts over and garnish with the lemon zest and black pepper to serve.

Serves 4   preparation: 25 minutes   cooking time: 20 minutes
per serving: 620 cals; 33g fat; 69g carhohydrate

Fast food

Spaghetti with Chilli and Garlic

400g (14oz) dried spaghetti
salt and pepper
5tbsp extra-virgin olive oil
1 red chilli, deseeded and finely chopped
1–2 garlic cloves, peeled and thinly sliced

50g (2oz) Parmesan cheese, grated,
  plus extra to serve
handful of flat-leafed parsley, roughly
  chopped

1 Cook the pasta in plenty of boiling salted water for the time stated on the packet.
2 When the pasta is nearly cooked, heat the olive oil in a small pan, add the chilli and garlic and cook for 1 minute.
3 Drain the pasta well, put back in the pan, then add the chilli and garlic oil, Parmesan and parsley. Season well and toss everything together. Spoon into bowls and serve with plenty of extra Parmesan grated over.

Serves 4   preparation: 5 minutes   cooking time: 10–12 minutes
per serving: 550 cals; 22g fat; 74g carbohydrate

09

Fast food

Sugarsnaps and Prosciutto Pasta Sauce

50g (2oz) pine nuts
150g (5oz) sugarsnap peas
125g (4oz) spinach

70g pack prosciutto, roughly torn
black pepper

1 Dry-fry the pine nuts in a frying pan until golden brown, then put to one side.
2 Cook conchiglioni pasta and add the sugarsnap peas to the water 4 minutes before the end of the cooking time.
3 Just before draining, add the spinach, then drain everything thoroughly and return to the pan. Add the pine nuts and prosciutto, season well with pepper and toss to mix.

Serves 4   preparation: 5 minutes   cooking time: 7 minutes
per serving: 150 cals; 11g fat; 3g carbohydrate

Pasta with Broccoli and Thyme

500g pack dried rigatoni pasta
salt and pepper
900g (2lb) tenderstem broccoli, ends
   trimmed, or 2 broccoli heads, chopped
   into florets and stalks peeled and sliced
150ml (¼ pint) hot vegetable stock

2 garlic cloves, peeled and crushed
2tbsp olive oil
250g tub mascarpone
2tbsp chopped thyme
100g (3½oz) pecorino cheese, grated

1 Cook the pasta in a large pan of boiling salted water for the time stated on the packet. Drain well, reserving about a ladleful of the cooking water.
2 Meanwhile, make the sauce: put the broccoli in a pan with the hot stock. Bring to the boil, then cover the pan, reduce the heat and simmer for 3–4 minutes until tender – the stock should have evaporated.
3 Add the garlic and olive oil to the pan and cook for 1–2 minutes to soften the garlic. Add the mascarpone, thyme and pecorino and carefully mix.
4 Return the pasta to the pan, then add the broccoli sauce. Toss everything together, adding a little of the reserved cooking water if necessary, then season to taste and divide among four warmed pasta bowls and serve.

Serves 4   preparation: 15 minutes   cooking time: 15 minutes
per serving: 950 cals; 48g fat;100g carbohydrate

Pasta with Creamy Pesto Sauce

450g (1lb) fresh tagliatelle pasta
salt and pepper
5tbsp freshly grated Parmesan cheese
25g (1oz) pine nuts, toasted
200ml carton low-fat fromage frais

2 garlic cloves, peeled
40g (1½oz) torn basil leaves
40g (1½oz) roughly chopped flat-leafed
  parsley

1 Cook the pasta in a large pan of boiling salted water for the time stated on the packet, then drain.
2 Meanwhile, put the Parmesan, pine nuts, fromage frais and garlic into a food processor and whiz to a thick paste. Scrape into a bowl and season generously. Add the herbs and whiz for 2–3 seconds.
3 Stir the pesto sauce into the drained pasta, check the seasoning and serve.

Serves 4   preparation: 8 minutes   cooking time: 5 minutes
per serving: 450 cals; 13g fat; 62g carbohydrate

Roast Tomato Pasta

400g (14oz) dried rigatoni pasta
salt and pepper
700g (1½lb) cherry tomatoes
few glugs of olive oil

50g (2oz) pine nuts
large handful of basil leaves, freshly torn
plenty of freshly grated Parmesan cheese,
   to serve

1   Preheat the oven to 240°C (220°C fan oven) mark 9. Cook the pasta in a large pan of boiling salted water for the time stated on the packet
2   Meanwhile, cut half the tomatoes in two and arrange them in a large roasting tin, cut side up. Add the remaining tomatoes, drizzle them with olive oil and season. Put the pine nuts on a separate roasting tray and roast both for 15 minutes until the tomatoes are softened and lightly caramelised.
3   Drain the pasta well and add to the roasting tin when the tomatoes are done. Scatter over the pine nuts and basil, then stir thoroughly so the pasta gets coated in all the juices. Taste and season again, if necessary, then stir in an extra glug or two of oil if the pasta needs it. Serve sprinkled with a generous amount of Parmesan.

Serves 4   preparation: 5 minutes   cooking time: 15 minutes
per serving: 560 cals; 19g fat; 80g carbohydrate

Fast food

Pasta with Leeks, Pancetta and Mushrooms

450g (1lb) dried conchiglie pasta
salt and pepper
50g (2oz) butter
125g (4oz) pancetta, diced

2 medium leeks, thickly sliced
225g (8oz) chestnut mushrooms, sliced
1 garlic clove, peeled and crushed
150g pack soft herb cream cheese

1 Cook the pasta in a large pan of boiling salted water for the time stated on the packet, then drain.
2 Meanwhile, melt the butter in a pan and add the pancetta, leeks, mushrooms and garlic. Cook over a medium heat for 5–10 minutes until the leeks are tender. Reduce the heat, add the herb cheese and season well. Add the pasta to the sauce, toss and serve.

Serves 4   preparation: 5 minutes   cooking time: 15–20 minutes
per serving: 790 cals; 43g fat; 85g carbohydrate

Spaghetti with Smoky Bacon and Tomato

350g (12oz) dried spaghetti
salt and pepper
250g (9oz) smoked streaky bacon rashers,
  roughly chopped
450g (1lb) vine-ripened tomatoes, roughly
  chopped

20g pack flat-leafed parsley, very
  roughly chopped
125g (4oz) full-flavoured melting cheese
  such as dolcelatte, Gorgonzola, Taleggio
  or Camembert, cut into rough chunks

1 Cook the pasta in plenty of boiling salted water for the time stated on the packet.
2 Meanwhile, stir-fry the bacon in a non-stick frying pan over a high heat until the fat begins to run and the bacon turns golden. Remove with a slotted spoon.
3 Add the tomatoes to the bacon fat in the pan and continue to stir over the heat until they just begin to soften and break up at the edges.
4 Drain the pasta well, then toss with the bacon, tomatoes and chopped parsley. Season with plenty of pepper.
5 Stir the chopped cheese into the pasta just before serving so it begins to melt in the heat of the pan.

Serves 4   preparation: 10 minutes   cooking time: 15 minutes
per serving: 670 cals; 34g fat; 68g carbohydrate

Penne with Leeks and Salami

400g (14oz) dried penne pasta
salt and pepper
150g (5oz) salami, cut into cubes
2 medium leeks, sliced
1 garlic clove, peeled and crushed

1tbsp olive oil
100ml (3½fl oz) crème fraîche
handful of flat-leafed parsley, chopped
freshly grated Parmesan cheese, to serve

1 Cook the pasta in a large pan of boiling salted water for the time stated on the packet.
2 Meanwhile, heat a non-stick pan over a medium heat and fry the salami for 2–3 minutes. There's no need for oil at this point – the heat will release the fat from the meat. Add the leeks and garlic to the pan with the olive oil and toss to coat. Reduce the heat to low, cover the pan and cook for 10 minutes or until the leeks are soft and translucent.
3 Add the crème fraîche to the pan and season well. Continue to cook on the lowest heat until the sauce is warmed through.
4 Drain the pasta, reserving a little of the cooking water. Tip the pasta back into the pan with the sauce, the parsley and a splash of the reserved water. Toss well to coat. Serve with plenty of grated Parmesan.

Serves 4   preparation: 5 minutes   cooking time: 15 minutes
per serving: 720 cals; 36g fat; 78g carbohydrate

09

Fast food

Spicy Mushroom Pasta

1tbsp olive oil
1 onion, peeled and finely chopped
1 garlic clove, peeled and crushed
250g (9oz) chestnut mushrooms, sliced
65g pack pancetta, diced
1 red chilli, sliced

1tbsp tomato purée
400g can chopped tomatoes
   in rich tomato juice
salt and pepper
500g pack dried penne pasta
2tbsp basil leaves, freshly torn

1   Heat the olive oil in a pan, add the onion, garlic, mushrooms, pancetta and chilli and cook over a medium heat for about 10 minutes until soft. Add the tomato purée and cook for 1 minute. Stir in the tomatoes, season well and simmer for 25 minutes.
2   Cook the pasta in boiling salted water for the time stated on the packet. Drain, reserving a little of the water and return the pasta to the pan. Add the basil leaves to the tomato sauce, then toss through the cooked penne, adding a little reserved pasta water if necessary, and serve.

Serves 4   preparation: 10 minutes   cooking time: 35 minutes
per serving: 570 cals; 12g fat; 100g carbohydrate

Speedy Macaroni Cheese

225g (8oz) short-cut macaroni
salt and pepper
50g (2oz) butter or margarine
50g (2oz) plain flour
900ml (1½ pints) milk

½ tsp grated nutmeg or mustard powder
225g (8oz) mature Cheddar cheese, grated
3 tbsp fresh white or wholemeal
   breadcrumbs

1   Cook the macaroni in a large pan of boiling salted water until *al dente*.
2   Meanwhile, melt the butter in a pan, stir in the flour and cook, stirring, for 1 minute. Remove from the heat and gradually stir in the milk. Bring to the boil and cook, stirring, until the sauce thickens. Remove from the heat. Season with salt and pepper, and add the nutmeg or mustard.
3   Drain the macaroni and add to the sauce, together with three quarters of the cheese. Mix well, then turn into an ovenproof dish.
4   Preheat the grill to high. Sprinkle the breadcrumbs and remaining cheese over the macaroni. Put under the grill for 2–3 minutes until golden brown on top and bubbling. Serve immediately.

Serves 4–6   preparation: 10 minutes   cooking time: 15 minutes
per serving: 680–460 cals; 34–23g fat; 67–45g carbohydrate

Fast food

Asparagus and Cheese Pasta

225g (8oz) wide-ribbon dried pasta,
  such as pappardelle
salt and pepper
350g (12oz) asparagus or French beans
175g (6oz) leeks, cut into fine shreds

284ml carton single cream
75g (3oz) mature Cheddar cheese, grated
25g (1oz) freshly grated Parmesan cheese
125g (4oz) thinly sliced cooked smoked
  ham, roughly chopped

1 Cook the pasta in a large pan of boiling salted water until just tender, then drain.
2 Meanwhile, cook the asparagus or French beans in boiling salted water for 7–10 minutes or until just tender. Add the leeks to the pan for the last 30 seconds, then drain the vegetables well and keep warm.
3 Put the cream into a small pan with half each of the Cheddar and Parmesan. Heat until just beginning to boil, stirring now and then to prevent it from boiling over.
4 Add the hot vegetables to the pasta and toss with the smoked ham and remaining cheese. Season with plenty of pepper (you won't need to add salt as the ham and cheese already make the dish quite salty).
5 Serve immediately on hot plates and hand the cream sauce around separately.

Serves 4   preparation: 15 minutes   cooking time: 15 minutes
per serving: 480 cals; 26g fat; 35g carbohydrate

Peppered Fettuccine

350g (12oz) dried pasta noodles
salt
125g (4oz) each peeled shallots and brown-
  cap mushrooms, sliced
25g (1oz) butter
275g (10oz) peppered salami, cut into strips

125g (4oz) soft cheese with garlic and herbs
142ml carton single cream
4tbsp milk
freshly grated Parmesan cheese, to serve
  (optional)

1 Cook the pasta in boiling salted water for the time stated on the packet.
2 Meanwhile, fry the shallots in the butter until golden. Add the mushrooms and fry for about 5 minutes or until beginning to soften. Add the salami and fry, stirring, for 1–2 minutes. Reduce the heat and stir in the soft cheese, cream and milk. Simmer, stirring, for about 2 minutes until piping hot.
3 Drain the pasta, put back in the pan and stir in the sauce. Serve immediately with a little Parmesan sprinkled over, if you like.

Serves 4   preparation: 15 minutes   cooking time: 15 minutes
per serving: 870 cals; 53g fat; 74g carbohydrate

Walnut and Creamy Blue Cheese Tagliatelle

400g (14oz) dried tagliatelle pasta
salt and pepper
1tsp olive oil
1 garlic clove, peeled and crushed
25g (1oz) walnut pieces, toasted

100g (3½oz) Gorgonzola cheese, chopped
into cubes
142ml carton single cream
50g (2oz) rocket

1   Cook the pasta in a large pan of boiling salted water for the time stated on the packet.
2   A few minutes before the pasta is ready, make the sauce. Heat the olive oil in a small pan, add the garlic and walnuts and cook for 1 minute – the garlic should be just golden. Add the Gorgonzola and cream and season with a little salt and plenty of pepper.
3   Drain the pasta well and return to the pan with a couple of spoonfuls of cooking water. Add the creamy sauce and the rocket, toss well and serve immediately.

Serves 4   preparation: 5 minutes   cooking time: 10–12 minutes
per serving: 550 cals; 26g fat; 60g carbohydrate

Fast food

Flash-in-the-pan Pork

700g (1½lb) new potatoes, scrubbed
salt
175g (6oz) runner beans, sliced
a little sunflower or olive oil
4 pork escalopes
150ml (¼ pint) each hot chicken stock
  and cider

2tbsp wholegrain mustard
150g tub Greek-style yogurt
leaves of 4 tarragon stems
squeeze of lemon juice

1 Cook the potatoes in a large pan of boiling salted water for 10 minutes. Add the beans and cook for 5 minutes or until tender. Drain and keep warm.
2 Meanwhile, heat the oil in a large non-stick frying pan and cook the pork over a medium heat for 3 minutes on each side until browned. Remove from the pan and keep warm. Add the hot stock, cider and mustard to the pan and increase the heat to reduce the liquid by half.
3 Just before serving, reduce the heat and add the yogurt, tarragon leaves and lemon juice to taste. Put the pork back into the pan to coat with sauce and warm through. Serve with the potatoes and beans.

Serves 4   preparation: 5 minutes   cooking time: 15 minutes
per serving: 430 cals; 17g fat; 31g carbohydrate

09

Fast food

Pesto Cod and Beans

4 small Icelandic cod fillets
4tbsp red pesto
generous glug of olive oil
2 x 410g cans butter beans, drained and rinsed

2 garlic cloves, peeled and crushed
225g (8oz) spinach
squeeze of lemon juice

1   Preheat the grill to medium. Spread each cod fillet evenly with 1tbsp red pesto and grill them for 10–15 minutes until the flesh is opaque and just cooked.
2   Meanwhile, heat the olive oil in a pan and add the beans and garlic. Cook for 10 minutes, stirring occasionally and mashing the beans lightly as you do.
3   A couple or so minutes before serving, add the spinach to the pan and allow it to wilt. Spoon the butter bean mash on to warmed plates and top with the cod and any juices from the tin. Squeeze a little lemon juice over each piece of fish and serve.

Serves 4   preparation: 5 minutes,   cooking time: 15 minutes
per serving: 410 cals; 13g fat; 26g carbohydrate

Sardines with Herbs

900g (2lb) sardines (at least 12), gutted
125ml (4fl oz) olive oil
3tbsp lemon juice, plus 2tsp grated lemon zest

4tbsp chopped mixed herbs, such as
    parsley, chervil and thyme
salt and pepper

1   Preheat the grill to medium-high. Rinse the sardines and pat dry with kitchen paper.
2   Pour the olive oil into a bowl and mix in the lemon juice, lemon zest, herbs and seasoning.
3   Lay the sardines on a grill rack, drizzle the herb dressing over them and grill for 5–7 minutes each side, basting frequently with the dressing. Serve hot or cold, accompanied by plenty of crusty bread.

Serves 4   preparation: 10 minutes   cooking time: 10 minutes
per serving: 340 cals; 25g fat; 0g carbohydrate

Smoked Trout Sandwich in Seconds

125g pack smoked trout, flaked
3tbsp Greek-style yogurt
salt and pepper

2 slices of Swedish-style rye bread
100g bag bistro salad

1   Put the smoked trout in a bowl, then mix in the yogurt. Season and spoon on to each slice of rye bread. Top with the salad and serve.

Serves 1–2   preparation: 5 minutes
per serving: 210 cals; 6g fat; 20g carbohydrate

Bacon and Egg Salad

4 eggs
250g (9oz) rindless smoked bacon rashers
150g (5oz) cherry tomatoes
2 slices of thick-cut bread
3tbsp mayonnaise

½ lemon
25g (1oz) freshly grated Parmesan cheese
black pepper
2 little gem lettuces

1 Heat a pan of water until simmering, add the eggs and boil for 6 minutes. Cool completely under cold water, then peel and put to one side.
2 Meanwhile, heat a griddle pan, then fry the bacon for 5 minutes until crisp. Remove from the pan, chop into large pieces and leave to cool.
3 Add the tomatoes and bread to the pan and fry in the bacon juices for 2–3 minutes until the bread is crisp and the tomatoes are starting to char. Remove from the heat, chop the bread into bite-sized croûtons and put to one side.
4 To make the dressing, put the mayonnaise into a bowl, squeeze in the lemon juice, add the Parmesan and mix. Season with pepper.
5 Separate the little gem leaves and put into a large serving bowl. Cut the eggs in half and add to the bowl with the bacon, tomatoes and croûtons. Drizzle over the dressing, toss lightly and serve.

Serves 4   preparation: 10 minutes   cooking time: about 10 minutes
per serving: 360 cals; 23g fat; 14g carbohydrate

Asparagus and Quail's Egg Salad

24 quail's eggs
24 asparagus spears, trimmed
salt and pepper
juice of ½ lemon
5tbsp olive oil

4 large spring onions, finely sliced
100g bag watercress, roughly chopped
few dill and tarragon sprigs

1 Add the quail's eggs to a pan of boiling water and cook for 2 minutes, then drain and plunge into cold water. Cook the asparagus in boiling salted water for 2 minutes or until just tender. Drain, plunge into cold water and leave to cool.
2 Whisk together the lemon juice, olive oil and seasoning. Stir in the spring onions and put to one side.
3 Peel the quail's eggs and cut in half. Put into a large bowl with the asparagus, watercress, dill and tarragon. Pour over the dressing and lightly toss all the ingredients together. Season and serve.

Serves 8   preparation: 30 minutes   cooking time: 2 minutes
per serving: 180 cals; 14g fat; 3g carbohydrate

Mixed Leaves with Avocado and Cherry Tomatoes

1tbsp cider or white wine vinegar
1tsp golden caster sugar
4tbsp walnut oil
salt and pepper

1 ripe avocado, peeled and flesh diced
150g (5oz) cherry tomatoes
about 200g (7oz) mixed salad leaves

1 Whisk together the vinegar, sugar and oil in a large bowl and season.
2 Toss the avocado in the dressing with the tomatoes and salad leaves. Serve at once.

Serves 6   preparation: 10 minutes
per serving: 150 cals; 14g fat; 3g carbohydrate

Spicy Noodle Salad

250g (9oz) cooked rice noodles
175g (6oz) each blanched broccoli and
  mangetout
2tsp sesame oil

2tbsp plum sauce
4tbsp dark soy sauce
sliced spring onions and chopped red
  chillies, to serve

1 Mix the noodles with the broccoli and mangetout, then toss with the oil, plum and soy sauces.
2 Sprinkle with the spring onions and chillies and serve.

Serves 4   preparation: 5 minutes   cooking time: 15 minutes
per serving: 110 cals; 3g fat; 16g carbohydrate

Hot Tomato Salad

700g (1½lb) mixed cherry tomatoes
   (red and yellow, if possible), halved
2 garlic cloves, peeled and sliced
2tbsp capers, drained and rinsed
1tsp golden caster sugar
salt and pepper

125ml (4fl oz) extra-virgin olive oil
1 ready-to-bake olive ciabatta loaf
2tbsp chopped basil
balsamic or red wine vinegar, to taste
basil sprigs, to garnish

1 Preheat the oven to 200°C (180°C fan oven) mark 6. Put the tomatoes, garlic, capers and sugar into a small roasting tin and stir to mix. Season well and pour on the olive oil.
2 Transfer to the oven and cook for 10–12 minutes or until the tomatoes are hot and beginning to soften. Pop the bread in the oven to bake alongside.
3 Remove the tomatoes from the oven and stir in the basil with a few drops of vinegar to taste. Slice the hot bread and spoon over the warm tomatoes and juices. Garnish with basil sprigs and serve.

Serves 6   preparation: 5 minutes   cooking time: 10–12 minutes
per serving: 310 cals; 20g fat; 27g carbohydrate

Warm Chicken Liver Salad

1–2tbsp balsamic vinegar
1tsp Dijon mustard
5tbsp olive oil
salt and pepper
2 x 225g tubs chicken livers

200g (7oz) streaky bacon rashers, de-rinded
   and cut into small pieces (lardons)
½ curly endive, about 175g (6oz)
100g (3½oz) rocket
1 bunch of spring onions, sliced

1 Unless you have very good, aged balsamic vinegar, put the vinegar in a small pan and reduce it by half. This will give the dressing a nice mellow flavour. To make the dressing, put the vinegar, mustard and 4tbsp olive oil in a small bowl and season. Whisk together and put to one side.
2 Drain the chicken livers, then trim them and cut into pieces.
3 Fry the lardons in a non-stick frying pan, until beginning to brown, stirring from time to time. Add the remaining oil and the chicken livers and stir-fry over a high heat for 2–3 minutes or until just pink in the centre. Season to taste.
4 Toss the endive, rocket and spring onions with the dressing in a large bowl. Quickly combine the warm livers and bacon and serve at once.

Serves 4   preparation: 20 minutes   cooking time: 8–10 minutes
per serving: 520 cals; 43g fat; 2g carbohydrate

Warm Spicy Chorizo Sausage and Chickpea Salad

5tbsp olive oil
200g (7oz) chorizo or spicy sausage,
  thinly sliced
225g (8oz) red onion, peeled and chopped
1 large red pepper, deseeded and
  roughly chopped
3 garlic cloves, peeled and finely chopped

1tsp cumin seeds
2 x 400g cans chickpeas,
  drained and rinsed
2tbsp chopped coriander
juice of 1 lemon
salt and pepper

1　Heat 1tbsp olive oil in a non-stick frying pan and cook the chorizo or spicy sausage over a medium heat for 1–2 minutes or until lightly browned. Remove the chorizo with a slotted spoon and put to one side. Fry the onion in the chorizo oil for 10 minutes or until browned.
2　Add the red pepper, garlic, cumin and chickpeas to the onion and cook for a further 5 minutes, stirring frequently to prevent sticking. Remove the pan from the heat and add the chorizo.
3　Add the coriander, lemon juice and remaining olive oil. Season well and serve immediately.

Serves 4　preparation: 15 minutes　cooking time: 17 minutes
per serving: 470 cals; 32g fat; 29g carbohydrate

Hummus with Rocket and Mint Salad

400g can chickpeas, drained and rinsed
juice of 1 lemon
4tbsp tahini
1 garlic clove, peeled and crushed
175ml (6fl oz) extra-virgin olive oil
salt and pepper

3tbsp sherry vinegar
3 x 50g bags wild rocket
12 small mint leaves
12 Peppadew sweet piquant peppers (mild)
6tbsp sliced jalapeño chillies
4 sesame seed flatbreads

1　To make the hummus, put the chickpeas, lemon juice, tahini, garlic and 75ml (3fl oz) olive oil in a food processor. Season generously, then whiz to a paste. Spoon the hummus into a non-metallic bowl, then cover and chill overnight.
2　To make the dressing, put the remaining olive oil, the sherry vinegar and a pinch of salt in a screw-topped jar. Tighten the lid and shake well to mix. Chill overnight.
3　To serve, divide the hummus between six small (150ml/¼ pint) pots. Put on to six plates. Put the rocket and mint leaves in a bowl, then drizzle the dressing over. Divide the salad, peppers, jalapeño chillies and sesame seed flatbreads among the six plates. Note: once the salad is dressed, you need to serve within 20 minutes.

Serves 6　preparation: 15 minutes　cooking time: 5 minutes
per serving: 470 cals; 31g fat; 39g carbohydrate

Lamb Steaks with Mixed Bean Salad

150g (5oz) sunblush tomatoes in oil
1 garlic clove, peeled and crushed
few rosemary sprigs
salt and pepper
4 x 175g (6oz) leg of lamb steaks

½ small red onion, peeled and finely sliced
2 x 400g cans mixed beans, drained
 and rinsed
large handful of rocket

1 Preheat the grill to high. Drain the sunblush tomatoes, reserving the oil. Put the garlic in a large shallow
   dish with 1tbsp oil from the tomatoes. Snip the rosemary leaves into small pieces and add half to the
   dish. Season, then add the lamb and toss to coat.

2 Grill the lamb for 3–4 minutes on each side until cooked but still just pink. Roughly chop the tomatoes
   and put into a pan with the onion, beans, remaining rosemary, rocket and a further 1tbsp oil from the
   tomatoes. Warm through until the rocket starts to wilt. Serve the lamb steaks with the salad on
   warmed plates.

Serves 4   preparation: 5 minutes   cooking time: about 10 minutes
per serving 370 cals; 16g fat; 15g carbohydrate

Egg and Pepper Pizza

150g (5oz) red and yellow marinated
  peppers in oil
8tbsp passata

4 small pizza bases
4 eggs
125g (4oz) watercress

1 Preheat the oven to 220°C (200°C fan oven) mark 7. Preheat two large baking sheets, big enough
   to fit two pizzas each.
2 Drain the peppers, reserving the oil, and chop them into thin strips. Spoon 2tbsp passata over each
   pizza base and scatter strips of pepper round the edges. Make a dip in the passata in the middle of
   each pizza and break an egg into it. Carefully slide the pizzas on to the preheated baking sheet.
   Transfer to the oven and cook for 12 minutes until the egg is thoroughly cooked.
3 Top the pizzas with the watercress, drizzle over a little of the reserved oil from the peppers and serve.

Serves 4 preparation: 5 minutes   cooking time: 12 minutes
per serving: 330 cals; 12g fat; 40g carbohydrate

Pan-fried Mushrooms and Feta Omelette

50g (2oz) butter
225g (8oz) large mushrooms, thinly sliced
3 garlic cloves, peeled and sliced
50g (2oz) sun-dried tomatoes, roughly
  chopped

4 large eggs, beaten
black pepper
100g (3½oz) feta cheese, crumbled
thyme sprigs, to garnish

1 Melt the butter in an 18cm (7 inch) diameter non-stick omelette pan and fry the mushrooms with the
   garlic until they're a deep golden brown and beginning to go crisp around the edges. Add the sun-
   dried tomatoes and stir over the heat for 1–2 minutes. Meanwhile, preheat the grill to high.
2 Roughly spread the mushroom mixture over the base of the pan. Beat 2tbsp cold water into the eggs
   and season with pepper (both feta cheese and sun-dried tomatoes can be salty so no extra salt
   should be needed to season the omelette). Pour over the mushrooms, gently swirling the pan to
   spread the eggs. Leave to set undisturbed on a low heat for 1–2 minutes, then sprinkle the feta over.
3 Put the pan under the grill for about 1–2 minutes or until the eggs are lightly cooked and the feta
   cheese is just beginning to melt.
4 Sprinkle the omelette with black pepper and scatter with thyme sprigs to garnish. Cut into wedges
   and serve immediately.

Serves 4 preparation: 5 minutes   cooking time: 15 minutes
per serving: 280 cals; 22g fat; 5g carbohydrate

15-minute Couscous

225g (8oz) couscous
75g (3oz) dates, roughly chopped
large pinch of saffron strands

40g (1½oz) butter
salt and pepper
25g (1oz) flaked almonds

1 Put the couscous, dates, saffron and 25g (1oz) butter in a bowl. Add 300ml (½ pint) boiling water, season and stir to mix. Cover and leave to soak for 10 minutes or until all the water is absorbed and the couscous is soft.
2 To make each portion, line a 300ml (½ pint) bowl with clingfilm, spoon in a quarter of the couscous and press down firmly. Invert a dinner plate on to the couscous and turn out, discarding the clingfilm. Repeat with the rest of the couscous.
3 Fry the almonds in the remaining butter until golden and scatter over each portion of couscous. Serve on its own or as an accompaniment.

Serves 4   preparation: 5 minutes, plus soaking
per serving: 350 cals; 12g fat; 55g carbohydrate

Posh Mushrooms on Toast

4 large flat mushrooms, such as portabello
4tbsp mascarpone
salt and pepper
8 slices of Parma ham

4 slices of good firm bread,
  such as sourdough
rocket or other salad leaves, to serve

1 Preheat the oven to 230°C (210°C fan oven) mark 8. Trim the mushroom stalks and put the mushrooms, stalk side up, on a roasting tray and spoon 1tbsp mascarpone on top of each. Season well, then put 2 slices of ham on top of each, arranging them so that the whole mushroom is covered. Cook in the oven for 10 minutes.
2 Meanwhile, toast the bread. Top each slice of toast with a mushroom and serve with a handful of rocket.

Serves 4   preparation: 5 minutes   cooking time: 10 minutes
per serving: 250 cals; 12g fat; 24g carbohydrate

Chèvre en Croute

½ short baguette
1–2tbsp hazelnut oil
1 small garlic clove, peeled and crushed
125g (4oz) chèvre log, about 2.5cm (1 inch)
   in diameter, cut into six slices

paprika
6 thyme sprigs

1 Preheat the oven to 180°C (160°C fan oven) mark 4. Cut six 1cm (½ inch) thick slices from the baguette. Mix the oil with the garlic and brush both sides of the baguette slices. Put on a baking sheet and bake for about 5 minutes.
2 Remove from the oven and put a slice of chèvre on each baguette slice and top with a sprinkling of paprika and a thyme sprig.
3 Return the croûtes to the oven for a further 7 minutes, or until the cheese is soft and spongy. Serve warm with a mixed leaf salad.

Serves 6 preparation: 5 minutes   cooking time: 12 minutes
per serving: 110 cals; 7g fat; 8g carbohydrate

Smoked Haddock Rarebit

4 x 150g (5oz) skinned smoked
   haddock fillets
salt and pepper
1 large ciabatta

200g (7oz) spinach
300g carton cheese sauce
2 large tomatoes, sliced

1 Preheat the grill. Season the haddock and put into a shallow ovenproof dish. Grill for 6–8 minutes until opaque and cooked through.
2 Slice the ciabatta in half lengthways, then halve again horizontally. Grill on both sides until golden.
3 Put the spinach in a pan, cover and cook for 1–2 minutes until starting to wilt. Season and tip into a bowl. Add the cheese sauce to the pan and bring to the boil, then reduce the heat and simmer for 1–2 minutes until hot.
4 Top each piece of ciabatta with a piece of fish, then add the spinach and tomato slices. Pour over the cheese sauce and grill for 2–3 minutes to heat through. Season well with pepper and serve.

Serves 4 preparation: 5 minutes   cooking time: 10–15 minutes
per serving: 500 cals; 16g fat; 43g carbohydrate

Cheese Bites

butter, to grease
225g (8oz) puff pastry
50g (2oz) olives, pitted and halved or
quartered
125g (4oz) firm buttery cheese, such as
Jarlsberg or Emmental, or a soft cheese
such as mozzarella, cut into small dice

50g (2oz) sun-dried tomatoes in oil, drained
and roughly chopped
50g (2oz) capers, roughly chopped
50g can anchovy fillets, roughly chopped
50g (2oz) pesto sauce
salt and pepper

1   Preheat the oven to 200°C (180°C fan oven) mark 6. Lightly grease a baking sheet. Roll out the pastry
to 3mm (⅛ inch), then, using a 5cm (2 inch) round cutter, stamp out 24 circles. Put them on the
baking sheet.
2   Arrange some olives, cheese, sun-dried tomatoes, capers and anchovies on each pastry circle.
Spoon over a little pesto sauce and season.
3   Transfer to the oven and cook for 10–15 minutes, until well risen and crisp. Serve immediately.

Makes about 24   preparation: 5 minutes   cooking time: 10–15 minutes
per bite: 80 cals; 6g fat; 4g carbohydrate

Easy Wrap

1tsp each salt and pepper
2 cooked chicken breasts, cut into bite-
sized pieces
1 carrot, peeled and grated
1 avocado, peeled and chopped

small handful of rocket
juice of ½ lemon
3tbsp mayonnaise
4 soft tortillas

1   Mix the salt with the pepper in a large bowl. Add the chicken, carrot, avocado and rocket and
mix well.
2   In a separate bowl, mix the lemon juice with the mayonnaise, then spread over the tortillas. Divide the
chicken mixture among the tortillas, roll up and serve in napkins.

Serves 4   preparation: 10 minutes   cooking time: about 10 minutes
per serving: 360 cals; 23g fat; 14g carbohydrate

Better than a takeaway

Sometimes nothing but a curry will do. And once the idea's in your head, it really gets the tastebuds going.

You might fancy an Indian – Prawn Madras served with Coconut Chutney, or a Thai Green Chicken Curry served with Thai Rice. Or perhaps noodles are more your thing. The Yellow Bean Noodles with Tiger Prawns are ready in no time, while the Chinese Speedy Beef Noodles are spiced up with chilli.

Curry doesn't necessarily mean hot – it can be aromatic and spicy, such as the Salmon Laksa Curry, where succulent salmon is simmered in laksa stock, its heat tempered by soothing coconut milk. The noodles are then stirred into the broth, making this a complete meal in one.

Classic Saag Aloo; Chicken Satay Skewers; Crispy Duck with Hot and Sweet Dip; Thai Crab Balls with Sweet Chilli Sauce; Fried Yellow Bean Pork with Cashews – so many to choose from, and to got with it all you need to do is rustle up some Easy Basmati Pilaf, Special Prawn Fried Rice, or Split Pea Roti, then sit back and enjoy.

So get out the chopsticks or put on some bangra, get cooking and prove that these are definitely 'better than a takeaway'.

Yellow Bean Noodles with Tiger Prawns

250g pack medium egg noodles
1tbsp stir-fry oil or sesame oil
1 garlic clove, peeled and sliced
1tsp peeled and freshly grated root ginger
1 bunch of spring onions, each cut into four

250g pack frozen peeled raw
  tiger prawns, thawed
200g pak choi, leaves removed and white
  base cut into thick slices
160g jar Chinese yellow bean stir-fry sauce

1 Put the noodles in a bowl, pour over 2 litres (3½ pints) boiling water and leave to soak for 4 minutes. Drain.
2 Heat the oil in a wok, add the garlic and ginger and stir-fry for 30 seconds. Add the spring onions and prawns and cook for 2 minutes.
3 Add the chopped white part of the pak choi and the yellow bean sauce. Pour boiling water to fill the sauce jar and pour this into the wok.
4 Add the noodles to the pan and cook for 1 minute, tossing every now and then to heat everything through. Finally, stir in the green pak choi leaves and serve.

Serves 4–6   preparation: 10 minutes   cooking time: 5 minutes, plus standing
per serving: 340 cals; 6g fat; 51g carbohydrate

Thai-style Tiger Prawns with Pak Choi

3tbsp Thai red curry paste
200ml (7fl oz) coconut milk
juice of 1 lime
24 raw tiger prawns, peeled with
  tail on and deveined
8 kaffir lime leaves
4 long lemon grass stalks, outer
  layer removed

2 x 200g packs pak choi, cut in
  half lengthways
1tbsp light soy sauce
salt and pepper
2tbsp sweet chilli sauce

1 Put the curry paste in a bowl and add the coconut milk, half the lime juice and the prawns. Stir to coat, then cover and chill for 15 minutes. Preheat the grill.
2 Carefully skewer six prawns and two lime leaves on to each lemon grass stalk. Cook under the grill for 5 minutes or until the prawns are pink and cooked through.
3 Meanwhile, put the pak choi in a steamer over a pan of boiling water, cover and cook for 3–4 minutes.
4 Toss the pak choi in the soy sauce and remaining lime juice and season. Serve with the prawn skewers, drizzled with sweet chilli sauce.

Serves 4–6   preparation: 10 minutes, plus marinating   cooking time: 5 minutes
per serving: 168 cals; 8g fat; 8 carbohydrate

Better than a takeaway

Sesame Chilli Prawns

40 ready-cooked tiger prawns, about 450g
  (1lb), peeled with tail on

5tbsp sweet chilli sauce
75g (3oz) toasted sesame seeds

1 Hold each prawn by the tail and dip into the chilli sauce, then into the sesame seeds.
2 Put on a tray lined with clingfilm, cover loosely and chill until required.

Makes 40   preparation: 40 minutes
per prawn 20 cals; 1g fat; Tr carbohydrate

Thai Noodles with Prawns

1–2tbsp Thai red curry paste
175g (6oz) medium egg noodles, preferably
  wholewheat
2 small red onions, peeled and chopped
1 lemon grass stalk, sliced
1 Thai red chilli, deseeded and finely
  chopped
300ml (½ pint) half-fat coconut milk, or use

half a can of full-fat coconut milk and
  make up the difference with water
  or stock
400g (14oz) peeled raw tiger prawns,
  deveined
salt and pepper
4tbsp chopped coriander, plus extra
  leaves to garnish

1 Put 2 litres (3½ pints) water into a large pan and bring to the boil. Add the curry paste, noodles, onions, lemon grass, chilli and coconut milk. Bring the mixture to the boil, then add the prawns and coriander, reduce the heat and simmer for 2–3 minutes or until the prawns turn pink.
2 Season and serve in large bowls sprinkled with coriander leaves.

Serves 4   preparation: 10 minutes   cooking time: 5 minutes
per serving: 340 cals; 11g fat; 38g carbohydrate

Thai Green Shellfish Curry

1tbsp vegetable oil
1 pack fresh Thai herbs (containing 1 lemon
grass, 2 Thai chillies, coriander leaves,
2 lime leaves), all chopped
1-2tbsp Thai green curry paste
400ml can coconut milk

450ml (¾ pint) vegetable stock
salt and pepper
375g (13oz) queen scallops with corals
250g (9oz) raw tiger prawns, peeled with
tails on and deveined
coriander leaves, to garnish

1 Heat the oil in a wok and fry the Thai herbs for 30 seconds. Add the curry paste and fry for 1 minute.
2 Add the coconut milk and stock and bring to the boil, then reduce the heat and simmer for
   5-10 minutes until reduced a little. Season well.
3 Add the scallops and prawns and bring to the boil, then reduce the heat and simmer gently for
   2-3 minutes or until cooked. Spoon into bowls of Thai jasmine rice and garnish with coriander.

Serves 6   preparation: 5 minutes   cooking time: 15 minutes
per serving: 230 cals; 14g fat; 2g carbohydrate

Thai Red Seafood Curry

1tbsp oil
3tbsp Thai red curry paste
450g (1lb) monkfish tail, filleted and
sliced into rounds, about 350g
(12oz) filleted weight
350g (12oz) peeled large raw prawns,
deveined
400ml can half-fat coconut milk, or use

half a can of full-fat coconut milk and make
up the difference with water or stock
200ml (7fl oz) fish stock
juice of 1 lime
1-2tbsp Thai fish sauce
125g (4oz) mangetout, sliced lengthways
3tbsp torn coriander
salt and pepper

1 Heat the oil in a large non-stick sauté pan or wok. Add the curry paste and cook, stirring, for 1-2 minutes.
2 Add the monkfish and prawns and stir well to coat in the curry paste. Add the coconut milk, stock,
   lime juice and fish sauce. Stir all the ingredients together and bring just to the boil.
3 Add the mangetout, reduce the heat and simmer for 5 minutes or until both mangetout and fish are
   tender. Stir in the coriander and season to taste. Serve with plain boiled rice.

Serves 4   preparation: 15 minutes   cooking time: 8-10 minutes
per serving: 350 cals; 19g fat; 5g carbohydrate

Thai Crab Balls with Sweet Chilli Sauce

2tsp sesame oil

1 large red chilli, deseeded and
  finely chopped

2.5cm (1 inch) piece fresh root ginger,
  peeled and finely grated, plus 2tbsp finely
  chopped fresh root ginger

2 garlic cloves, peeled and crushed

8tbsp light muscovado sugar

3tsp Thai fish sauce

2tbsp light soy sauce

juice of 2 limes

1tbsp sunflower oil, plus extra for
  deep-frying

4 spring onions, finely chopped

1 lemon grass stalk, outer leaves discarded
  and remainder finely chopped

350g (12oz) fresh or frozen crab meat

2tbsp chopped coriander

75g (3oz) white breadcrumbs

3 eggs

black pepper

50g (2oz) plain flour

coriander sprigs and shredded red chilli,
  to garnish

1 To make the chilli sauce, put the sesame oil in a pan and heat gently. Add ½tsp chopped chilli, the 2tbsp chopped ginger and 1 garlic clove and cook for 1–2 minutes until softened. Add the sugar, 2tsp fish sauce and the soy sauce, then bring to the boil, reduce the heat and simmer for 2 minutes. Remove from the heat and stir in 8tbsp water and the lime juice. Pour into a serving bowl, cover and put to one side.

2 To make the crab balls, heat the sunflower oil in a small pan and add the spring onions, remaining garlic, the grated ginger, remaining chilli and the lemon grass. Cook gently for 2–3 minutes or until soft. Transfer to a bowl and cool, then stir in the crab meat, coriander, remaining fish sauce, 6tbsp breadcrumbs and 1 egg. Mix and season with pepper only. Shape tablespoonfuls of the mixture into 18 balls, put on a baking sheet and chill for 20 minutes.

3 Beat the remaining eggs. Coat each ball lightly with flour, roll in the beaten eggs, then in the remaining breadcrumbs. Heat the sunflower oil in a large pan and deep-fry the crab balls in batches for 3–4 minutes or until golden. Drain on kitchen paper and keep warm while frying the remaining balls. Garnish with coriander sprigs and shredded red chilli and serve with the sweet chilli sauce.

Makes 18 balls   preparation: 30 minutes, plus chilling   cooking time: 20 minutes
per ball with sauce: 120 cals; 6g fat; 12g carbohydrate

Thai Fishcakes with Chilli Mayo

1 bunch of spring onions

2.5cm (1 inch) piece fresh root ginger,
   peeled and roughly chopped

1 lemon grass stalk, roughly chopped

20g pack coriander

½ red chilli, deseeded

1tsp Thai fish sauce (optional)

½ quantity Five-minute Mayonnaise
   (page 17)

75g (3oz) fresh white breadcrumbs

225g (8oz) each haddock and cooked
   peeled prawns

oil, for frying

2tbsp Thai sweet chilli sauce

20g pack basil, roughly chopped

1 fat garlic clove, crushed (optional)

2 limes, halved

120g bag baby leaf spinach

1 Put the spring onions, ginger, lemon grass, coriander, chilli and fish sauce, if using, in a food processor and whiz to a rough paste. Add 3tbsp mayonnaise, the breadcrumbs, fish and prawns and whiz for 5 seconds.

2 With wet hands, shape into eight patties, each about 5cm (2 inches) in diameter.

3 Heat a drizzle of oil in a non-stick frying pan. Fry the patties for 3–4 minutes on each side until crisp and golden.

4 Mix the chilli sauce, basil and garlic, if using, into the remaining mayonnaise. Serve with the fishcakes, lime and spinach leaves.

Serves 4   preparation: 25 minutes   cooking time: 8–10 minutes
per serving: 470 cals; 29g fat; 11g carbohydrate

Prawn and Vegetable Pilau

250g (9oz) long-grain rice

1 broccoli head, broken into florets

150g (5oz) baby sweetcorn, halved

200g (7oz) sugarsnap peas

1 red pepper, halved, deseeded and cut into
   thin strips

400g (14oz) cooked peeled king prawns

1tbsp sesame oil

5cm (2 inch) piece fresh root ginger,
   peeled and grated

juice of 1 lime

1–2tbsp soy sauce

1 Put the rice in a very large, wide pan. Add 600ml (1 pint) boiling water. Cover and bring to the boil, then reduce the heat to low and cook the rice for the time stated on the packet.

2 About 10 minutes before the end of the rice cooking time, add the broccoli, sweetcorn, sugarsnaps and red pepper. Stir well, then cover and cook until the vegetables and rice are just tender.

3 Meanwhile, put the prawns into a bowl and add the sesame oil, ginger, lime juice and soy sauce. Stir the prawns and dressing into the cooked vegetables and rice and toss well.

Serves 4   preparation: 10 minutes   cooking time: 15–20 minutes
per serving: 390 cals; 5g fat; 57g carbohydrate

Salmon Laksa Curry

1tbsp olive oil
1 onion, peeled and finely sliced
3tbsp laksa paste
200ml (7fl oz) coconut milk
900ml (1½ pints) hot vegetable stock
200g (7oz) baby sweetcorn, halved
  lengthways
salt and pepper

600g (1lb 6oz) piece skinless salmon fillet,
  cut into 1cm (½ inch) slices
225g pack baby spinach leaves
250g pack medium rice noodles
2 spring onions, sliced diagonally
2tbsp chopped coriander
1 lime, cut into four wedges

1 Heat the olive oil in a large pan, add the onion and fry over a medium heat for 10 minutes, stirring, until golden. Add the laksa paste and cook for 2 minutes. Add the coconut milk, hot stock and baby sweetcorn and season. Bring to the boil, then reduce the heat and simmer for 5 minutes. Add the salmon and spinach and immerse them in the liquid. Cook for 4 minutes until the fish is opaque to the centre.
3 Meanwhile, put the noodles in a large bowl, pour boiling water over and soak for 30 seconds. Drain, then stir into the curry. Pour into bowls, garnish with the spring onions, coriander and lime and serve.

Serves 4 preparation: 15 minutes   cooking time: 22 minutes
per serving: 680 cals; 33g fat; 58g carbohydrate

Salmon and Coconut Curry

1tbsp olive oil
1 red onion, peeled and sliced
2tbsp tikka masala curry paste
4 x 100g (3½oz) salmon steaks

400ml can coconut milk
juice of 1 lime
handful of coriander, roughly chopped

1 Heat the olive oil in a pan. Add the onion and cook over a medium heat for 10 minutes until golden and softened.
2 Add the curry paste to the pan and cook for 1 minute to warm the spices. Add the fish and cook for 2 minutes, turning it once to coat it in the spices.
3 Pour in the coconut milk and bring to the boil, then reduce the heat and simmer for 5 minutes or until the fish is cooked through. Squeeze over the lime juice, sprinkle with coriander and serve with boiled rice or naan bread to soak up the creamy sauce.

Serves 4 preparation: 2 minutes   cooking time: 18 minutes
per serving: 400 cals; 33g fat; 6g carbohydrate

Prawn Madras with Coconut Chutney

1 small and 2 medium onions, peeled

2.5cm (1 inch) piece fresh root ginger,
  peeled and finely chopped

2 garlic cloves, peeled and crushed

juice of ½ lemon

1tbsp each cumin seeds and coriander seeds

1tsp cayenne pepper

2tsp each ground turmeric and
  garam masala

salt

3tbsp groundnut oil

1tbsp black mustard seeds

125g (4oz) desiccated coconut

1 red chilli, deseeded and diced

1 green chilli, deseeded and finely chopped

600ml (1 pint) vegetable stock

450g (1lb) raw king prawns, peeled
  and deveined

2 bay leaves

coriander leaves, to garnish

1　To make the madras paste, finely chop 1 small onion and put into a food processor with the ginger, garlic, lemon juice, cumin and corianders seeds, cayenne pepper, turmeric and garam masala, 1tsp salt and 2tbsp water and whiz until smooth. Divide the paste into three equal portions, freeze two parts in separate bags to use within 3 months (see below) and put the rest into a large bowl.

2　To make the coconut chutney, grate 1 onion. Heat 1tbsp oil in a pan and add the mustard seeds. Cover the pan with a lid and cook over a medium heat until the seeds pop – you'll hear them jumping against the lid. Add the grated onion, coconut and red chilli and cook for 3–4 minutes to toast the coconut. Take off the heat and put to one side.

3　To make the curry, finely slice the remaining onion. Heat the remaining oil in a pan, add the sliced onion and fry for 10 minutes until soft and golden. Add the madras paste and green chilli and cook for 5 minutes. Add the stock and bring to the boil.

4　Reduce to a simmer and add the prawns and bay leaves. Cook for 3–5 minutes or until the prawns turn pink and are cooked. Garnish with coriander and serve with the coconut chutney and basmati rice.

Serves 4　preparation: 10 minutes　cooking time: 25 minutes
per serving: 430 cals; 31g fat; 13g carbohydrate

To use the frozen paste: Put the paste in a microwave and cook on Defrost for 1 minute 20 seconds (based on 900W oven), or thaw at cool room temperature for 1 hour.

Easy Thai Red Chicken Curry

1tbsp vegetable oil

3tbsp Thai red curry paste

4 skinless boneless chicken breasts, about
 600g (1lb 6oz), sliced

400ml can coconut milk

300ml (½ pint) hot chicken or

vegetable stock

juice of 1 lime

200g pack mixed baby sweetcorn
 and mangetout

2tbsp chopped coriander

1 Heat the oil in a wok or large pan. Add the curry paste and cook for 2 minutes. Add the chicken breasts and fry gently until browned.
2 Add the coconut milk, hot stock, lime juice and baby corn to the pan and bring to the boil. Add the mangetout, reduce the heat and simmer for 4–5 minutes until the chicken is cooked. Add the coriander and serve immediately with plain rice noodles.

Serves 4   preparation: 5 minutes   cooking time: 20 minutes
per serving: 410 cals; 28g fat; 5g carbohydrate

Thai Green Chicken Curry

1tsp olive oil

1 small onion, peeled and finely sliced

1cm (½ inch) piece fresh root ginger,
 peeled and diced

½ small red chilli, deseeded and
 finely chopped

2 skinless boneless chicken breasts,
 about 250g (9oz), sliced

1tbsp Thai green curry paste

200ml (7fl oz) each coconut milk
 and hot vegetable stock

50g (2oz) Thai jasmine rice

1 pak choi, sliced into three pieces

125g (4oz) broccoli, cut into florets

125g (4oz) mangetout

1 Heat the olive oil in a pan and fry the onion until soft. Add the ginger, chilli and chicken and stir-fry for 5 minutes.
2 Add the curry paste, coconut milk and hot stock and bring to the boil, then reduce the heat and simmer for 15 minutes or until the chicken is cooked.
3 Meanwhile, put the rice in a pan, stir in 125ml (4fl oz) cold water and bring to the boil. Cover the pan, reduce the heat and simmer for about 8 minutes. Turn off the heat, cover with a tea-towel and replace the lid to absorb the steam.
4 Add the pak choi, broccoli and mangetout to the curry, then cover and cook for about 5 minutes.
5 Fluff up the rice with a fork and serve with the chicken curry.

Serves 2   preparation: 15 minutes   cooking time: 25 minutes
per serving: 475 cals; 8g fat; 34g carbohydrate

Coconut Thai Chicken

1tbsp Thai red curry paste

4tbsp coconut milk

salt and pepper

2 chicken breasts, with skin on

1 Put the curry paste and coconut milk in a bowl, season and mix well. Place the chicken breasts in the marinade, cover and leave for at least 30 minutes. Heat the grill to high.

2 Drain the chicken, reserving the marinade and grill the chicken, skin side down, for 5 minutes. Turn the chicken, brush with marinade and cook for 5 minutes or until golden and cooked through. (Insert a skewer into the thickest part of the chicken: if the juices run clear, it's done.) To crisp the skin, move the chicken closer to the heat.

3 Just before serving, spoon the reserved marinade over and return the chicken to the grill for 1 minute. Slice the chicken and serve.

Serves 2   preparation: 5 minutes, plus marinating   cooking time: 10 minutes
per serving: 320 cals; 22 fat; 1g carbohydrate

Chicken Glazed in Hoisin Sauce

450g (1lb) skinless boneless
    chicken breasts

½tsp salt

pinch of white pepper

8tsp medium-dry sherry

1tsp cornflour

1 egg white, lightly beaten

2tsp sesame oil

2tbsp vegetable oil

5 garlic cloves, peeled and roughly chopped

5 spring onions, roughly chopped

227g can sliced bamboo shoots, drained

227g can whole water chestnuts, drained

juice of 1 orange

244g jar hoisin sauce

50g (2oz) cashew nuts

1tbsp sesame seeds

1 Cut the chicken into 2cm (¾ inch) pieces. Put in a bowl with the salt, pepper and 2tsp sherry. Sprinkle with the cornflour and stir in the egg white. Leave for 15–20 minutes; stir in the sesame oil.

2 Heat 1tbsp vegetable oil in a wok. Add the chicken and cook for 2 minutes, then transfer to a plate.

3 Add the remaining oil to the wok and, when hot, add the garlic, spring onions, bamboo shoots and water chestnuts and stir-fry for 2 minutes. Pour the remaining sherry around the side of the wok and when the sizzling has stopped, return the chicken to the wok with the orange juice and hoisin sauce. Heat through gently, then stir in the cashew nuts and sesame seeds. Transfer to a warmed dish and serve immediately.

Serves 4   preparation: 5 minutes, plus standing   cooking time: 10 minutes
per serving: 470 cals; 23g fat; 35g carbohydrate

Chicken Satay Skewers

1tbsp each coriander seeds and
  cumin seeds
2tsp ground turmeric
4 garlic cloves, peeled and roughly chopped
zest and juice of 1 lemon
2 bird's eye chillies, deseeded and
  finely chopped
3tbsp vegetable oil
1tsp salt

4 boneless, skinless chicken breasts, about
  600g (1¼lb), cut into finger-length strips
200g (7oz) salted peanuts
1tbsp molasses sugar
½ lemon grass stalk, chopped
2tbsp dark soy sauce
juice of ½ lime
200ml pack coconut cream
½ cucumber, thinly sliced, to serve

1 Soak 24 x 15cm (6 inch) bamboo skewers in water. Put the coriander and cumin seeds and the turmeric in a dry frying pan and heat for 30 seconds. Tip into a processor and add the garlic, lemon zest and juice, chillies, 1tbsp oil and the salt. Whiz for 1–2 minutes to a paste.

2 Put the paste in a large shallow dish, add the chicken and toss everything together. Cover and chill for at least 20 minutes or up to 12 hours.

3 To make the sauce, put the peanuts, sugar, lemon grass, soy sauce, lime juice and coconut cream in a processor and add 2tbsp water. Whiz to make a thick, chunky sauce and spoon into a dish.

4 Preheat the grill to high. Thread the chicken on to the skewers, drizzle with the remaining oil and grill for 4–5 minutes on each side or until the juices run clear. Serve with the sauce and the cucumber.

Serves 4 preparation: 30 minutes, plus chilling cooking time: 40 minutes
per serving: 610 cals; 47g fat; 9g carbohydrate

Chicken Tikka Masala

2tbsp oil
1 onion, peeled and finely sliced
2 garlic cloves, peeled and crushed
6 skinless boneless chicken thighs, cut
  into strips

2tbsp tikka masala curry paste
200g can chopped tomatoes
450ml (¾ pint) hot vegetable stock
225g (8oz) baby spinach leaves

1 Heat the oil in a large pan, add the onion and fry over a medium heat for 5–7 minutes until golden. Add the garlic and chicken and stir-fry for about 5 minutes until golden.

2 Stir in the curry paste, then add the tomatoes and hot stock. Bring to the boil, then reduce the heat, cover the pan and simmer over a low heat for 15 minutes or until the chicken is cooked through.

3 Add the spinach to the curry, stir and cook until the leaves have just wilted. Serve with plain boiled rice, mango chutney and poppadoms.

Serves 4 preparation: 15 minutes cooking time: 25 minutes
per serving: 270 cals; 14g fat; 10g carbohydrate

Tandoori Chicken with Cucumber Raita

24 garlic cloves, about 125g (4oz), peeled
  and crushed
5cm (2 inch) piece fresh root ginger, peeled
  and chopped
3tbsp each coriander seeds, cumin seeds,
  ground fenugreek and paprika
3 red chillies, deseeded and chopped
3tsp English mustard
2tbsp tomato purée

1tsp salt
4tbsp groundnut oil, plus extra to oil
3 x 150ml cartons natural yogurt
juice of ½ lemon
4 skinless boneless chicken breasts, about
  600g (1¼lb), cut into finger-width pieces
½ cucumber
salt and pepper
mint sprigs, to garnish

1 To make the tandoori paste, put the garlic, ginger, coriander and cumin seeds, fenugreek, paprika, chillies, mustard, tomato purée and salt into a mini processor with 8tbsp water and whiz to a paste. Divide the paste into three equal portions, freeze two parts in separate bags to use within 3 months (see below) and put the rest into a large bowl.
2 To make the tandoori chicken, add half the oil, 2 cartons yogurt and the lemon juice to the paste. Add the chicken to it and stir well to coat. Cover the bowl, chill and marinate the chicken for at least 4 hours.
3 Preheat the oven to 220°C (200°C fan oven) mark 7. Oil a roasting tin. Put the chicken in it, drizzle the remaining oil over it and roast the chicken for 20 minutes or until cooked through.
4 Meanwhile, prepare the raita. Whisk the remaining carton of yogurt. With a vegetable peeler, scrape the cucumber into very thin strips. Put the strips in a bowl and pour the whisked yogurt over them. Season, then chill. Garnish the cucumber raita with mint sprigs and serve it with the chicken.

To use the frozen paste: Put the paste in a microwave and cook on Defrost for 1 minute 20 seconds (based on 900W oven), or thaw at cool room temperature for 1 hour.

Serves 4 preparation: 45 minutes, plus marinating   cooking time: 20 minutes
per serving: 360 cals; 20g fat; 10g carbohydrate

10-minute Thai Curry

1tbsp vegetable oil
4 skinless boneless chicken breasts, about
  600g (1¼lb), thinly sliced

400ml can Gang Musman red curry
200ml (7fl oz) coconut milk
150g (5oz) sugarsnap peas

1 Heat the oil in a large pan and fry the chicken over a medium-high heat for 5 minutes until golden.
2 Add the red curry, coconut milk and sugarsnap peas. Heat for 5 minutes or until the meat is cooked and the sauce is heated through, then serve with jasmine rice.

Serves 4 preparation: 5 minutes   cooking time: 12 minutes
per serving: 240 cals; 16g fat; 10g carbohydrate

Chicken Curry

1tbsp oil
4 chicken legs, skinned
1 onion, peeled and finely chopped
2tbsp mild or medium curry paste
2 leeks, sliced

200g can chopped tomatoes
1 small cauliflower, broken into florets
250g (9oz) small new potatoes
600ml (1 pint) hot chicken stock
150g (5oz) each spinach and frozen peas

1 Heat the oil in a large non-stick casserole dish and brown the chicken all over. After 5 minutes, add the onion to the pan and cook for 5–10 minutes until golden.
2 Add the curry paste and cook for 1 minute, then add the leeks, tomatoes, cauliflower, potatoes and hot stock. Bring to the boil, then reduce the heat, cover the pan and simmer for 20–30 minutes until the chicken is cooked and the potatoes are tender.
3 Add the spinach and peas and cook for 5 minutes until heated through. Serve with rice.

Serves 4   preparation: 20–25 minutes   cooking time: about 50 minutes
per serving: 270 cals; 10g fat; 22g carbohydrate

Chicken Tikka with Coconut Dressing

125ml (4fl oz) crème fraîche
5tbsp coconut milk
4 pitta bread
200g bag mixed salad leaves
2 x 210g packs cooked chicken tikka
    fillets, sliced

2 spring onions, finely sliced
2tbsp mango chutney
15g (½oz) flaked almonds
25g (1oz) raisins

1 Mix the crème fraîche and coconut milk in a bowl and put to one side.
2 Split each pitta bread to form a pocket, then fill each pocket with a generous handful of salad leaves. Put the chicken tikka on top of the salad, sprinkle the spring onions over, add the mango chutney, drizzle with the crème fraîche mixture, then top with a sprinkling of flaked almonds and raisins. Serve.

Serves 4   preparation: 10 minutes
per serving: 560 cals; 23g fat; 54g carbohydrate

Quick Chicken Pilau

50g (2oz) butter
2 medium onions, peeled and finely sliced
600g tub cooked pilau rice

300g pack spicy fried chicken pieces
4tbsp chopped coriander

1   Melt the butter in a large non-stick frying pan or wok and cook the onions over a gentle heat for 15 minutes or until golden and caramelised.
2   Add the rice to the pan, stir to coat in the butter, then add the chicken pieces. Cook for 5 minutes to heat through, then stir in the coriander and serve.

Serves 4   preparation: 5 minutes   cooking time: 20 minutes
per serving: 450 cals; 16g fat; 54g carbohydrate

Thai Red Turkey Curry

3tbsp vegetable oil
450g (1lb) onions, peeled and
   finely chopped
200g (7oz) French beans, trimmed
125g (4oz) baby sweetcorn, cut on
   the diagonal
2 red peppers, halved, deseeded and
   cut into thick strips
1tbsp Thai red curry paste, or to taste
1 red chilli, deseeded and finely chopped
1 lemon grass stalk, trimmed and very
   finely chopped

4 kaffir lime leaves, bruised
2tbsp peeled and finely chopped
   fresh root ginger
1 garlic clove, peeled and crushed
400ml can coconut milk
600ml (1 pint) chicken or turkey stock
450g (1lb) cooked turkey, cut into strips
150g (5oz) beansprouts
fresh coriander sprigs and lime zest,
   to garnish

1   Heat the oil in a large frying pan or wok, add the onions and cook for 4–5 minutes or until soft. Add the French beans, baby sweetcorn and red peppers to the pan and stir-fry for 3–4 minutes. Add the curry paste, chilli, lemon grass, lime leaves, ginger and garlic and cook for 2 minutes, stirring. Remove from the pan and put to one side.
2   Add the coconut milk and stock to the pan, bring to the boil and bubble vigorously for 5–10 minutes or until reduced by a quarter. Return the vegetables to the pan with the turkey and beansprouts. Bring back to the boil and cook for 1–2 minutes, then serve immediately, garnished with coriander sprigs and lime zest.

Serves 6   preparation: 35 minutes   cooking time: 25 minutes
per serving: 300 cals; 16g fat; 11g carbohydrate

Crispy Duck with Hot and Sweet Dip

8 small duck legs
2 pieces star anise
4 fat garlic cloves, peeled and sliced
1 dried red chilli
grated zest and juice of 1 orange

1tbsp fresh tamarind or lemon juice
fried garlic slivers, fried chilli pieces and
  star anise, to garnish
Hot and Sweet Dip (see below), to serve

1 Prick the duck legs all over with a skewer or fork. Put them in a large pan, cover with cold water and bring to the boil, then reduce the heat and simmer for 45 minutes.
2 Meanwhile, put the star anise, garlic, chilli, orange zest and juice and tamarind or lemon juice in a blender and whiz to paste. Preheat the grill.
3 Drain the duck and put, skin side down, on a foil-lined grill pan. Brush half the spice paste over the duck, grill for 5 minutes, then turn skin side up and brush the remaining paste over. Grill for a further 5–7 minutes or until the duck skin is well charred and crisp. Garnish with the fried garlic slivers, fried chilli pieces and star anise and serve with Hot and Sweet Dip.

Serves 4   preparation: 10 minutes   cooking time: 55 minutes
per serving: 420 cals; 36g fat; trace carbohydrate

Hot and Sweet Dip

200ml (7fl oz) white wine vinegar
150g (5oz) golden caster sugar
75g (3oz) each cucumber, spring onion and
  mango, cut into fine shreds

1 dried red chilli or ¼tsp deseeded and
  shredded red chilli

1 Boil the vinegar and sugar together in a pan for 2 minutes, then stir in the cucumber, spring onion, mango and chilli. Put the mixture to one side and leave to cool. Allow the dip to come to room temperature before serving.

Serves 4   preparation: 5 minutes   cooking time: 2 minutes
per serving: 170 cals; trace fat; 43g carbohydrate

Oriental Crisp Duck Breast with Citrus Sauce

3 small whole ducks, each about 2.3kg (5lb),
  with legs removed
sea salt and black pepper
3 bunches of thyme
3 small oranges, cut into quarters, plus
  pared zest and juice of 4 oranges
125g (4oz) golden caster sugar

2tsp coriander seeds, roasted and crushed
3tbsp lemon juice
300ml (½ pint) balsamic vinegar or 150ml
  (¼ pint) each balsamic vinegar and stock
fresh rosemary sprigs, watercress and
  orange julienne strips, to garnish

1   Put the ducks on racks and pour boiling water over them until the skin becomes taut. Leave in a cool place for 4 hours and, once cold, store uncovered in the fridge overnight.

2   Preheat the oven to 200°C (180°C fan oven) mark 6. Season the ducks inside and out and insert a bunch of thyme and 4 orange quarters into each cavity. Put the ducks on racks over roasting tins and roast for 1–1½ hours or until the juices run clear when the thickest part of the duck is pierced. If necessary, transpose the roasting tins halfway through cooking time.

3   Meanwhile, make the sauce. Put the orange zest and juice and the sugar in a pan, bring to the boil, then reduce the heat and simmer for 5 minutes. Remove the zest. Add the coriander seeds and bubble for 4–5 minutes or until well reduced and a pale golden brown. Immediately add the lemon juice and vinegar, season, then bring to the boil and bubble until syrupy – about 10 minutes.

4   Transfer the ducks to a board. Cut the breasts from the carcass, garnish with rosemary, watercress and orange julienne strips and serve with the citrus sauce.

Serves 6   preparation: 30 minutes, plus standing   cooking time: 1½ hours
per serving: 390 cals; 17g fat; 29g carbohydrate

10

Better than a takeaway

Crispy Duck Pancakes

2.3kg (5lb) fresh oven-ready duckling
2 bay leaves
1tsp salt
10 black peppercorns
75g (3oz) butter
350g (12oz) onions, peeled and finely sliced
2 garlic cloves, peeled and finely sliced
2 red chillies, deseeded and finely sliced
2.5cm (1 inch) piece fresh root ginger,
    peeled and chopped
2 red peppers

175g (6oz) cucumber, deseeded
4 spring onions
125ml (4fl oz) hoisin sauce
3tsp teriyaki sauce
6tbsp chopped coriander
18 sheets filo pastry, about 225g (8oz)
1 egg, beaten
oil, for deep-frying
deep-fried spring onions and red chillies,
    to garnish
sweet chilli sauce, to serve

1   Put the duck, bay leaves, salt and peppercorns in a large pan with cold water to cover. Bring to the boil, reduce the heat, cover the pan and simmer for 2 hours. Drain off the resulting stock and cool. Strip the meat from the duck, discarding the skin and bones. Cut the flesh into long strips.

2   Heat 25g (1oz) butter in a medium-sized pan and cook the onions, garlic, chillies and ginger over a low heat for 30 minutes or until soft and golden, then cool slightly. Preheat the grill to high.

3   Cook the red peppers under the hot grill for about 10–15 minutes or until the skin is well blackened. Put to one side to cool, then skin, discard the seeds and slice into strips. Cut the cucumber and spring onions into 5cm (2 inch) fine matchsticks.

4   Mix the duck meat with the cooked onion mixture, the hoisin and teriyaki sauces and the coriander.

5   Melt the remaining butter in a small pan. Lay a sheet of filo pastry on a work surface and brush lightly with melted butter; repeat with two more sheets of filo pastry. Cut the filo into squares measuring about 15 x 15cm (6 x 6 inches). Complete the same process with the remaining filo pastry. Cover the pastry with a damp tea-towel or clingfilm as you work to prevent it drying out.

6   Lay a few red pepper strips diagonally across the centre of each filo square, top with a little duck mixture, then with spring onions and cucumber. Lightly brush two opposite corners of pastry with beaten egg, then roll up into a cigar shape. Put to one side and continue until all the filling mixture and filo pastry are used up.

7   Heat the oil in a deep-fat fryer or large pan to 160°C or until a cube of bread begins to sizzle. Deep-fry each parcel for 3–4 minutes or until golden. Serve the pancakes immediately, allowing two per person, garnished with deep-fried spring onions and red chillies and accompanied by a small bowl of sweet chilli sauce for dipping.

Serves 6   preparation: 30 minutes   cooking time: 2¼ hours
per serving: 640 cals; 34g fat; 37g carbohydrate

Better than a takeaway

Chow Mein

250g (9oz) dried medium egg noodles
1tbsp toasted sesame oil
2 skinless boneless chicken breasts, cut
   into thin strips
bunch of spring onions, thinly sliced on the
   diagonal

150g (5oz) mangetout, thickly sliced
   on the diagonal
125g (4oz) beansprouts
100g (3½oz) cooked ham, finely shredded
120g sachet chow mein sauce
salt and pepper
light soy sauce, to serve

1 Cook the noodles in boiling water for the time stated on the packet. Drain, rinse thoroughly under cold water and put to one side.

2 Meanwhile, heat a wok or large frying pan until hot, then add the oil. Add the chicken and stir-fry over a high heat for 3–4 minutes until browned all over. Add the spring onions and mangetout, stir-fry for 2 minutes, then stir in the beansprouts and ham and cook for 2 minutes.

3 Add the drained noodles, then pour over the chow mein sauce and toss together to coat evenly. Stir-fry for 2 minutes or until piping hot. Season to taste and serve with light soy sauce to drizzle over.

Serves 4   preparation: 10 minutes   cooking time: 10 minutes
per serving: 380 cals; 9g fat; 46g carbohydrate

Chinese Spare Ribs

10tbsp hoisin sauce
3tbsp tomato ketchup
1 garlic clove, peeled and crushed
salt and pepper

2 x 10-bone baby rack of pork ribs
   (available from butchers), cut in half to
   make 4 x 5-bone racks

1 Put the hoisin sauce, ketchup and garlic in a large shallow dish. Season and stir everything together until combined.

2 Add the pork ribs and toss to coat, spooning over the marinade to cover completely. You can either cook the ribs immediately or, if you have time, cover and chill them for 2 hours or overnight.

3 Preheat a grill until medium-high. Alternatively, preheat the barbecue – it's ready to use when the coals glow and are covered with light ash. Lift the ribs from the marinating dish and grill or barbecue for 10–12 minutes on each side. Alternatively, roast in a preheated oven at 200°C (180°C fan oven) mark 6 for 45 minutes.

Serves 4   preparation: 10 minutes, plus marinating (optional)   cooking time: 20–45 minutes
per serving: 330 cals; 20g fat; 7g carbohydrate

Indonesian Pork Satay

3tbsp chilli soy sauce
1tbsp molasses sugar
1 garlic clove, peeled and grated
salt and pepper
500g (1lb 2oz) pork fillet, cut into finger-
  length strips
250g (9oz) crunchy peanut butter

100ml (3½ fl oz) half-fat coconut milk,
  or use half a can of full-fat coconut
  milk and make up the difference with
  water or stock
1tbsp chilli soy sauce
1tbsp vegetable oil

1   Soak 16 x 15cm (6 inch) bamboo skewers in cold water for 30 minutes. Meanwhile, put the soy
    sauce, sugar and garlic into a shallow dish, season and mix to dissolve the sugar. Add the pork, coat
    evenly, then cover and chill for at least 30 minutes or up to 12 hours.
2   To make the sauce: put the peanut butter into a bowl and gradually stir in 6tbsp hot water. Slowly add
    the coconut milk, stir until thinned, then add the soy sauce. Season, cover and chill for up to one day.
3   Thread the pork on to the skewers. Cook in batches on a hot, oiled griddle for 3–4 minutes on each
    side. Serve with the satay sauce, jasmine rice and cucumber batons.

Serves 4   preparation: 15 minutes, plus marinating   cooking time: 12–16 minutes
per serving: 620cals; 48g fat; 8g carbohydrate

Better than a takeaway

Garlic and Soy Ribs with Sweet Potatoes

450g (1lb) rack of pork ribs, cut in half
½ lemon
1tbsp chicken seasoning
4tbsp soy sauce
3tbsp malt vinegar
3tbsp light muscovado sugar
2 garlic cloves, peeled and crushed
½tsp peeled and freshly grated root ginger

1tsp Chipotle Tabasco (if you have only the
   regular variety, just add a couple of drops
125ml (4fl oz) beef stock, cooled
4 sweet potatoes, scrubbed
olive oil and sea salt (optional)
4tbsp Greek-style yogurt
2 spring onions, roughly chopped

1   Put the pork ribs into a shallow dish. Rub the lemon over the meat, squeezing out the juice as you go, then sprinkle over the chicken seasoning, soy sauce, vinegar, sugar, garlic, ginger and Tabasco. Turn the ribs to coat evenly in the marinade. If you have time, cover and chill to marinate for at least 2 hours.
2   Preheat the oven to 200°C (180°C fan oven) mark 6. Put the ribs and marinade into a roasting tin and pour over the beef stock. Roast for 50–55 minutes, turning the ribs during cooking to coat in the sauce.
3   Meanwhile, drizzle the sweet potatoes with a little olive oil and sprinkle the skins with sea salt, if using, then wrap in foil and bake for 50–55 minutes until they are just tender.
4   To serve, transfer the ribs to a board and cut between each rib to separate. Slash the top of each potato and squeeze the sides to push up the sweet flesh. Top each potato with a dollop of yogurt, sprinkle over the spring onions and serve with the ribs.

Serves 4   preparation: 15 minutes   cooking time: 55 minutes
per serving: 440 cals; 17g fat; 49g carbohydrate

Fried Yellow Bean Pork with Cashews

6 cardamom pods, split
2.5cm (1 inch) piece fresh root ginger,
   peeled and finely chopped
1tbsp five-spice powder
450g (1lb) pork tenderloin, thinly sliced
2tbsp oil

225g (8oz) small oyster mushrooms
125g (4oz) leek or spring onions, sliced
3 garlic cloves, peeled and sliced
2tbsp yellow bean sauce
pared zest and juice of 1 small orange
50g (2oz) toasted cashew nuts

1   Rub the cardamom, ginger and five-spice powder into the pork and put to one side.
2   Heat half the oil in a wok or frying pan and fry the mushrooms quickly for about 1 minute. Remove the mushrooms with a slotted spoon before they begin to wilt. Add the remaining oil and, when hot, stir the pork, leek and garlic into the pan and stir-fry over a high heat for 5 minutes.
3   Return the mushrooms to the pan with the yellow bean sauce, orange zest and juice and the cashew nuts and cook, stirring over a high heat, until all the ingredients are coated in sauce and hot through. Serve immediately.

Serves 4   preparation: 10 minutes   cooking time: 10 minutes
per serving: 320 cals; 21g fat; 7g carbohydrate

Red Lamb Curry with Pumpkin and Coconut

1tbsp oil, preferably stir-fry oil
550g (1¼lb) diced leg of lamb
225g (8oz) red onion, peeled and chopped
125g (4oz) block creamed coconut
2tsp Thai red curry paste
2.5cm (1 inch) piece fresh root ginger,
  peeled and chopped

salt
225g (8oz) pumpkin, peeled and
  cut into thin wedges
4tbsp mango chutney
basil leaves and fried red onion rings,
  to garnish

1 Heat the oil in a large pan and fry the lamb over a high heat until deep golden brown. Reduce the heat, add the onion and continue to fry, stirring, until the onion is soft and golden. Take a good 10 minutes to do this as it brings out the natural sweetness of the onions and adds to both the flavour and colour of the finished recipe.

2 Meanwhile, pour 600ml (1 pint) boiling water over the creamed coconut and leave to dissolve.

3 Add the curry paste and ginger to the lamb and fry for 1–2 minutes. Stir in the coconut liquid and bring to the boil. Season with salt, then cover the pan, reduce the heat and simmer on a very low heat for 30 minutes.

4 Stir the pumpkin and chutney into the lamb, cover again and cook for 30 minutes or until the lamb and pumpkin are tender. Garnish with basil leaves and onion rings, then serve with basmati rice.

Serves 4   preparation: 10 minutes   cooking time: 1 hour 20 minutes
per serving: 530 cals; 38g fat; 17g carbohydrate

Lamb Korma with Red Onion Cachumber

0tbsp ground cinnamon

36 green cardamoms

30 cloves

18 bay leaves

1tbsp fennel seeds

salt and pepper

150ml carton natural yogurt

700g (1½lb) boneless lamb, cut into 2.5cm (1 inch) pieces

1tbsp golden caster sugar

3tbsp groundnut oil

1tsp ground turmeric

2tsp ground coriander

1 small onion, peeled and finely chopped

4 garlic cloves, peeled and crushed

1cm (½ inch) piece fresh root ginger, peeled and finely chopped

1 red onion, peeled and finely sliced

1 tomato, deseeded and diced

1tbsp chopped mint, plus sprigs to garnish

juice of ½ lime

50g (2oz) ground almonds

142ml carton double cream

large pinch of saffron

1 For the korma paste, put the cinnamon, cardamoms, cloves, bay leaves, fennel seeds and 1tsp salt into a mini processor and whiz to a powder. Tip the powder into a bowl and add 4tbsp water, stirring well to make a paste. Divide into three equal portions, then freeze two portions in separate bags to use within 3 months (see below) and put the remainder into a large bowl.

2 To make the curry, add the yogurt, lamb and sugar to the paste in the bowl and mix well. Cover the bowl, chill and marinate the lamb for at least 4 hours, preferably overnight.

3 Preheat the oven to 190°C (170°C fan oven) mark 5. Heat the oil in a flameproof casserole, add the turmeric and coriander and fry for 30 seconds. Add the chopped onion and stir-fry over a high heat for 10 minutes until softened and golden. Add the garlic and ginger and cook for 1–2 minutes, then add the lamb, cover the casserole and cook in the oven for 20 minutes.

4 Meanwhile, make the red onion cachumber. Put the sliced onion, tomato, mint and lime juice in a small bowl and toss them together, then season well with salt and chill until needed.

5 Take the casserole out of the oven, and reduce the oven temperature to 170°C (150°C fan oven) mark 3. Add the ground almonds, cream, saffron and 100ml (3½fl oz) water. Season well with salt and pepper and stir together. Cover the casserole, return to the oven and cook for 1½ hours or until tender.

6 Serve the lamb korma, garnished with mint sprigs, in deep, warmed bowls, with the red onion cachumber in a separate dish, and some naan bread to wipe the bowl clean.

To use the frozen paste: Put the paste in a microwave and cook on Defrost for 1 minute 20 seconds (based on a 900W oven), or thaw at cool room temperature for 1–1½ hours.

Serves 4   preparation: 20 minutes, plus marinating   cooking time: 2 hours
per serving: 660 cals; 49g fat; 15g carbohydrate

Curried Lamb with Lentils

500g (1lb 2oz) stewing lamb on the bone, cut into eight (ask your butcher to do this)
1tbsp ground cumin
1tsp ground turmeric
2 garlic cloves, peeled and crushed
1 red chilli, deseeded and chopped
2.5cm (1 inch) piece fresh root ginger, peeled and grated
1tsp salt
2tbsp sunflower oil
1 onion, peeled and chopped
400g can chopped tomatoes
2tbsp vinegar
175g (6oz) red lentils, rinsed
traditional Mediterranean wraps
chopped coriander leaves, to serve

1 Put the lamb into a shallow sealable container, add the spices, garlic, chilli, ginger and salt. Stir well to mix, then cover and chill for 30 minutes or more.
2 Heat the oil in a large flameproof casserole. Add the onion and cook over a gentle heat for 5 minutes. Add the lamb and cook for 10 minutes, turning regularly, until the meat is evenly browned.
3 Add the tomatoes, vinegar, 450ml (¾ pint) boiling water and the lentils and bring to the boil. Reduce the heat, cover the casserole and simmer for 1 hour. Remove the lid and cook uncovered for 30 minutes, stirring occasionally, until the sauce is thick and the lamb is tender.
4 Remove the wraps from their plastic packaging and roll up together, then wrap in greaseproof paper or baking parchment, twisting the ends to secure. Microwave on High for 1½ minutes (based on a 900W oven) until warmed through. Spread the lamb curry on to the wraps, sprinkle with coriander and roll up individually to serve.

Serves 4   preparation: 15 minutes   cooking time: 1 hour 50 minutes
per serving (not including wraps): 340 cals; 18g fat; 14g carbohydrate

10

Better than a takeaway

Split Pea Roti

125g (4oz) yellow split peas, soaked in cold
  water overnight
¼tsp ground turmeric
1tsp ground cumin
1 garlic clove, peeled and finely sliced

1½tsp salt
225g (8oz) plain flour, sifted, plus extra to dust
1½tsp baking powder
1tbsp vegetable oil, plus extra to fry
125–150ml (4–5fl oz) full-fat milk

1 Drain the split peas and put into a small pan with the turmeric, cumin, garlic and 1tsp salt. Add 200ml (7fl oz) cold water and bring to the boil, then reduce the heat and simmer for 30 minutes or until the peas are soft, adding a little more water if necessary. Take off the heat and leave to cool.
2 Sift the flour, baking powder and remaining salt into a large bowl. Make a well in the centre, add the oil and gradually mix in enough milk to form a soft dough. Transfer to a lightly floured surface and knead until smooth. Cover with a damp tea-towel and leave to rest for 30 minutes.
3 Whiz the cooled peas in a food processor or blender until smooth, adding 1tbsp water.
4 Divide the dough into eight. Roll each piece out on a lightly floured surface to a 20cm (8 inch) round. Divide the pea mixture between 4 rounds, placing it in the centre, then top with the other rounds and press the edges together to seal.
5 Heat a large heavy-based frying pan until really hot. Brush each roti with a little oil and fry one or two at a time, for 1 minute on each side or until lightly brown. Keep warm while you cook the rest. Serve with a vegetable curry.

Serves 4 preparation: 25 minutes, plus soaking and resting cooking time: 40 minutes
per serving: 170 cals; 3g fat; 32g carbohydrate

Speedy Beef Noodles

250g pack fine rice noodles
4tbsp sesame oil, plus a little extra
300g (11oz) beef fillet
4tbsp soy sauce with chilli
juice of 1 lime

2 red peppers, halved, deseeded and cut
  into thin strips
200g pack mangetout, sliced
4tbsp chopped coriander

1 Put the noodles into a large bowl and cover with boiling water. Leave to soak for 4 minutes, then rinse under cold running water and put to one side.
2 Meanwhile, brush a large frying or griddle pan with a little sesame oil and heat until hot. Fry the beef over a medium-high heat for 3–4 minutes on each side (4–5 minutes if you like it well done). Remove from the pan and keep warm.
3 Add 4tbsp oil to the pan with the soy sauce, lime juice, red peppers, mangetout and coriander and stir to mix. Add the noodles and use two large spoons to toss them over the heat to combine with the sauce and warm through. Cut the beef into thin slices and serve on a bed of noodles.

Serves 4 preparation: 5 minutes cooking time: 10 minutes
per serving: 450 cals; 19g fat; 47g carbohydrate

Thai Beef Curry

4 cloves
1tsp each coriander seeds and cumin seeds
seeds from 3 cardamom pods
2 garlic cloves, peeled and roughly chopped
2.5cm (1 inch) piece fresh root ginger,
  peeled and roughly chopped
1 small onion, peeled and roughly chopped
2tbsp sunflower oil
1tbsp sesame oil
1tbsp Thai red curry paste
1tsp ground turmeric

450g (1lb) sirloin steak, cut into 3cm
  (1¼ inch) cubes
225g (8oz) potatoes, peeled and quartered
4 tomatoes, quartered
1tsp sugar
1tbsp light soy sauce
300ml (½ pint) coconut milk
150ml (¼ pint) beef stock
4 red chillies, bruised
50g (2oz) cashew nuts

1 Put the cloves, coriander, cumin and cardamom seeds into a small heavy-based frying pan over a high heat for 1–2 minutes until the spices release their aroma. Leave to cool slightly, then grind to a powder in a spice grinder or blender.
2 Purée the garlic, ginger and onion in a blender or food processor to form a smooth paste. Heat the two oils together in a deep frying pan. Add the onion purée with the curry paste and stir-fry for 5 minutes, then add the roasted ground spices and the turmeric and fry for 5 minutes.
3 Add the beef to the pan and fry for 5 minutes until browned on all sides. Add all the remaining ingredients, except the cashew nuts. Bring to the boil, then reduce the heat, cover the pan and simmer gently for 20–25 minutes until the beef is tender and the potatoes are cooked.
4 Stir in the cashew nuts and serve the curry with plain boiled rice or noodles and stir-fried vegetables.

Serves 4   preparation: 30 minutes   cooking time: 40–45 minutes
per serving: 500 cals; 34g fat; 22g carbohydrate

Classic Saag Aloo

2–3tbsp oil
1 onion, peeled and finely sliced
2 garlic cloves, peeled and finely chopped
1tbsp black mustard seeds
2tsp ground turmeric

900g (2lb) potatoes, peeled and cut into
  4cm (½ inch) chunks
1tsp salt
4 handfuls baby spinach leaves

1 Heat the oil in a pan and fry the onions over a medium heat for 10 minutes until golden, taking care not to burn them.
2 Add the garlic, mustard seeds and turmeric and cook for 1 minute. Add the potatoes, salt and 150ml (¼ pint) water and cover the pan. Bring to the boil, then reduce the heat and cook gently for 35–40 minutes or until tender. Add the spinach and cook until the leaves just wilt. Serve immediately.

Serves 4   preparation: 15 minutes   cooking time: 55 minutes
per serving: 260 cals; 9g fat; 43g carbohydrate

Aubergine and Coconut Curry

5–6tbsp olive oil
1 medium aubergine, cut into chunks a bit
  bigger than bite-sized
1 medium onion, peeled and chopped
thumb-sized piece fresh root ginger, peeled
2tbsp garam masala or mild curry paste
400g can chickpeas, drained and rinsed
1 large sweet potato, peeled and cut into

bite-sized chunks
400g can chopped tomatoes
400ml can coconut milk
salt and pepper
small bunch of coriander, roughly torn
about 125g (4oz) spinach leaves,
150g tub Greek-style natural yogurt
  (optional)

1 Heat about 4tbsp olive oil in a large non-stick pan and fry the aubergine until golden brown and beginning to soften. Transfer to a plate with a draining spoon, then add another 1–2tbsp olive oil to the pan and fry the onion over a medium heat for at least 10 minutes until soft and deep golden.
2 Coarsely grate the ginger into the onion, stir for 2 minutes, then add the garam masala or curry paste. Reduce the heat and cook for 1–2 minutes. Add the aubergine, chickpeas, sweet potato, tomatoes and coconut milk, bring to the boil, then reduce the heat and simmer gently until the sweet potato is just tender – about 10–12 minutes. Taste and add seasoning. To serve, add the coriander and spinach leaves – they'll wilt in the heat of the pan. If you want to, top with generous spoonfuls of yogurt.

Serves 4   preparation: 15 minutes   cooking time: 30–35 minutes
per serving: 570 cals; 43g fat; 34g carbohydrate

Vegetable Curry

3tbsp vegetable oil
1 onion, peeled and finely sliced
4 garlic cloves, peeled and crushed
2.5cm (1 inch) piece fresh root ginger,
  peeled and grated
3tbsp medium curry powder
6 curry leaves
150g (5oz) potatoes, peeled and cut into
  1cm (½ inch) cubes
125g (4oz) aubergine, cut into 2cm (¾ inch)

long, 5mm (¼ inch) wide sticks
150g (5oz) carrots, peeled and cut into 5mm
  (¼ inch) dice
900ml (1½ pints) hot vegetable stock
pinch of powdered saffron
salt and pepper
150g (5oz) green beans
75g (3oz) frozen peas
3tbsp chopped coriander leaves

1 Heat the oil in a large heavy-based pan. Add the onion and fry over a low heat for 5–10 minutes until softened and golden. Add the garlic, ginger, curry powder and curry leaves and fry for 1 minute. Add the potatoes and aubergine and fry, stirring, for 2 minutes. Add the carrots, hot stock, saffron, 1tsp salt and plenty of pepper. Cover and cook for 10 minutes until the vegetables are almost tender.
2 Add the beans and peas to the pan and cook for 4 minutes. Scatter with coriander and serve.

Serves 4   preparation: 20 minutes   cooking time: 30 minutes
per serving: 190 cals; 11g fat; 19g carbohydrate

Thai Vegetable Curry

2tbsp vegetable oil
1 large onion, peeled and finely chopped
4tsp Thai green curry paste
600ml (1 pint) vegetable stock
200g (7oz) washed new potatoes, cut in half
225g (8oz) easy-cook long-grain rice
200g (7oz) courgettes, cut on the diagonal

200g (7oz) carrots, peeled and cut on
   the diagonal
150g (5oz) broccoli, divided into florets
125g (4oz) tomatoes, cut in quarters
150g (5oz) frozen spinach, thawed
300ml (½ pint) coconut milk
coriander sprigs, to garnish (optional)

1   Heat the oil in a large frying pan. Add the onion and green curry paste, then cook for 4–5 minutes. Add the stock and potatoes, bring to the boil, then reduce the heat, cover the pan and cook for 20 minutes or until the potatoes are just tender.
2   Meanwhile, cook the rice for the time stated on the packet. Add the courgettes, carrots and broccoli to the curry. Cook for 3–4 minutes or until the vegetables are tender. At the last minute, add the tomatoes, spinach and coconut milk and heat through thoroughly. Serve the curry on a bed of rice and garnish with coriander sprigs.

Serves 4   preparation: 15 minutes   cooking time: 35 minutes
per serving: 480 cals; 19g fat; 69g carbohydrate

Saffron Rice

500g (1lb 2oz) basmati rice
900ml (1½ pints) stock made with 1½
   chicken stock cubes
5tbsp sunflower or light vegetable oil
salt

½tsp saffron
75g (3oz) blanched almonds and pistachio
   nuts, coarsely chopped, to garnish
   (optional)

1   Put the rice into a bowl and cover with warm water, then drain well through a sieve.
2   Put the stock, oil and a good pinch of salt into a pan, then cover and bring to the boil. Add the saffron and the rice.
3   Cover the pan and bring the stock back to the boil, then stir, reduce the heat to low and cook, covered, gently for 20 minutes until little holes appear all over the surface of the cooked rice and the grains are tender.
4   Fluff up the rice with a fork and transfer it to a warmed serving dish. Sprinkle the chopped almonds and pistachios on top, if using, and serve.

Serves 8   preparation: 5–10 minutes   cooking time: 25 minutes
per serving: 350 cals; 13g fat; 50g carbohydrate

Thai Rice

500g (1lb 2oz) Thai rice
salt

handful of mint leaves

Cook the rice and mint in boiling salted water for 10–12 minutes or until tender. Drain well and serve.

Serves 6   cooking time: 10–12 minutes
per serving: 300 cals; Tr fat; 67g carbohydrate

Basic Pilau Rice

50g (2oz) butter
225g (8oz) long-grain white rice
750ml (1¼ pints) hot chicken stock

salt and pepper
generous knob of butter, to serve

1   Melt the butter in a pan, add the rice and fry gently for 3–4 minutes until translucent.
2   Slowly pour in the hot stock, season, stir and cover with a tight-fitting lid. Leave, undisturbed, over a very low heat for about 15 minutes until the water has been absorbed and the rice is just tender.
3   Remove the lid and cover the surface of the rice with a clean cloth. Replace the lid and leave to stand in a warm place for about 15 minutes to dry the rice before serving.
4   Fork through and add a knob of butter to serve.

Serves 4   preparation: 5 minutes   cooking time: 20 minutes, plus standing
per serving: 320 cals; 13g fat; 45g carbohydrate

Easy Basmati Pilaf

50g (2oz) butter
1 onion, peeled and finely chopped
1 garlic clove, peeled and crushed
225g (8oz) basmati rice

750ml (1¼ pints) chicken stock
salt and pepper
1tbsp chopped flat-leafed parsley

1   Preheat the oven to 170°C (150°C fan oven) mark 3. Melt the butter in a heavy-based casserole, add the onion and cook over a low heat for 10–12 minutes or until soft. Add the garlic and rice and stir over a low heat for 1–2 minutes. Add the stock and season lightly.
2   Bring to the boil, cover with a tight-fitting lid and cook in the oven for 20–25 minutes. Stir with a fork halfway through the cooking time. The rice is cooked when it's just soft to the centre and all the liquid has been absorbed. Remove from the oven, add the parsley and serve.

Serves 4   preparation: 15 minutes   cooking time: 40 minutes
per serving: 310 cals; 11g fat; 48g carbohydrate

Curried Vegetable Rice

1tbsp vegetable oil
1 small onion, peeled and chopped
½tsp Balti curry paste
1 large carrot, peeled and grated
150ml (¼ pint) rice

1 vegetable or chicken stock cube,
 crumbled
salt and pepper
handful of broccoli or cauliflower florets

1 Heat the oil in a large pan and fry the onion for 15 minutes until tender.
2 Add the curry paste and cook for 2–3 minutes.
3 Add the carrot and rice, then immediately add 300ml (½ pint) boiling water, the stock cube and plenty
    of seasoning. Cover the pan and bring to the boil, then reduce the heat and simmer for 10 minutes.
4 Add the broccoli or cauliflower florets and cook for 5 minutes, then serve.

Serves 2   preparation: 5 minutes   cooking time: 35 minutes
per serving: 390 cals; 8g fat; 70g carbohydrate

Variation

Thai curried vegetable rice: Use 1–2tbsp of Thai curry paste instead of the regular Indian variety and
substitute a 400g can of coconut milk in place of the tomatoes.

Special Prawn Fried Rice

1tbsp sesame oil
6tbsp nasi goring paste
250g (9oz) cooked king prawns
200g (7oz) green cabbage, shredded
2 x 250g packs microwave rice

2tbsp soy sauce
1tbsp sunflower oil
2 eggs, beaten
2 spring onions, finely sliced
1 lime, quartered

1 Heat the sesame oil in a wok and fry the nasi goring paste for 1–2 minutes. Add the prawns and
    cabbage and fry for 2–3 minutes. Next, add the rice and soy sauce and cook for 5 minutes, stirring
    occasionally.
2 To make the omelette, heat the sunflower oil in a non-stick frying pan (about 25.5cm/10 inches in
    diameter) and add the eggs. Swirl around to cover the base in a thin layer and cook for 2–3 minutes
    until set.
3 Roll up the omelette and cut into slivers. Serve the rice scattered with the egg and spring onions, with
    the lime quarters to squeeze over.

Serves 4   preparation: 5 minutes   cooking time: 8–10 minutes
per serving: 380 cals; 15g fat; 43g carbohydrate

Vegetables

With their fresh clean taste and inherent goodness, vegetables really are the jewels in the kitchen. Steamed, baked, roasted, stir-fried, braised – cook them however you want, they're so versatile. And there are so many to choose from.

Big bowlfuls of creamy mash are just right for soaking up the last warm lashings of gravy on your plate. And we're not talking just mashed potatoes – try Parsnip Mash with Crisp Bacon, or Vegetable and Mustard Mash. But potatoes are great comfort food: pile a dish high with crispy Potato Croquettes with Bacon and Cheese, or crunchy Potato Frites and see how long you can resist them.

Perhaps it's time to try out something different. What about Braised Chicory in White Wine; Stir-fried Kale; Roasted Fennel with Oranges and Dill Mash; or Gratin of Chard? New and enticing smells will be wafting round your kitchen in no time.

Then there's cabbage – red, white or green, cooked with the sweetness of onions and cranberries, the pungency of garlic, or the earthiness of caraway. Simple, tasty and good for you. Vegetables don't have to be just an accompaniment – eat and enjoy them on their own.

Brussels Sprouts with Shallots and Pancetta

200g (7oz) diced pancetta
salt and pepper
900g (2lb) Brussels sprouts, peeled
200g (7oz) shallots, blanched in boiling
   water, drained and peeled

2tsp golden caster sugar
4tbsp red wine vinegar
150ml (¼ pint) red wine
1tsp juniper berries
1tbsp chopped thyme

1 Heat a large frying pan and dry-fry the pancetta for 5 minutes until golden. Remove with a slotted spoon and put to one side.
2 Bring a pan of salted water to the boil, add the sprouts and cook for 5 minutes. Drain the sprouts, plunge them into cold water for 10 minutes, then drain and put to one side.
3 Fry the shallots in the pancetta pan for 5 minutes. Add the sugar and cook for 5 minutes until caramelised. Add the vinegar, wine, juniper berries and thyme, cover and simmer for 10 minutes until almost tender. Uncover the pan, bring to the boil and reduce the liquid until syrupy.
4 Add the pancetta and sprouts to the pan and cook for 3–4 minutes until heated through, then season.

Serves 8   preparation: 15 minutes   cooking time: 40 minutes
per serving: 210 cals; 17g fat; 8g carbohydrate

Brussels Sprouts with Chestnuts and Shallots

salt and pepper
900g (2lb) small Brussels sprouts, trimmed
1tbsp olive oil
8 shallots, blanched in boiling water,
   drained, peeled and finely chopped

200g pack peeled cooked chestnuts
15g (½oz) butter
pinch of freshly grated nutmeg

1 Bring a pan of salted water to the boil, add the Brussels sprouts and blanch for 2 minutes. Drain the sprouts and refresh with cold water.
2 Heat the olive oil in a wok or sauté pan. Add the shallots and stir-fry for 5 minutes until almost tender.
3 Add the sprouts to the pan with the chestnuts and stir-fry for about 4 minutes to heat through.
4 Add the butter and nutmeg and season generously. Serve immediately.

Serves 8   preparation: 15 minutes   cooking time: 10 minutes
per serving: 140 cals; 5g fat; 18g carbohydrate

Herby Buttered Brussels Sprouts

salt and pepper
900g (2lb) Brussels sprouts, trimmed
125g (4oz) unsalted butter

4tbsp red wine vinegar
4tbsp each chopped chives and tarragon

1 Bring a pan of salted water to the boil, add the Brussels sprouts and cook for 5 minutes or until nearly tender. Drain the sprouts, plunge into cold water for 5 minutes, then drain again thoroughly and put to one side.
2 To make the beurre noisette sauce, melt the butter in a small pan and cook until brown. Add the vinegar and cook for 2 minutes. Stir in the herbs.
3 Heat a large frying pan and stir-fry the sprouts for 2–3 minutes, then season. Pour the beurre noisette sauce over, making sure the sprouts are evenly coated in butter and are thoroughly heated through.

Serves 8   preparation: 10 minutes, plus standing   cooking time: 8–10 minutes
per serving: 160 cals; 14g fat; 4g carbohydrate

Creamy Brussels Sprouts

600ml (1 pint) milk
1 thick slice each onion and celery
6 peppercorns
1 small bay leaf
1.1kg (2½lb) Brussels sprouts, lightly
  trimmed
salt and pepper

40g (1½oz) butter
40g (1½oz) plain flour
½ whole nutmeg, grated, about 1tsp
4tbsp single cream
oregano sprigs, flat-leafed parsley and
  freshly grated nutmeg, to garnish

1 Put the milk in a pan with the onion, celery, peppercorns and bay leaf. Bring to the boil, remove from the heat and leave to infuse for 20–30 minutes.
2 Meanwhile, cook the sprouts in a pan of boiling salted water for 10–15 minutes until just tender. Drain and plunge into a bowl of icy cold water. Drain again and dry well.
3 Strain and reserve the milk. Melt the butter in a heavy-based pan. Take the pan off the heat, add the flour and stir until smooth. Stir in the milk and mix until smooth. Return to the heat and bring to the boil, stirring. Reduce the heat and simmer for 1–2 minutes, then add the nutmeg and season. Float the cream on top.
4 Pulse the sprouts briefly in a food processor until roughly chopped. Combine with the sauce, put in a pan over a low heat and stir until hot. Garnish with the oregano, parsley and nutmeg and serve.

Serves 8–10   preparation: 15 minutes   cooking time: 25 minutes, plus infusing
per serving: 170–140 cals; 10–8g fat; 13–10g carbohydrate

11

Vegetables

Crisp Parsnip Cakes

700g (1½lb) parsnips, peeled and diced
salt and pepper
25g (1oz) unsalted butter
3tbsp plain flour, plus extra to dust

several pinches of ground mace
1 large egg, beaten
100g (3½oz) fresh white breadcrumbs
1tbsp oil

1 Cook the parsnips in boiling salted water for about 10 minutes until tender. Drain well and return to the pan. Add the butter and 1tbsp flour. Mash well, adding the mace and seasoning to taste. Leave to cool for 10 minutes.

2 Put the remaining flour on a plate. Pour the beaten egg into a shallow bowl. Scatter the breadcrumbs on to another plate. With lightly floured hands, divide the parsnip mash into six and roll into balls. Flatten slightly to form cakes.

3 Take one parsnip cake and dust with a little flour, then dip in the beaten egg and then roll it in the breadcrumbs to coat, shaking off any excess. Repeat with the remaining cakes. Chill for 15 minutes (or overnight if preparing ahead).

4 To cook, heat the oil in a large non-stick frying pan. Add the parsnip cakes and fry for 15 minutes, turning halfway through, until crisp and golden all over.

Serves 6 preparation: 10 minutes, plus chilling   cooking time: 25 minutes
per serving: 190 cals; 8g fat; 26g carbohydrate

Crushed Roast Parsnip and Apple

900g (2lb) even-sized parsnips, peeled and
  cut into large chunks
700g (1½lb) old potatoes, peeled and cut
  into large chunks
2 crisp, tart eating apples, peeled, cored
  and chopped

salt and pepper
3tbsp oil
50g (2oz) butter
2tbsp chopped chives

1 Preheat the oven to 220°C (200°C fan oven) mark 7. Cook the parsnips, potatoes and apples together in boiling salted water for 3 minutes, then drain well.

2 Heat the oil in a small roasting tin and add the parsnip mixture. Stir to coat in the oil. Roast for 45 minutes or until very tender.

3 Roughly crush the mixture with the butter. Sprinkle with chives, season and serve.

Serves 6 preparation: 25 minutes   cooking time: 50 minutes
per serving: 310 cals; 15g fat; 41g carbohydrate

Parmesan and Mustard Parsnips

700g (1½lb) small parsnips, peeled
and halved
salt and pepper
50g (2oz) butter

2tbsp olive oil
100g (3½oz) freshly grated
Parmesan cheese
5tbsp English mustard powder

1 Cook the parsnips in boiling salted water for 5 minutes, then drain well and keep warm.
2 Preheat the oven to 200°C (180°C fan oven) mark 6. Put the butter and olive oil in a roasting tin and heat in the oven for 5 minutes.
3 Mix the Parmesan with the mustard powder and season well. Coat the warm parsnips in the mixture, pressing the coating on well.
4 Put into the preheated roasting tin and cook in the oven for 30–40 minutes or until golden.

Serves 8   preparation: 20 minutes   cooking time: 40–45 minutes
per serving: 190 cals; 13g fat; 11g carbohydrate

Parsnip, Potato and Cheese Rösti

350g (12oz) waxy potatoes, such as
Desirée, peeled
225g (8oz) parsnips, peeled
1 onion, peeled and sliced
1 garlic clove, peeled and crushed
1tbsp chopped sage

salt and pepper
1 large egg, beaten
2tbsp sunflower oil
175g (6oz) fontina or Cheddar
cheese, grated

1 Using the medium grater attachment of a food processor or the coarse side of a grater, grate the potatoes and parsnips, then squeeze out any excess liquid.
2 Place the grated vegetables, onion, garlic and sage in a large bowl and season generously. Stir in the egg until the mixture is well combined.
3 Heat the oil in a large non-stick frying pan. When it's hot, spread half the vegetable mixture over the base of the pan. Scatter over the cheese, then top with the remaining vegetable mixture, spreading it flat.
4 Cook over a low heat for about 10 minutes until golden underneath. Using a palette knife, slide the rösti out on to a large plate, then flip back into the pan and cook for 10 minutes until the underside is browned and the vegetables are tender and cooked through.
5 Serve the rösti immediately, cut into wedges.

Serves 4   preparation: 10 minutes   cooking time: 20 minutes
per serving: 370 cals; 24g fat; 25g carbohydrate

Parsnip Mash with Crisp Bacon

900g (2lb) parsnips, peeled
salt and pepper
25g (1oz) butter

1–2tbsp single cream
4 streaky bacon rashers

1 Cook the parsnips in boiling salted water for 15 minutes or until tender. Meanwhile, preheat the grill. Drain the parsnips well, return to the pan and roughly mash with the butter. Beat in the cream and season with pepper.
2 Grill the bacon until crisp, then crumble and stir through the mash just before serving.

Serves 4   preparation: 5 minutes   cooking time: 15 minutes
per serving: 290 cals; 17g fat; 27g carbohydrate

Roasted Parsnips with Leeks, Apple and Bacon

2 parsnips, peeled and cut into
  six lengthways
175g pack baby leeks, cut in half crossways
2 medium red apples, unpeeled and cored,
  each cut into six wedges

50g (2oz) butter, diced
4 rindless streaky bacon rashers

1 Preheat the oven to 220°C (200°C fan oven) mark 7. Put the parsnips, leeks and apples in a single layer in a roasting tin and dot the butter over them.
2 Lay the bacon on top of the vegetables, put in the oven and roast for about 25 minutes or until the parsnips are soft and the bacon is crisp.

Serves 2   preparation: 10 minutes   cooking time: 30 minutes
per serving: 500 cals; 41g fat; 23g carbohydrate

Creamy Kale

450g (1lb) curly kale
25g (1oz) unsalted butter
5tbsp double cream

¼tsp freshly grated nutmeg
salt and pepper

1 Remove and discard the tough central stem from each kale leaf, then wash thoroughly and drain. Put the kale into a large pan with a drizzle of water and simmer, covered, for 5 minutes until bright green and almost cooked. Drain off any liquid.
2 Return the kale to the pan. Add the butter and cream and heat through, stirring, for 2 minutes. Add the grated nutmeg, season generously and serve.

Serves 6   preparation: 10 minutes   cooking time: 7 minutes
per serving: 100 cals; 10g fat; 1g carbohydrate

Roast Parsnips with Honey Glaze

2tbsp oil
700g (1½lb) each parsnips and sweet
    potatoes, peeled and cut into large
    chunks

salt and pepper
4tbsp runny honey

1 Preheat the oven to 200°C (180°C fan oven) mark 6. Heat the oil in a roasting tin on the hob. Add the parsnips and sweet potatoes and shake the tin to coat them with oil, then season. Roast for 45 minutes, turning the parsnips from time to time.
2 Remove from the oven and mix in the honey, then return to the oven and roast for a further 10–15 minutes or until the vegetables are glazed, sticky and a deep golden brown. Season and turn out into a serving dish. (Don't leave the vegetables in the tin as they may stick to the bottom.)

Serves 8–10   preparation: 10 minutes   cooking time: 1 hour
per serving: 150–120 cals; 3–2g fat; 32–25g carbohydrate

Curly Kale With Crispy Bacon

1.1kg (2½lb) curly kale, any tough or
　discoloured outer leaves discarded, or
　1.1–1.4kg (2½–3lb) Savoy cabbage,
　quartered, cored and coarsely shredded

salt and pepper
25g (1oz) butter
6 dry cure, rindless streaky bacon
　rashers, cut into strips

1　Blanch the curly kale or cabbage for 20 seconds in boiling salted water; blanch the cabbage for 1–2 minutes. Drain and immediately plunge into cold water to stop further cooking. Drain again and tip out on to kitchen paper to dry. Put to one side.
2　Melt the butter in a wok or large frying pan. Add the bacon and fry gently for 3–4 minutes or until turning golden brown. Toss in the curly kale or cabbage and stir-fry for 3–4 minutes until coated with butter and heated through. Season well and serve.

Serves 6　preparation: 5 minutes, plus cooling and draining　cooking time: 5 minutes
per serving: 190 cals; 16g fat; 3g carbohydrate

Stir-fried Kale

1tbsp sesame oil
1 garlic clove, peeled and crushed
1tbsp sesame seeds

450g (1lb) curly kale, finely sliced
2tbsp soy sauce

1　Heat the oil in a non-stick wok. Add the garlic and sesame seeds and cook for 30 seconds until golden. Add the cury kale and stir-fry for 5 minutes.
2　Add the soy sauce, bring to the boil, bubble to reduce slightly. Transfer to a dish and serve.

Serves 4　preparation: 5 minutes　cooking time: 6–7 minutes
per serving: 90 cals; 7g fat; 2g carbohydrate

Vegetables

Stir-fried Vegetables with Oyster Sauce

100ml (3½fl oz) vegetable stock
2tbsp oyster sauce
1tbsp light soy sauce
2tsp runny honey
1tsp cornflour
oil, for deep-frying
175g (6oz) tofu, drained, dried and cut into
   large cubes
2 garlic cloves, peeled and thinly sliced

1 green pepper, deseeded and sliced
225g (8oz) broccoli, cut into small florets,
   stalk sliced
125g (4oz) yard-long beans or French
   beans, trimmed and cut into short lengths
50g (2oz) beansprouts, washed and dried
50g can straw mushrooms, drained
125g (4oz) canned water chestnuts, drained
2tbsp chopped coriander, to garnish

1   To make the sauce, blend the stock, oyster and soy sauces, honey and cornflour together until smooth and put to one side.
2   Heat a 10cm (4 inch) depth of oil in a deep pan until a cube of bread dropped into the oil browns in 30 seconds. Add the tofu and deep-fry for 1–2 minutes until golden. Drain and put to one side.
3   Heat 2tbsp oil, add the garlic and fry for 1 minute then discard. Add the green pepper, broccoli and beans and stir-fry for 3 minutes. Add the beansprouts, mushrooms and water chestnuts and stir-fry for 1 minute.
4   Add the tofu and sauce to the vegetables and simmer, covered, for 3–4 minutes. Garnish with the coriander and serve.

Serves 4   preparation: 30 minutes   cooking time: 12–15 minutes
per serving: 300 cals; 15g fat; 21g carbohydrate

11

Vegetables

Colcannon

900g (2lb) potatoes, cut into
  even-sized chunks
salt and pepper

50g (2oz) butter
¼ Savoy cabbage, shredded
100ml (3½fl oz) semi-skimmed milk

1 Put the potatoes in a pan of lightly salted water, bring to the boil, then reduce the heat and simmer, partially covered, for 15–20 minutes or until the potatoes are tender.
2 Meanwhile, melt the butter in a large frying pan. Add the cabbage and stir-fry for 3 minutes.
3 Drain the potatoes well, then tip back into the pan and put over a medium heat for 1 minute to drive off excess moisture. Turn into a colander and cover to keep warm.
4 Pour the milk into the potato pan and bring to the boil, then take off the heat. Add the potatoes and mash well until smooth.
5 Add the cabbage and any butter from the pan to the mash and mix well. Season to taste and serve immediately.

Serves 4   preparation: 10 minutes   cooking time: 20 minutes
per serving: 310 cals; 12g fat; 45g carbohydrate

Layered Potato and Tomato Gratin

2 medium waxy potatoes, such as Desirée,
  peeled and cut into 5cm (¼ inch) slices
450ml (¾ pint) vegetable stock
oil, to oil
350g (12oz) tomatoes, sliced

1 garlic clove, peeled and crushed
1tsp dried thyme
salt and pepper
2tbsp grated low-fat Cheddar cheese

1 Put the potatoes into a pan and cover with the stock. Bring to the boil, reduce the heat and simmer until just tender, then drain and reserve.
2 Preheat the oven to 200°C (180°C fan oven) mark 6. Lightly oil an ovenproof dish. Layer the potatoes with the tomatoes in the dish, sprinkling each layer with the garlic, thyme and seasoning. Sprinkle with the Cheddar.
3 Bake for 40–45 minutes, then serve.

Serves 2   preparation: 5 minutes   cooking time: 1 hour–1 hour 5 minutes
per serving: 230 cals; 3g fat; 44g carbohydrate

Potato Gratin

450ml (¾ pint) milk
150ml (¼ pint) double cream
2 bay leaves, bruised
2 strips of lemon zest, bruised
pinch of saffron strands

900g (2lb) even-sized, small waxy potatoes
1 small onion, peeled and grated
2 garlic cloves, peeled and finely chopped
25g (1oz) butter, diced
salt and pepper

1 Put the milk, cream, bay leaves and lemon zest into a pan. Bring slowly to the boil, then remove from the heat, add the saffron and put to one side to infuse for 10 minutes. Preheat the oven to 200°C (180°C fan oven) mark 6.
2 In the meantime, peel the potatoes, then cut into even, thin slices, preferably using a mandolin or food processor fitted with a fine slicing blade.
3 Arrange a layer of potato slices over the base of a 1.5 litre (2¼–2½ pint) gratin dish. Scatter over some of the onion, garlic and butter and season generously. Repeat the layers, finishing with potatoes and a few pieces of butter.
4 Strain the infused cream over the potatoes, pressing the herbs and lemon to extract as much flavour as possible. Cover the dish with foil, put on a baking sheet and bake for 1 hour.
5 Remove the foil and bake for 15–20 minutes until the potatoes are softened and golden brown on top.

Serves 4–6 preparation: 15–20 minutes   cooking time: 1¼ hours
per serving: 450–300 cals; 25–17g fat; 49–33g carbohydrate

Creamed Cumin and Turmeric Potatoes

575g (1¼lb) potatoes, peeled and
  roughly cut
¼tsp salt, plus extra for boiling water
½tsp each ground turmeric and red
  chilli powder

2tbsp vegetable oil
1tsp cumin seeds
200g (7oz) Greek-style yogurt
100ml (3½fl oz) milk

1 Put the potatoes in a pan of lightly salted water, bring to the boil, then reduce the heat and simmer for about 10–15 minutes until tender. Drain and immediately mix with the turmeric and chilli powder.
2 Heat the oil in a heavy-based pan, add the cumin seeds and cook for 1 minute until they turn nut brown. Add the potatoes and cook for 10 minutes until lightly golden.
3 Add the yogurt, milk and ¼tsp salt, reduce the heat, cover the pan and cook for 5 minutes. Serve immediately.

Serves 4 preparation: 10 minutes   cooking time: about 25 minutes
per serving: 240 cals; 13g fat; 26g carbohydrate

Mustard Mash

1.25kg (2¾lb) old potatoes,
  peeled and chopped
salt and pepper
100ml (3½fl oz) warm milk

100ml (3½fl oz) olive oil, plus extra
  to drizzle
2tbsp Dijon mustard

1 Put the potatoes in a pan of lightly salted water, bring to the boil, then reduce the heat and simmer for 15–20 minutes until tender. Drain the potatoes well and return to the hot pan to dry off any excess moisture, then mash.
2 Put the pan back over a low heat, push the potatoes to one side of the pan and add the milk to warm through. Add the olive oil and mustard, season well and mash into the potatoes. Serve drizzled with olive oil.

Serves 6   preparation: 5 minutes   cooking time: 12 minutes
per serving: 290 cals; 17g fat; 32g carbohydrate

Saffron Mash

900g (2lb) potatoes, peeled
salt
pinch of saffron strands

50g (2oz) butter
coarse sea salt, to sprinkle

1 Put the potatoes in a pan of lightly salted water, bring to the boil, then reduce the heat and simmer for 20–30 minutes until tender. Meanwhile, soak the saffron strands in 2tbsp boiling water.
2 Drain the potatoes well and return to the hot pan to dry off any excess moisture.
3 Mash the potatoes with the butter and beat in the saffron with its soaking liquid. Sprinkle with coarse sea salt and serve.

Serves 4–6   preparation: 5 minutes   cooking time: about 20–30 minutes
per serving: 250–170 cals; 11–7g fat; 37–24g carbohydrate

Butter and Dill Baked Potatoes

40g (1½oz) butter, plus extra to grease
1.7 litres (3 pints) vegetable stock
700g (1½lb) Desirée potatoes, scrubbed
  and very finely sliced

1 onion, peeled and finely sliced
salt and pepper
3tbsp roughly chopped dill

1 Preheat the oven to 200°C (180°C fan oven) mark 6. Grease a large baking sheet. Cut out six 9 x 00.5cm (3½ x 12 inch) pieces of foil. Fold one in half lengthways and then wrap around a 7cm (2¾ inch) cutter and secure the foil with a paperclip. Remove the foil ring and do the same with the other pieces of foil. (Or use six 7cm (2¾ inch) cooking rings.) Grease the inside of each foil ring with butter, then put the foil rings on to the baking sheet.

2 Put the stock into a pan and bring to the boil. Add the potatoes and onion, reduce the heat and simmer for 5 minutes. Drain, discarding the stock, then use a palette knife to divide the potatoes and onion equally among the foil rings, layering them up, and seasoning well between each layer.

3 Melt the butter in a pan, add the dill and spoon over each potato stack. Cover the whole roasting tin with foil and bake for 40 minutes or until tender. Remove from the oven and use a palette knife to loosen the sides of the potato stacks from the foil or rings and lift off. Serve.

Serves 6 preparation: 15 minutes cooking time: 50 minutes
per serving: 150 cals; 6g fat; 22g carbohydrate

Crispy Better-than-baked Potatoes

4 sweet potatoes, each about 175g (6oz)
200g pack cream cheese
4tbsp finely chopped chives

salt and pepper
55g pack smoked crispy bacon

1 Preheat the oven to 220°C (200°C fan oven) mark 7. Put the potatoes in a roasting tin and bake for 50–60 minutes or until soft.

2 Meanwhile, mix the cream cheese and chives and season.

3 Remove the tin from the oven, cut the potatoes in half, spoon in the cream cheese and chives and top with the crispy bacon.

Serves 4 preparation: 5 minutes cooking time: 50 60 minutes
per serving: 430 cals; 29 fat; 37g carbohydrate

Mini Baked Potatoes with Caraway Seeds

18 small potatoes, scrubbed
2tbsp olive oil

1tbsp each caraway seeds and sea salt
black pepper

1 Preheat the oven to 220°C (200°C fan oven) mark 7. Toss the potatoes in the olive oil and sprinkle over the caraway seeds and sea salt. Season with pepper.
2 Roast the potatoes for 35–45 minutes or until golden and cooked through. Serve with crispy bacon and soured cream.

Serves 6   preparation: 5 minutes   cooking time: 35–45 minutes
per serving: 170 cals; 5g fat; 29g carbohydrate

Creamy Baked Potatoes with Mustard Seeds

6 baking potatoes, about 1.4kg (3lb)
2tbsp sunflower oil
1tbsp coarse sea salt
4–5 plump garlic cloves, unpeeled
50g (2oz) butter

6tbsp crème fraîche
2tbsp mustard seeds, toasted and
  lightly crushed
salt and pepper
oregano sprigs, to garnish

1 Preheat the oven to 200°C (180°C fan oven) mark 6. Prick the potato skins, rub with the oil and sprinkle with the salt. Put on a baking tray and bake for 40 minutes. Add the garlic and cook for 20 minutes.
2 Remove the tray from the oven. Slice the tops off the potatoes, scoop the flesh into a warm bowl, squeeze the garlic out of the skin and add to the potato with the butter, crème fraîche and mustard seeds. Mash and season. Spoon the mixture into the hollowed skins and put back on the tray.
3 Return to the oven and bake for 15 minutes or until golden brown. Garnish with oregano sprigs and serve.

Serves 6   preparation: 15–20 minutes   cooking time: 1¼ hours
per serving: 450 cals; 19g fat; 69g carbohydrate

11

Vegetables

Crushed Potatoes with Feta and Olives

700g (1½lb) new potatoes, unpeeled
salt and pepper
75ml (3fl oz) olive oil

75g (3oz) pitted black olives, shredded
2tbsp chopped flat-leafed parsley
200g (7oz) feta cheese, crumbled

1 Put the potatoes in a pan of lightly salted water, bring to the boil, then reduce the heat and simmer for 15 minutes or until tender. Drain, put back in the pan and crush roughly.
2 Add the olive oil, olives, parsley and feta cheese. Season and toss together – don't over-mix or the potatoes will become glutinous. Serve.

Serves 4   preparation: 20 minutes   cooking time: 15 minutes
per serving: 410 cals; 29g fat; 29g carbohydrate

Cracked Potatoes

700g (1½lb) new potatoes
salt and pepper
2tbsp olive oil
1 medium red onion, peeled and chopped

3 garlic cloves, peeled and crushed
150ml (¼ pint) white wine
6 rosemary sprigs
salt and pepper

1 Put the potatoes in a pan of lightly salted water, bring to the boil, then reduce the heat and simmer for 15 minutes or until just tender. Drain and put to one side.
2 Meanwhile, heat the olive oil in a frying pan, add the onion and cook for 4 minutes or until soft. Add the garlic and potatoes. Using the back of a spoon, flatten each potato so it looks as though it's cracking. Add the wine and rosemary, bring to the boil, then reduce the heat and simmer until the wine is reduced to nothing. Season and serve.

Serves 6   preparation: 5 minutes   cooking time: 20 minutes
per serving: 130 cals; 5g fat; 21g carbohydrate

Vegetables

Roasted Potatoes with Shallots and Rosemary

900g (2lb) potatoes, peeled and cut
  into 2.5cm (1 inch) pieces
salt and pepper
1 rosemary sprig or 1tbsp dried
4 tbsp olive oil

150g (5oz) shallots, blanched in boiling
  water, drained, peeled and quartered
2 garlic cloves, peeled and finely sliced
sea salt, to sprinkle

1 Preheat the oven to 200°C (180°C fan oven) mark 6. Put the potatoes in a pan of lightly salted water, bring to the boil, then reduce the heat and simmer for about 15 minutes until just tender. Meanwhile, strip the rosemary off the stem.
2 Heat the olive oil in a roasting tin. Drain the potatoes and add to the tin with the rosemary. Transfer to the oven and cook for about 35 minutes, turning occasionally.
3 Add the shallots and garlic and cook for 10–15 minutes or until golden. Season and serve sprinkled with sea salt.

Serves 6   preparation: 10 minutes   cooking time: 1 hour
per serving: 190 cals; 9g fat; 26g carbohydrate

Vegetables

Roasted New Potatoes with Herby Cheese

750g bag baby new potatoes
salt and pepper
olive oil

80g pack soft herb cheese
1tbsp finely chopped chives

1 Preheat the oven to 200°C (180°C fan oven) mark 6. Put the potatoes in a pan of lightly salted water, then reduce the heat and simmer for 10–15 minutes until tender. Drain well.
2 Tip the potatoes into a roasting tin, add a little olive oil and seasoning and toss well. Transfer to the oven and roast for 25 minutes, then remove from the oven and cool for 5–10 minutes.
3 Cut a cross in the top of each potato. Squeeze them a little and spoon $\frac{1}{3}$tsp cheese into each and sprinkle with chives. Serve warm or at room temperature.

Makes 24   preparation: 10 minutes, plus cooling   cooking time: 35 minutes
per serving: 240 cals; 2g fat; 5g carbohydrate

Roasted Parma Potatoes

about 50 sage leaves
900g (2lb) new potatoes, about 25
2 x 85g packs Parma ham, torn into strips

4tbsp olive oil
salt and pepper

1 Preheat the oven to 200°C (180°C fan oven) mark 6. Put two sage leaves on each potato and wrap a strip of Parma ham around. Repeat until all the potatoes are wrapped up.
2 Put half the olive oil in an ovenproof dish. Add the potatoes, drizzle with the remaining oil and season well. Roast for 45–50 minutes until tender.

Serves 6   preparation: 15 minutes   cooking time: 45–50 minutes
per serving: 250 cals; 13g fat; 24g carbohydrate

Mustard Roast Potatoes and Parsnips

1.5kg (3¼lb) small even-sized
  potatoes, peeled
800g (1¾lb) small parsnips, peeled
salt

50g (2oz) goose fat
1–2tbsp black mustard seeds
2–3tsp sea salt flakes

1 Preheat the oven to 200°C (180°C fan oven) mark 6. Cut out a small wedge from one side of each potato and parsnip (this will help make them extra crispy). Put them into a pan of lightly salted water, bring to the boil and cook for 6 minutes. Drain thoroughly.
2 Heat the goose fat in a roasting tin in the oven for 4 minutes until sizzling hot. Add the potatoes, toss in the hot melted fat and roast for 30 minutes.
3 Add the parsnips and sprinkle over the mustard seeds and sea salt. Return to the oven and roast for 30–35 minutes, turning halfway, or until golden. Serve at once.

Serves 8   preparation: 25 minutes   cooking time: about 1 hour
per serving: 220 cals; 5g fat; 41g carbohydrate

Fantail Potatoes

1.8kg (4lb) large potatoes, such as King
  Edward, scrubbed
6tbsp olive oil

2tsp sea salt flakes
black pepper

1 Preheat the oven to 220°C (200°C fan oven) mark 7. Halve any very large potatoes lengthways. Using a sharp knife, slice down each potato widthways, three-quarters of the way through, at 5mm (¼ inch) intervals. If you push a skewer through the base of the potato along its length it will stop you cutting all the way through.
2 Put on a baking tray, drizzle with the olive oil and season with the salt and pepper.
3 Transfer to the oven and cook for 1 hour, basting every 10 minutes until the potatoes are crisp and cooked all the way through.

Serves 8–10   preparation: 15 minutes   cooking time: 1 hour
per serving: 260–210 cals; 13–10g fat; 34–28g carbohydrate

Soufflé Potatoes

700g (1½lb) floury potatoes, such as King
  Edward, peeled and cut into chunks
salt and pepper
butter, to grease

6tbsp finely grated Parmesan cheese
300g carton fresh four-cheese sauce
1tbsp wholegrain mustard
3 eggs, separated

1 Put the potatoes in a pan of lightly salted water, bring to the boil, then reduce the heat and simmer for 20 minutes or until tender. Drain, put back in the pan and mash over a low heat for 1–2 minutes to dry a little. Put in a bowl and cool for 10 minutes.
2 Preheat the oven to 200°C (180°C fan oven) mark 6. Grease six 225ml (8fl oz) ramekins, sprinkle each with 1tbsp Parmesan and put them on a baking sheet.
3 Add the cheese sauce, mustard and egg yolks to the potato, season well and beat together.
4 Whisk the egg whites in a clean grease-free bowl until they stand in stiff peaks, then fold into the mashed potato. Spoon into the prepared dishes and bake for 30 minutes until well risen. Serve immediately.

Serves 6   preparation: 10–15 minutes   cooking time: 50 minutes
per serving: 270 cals; 13g fat; 25g carbohydrate

Vegetables

Potato and Onion Pan-fry

500g (1lb 2oz) potatoes, peeled and
thickly sliced
salt and pepper

2–3tbsp olive oil
1 onion, peeled and cut into 8 wedges
1tbsp chopped flat-leafed parsley

1 Put the potatoes in a pan of lightly salted water and boil for 2–3 minutes. Meanwhile, heat the olive oil in a pan and fry the onion for 5 minutes. Drain the potatoes and add to the pan.
2 Cook for 5–10 minutes until golden and crisp, then season well and toss through the parsley to serve.

Serves 4 preparation: 5 minutes cooking time: 10–15 minutes
per serving: 170 cals; 8g fat; 23g carbohydrate

Potato Croquettes with Bacon and Cheese

1kg (2¼lb) floury potatoes, such as King
Edward, peeled and cut into large chunks
salt and pepper
125g (4oz) streaky bacon rashers, de-rinded
and cut into narrow strips
125g (4oz) Lancashire cheese, crumbled, or
Cheddar cheese, coarsely grated

50g (2oz) butter
2tbsp chopped flat-leafed parsley
2 large eggs, separated
125g (4oz) fine fresh breadcrumbs
vegetable oil, for frying
sea salt and marjoram sprigs, to garnish

1 Put the potatoes in a pan of lightly salted water, bring to the boil, then reduce the heat and simmer for 15–20 minutes until tender. Drain and return the potatoes to the pan. Meanwhile, fry the bacon in a non-stick frying pan until brown and crisp.
2 Mash the potatoes over a low heat to dry them out. Mix the potato, bacon, cheese, butter and parsley thoroughly and season well. Leave to cool.
3 Once the mixture is cold, add the egg yolks. Shape into 20 golf ball-sized portions. Lightly whisk the egg whites in a clean grease-free bowl. Dip the potato balls in the egg white, then in the breadcrumbs, making sure the coating covers the potato balls evenly. Arrange on a flat dish and chill, uncovered, until ready to fry.
4 Heat the oil in a deep frying pan until very hot. Carefully lower the potato balls into the oil in batches and cook for 2–3 minutes or until crisp and a chestnut brown colour. Drain on kitchen paper. Garnish with sea salt and marjoram sprigs and serve.

Makes 20 preparation: 30 minutes cooking time: 35 minutes, plus cooling
per croquette: 140 cals; 9g fat; 11g carbohydrate

Paprika Potato Wedges

700g (1½lb) potatoes, peeled and cut into
 chunky wedges
salt and pepper

3tbsp oil
1tsp ground paprika

1 Preheat the oven to 200°C (180°C fan oven) mark 6. Cook the potatoes in boiling salted water for 3 minutes, then drain, put into a roasting tin and toss in the oil, plenty of seasoning and the paprika.
2 Roast for 35–40 minutes, turning occasionally to brown evenly.

Serves 4   preparation: 5 minutes   cooking time: 40–45 minutes
per serving: 220 cals; 10g fat; 30g carbohydrate

Rösti Potatoes

4 medium potatoes, such as Desirée, about
 1kg (2¼lb) in total, scrubbed
salt and pepper

50g (2oz) butter, melted, plus extra to
 grease
4 slices Emmental cheese

1 Put the potatoes in a large pan of cold salted water, cover and bring to the boil. Cook for 5–8 minutes, then drain, transfer to a bowl and leave to cool for 10 minutes.
2 Preheat the oven to 220°C (200°C fan oven) mark 7. Grease two large baking trays. Peel the potatoes, then grate coarsely into long strands by rubbing each one lengthways along a coarse grater. Divide into four.
3 Shape each portion into a mound and put well apart on the baking trays. Drizzle the melted butter over each mound, season generously and cook in the oven for about 30 minutes until golden.
4 Put a slice of cheese on each rösti and return to the oven for 10 minutes or until golden and bubbling. Serve immediately.

Serves 4   preparation: 20 minutes, plus cooling   cooking time: 40 minutes
per serving: 380 cals; 18g fat; 43g carbohydrate

Vegetables

Potato Frites

**700g (1½lb) baking potatoes, peeled and
cut into long, very thin sticks**

**oil, for frying
sea salt flakes and black pepper**

1 Dry the potatoes thoroughly in a clean tea-towel. Heat 1cm (½ inch) oil in a deep frying pan and fry the potatoes in batches for 3–4 minutes or until golden brown and very crisp.
2 Drain on kitchen paper, season with sea salt flakes and pepper and keep warm. Continue to fry the potato sticks in batches until all the potatoes are used up. Serve immediately.

Serves 4   preparation: 15 minutes   cooking time: 15 minutes
per serving: 280 cals; 6g fat; 52g carbohydrate

Potato Wedges with Dill Cream

**2tbsp chopped dill
142ml carton soured cream
700g (1½lb) Desirée potatoes, scrubbed
and cut into wedges**

**2tbsp olive oil
salt**

1 Preheat the oven to 200°C (180°C fan oven) mark 6. Stir the dill into the soured cream. Put the potatoes in a roasting tin, drizzle with the olive oil and sprinkle with salt.
2 Roast for 40–50 minutes, then remove from the oven and serve with the dill cream.

Serves 4   preparation: 5 minutes   cooking time: 40–50 minutes
per serving: 250 cals; 12g fat; 31g carbohydrate

11

Vegetables

Grilled Sweet Potatoes with Harissa

350g (12oz) scrubbed, sliced
  sweet potatoes
salt and pepper
1tbsp olive oil

1tsp harissa paste
50g (2oz) unsalted butter, chilled and diced
coriander sprigs, to garnish

1 Put the potatoes in a pan of lightly salted water, bring to the boil, then reduce the heat and simmer for about 15–20 minutes or until just tender but still firm. Drain and slice thickly. Meanwhile, preheat the grill.
2 Toss the potatoes with the olive oil and harissa. Spread out in a single layer on a grill pan and grill for 2 minutes on each side.
3 Season with pepper. Dot with the butter, garnish with coriander sprigs and serve.

Serves 4   preparation: 5 minutes   cooking time: about 20 minutes
per serving: 200 cals; 14g fat; 19g carbohydrate

Sweet Potato Mash

2 medium potatoes, about 400g (14oz),
  such as King Edward, peeled and cut
  into chunks
900g (2lb) sweet potatoes, peeled and cut
  into chunks

salt and pepper
50g (2oz) butter

1 Put all the potatoes in a large pan of lightly salted water. Bring to the boil, then reduce the heat and simmer, half covered, for 15–20 minutes until tender.
2 Drain well, add the butter and season generously. Mash until smooth, then serve.

Serves 6   preparation: 10 minutes   cooking time: 20 minutes
per serving: 240 cals; 7g fat; 42g carbohydrate

Vegetables

Braised Celery with Pancetta and Cheese

1 head of celery, about 450g (1lb)
  trimmed weight
125g (4oz) smoked pancetta or rindless
  streaky bacon rashers, diced
25g (1oz) butter

1 large onion, peeled and chopped
2 garlic cloves, peeled and crushed
150ml (¼ pint) single cream
salt and pepper
125g (4oz) Gruyère cheese, grated

1 Separate the celery sticks and cut each into 5cm (2 inch) lengths, on the diagonal.
2 Preheat a large sauté pan suitable for use under the grill. Add the pancetta or bacon and stir-fry over
   a high heat until it releases its fat and browns. Remove with a slotted spoon and put to one side.
3 Melt the butter in the pan, add the onion and garlic and fry gently for 10 minutes until softened. Add
   the celery and cook for 5 minutes.
4 Preheat the grill to its highest setting. Return the pancetta to the pan, add the cream and bring to the
   boil. Cover the pan, reduce the heat and simmer for 5 minutes; season to taste.
5 Scatter the cheese over the celery and put under the grill for 1–2 minutes until golden. Serve at once.

Serves: 4–6   preparation: 10 minutes cooking time: 25 minutes
per serving: 410–270 cals; 36–24g fat; 6–4g carbohydrate

Celeriac Dauphinoise

700g (1½lb) potatoes, peeled and
  thinly sliced
450g (1lb) celeriac, peeled and thinly sliced
2 bay leaves
600ml (1 pint) milk

25g (1oz) diced butter, plus extra to grease
salt and pepper
2 garlic cloves, peeled and crushed
284ml carton double cream

1 Put the potatoes and celeriac in a large pan with the bay leaves and milk. Bring just to the boil, then
   reduce the heat and cook for 5–8 minutes until tender. Drain, then discard the milk and bay leaves.
2 Preheat the oven to 180°C (160°C fan oven) mark 4. Grease a 1.4 litre (2½ pint) gratin dish with a
   little butter. Season the potatoes and celeriac well, then arrange in layers in the dish. Add the garlic
   and cream and dot with the diced butter.
3 Cover with foil and bake for 1 hour. Remove the foil and bake for another 15–20 minutes until golden,
   then serve.

Serves 6   preparation: 20 minutes   cooking time: 1 hour 25 minutes
per serving: 380 cals; 28g fat; 26g carbohydrate

Creamed Spinach

900g (2lb) spinach leaves, stalks removed   salt and pepper
4tbsp crème fraîche

1   Cook the spinach with just the water clinging to the leaves after washing in a covered pan for 3–4 minutes or until just wilted.
2   Stir in the crème fraîche and season to taste. Serve at once.

Serves 6   preparation: 15 minutes   cooking time: 5 minutes
per serving: 80 cals; 5g fat; 3g carbohydrate

Spinach with Tomatoes

50g (2oz) butter   250g bag baby spinach leaves
2 garlic cloves, peeled and crushed   salt and pepper
450g (1lb) baby plum tomatoes, halved   freshly grated nutmeg, to serve

1   Melt 25g (1oz) butter in a pan and cook the garlic until just soft.
2   Add the tomatoes and cook for 4–5 minutes.
3   Put the spinach leaves and a little water in a clean pan, cover and cook for 2–3 minutes. Drain well, chop roughly and stir into the tomatoes.
4   Add the remaining butter and gently heat through. Season well, stir in a large pinch of nutmeg and serve.

Serves 6   preparation: 10 minutes   cooking time: 10 minutes
per serving: 90 cals; 7g fat; 3g carbohydrate

Beetroot and Dill Salad

900g (2lb) beetroot   juice of 1 lemon
salt and pepper   2tbsp chopped dill
4tbsp olive oil

1   Trim the stalks from the beetroot and discard, then rinse well. Put in a pan of cold salted water. Cover and bring to the boil, then reduce the heat and simmer, half-covered, for 20–25 minutes or until tender. Drain well, then slip the skins off the beetroot.
2   Halve each beetroot and put in a bowl. Add the olive oil, lemon juice and dill and season well. Toss together and serve.

Serves 6   preparation: 5 minutes   cooking time: 30–35 minutes
per serving: 130 cals; 9g fat; 12g carbohydrate

Minted Peas with Spring Onions and Courgettes

450g (1lb) shelled fresh peas
225g (8oz) French beans
25g (1oz) butter
1 bunch of spring onions, thickly sliced
225g (8oz) courgettes, cut lengthways
   into wedges

200ml carton crème fraîche
1tsp sugar (optional)
3tbsp roughly chopped mint leaves
salt and pepper

1 Cook the peas and French beans in a pan of boiling water for 5 minutes or until tender, then drain.
2 Heat the butter in a frying pan and sauté the spring onions and courgette wedges for 3 minutes. Add the crème fraîche, bring to a simmer and leave to bubble for 2 minutes.
3 Stir in the peas, French beans, sugar, if using, and mint. Season to taste and serve at once.

Serves 6 preparation: 15 minutes cooking time: 10 minutes
per serving: 240 cals; 8g fat; 13g carbohydrate

Minted Peas with Cucumber

450g (1lb) podded fresh or frozen peas
50g (2oz) butter
1 bunch of spring onions, sliced
175g (6oz) cucumber, halved lengthways,
   deseeded and thickly sliced
142ml carton crème fraîche

3tbsp vermouth, such as Noilly Prat
2tbsp chopped mint
salt and pepper
½tsp golden caster sugar
mint sprigs, to garnish

1 Bring a pan of water to the boil, add the peas and simmer for 5 minutes or until tender and just cooked through. Drain, return to the pan and keep warm.
2 Heat the butter in a frying pan. Add the spring onions and cucumber and sauté for 3 minutes. Add the crème fraîche and vermouth and bring to the boil, then bubble for 2–3 minutes. Add the peas and mint, season generously and add the sugar. Serve garnished with mint sprigs.

Serves 4–6 preparation: 5 minutes cooking time: 10 minutes
per serving: 330–220 cals; 26–17g fat; 16–11g carbohydraate

Braised Chicory in White Wine

50g (2oz) butter, softened
6 heads of chicory, trimmed
salt and pepper

100ml (3½fl oz) white wine
snipped chives, to serve

1 Preheat the oven to 190°C (170°C fan oven) mark 5. Grease a 1.7 litre (3 pint) ovenproof dish with 15g (½oz) butter and lay the chicory in the dish.
2 Season to taste, add the wine and dot the remaining butter over the top. Cover with foil and cook in the oven for 1 hour or until soft. Scatter with chives to serve.

Serves 6 preparation: 5 minutes   cooking time: about 1 hour
per serving: 80 cals; 7g fat; 3g carbohydrate

Spicy Red Cabbage with Apples

1tbsp olive oil
1 small red onion, peeled and sliced
2 garlic cloves, peeled and crushed
½ red cabbage, about 500g (1lb 2oz),
   shredded
1tbsp light muscovado sugar
1tbsp red wine vinegar

4 juniper berries
¼tsp each freshly grated nutmeg and
   ground allspice
150ml (¼ pint) vegetable stock
salt and pepper
50g (2oz) sultanas
2 eating apples, cored and sliced

1 Heat the olive oil in a large heavy-based pan, add the onion and cook gently for 3–4 minutes to soften.
2 Add the garlic, cabbage, sugar, vinegar, juniper berries, nutmeg, allspice and stock. Season well. Bring to the boil, reduce the heat, then cover the pan and simmer for 30 minutes.
3 Add the sultanas and apples and stir through. Cook for a further 15 minutes or until the cabbage is just tender and nearly all the liquid has evaporated. The flavour of this dish improves with keeping, so make it a day ahead and reheat to serve.

Serves 8 preparation: 10 minutes   cooking time: 50 minutes
per serving: 270 cals; 2g fat; 12g carbohydrate

Red Cabbage with Caraway Seeds

1 red cabbage, about 700g (1½lb), cored
  and finely shredded
juice of ½ lemon
1 medium red onion, peeled and sliced
1 garlic clove, peeled and crushed
1 apple, cored and thinly sliced

2tbsp white wine vinegar
150ml (¼ pint) dry cider
1tsp caraway seeds
1tbsp runny honey
salt and pepper

1 Combine all the ingredients in a heavy-based pan, cover and bring to the boil.
2 Reduce the heat to a gentle simmer and cook slowly for 45 minutes–1 hour.

Serves 8 preparation: 15 minutes cooking time: 1 hour
per serving: 40 cals; trace fat; 7g carbohydrate

Pan-fried Red Cabbage with Red Onion and Cranberries

1tbsp olive oil
1 small red onion, peeled and finely sliced
½ small red cabbage, cored and finely sliced

25g (1oz) dried cranberries
salt and pepper
1tbsp balsamic vinegar

1 Heat the olive oil in a non-stick wok or frying pan. Add the onion and stir-fry over a medium heat for about 5 minutes.
2 Add the cabbage, cranberries and 1tbsp water. Season and continue to cook for 10 minutes, tossing every now and then until the cabbage is just tender.
3 Drizzle over the balsamic vinegar, toss again to mix, then tip into a warm serving bowl and serve.

Serves 2 preparation: 10 minutes cooking time: 17 minutes
per serving: 120 cals; 7g fat; 12g carbohydrate

Braised Garlic Cabbage

2tbsp olive oil
2 garlic cloves, peeled and crushed
1 small Savoy cabbage, quartered, cored
  and shredded

salt and pepper
2tbsp chopped flat-leafed parsley

1 Heat the olive oil in a heavy-based pan, add the garlic and cook for 30 seconds. Add the cabbage and cook, stirring, for 5 minutes. Season, stir in the parsley and serve.

Serves 4 preparation: 10 minutes cooking time: 6 minutes
per serving: 90 cals; 7g fat; 5g carbohydrate

Red Cabbage with Ginger

2tbsp white wine vinegar
2.5cm (1 inch) piece fresh root
  ginger, peeled
1.4kg (3lb) red cabbage, outer leaves
  discarded, cored and finely shredded

salt
olive oil, to drizzle
thyme sprigs, to garnish

1 Add the vinegar and ginger to a large pan of water and bring to the boil. Add the cabbage, season with salt and cook for 5–10 minutes.
2 Drain and discard the ginger. Serve drizzled with olive oil and garnished with thyme sprigs.

Serves 6   preparation: 5 minutes   cooking time: 5–10 minutes
per serving: 50 cals; 3g fat; 5g carbohydrate

Savoy Cabbage Parcels

3tbsp olive oil
125g (4oz) onion, peeled and finely chopped
1 garlic clove, peeled and crushed
125g (4oz) each aubergine and
  courgette, diced

½ red and ½ yellow pepper, diced
6 young Savoy cabbage leaves

1 To make the ratatouille stuffing, heat the olive oil in a frying pan, add the onion and cook until soft. Add the garlic and aubergine and cook for 2–3 minutes, stirring from time to time. Add the courgettes and diced peppers and continue to cook for 2–3 minutes or until the vegetables are soft. Put to one side.
2 Preheat the oven to 180°C (160°C fan oven) mark 4. Plunge the cabbage leaves into boiling water for 1–2 minutes, drain, plunge into cold water and drain again. Dry on kitchen paper. Place a spoonful of the ratatouille in each cabbage leaf and shape into a parcel. Place in an ovenproof dish, cover and heat through in the oven for 7–10 minutes.

Serves 6   preparation: 10 minutes   cooking time: about 28 minutes
per serving: 80 cals; 7g fat; 4g carbohydrate

Buttered Cabbage with Caraway Seeds

450g (1lb) finely shredded cabbage
½tsp caraway seeds

50g (2oz) butter
juice of ½ lemon

1 Cook the cabbage in boiling salted water until just tender. Drain well.
2 Meanwhile, fry the caraway seeds in a dry pan until toasted. Take the pan off the heat, add the butter and leave to melt in the heat of the pan.
3 Toss the butter through the cabbage and serve with a squeeze of lemon juice.

Serves 4   preparation: 5 minutes   cooking time: about 10 minutes
per serving: 120 cals; 11g fat; 4g carbohydrate

Spring Vegetables with Prosciutto

8 small baby globe artichokes with stalks
500g (1lb 2oz) each frozen broad beans and
   frozen peas
50g (2oz) butter
4tbsp olive oil
2 medium red onions, peeled and finely
   chopped

1 thick slice prosciutto
2 large handfuls mint leaves, half roughly
   chopped
salt and pepper
8 thin slices proscuitto

1 Bring a large pan of water to the boil and blanch the artichokes for 5 minutes or until you can pull off an outer leaf with a sharp tug – they shouldn't be completely cooked at this stage. Drain and leave to cool on a plate.
2 Fill the pan with fresh water, bring to the boil and blanch the broad beans for 2 minutes. Drain and leave to cool.
3 Put the butter in a large heavy-based pan with 2tbsp olive oil, then gently fry the onions for 6–8 minutes until golden. Add the peas and stir gently for 2 minutes to coat with the oil and onion. Pour in just enough water to cover, then add the thick slice of prosciutto and simmer gently for 20 minutes.
4 When the artichokes have cooled, peel off the tough outer leaves, then cut off the stalks about 5cm (2 inches) from the base. If the stalk seems stringy, scrape away the outer layer – the core is always tender. Cut off the tough top part of the cone, then slice each artichoke lengthways into eighths.
5 Heat the remaining oil in a separate pan, add the sliced artichokes and fry, stirring, until they are lightly browned. Add the whole mint leaves, seasoning and a ladleful of water. Cook for 1–2 minutes.
6 Remove and discard the prosciutto from the peas. Add the fried artichokes and their juices to the peas, along with the broad beans and chopped mint. Heat through gently but don't cook as this will toughen the beans. Take off the heat, chop the thin slices of prosciutto into ribbons and stir them into the vegetables. Spoon into a warm serving dish and serve.

Serves 8   preparation: 30 minutes   cooking time: 50 minutes
per serving: 250 cals; 14g fat; 18g carbohydrate

Buttered Asparagus with Roasted Garlic

6 garlic bulbs
3tbsp olive oil
salt and pepper
125g (4oz) unsalted butter
1.4kg (3lb) asparagus spears, trimmed

juice of ½ lemon
1tbsp chopped chervil, plus six sprigs
to garnish
1 ciabatta loaf, sliced

1 Preheat the oven to 200°C (180°C fan oven) mark 6. Peel off one layer of papery skin from each garlic bulb and discard. Put the bulbs in a roasting tin, drizzle with 1tbsp water and the olive oil and season. Cover with foil and roast for 40 minutes or until soft and golden.

2 Melt the butter in a small pan, bring to the boil, take off the heat and cool. Skim the milky solids from the surface and discard.

3 Cook the asparagus in a deep frying pan of boiling water for 4–5 minutes or until tender, then drain. Add the lemon juice to the butter, season, then add the chopped chervil.

4 Remove the garlic from the roasting tin and slice off the tops.

5 Divide the asparagus and garlic bulbs between each plate, drizzle over the butter and garnish with chervil sprigs. To eat, squeeze the sweet garlic purée from individual cloves on to the ciabatta.

Serves 6   preparation: 5 minutes   cooking time: 40 minutes
per serving: 390 cals; 27g fat; 28g carbohydrate

Vegetables

Asparagus with Lemon Dressing

finely grated zest of ½ lemon
2tbsp lemon juice
3tbsp extra-virgin olive oil
pinch of golden caster sugar

salt and pepper
250g (9oz) fine-stemmed asparagus,
ends trimmed

1 To make the dressing, put the lemon zest into a screw-topped jar, add the lemon juice, olive oil and pinch of sugar, then shake to mix.
2 Half fill a frying pan with boiling salted water. Add the asparagus, then cover and simmer for 5 minutes or until just tender.
3 Remove the asparagus with a large draining spoon. If serving the asparagus cold, plunge it into a large bowl of iced water – this will help keep its bright green colour – then drain.
4 To serve, arrange the asparagus in a concentric pattern in a large shallow bowl, with tips outwards and ends overlapping in the centre. Season generously and drizzle with the dressing.

Serves 5   preparation: 15 minutes   cooking time: 5 minutes
per serving: 90 cals; 8g fat; 3g carbohydrate

11

Vegetables

Roasted Root Vegetables

1 large potato and 1 large sweet potato,
each peeled and cut into large chunks
2 carrots and 2 parsnips, each peeled and
cut into large chunks

1 small swede, peeled and cut into
large chunks
3tbsp olive oil
2 rosemary and 2 thyme sprigs
salt and pepper

1 Preheat the oven to 200°C (180°C fan oven) mark 6. Put all the vegetables in a large roasting tin. Add the olive oil.
2 Use scissors to snip the herbs over the tin, then season well and toss everything together. Roast for 1 hour or until tender.

Serves 4   preparation: 15 minutes   cooking time: 1 hour
per serving: 240 cals; 11g fat; 35g carbohydrate

Roast Vegetables with Tabbouleh

2 red peppers, deseeded and cut into 2cm
(¾ inch) chunks
4 courgettes, about 450g (1lb), cut into 2cm
(¾ inch) chunks
1 aubergine, about 350g (12oz), cut into
2cm (¾ inch) chunks
2 red onions, about 350g (12oz), peeled and
cut into 2cm (¾ inch) chunks
6 garlic cloves, unpeeled

3tbsp olive oil
salt and pepper
375g pack bulgur wheat
½ cucumber, diced
6tbsp each roughly chopped mint and
flat-leafed parsley
zest and juice of 2 lemons
6tbsp extra-virgin olive oil
2tsp harissa paste

1 Preheat the oven to 200°C (180°C fan oven) mark 6. Put the peppers, courgettes, aubergine, onions and garlic in a roasting tin, add the olive oil, toss well and season. Roast for 1 hour or until tender and starting to char.
2 Meanwhile, put the bulgur wheat in a bowl, add 1.1 litres (2 pints) boiling water and soak for 30 minutes.
3 Drain the bulgur in a sieve, then tip into a clean tea-towel. Wrap up tight and squeeze over the sink to extract the water. Tip into a large glass serving bowl, season and stir in the cucumber, mint and parsley.
4 Take the roasting tin out of the oven, remove the garlic from the tin and put to one side. Spoon the remaining roasted vegetables on top of the bulgur.
5 To make the dressing, squeeze the purée from the garlic cloves into a food processor, then add the lemon zest and juice, the extra-virgin olive oil and harissa. Season, then whiz for 1–2 minutes. Drizzle the dressing over the vegetables and toss everything together.

Serves 6   preparation: 30 minutes   cooking time: 1 hour
per serving: 430 cals; 19g fat; 57g carbohydrate

Vegetable and Mustard Mash

1.4kg (3lb) floury potatoes, such as Maris
   Piper, peeled and cut into large chunks
900g (2lb) parsnips or celeriac, peeled and
   cut into large chunks
salt and pepper

50g (2oz) butter
4tbsp snipped chives or chopped flat-
   leafed parsley
200g tub crème fraîche
3tbsp Dijon mustard

1 Put the potatoes and parsnips or celeriac in a pan of lightly salted water, bring to the boil, then reduce the heat and simmer for 20–25 minutes or until tender.
2 Meanwhile, melt the butter in a small pan, bring to the boil, take off the heat and skim off the white surface with a slotted spoon. Carefully pour the butter into a jug, discarding the milky substance at the bottom. Add the herbs and season well.
3 Drain the vegetables. Return them to the pan and put over a low heat for 1–2 minutes to dry, then crush with a potato masher. Beat in the crème fraîche and mustard and season well. Using two dessertspoons, shape the mash into ovals, spoon into a warm serving dish and drizzle with the herb butter.

Serves 10   preparation: 30 minutes   cooking time: 30 minutes
per serving: 240 cals; 13g fat; 29g carbohydrate

Vegetables

Stir-fried Green Vegetables

2tbsp oil
225g (8oz) courgettes, thinly sliced
175g (6oz) mangetout, trimmed

25g (1oz) butter
175g (6oz) frozen peas, thawed
salt and pepper

1 Heat the oil in a large frying pan or wok, add the courgettes and cook for 1–2 minutes. Add the mangetout and cook for 1 minute. Add the butter and peas and cook for 1 minute. Season and serve.

Serves 6   preparation: 5 minutes   cooking time: 3–4 minutes
per serving: 110 cals; 8g fat; 5g carbohydrate

Ratatouille

4tbsp olive oil

2 onions, peeled and thinly sliced

1 large garlic clove, peeled and crushed

350g (12oz) small aubergine, thinly sliced

450g (1lb) small courgettes, thinly sliced

450g (1lb) tomatoes, skinned, deseeded and
  roughly chopped

1 green and 1 red pepper, each cored,
  deseeded and sliced

1tbsp chopped basil

2tsp chopped thyme

2tbsp chopped flat-leafed parsley

2tbsp sun-dried tomato paste

salt and pepper

1 Heat the olive oil in a large pan, add the onions and garlic and fry gently for 10 minutes or until softened and golden.
2 Add the aubergine, courgettes, tomatoes, sliced peppers, herbs, tomato paste and seasoning. Fry, stirring, for 2–3 minutes.
3 Cover the pan tightly and simmer for 30 minutes or until all the vegetables are just tender. If necessary, uncover towards the end of the cooking time to evaporate some of the liquid.
4 Taste and adjust the seasoning. Serve the ratatouille hot or cold.

Serves 4–6   preparation: 20 minutes   cooking time: about 45 minutes
per serving: 220–150 cals; 15–10g fat; 18–12g carbohydrate

Oven-baked Root Vegetable Chips

700g (1½lb) large Maris Piper potatoes,
  peeled and cut lengthways into 1cm
  (½ inch) wide x 7.5cm (3 inch) long chips

300g (11oz) large carrots, peeled and cut
  lengthways into 1cm (½ inch) wide x
  7.5cm (3 inch) long chips

3 large parsnips, about 700g (1½lb) in total,
  peeled and cut lengthways into 1cm
  (½ inch) wide x 7.5cm (3 inch) long chips

4tbsp olive oil

2tsp all-purpose seasoning

½tsp sea salt

1 Preheat the oven to 220°C (200°C fan oven) mark 7. Put the vegetables in a bowl and toss with the olive oil, all-purpose seasoning and the salt, then transfer to two roasting tins.
2 Bake for 50–55 minutes or until the vegetables are tender and golden. Toss frequently and swap the tins over occasionally, so that the vegetables cook evenly.
3 Drain the vegetables on kitchen paper and serve warm with tomato ketchup.

Serves 6   preparation: 30 minutes   cooking time: 55 minutes
per serving: 200 cals; 6g fat; 32g carbohydrate

Sweet Roasted Fennel

700g (1½lb) fennel bulbs, about 3 bulbs,
  quartered
3tbsp olive oil
50g (2oz) butter, melted

1 lemon, halved
1tsp golden caster sugar
salt and pepper
2 large thyme sprigs

1 Preheat the oven to 200°C (180°C fan oven) mark 6. Put the fennel in a large roasting tin and drizzle with the olive oil and melted butter, then squeeze the lemon juice over. Add the lemon halves to the tin. Sprinkle with the sugar and season generously. Add the thyme and cover with a damp piece of non-stick baking parchment.
2 Transfer to the oven and cook for 30 minutes, then remove the baking parchment and cook for 20–30 minutes or until lightly charred or tender.

Serves 4–6 preparation: 10 minutes cooking time: 1 hour
per serving: 210–140 cals; 20–14g fat; 4–3g carbohydrate

Florentine Fennel with White Wine

3tbsp olive oil
750g (1lb 10oz) fennel, sliced

150ml (¼ pint) white wine
salt and pepper

1 Heat the olive oil in a deep, lidded frying pan. Add the fennel and wine, then season generously.
2 Cover with a tight-fitting lid and bring to the boil, then reduce the heat and simmer gently for 30 minutes or until the fennel is very tender and the liquid is reduced.

Serves 6 preparation: 5 minutes cooking time: 35 minutes
per serving: 90 cals; 7g fat; 2g carbohydrate

Roasted Fennel with Oranges and Dill Mash

2 fennel bulbs, cut into wedges
2 red onions, peeled and cut into wedges
2tbsp olive oil
salt and pepper
1.1kg (2½lb) floury potatoes, such as King
   Edward, peeled and cut into chunks

50g (2oz) butter
2 oranges, peeled and segmented
50g (2oz) walnut halves, roughly chopped
juice of 1 orange
4tbsp chopped dill

1 Preheat the oven to 220°C (200°C fan oven) mark 7. Put the fennel in a large roasting tin, add the onions and half the olive oil and season well. Roast for 45 minutes or until soft.
2 Meanwhile, put the potatoes in a large pan of lightly salted water, bring to the boil, then reduce the heat and simmer gently for 15–20 minutes or until tender. Drain well, then return to the hot pan to dry off any moisture. Add the butter, season and mash until smooth. Keep warm.
3 Add the orange segments and walnuts to the vegetables in the roasting tin and cook for a further 5 minutes.
4 Mix the orange juice with the remaining oil and season well to taste. Fold the dill through the mash, then spoon on to four warm plates and top with the roasted vegetables. Drizzle over the orange juice and olive oil dressing and serve immediately.

Serves 4   preparation: 30 minutes   cooking time: 50 minutes
per serving: 370 cals; 18g fat; 49g carbohydrate

Roasted Pepper, Fennel and Cherry Tomatoes

125g (4oz) butter, softened at room
   temperature
1tbsp rosemary, stripped from the woody
   stem and chopped
2tbsp chopped mint
salt and pepper

olive oil, to brush
3 red peppers, cut into quarters, with the
   stalks still attached and deseeded
9 baby fennel, halved
6 sprigs of cherry tomatoes on the vine

1 Put the butter in a bowl and beat in the rosemary and mint, then season. Put the butter on to a piece of greaseproof paper and shape into a log. Wrap up and chill in the fridge.
2 Preheat the oven to 200°C (180°C fan oven) mark 6. Oil one large roasting tin and one smaller tin. Put the red peppers in the large tin and the fennel in the smaller tin. Brush the vegetables with olive oil and season. Divide the chilled butter among the pepper quarters, the roast the peppers and fennel for 20 minutes.
3 Put the tomatoes in the roasting tin with the peppers and put back in the oven to roast for 20 minutes. Serve with any buttery juices drizzled over.

Serves 6   preparation: 15 minutes   cooking time: 40 minutes
per serving: 190 cals; 17g fat; 6g carbohydrate

Leeks with Red Wine

3–4tbsp olive oil
450g (1lb) small leeks (white part only), all
   of similar size

salt
1 wine glass of red wine
2tbsp good meat stock or water

1　Heat the olive oil in a large frying pan. Put the leeks in the pan and as soon as they have taken colour on one side, turn them over. Season with very little salt.

2　Pour over the wine (watch out for spluttering), let it bubble, then add the stock – or water if no stock is available. Cover the pan and cook at a moderate pace for 7–10 minutes, turning the leeks over once during the process. They are done when a skewer pierces the root end quite easily.

3　Transfer the leeks to a shallow oval dish. Cook the sauce for a minute or two until slightly reduced, then pour it over the leeks. Serve hot or cold.

Serves 4–6　preparation: 10 minutes　cooking time: 15 minutes
per serving: 130–90 cals; 10–7g fat; 4–2g carbohydrate

Leek and Broccoli Bake

2tbsp olive oil
1 large red onion, peeled and cut
   into wedges
1 aubergine, chopped
2 leeks, cut into chunks
1 broccoli head, cut into florets and
   stalks chopped

3 large flat mushrooms, chopped
3 rosemary sprigs, chopped
2 x 400g cans cherry tomatoes
salt and pepper
50g (2oz) freshly grated Parmesan cheese

1　Preheat the oven to 200°C (180°C fan) mark 6. Heat the olive oil in a large flameproof dish. Add the onion, aubergine and leeks and cook on the hob for 10–12 minutes until golden and softened.

2　Add the remaining vegetables, half the rosemary, the tomatoes and 300ml (½ pint) boiling water. Season. Stir well, then cover and bake for 30 minutes.

3　Meanwhile, put the Parmesan in a bowl. Add the remaining rosemary and season with pepper. When the vegetables are cooked, remove from the oven, uncover and sprinkle the Parmesan mixture over. Return to the oven and cook, uncovered, for 5–10 minutes until the topping is golden.

Serves 4　preparation: 20 minutes　cooking time: 45–55 minutes
per serving: 220 cals; 12g fat; 15g carbohydrate

Buttery Runner Beans

450g (1lb) runner beans, de-stringed and
  sliced thickly on the diagonal
1 shallot, blanched in boiling water, drained,
  peeled and finely chopped

knob of butter
salt and pepper

1 Cook the beans in boiling water for 3 minutes until tender.
2 Drain well, then add the shallot and butter and season well. Toss together and serve.

Serves 4   preparation: 5 minutes   cooking time: 3 minutes
per serving: 50 cals; 2g fat; 6g carbohydrate

French Beans with Black Mustard Seeds

1tbsp olive oil
1 garlic clove, peeled and crushed
1tbsp black mustard seeds

450g (1lb) French beans
salt

1 Heat the olive oil in a large frying pan or wok for 30 seconds. Add the garlic and mustard seeds and cook for 30 seconds.
2 Add the beans to the pan and stir-fry for 5–7 minutes until just tender, yet still bright green. Season with salt and serve.

Serves 6   preparation: 5 minutes   cooking time: 5–7 minutes
per serving: 40 cals; 3g fat; 2g carbohydrate

11

Vegetables

Pumpkin and Tomato Gratin

900 kg (2lb) piece pumpkin, peeled,
  deseeded and cored
40g (1½oz) butter
2 celery sticks or tops of a whole small
  head, chopped
1tbsp salt

450g (1lb) tomatoes, skinned and chopped
1 garlic clove, peeled and crushed
  (optional)
chopped flat-leafed parsley, plus a sprig
  to garnish
about 1tbsp coarse breadcrumbs

1 Cut the pumpkin into small chunks.
2 Heat 25g (1oz) butter in a large heavy-based frying pan, then add the celery, pumpkin and most of the salt. Cook gently, uncovered, until the pumpkin is soft and just beginning to look slightly jammy. Transfer it to a shallow ovenproof gratin dish.
3 Preheat the oven to 180°C (160°C fan oven) mark 4. Cook the tomatoes and the garlic, if using, in the same pan with the remaining salt and the parsley. When most of the moisture has evaporated and the tomatoes are almost a purée, mix with the pumpkin, then smooth down the top (the dish should be quite full).
4 Cut the remaining butter cut into tiny knobs. Cover the pumpkin mixture with the breadcrumbs and dot over the butter. Stand the gratin dish on a baking sheet and cook near the top of the oven for 35–40 minutes until the surface is golden and crisp. Remove from the oven, garnish with the parsley sprig and serve.

Serves 4–6 preparation: 20 minutes cooking time: 50 minutes–1 hour
per serving: 140–100 cals; 10–7g fat; 11–7g carbohydrate

Butter-baked Pumpkin

900g (2lb) pumpkin, peeled, deseeded and
  cut into large chunks
2tbsp olive oil

25g (1oz) butter
salt and pepper
chopped flat-leafed parsley, to garnish

1 Preheat the oven to 220°C (200°C fan oven) mark 7. Put the pumpkin in a single layer in a roasting tin with 50ml (2fl oz) hot water, drizzle with the olive oil and dot with the butter. Season well and bake for about 30 minutes or until tender and golden, turning occasionally. The liquid will have evaporated by the time the pumpkin is cooked.
2 Remove the tin from the oven, sprinkle with the parsley and serve.

Serves 4 preparation: 5 minutes cooking time: about 30 minutes
per serving: 130 cals; 12g fat; 5g carbohydrate

Mushrooms with Cherry Tomatoes

oil, to oil

6 portabello or large flat mushrooms

2 garlic cloves, peeled and finely sliced

6 sprigs of cherry tomatoes on the vine,
   each sprig weighing about 125g (4oz)

3tbsp olive oil

salt and pepper

1 Preheat the oven to 200°C (180°C fan oven) mark 6. Lightly oil a large roasting tin. Put the mushrooms into the tin, scatter over the garlic, arrange a sprig of cherry tomatoes – still on the vine – on top of each mushroom, easing to fit, then drizzle with the olive oil.

2 Season well, cover with foil and bake for 15 minutes. Remove the foil and continue to roast, uncovered, for a further 15 minutes.

Serves 6   preparation: 5 minutes   cooking time: 30 minutes
per serving: 120 cals; 8g fat; 8g carbohydrate

Turkish Tomatoes

36 cherry tomatoes on the vine,
  picked from the stem
3tbsp extra-virgin olive oil
1tsp sea salt

½tsp dried chilli flakes
juice of 1 small lemon
3tbsp chopped dill

1   Heat a frying pan and, when moderately hot, add the tomatoes, 1tbsp olive oil and the salt. Cook, shaking the pan, until the tomatoes begin to colour and the skins of around six of them have burst.
2   Add the chilli flakes and lemon juice to the pan and shake for a few seconds. Add the remaining oil, count to 20, then take off the heat.
3   Tip the tomatoes into a bowl and cool for 10 minutes, then stir in the dill, cover with clingfilm and put to one side so that the flavours can mature.

Serves 6   preparation: 5 minutes, plus infusing   cooking time: 5 minutes
per serving: 70 cals; 7g fat; 2g carbohydrate

Grilled Cherry Tomatoes

450g (1lb) cherry tomatoes
1tbsp each olive oil and balsamic vinegar

salt and pepper
pinch of sugar

1 Preheat the grill to its highest setting. Put the tomatoes in the grill tray and drizzle with the olive oil and vinegar. Season and add a pinch of sugar.
2 Grill for 4–5 minutes or until the skins just begin to turn brown and burst. Serve or keep warm until required.

Serves 8–10   preparation: 2 minutes   cooking time: 4–5 minutes
per serving: 30–20 cals; 2–1g fat; 2–2g carbohydrate

Grilled Peppers with Pine Nuts

2 yellow peppers, halved and deseeded
olive oil, to brush
1tsp crushed coriander seeds
2tbsp mixed pine nuts and flaked almonds

salt and pepper
oregano sprigs, to garnish
soured cream, to serve

1 Preheat the grill to high. Brush the yellow peppers with a little olive oil and sprinkle with the coriander seeds. Put in a grill pan and grill for 5–10 minutes until charred and tender, adding the pine nuts and flaked almonds for the last 2 minutes of the cooking time.
2 Transfer the peppers to a serving dish and season. Garnish with oregano sprigs and serve with soured cream.

Serves 4   preparation: 5 minutes   cooking time: about 5–10 minutes
per serving (without cream): 80 cals; 7g fat; 3g carbohydrate

Mixed Pepper Salad

700g (1½lb) red and yellow peppers, halved
  and deseeded
4tbsp olive oil
1 garlic clove, peeled and finely chopped

50g (2oz) pitted black olives
basil leaves
salt and pepper

1 Preheat the oven to 200°C (180°C fan oven) mark 6. Put the peppers in a roasting tin, drizzle with 2tbsp oil and cook for 45 minutes. Remove from the oven, skin the peppers and cut into thick slices.
2 Mix the garlic with the pepper slices, the remaining oil, the olives and basil. Season and serve.

Serves 6   preparation: 5 minutes   cooking time: 45 minutes
per serving: 120 cals; 10g fat; 7g carbohydrate

Lemon and Orange Carrots

900g (2lb) carrots, peeled and cut
  into long batons
150ml (¼ pint) orange juice
juice of 2 lemons

150ml (¼ pint) dry white wine
50g (2oz) butter
3tbsp light muscovado sugar
4tbsp coriander, roughly chopped

1 Put the carrots, orange and lemon juice, wine, butter and sugar in a pan. Cover and bring to the boil.
2 Remove the lid and cook until almost all the liquid has evaporated – this should take about 10 minutes.
3 Serve sprinkled with the coriander.

Serves 8 preparation: 5 minutes cooking time: 10–15 minutes
per serving: 120 cals; 5g fat; 16g carbohydrate

Baby Carrots and Fennel

450g (1lb) each baby carrots and fennel   salt

1 Cook the carrot and fennel in boiling salted water for 4–5 minutes or until just tender.
2 Drain well and serve.

Serves 4 preparation: 2 minutes cooking time: 4–5 minutes
per serving: 50 cals; 1g fat; 9g carbohydrate

Chilli Red Onions with Goat's Cheese

75g (3oz) unsalted butter, softened
2 medium red chillies, deseeded and finely
  diced
1tsp crushed chillies

salt and pepper
6 small red onions, peeled
3 x 100g Somerset goat's cheese
balsamic vinegar, to serve

1 Preheat the oven to 200°C (180°C fan oven) mark 6. Put the butter in a small bowl, beat in the diced and crushed chillies and season well.
2 Cut the root off one of the onions, sit it on its base, then make several deep cuts in the top to create a star shape, slicing about two-thirds of the way down the onion. Do the same with the other five onions, then divide the chilli butter equally among them, pushing it down into the cuts. Put the onions in a small roasting tin, cover with foil and bake for 40–45 minutes or until soft.
3 About 5 minutes before the onions are ready, slice each goat's cheese in two, leaving the rind intact, then put on a baking sheet and bake for 2–3 minutes. Put the onion on top of the goat's cheese and serve drizzled with balsamic vinegar.

Serves 6 preparation: 10 minutes cooking time: 40–45 minutes
per serving: 230 cals; 18g fat; 10g carbohydrate

Glazed Shallots with Balsamic Vinegar

1kg (2¼lb) medium-sized shallots,
blanched in boiling water, drained
and peeled, root left intact
50g (2oz) butter

1tbsp golden caster sugar
salt and pepper
2tbsp balsamic vinegar

1   Put the shallots in a pan of cold water, bring to the boil and cook for 5 minutes or until just soft; drain.
2   Heat the butter in a wide heavy-based pan. Add the shallots, sugar and seasoning. Cook over a medium heat, stirring occasionally, for 15–20 minutes or until shallots are brown, shiny and cooked to the centre. Add the vinegar, bring to the boil and bubble until the liquid has evaporated.

Serves 8–10   preparation: 20 minutes   cooking time: 15–20 minutes
per serving: 100–80 cals; 5–4g fat; 12–9g carbohydrate

Gratin of Chard

600ml (1 pint) milk
½ onion, peeled
1 bay leaf
6 peppercorns
50g (2oz) butter, plus extra to grease
1kg (2¼lb) chard, green leaves separated
from white stalks

salt and pepper
40g (1½oz) plain flour
pinch of freshly grated nutmeg
¼tsp French mustard
125g (4oz) freshly grated Parmesan cheese
142ml carton double cream

1   Pour the milk into a pan, add the onion, bay leaf and peppercorns, bring to the boil and remove from the heat. Cover and put to one side for 20 minutes to infuse.
2   Preheat the oven to 200°C (180°C fan oven) mark 6. Grease a 1.7 litre (3 pint) ovenproof dish. Tear the chard leaves into shreds, trim the ends of the stalks and slice. Cook the stalks in a pan of boiling salted water for about 4 minutes until just tender. Add the leaves to the pan for the last 30 seconds. Drain, then plunge into a bowl of icy cold water.
3   Melt the butter in a pan and stir in the flour. Cook for 30 seconds, then add the strained milk, discarding the onion, bay leaf and peppercorns. Bring the sauce to boil, stirring, then reduce the heat and simmer until creamy. Stir in a pinch of nutmeg, the mustard, 50g (2oz) Parmesan and the cream and season well.
4   Drain the chard well and mix with the sauce. Pour the mixture into the prepared dish. Sprinkle with the remaining Parmesan and bake for 25–30 minutes or until golden brown and bubbling.

Serves 6   preparation: 10 minutes   cooking time: 35–40 minutes, plus infusing
per serving: 380 cals; 29 fat; 15g carbohydrate

Cooking
to impress

There comes a time when you really want to throw a good bash. It might be casual or you might want to make it extra special, but either way you'll want to impress.

Catering for crowds needn't be daunting – keep it simple, get organised and don't panic! The Entertaining Menu for 10 has a simple but tasty starter that can be assembled ahead of time, then an amazing chilled chicken, prawn and rice dish, followed by fruit salads and a delicious cake that will be truely memorable.

And that goes for the Winter Menu for 20, too. With two sides of roasted salmon as its centrepiece, the menu also includes easy bites and salads with a grand finale of a luscious black cherry and mascarpone gateau.

The thought of cooking a full Christmas lunch can send some cooks running for the gin, but the Perfect Christmas Lunch for 8 will be just that – perfect. The turkey is the star of the show, but its co-stars all play their part, from the Crisp and Crunchy Roast Potatoes, to the Sweet-glazed Chipolatas and Brussels Sprouts with Hazelnut Butter. And then – the grand finale: a fabulous Christmas pudding, flamed in brandy and served with Boozy Cream and Muscovado Butter. Impressive, indeed.

Brunch Menu for 8

Soft-boiled Eggs with Rosemary and Garlic Fingers

American Pancakes with Secret Muscovado Bacon

Sweet Spiced Oranges

Soft-boiled Eggs with Rosemary and Garlic Fingers

8 large eggs
2 rosemary and garlic focaccia, each cut
  into 8 slices

butter

1 Bring a large pan of water to the boil. Prick the bottom of each egg with a pin. Once the water is boiling, lower in the eggs. Cook for 4 minutes for soft and runny or 6 minutes for medium-boiled.
2 Meanwhile, toast the focaccia slices, then spread with butter. Serve with the eggs.

Serves 8   preparation: 5 minutes   cooking time: 10 minutes
per serving: 400 cals; 24g fat; 33g carbohydrate

American Pancakes

175g (6oz) self-raising flour, sifted
2tsp baking powder
1 pinch of salt

142ml carton soured cream
3 large eggs, beaten
75g (3oz) unsalted butter

1 Put the flour in a large bowl. Stir in the baking powder and salt and make a well in the centre.
2 Whisk the soured cream, 100ml (3½fl oz) cold water and the eggs together in a jug. Gradually whisk this mixture into the flour until you have a smooth, slightly thick batter.
3 Put a large solid non-stick frying pan over a medium heat. Add 1tsp butter and heat until it shimmers. Spoon half a ladle of batter into the middle of the pan to make a thickish pancake.
4 After about 1 minute bubbles will appear on the surface of the pancake, at which point it's ready to be turned. Flip it over and cook for 45 seconds on the other side – it should puff up like a little soufflé. Lift the pancake on to a warm plate and continue with the remaining batter mixture and butter.
5 Serve the pancakes with the muscovado bacon (opposite) and a drizzle of maple syrup, or with Greek-style yogurt and honey.

Serves 8   preparation: 10 minutes   cooking time: 15 minutes
per serving: 210 cals; 14g fat; 17g carbohydrate

Secret Muscovado Bacon Recipe

vegetable oil, to oil
700g (1½lb) smoked back bacon rashers

4tbsp light muscovado sugar

1 Preheat the grill. Lightly oil a baking sheet and put the bacon in a single layer on top – you may need to do two batches.
2 Sprinkle the bacon with sugar and grill until crisp.

Serves 8   preparation: 5 minutes   cooking time: 20 minutes
per serving: 330 cals; 26g fat; 5g carbohydrate

Sweet Spiced Oranges

3 cloves
1 cinnamon stick
small piece fresh root ginger, peeled and
   bruised

225g (8oz) golden caster sugar
300ml (½ pint) distilled malt vinegar
6 large navel oranges, thinly sliced
150ml (¼ pint) maple syrup

1 Put the spices, sugar and vinegar in a large pan with 600ml (1 pint) cold water. Heat gently until the sugar has completely dissolved, then bring to the boil and bubble for 10 minutes to make a thin syrup.
2 Put the orange slices in the pan, reduce the heat and simmer for 5 minutes until tender but not broken down. Lift out the oranges and pack into a sterilised jar.
3 Boil the syrup until reduced by half, then stir in the maple syrup and pour over the oranges to cover. Seal and cool. Keep in a cool place for up to two months.

Serves 8   preparation: 10 minutes   cooking time: 25 minutes
per serving: 210 cals; Trace fat; 55g carbohydrate

12

Cooking to impress

Friday-night Menu for 8

Smoked Haddock Fish Pie

Green Bean and Pea Salad

Caramelised Pineapple

Smoked Haddock Fish Pie

1.8kg (4lb) large floury potatoes, preferably
  Maris Piper or Desirée, peeled and
  roughly chopped
salt and pepper
3 medium-sized undyed smoked haddock
  or cod fillets, about 1.1kg (2½lb), cut into
  5 x 5cm (2 x 2 inch) pieces

2 x 20g packs flat-leafed parsley, or
  1 medium bunch, roughly chopped
2 fat garlic cloves, peeled and crushed
about 175g (6oz) unsalted butter
olive oil, to fry
1tbsp Dijon mustard
500ml carton full-fat crème fraîche

1 Put the potatoes into a large pan of lightly salted water and bring to the boil, then reduce the heat and simmer for about 20 minutes until very tender.
2 Meanwhile, put the fish into a bowl, add the parsley and garlic and toss gently to coat.
3 Heat 40g (1½oz) butter in a large frying pan with a drizzle of olive oil until it starts to foam. Put half the fish pieces into the pan and fry over a very high heat for about 1 minute until they form a golden crust on the underside. Turn over and fry on the other side until the fish is opaque – just 2–3 minutes or it will overcook.
4 Take the pan off the heat and add half the mustard and half the crème fraîche to the fish. Leave it to melt in the heat of the pan (without stirring, to prevent the fish from breaking up), then spoon the mixture into a large ovenproof serving dish.
5 Wipe out the pan and repeat steps 3 and 4 with another 40g (1½oz) butter and the remaining fish, mustard and crème fraîche. The fish mixture will look quite liquid at this stage, but that's fine.
6 Preheat the grill. Drain the potatoes, tip them back into the pan and return to the heat for 1–2 minutes to dry off. Mash with the remaining butter, plenty of pepper and about 6tbsp of the cooking liquid from the fish. Give the potatoes a good beat, taste for seasoning, then spoon the mash over the fish.
7 Pop the dish under the grill for a few minutes until the potato is golden, then serve immediately.

Serves 8   preparation: 30 minutes   cooking time: 30 minutes
per serving: 670 cals; 46g fat; 37g carbohydrate

Green Bean and Pea Salad

3 slices ready-made garlic bread
200g (7oz) fine French beans
salt
190g pack shelled peas
2 x 120g bags salad leaves
6tbsp extra-virgin olive oil

1tbsp white wine vinegar
1tbsp wholegrain mustard
½ small garlic clove, peeled and crushed
pinch of golden caster sugar
mint sprigs, to garnish

1 Preheat the grill. Toast the garlic bread on both sides under a hot grill until golden and crisp. Leave to cool, then put into a food processor or blender and whiz to make rough breadcrumbs.
2 Cook the French beans in boiling salted water for 5 minutes, then add the peas. Bring back to the boil and bubble for 2 minutes until the beans are just tender. Drain the vegetables well, then drop into a bowl of iced water to cool immediately and keep their fresh green colour; drain well again.
3 Put the vegetables into a large bowl, then put the salad leaves on top. Cover with clingfilm and chill.
4 To make the dressing, whisk together the remaining ingredients in a bowl, then toss with the salad leaves, vegetables and breadcrumbs. Garnish with mint sprigs and serve.

Serves 8   preparation: 25 minutes   cooking time: 10 minutes
per serving: 140 cals; 10g fat; 10g carbohydrate

Caramelised Pineapple

1 large, ripe pineapple
4 passion fruit

juice of 1 orange
4tbsp light muscovado sugar

1 Using a sharp knife, cut the top and tail off the pineapple. Stand the fruit on a board and cut away all the peel, slicing from top to bottom. Slice the flesh into 12 rounds, then cut each in half.
2 Preheat the grill. Halve the passion fruit and spoon the juice and seeds into a sieve resting over a bowl. Stir well to extract the juice. Discard the seeds, then add the orange juice to the bowl.
3 Lay half the pineapple slices in a single layer on a baking sheet, then sprinkle with half the sugar and half the fruit juice. Grill for about 2–3 minutes until the sugar begins to bubble and caramelise, then spoon the pineapple and juices into a dish. Grill the rest of the pineapple with the remaining sugar and juice.
4 Put three pieces of pineapple on each serving plate with some of the cooking juices. Delicious served with a scoop or two of mango sorbet.

Serves 8   preparation: 20 minutes   cooking time: 10 minutes
per serving: 120 cals; 0g fat; 31g carbohydrate

Saturday Dinner For 8

Prawn and Guacamole Cocktail

Sticky Honey and Ginger Chicken
Mango and Red Pepper Relish
Coconut Rice

Apricot and Coconut Tart

Prawn and Guacamole Cocktail

400g (14oz) cooked, peeled king prawns
150ml (¼ pint) salad dressing, such as
  Roasted Red Pepper Dressing
2 ripe avocados, peeled, stoned and sliced
16 cherry tomatoes, quartered

4 little gem lettuces, halved and shredded
2 x 300g tubs fresh guacamole dip
2 limes, cut into wedges
black pepper

1 Put the prawns and 6tbsp dressing in a bowl, stir, then cover. Put the avocado and tomatoes in a separate small bowl, stir in the remaining dressing, then cover. Chill both bowls in the fridge for 2 hours.
2 To serve, put the lettuce leaves in the base of eight dishes. Spoon the avocado and tomatoes on top, then the prawns and a dollop of guacamole. Finish with a lime wedge and a grinding of black pepper.

Serves 8   preparation: 20 minutes, plus marinating
per serving: 460 cals; 42g fat; 9g carbohydrate

Sticky Honey and Ginger Chicken

2tsp ground turmeric
250g (9oz) runny honey
10cm (4 inch) piece fresh root ginger,
  peeled and finely grated
2 fat garlic cloves, peeled and crushed

grated zest and juice of 2 large limes
175g (6oz) sweet Thai chilli dipping sauce
8 chicken breasts, skin on
600ml (1 pint) white wine

1   To make the marinade, put the turmeric, honey, ginger, garlic, lime zest and juice and chilli sauce into a bowl, then whisk to combine. Make several deep slashes through the skin and flesh of each chicken breast, then add them to the bowl and stir to coat in the mixture. Cover with clingfilm and leave in the fridge overnight.
2   Preheat the oven to 220°C (200°C fan oven) mark 7. Lift the chicken breasts from the marinade and put them, skin side up, in a roasting tin just large enough to hold them in a single layer (any larger and the marinade will burn). Spoon over 4tbsp of the marinade and roast for 30–35 minutes until the chicken is golden and cooked through. Keep warm.
3   Put the remaining marinade into a pan with the wine and bring to the boil. Bubble for 10–12 minutes until reduced by half and syrupy. Serve the chicken with the sauce and Mango and Red Pepper Relish (below).

Serves 8   preparation: 15 minutes, plus marinating   cooking time: 40–50 minutes
per serving: 400 cals; 18g fat; 25g carbohydrate

Mango and Red Pepper Relish

2 ripe mangoes, peeled and chopped
125g (4oz) roasted red peppers from a jar,
  halved, deseeded and sliced
2 small red onions, peeled and finely sliced

4tbsp sweet Thai chilli dipping sauce
grated zest of 2 limes, plus the juice
  of 3 limes
20g pack of coriander

1   Put the mango in a bowl with the red peppers and onions. Add the dipping sauce, lime zest and juice, toss together, cover and chill until needed.
2   Just before serving, roughly chop the coriander leaves, add to the relish and mix well.

Serves 8   preparation: 10 minutes
per serving: 50 cals; trace fat; 11g carbohydrate

Coconut Rice

25g (1oz) butter
450g (1lb) long-grain rice, rinsed
and drained

1tsp salt
50g (2oz) creamed coconut

1 Melt the butter in a large pan, add the rice and stir to coat all the rice in butter. Add 1.1 litres (2 pints) cold water and the salt. Cover the pan and bring to the boil, then reduce the heat and simmer for 20–25 minutes (or as stated on the packet) until all the water has been absorbed.
2 Once cooked, remove the pan from the heat and add the creamed coconut. Cover the pan with a clean tea-towel and replace the lid to allow the coconut to melt and the rice to absorb any steam. Fluff up with a fork before serving.

Serves 8   preparation: 5 minutes   cooking time: 20–25 minutes
per serving: 270 cals; 7g fat; 45g carbohydrate

12

Cooking to impress

Apricot and Coconut Tart

375g pack Saxby's dessert pastry
flour, to dust
125g (4oz) butter, softened
125g (4oz) golden caster sugar
2 eggs
75g (3oz) ground almonds

25g (1oz) desiccated coconut, plus extra
to sprinkle
zest and juice of ½ small orange
400g can apricot halves in juice, drained
1tbsp golden icing sugar, to glaze, plus a
little to dust

1   Preheat the oven to 190°C (170°C fan oven) mark 5 and put a heavy flat baking sheet in to preheat.
Roll the pastry out on a lightly floured surface and use to line a 23cm (9 inch) fluted flan tin. Prick the
base of the pastry with a fork, then line with greaseproof paper and fill with baking beans.

2   Put the pastry case on the baking sheet and bake for 15 minutes, then remove the baking beans and
cook for 10 minutes until dry and pale golden. Leave the baking sheet in the oven and put the pastry
case aside to cool.

3   Using an electric whisk, beat together the butter and caster sugar until light and creamy, then gradually
beat in the eggs. Using a wooden spoon, stir in the ground almonds, coconut and orange zest.

4   Spoon the filling into the pastry case, then top with the apricots, skin side up. Put the tart back on
the baking sheet and bake for 40–45 minutes until golden (cover with foil if the top gets too dark). The
filling won't be totally set but will firm up as it cools.

5   Mix the icing sugar and orange juice in a bowl to a thin icing. Remove the tart from the oven and
spoon the icing evenly over the tart, then sprinkle with coconut. Return to the oven for 5–10 minutes
to glaze the top. To serve, dust with icing sugar and a little coconut.

Serves 8   preparation: 35 minutes   cooking time: 1 hour 10 minutes–1 hour 20 minutes
per serving: 530 cals; 35g fat; 51g carbohydrate

12

Cooking to impress

Faster Menu for 8

Stuffed Leg of Lamb with Redcurrant and Red Wine Sauce
Sweet Roasted Carrots
Purple Sprouting Broccoli with Pine Nuts
Minted Sugarsnaps
Saffron-baked Potatoes
Chocolate Truffle Torte

Stuffed Leg of Lamb with Redcurrant and Red Wine Sauce

25g (1oz) butter
75ml (3fl oz) olive oil
1 small red onion, peeled and finely
    chopped
450g (1lb) chestnut mushrooms, finely
    chopped
1tbsp chopped oregano

½ x 20g pack thyme, leaves stripped, plus
    extra sprigs to garnish
20g pack flat-leafed parsley, finely chopped
salt and pepper
1 leg of new-season lamb, about 2.7kg (6lb),
    knucklebone removed but end bone left in
2 medium garlic bulbs

1   First make the stuffing. Melt the butter in a frying pan with 2tbsp olive oil. Add the onion and fry gently for 10–15 minutes until soft and golden. Add the mushrooms and cook over a brisk heat for 15–20 minutes – the juices will evaporate and the mixture become dryish, but continue to cook, stirring all the time, until the mushrooms begin to turn golden brown at the edges. Add the herbs and cook for 1 minute. Remove from the heat, season and leave to cool.

2   Preheat the oven to 190°C (170°C fan oven) mark 5. Open out the lamb and spread the mushroom stuffing over the meat. Reshape the lamb and sew securely with string. Weigh the lamb and calculate the cooking time. Allow 25 minutes per 450g (1lb) for lamb with just a tinge of pink – for this leg it should be about 2½–3 hours.

3   Put the lamb in a roasting tin and season. Transfer to the oven and baste occasionally to keep the meat succulent. Halfway through the cooking time, put a few thyme sprigs on top.

4   About 1 hour before the end of the cooking time, rub the whole garlic bulbs with a little oil and put them in the oven alongside the lamb for 45 minutes–1 hour until very soft. Remove from the oven and keep them warm until ready to serve.

5   To tell if the lamb is cooked to your liking, insert a skewer into the centre, remove it, then press the flat of the skewer against the meat: the pinker the juice that runs out, the rarer the meat. When it's sufficiently cooked, remove the lamb to a carving board and cover with a tent of foil to keep warm while you make the Redcurrant and Red Wine Sauce (page 478).

6   To serve, carve the lamb and garnish with the roasted garlic, broken into cloves. Drizzle with a little of the sauce and hand the rest round in a jug.

Serves 8   preparation: 40 minutes   cooking time: 3 hours–3 hours 40 minutes, plus resting
per serving: 400 cals; 23g fat; 2g carbohydrate

Redcurrant and Red Wine Sauce

600ml (1 pint) fruity red wine
6tbsp redcurrant jelly
3tbsp Worcestershire sauce
juice of 1 lemon and 1 orange

roasting juices from the lamb
2tbsp plain flour
2tsp English mustard powder

1 Pour the wine into a small pan and add the redcurrant jelly, Worcestershire sauce and lemon and orange juice. Heat very gently until the jelly melts.

2 Spoon off the fat from the tin the lamb was roasted in until 2tbsp remains. Put the tin over a low heat and stir in the flour and mustard powder to make a smooth paste.

3 Increase the heat and pour in the wine mixture a little at a time. Mix with a wooden spoon after each addition, scraping up any crusty bits. Once all the wine is in, swap the spoon for a whisk and whisk until the sauce is smooth. Reduce the heat and bubble gently for 10 minutes, then pour into a warm jug.

Serves 8   preparation: 10 minutes   cooking time: 25 minutes
per serving: 120 cals; 4g fat; 12g carbohydrate

Cooking to impress

Sweet Roasted Carrots

900g (2lb) whole new baby carrots, trimmed   **salt and pepper**
4tbsp fat and roasting juices from the lamb

1   After the lamb has been in the oven for 2 hours, put the carrots in a roasting tin. Spoon over the fat and roasting juices from the lamb and toss to coat. Season well, then roast for 45 minutes–1 hour.
2   Remove from the oven and transfer to a serving dish.

Serves 8   preparation: 10 minutes   cooking time: 45 minutes–1 hour
per serving: 60 cals; 4g fat; 7g carbohydrate

Purple Sprouting Broccoli with Pine Nuts

50g (2oz) pine nuts   **50g (2oz) raisins**
1.1kg (2½lb) purple sprouting broccoli   **small knob of butter**

1   Put the pine nuts in a frying pan and dry-fry them for 2–3 minutes until golden. Put to one side.
2   Bring a large pan of water to the boil. Trim the ends off the broccoli and chop any large stems in two. Add to the water and cook for 5–6 minutes. Add the raisins and cook for another 2–3 minutes until the broccoli is tender.
3   Drain the broccoli and raisins, then toss with the pine nuts and the butter. Serve immediately.

Serves 8   preparation: 5 minutes   cooking time: about 10 minutes
per serving: 110 cals; 7g fat; 8g carbohydrate

12

Cooking to impress

Minted Sugarsnaps

500g (1lb 2oz) sugarsnap peas
2 mint sprigs

15g (½oz) butter
salt and pepper

1   Bring a large pan of water to the boil, then add the peas and one mint sprig. Bring back to the boil, then reduce the heat and simmer for 3–4 minutes. Drain well and return to the warm pan.
2   Add the butter and seasoning, then toss to coat. Tip the peas into a warm serving bowl and garnish with the remaining mint sprig.

Serves 8   preparation: 2 minutes   cooking time: about 10 minutes
per serving: 40 cals; 2g fat; 3g carbohydrate

Saffron-baked Potatoes

generous pinch of saffron strands
600ml (1 pint) hot vegetable stock
50g (2oz) butter, melted, plus extra to
   grease

12 medium-sized baking potatoes,
   preferably Desirée, peeled
salt and pepper
leaves from ½ x 20g pack thyme

1   Preheat the oven to 190°C (170°C fan oven) mark 5. Put the saffron strands in a small bowl, add 2tbsp hot stock and leave to soak for 10 minutes, then stir into the remaining stock.
2   Meanwhile, grease a deep ovenproof dish. Cut the potatoes into thin slices and arrange in the dish in layers, sprinkling each layer with thyme and seasoning well.
3   Spoon the melted butter over the potatoes, then pour the hot saffron stock over the top. Transfer to the oven and cook uncovered for 1–1¼ hours, basting occasionally, until the liquid is completely absorbed and the potatoes are crisp and golden brown. Season, then serve immediately.

Serves 8   preparation: 30 minutes   cooking time: 1–1¼ hours
per serving: 270 cals; 6g fat; 52g carbohydrate

Cooking to impress

Chocolate Truffle Torte

flavourless oil, such as safflower, to oil
3 large eggs, plus 3 large egg yolks
150g (5oz) golden caster sugar
25g (1oz) plain flour
1tbsp cocoa powder, plus extra to dust
3tbsp Tia Maria
300g (11oz) good-quality plain dark
   chocolate (with minimum 50% cocoa
solids), broken into chunks
200g (7oz) good-quality plain chocolate,
   semi-sweet such as Bournville, broken
   into chunks
568ml carton double cream
1tbsp instant espresso coffee
chocolate mini eggs and cocoa-dusted
   almonds, to decorate

1   Preheat the oven to 180°C (160°C fan oven) mark 4. Oil a 20.5cm (8 inch) loose-based cake tin and line the base with non-stick baking parchment.
2   To make the cake base, put the whole eggs into the bowl of a food mixer, add 75g (3oz) sugar, then mix on high speed until doubled in volume and very thick. (Or beat, using a hand-held electric whisk, in a large heatproof bowl set over a pan of simmering water until thick, then remove from the heat and whisk until cool.)
3   Sift the flour and cocoa powder together over the mixture and fold in carefully. Don't overfold, as you'll knock out the air and create a flat cake.
4   Pour the cake mixture into the prepared tin and bake for 25–30 minutes until well risen and shrinking away from the sides of the tin. Remove from the oven and leave the cake base in the tin for 10 minutes, then turn out and put on a wire rack, keeping the parchment on. Drizzle with the Tia Maria and put to one side to cool.
5   Remove the parchment and put the paper upside down in the cake tin. Brush with oil and return the cake base to the tin, turning it upside down and pressing firmly to fit.
6   Next, make the truffle mixture. Put all the chocolate in a heatproof bowl with half the cream and the espresso coffee, then set over a pan of simmering water. Once the chocolate has melted, stir gently to combine. Leave to cool.
7   Whip the remaining cream in a large bowl until soft peaks form. In another bowl, beat together the egg yolks and remaining sugar, using an electric whisk, until pale and fluffy. Whisk this mixture into the cooled chocolate, then fold gently into the whipped cream. Immediately pour over the cake base in the tin, then chill for at least 3 hours, or preferably overnight, until the truffle mixture has set firm.
8   To serve, run a warm knife around the edge of the torte and carefully remove from the tin. Dust with cocoa and decorate with mini eggs and cocoa-dusted almonds. Cut into slices to serve. The torte will keep in the fridge for up to five days.

Serves 10   preparation: 40 minutes, plus chilling   cooking time: 30–35 minutes
per serving: 690 cals; 52g fat; 45g carbohydrate

Cooking to impress

Entertaining Menu for 10

Easiest Ever Canapés

Spicy Chicken and Prawn Rice with Crisp Fried
Shallots and Coconut Mayonnaise

Fresh Mango and Pineapple Salad
Poached Peaches in Strawberry Syrup
Orange and White Chocolate Cake

Easiest Ever Canapés

200g (7oz) smoked salmon slices
100g (3½oz) full-fat soft cheese or
  goat's cheese
1tbsp dill-flavoured mustard or creamed
  horseradish
200g pack prosciutto (lightly smoked,
  Italian dry-cured ham)

about 2tbsp smooth fruity chutney, such
  as mango
1 large courgette
about 2tbsp hummus
20g pack chives, finely chopped
1 roasted red pepper, finely chopped
black pepper

1 Lay the salmon slices out on a sheet of greaseproof paper. Spread thinly with a little soft cheese or goat's cheese, then very thinly with mustard or horseradish. Roll up into bite-sized rolls.
2 Lay the prosciutto on a board. Spread thinly with the cheese, then with chutney and roll up into bite-sized rolls.
3 Pare the courgette into wafer-thin strips with a vegetable peeler. Lay them on a board, spread with the cheese and hummus, then roll up.
4 Stand the rolls on end on a flat plate or greaseproof-lined baking sheet (trim bases if necessary). Cover with clingfilm and chill.
5 About 2 hours before serving, top each roll with a little cheese. Dip the salmon rolls into the chopped chives, the prosciutto rolls into the red pepper, and the courgette rolls into a little coarsely ground black pepper. Chill until ready to serve.

Serves 10 preparation: 20 minutes
per serving: 140 cals; 9g fat; 3g carbohydrate

Cooking to impress

Spicy Chicken and Prawn Rice with Crisp-fried Shallots

4 small skinless boneless chicken breasts,
  cut into bite-sized pieces
150ml (¼ pint) olive oil
2tsp ground turmeric
salt
450g (1lb) long-grain rice, washed
425g (15oz) shallots, blanched in boiling
  water, drained, peeled
4 garlic cloves, peeled and crushed
10cm (4 inch) piece fresh root ginger,
  peeled and finely grated
2tbsp garam masala

100g (3½oz) shelled pistachio nuts
150ml carton natural yogurt
150ml (¼ pint) chicken stock
200ml (7fl oz) vegetable oil
450g (1lb) cooked, peeled tiger prawns
6tbsp mild lime pickle
juice of 2 limes, about 6tbsp
6tbsp runny honey
2 x 20g packs basil, roughly torn
small bunch of flat-leafed parsley,
  roughly chopped
20g pack coriander, roughly chopped

1 Put the chicken in a bowl and stir in 2tbsp olive oil and the turmeric.

2 Put 1.7 litres (3 pints) cold water into a large pan, bring to the boil and add a good pinch of salt. Add the rice a little at a time so the water stays boiling. Stir once, then boil for 8 minutes and drain well.

3 In another large pan heat 2tbsp olive oil. Slice 225g (8oz) shallots thinly into rounds and add to the pan. Fry for 10 minutes or until soft and golden. Add the garlic and ginger and fry for 3–4 minutes, then remove the shallot mixture from the pan. Fry the chicken in batches for 10 minutes or until golden brown. Return all the chicken and the shallot mixture to the pan.

4 Stir in the garam masala and cook for 1–2 minutes, then add the nuts, yogurt and stock and stir over the heat for 1 minute.

5 Spoon the rice on to the chicken, then cover the pan with foil and a tight-fitting lid. Reduce the heat and cook gently for 10 minutes. Remove from the heat and let the rice rest (still covered) for 5 minutes. Uncover and leave to cool. Transfer to a bowl, cover and chill.

6 To make the crisp-fried shallots, heat the vegetable oil in a small pan. Finely slice the remaining shallots, add a spoonful to the pan and deep-fry until golden. Remove with a slotted spoon and drain on kitchen paper. Repeat until all the shallots are cooked.

7 Mix the prawns with the lime pickle, lime juice, honey and remaining olive oil.

8 When ready to serve, stir the herbs and the prawn mixture into the rice. Garnish with the crisp-fried shallots and serve with Coconut Mayonnaise (see opposite).

Serves 10   preparation: 25 minutes   cooking time: 55 minutes, plus resting
per serving: 600 cals; 32g fat; 52g carbohydrate

Coconut Mayonnaise

¼ quantity chilli lime dressing (reserved
from the Fresh Mango and Pineapple
Salad, below)

125g (4oz) mayonnaise
175g (6oz) Greek-style yogurt
200ml carton coconut cream

1 Put all the ingredients in a bowl and, using a balloon whisk, beat everything together until well
combined. Cover with clingfilm and store in the fridge until needed. Serve with the Spicy Chicken.

Serves 10 preparation: 5 minutes
per serving: 200 cals; 20g fat; 3g carbohydrate

Fresh Mango and Pineapple Salad

¼ large red chilli, deseeded and
finely chopped
2 garlic cloves, peeled and crushed
2.5cm (1 inch) piece fresh root ginger,
peeled and finely grated
juice of 3 large limes, about 9tbsp
125ml (4fl oz) olive oil
3tbsp light muscovado sugar
leaves from 20g pack coriander
leaves from 2 x 20g packs mint
1 ripe, firm mango, peeled, stoned and cut

into fine slices
½ ripe pineapple, peeled, cored and cut into
fine shards
200g (7oz) small pak choi
225g bag baby spinach leaves, or a mixture
of spinach, watercress and rocket
leaves from 20g pack flat-leafed parsley
1tbsp salted peanuts, toasted under the
grill and finely chopped
1 bunch of spring onions, finely shredded

1 First, make the dressing. Put the chilli, garlic, ginger, lime juice, olive oil and sugar into a food processor
or blender and whiz for 10 seconds to combine. Add the coriander and half the mint and whiz together
for 5 seconds to chop roughly.
2 Put the mango and pineapple in a large bowl and pour over half the dressing. Put the remainder in a
bowl and reserve for the Coconut Mayonnaise (above). Cover both with clingfilm and chill for at least
2 hours or up to 24 hours.
3 Chop the green pak choi leaves off the top of the stalks and roughly chop the white fleshy part. Add
all of it to the bowl of marinated fruit with the spinach, parsley and remaining mint. Sprinkle with the
peanuts and spring onions and serve immediately.

Serves 10 preparation: 25 minutes, plus chilling
per serving: 190 cals; 12g fat; 20g carbohydrate

Poached Peaches in Strawberry Syrup

75cl dry white wine
175g (6oz) golden caster sugar
2.5cm (1 inch) piece fresh root ginger,
   peeled and sliced

450g (1lb) strawberries, hulled
8 ripe, firm peaches
lemon juice, to taste

1   Put the wine, sugar and ginger in a large pan. Thinly slice 125g (4oz) strawberries and add them to the pan. Bring to the boil, stirring to dissolve the sugar.
2   Add the peaches to the pan and cover with a piece of greaseproof paper and a lid. Bring the liquid back to the boil, then reduce the heat and simmer the fruit for 5 minutes or until tender. Take off the heat and leave in the pan to cool.
3   Take the cooled peaches out of the pan with a slotted spoon and ease off the skins. Cut in half, discard the stones, and put in a large serving bowl. Halve the remaining strawberries and add to the bowl.
4   Bring the poaching liquid to the boil and bubble for 20–25 minutes or until well reduced and syrupy. Add a squeeze of lemon juice to taste. Allow the syrup to cool, then strain through a sieve over the fruit. Cover with clingfilm and chill overnight.

Serves 10   preparation: 10 minutes   cooking time: 35–40 minutes, plus chilling
per serving: 140 cals; 0g fat; 29g carbohydrate

12

Cooking to impress

Orange and White Chocolate Cake

oil, to oil
6 large eggs, separated
250g (9oz) golden caster sugar
150g (5oz) each self-raising flour and
   ground almonds
grated zest of 2 and juice of 3 large oranges
100g (3½oz) golden granulated sugar

250ml (8fl oz) sweet white wine
225g (8oz) good-quality white chocolate,
   chopped
568ml carton double cream
350g (12oz) strawberries, hulled and
   thinly sliced

1   Preheat the oven to 180°C (160°C fan oven) mark 4. Oil a deep 23cm (9 inch) round cake tin and line the base with greaseproof paper.
2   Put the egg whites in a clean grease-free bowl and whisk until soft peaks form. Gradually beat in 50g (2oz) caster sugar and whisk until the mixture stands in stiff peaks and looks glossy.
3   Put the egg yolks and remaining caster sugar in another bowl. Whisk until soft and moussey, then carefully stir in the flour to make a paste.
4   Using a clean metal spoon, add a third of the egg white to the paste and fold in carefully. Put the remaining egg white, ground almonds and orange zest in the bowl and fold in, taking care not to knock too much volume out of the egg whites. You should end up with a smooth batter.
5   Spoon into the prepared tin and bake for 35 minutes or until a skewer inserted in the centre comes out clean. Remove from the oven and cool in the tin for 10 minutes, then turn out on to a wire rack to cool completely.
6   To make the syrup, put the granulated sugar, wine and orange juice in a small pan and stir over a gentle heat until the sugar has dissolved. Bring to the boil and bubble for 5 minutes or until syrupy. Cool and put to one side.
7   To make the ganache, put the chocolate in a heatproof bowl with half the cream and set over a pan of simmering water. Leave until the chocolate has melted, then stir. (Don't stir the chocolate until it has completely melted.) Cool until beginning to thicken, then beat with a wooden spoon until cold and thick. Put the remaining cream into a bowl and whip lightly. Beat a large spoon of the whipped cream into the chocolate cream to loosen it, then fold in the remainder. Cover and chill for 2 hours.
8   Cut the cake in half horizontally, pierce all over with a skewer and put it, cut sides up, on an edged tray or baking sheet. Spoon over the syrup and leave to soak in.
9   Spread a quarter of the ganache over the base cake and scatter with 225g (8oz) strawberries. Cover with the top half of the cake and press down lightly. Using a palette knife, smooth the remaining ganache over the top and sides of the cake. Cover loosely and chill for up to 4 hours. Decorate with the remaining strawberries and serve.

Serves 14   preparation: 35 minutes   cooking time: 35–40 minutes, plus chilling
per serving: 530 cals; 34g fat; 48g carbohydrate

Cooking to impress

The Perfect
Christmas Lunch for 8

Smoked Salmon with Prawn and Avocado Salsa

Bacon-roasted Turkey with Chestnut, Shallot and Orange Stuffing

Crisp and Crunchy Roast Potatoes
Brussels Sprouts with Hazelnut Butter
Roast Roots with Garlic and Pepper
Spiced Red Cabbage
Sweet-glazed Chipolatas
Cranberry, Honey and Ginger Sauce (page 665)
Special Bread Sauce (page 652)

The Ultimate Christmas Pudding with Boozy Cream and Muscovado Butter

Smoked Salmon with Prawn and Avocado Salsa

2 large ripe but firm avocados, peeled,
  stoned and roughly chopped
350g (12oz) cooked, peeled king prawns
6 small spring onions, finely sliced
3tbsp chopped coriander

zest and juice of 3 limes, plus extra wedges
  to garnish
8tbsp olive oil
salt and pepper
225g (8oz) smoked salmon slices

1   To make the salsa, put the avocados into a large bowl, then add the prawns, spring onions, coriander, lime zest and juice and olive oil. Mix well, season, cover and chill until ready to serve with the salmon.
2   Divide the salmon among eight serving plates and top each with some salsa. Garnish each with a lime wedge and serve.

Serves 8   preparation: 15 minutes
per serving: 290 cals; 23g fat; 1g carbohydrate

Bacon-roasted Turkey

5.4–6.3kg (12–14lb) turkey with giblets
  removed to make stock
Chestnut, Shallot and Orange Stuffing,
  (page 490)
125g (4oz) butter, softened, plus extra
  to grease

salt and pepper
3 rosemary sprigs
300g (11oz) rindless smoked streaky
  bacon rashers

1 Take the turkey out of the fridge 30 minutes before stuffing to take the chill off it. Preheat the oven to 220°C (200°C fan oven) mark 7.
2 Put the turkey on a board, breast side down. Use your hands to push some of the stuffing into the neck end of the turkey, easing it up between the flesh and the skin towards the breast. Don't pack it in too tightly as it will expand on cooking.
3 Shape the protruding stuffing into a neat round, then tuck the neck skin under the bird and secure with a skewer. Weigh the bird and calculate the cooking time if outside the range given for this recipe (see below).
4 Put any leftover stuffing into a greased ovenproof dish. Cover with buttered foil.
5 Put one or two large sheets of strong foil across a large roasting tin. Put the turkey in the middle and spread the butter all over it. Season with a little salt and plenty of pepper and pop two rosemary sprigs inside the cavity. Overlap the bacon rashers across the turkey breast, snip over the remaining rosemary and tie the legs together with string.
6 Bring the edges of the foil together and make into a pleat along the length of the breastbone, but well above it to make a 'tent' with plenty of air space above the breast.
7 Put the turkey on a low shelf in the main oven and roast for about 30 minutes. Reduce the oven temperature to 170°C (150°C fan oven) mark 3 and cook for a further 3½ hours.
8 Fold back the foil from the top and sides of the turkey and push the bacon slices off the breast to allow the skin to brown. Increase the oven temperature to 200°C (180°C fan oven) mark 6 and cook the turkey for 30–40 minutes, basting it with the juices twice during this time.
9 When the bird is cooked, transfer it to a warm carving platter – you'll need help at this stage, so you can tip the bird upright and let the cooking juices run back into the roasting tin.
10 Cover the turkey with foil and leave to rest for 30–40 minutes before carving, while you make the gravy and finish the vegetables.

Serves 8 (with leftovers)   preparation: 15 minutes   cooking time: about 4 hours 40 minutes
per 125g (4oz) meat: 250 cals; 10g fat; 0g carbohydrate

Is your turkey a different size?
3.5–4.9kg (8–11lb) Cook for 30 minutes at 220°C (200°C fan oven) mark 7,
then for 2½–3 hours at 170°C (150°C fan oven) mark 3.
Finally, cook for 30 minutes uncovered at 200°C (180°C fan oven) mark 6.
6.8–9kg (15–20lb) Cook for 50 minutes at 220°C (200°C fan oven) mark 7.
Reduce the temperature to 170°C (150°C fan oven) mark 3 and cook for 4–5 hours.
Finally, cook for 30 minutes uncovered at 200°C (180°C fan oven) mark 6.

Chestnut, Shallot and Orange Stuffing

50g (2oz) butter
6 shallots, blanched in boiling water,
  drained and roughly chopped
4 celery sticks, roughly chopped
1 rosemary sprig, snipped
1tbsp chopped flat-leafed parsley
175g (6oz) firm white bread, cut into
  rough dice

2 cooking apples, about 225g (8oz), peeled,
  cored and chopped
125g (4oz) cooked, peeled chestnuts,
  roughly chopped
zest of 1 large orange
salt and pepper
450g (1lb) good-quality coarse pork
  sausagemeat

1   Melt the butter in a large frying pan and gently fry the shallots, celery and rosemary for 10–12 minutes until the vegetables are golden and softened. Tip into a large bowl (there's no need to wash the pan). Add the parsley, bread, apples, chestnuts and orange zest to the bowl. Season and mix well.
2   Divide the sausagemeat into walnut-sized pieces. Fry in batches in the pan until golden and cooked through. Add to the bowl with the stuffing mix and stir. Cool, then use to stuff the turkey (page 491). Put any leftover stuffing into a greased ovenproof dish, cover with foil and cook with the chipolatas (page 494).

Makes enough to stuff a 5.4–6kg (12–14lb) turkey   preparation: 15 minutes   cooking time: 20–25 minutes
per serving: 100 cals; 6g fat; 9g carbohydrate

Crisp and Crunchy Roast Potatoes

1.8kg (4lb) potatoes, preferably King
  Edward, cut into two bite-sized pieces
salt

2tsp paprika
2–3 tbsp goose or white vegetable fat

1   Put the potatoes in a pan of lightly salted water, bring to the boil and boil for 7 minutes, then drain well in a colander. Add the paprika to the colander, then cover and shake the potatoes roughly, so they become fluffy around the edges.
2   Melt the fat in a large roasting tin on the hob. When it sizzles, add the potatoes and tilt the tin to coat, taking care because the fat will splutter.
3   Roast the potatoes above the turkey at 170°C (150°C fan oven) mark 3 for about 30 minutes. Then roast at 200°C (180°C fan oven) mark 6 for a further 40 minutes. Move the potatoes only once or twice during cooking, otherwise the edges won't crisp and brown. Season with a little salt before serving.

Serves 8   preparation: 20 minutes   cooking time: 1 hour 10 minutes
per serving: 250 cals; 10g fat; 39g carbohydrate

Brussels Sprouts with Hazelnut Butter

50g (2oz) butter, at room temperature
100g (3½oz) blanched hazelnuts, toasted
   and roughly chopped
freshly grated nutmeg
salt and pepper

1.4kg (3lb) Brussels sprouts
lemon juice
cooked bacon from turkey (page 491), or
   300g (11oz) rindless smoked streaky
   bacon rashers

1 To make the hazelnut butter, put the butter into a bowl and beat to soften. Add the hazelnuts and nutmeg and season. Mix well, then wrap the butter in greaseproof paper and foil and chill until needed.
2 Cook the sprouts in boiling salted water for 7–10 minutes or until tender but with a slight bite. Drain well then toss in the hazelnut butter. Add a squeeze of lemon juice, crumble the bacon from the turkey over and tip into a serving dish. Alternatively, grill the uncooked bacon until crisp and crumble over the sprouts.

Serves 8 preparation: 5 minutes
per serving: 190 cals; 15g fat; 8g carbohydrate

Roast Roots with Garlic and Pepper

1.4kg (3lb) mixed carrots and parsnips,
   peeled and cut into 5cm (2 inch) wedges
3 fat garlic cloves, peeled and cut in half

1tsp black peppercorns, crushed
4tbsp olive oil
chopped flat-leafed parsley, to garnish

1 Preheat the second oven to 200°C (180°C fan oven) mark 6. Put the carrots and parsnips into a large pan of boiling water and cook for 10 minutes. Drain, put back into the pan and add the garlic, pepper and olive oil. Toss for 2–3 minutes.
2 Roast the vegetables for 1 hour. Transfer to a serving dish, garnish with parsley and serve.

Serves 8 preparation: 15 minutes   cooking time: 1 hour 25 minutes
per serving: 130 cals; 6g fat; 16g carbohydrate

Spiced Red Cabbage

25g (1oz) butter
3 red onions, peeled and finely chopped
900g (2lb) red cabbage, shredded
2 Bramley cooking apples, peeled, cored
and chopped
4tbsp each redcurrant jelly (or light
muscovado sugar if you prefer) and
red wine vinegar

1 each cinnamon stick and clove
2 thyme sprigs
salt and pepper

1 Preheat the oven to 170°C (150°C fan oven) mark 3. Melt the butter in a large flameproof casserole, then fry the onions for 7–10 minutes until beginning to soften.
2 Add the remaining ingredients and stir together. Season the mixture well, then cover the casserole and cook in the oven for 2 hours, stirring once or twice during cooking.
3 Remove from the oven, tip the cabbage into a serving dish and discard the thyme, cinnamon stick and cloves.

Serves 8   preparation: 20 minutes   cooking time: 2 hours 10 minutes
per serving: 100 cals; 3g fat; 17g carbohydrate

Sweet-glazed Chipolatas

450g (1lb) chipolata sausages
3tbsp home-made Cranberry, Honey and
Ginger Sauce (page 665)

1tbsp olive oil
rosemary sprigs, to garnish (optional)

1 Put the sausages into a plastic container and add the sauce and olive oil. Toss together, then cover and chill until ready to cook.
2 Preheat the second oven to 200°C (180°C fan oven) mark 6. Spread the chipolatas out on a baking sheet and cook for 30–40 minutes. Remove from the oven and arrange the chipolotas around the turkey. Garnish with rosemary sprigs, if you like.

Serves 8   preparation: 5 minutes   cooking time: 30–40 minutes
per serving: 230 cals; 20g fat; 6g carbohydrate

The Ultimate Christmas Pudding

200g (7oz) each currants, sultanas
  and raisins
75g (3oz) whole candied peel, finely
  chopped
1 small apple, peeled, cored and grated
1tsp each ground cinnamon, cloves and
  freshly grated nutmeg
¼tsp mixed spice
1tbsp each brandy and rum

125ml (4fl oz) beer
175g (6oz) breadcrumbs
175g (6oz) suet
100g (3½oz) each sifted flour and light
  muscovado sugar
2 eggs, beaten
butter, to grease
25ml (1fl oz) brandy, to flame

1   Put the currants, sultanas, raisins, candied peel, apple, ground cinnamon, cloves, nutmeg and mixed spice into a large bowl. Pour in the brandy, rum and beer. Stir everything together, then cover and leave to soak in a cool place for at least 1 hour – preferably overnight.
2   Add the breadcrumbs, suet, flour, sugar and beaten eggs to the bowl and mix really well. Don't forget to let everyone have a stir and make a wish.
3   Grease a 1 litre (1¾ pint) pudding basin and line with a 60cm (24 inch) square piece of muslin. Spoon the mixture into the basin and flatten the surface. Gather the muslin over the top of the mixture, then secure with string. Tie a piece of string around the basin just under the rim and knot. Don't cut the string, but bring the ends over the top of the bowl and secure to the string on the other side to make a handle. Trim the muslin.
4   To cook the pudding, put the basin on an upturned, heatproof plate in a deep pan. Fill the pan with water to come halfway up the side of the basin and bring to a simmer. Cover the pan with a tight-fitting lid and steam for 6 hours. Keep an eye on the water level and top up as necessary with boiling water – probably every hour. Remove the bowl from the pan. Cool the pudding in the bowl, then lift it out of the bowl, still in its muslin. Wrap in clingfilm and a double layer of tin foil and keep in a cool, dark place until Christmas.
5   To serve, steam the pudding for 2½ hours, checking the water level every 40 minutes and topping up, if necessary, with boiling water. Unmould the pudding on to a serving plate, garnish with a holly sprig and take to the table. Warm the brandy in a small pan until hot, pour into a small ladle, light with a match and pour over the pudding. The flames will disappear almost immediately and the pudding is then ready to serve.

Serves 12   preparation: 30 minutes, plus soaking   cooking time: 6 hours, plus reheating
per serving: 387 cals; 14g fat; 62g carbohydrate

Cooking to impress

Boozy Cream

125g (4oz) chopped dried fruit, such as figs
or prunes
125ml (4fl oz) crème de cacao or
Grand Marnier

568ml carton double cream
100ml (3½fl oz) brandy
pinch of freshly grated nutmeg
about 1tbsp golden icing sugar

1 Put the fruit in a bowl, add the crème de cacao or Grand Marnier and soak for 10 minutes.
2 Lightly whip the cream in a large bowl until thickened. Fold in the brandy, nutmeg, fruit and juices and
   a little icing sugar to taste. Transfer to a serving bowl and chill until ready to serve.

Serves 8   preparation: 15 minutes
per serving: 400 cals; 36g fat; 12g carbohydrate

Muscovado Butter

250g (9oz) unsalted butter, softened
225g (8oz) light muscovado sugar

8tbsp Grand Marnier or Cointreau

1 Put the butter into a large bowl and add the sugar. Using an electric hand whisk, cream together
   until smooth and pale.
2 Add the Grand Mariner or Cointreau, a little at a time, and continue to whisk for about 5 minutes until
   thick and mousse-like. Transfer to a serving bowl and chill until needed.

Serves 8   preparation: 10 minutes
per serving: 380 cals; 26g fat; 34g carbohydrate

12

Cooking to impress

Alternative
Christmas Lunch for 8

Goose with Roasted Apples and Onions

Cranberry and Lemon Stuffing Balls
Buttery Potatoes and Celeriac
Braised Shallots and Chestnuts with Pancetta and Sage
Braised Red Cabbage

Grand Marnier Oranges and Passion fruit

Goose with Roasted Apples and Onions

giblets removed from the goose
1 carrot, peeled and chopped
1 celery stick, chopped
1 onion, peeled and quartered
1 bouquet garni (1 bay leaf, 1 thyme sprig,
  1 parsley sprig)
6 black peppercorns
5kg (11lb) oven-ready goose

salt and pepper
6 small red onions, peeled
7 small red eating apples
small bunch each of sage and rosemary
1 bay leaf
30g pack Madeira Wine Gravy Mix
300ml (½ pint) red wine
bunch of watercress, to garnish

1 To make the stock, put the giblets into a pan, add the carrot, celery, quartered onion, bouquet garni and peppercorns, then cover with 1.1 litres (2 pints) cold water. Cover and bring slowly to the boil, then reduce the heat and simmer for 1 hour. Strain and reserve the stock.

2 Wash the goose and pat dry with kitchen paper, then season the bird inside and out.

3 Cut one of the red onions and two of the apples into quarters and put into the cavity of the goose with half the sage, half the rosemary and the bay leaf. Tie the legs together with string and push a long skewer through the wings to tuck them close to the body. Put the goose, breast side up, on to a rack in a large roasting tin. Use a metal skewer to prick the breast all over to help release the fat during cooking. Season generously. Put the remaining onions around the goose. Cover the goose and tin with foil, then chill until required. Take the goose out of the fridge 30 minutes before cooking it.

4 When you're ready to cook, preheat the oven to 230°C (210°C fan oven) mark 8. Calculate the cooking time and cook the goose for 15 minutes per 450g (1lb) plus 15 minutes – this works out at 3 hours for a 5kg (11lb) goose. Roast for 30 minutes.

5 Reduce the oven temperature to 190°C (170°C fan oven) mark 5. Use a baster to remove the fat from the base of the tin, drizzling some over the goose to keep the flesh moist. Put the remaining fat into a heatproof glass jar and put to one side for the braised shallots (see page 500). Roast the goose for a further 1 hour, then remove and reserve the excess fat again from the base of the tin.

6 Cook the bird for 30 minutes, then remove the foil. Extract and reserve the fat again, then add the remaining apples to the tin. Sprinkle the goose with the remaining sage and rosemary sprigs, then return it to the oven and roast for 1 hour. To test whether the goose is cooked, pierce the thigh with a skewer – it's ready when the juices run clear. Transfer the cooked bird to a warm platter, cover tightly with foil and leave to rest for 30 minutes. Remove the apples and onions, cover and keep warm.

7 To make the gravy, pour out and reserve all but 1tbsp of the fat from the tin, then sprinkle in the gravy mix and whisk in the wine. Put the tin directly on to the hob and bubble the gravy for 5 minutes to reduce it slightly. Stir regularly, scraping up the goodness from the base of the tin, then whisk in 200ml (7fl oz) giblet stock and bring to the boil.

8 Take one roast apple and onion and add them to the gravy, pressing them down with the back of a wooden spoon. Simmer the gravy for 10 minutes, then strain it through a metal sieve into a clean pan, squeezing the onion and apple with the spoon to extract as much flavour as possible.

9 Cut the remaining apples and onions into wedges and serve with the goose, garnished with watercress.

Serves 8   preparation: 30 minutes   cooking time: 4 hours
per serving: 450 cals; 28g fat; 6g carbohydrate

12

Cooking to impress

Cranberry and Lemon Stuffing Balls

25g (1oz) butter
1 large onion, peeled and finely chopped
1 garlic clove, peeled and crushed
450g (1lb) best-quality Lincolnshire
  sausages
4tbsp chopped flat-leafed parsley

2tbsp chopped sage, plus a few leaves
  to garnish
zest of 2 lemons
1tbsp brandy or Calvados (optional)
75g (3oz) dried cranberries
salt and pepper

1 Melt the butter in a pan and sauté the onion for about 10 minutes until soft but not coloured. Add the garlic and cook for 1 minute. Transfer to a bowl and cool.
2 Squeeze the meat from the sausages into the bowl with the cooled onion and garlic, discarding the sausage skins. Add the parsley and sage, lemon zest, brandy or Calvados, if using, and cranberries. Season well, then mix well to combine – you may find it easiest to do this with clean hands.
3 Shape the mixture into 18 balls and put into mini paper muffin cases (to prevent it from sticking), then into mini muffin tins, if you like. Cook immediately or cover and freeze for up to one month.
4 Preheat the oven to 190°C (170°C fan oven) mark 5. Bake the stuffing balls for 20–25 minutes, or from frozen for 35–40 minutes, until cooked and golden. Garnish with sage leaves and serve with the goose.

Makes 18 balls preparation: 35 minutes   cooking time: 20–25 minutes (35–40 minutes from frozen)
per serving: 200 cals; 15g fat; 8g carbohydrate

Buttery Potatoes and Celeriac

175g (6oz) unsalted butter
900g (2lb) potatoes, peeled and very thinly
  sliced (slices not washed)
1 celeriac head, about 700g (1½lb), peeled
  and thinly sliced

salt and pepper
freshly grated nutmeg

1 Preheat the oven to 190°C (170°C fan oven) mark 5. Melt the butter in a heavy-based pan.
2 Line the base of a 25cm (10 inch) loose-based cake tin with baking parchment and brush with a little melted butter. Layer up the potato and celeriac slices, slightly overlapping, seasoning each layer well with salt, pepper and nutmeg. Finish by drizzling with butter and seasoning generously again.
3 Cover with baking parchment, then put a 23cm (9 inch) cake tin filled with baking beans on top to compact the cake, making it easier to slice. Bake for 1 hour 10 minutes or until the potatoes are tender. Remove from the oven, cool, cover and chill overnight.
4 To heat up, invert the tin on to a heatproof serving plate and warm in the oven at 190°C (170°C fan oven) mark 5 for 10 minutes, then brown under a preheated grill for 5–10 minutes. Serve sliced into wedges.

Serves 8 preparation: 30 minutes   cooking time: 1 hour 10 minutes
per serving: 250 cals; 19g fat; 19g carbohydrate

Braised Shallots and Chestnuts with Pancetta and Sage

130g pack cubed pancetta

1tbsp goose fat or olive oil

500g (1lb 2oz) shallots, blanched in boiling
water, drained and peeled

1tbsp golden caster sugar

150ml (¼ pint) red wine

2tbsp red wine vinegar

a few thyme sprigs

4 sage leaves, shredded, plus a few extra
leaves to garnish

300ml (½ pint) hot giblet or chicken stock

salt and pepper

400g (14oz) whole cooked chestnuts

1 Dry-fry the pancetta for 5 minutes until cooked and golden, then put to one side.
2 Add the goose fat or olive oil to the pan and gently fry the shallots for 10 minutes or until golden.
3 Add the sugar to the pan and stir to dissolve, then heat for 1–2 minutes until it begins to caramelise. Add the wine and vinegar, scraping the base of the pan to dissolve any rich sticky bits, and gently simmer until the liquid has reduced slightly.
4 Add the thyme, shredded sage and hot stock, then season and cook for 20 minutes.
5 Add the chestnuts and cook for 10 minutes until there's just enough liquid left to glaze. Transfer to a serving dish and serve.

Serves 8   preparation: 10 minutes   cooking time: 50 minutes
per serving: 200 cals; 10g fat; 25g carbohydrate

Braised Red Cabbage

½ medium red cabbage, about 500g
(1lb 2oz), shredded

1 red onion, peeled and finely chopped

1 Bramley apple, peeled, cored and
chopped

25g (1oz) light muscovado sugar

1 cinnamon stick

pinch of ground cloves

¼tsp freshly grated nutmeg

2tbsp each red wine vinegar and red wine

juice of 1 orange

salt and pepper

1 Put all the ingredients into a large pan and stir to mix well.
2 Put the pan, covered, over a low heat and cook gently for about 1½ hours, stirring the cabbage from time to time to prevent it from burning on the bottom.
3 When the cabbage is tender, remove the pan from the heat and discard the cinnamon stick. Serve at once, or cool, put into a bowl, cover and chill the cabbage overnight.
4 To reheat, put the cabbage into a pan, add 2tbsp cold water and cover with a tight-fitting lid. Bring to the boil, then reduce the heat and simmer for 25 minutes.

Serves 8   preparation: 10 minutes   cooking time: 1½ hours
per serving: 40 cals; trace fat; 10g carbohydrate

Grand Marnier Oranges and Passion Fruit

8 large sweet oranges
6 passion fruit

150g (5oz) golden caster sugar
6tbsp Grand Marnier

1 Use a vegetable peeler to pare strips of peel from two oranges. Cut the strips into needle-fine shreds, then put into a heavy-based pan.
2 Cut the top and bottom off each orange, then use a sharp knife to remove all the skin and pith, then discard. Slice the fruit into rounds, saving the juice, then put the fruit into a bowl. Add the juice to the pan.
3 Cut each passion fruit in half, scooping the juice and seeds of three into the pan. Push the seeds and pulp of the remaining fruit through a sieve held over the pan, so the juice drips through; discard the seeds.
4 Add the sugar to the pan, set it over a medium heat and leave to dissolve completely. Increase the heat and, swirling the pan occasionally, allow the sugar to caramelise gently – it should take about 10 minutes to become syrupy.
5 Remove the pan from the heat and add the Grand Marnier to the syrup – it may splutter as you do this, so protect your hands with a cloth. Cool the syrup, then pour it over the oranges. Cover and chill for up to two days before serving.

Serves 8   preparation: 30 minutes   cooking time: 10 minutes
per serving: 160 cals; 0g fat; 36g carbohydrate

12

Cooking to impress

Boxing Day Menu for 10

Honey and Mustard Glazed Ham

Carrot, Peanut and Coriander Salad
Avocado, Clementine and Chicory Salad
Cannellini Bean and Sunblush Tomato Salad

Apricot and Peach Trifle

Honey and Mustard Glazed Ham

4kg (9lb) ham, bone in
1 onion, peeled and quartered
1 carrot, peeled and chopped into three
1 celery stick, chopped into three
1 sprig each parsley, rosemary and thyme

1 bay leaf
handful of cloves
4tbsp runny honey
4tbsp Dijon mustard

1 Put the ham into a large pan. Add the onion, carrot, celery and herbs. Cover with water and bring to the boil, then reduce the heat and simmer, half-covered with a lid, for 2¼ hours or 15 minutes per 450g (1lb).
2 Lift the ham out of the pan and put into a roasting tin. Preheat the oven to 220°C (200°C fan oven) mark 7. Using a sharp knife, remove and discard the skin to leave a thin layer of fat behind.
3 Score the fat lightly in a diamond pattern and stud each diamond with a clove. Put the honey into a small bowl, add the mustard and mix well. Brush the mixture all over the exposed fat. Roast the ham for 15 minutes until golden.

Serves 10 with plenty for leftovers   preparation: 15 minutes   cooking time: 2½ hours
per 150g (5oz) serving: 180 cals; 8g fat; 0g carbohydrate

Cooking to impress

Carrot, Peanut and Coriander Salad

900g (2lb) carrots, peeled and grated or
  shredded
100g (3½oz) unsalted peanuts, toasted and
  roughly chopped
100g (3½oz) sultanas

2 x 20g packs coriander, chopped
7tbsp olive oil
3tbsp white wine vinegar
1tbsp runny honey
salt and pepper

1 Put the carrots, peanuts, sultanas and coriander into a large bowl and mix well.
2 To make the dressing, put the olive oil, vinegar and honey into a small bowl and season well to taste.
   Whisk everything together.
3 Pour the dressing over the salad and toss well. Leave at room temperature for 30 minutes for the flavours
   to mingle.

Serves 10   preparation: 10 minutes, plus marinating
per serving: 200 cals; 14g fat; 14g carbohydrate

Avocado, Clementine and Chicory Salad

juice of 1 orange
8tbsp olive oil
20g pack dill, finely chopped
salt and pepper
6 chicory heads, leaves separated

4 ripe avocados, peeled, stoned and sliced
6 clementines or satsumas, peeled and
  thinly sliced into rounds
50g (2oz) pine nuts, toasted

1 To make the dressing, put the orange juice into a bowl and add the olive oil and dill. Season and
   whisk everything together.
2 Divide the chicory among two platters and arrange the avocados and clementines or satsumas on
   top. Just before serving, sprinkle over the pine nuts and spoon the dressing on top.

Serves 10   preparation: 10 minutes
per serving: 280 cals; 27g fat; 7g carbohydrate

Cannellini Bean and Sunblush Tomato Salad

1 small red onion, peeled and very finely
   sliced
3tbsp red wine vinegar
handful each chopped mint and flat-leafed
   parsley
4 x 400g cans cannellini beans, well drained
   and rinsed

6tbsp extra-virgin olive oil
6 celery sticks, finely sliced
100g (3½oz) sunblush tomatoes, snipped
   in half

1   Put the onion into a small bowl, add the vinegar and toss. Leave to marinate for 30 minutes – this stage is important as it takes the astringency out of the onion.
2   Add the remaining ingredients and toss everything together.

Serves 10   preparation: 5 minutes, plus marinating
per serving: 130 cals; 8g fat; 11g carbohydrate

Apricot and Peach Trifle

2 x packs trifle sponges, each containing
   eight sponges, or 1 x 440g ready-made
   Madeira cake
6tbsp apricot jam
4tbsp sherry
4 x 415g cans apricots in natural fruit juice,
   drained

2 x 415g cans peaches in natural fruit juice,
   drained
568ml carton double cream
500g carton fresh custard
250g tub mascarpone
50g (2oz) pecan nuts, toasted

1   Cut the trifle sponges in half horizontally and spread one half with the apricot jam. Cover with the other half to make mini sandwiches. If using cake, cut into slices first, then sandwich together in pairs with jam. Use to line a large glass serving bowl. Drizzle over the sherry, then add the apricots.
2   Put the peaches into a food processor or blender and whiz to a purée. Pour over the apricots in an even layer.
3   Put the cream into a large bowl and whisk until soft peaks form. Chill. Put the whisk to one side – you needn't rinse it.
4   Put the custard and mascarpone into a large bowl and whisk together briefly to mix well. Pour over the fruit in an even layer.
5   Spoon the whipped cream over the custard mix and scatter the top with pecan nuts.

Serves 10   preparation: 20 minutes
per serving: 830 cals; 51g fat; 90g carbohydrate

Winter Menu for 20

Mozzarella Nibbles
Tangy Chicken Bites

Roasted Salmon
Winter Leaf Salad
Roasted Root Vegetable Salad
Classic Coleslaw
Cheese and Onion tart

Cheat's Gateau
Boozy Oranges with Orange Cream

Mozzarella Nibbles

85g pack Parma ham
2 x 125g tubs bocconcini (mini mozzarella
balls), drained
397g jar pitted black and green olives,
drained and halved

125g (4oz) each roast artichokes and
peppers, cut into small pieces
bunch of basil leaves

1 Wrap a little Parma ham around each mozzarella ball.
2 Push a halved olive on to a cocktail stick, then add a piece each of artichoke and pepper, a basil leaf,
then the Parma and mozzarella ball. Repeat to make 30 nibbles. Serve immediately or cover and chill
for up to 1 hour.

Makes 30 preparation: 15 minutes per nibble: 40 cals; 3g fat; trace carbohydrate

Tangy Chicken Bites

2 x 50g pack mini croustades
about 275g (10oz) fruity chutney
2 roast chicken breasts, skinned and torn
into small pieces

275ml (9fl oz) crème fraîche
thyme sprigs

1 Spread out the croustades on a board and spoon about ½tsp chutney into each one.
2 Top with a few shreds of chicken, a small blob of crème fraîche and a few thyme leaves. Serve
immediately.

Makes 48 preparation: 10 minutes per bite: 50 cals; 3g fat; 4g carbohydrate

Roasted Salmon

3 lemons, 2 sliced and the juice of ½
2 salmon sides, filleted, each 1.4kg (3lb),
  skin on, boned and trimmed
salt and pepper
2tbsp dry white wine
500ml carton crème fraîche
500g carton natural yogurt
2tbsp horseradish sauce

3tbsp chopped tarragon
4tbsp capers, roughly chopped, plus extra
  to garnish
¼ cucumber, deseeded and diced, plus
  extra to garnish
2 large bunches of watercress, to serve
lemon and cucumber slices, to garnish

1   Preheat the oven to 190°C (170°C fan oven) mark 5. Take two big pieces of foil, each large enough to wrap a salmon side, and put a piece of greaseproof paper on top of each.

2   Divide the lemon slices among each piece of greaseproof and lay each salmon side on top, skin side up. Season well, then pour over the lemon juice and wine.

3   Score the skin at 4cm (1½ inch) intervals across the width of each salmon fillet, keeping the side in one piece, to mark 10 portions.

4   Scrunch the foil around each salmon, keeping it loose so the fish doesn't stick. Put on to two separate racks in the oven and cook for 45 minutes until the flesh is just opaque.

5   Unwrap the foil and cook for 20 minutes until the skin crisps up and the fish is cooked. To check, ease a knife into one of the slashes in the skin. Remove from the oven and cool quickly in a cold place. Re-wrap and chill.

6   To make the dressing, put the crème fraîche, yogurt, horseradish sauce, tarragon, capers and diced cucumber in a large bowl. Season and mix well, then cover and chill.

7   To serve, cut through the slashes in each salmon side to make 10 portions. Put on a bed of watercress and garnish with the lemon and cucumber slices. Serve with the dressing, garnished with capers and diced cucumber.

Serves 20   preparation: 15 minutes   cooking time: 1 hour 5 minutes
per serving: 370 cals; 27g fat; 3g carbohydrate

Cooking to impress

Winter Leaf Salad

3tbsp each white wine vinegar and
  walnut oil
6tbsp olive oil
salt and pepper
100g (3½oz) lamb's lettuce

2 heads radicchio
4 heads red chicory
200g (7oz) walnuts, toasted and roughly
  chopped

1 Put the vinegar, walnut and olive oils in a screw-topped jar, season and shake well to mix.
2 Tear all the salad leaves into bite-sized pieces and put in a large bowl. Add the walnuts and toss to mix.
3 To serve, shake the dressing again, then pour over the salad and toss well. Divide among two large bowls.

Serves 20   preparation: 20 minutes
per serving: 110 cals; 11g fat; 1g carbohydrate

Roasted Root Vegetable Salad

4 butternut squash, halved, deseeded
  and cubed
6 large carrots, peeled and cut into chunks
10 thyme sprigs
6tbsp olive oil
salt and pepper

8 red onions, peeled and cut into wedges
4tbsp balsamic vinegar
4 x 410g cans chickpeas, drained
  and rinsed
100g (3½oz) pine nuts, toasted
4 x 100g bags wild rocket

1 Preheat the oven to 190°C (170°C fan oven) mark 5. Divide the squash and carrots among two large deep roasting tins. Scatter over the thyme and drizzle each with 2tbsp olive oil, then season and roast for 20 minutes.
2 Remove the tins from the oven, give them a good shake to make sure the vegetables aren't sticking, then divide the onions among the tins. Drizzle 1tbsp oil over each and toss to coat. Continue to roast for 20 minutes or until all the vegetables are tender.
3 Remove the roasted vegetables from the oven and discard any twiggy bits of thyme. Drizzle 2tbsp vinegar over each tin, stir in and put to one side to cool.
4 To serve, put the chickpeas into a large bowl. Add the cooled vegetables, pine nuts and rocket (reserving some for a garnish). Toss everything together. Divide among two large serving dishes and garnish each with a little rocket.

Serves 20   preparation: 20 minutes   cooking time: 40 minutes
 per serving: 170 cals; 8g fat; 19g carbohydrate

Classic Coleslaw

5tbsp red wine vinegar	1 small red and 1 small white cabbage,
250ml (8fl oz) olive oil	each shredded
2tbsp Dijon mustard	4 carrots, peeled and grated
salt and pepper	75g (3oz) flat-leafed parsley, finely chopped

1 First, make the dressing. Pour the vinegar into a large screw-topped jar. Add the olive oil and mustard and season well. Screw on the lid and shake well.
2 Put the cabbage and carrots into a large bowl. Toss together so the vegetables are well mixed, then add the parsley.
3 Shake the dressing again, pour over the cabbage mixture and toss well to coat. Divide the coleslaw among two large bowls to serve.

Serves 20 preparation: 20 minutes
per serving: 140 cals; 10g fat; 8g carbohydrate

Cheese and Onion Tart

40g (1½oz) unsalted butter	375g pack ready-rolled puff pastry
4 red onions, peeled and thinly sliced	2tbsp milk, to glaze
2tbsp golden caster sugar	200g (7oz) soft goat's cheese,
1tbsp sherry vinegar	roughly crumbled
juice of ¼ lemon	basil leaves, to garnish

1 Melt the butter in a pan. Add the onions and sugar, then cover and cook over a low heat for 20 minutes, stirring occasionally, or until softened. Stir in the vinegar and lemon juice and cook, uncovered, for 5–10 minutes. Take off the heat and cool.
2 Preheat the oven to 180°C (160°C fan oven) mark 4. Put the pastry on a non-stick baking sheet and roll out to measure 28 x 38cm (11 x 15 inches). Score around the edge leaving a 2.5cm (1 inch) border, then brush the edge with milk. Bake for 15–20 minutes until golden. Remove from the oven and leave to cool.
3 Use a palette knife to push down the middle square of pastry. Spread the onion mixture evenly over the central square, then scatter over the cheese. Return to oven for 10 minutes until the cheese is golden and the tart is warm. Scatter the basil leaves on top, then cut the tart into pieces and serve.

Serves 10 preparation: 15 minutes cooking time: 50 minutes–1 hour
per serving: 290 cals; 20g fat; 24g carbohydrate

Cheat's Gateau

500g tub mascarpone
1tbsp golden icing sugar, sifted, plus extra
to dust
2 x 425g cans pitted black cherries in
syrup, drained

1kg box of panettone
50g (2oz) good-quality plain dark chocolate
(with minimum 50% cocoa solids), broken
into pieces

1 Put the mascarpone in a bowl, add the sugar and mix well. Gently stir in the cherries.
2 Put the panettone on a board and slice horizontally through the middle into three slices. Using a
   palette knife, spread half the mascarpone mixture over the base of the panettone, then spread the
   rest on to the middle layer. Carefully sandwich the cake together and leave standing on the board.
3 Melt the chocolate in a small heatproof bowl set over a pan of barely simmering water. Dust the
   panettone with a little icing sugar, then drizzle the melted chocolate on top. Put on a serving plate or
   cake stand to serve.

Serves 20   preparation: 10 minutes   cooking time: 3 minutes
per serving: 300 cals; 19g fat; 32g carbohydrate

Boozy Oranges with Orange Cream

8 large juicy oranges
6tbsp Cointreau (optional)

568ml carton double cream
1tbsp golden icing sugar, sifted

1 Grate the zest from 2 oranges, put in a small bowl and put to one side.
2 Put the oranges on a board and use a sharp knife to cut the top and bottom off each. Next, cut off
   all the peel and white pith. Cut the flesh into rounds, pouring any juice into a large serving bowl. Put
   the slices in the bowl, add 3tbsp Cointreau, if using, and put to one side.
3 Whip the cream in a bowl until just thick, then stir in the remaining Cointreau, almost all the orange
   zest and the sugar. Scatter over the remaining zest and serve with the oranges.

Serves 20   preparation: 15 minutes
per serving: 160 cals; 14g fat; 7g carbohydrate

Cooking to impress

Cold desserts

You've had a great meal so far and now you're anticipating the dessert. What do you fancy – meringues, fools, ice cream, trifles, jellies, fruit? Something thick and creamy, or delicate and aromatic? A solid chunk of cheesecake, or a sublime slice of panna cotta?

If ice cream is what you're after, then there are so many to choose from: Apricot and Ginger; Cinnamon and Nutmeg; Ginger, Rum and Raisin, to mention just three, plus Banana and Chocolate Ice Cream Pie and Italian Ice Cream Cake.

What about fruit? Take your pick from Nectarines and Apricots with Pistachios; Marinated Strawberries; or Spiced Caramelised Clementines, for starters.

Perhaps jellies are more your thing. Sparkling Fruit Jellies capture grapes and raspberries in their depths; Port and Orange Jellies are what it says on the label; while, for something a bit posher, Champagne and Ginger Jelly with Ginger Cream is an exciting combination.

Finally, an old favourite: trifle – layers of alcohol-soaked sponge, cream, custard and fruit. Make it as simple as a Crème Anglaise Trifle, or as seductive as a Tropical Fruit Trifle, with pawpaw, mango and rum. The perfect way to spoil yourself.

Amaretti with Lemon Mascarpone

juice from ¼ lemon, plus the rind pared
from ¼ lemon, white skin removed, and
sliced finely into long strips, or lemon zest

1tbsp golden caster sugar, plus a little extra
to sprinkle
50g (2oz) mascarpone
13 single Amaretti biscuits

1 Put the lemon juice in a small pan. Add the sugar and dissolve over a low heat. Add the finely sliced lemon rind and cook for 1–2 minutes – it will curl up. Lift out, using a slotted spoon and put on to a sheet of baking parchment, reserving the syrup. Sprinkle with sugar to coat.
2 Beat the mascarpone in a bowl to soften, then stir in the sugar syrup.
3 Crush one of the Amaretti biscuits and put to one side, ready to dust.
4 Put a blob of mascarpone on to each remaining Amaretti biscuit, then top with a couple of strips of the crystallised lemon peel, or the lemon zest, if using. Sprinkle over the crushed Amaretti crumbs.

Makes 12   preparation: 15 minutes   cooking time: 5 minutes   per serving: 20 cals; 1g fat; 2g carbohydrate

Apricot Fool

410g can apricots, drained
200g (7oz) Greek-style yogurt

25g golden caster sugar, to taste

1 Put the apricots in a food processor and blend until smooth.
2 Stir the purée into the yogurt and sweeten to taste. Chill for 2 hours before serving.

Serves 4–6   preparation: 5 minutes, plus chilling
per serving: 160–100 cals; 5–3g fat; 27–18g carbohydrate

Oh-so-fruity Fool

500g carton Summer Fruit Compôte

500g carton fresh custard sauce

1 Divide half the compôte among six serving glasses and add a thin layer of custard sauce. Repeat the process to use up all the compôte and sauce.
2 Stir each fool once to swirl the custard and compôte together, then serve.

Serves 6   preparation: 5 minutes
per serving: 154 cals; 4g fat; 27g carbohydrate

Passion Fruit and Lime Cream Pots

12 ripe passion fruit
568ml carton double cream
50g (2oz) golden caster sugar

zest and juice of 1 lime
biscuits to serve, such as biscuit curls or
   cigarette russe

1 Rest a sieve over a large bowl. Halve the passion fruit and scrape the juice and seeds into the sieve. Stir the seeds with a spoon to extract all the juice, then discard the seeds.
2 Pour the cream into a heavy-based pan and add all but 1tbsp sugar. Heat gently until the sugar has dissolved, then bring to the boil and cook for 5–8 minutes, stirring continuously with a wooden spoon, making sure it doesn't catch on the bottom, until it has reduced a little.
3 Pour the mixture into a large jug, add the lime zest, 2tsp lime juice and a quarter of the passion fruit juice – it will thicken immediately, so stir it well to stop it going lumpy.
4 Pour the mixture into six 200ml (7fl oz) serving glasses. Leave to cool a little, then chill in the fridge for 1 hour for a soft set or overnight for a firm set.
5 Pour the remaining passion fruit and lime juice into a pan, add the remaining 1tbsp sugar and bring to the boil. Cook for 3 minutes until syrupy. Leave to cool.
6 About 20–30 minutes before serving, remove the creams from the fridge. When ready, pour a little passion fruit syrup on top of each set cream and serve with the biscuits.

Serves 6   preparation: 15 minutes, plus chilling   cooking time: 8–11 minutes
per serving: 470 cals; 45g fat; 13g carbohydrate

Atholl Brose

125g (4oz) raspberries, plus extra
   to decorate
pinch of ground cinnamon
1tsp lemon juice
25g (1oz) golden caster sugar

300ml (½ pint) double cream
3tbsp thin honey
25–50ml (1–2fl oz) whisky, to taste
50g (2oz) coarse oatmeal, toasted

1 Put the raspberries, cinnamon, lemon juice, sugar and 2tbsp water into a small pan and heat gently for 1–2 minutes until the raspberries just soften. Remove from the heat and leave to cool.
2 Whip the cream in a bowl with the honey until it just begins to hold its shape, then beat in the whisky. Fold in the oatmeal.
3 Divide the raspberries among serving glasses and spoon the oatmeal cream on top. Chill in the fridge for 30 minutes.
4 Decorate each serving with a few raspberries and serve with crisp dessert biscuits, if you like.

Serves 4   preparation: 10 minutes, plus chilling   cooking time: 2 minutes
per serving: 470 cals; 37g fat; 28g carbohydrate

Iced Plum Creams

450g (1lb) dark-skinned plums, halved with stones intact	2 large eggs
200ml (7fl oz) sloe gin	150g (5oz) mascarpone
75g (3oz) golden caster sugar	light sunflower oil, to grease
	redcurrants, to decorate

1 Put the plums in a pan with the sloe gin and 40g (1½oz) sugar, cover with a tight-fitting lid and bring to the boil. Reduce the heat and simmer until the plums are tender – about 20 minutes. Cool and drain, reserving the juice. Remove the stones from the cooled plums and whiz the plums in a food processor until smooth, then put to one side.
2 Separate the eggs, reserve one white (discard the other). Whisk the yolks with the remaining sugar and the reserved plum juice for 2–3 minutes or until pale and lightly thickened. Whisk the plum purée and mascarpone together, then carefully fold in the egg yolk mixture. Whisk the reserved egg white in a clean grease-free bowl until stiff peaks form and carefully fold into the mixture.
3 Divide the plum mixture between six or eight 150ml (¼ pint) lightly oiled dariole moulds or ramekins. Cover and put in the freezer for 4 hours.
4 To serve, invert the creams on to plates and unmould. (You can eat the creams straight away, but it's better to give them 5–10 minutes in the fridge before serving.) Decorate with redcurrants and serve.

Makes 6–8 servings   preparation: 40 minutes, plus freezing   cooking time: 20 minutes
per serving: 310–230 cals; 14–11g fat; 30–23g carbohydrate

Baked Raspberry Creams

2 large eggs, plus 2 large egg yolks	284ml carton double cream
50g (2oz) golden caster sugar	flavourless oil, such as safflower, to grease
250g (9oz) puréed raspberries (whiz the raspberries in a food processor, then press through a sieve with the back of a spoon to remove the pips)	450g (1lb) mixed raspberries, strawberries and redcurrants
	icing sugar, to dust

1 Preheat the oven to 170°C (150°C fan oven) mark 3. Whisk the eggs and egg yolks with the sugar. Strain into the raspberries, then pour in the cream and stir well. Divide the mixture between six 150ml (¼ pint) ramekins, put them in a roasting tin and pour in enough boiling water to come halfway up their sides.
2 Cover with oiled greaseproof paper and bake for 30–35 minutes or until just set. Remove from the oven and lift the dishes out of the roasting tin. Cool, cover and chill overnight.
3 Spoon the raspberries, strawberries and redcurrants on top of the creams and dust with icing sugar, then serve.

Serves 6   preparation: 10 minutes, plus chilling   cooking time: 30 minutes
per serving: 370 cals; 27g fat; 27g carbohydrate

Passion Fruit and Mango Brûlée

1 large ripe mango, peeled
2 passion fruit, halved
500ml carton reduced-fat crème fraîche

200g (7oz) mascarpone
2tbsp light muscovado sugar

1 Preheat the grill to high. Slice the mango flesh away from either side of the stone, then cut into cubes. Put into the base of four ramekin dishes.
2 Scoop out the passion fruit juice and seeds into a bowl and add the crème fraîche and mascarpone. Beat together with a wooden spoon to form a thick creamy mixture.
3 Spoon this mixture over the mango in the ramekins, then sprinkle the sugar over the top.
4 Put under the grill and cook until the sugar melts and forms a dark caramel. Cool slightly before serving.

Serves 4   preparation: 6 minutes   cooking time: 4 minutes
per serving: 500 cals; 42g fat; 22g carbohydrate

Roasted Apricot and Pistachio Creams

700g (1½lb) ripe apricots or peaches,
  halved and stoned
2.5cm (1 inch) piece stem ginger in syrup,
  drained and chopped, plus 1tbsp of
  the syrup
4tbsp maple syrup
25g (1oz) pistachio nuts, roughly chopped

25g (1oz) ground rice
1tbsp cornflour
25g (1oz) golden caster sugar
600ml (1 pint) full-fat milk
1tbsp rosewater or orange flower water
25g (1oz) ground almonds

1 Preheat the oven to 200°C (180°C fan oven) mark 6. Put the apricots or peaches in a large shallow ovenproof dish with the ginger, ginger syrup and maple syrup. Bake, uncovered, for 30 minutes or until tender and slightly caramelised, basting occasionally.
2 Meanwhile, put the pistachios on a baking tray and cook below the apricots for 2–3 minutes or until they're lightly toasted. Remove the apricots or peaches from the oven and, using a fork or potato masher, mash until they're lightly crushed, then leave to cool.
3 Mix the ground rice, cornflour and sugar in a small bowl to a smooth paste with 4tbsp milk. Pour the remaining milk into a heavy-based pan, bring to the boil, then pour half on to the paste, stirring until well combined. Return to the pan and bring back to the boil. Reduce the heat and simmer, stirring constantly to prevent it from catching on the bottom of the pan, for 10 minutes or until the mixture has thickened. Stir in the rosewater or orange flower water and the ground almonds. Simmer for 5 minutes, then remove the pan from the heat and leave to cool.
4 To assemble, spoon half the apricot or peach mixture into glass serving dishes, top with half the almond cream, then sprinkle with half the chopped pistachio nuts. Cover with the remaining fruit, almond cream and sprinkle with remaining pistachio nuts. Cover and chill for at least 2–3 hours or overnight.

Serves 6   preparation: 15 minutes, plus chilling   cooking time: 45 minutes
per serving: 220 cals; 8g fat; 31g carbohydrate

Iced Pistachio and Orange Parfait

flavourless oil, such as safflower, to grease

75g (3oz) shelled, unsalted pistachio nuts, lightly toasted and finely chopped by hand, plus extra to decorate

200ml (7fl oz) double cream

4 large egg whites

75g (3oz) icing sugar, sieved

2tbsp orange-flavoured liqueur, such as Grand Marnier

75g (3oz) white chocolate

white chocolate curls (page 000), to decorate

1 Lightly oil six 150ml (¼ pint) ramekins and line the bases with greaseproof paper. Sprinkle each base lightly with chopped pistachio nuts. Cut six 5 x 25.5cm (2 x 10 inch) strips of greaseproof paper. Lightly oil one side of the paper and sprinkle with nuts. Reserve the remaining nuts. With the nut side facing inwards, curl the paper around the insides of the ramekins.

2 Lightly whip the cream. Whisk the egg whites in a clean grease-free bowl until stiff, then gradually whisk in the sugar. Fold in the reserved nuts, the liqueur and cream. Don't over-mix.

3 Divide the mixture between the ramekins and freeze for 4 hours, preferably overnight.

4 Melt the chocolate in a heatproof bowl set over a pan of simmering water. Cut six 5 x 25.5cm (2 x 10 inch) strips of non-stick baking parchment. Spread the chocolate thinly over each strip and leave to firm slightly. Unmould the parfaits and remove the lining papers. Lift the chocolate-covered strips and wrap around the parfaits, chocolate side inside. Freeze until set – about 30 minutes.

5 Peel away the parchment from the parfaits. Decorate with pistachio nuts and chocolate curls and serve.

Serves 6 preparation: 1 hour, plus freezing
per serving: 420 cals; 31g fat; 27g carbohydrate

Spiced Caramelised Clementines

225g (8oz) golden caster sugar

2 cinnamon sticks, halved

15 cloves

2 star anise

pared zest of 1 lemon

16 clementines or 8 satsumas, peeled and membrane removed

1 Heat the sugar with 300ml (½ pint) cold water very slowly in a heavy-based pan until the sugar has dissolved, then bring to the boil and bubble until the syrup turns a dark caramel.

2 Remove from the heat and carefully add 300ml (½ pint) warm water – it may splutter. Return to the heat to dissolve any hardened caramel.

3 Add the cinnamon sticks, cloves, star anise and lemon zest. Remove from the heat and leave to cool.

4 Slice each clementine or satsuma into five and spear with a cocktail stick to hold together. Put into a bowl, pour over the warm caramel and chill for at least 4 hours, preferably 2–3 days.

Serves 8 preparation: 15 minutes   cooking time: 25 minutes, plus chilling
per serving: 130 cals; 0g fat; 35g carbohydrate

Cold desserts

Crema Catalana With Berries In Cassis

450ml (¾ pint) full-fat milk
200ml (7fl oz) double cream
zest of 1 lemon
1tsp fennel seeds, crushed
6 large egg yolks
175g (6oz) golden caster sugar, plus 4tsp
2tbsp cornflour

450g (1lb) strawberries, hulled, halved
 or quartered
200g (7oz) mixture of blueberries and wild
 strawberries, halved or quartered
4tbsp crème de cassis
juice of ½ lemon
¼tsp ground cinnamon

1 Put the milk, cream, lemon zest and fennel seeds in a heavy-based pan. Heat to boiling point, then leave for 30 minutes to infuse.
2 Beat together the egg yolks, 125g (4oz) sugar and the cornflour in a small bowl until the mixture is light and fluffy.
3 Strain the infused milk on to the egg yolk mixture, a little at a time, stirring constantly. Pour the mixture back into the clean pan. Cook over a low heat for 6–8 minutes, stirring, until the cream just comes to the boil and is thick and leaves a trail.
4 Pour into six 150ml (¼ pint) ramekins or heatproof pots. Cool, cover loosely with foil and chill overnight to set.
5 To make the berries in cassis, put the strawberries, blueberries and wild strawberries in a bowl. Sprinkle the 4tsp sugar, the cassis and lemon juice over, toss together, then cover and chill.
6 It's a good idea to put the custard in the freezer for 30 minutes before grilling to prevent the set custard curdling. Preheat the grill to high. Mix the remaining 50g (2oz) sugar with the cinnamon and sprinkle evenly over each of the custards. Put under the hot grill until the sugar has caramelised. Leave to stand for at least 20 minutes, then serve with the berries in cassis.

Serves 6   preparation: 10 minutes, plus infusing and chilling   cooking time: 10 minutes
per serving: 460 cals; 25g fat; 52g carbohydrate

Rum Sabayon

75g (3oz) golden caster sugar
3 egg yolks
142ml carton double cream

2tbsp dark rum
zest of 1 lemon, plus 2tbsp lemon juice

1 Put the sugar in a pan with 100ml (4fl oz) water and heat to dissolve the sugar. Boil for 7–8 minutes until syrupy but not coloured.
2 Beat the egg yolks until thick and pale, adding the hot syrup while whisking. Whisk until cool.
3 Whip the cream until stiff, then add the rum, lemon zest and juice and whisk together again until soft peaks form. Fold into the mousse. Cover and chill until ready to serve.

Serves 8   preparation: 10 minutes   cooking time: 10 minutes
per serving: 150 cals; 11g fat; 10g carbohydrate

Cold desserts

Turkish Delight Crème Brûlée

750ml (1¼ pints) double cream
1 vanilla pod, split lengthways, seeds
   removed and reserved
6 pieces Turkish delight cut into small
   pieces (optional)

8 large egg yolks
75g (3oz) golden caster sugar
2tbsp rosewater
demerara sugar, to sprinkle

1 Put the cream in a heavy-based pan with the vanilla pod seeds, bring to the boil slowly, then put to one side for 20 minutes. If using, put the pieces of Turkish delight into the base of six 150ml (¼ pint) earthenware dishes.

2 In a separate bowl, beat together the egg yolks, caster sugar and rosewater. Pour the vanilla flavoured cream on to the egg mixture and mix until thoroughly combined.

3 Return the cream and egg mixture to the heavy-based pan and cook, stirring constantly, over a low to moderate heat until bubbles start to appear on the surface, but don't allow the custard to boil. Pour immediately into the earthenware dishes. Set aside to cool, then chill overnight. Don't cover the dishes as you want a skin to form on the top of the custard.

4 Liberally sprinkle the custards with demerara sugar. Preheat the grill and, when hot, put the dishes underneath until the sugar has melted and is a deeper brown. Leave the dissolved sugar to set hard for 10 minutes before serving.

Serves 6 preparation: 15 minutes, plus infusion and chilling   cooking time: 10 minutes
per serving: 800 cals; 68g fat; 44g carbohydrate (without Turkish Delight: 760 cals; 68g fat; 32g carbohydrate)

Mocha Panna Cotta

142ml carton double cream
150ml (¼ pint) full-fat milk
3tbsp light muscovado sugar
1tbsp instant espresso coffee powder
1tsp vanilla extract
50ml miniature bottle Tia Maria

40g (1½oz) good-quality plain dark
   chocolate (with minimum 50% cocoa
   solids), chopped
1½tsp powdered gelatine
4 chocolate-coated coffee beans
flavourless oil, such as safflower, to grease

1 Line two 150ml (¼ pint) individual pudding basins with clingfilm. Put 100ml (3½fl oz) cream into a small pan with the milk, sugar, coffee, vanilla extract, 1tbsp Tia Maria and the chocolate and heat gently until the chocolate has melted. Bring to the boil, then remove the pan from the heat, sprinkle the gelatine over the liquid and leave for 5 minutes.

2 Stir well, then strain the mixture into a jug and pour into the lined moulds. Put in the freezer for 1 hour to cool quickly or chill for 2 hours.

3 To serve, invert the moulds on to plates and remove the clingfilm. Drizzle around the rest of the Tia Maria and cream and top each with two chocolate coffee beans.

Serves 2 preparation: 10 minutes, plus chilling
per serving: 640 cals; 45g fat; 39g carbohydrate

Tropical Lemon Mousse

flavourless oil, such as safflower, to grease
2tsp powdered gelatine
pared zest of 2 lemons, plus 175ml (6fl oz)
  lemon juice
100ml (4fl oz) double cream
5 eggs, separated
175g (6oz) golden caster sugar
20g (¾oz) plain white flour

icing sugar, to dust
1 small pineapple, peeled and sliced
6–8 kiwi fruit, peeled and thickly sliced
Strawberry Sauce and Passion Fruit Sauce
  (pages 075 and 674), to serve
kiwi fruit, passion fruit, physalis, thin lemon
  slices and fresh mint sprigs, to decorate

1   Grease six 200ml (7fl oz) ramekins. Spoon 3tbsp cold water into a bowl, sprinkle the gelatine over and put to one side. Put the lemon zest, lemon juice and cream in a pan, bring to the boil and put to one side.
2   Beat the egg yolks and 40g (1½oz) caster sugar together in a bowl until thick and light, then mix in the flour until smooth. Strain the lemon and cream mixture into the bowl and mix until smooth, then return to the clean saucepan.
3   Cook, stirring, for about 30 seconds until the mixture comes to the boil. Remove from the heat and cool. Add the gelatine and stir until melted. Cover and set aside.
4   Place the remaining caster sugar with 100ml (7fl oz) water in a pan and dissolve over a low heat. Bring to the boil and bubble for 10 minutes or until the temperature reaches 117°C. When the syrup is almost at the correct temperature, whisk the egg whites in a clean grease-free bowl until stiff peaks form. Pour in the sugar syrup and slowly whisk until the mixture is cool. Fold the mixture into the custard.
5   Pour the lemon mousse mixture into the ramekins, smooth the tops and chill for 2–3 hours or until set. Half an hour before serving, place the mousses in the freezer.
6   Preheat the grill. Unmould the mousses and dust with icing sugar, put on a baking sheet under the grill and cook until lightly browned. Return them to the freezer for 15 minutes, if necessary.
7   To serve, arrange the pineapple and kiwi fruit on plates and top with a lemon mousse. Spoon the sauces around the plate, then decorate and serve.

Serves 6   preparation: 45 minutes, plus cooling, chilling and freezing   cooking time: 15 minutes
per serving (without sauce): 380 cals; 14g fat; 59g carbohydrate

13

Cold desserts

Cherry Crush

400g can pitted cherries
500g tub Greek-style yogurt

150g pack ratafia biscuits
4tbsp cherry brandy

1   Spoon some cherries into the base of four 400ml (14fl oz) dessert glasses. Top with a dollop of yogurt, some ratafia biscuits and a drizzle of cherry brandy.
2   Continue layering up each glass until all the ingredients are used up. Chill for 15 minutes–2 hours before serving.

Serves 4   preparation: 10 minutes, plus chilling   per serving: 390 cals; 14g fat; 51g carbohydrate

Tropical Fruit Salad

4 passion fruit, halved
100g (3½oz) golden caster sugar
50ml (2fl oz) white rum or Malibu
grated zest and juice of 1 lime
125g (4oz) cranberries

1 small pineapple, peeled, halved and cored
1 papaya, peeled and halved
1 large ripe mango, peeled
1 large banana

1 Scoop out the pulp from the passion fruit into a sieve set over a small pan and press with the back of a wooden spoon to extract the juice. Discard the seeds.
2 Add the sugar, rum, lime zest and juice to the passion fruit juice in the pan and heat gently to make a syrup. Add the cranberries and cook over a medium heat for 5 minutes. Leave to cool.
3 Slice the pineapple lengthways. Scoop out and discard the papaya seeds and slice lengthways. Slice the mango flesh away from either side of the stone, then slice lengthways. Slice the banana on the diagonal.
4 Put the pineapple, papaya, mango and banana into a large bowl, then add the cranberries and syrup. Leave to stand at room temperature for at least 30 minutes before serving to let the flavours develop.

Serves 8   preparation: 20 minutes, plus standing   cooking time: 7 minutes
per serving: 120 cals; trace fat; 28g carbohydrate

Ginger and Mint Fruit Salad

70cl bottle ginger wine
225g (8oz) golden caster sugar
25g (1oz) piece fresh root ginger, peeled
3 large mangoes, peeled and roughly chopped
3 large papaya, peeled and roughly chopped

2 Charentais melons, peeled and roughly chopped
450g (1lb) seedless red grapes, removed from stalks
2 mint sprigs, plus extra to decorate

1 Put the wine, sugar and ginger in a pan with 600ml (1 pint) cold water and heat gently until the sugar has dissolved. Increase the heat and bring to the boil, then reduce the heat and simmer gently for 20–30 minutes. Leave to cool.
2 Put all the fruit in a large serving bowl and strain the cooled syrup over. Chill for at least 2 hours, preferably overnight.
3 To serve, chop the mint leaves and add to the fruit salad. Decorate with mint sprigs.

Serves 12   preparation: 50 minutes, plus cooling and chilling   cooking time: 30 minutes
per serving: 205 cals; 0g fat; 42g carbohydrate

Exotic Fruit Salad

125g (4oz) golden caster sugar
6 mint sprigs
¼tsp Chinese five-spice powder
2 small bay leaves
4 lemon grass stalks, split in half and
crushed, plus whole stalks to decorate
(optional)

½tsp peeled and grated fresh root ginger
1 ripe medium pineapple, about 900g (2lb),
flesh cored and cut into chunks
2 ripe papaya, deseeded, peeled and sliced
1 Galia melon, deseeded, the flesh cut into
chunks

1   To make the syrup, put the sugar in a pan with 600ml (1 pint) water and the mint, five-spice powder, bay leaves, lemon grass and ginger. Heat gently until the sugar has dissolved. Bring to the boil, then reduce the heat and simmer for 5 minutes. Remove from the heat and leave to infuse for at least 1 hour, preferably longer.
2   Put all the fruit in a bowl, strain the cooled syrup on top, then cover and chill for at least 2 hours. If you want to, decorate with lemon grass stalks to serve.

Serves 6   preparation: 30 minutes, plus infusing and chilling   cooking time: 7 minutes
per serving: 200 cals; Trace fat; 51g carbohydrate

Raspberries With Chocolate Mallow

225g (8oz) raspberries
grated zest of ½ orange
125g (4oz) golden caster sugar, plus 1tbsp
3 large egg whites

1tbsp cocoa powder, sifted
15g (½oz) hazelnuts, toasted and roughly
chopped

1   Preheat the oven to 150°C (130°C fan oven) mark 2. Divide the raspberries, orange zest and 1tbsp sugar among six 150ml (¼ pint) ramekins.
2   Put the egg whites and the 125g (4oz) sugar in a heatproof bowl set over a pan of gently simmering water and whisk, using an electric hand whisk, until the mixture is very stiff and shiny. Remove the bowl from the heat and whisk for 4–5 minutes or until the bowl is cool. At the last moment, fold in the cocoa powder.
3   Spoon the meringue over the fruit and sprinkle the chopped hazelnuts on top. Bake for 20–25 minutes or until the meringue is lightly coloured, crisp on the outside and soft in the middle. Serve immediately.

Serves 6   preparation: 15 minutes   cooking time: 20–25 minutes
per serving: 120 cals; 1g fat; 27g carbohydrate

Marinated Strawberries

350g (12oz) strawberries, hulled and cut in
  half if large

juice of ¼ lemon
2tbsp golden caster sugar

1   Put the strawberries into a bowl with the lemon juice and sugar. Stir to mix, then put to one side for 30 minutes. Serve with vanilla ice cream.

Serves 4   preparation: 5 minutes, plus infusing
per serving: 50 cals; 0g fat; 13g carbohydrate

Watermelon with Feta Cheese and Honey

½ watermelon, peeled, pipped and sliced
100g (3½oz) feta cheese

2tbsp clear honey

1   Arrange the watermelon on a serving plate, then crumble over the feta and drizzle with the honey. Serve.

Serves 4   preparation: 5 minutes
per serving: 130 cals; 5g fat; 17g carbohydrate

Fresh Fruit with Feta

1 melon, peeled and sliced
450g (1lb) strawberries, washed and hulled

225g (8oz) feta or goat's cheese

1   Put all the fruit into a bowl and mix gently. Serve with the feta or goat's cheese.

Serves 4   preparation: 5 minutes
per serving: 220 cals; 11g fat; 18g carbohydrate

Nectarines and Apricots with Pistachios

6 apricots, quartered and stoned
2 nectarines, quartered and stoned
2tbsp clear honey

50g (2oz) chopped or shelled whole
  pistachio nuts

1   Arrange the apricots and nectarines on a plate. Drizzle over the honey and scatter over the pistachio nuts. Serve.

Serves 4   preparation: 5 minutes
per serving: 140 cals; 7g fat; 18g carbohydrate

Orange Poached Peaches

100g (3½oz) golden caster sugar
grated zest and juice of 2 oranges

10 ripe peaches
2 vanilla pods, to decorate

1 Put the sugar in a pan with 600ml (1 pint) water, the orange zest and juice, bring to the boil and bubble for 5 minutes. Add the peaches to the pan, bring back to the boil, then reduce the heat, cover the pan and simmer for 10–15 minutes until they're almost soft, turning the peaches from time to time.

2 Remove the pan from the heat, carefully lift out the peaches with a slotted spoon, reserving the liquid, and allow them to cool. Remove the skin and place the peaches in a serving dish.

3 Bring the reserved liquid to the boil and bubble for 10 minutes or until it reaches a syrupy consistency. Strain the syrup over the peaches and leave to cool. Decorate the peaches with the vanilla pods and serve with crème fraîche.

Serves 10   preparation: 5 minutes, plus cooling   cooking time: 30 minutes
per serving: 80 cals; 0g fat; 21g carbohydrate

13

Cold desserts

Port and Orange Jellies

125g (4oz) golden granulated sugar	**2tbsp powdered gelatine**
450ml (¾ pint) ruby port	**8 oranges**

1 Line eight 150ml (¼ pint) individual fluted moulds with clingfilm and chill. Put the sugar in a large pan with 600ml (1 pint) cold water. Heat gently to dissolve, then bring to the boil and bubble until the liquid has reduced by half – this will take about 15 minutes.
2 Meanwhile, pour 6tbsp port into a bowl and sprinkle over the gelatine, then put to one side until spongy.
3 In the meantime, using a large sharp knife, cut away the peel and white pith from the oranges, then carefully cut the segments free from the membrane. Discard any pips.
4 Add the rest of the port to the sugar syrup and bring to a simmer. Remove from the heat, add the soaked gelatine mixture and stir until completely dissolved.
5 Stand the orange segments in the flutes of the moulds so they are upright and rest against the edge of the mould. Pour in enough liquid to come halfway up the sides. Chill to set, then pour in the rest of the liquid and chill again.
6 To serve, dip each mould briefly in a bowl of hot water to loosen the surface. Upturn on to individual plates and carefully remove the moulds. Serve at once, with pouring cream.

Serves 8   preparation: 25 minutes, plus setting   cooking time: 15 minutes
per serving: 200 cals; 0g fat; 34g carbohydrate

Sparkling Fruit Jellies

75cl bottle demi-sec or dry sparkling wine	**5tsp powdered gelatine**
300ml (½ pint) red grape juice or cranberry	**125g (4oz) small seedless grapes, halved**
juice	**225g (8oz) raspberries or small strawberries**

1 Pour the sparkling wine into a bowl. Put 4tbsp grape or cranberry juice into a small pan, sprinkle over the gelatine and leave to soak for 5 minutes, then heat very gently until the gelatine is completely dissolved. Stir in the remaining juice, then stir this mixture into the wine.
2 Divide the grapes and raspberries or strawberries among serving glasses, pour in enough of the wine mixture to cover them and chill until just set.
3 Pour on the remaining wine mixture and chill for a further 3–4 hours until set.

Serves 8   preparation: 10 minutes, plus chilling
per serving: 110 cals; trace fat; 10g carbohydrate

13

Cold desserts

Champagne and Ginger Jelly with Ginger Cream

8 gelatine leaves, about 25g (1oz)
175g (6oz) golden caster sugar
pared zest of 2 unwaxed lemons (use a
   vegetable peeler to remove zest in
   long strips)

75cl bottle champagne or sparkling wine
6–8tbsp ginger wine
284ml carton double cream
7 balls stem ginger in syrup, drained,
   plus 2tsp of the syrup

1   Pour 600ml (1 pint) cold water into a bowl. Break up the gelatine, add to the bowl and soak for 5 minutes.
2   Put the sugar in a pan and add the lemon zest and 400ml (14fl oz) cold water. Heat gently to dissolve the sugar, then simmer for 2–3 minutes. Remove from the heat and cool a little, then remove the lemon zest.
3   Lift the soaked gelatine out of the water and add it to the pan. Stir until melted.
4   Stir in the champagne and ginger wine. Ladle the jelly into 10 wine glasses and chill until set.
5   Meanwhile, make the ginger cream. Whip the cream in a bowl until soft peaks form. Chop 3 stem ginger balls and fold into the cream with the ginger syrup. Spoon into a serving dish and chill until ready to serve.
6   Just before serving, cut the remaining stem ginger balls into slivers and sprinkle on to the jellies. Serve with the ginger cream.

Serves 10   preparation: 15 minutes   cooking time: 20 minutes
per serving: 150 cals; 0g fat; 20g carbohydrate

Sloe Gin Jelly

350g (12oz) small black seedless grapes or
   strawberries
300ml (½ pint) sloe gin

125g (4oz) kumquats
2tsp powdered gelatine
75g (3oz) granulated sugar

1   Lightly prick the grapes with a cocktail stick and put in a bowl. Reserve 4tbsp sloe gin and pour the remainder over the grapes; cover and refrigerate for at least 2 hours or overnight.
2   Slice the kumquats. Put the reserved 4tbsp sloe gin in a bowl, sprinkle the gelatine over and leave to soak for 5 minutes.
3   Put 600ml (1 pint) water in a saucepan, add the sugar and cook over a low heat until the sugar has dissolved. Bring to the boil and bubble until the liquid has reduced by half, then leave to cool for 1 minute. Add the soaked gelatine, then stir until melted.
4   Add the macerated grapes and their liquid to the syrup with the kumquats and stir until well mixed. Place in a bowl and refrigerate until the jelly begins to set – about 1 hour.
5   Spoon the jelly into six or eight champagne flutes, then cover and refrigerate for 1 hour or until set. Take the glasses of sloe gin jelly out of the fridge about 30–45 minutes before serving to allow the jelly to soften slightly.

Serves 6–8   preparation: 30 minutes, plus marinating and chilling   cooking time: 15 minutes
per serving: 220–160 cals; trace fat; 36–27g carbohydrate

Strawberry 'Jelly and Ice Cream'

1 pack strawberry jelly cubes
2tbsp kirsch
450g (1lb) strawberries, hulled, plus
   quartered strawberries to decorate

500ml tub good-quality strawberry
   ice cream
mint leaves, to decorate

1 Cut the jelly up and put in a 600ml (1 pint) measuring jug. Pour on 450ml (¾ pint) boiling water and stir until melted. Cool, then add the kirsch.
2 Halve or quarter the strawberries if large. Put them in the base of a 2 litre (3½ pint) serving dish, then pour the jelly over and refrigerate until set.
3 Just before serving, scoop the strawberry ice cream on top of the jelly and decorate with quartered strawberries and mint.

Serves 6   preparation: 20 minutes, plus chilling
per serving: 180 cals; 4g fat; 32g carbohydrate

Tropical Smoothie Jelly

750ml bottle mango and passion fruit
   smoothie

11.7g sachet powdered gelatine
4tbsp half-fat crème fraîche

1 Pour the smoothie into a pan and sprinkle over the gelatine. Heat gently for 3 minutes until hot but not boiling, stirring constantly to dissolve the gelatine.
2 Pour the mixture into a large jug, then divide among four 350ml (12fl oz) tumblers. Cool for 15 minutes, then chill for 3½ hours or until just set.
3 Spoon 1tbsp crème fraîche on top of each jelly and serve.

Serves 4   preparation: 5 minutes, plus chilling   cooking time: 3 minutes
per serving: 120 cals; 3g fat; 23g carbohydrate

Last of the Summer Berries

700g (1½lb) mixed soft fruit, such as
   cherries, blackberries and blueberries
juice of 1 orange

2tbsp golden icing sugar
6tbsp mascarpone
demerara sugar, to sprinkle

1 Put the fruit in a bowl, add the orange juice and icing sugar and stir to mix. Cover and leave to marinate in the fridge for up to 3 hours.
2 Serve with the mascarpone and a sprinkle of demerara sugar.

Serves 6   preparation: 10 minutes, plus marinating
per serving: 150 cals; 7g fat; 21g carbohydrate

Foolproof Meringue

100g (3½oz) egg whites, about 3 eggs   **225g (8oz) golden caster sugar**

1 Put the egg whites and sugar in a large heatproof grease-free bowl set over a pan of very gently simmering water, making sure the base of the bowl doesn't touch the water. Using a wooden spoon, stir the mixture until the sugar has dissolved and the egg white is warm to the touch – about 10 minutes.
2 Remove the bowl from the heat and sit it on a tea-towel on a work surface to prevent it slipping about. Using an electric whisk, beat the egg whites until the mixture is cold, glossy and stands in stiff, shiny peaks when the whisk is lifted from the bowl. This will take a good 15 minutes – any less and the meringue won't hold its shape in the oven.
3 Preheat the oven to 170°C (150°C fan oven) mark 3. Cover one large baking sheet with non-stick baking parchment or a silicone mat. To shape the meringues, hold one dessertspoon in each hand and take a scoop of mixture. With the other spoon, scrape it against the first spoon to lift the mixture off. Repeat twice more to make a rough oval shape, then push on to the lined baking sheet. Repeat to use up all the mixture – you should end up with 12 meringues. Bake for 15 minutes, then turn off the heat and leave the meringues in the oven to dry out overnight.

Makes 12 small meringues   preparation: 25 minutes, plus cooling   cooking time: 15 minutes
per meringue: 80 cals; 0g fat; 20g carbohydrate

Almond Toffee Meringues

flavourless oil, such as safflower, to oil   **1 quantity uncooked Foolproof Meringue**
25g (1oz) light muscovado sugar   **Mixture (above)**
                                         25g (1oz) flaked almonds

1 Preheat the oven to 170°C (150°C fan oven) mark 3 and preheat the grill. Lightly oil a baking sheet and sprinkle over the sugar. Grill for 2–3 minutes or until the sugar has melted and begins to bubble and caramelise. Cool for about 15 minutes, then break the hardened sugar into a food processor or blender and whiz to a coarse powder.
2 Cover two large baking sheets with non-stick baking parchment or silicone mats. Using a large metal spoon, fold half the powdered sugar into the meringue mixture. Spoon four very rough oval mounds of meringue on to the baking sheets, leaving plenty of space between each for them to spread out. Sprinkle with flaked almonds and the remaining powdered sugar.
3 Bake for 20 minutes, then turn off the heat and leave the meringues in the oven to dry out overnight. Serve with marinated fruit and lightly whipped cream – or, for a sharper flavour, a mix of lightly whipped cream and crème fraîche.

Makes 4   preparation: 35 minutes, plus cooling   cooking time: 22–23 minutes
per meringue: 290 cals; 3g fat; 6g carbohydrate

13

Cold desserts

Iced Maple and Walnut Meringue Cake

50g (2oz) walnut pieces, toasted and
   chopped by hand
1 quantity uncooked Foolproof Meringue
   Mixture (page 535)
3 eggs, separated

8tbsp maple syrup
200g (7oz) Greek-style yogurt
12 ripe apricots
juice of ½ orange and ½ lemon

1   Preheat the oven to 170°C (150°C fan oven) mark 3. Line two baking sheets with non-stick baking parchment. Using a felt-tip pen, mark out two 20.5cm (8 inch) diameter circles, then turn the paper over.

2   Fold the nuts into the meringue mixture and spoon about one-third of the mixture on to one of the marked circles. Using a palette knife, smooth the meringue over the circle to fill it evenly. Fill the second circle with rough dollops of the remaining meringue, making sure there are no holes. Bake for 15 minutes, then turn off the heat and leave the meringues in the oven to dry out overnight.

3   To make the filling, put the egg yolks and half the maple syrup in a bowl set over a pan of simmering water. Whisk until thick and moussey, then fold in the yogurt.

4   Whisk the egg whites in a clean grease-free bowl until soft peaks form, then fold them into the yogurt mixture. Pour into a freezerproof container and freeze for 30 minutes. Beat the mixture to break down the ice crystals and freeze again for 30 minutes. Beat the mixture once more and freeze for another 30 minutes.

5   Put the thin meringue base on to a large sheet of foil and spoon on the frozen yogurt mixture. Press the second meringue round lightly on top, wrap in clingfilm and return to the freezer for at least 1 hour or up to one week.

6   To serve, halve and stone the apricots and put in a bowl with the remaining maple syrup and the orange and lemon juice. Stir, then cover and chill until needed. About 2 hours before serving, put the cake in the fridge to soften. Cut into wedges and serve with the fruit.

Serves 8   preparation: 45 minutes, plus cooling and freezing   cooking time: 15 minutes
per serving: 260 cals; 6g fat; 47g carbohydrate

Strawberry and Meringue Sundae

700g (1½lb) strawberries, hulled and
   quartered
75g (3oz) ready-made meringue nests,
   roughly crushed

142ml carton double cream, lightly whipped
500ml tub good-quality strawberry ice
   cream or frozen yogurt

1   Layer the strawberries, meringue, whipped cream and the ice cream or frozen yogurt in six large sundae glasses, finishing with a layer of strawberries. Serve the sundae immediately.

Serves 6   preparation: 5 minutes
per serving: 335 cals; 24g fat; 36g carbohydrate

Cold desserts

Strawberry Meringue Crush

150ml (¼ pint) double cream
200g (7oz) thick Greek-style yogurt
500g (1lb 2oz) strawberries, hulled

2tbsp crème de cassis
5 ready-made meringue nests

1   Lightly whip the cream until soft peaks form, then fold in the yogurt and chill for 30 minutes. Put half the strawberries into a food processor, whiz to a purée, then stir in the crème de cassis. Reserve 6tbsp of the purée for decoration.
2   Slice the remaining strawberries, reserving six for decoration, and put into a bowl. Pour the strawberry purée over them, cover and leave to macerate in the fridge for 20 minutes.
3   Break up the meringue nests and carefully fold into the cream mixture, with the strawberry mixture. Divide among glass serving bowls. Drizzle 1tbsp reserved strawberry purée over each serving and top with a halved strawberry.

Serves 6   preparation: 15 minutes, plus chilling
per serving: 270 cals; 15g fat; 28g carbohydrate

Lemon and Mango Meringue Cake

5 egg whites
300g (11oz) golden caster sugar
25g (1oz) flaked almonds, toasted
125g (4oz) mascarpone

1 each 284ml and 142ml cartons
   double cream
125g (4oz) good-quality lemon curd
1 small mango, peeled and sliced

1   Preheat the oven to 140°C (120°C fan oven) mark 1. Put the egg whites in a clean grease-free bowl and whisk until stiff peaks form. Whisk in 3tbsp sugar, then gently fold in the remaining sugar with a metal spoon.
2   Line three baking sheets with baking parchment. Using a plate or cake tin as a template, mark a 20.5cm (8 inch) circle in the middle of each piece of parchment. Turn the sheets over and put two large spoonfuls of the meringue mixture into the middle of each circle. Using the back of a metal spoon or a palette knife, spread the mixture roughly to fill the circles, then sprinkle a few almonds over the top of each meringue circle. Bake for 1½–2 hours or until firm. Remove from the oven, carefully peel off the parchment paper, then cool the meringue circles on a wire rack.
3   Put the mascarpone in a bowl and beat to loosen it. In a separate bowl, whip the cartons of cream until soft peaks form. Add half the cream to the mascarpone and, using a metal spoon, fold it in, then add the remaining cream along with the lemon curd. Fold carefully into the mixture.
4   Spread the cream mixture evenly over two of the meringue circles and top each one with some slices of mango. Sandwich the circles together carefully, placing the third meringue on top, and serve.

Serves 8   preparation: 25 minutes   cooking time: 1½–2 hours
per serving: 560 cals; 38g fat; 52g carbohydrate

13

Cold desserts

Brown Sugar Meringue Roulade

5 large egg whites
175g (6oz) golden caster sugar
125g (4oz) light muscovado sugar
50g (2oz) shelled, unsalted pistachio nuts,
 roughly chopped
284ml carton double cream
50g (2oz) stem ginger in syrup, drained and
 sliced, plus 1tbsp of the syrup

1 tbsp dark rum (optional)
150g (5oz) fresh pineapple, peeled and
 roughly chopped
1 small ripe mango, peeled and roughly
 chopped
icing sugar, to dust

1 Preheat the oven to 200°C (180°C fan oven) mark 6. Line a 23 x 33cm (9 x 13 inch) Swiss roll tin with non-stick baking parchment. Using an electric whisk, beat the egg whites in a clean grease-free bowl until stiff, then add both sugars, 1tbsp at a time, whisking well after each addition until the mixture is stiff and glossy.
2 Spoon into the prepared tin and level the surface with a round-bladed knife. Sprinkle over half the nuts. Bake for 10–15 minutes or until golden brown and puffed, then reduce the oven temperature to 170°C (150°C fan oven) mark 3 and bake for 20–25 minutes or until firm to the touch. Remove from the oven and cool for 5 minutes, then invert on to a sheet of greaseproof paper and cool for 15 minutes.
3 Whip the cream until soft peaks form, then fold in the ginger, ginger syrup and rum, if using. Trim the edges of the meringue, spread the cream just to the edges and top with the fruit.
4 With a long edge facing you, carefully roll up the meringue, using the greaseproof paper to help. Chill for at least 2 hours. The roulade will keep for a day, or can be frozen at this stage.
5 To serve, sprinkle over the rest of the nuts and dust with icing sugar.

Serves 8   preparation: 45 minutes, plus cooling and chilling   cooking time: 40 minutes
per serving: 410 cals; 20g fat; 56g carbohydrate

13

Cold desserts

Apricot and Almond Roulade

butter, to grease
25g (1oz) flaked almonds
5 large eggs, separated
150g (5oz) golden caster sugar, plus extra
   to dust
1tsp vanilla extract

125g (4oz) white almond paste, grated
3tbsp plain white flour
3tbsp Amaretto liqueur
6 ripe apricots
300ml (½ pint) crème fraîche

1 Preheat the oven to 180°C (160°C fan oven) mark 4. Grease a 33 x 23cm (13 x 9 inch) Swiss-roll tin with butter and line with greased non-stick baking parchment. Scatter the flaked almonds evenly over the paper.

2 Whisk the egg yolks with 125g (4oz) sugar until pale and fluffy. Stir in the vanilla extract and grated almond paste. Sift the flour over the mixture then, using a metal spoon, fold in lightly.

3 Whisk the egg whites in another bowl until they are stiff but not dry. Gradually whisk in the remaining caster sugar. Using a large metal spoon, fold a quarter of the egg whites into the almond mixture to loosen it, then carefully fold in the remainder.

4 Turn the mixture into the prepared tin, gently easing it into the corners. Bake for about 20 minutes or until well risen and just firm to the touch. Remove from the oven, cover with a sheet of non-stick baking parchment and a damp tea-towel and leave until cool.

5 Remove the tea-towel and invert the roulade (and the paper) on to a sugar-dusted piece of baking parchment. Peel off the lining paper very slowly and carefully. Drizzle the roulade with the amaretto liqueur.

6 For the filling, halve and stone the apricots, then cut them into small pieces. Spread the roulade evenly with the crème fraîche and scatter the apricots over the top.

7 Starting from one of the narrow ends, carefully roll up the roulade, using the baking parchment to help. Transfer the roulade to a serving plate and dust with sugar to serve.

Serves 8 preparation: 20 minutes, plus standing   cooking time: 20 minutes
per serving: 420 cals; 25g fat; 39g carbohydrate

Cold desserts

Easy Vanilla Ice Cream

6 eggs, separated
125g (4oz) golden syrup
568ml carton double cream, chilled

seeds from 2 split vanilla pods, or 2tbsp
vanilla paste

1 Put the egg yolks and syrup into a large bowl. Using an electric hand whisk or freestanding mixer, whisk together for 4–6 minutes until the mixture leaves a ribbon-like trail when you lift the whisk. Pour the cream into a separate bowl and whisk until it starts to thicken and hold its shape, then use a large metal spoon to fold it into the egg mixture. Whisk briefly to combine, then chill.
2 Wash the whisk well. Put the egg whites in a clean grease-free bowl and whisk until soft peaks form. Using a large metal spoon, add one spoonful of egg white to the chilled egg yolk, syrup and cream mixture and stir thoroughly. Add the remaining egg white and the vanilla seeds or paste and fold in, taking care not to knock out the air.
3 Pour the mixture into a 1 litre (1¾ pint) shallow freezerproof container and freeze for at least 6 hours until firm. Leave to soften in the fridge for up to 20 minutes before serving.

Serves 10   preparation: 15 minutes, plus freezing
per serving: 350 cals; 31g fat; 11g carbohydrate

Cinnamon and Nutmeg Ice Cream

½tsp each ground cinnamon and freshly
   grated nutmeg
50g (2oz) golden caster sugar

142ml carton double cream
250g tub mascarpone
400g carton fresh custard

1 Put the cinnamon, nutmeg, sugar and cream in a small pan, bring slowly to the boil, then put to one side to cool.
2 Put the mascarpone in a large bowl and beat until smooth. Stir in the custard and the cooled spiced cream. Pour the mixture into a shallow freezer container and freeze for 2–3 hours.
3 Beat to break up the ice crystals and freeze for a further 2–3 hours before using. The ice cream will keep in the freezer for up to one month.

Serves 8   preparation: 10 minutes, plus freezing   cooking time: 5 minutes
per serving: 290 cals; 24g fat; 17g carbohydrate

13

Cold desserts

Burnt Honey and Thyme Ice Cream

600ml (1 pint) full-fat milk
568ml carton double cream
8 thyme sprigs

150ml (¼ pint) dark clear honey, plus extra
to drizzle
6 large egg yolks

1 Put the milk, cream and thyme sprigs in a pan and bring to the boil. Remove from the heat and leave for 20–30 minutes to infuse. Strain the milk and discard the thyme sprigs.

2 Put the honey in a small pan and heat gently. Bring to the boil and bubble for 4–5 minutes or until it has a slight burnt caramel smell. Remove from the heat and immediately place the saucepan in a bowl of cold water to stop the cooking process. Put aside.

3 Put the egg yolks in a bowl and slowly whisk in the infused milk until thoroughly combined. Return the mixture to the clean pan and cook over a gentle heat, stirring until thickened (don't boil). Strain the mixture into the honey and stir until well combined. (It may be necessary to warm the mixture gently.) Leave the custard mixture to cool, then cover and chill for 30 minutes.

4 Put the chilled mixture in an ice cream machine and freeze according to the manufacturer's instructions. Alternatively, put the custard mixture in a clean enamelled or stainless steel roasting tin and freeze for about 1 hour. Stir the ice cream as it begins to set around the edges and return to the freezer (this will take 4–6 hours). Repeat until the ice cream is completely frozen, then transfer to a freezerproof container and return to the freezer. Serve the ice cream drizzled with honey and accompanied by crisp sweet biscuits.

Serves 6   preparation: 5 minutes, plus infusing, chilling and freezing   cooking time: 20 minutes
per serving: 660 cals; 55g fat; 34g carbohydrate

13

Cold desserts

Apricot and Ginger Ice Cream

600g (1¼lb 0oz) ripe apricots, stoned
3tbsp golden caster sugar
250g tub mascarpone
284ml carton double cream
200g (7oz) golden icing sugar

50g (2oz) brown breadcrumbs
50g (2oz) stem ginger in syrup, drained and
   finely chopped, plus 6tbsp of the syrup
mango and lime coulis

1 Line a 900g (2lb) loaf tin with clingfilm. Put 400g (14oz) apricots in a blender, add the caster sugar and whiz to a coarse purée.
2 Put the mascarpone, cream and icing sugar into a large bowl and whisk with an electric hand whisk until smooth.
3 Add the breadcrumbs and half the purée, then fold in. Add the remaining purée, the chopped ginger and syrup and fold in gently. Pour into the lined loaf tin and freeze for at least 6 hours.
4 Transfer to the fridge 30 minutes before serving. Slice the remaining apricots.
5 Unwrap the clingfilm, upturn the ice cream on to a board and slice. Put one slice on each plate, drizzle with the coulis, decorate with the apricots and serve.

Serves 6–8   preparation: 15 minutes, plus freezing and chilling
per serving: 480 cals; 32g fat; 50g carbohydrate

Spicy Ginger Ice Cream

568ml carton double cream
175g (6oz) golden caster sugar, plus 1tbsp
4 eggs, separated
2tsp ground ginger

50g (2oz) unsalted butter
2tbsp whisky
4 balls stem ginger in syrup, drained and
   roughly chopped, plus 2tbsp of the syrup

1 Whisk the cream until just thickened, then chill. Whisk 125g (4oz) sugar with the egg yolks until pale and creamy.
2 Beat the egg whites in a clean grease-free bowl until stiff peaks form. Beat in the 1tbsp sugar.
3 Fold the cream into the egg and sugar mixture with the ground ginger, then quickly fold in the beaten egg whites. Pour into a freezerproof container and freeze for 4 hours.
4 To make the sauce, put the butter, remaining sugar, the whisky and ginger syrup in a pan and heat gently. Bring to the boil, then reduce the heat and simmer for 5 minutes until thick. Take off the heat and leave to cool.
5 Fold the stem ginger through the ice cream and drizzle the sauce over. Stir once or twice to create a ripple effect and continue to freeze for 4 hours or overnight. Serve with brandy snaps.

Serves 8   preparation: 30 minutes, plus freezing   cooking time: 5 minutes
per serving: 520 cals; 43g fat; 28g carbohydrate

13

Cold desserts

Zabaglione Ice Cream

50g (2oz) golden caster sugar
4 large egg yolks
250ml (8fl oz) double cream
4tbsp Malmsey Madeira or dark
cream sherry

50g (2oz) macaroons or ratafia biscuits,
roughly crushed
25g (1oz) shelled pistachio nuts, chopped

1 Line a 450g (1lb) loaf tin with clingfilm or non-stick baking parchment. Put the sugar in a small pan with 125ml (8fl oz) water and bring slowly to the boil, making sure the sugar is dissolved before boiling. Bubble for 3 minutes.
2 Put the egg yolks in a heatproof bowl and whisk until light and fluffy. Gradually whisk in the hot sugar syrup.
3 Sit the bowl over a pan of barely simmering water with the water just touching the bowl. Cook, stirring, for about 15 minutes or until the mixture is thickened and coats the back of the spoon. Be careful the mixture doesn't get too hot or the eggs will scramble.
4 Remove the bowl from the heat and, using an electric whisk, whisk for 10 minutes or until the mixture is thick, glossy, cold and almost doubled in volume. Cover and chill for 30 minutes.
5 Whisk the cream with the Madeira or sherry until it holds soft peaks. Carefully fold into the chilled egg mixture. Spoon into the prepared tin and freeze overnight.
6 Just before serving, turn the ice cream out on to a chilled serving dish and peel away the clingfilm. Mix the macaroons with the pistachios and gently press them over the top and the long sides of the ice cream. Cut into slices and serve.

13

Serves 4 preparation: 15 minutes, plus chilling and freezing cooking time: 30 minutes
per serving: 510 cals; 40g fat; 27 carbohydrate

Cold desserts

Pistachio and Date Ice Cream

100g (3½oz) shelled pistachio nuts
218g can condensed milk
284ml carton double cream
1tbsp orange flower water

125g (4oz) fresh Medjool dates, pitted and
roughly chopped
3 pomegranates

1   Reserve 15g (½oz) pistachio nuts and put the rest in a food processor. Add the condensed milk and whiz for 1–2 minutes to roughly chop the nuts and flavour the milk.
2   Pour the cream into a bowl and whip until soft peaks form. Stir in the chopped pistachios and condensed milk, orange flower water and dates.
3   Line six 150ml (¼ pint) dariole moulds or empty, clean yogurt pots with heavy-duty clingfilm (leave the edges overhanging). Spoon in the cream mixture and freeze for at least 5 hours.
4   Cut the pomegranates in half, scoop out the seeds and push them through a sieve to extract the juice. Put the liquid in a pan and bring to the boil, then simmer for 8 minutes until reduced to a syrup. Cool, put in a small airtight container and chill until needed.
5   To serve, ease the ice cream out of the moulds and remove the clingfilm. Cut each in half vertically and arrange on serving plates. Chop the remaining pistachios and sprinkle them over, then drizzle around some pomegranate sauce.

Serves 6   preparation: 15 minutes, plus freezing
per serving: 460 cals; 32g fat; 38g carbohydrate

Cognac and Crème Fraîche Ice Cream

500ml carton full-fat crème fraîche
175g (6oz) golden icing sugar, sifted

4tbsp special reserve Cognac

1   Whisk the crème fraîche, sugar and Cognac together – it will become thin, but continue whisking until it thickens slightly.
2   Pour into a 450g (1lb) loaf tin lined with clingfilm, cover and freeze for up to one month.

Serves 8   preparation: 5 minutes, plus freezing
per serving: 340 cals; 25g fat; 25g carbohydrate

13

Cold desserts

Brandy and Toffee Mascarpone Ice Cream

4 x 250g tubs mascarpone	250g (9oz) golden icing sugar
2 vanilla pods, split lengthways	4tbsp brandy or bourbon
4 eggs	8tbsp banoffee toffee dulce de leche

1 Turn your freezer to the fast-freeze setting. Empty the four tubs of mascarpone into a large mixing bowl. Using the pointed end of the knife, scrape all the tiny seeds out of the vanilla pods, then add these to the mascarpone.

2 Whisk the eggs and sugar in a heatproof bowl set over a pan of simmering water for about 15 minutes until pale, thickened, moussey and almost tripled in volume. Pour on to the vanilla and mascarpone mixture, then add 2tbsp brandy or bourbon and combine with a hand held electric mixer. Pour into a clean roasting tin and freeze in the tin for 1–1½ hours.

3 Put the banoffee toffee sauce into a small heavy-based pan with the remaining brandy or bourbon. Heat gently and stir to combine, then leave to cool for 3–4 minutes. Alternatively, half fill a bowl with boiling water, then rest another bowl on top. Put the banoffee toffee and remaining brandy or bourbon into the top bowl and mix well. Leave to cool for 3–4 minutes.

4 Remove the ice cream from the freezer, whisk to break up the ice crystals and put half into a 1.8kg (4lb) loaf tin. Drizzle half the cooled brandy sauce mixture on to the ice cream, drag a skewer through it several times to create a swirled effect, then repeat using the remaining ice cream and brandy sauce. Drag the skewer through the sauce again, then cover and freeze for at least 5 hours. Use within a month.

Serves 16   preparation: 15 minutes, plus cooling and freezing   cooking time: 20 minutes
per serving: 255 cals; 33g fat; 44g carbohydrate

Cold desserts

Orange Ice Cream

4 large egg yolks
300g (11oz) golden caster sugar, plus extra
    to dust
284ml carton single cream

450ml (¾ pint) double cream
8 large unwaxed oranges
2tbsp Grand Marnier or orange liqueur
1tsp orange flower water

1 Beat together the egg yolks and 175g (6oz) sugar until pale and creamy. Pour the single and double creams into a pan and bring to the boil, then beat into the egg and sugar mixture.
2 Return the custard to a clean pan and heat gently until the mixture thickens slightly – about 5 minutes. Take off the heat and cool.
3 Cut about 1cm (½ inch) off the top of each orange and reserve, then cut the flesh away from the inside, leaving a shell. Cut about 5mm (¼ inch) off the bottom.
4 Use a canelle knife to carve a pattern on the orange shells, then freeze them. Put the top and bottom peels to one side. Whiz the orange flesh in a processor, then sieve to extract all the juice – you should end up with about 400ml (14fl oz).
5 Add the juice to the custard mixture and stir in the liqueur. Churn in an ice cream machine until frozen, spoon into a freezerproof container and freeze for 1 hour. Alternatively, pour into a freezerproof container and freeze, beating every hour until frozen (about 4 hours).
6 Put the remaining sugar in a pan with 100ml (3½fl oz) cold water. Heat gently to dissolve the sugar, bring to the boil and boil for 4–5 minutes until syrupy. Add the reserved orange peel and cook for 2 minutes. Lift the peel out, place on greaseproof paper and dust immediately with sugar. Leave to dry, then pack in an airtight container.
7 Once the ice cream is frozen, spoon into the orange shells and freeze. Put the leftover ice cream in a freezerproof container and freeze.
8 Take the orange shells out of freezer 10–15 minutes before serving. To serve, scoop a ball of ice cream on top of each orange shell and decorate with the orange peel.

Serves 8 preparation: 45 minutes, plus freezing   cooking time: 12 minutes
per serving: 310 cals; 10g fat; 52g carbohydrate

Yogurt Ice Cream

4 large egg yolks
125g (4oz) icing sugar

142ml carton double cream
300g (10oz) Greek-style yogurt

1 Beat the egg yolks and the sugar with a whisk until thick.
2 In a separate bowl, whip the cream until it begins to thicken, then fold in the yogurt. Fold this into the egg mixture. Pour into a shallow container, cover and freeze.

Serves 4–6 preparation: 20 minutes, plus freezing
per serving: 440–290 cals; 30–20g fat; 35–24g carbohydrate

Ginger, Rum and Raisin Ice Cream

75g (3oz) raisins
3tbsp dark rum
4 balls stem ginger in syrup, drained and
diced, plus 2tbsp of the syrup, plus extra
chopped stem ginger to serve (optional)

1 quantity Easy Vanilla Ice cream
(page 545), frozen for 4 hours until
almost firm

1 Put the raisins in a small bowl, add the rum and leave to soak for 30 minutes.
2 Using a wooden spoon, beat the rum, raisins, ginger and syrup into the ice cream. Return to the freezer for at least 2 hours until firm.
3 Leave the ice cream to soften in the fridge for about 20 minutes before serving. Serve with thin ginger biscuits and sprinkle extra chopped stem ginger on top, if you want to.

Serves 10 preparation: 20 minutes, plus soaking and freezing
per serving: 380 cals; 31g fat; 18g carbohydrate

Cinnamon Crumble Ice Cream Sundae

150g (5oz) plain flour
75g (3oz) light muscovado sugar
75g (3oz) butter
2tsp ground cinnamon

1 quantity Easy Vanilla Ice Cream
(page 545), frozen for 2½ hours until
starting to firm up
sliced bananas, chocolate sauce and grated
chocolate, to sprinkle

1 Preheat the oven to 190°C (170°C fan oven) mark 5. Put the flour in a large bowl, add the sugar, butter and cinnamon and rub in until the mixture looks like crumbs. Spread out the crumble on a non-stick baking sheet and bake for 10 minutes or until golden. Cool for 10 minutes, then break into pea-sized pieces – any larger and the finished ice cream will be too lumpy, any smaller and they'll disappear – and set aside one-third.
2 Using a wooden spoon, stir the remaining crumble into the ice cream. Return to the freezer for at least 2 hours until firm.
3 Soften the ice cream in the fridge for about 20 minutes before serving. Put a layer each of bananas, chocolate sauce and ice cream in tall sundae glasses. Decorate with a sprinkling of reserved crumble and grated chocolate and serve at once.

Serves 10 preparation: 25 minutes, plus freezing   cooking time: 10 minutes
per serving (ice cream only): 520 cals; 37g fat; 37g carbohydrate

13

Cold desserts

Mascarpone Ice Cream Cake

2tsp instant espresso coffee powder
4tbsp Tia Maria
12–16 sponge fingers
2 eggs, separated
75g (3oz) golden caster sugar

250g tub mascarpone
4tbsp Marsala
1tsp vanilla extract
25g (1oz) plain dark chocolate, grated

1 Double-line a 900g (2lb) loaf tin with clingfilm. Dissolve the coffee in 4tbsp boiling water, add the Tia Maria and set aside. Use half the sponge fingers, placed widthways and sugared-side down, to line the base of the loaf tin – you may need to trim them – then put to one side.
2 Put the egg whites in a clean grease-free bowl and whisk until stiff. Add the sugar 1tbsp at a time and continue to whisk until the mixture stands in stiff peaks.
3 In a separate bowl, beat together the mascarpone, egg yolks, Marsala and vanilla extract. Using a metal spoon, mix in a large spoonful of the egg whites, then carefully fold in the rest. Drizzle two-thirds of the coffee mixture over the sponge fingers and sprinkle the chocolate over. Spoon the mascarpone mixture into the tin and smooth the top. Arrange the remaining sponge fingers widthways on top and finish by drizzling over the remaining coffee mixture. Cover and freeze for 5 hours.
4 To serve, unwrap and upturn on to a large serving plate, then carefully lift off the loaf tin, remove the clingfilm and cut into slices.

Serves 6 preparation: 15 minutes, plus freezing
per serving: 370 cals; 23g fat; 28g carbohydrate

Banana and Chocolate Ice Cream Pie

500ml tub good-quality chocolate ice cream
flavourless oil, such as safflower, to oil
75g (3oz) butter or olive oil spread
200g pack plain chocolate digestive
  biscuits

2 large bananas
juice of ½ lemon
1 king-size Mars bar, cut into thin
  slivers and chilled

1 Take the ice cream out of the freezer and let it soften. Oil a 20.5cm (8 inch) loose-based fluted flan tin and line the base with greaseproof paper. Put the butter or olive oil spread in a bowl and microwave on High for 1 minute (based on a 900W oven).
2 Put the biscuits into a food processor and whiz until they resemble coarse breadcrumbs. Pour the melted fat into the processor and blend with the biscuits to combine. Press into the base of the prepared tin.
3 Peel and slice the bananas and toss in the lemon juice, then scatter over the biscuit base. Upturn the ice cream tub on to the bananas and use a palette knife to spread it evenly, covering the fruit.
4 Scatter the Mars bar slices over the ice cream and freeze for at least 1 hour before slicing.

Serves 8 preparation: 15 minutes, plus freezing
per serving: 330 cals; 19g fat; 39g carbohydrate

Mango Ice Cream Terrine

flavourless oil, such as safflower, to oil
2 small mangoes, peeled and chopped
2 eggs
125g (4oz) golden caster sugar

284ml carton double cream, whipped
1½tbsp Malibu
4 ratafia biscuits

1   Lightly oil a 900g (2lb) loaf tin, then line with clingfilm, leaving enough to hang over the edges and smoothing any creases.
2   Whiz the mangoes in a food processor until smooth, then put to one side.
3   Put the eggs and sugar into a large bowl and, using an electric hand whisk, mix until thick – this should take 5 minutes.
4   Add the whipped cream to the mixture and fold together with a large metal spoon. Fold in three-quarters of the puréed mango and the Malibu. Spoon the remaining mango purée into the lined tin to cover the base, then pour in the ice cream mixture. Cover with the overhanging clingfilm and freeze overnight (or for up to one month).
5   Remove the ice cream from the freezer 5 minutes before serving. Roughly crush the biscuits. Unwrap the clingfilm, turn the terrine out on to a serving dish, cover with the biscuits, slice and serve.

Serves 8   preparation: 20–25 minutes, plus freezing
per serving: 280 cals; 19g fat; 26g carbohydrate

13

Blueberry Cheesecake

1 large sponge flan case
flavourless oil, such as safflower, to oil
300g pack cream cheese
1tsp vanilla extract
100g (3½oz) golden caster sugar

142ml carton soured cream
2 eggs
2tbsp cornflour
150g (5oz) blueberries
2tbsp redcurrant jelly

1   Preheat the oven to 180°C (160°C fan oven) mark 4. Use the base of a 20.5cm (8 inch) spring-release cake tin to cut out a circle from the flan case, discarding (or eating!) the edges. Oil the tin and line the base with greaseproof paper, then put the flan base into it. Press down with your fingers.
2   Put the cream cheese, vanilla, sugar, soured cream, eggs and cornflour into a processor and whiz until evenly combined.
3   Pour the mixture over the flan base and shake gently to level. Bake for 45 minutes until just set and pale golden. Turn off the oven and leave the cheesecake inside with the door ajar for about 30 minutes. Remove from the oven, cool and chill.
4   To serve, put the blueberries into a pan with the redcurrant jelly and heat through until the jelly has melted and the blueberries have softened slightly, or microwave on High for 1 minute (based on a 900W oven). Spoon on top of the cheesecake. Cool and chill for 15 minutes before serving.

Serves 8   preparation: 15 minutes, plus chilling   cooking time: 45 minutes
per serving: 430 cals; 31g fat; 34g carbohydrate

Italian Ice Cream Cake

400g (14oz) fresh cherries, pitted and quartered

4tbsp Amaretto liqueur

10tbsp crème de cacao

200g pack (containing 24) Savoiardi biscuits or sponge fingers

5 egg yolks

150g (5oz) golden caster sugar

450ml (¾ pint) double cream, lightly whipped

1tbsp vanilla extract

75g (3oz) pistachios or hazelnuts, roughly chopped in a food processor

75g (3oz) plain dark chocolate, roughly chopped in a food processor

2–3tbsp cocoa powder

2–3tbsp golden icing sugar

1 Put the cherries and Amaretto in a bowl, stir, cover with clingfilm and leave while you assemble the other ingredients.

2 Pour the crème de cacao into a shallow dish and take out a large chopping board. Quickly dip a sponge finger into the liqueur – on one side only, so it doesn't go soggy and fall apart – then put on to the board and cut in half lengthways to separate the sugary side from the base. Repeat with each biscuit.

3 Double-line a 24 x 4cm (9½ x 1½ inch) round tin with clingfilm. Arrange the sugar-coated sponge finger halves, sugar side down, on the base of the tin. Drizzle with any remaining crème de cacao.

4 Put the egg yolks and sugar into a bowl and whisk with an electric mixer until pale, light and fluffy. Fold in the cream, vanilla extract, pistachios or hazelnuts, chocolate and cherries, plus any remaining Amaretto. Spoon the mixture on top of the sponge fingers in the tin.

5 Cover the ice cream filling with the remaining sponge finger halves, cut side down. Cover with clingfilm and freeze for at least 5 hours.

6 Before serving, upturn the cake on to a serving plate, ease away the clingfilm and discard. Leave at room temperature for 20 minutes, if the weather is warm, 40 minutes at cool room temperature, or 1 hour in the fridge to allow the cherries to defrost and the ice cream to become 'semi-freddo' – half-frozen yet moussey. Sift cocoa and icing sugar over the top of the cake and cut into wedges.

Serves 10 preparation: 40 minutes, plus freezing
per serving: 540 cals; 32g fat; 54g carbohydrate

13

Cold desserts

Coconut and Mango Tart

125g (4oz) plain flour, plus extra to dust

65g (2½oz) firm, unsalted butter, diced

3tbsp golden caster sugar, plus 75g (3oz)

40g (1½oz) desiccated coconut

1 egg yolk, plus 3 whole eggs

2 small ripe mangoes

75ml (3fl oz) freshly squeezed orange juice

15g (½oz) cornflour

400ml can coconut milk

142ml carton double cream

toasted coconut shreds, to decorate

icing sugar, to dust

1 To make the pastry, sift the flour into a bowl, then rub in the diced butter using your fingertips. Stir in 1tbsp caster sugar and the desiccated coconut. Add the egg yolk and about 2tbsp cold water and mix to a firm dough. Knead lightly, wrap and chill for 30 minutes.

2 Preheat the oven to 200°C (180°C fan oven) mark 6. Roll out the pastry thinly on a lightly floured surface and use to line a 24 x 4cm deep (9½ x 1½ inch) loose-based flan tin, pressing the pastry into the tin. Line the pastry case with greaseproof paper and fill with baking beans and bake for 15 minutes. Remove the paper and beans and bake for 5 minutes. Remove from the oven and reduce the oven temperature to 150°C (130°C fan oven) mark 2.

3 Meanwhile, make the filling. Cut the mangoes into thin slices, discarding the skin and stones. Place the slices in a heavy-based pan with the orange juice and 2tbsp caster sugar. Bring to a simmer and cook gently for 3–5 minutes until the mango slices are softened but still retain their shape. Cool slightly.

4 Beat the whole eggs and the remaining caster sugar together in a bowl. Blend the cornflour with a little of the coconut milk in a pan. Add the remaining coconut milk and bring to the boil, stirring until thickened. Remove from the heat and stir in the double cream. Pour over the egg mixture, stirring constantly until smooth.

5 Drain the mangoes, reserving the juice, and arrange evenly in the pastry case. Stir the reserved juice into the coconut custard and ladle it over the mangoes. Bake for about 30 minutes until the custard is just set, then remove from the oven – it will continue to firm up as it cools. Leave to cool, then chill for several hours, preferably overnight. Decorate the tart with toasted coconut shreds and dust with icing sugar to serve.

Serves 10   preparation: 35 minutes, plus chilling   cooking time: 50 minutes
per serving: 380 cals; 25g fat; 37g carbohydrate

Cold desserts

Lemon and Strawberry Cheesecake

flavourless oil, such as safflower, to oil
75g (3oz) almonds, toasted
175g (6oz) ginger biscuits
50g (2oz) butter, melted
4 large lemons

2 x 405g cans condensed milk
568ml carton double cream
700g (1½lb) strawberries, hulled
2tbsp icing sugar

1 Lightly brush a 23cm (9 inch) spring-release tin with oil and line the base with baking parchment. Alternatively, oil a similar-sized deep flan ring and place on an oiled baking sheet.
2 Put the toasted almonds in a food processor and whiz until roughly chopped. Add the biscuits and whiz until almost smooth. Pour in the melted butter and mix well. Press the biscuit mixture into the base of the tin and chill for at least 30 minutes.
3 Meanwhile, grate the zest and squeeze the juice of the lemons – there should be about 200ml (7fl oz) juice. Pour the condensed milk into a bowl and slowly whisk in the cream. Stirring constantly, add the lemon zest and juice a little at a time (the mixture should thicken dramatically as you do this). Pour the lemon mixture over the biscuit base, then smooth the top and refrigerate for several hours, or overnight, to set.
4 To make the strawberry sauce, put 450g (1lb) strawberries in a food processor with the sugar. Whiz until the strawberries are well broken down, then sieve. Cut the remaining strawberries into small pieces and stir into the sauce.
5 Carefully remove the chilled cheesecake from the tin and serve with the strawberry sauce.

Serves 8 preparation: 40 minutes, plus chilling
per serving: 830 cals; 48g fat; 90g carbohydrate

13

Cold desserts

Caramelised Orange Trifle

125g (4oz) light muscovado sugar
2 x 135g packs orange jelly, broken into
  cubes
100ml (3½fl oz) brandy
10 oranges
150g pack ratafia biscuits
4tbsp sweet sherry

500g carton fresh custard
2 x 250g tubs mascarpone
284ml carton double cream
¼tsp vanilla extract
flavourless oil, such as safflower, to oil
125g (4oz) granulated sugar

1 Put the muscovado sugar in a large heavy-based pan, add 100ml (3½fl oz) water and dissolve the sugar over a low heat. Increase the heat and cook for about 5 minutes until the sugar is syrupy and thick.

2 Remove the pan from the heat (stand back as sugar will splutter) and add 450ml (¾ pint) boiling water. Add the jelly and stir until dissolved, then add the brandy and put to one side.

3 Cut the peel off each orange, removing all pith. Slice the flesh into rounds, reserving any juice. Add the juice – about 125ml (4fl oz) – to the jelly and leave to cool.

4 Tip the ratafias into a 3.5 litre (6¼ pint) bowl and drizzle with sherry. Put the orange rounds on top, then pour the jelly over. Chill for 4 hours until set.

5 Pour the custard on top and smooth over. Put the mascarpone, cream and vanilla extract in a bowl and combine with an electric hand mixer. Spoon three-quarters of the mixture on to the custard and smooth the surface. Put the remainder in a piping bag and pipe ten swirls around the edge. Chill.

6 Line a large baking sheet with baking parchment and grease it with oil. Half-fill the sink with cold water. Put the granulated sugar in a heavy-based pan and heat gently until it has dissolved. Increase the heat and cook the sugar to a golden caramel. Immediately plunge the base of the pan into the sink. Take the pan out of the sink and rest it next to the parchment. Dip a fork into the caramel to pick up the syrup, then hold it high over the parchment and flick backwards and forwards over the paper – as the sugar cools it will form very thin threads and build up a golden nest of spun sugar. Leave on the parchment until ready to serve, then lift on to the trifle.

Serves 16   preparation: 45 minutes, plus setting   cooking time: 5 minutes
per serving: 440 cals; 25g fat; 49g carbohydrate

13

Cold desserts

Tropical Fruit Trifle

1 small ripe mango and 1 small pineapple, each peeled and sliced	425g can mango slices in syrup, drained
1 ripe papaya, peeled, deseeded and sliced	500g carton fresh custard
1 banana, peeled, sliced and tossed in juice of 1 lemon	200g (7oz) mascarpone
	1tbsp golden icing sugar
125g (4oz) amaretti biscuits	142ml carton double cream
4tbsp dark rum	flavourless oil, such as safflower, to oil
	125g (4oz) granulated sugar

1 Layer the mango, pineapple, papaya and banana in a 3 litre (5 pint) glass bowl, then top with the biscuits. Pour the rum over.
2 Purée the mango slices in a food processor until smooth, then pour in the custard and whiz to mix. Spoon over the fruit.
3 Beat the mascarpone with the icing sugar, add the cream and beat until thick. Spread over the custard and chill.
4 Line a large baking sheet with baking parchment and grease it with oil. Half-fill the sink with cold water.
5 Put the granulated sugar in a pan and heat gently to dissolve. Increase the heat and cook until the sugar turns a deep golden brown. Plunge the base of the pan immediately into a sink of cold water to cool quickly. Take the pan out of the sink and rest it next to the parchment. Dip a fork into the caramel to pick up the syrup, then hold it high over the parchment and flick backwards and forwards over the paper – as the sugar cools it will form very thin threads and build up a golden nest of spun sugar. Leave on the parchment until ready to serve, then lift on to the trifle.

Serves 8 preparation: 30 minutes, plus chilling cooking time: 5–10 minutes
per serving: 520 cals; 24g fat; 69g carbohydrate

13

Cold desserts

Blueberry Trifle

1 ready-made all-butter Madeira cake, cut
   into cubes
6tbsp white wine
4tbsp elderflower cordial
3tbsp blueberry conserve

500g carton fresh custard
284ml carton double cream
125g (4oz) blueberries
1tbsp pistachio nuts, roughly chopped

1 Put the cake into a 2.3 litre (4 pint) glass serving bowl. Mix the wine with 2tbsp cordial, then pour over the cake.
2 Dot the blueberry conserve over the cake, then pour the custard on top. Whip the cream until soft peaks form, then fold in the remaining cordial and half the blueberries. Add to the trifle.
3 Cover and chill for at least 1 hour, but preferably overnight since the trifle tastes better the day after making it.
4 Just before serving, scatter the remaining blueberries and the nuts over the top.

Serves 6   preparation: 15 minutes, plus chilling
per serving: 540 cals; 34g fat; 52g carbohydrate

Crème Anglaise Trifle

450ml (¾ pint) full-fat milk
1 vanilla pod, split lengthways
1 large egg, plus 2 large egg yolks
4tbsp golden caster sugar, plus extra to
   sprinkle
200ml (7fl oz) double cream

200ml (7fl oz) crème de cassis or
   sweet sherry
8 trifle sponges, Madeira sponge
   or madeleines
450g (1lb) cherries, pitted, plus extra
   to decorate

1 Put the milk in a pan with the vanilla pod and bring slowly to the boil. Remove from the heat, then cover and leave to infuse for 20 minutes.
2 Whisk the egg, yolks and sugar together and add the milk. Return to a clean pan and cook gently without boiling until the custard thickens. Strain into a bowl and cool for 1 hour, then chill for 3 hours. To prevent a skin forming, sprinkle the surface with sugar.
3 Lightly whip the cream until just stiff, then whisk in the chilled custard. Pour 1tbsp crème de cassis or sherry into the base of four tall glasses. Make layers with sponge cake, custard, cherries and cassis, finishing with the custard. Decorate with cherries and serve.

Serves 4   preparation: 20 minutes, plus infusing, cooling and chilling   cooking time: 6 minutes
per serving: 660 cals; 34g fat; 67g carbohydrate

Vanilla Chilled Risotto

900ml (1½ pints) full-fat milk
1 vanilla pod, split lengthways
75g (3oz) risotto rice

40g (1½oz) golden caster sugar
200ml (7fl oz) double cream
ground cinnamon, to sprinkle

1 Pour the milk into a large pan, add the vanilla pod and bring slowly to the boil.
2 Stir in the rice, reduce the heat and simmer gently for about 40 minutes, stirring from time to time, until the rice is soft and most of the liquid has been absorbed. You might need to add a little more milk during the cooking time.
3 Stir in the sugar, remove the vanilla pod and leave to cool.
4 Stir the cream into the cooled mixture, pour into a large bowl, cover and chill.
5 Sprinkle with a little ground cinnamon and serve.

Serves 10   preparation: 5 minutes, plus cooling and chilling   cooking time: 50 minutes
per serving: 180 cals; 14g fat; 11g carbohydrate

Jewelled Cheesecake

butter, to grease
1 large sponge flan case
2tbsp orange-flavoured liqueur, such as
  Cointreau or Grand Marnier (optional)
500g (1lb 2oz) cream cheese
125g (4oz) golden caster sugar
3 eggs

zest of ½ orange
40g (1½oz) chopped mixed peel
50g (2oz) natural colour glacé cherries,
  thinly sliced
25g (1oz) pistachio nuts, chopped
golden icing sugar, to dust
raspberry coulis, to serve

1 Preheat the oven to 180°C (160°C fan oven) mark 4. Grease a 23cm (9 inch) spring-release cake tin and line with greaseproof paper. Cut off the raised edge of the sponge flan case so that it fits snugly inside the tin. You can reserve the edges for a trifle or just eat them – the cook's perk! If using, drizzle the liqueur over the sponge base.
2 Put the cream cheese in a large bowl, add the caster sugar and beat together, then mix in the eggs. Add the orange zest, mixed peel, glacé cherries and pistachio nuts, mixing well. Spoon into the tin on top of the sponge and smooth the top. Bake for 50–55 minutes until slightly risen and firm to the touch. Remove from the oven and leave to cool in the tin.
3 Carefully remove the cheesecake from the tin. Put it on a plate, then dust thickly with icing sugar. Cut it into slices, drizzle with a little raspberry coulis and serve.

Serves 8   preparation: 20 minutes   cooking time: 50–55 minutes
per serving: 560 cals; 42g fat (of which 24g saturates); 39g carbohydrate

Cold desserts

Iced Raspberry Soufflés

1 orange and 1 lemon	2 large egg whites
700g (1½lb) raspberries	400g (14oz) plain dark chocolate
225g (8oz) golden caster sugar	350g (12oz) mixed berries, such as
450ml (¾ pint) double cream	redcurrants, blueberries and blackberries

1 Line eight 125ml (4fl oz) ramekins with 6 x 25.5cm (2½ x 10 inch) strips of non-stick baking parchment, to form a collar above the rim. Squeeze the juice of the orange and lemon and put 2tbsp of each in a processor with the raspberries and sugar; whiz until smooth.

2 Sieve the sauce. Set aside 150ml (¼ pint) of the sauce, then cover and refrigerate. Place the remaining sauce in a large bowl. Whip the cream until it just holds its shape – don't over-whip as the acidity of the raspberries will help to thicken it, aim for a soft, dropping consistency. Using a large spoon, fold the cream into the sauce in the bowl.

3 Whisk egg whites to a soft peak and fold into raspberry cream mixture using a large metal spoon. Spoon mixture into the prepared ramekins, tapping them gently to level the surface. Freeze for at least 3–4 hours or overnight. Dip soufflé bases in hot water for 10 seconds, then turn out on to a baking sheet, remove parchment and return soufflés to the freezer.

4 Cut out eight strips of non-stick baking parchment, about 6.5cm (2½in) x 25.5cm (10in). In a bowl over a pan of barely simmering water, melt 225g (8oz) of the chocolate. Allow the melted chocolate to cool slightly, then brush over the parchment strips, covering them completely. Remove the soufflés from the freezer.

5 Carefully wrap the chocolate-covered strips around the soufflés (work quickly as the chocolate will set on contact with the frozen soufflés) and return to the freezer for 5 minutes to set. Peel the baking parchment away from the chocolate and return the soufflés to the freezer while you make decorative curls with the remaining chocolate.

6 Melt the remaining chocolate as before, then spread it over a marble slab or worksurface. When it has just set, push the blade of a knife at a 25° angle across the chocolate to form curls. Put soufflés in the fridge for 25 minutes before serving. Serve decorated with the mixed berries and chocolate curls and the reserved sauce.

Serves 8   preparation: 1¼ hours, plus freezing
per serving: 660 cals; 42g fat; 71g carbohydrate

13

Cold desserts

Hot puddings

Warm, comforting and homely is how we think of hot puds. Eating a Date and Walnut Pudding with Chocolate Sauce is almost as good as having a cuddle – wedges of sticky sponge pudding anointed with hot chocolate fudge sauce. Heaven.

But they don't all need to be guaranteed to have you snoozing in front of the fire. That golden oldie Baked Egg Custard will take you right back to the nursery and remind you just how good a simple pudding can be.

For something a bit sexier, Hot Orange Soufflé is simple and impressive. Just get it to the table as soon as it's cooked and you've cracked it. Home-made pies and tarts served with lashings of hot custard are dead easy, but terrific to eat – Rustic Blackberry and Apple; Rhubarb and Orange Crumble Tart; Plum and Cardamom Pie; and Maple Pecan Pie: all great favourites.

As are pancakes and fritters – Mango Pancakes are filled with fresh mango and passion fruit and bathed in a pineapple juice and Malibu sauce for an irresistible hot pud.

So forget the diet, and indulge yourself!

Baked Apricots with Almonds

12 apricots, halved and stoned
6tbsp golden caster sugar
2tbsp Amaretto liqueur

25g (1oz) unsalted butter
25g (1oz) flaked almonds

1   Preheat the oven to 200°C (180°C fan oven) mark 6. Put the apricot halves, cut side up, in an ovenproof dish. Sprinkle with the sugar, drizzle with the liqueur, then dot each apricot half with a little butter. Scatter over the flaked almonds.
2   Bake for 20–25 minutes until the apricots are soft and the juices are syrupy. Serve warm, with crème fraîche.

Serves 6   preparation: 10 minutes   cooking time: 20–25 minutes
per serving: 160 cals; 6g fat; 26g carbohydrate

Ginger-glazed Pineapple

2 medium-sized ripe pineapples, cut into
   four lengthways, with the stalk on
2tbsp light muscovado sugar

2tsp ground ginger, plus extra to dust
yogurt, to serve
1tsp runny honey (optional)

1   Remove the fibrous core from each pineapple quarter and cut along the skin to loosen the flesh, reserving the skin 'shells'. Cut the flesh into pieces and put back in the pineapple 'shell'. Wrap the green leaves of the stalk in foil so that they don't burn while grilling. Mix the sugar with the ground ginger.
2   Preheat the grill. Sprinkle each pineapple quarter with the sugar mixture, put on foil-lined baking sheets and cook under the grill for 10 minutes or until golden and caramelised.
3   Mix the yogurt with the honey, if using. Serve the pineapple with the yogurt and dust with ginger.

Serves 8   preparation: 30 minutes   cooking time: 10 minutes
per serving: 100 cals; 0g fat; 27g carbohydrate

14

Hot puddings

Pineapple Fritters

1 large ripe pineapple, peeled and cored,
   plus extra pineapple slices to decorate
450g (1lb) papaya, peeled, deseeded and
   sliced
1½tbsp golden caster sugar
50g (2oz) plain flour

pinch of salt
finely grated zest of ½ lemon
1 egg, separated
1tsp sunflower oil
oil, for deep-frying
lemon zest, to decorate

1 Slice the pineapple into 1cm (½ inch) thick rings. Cut each ring into three or four pieces and dry on kitchen paper.

2 To make the sauce, put the papaya in a blender or food processor and whiz until smooth. Stir in the sugar, pour into a bowl and put to one side.

3 To make the batter, sift the flour and salt into a bowl. Stir in the lemon zest and make a well in the centre. Put the egg yolk and 4tbsp water in the well and gradually incorporate the flour mixture, adding enough extra water to produce the consistency of single cream.

4 Whisk the egg white in a clean grease-free bowl until stiff peaks form, then fold into the batter with the sunflower oil.

5 Heat the oil in a deep-fat fryer to 190°C or until a cube of day-old bread dropped into the oil browns in 30 seconds. Spear six pieces of pineapple on to a skewer and dip them in the batter to coat. Lower the pieces into the hot oil and fry for 3–4 minutes until puffed, golden and crisp. Remove the pineapple pieces with a slotted spoon, drain on kitchen paper and keep them warm while you cook the remaining pineapple in the same way.

6 Decorate with pineapple slices and lemon zest and serve at once with the papaya sauce.

Serves 4–6   preparation: 30 minutes   cooking time: 10 minutes
per serving: 340–230 cals; 15–10g fat; 50–33g carbohydrate

14

Hot puddings

Sticky Maple Syrup Pineapple

**1 large pineapple, peeled and cut
lengthways into quarters**

200ml (7fl oz) maple syrup

1 Remove the fibrous core from each pineapple quarter. Slice each quarter lengthways into four to make sixteen wedges.
2 Pour the maple syrup into a large non-stick frying pan and heat for 2 minutes. Add the pineapple and fry for 3 minutes, turning once, until warmed through.
3 Arrange the pineapple on serving plates, drizzle the maple syrup over and around it and serve.

Serves 4   preparation: 10 minutes   cooking time: 5 minutes
per serving: 230 cals; 0g fat; 57g carbohydrate

14

Hot puddings

Fruit Kebabs with Spiced Pear Dip

150g (5oz) ready-to-eat dried pears, soaked
in hot water for about 30 minutes
juice of 1 orange
1tsp peeled and finely chopped fresh
root ginger
½tsp vanilla extract
50ml (2fl oz) very low-fat natural yogurt
½tsp ground cinnamon, plus extra to dust

1tsp dark runny honey, plus 1tbsp
25g (1oz) hazelnuts, toasted and
roughly chopped
3 large fresh figs, each cut into quarters
1 large ripe mango, skin and stone
removed, flesh cut into cubes
1 baby pineapple or 2 thick slices, skin
removed and flesh cut into cubes

1 To make the dip, drain the pears and put in a food processor or blender with the orange juice, ginger, vanilla extract, yogurt, cinnamon and 50ml (2fl oz) water and whiz until smooth. Spoon the dip into a bowl. Drizzle with 1tsp honey, sprinkle with the hazelnuts and dust with a little cinnamon. Cover and put to one side in a cool place until ready to serve. Meanwhile, soak six 20.5cm (8 inch) wooden kebab skewers in water for 30 minutes to stop them burning when cooking.

2 Preheat the grill to its highest setting. To make the kebabs, thread alternate pieces of fruit on to each skewer, using at least two pieces of each type of fruit per skewer. Place the skewers on a foil-covered tray and cover the ends of the skewers with strips of foil to prevent them burning. Drizzle with 1tbsp honey and grill for about 4 minutes on each side, close to the heat, until lightly charred. Serve warm or at room temperature with the dip.

Makes 6 kebabs   preparation: 20 minutes, plus soaking   cooking time: 8 minutes
per kebab, including dip: 90 cals; 2g fat; 17g carbohydrate

14

Hot puddings

Hot Orange Soufflé

65g (2½oz) unsalted butter
2tbsp dried breadcrumbs
40g (1½oz) plain flour
grated zest and juice of 2 small (or 1 large)
   oranges and 1 lemon

200ml (7fl oz) full-fat milk
125g (4oz) golden caster sugar
3tbsp Grand Marnier
4 large eggs, separated
icing sugar, to dust

1 Preheat the oven to 190°C (170°C fan oven) mark 5. Melt 15g (½oz) butter and use to grease a 1.4 litre (2½ pint) soufflé dish. Coat the dish with the breadcrumbs and put to one side.
2 Melt the remaining butter in a pan, add the flour, orange and lemon zest and cook for 30 seconds. Take the pan off the heat and gradually beat in the milk until smooth. Cook, stirring, over a low heat until the sauce is thickened and smooth. Continue to cook for a further 2 minutes.
3 Remove from the heat and stir in the sugar, orange and lemon juices and Grand Marnier, then beat in the egg yolks.
4 Whisk the egg whites in a clean grease-free bowl until stiff peaks form, then, using a large metal spoon, carefully fold into the sauce until evenly incorporated. Spoon into the soufflé dish and run a knife around the outside of the mixture.
5 Immediately bake for 25–30 minutes until the soufflé is risen and golden. Remove from the oven, dust with icing sugar and serve at once.

Serves 6   preparation: 20 minutes   cooking time: 25–30 minutes
per serving: 310 cals; 14g fat; 38g carbohydrate

Roast Apples with Butterscotch Sauce

125g (4oz) sultanas
6tbsp brandy
6 large Bramley cooking apples, cored
4tbsp light muscovado sugar, plus 125g
   (4oz)
2tbsp apple juice

125g (4oz) butter
2tbsp each golden syrup and black treacle
284ml carton double cream
125g (4oz) chopped and toasted hazelnuts
ricotta cheese, to serve

1 Preheat the oven to 220°C (200°C fan oven) mark 7. Soak the sultanas in 2tbsp brandy for 10 minutes, then stuff each apple with equal amounts.
2 Put the apples in a roasting tin, sprinkle over 4tbsp sugar and the apple juice. Bake for 15–20 minutes or until soft.
3 Meanwhile, make the sauce. Melt the butter, remaining sugar, the golden syrup and treacle in a heavy-based pan, stirring constantly. When the sugar has dissolved and the mixture is bubbling, stir in the remaining brandy and the cream. Bring back to the boil and set aside.
4 Remove the apples from the oven and serve with the sauce, hazelnuts and a dollop of ricotta cheese.

Serves 6   preparation: 5 minutes, plus soaking   cooking time: 15–20 minutes
per serving (without ricotta): 780 cals; 47g fat; 85g carbohydrate

Barbecued Figs with Honey and Marsala

12 large ripe figs
melted butter, to brush
1 cinnamon stick, roughly broken

6tbsp runny Greek-style honey
6tbsp Marsala
crème fraîche, to serve

1 Make a small slit in each fig, three-quarters of the way through. Take two sheets of foil large enough to hold the figs in one layer. With the shiny side uppermost, lay one piece on top of the other and brush the top piece all over with the melted butter.
2 Stand the figs in the middle of the foil and scatter over the broken cinnamon stick. Bring the sides of the foil together loosely, leaving a gap at the top, and pour in the honey and Marsala. Scrunch the edges of the foil together so that the figs are loosely enclosed.
3 Put the foil parcel on the barbecue and cook over medium hot coals for about 10–15 minutes, depending on how ripe the figs are, until very tender.
4 Just before serving, open up the foil slightly at the top and barbecue for a further 2–3 minutes to allow the juices to reduce and become syrupy.
5 Serve the figs immediately with a large dollop of crème fraîche and the syrupy juices spooned over.

Serves 6   preparation: 10 minutes   cooking time: 13–18 minutes
per serving: 140 cals; 3g fat; 24g carbohydrate

Spiced Cherries in Madeira Syrup

150g (5oz) golden caster sugar
600ml (1 pint) Madeira or sweet sherry
1 vanilla pod
1 basil sprig

zest of 1 lemon, plus a splash of juice
2 x 454g cans pitted cherries, drained
lemon zest, to decorate (optional)

1 Make a syrup by dissolving the sugar in the Madeira or sherry over a low heat. Add the vanilla pod, basil and lemon zest. Bring to the boil, then reduce the heat and simmer until slightly thick – about 5 minutes.
2 Pour into a serving dish, add the cherries and a splash of lemon juice to taste, then chill.
3 Decorate the cherries with lemon zest if you like and serve with a spoonful of crème fraîche, accompanied by shortbread biscuits.

Serves 6   preparation: 10 minutes, plus chilling   cooking time: 10 minutes
per serving: 280 cals; 0g fat; 50g carbohydrate

14

Hot puddings

Roast Pears with Butterscotch Sauce

40g (1½oz) butter
125g (4oz) golden caster sugar
2tbsp lemon juice
200ml (7fl oz) double cream
1tsp ground cinnamon

75g (3oz) pecan nuts, roughly chopped and
   lightly toasted
6 large ripe pears, such as Williams or
   Comice

1 Melt the butter in a small heavy-based pan, add the sugar and cook, stirring, to a dark caramel. Take off the heat and stir in 5tbsp hot water and the lemon juice – take care when you add the liquid as the mixture will probably splutter. Return the pan to the heat, stir until smooth, then add the cream and cinnamon. Simmer, stirring, for 1–2 minutes or until evenly combined. Take off the heat and add the pecan nuts.
2 Preheat the oven to 200°C (180°C fan oven) mark 6. Peel the pears, hollow out the core if you want to and place them upright, packed closely together, in an ovenproof dish. Spoon the butterscotch sauce over the pears and bake for 40–50 minutes or until the pears are tender.
3 To serve, put the pears on individual plates, together with some butterscotch sauce and a scoop of vanilla ice cream if wished. Decorate with broken pieces of Mixed Nut Caramel (see below).

Mixed Nut Caramel

Put 125g (4oz) golden caster sugar in a heavy-based non-stick pan. Cook over a low heat until the sugar turns a golden liquid caramel. Shake the pan – but don't stir – to encourage the sugar to dissolve evenly. As soon as it has turned to a caramel, immediately stir in 25g (1oz) mixed nuts and pour on to a lightly oiled baking sheet. Leave the caramel to cool, then break it up into shreds and use to decorate the pears.

Serves 6   preparation: 30 minutes   cooking time: 45–55 minutes
per serving: 110 cals; 2g fat; 22g carbohydrate

Roast Oranges with Caramel Sauce

6 small oranges, peeled and pithed, plus
   grated zest and juice of 1 large orange
25g (1oz) butter

2tbsp each golden caster sugar, Grand
   Marnier, marmalade
crème fraîche, to serve

1 Preheat the oven to 200°C (180°C fan oven) mark 6. Put the small oranges in a roasting tin just large enough to hold them. Melt the butter in a pan and add the remaining ingredients with the orange zest and juice. Heat gently to dissolve the sugar.
2 Pour the sauce over the oranges and bake for 30–40 minutes. Serve with crème fraîche.

Serves 6   preparation: 30 minutes   cooking time: 10 minutes
per serving: 120 cals; 3g fat; 22g carbohydrate

Baked Pears with Apricots and Almonds

50g (2oz) ready-to-eat dried apricots, roughly chopped

50g (2oz) each ground almonds and raisins

50g (2oz) golden caster sugar

1 large egg white

2 large ripe pears, halved lengthways and cored

Greek-style yogurt and a little warm honey, to drizzle (optional)

1 Preheat the oven to 180°C (160°C fan oven) mark 4. Put the apricots in a small bowl with the almonds, raisins and sugar. Add the egg white and mix well.

2 Pile the almond mixture into the centre of the pears. Put the pears in an ovenproof dish and bake for 25–30 minutes or until soft. Serve immediately with a spoonful of yogurt drizzled with honey, if you like.

Serves 4   preparation: 15 minutes   cooking time: 25–30 minutes
per serving: 220 cals; 7g fat; 37g carbohydrate

Hot Fudge Pears

75g (3oz) butter

1tbsp golden syrup

75g (3oz) light muscovado sugar

4tbsp evaporated milk or single or double cream

4 pears, cored, sliced and chilled

1 Melt the butter, syrup, sugar and evaporated milk together over a very low heat.

2 Stir thoroughly until all the sugar has dissolved completely, then bring the fudge mixture to the boil without any further stirring, and pour over the pears. Serve immediately with frozen yogurt or ice cream.

Serves 4   preparation: 5 minutes   cooking time: 15 minutes
per serving: 320 cals; 16g fat; 46g carbohydrate

Lime Fruits

zest and juice of 4 limes, about 150ml (¼ pint)

3tbsp golden caster sugar

6 pieces tropical fruit, such as papaya, melon or mango, peeled and sliced

1 Heat the lime juice in a small pan with the sugar. Bring to the boil and allow to bubble for 2–3 minutes or until all the sugar has dissolved.

2 Just before serving, add the lime zest to the warm syrup. Arrange the tropical fruits on serving plates and spoon over the lime syrup. Serve immediately.

Serves 4   preparation: 6 minutes   cooking time: 5 minutes
per serving: 120 cals; 0g fat; 31g carbohydrate

Mango Pancakes

125g (4oz) plain flour	150ml (¼ pint) pineapple juice
pinch of salt	juice of ½ lime
1 egg	2tbsp Malibu (optional)
300ml (½ pint) semi-skimmed milk	golden caster sugar
2 large mangoes	oil, to fry
6 passion fruit	icing sugar, to dust
2tsp arrowroot	

1 Put the flour, salt, egg and milk in a food processor and whiz until smooth. Cover and leave for 30 minutes.
2 To make the filling, peel and slice the mangoes. Halve the passion fruit and remove the pulp. Mix the arrowroot with 2tbsp cold water.
3 To make the sauce, put the pineapple juice in a small pan and warm gently. Stir in the arrowroot and bring to the boil. Remove from the heat and stir in the passion fruit pulp, lime juice and Malibu, if using. Sweeten to taste and put to one side.
4 Lightly brush an 18cm (7 inch) non-stick pancake pan with oil and heat. When hot, add enough batter to coat the base of the pan thinly – about 3tbsp. Cook for about 3 minutes or until golden, then flip over and cook for 1–2 minutes. Transfer to a plate, cover and keep warm. Cook the remaining pancakes in the same way.
5 Fold the pancakes in half, fill with the sliced mango and then fold in half again. Dust with icing sugar and serve with the warm sauce.

Makes 8–12 pancakes preparation: 15 minutes, plus standing cooking time: 15 minutes
per pancake: 140–90 cals; 2–1g fat; 30–20g carbohydrate

Barbecued Apple Bananas with Rum Mascarpone

250g tub mascarpone, chilled	12 apple bananas
2–3tsp light muscovado sugar	75g (3oz) dark chocolate, chopped
2–3tbsp dark rum	

1 Spoon the mascarpone into a bowl and stir in the sugar and rum. Cover and leave in a cool place.
2 Barbecue the unpeeled bananas over medium-hot coals for 8–10 minutes, turning frequently until tender and blackened.
3 Split the bananas open, sprinkle a little chocolate inside each and top with the mascarpone. Sprinkle over the remaining chocolate before serving.

Serves 6 preparation: 10 minutes cooking time: 8–10 minutes
per serving: 370 cals; 23g fat; 38g carbohydrate

Hot Mango and Banana Salad

2 large oranges
2 firm but ripe mangoes, about 700g (1½lb)
   total weight
4 small bananas

25g (1oz) very low-fat spread
1tsp light muscovado sugar
2tbsp rum
2tbsp lemon or lime juice

1 Coarsely grate the zest of 1 orange and squeeze the juice. Peel the remaining orange and slice thickly. Cut the mango across either side of the stone, then cut the flesh into large pieces and peel. Remove any flesh from around the stone and cut all the flesh into bite-sized pieces. Peel and thickly slice the bananas.

2 Melt the low-fat spread in a large non-stick frying pan. Add the sugar, mango and banana and cook for 2–3 minutes until just beginning to soften.

3 Pour in the rum, orange and lemon or lime juices and the orange slices. Bring to the boil, then serve immediately, decorated with the grated orange zest.

Serves 4   preparation: 10 minutes   cooking time: 5 minutes
per serving: 170 cals; 2g fat; 34g carbohydrate

Toffee Bananas

3 firm bananas, peeled and cut into chunks
3tbsp plain flour
1½tsp cornflour
1 egg white

oil, to deep-fry
125g (4oz) sugar
2tbsp sesame seeds

1 Dust the bananas with a little flour. Mix the remaining flour with the cornflour and egg white and stir well to form a paste.

2 Half-fill a deep pan with oil and heat to 180°C or until a cube of day-old bread dropped into the oil browns in 30 seconds.

3 Dip the banana chunks in the paste and then fry, a few at a time, in the hot oil until golden. Remove the bananas with a slotted spoon, drain on kitchen paper and keep them warm while you cook the remaining bananas in the same way.

4 To make the sesame caramel, put the sugar and 2tbsp water in a heavy-based pan and heat gently until the sugar dissolves. Bring to the boil, without stirring, and boil until the mixture is straw-coloured. Sprinkle in the sesame seeds and cook briefly until the mixture turns golden. Immediately remove the pan from the heat, add the fried bananas and stir to coat.

5 Have ready a bowl of iced water. Dip the bananas into the water to set the caramel. Remove at once with a slotted spoon and serve.

Serves 4   preparation: 10 minutes   cooking time: 20 minutes
per serving: 320 cals; 9g fat; 58g carbohydrate

Hot puddings

Bananas Grilled with Cardamom Butter

2 green cardamom pods, split	50g (2oz) light muscovado sugar
50g (2oz) butter	4 bananas, unpeeled, slit along their length

1 Beat the seeds of the cardamom pods into the butter and sugar.
2 Preheat the grill. Open out the bananas a little and put on a grill pan. Spoon a little of the flavoured butter into each one. Grill for 3–5 minutes, basting with the butter, until the bananas are soft and beginning to caramelise.
3 Serve the bananas piping hot with a little of the buttery sauce and some vanilla ice cream.

Serves 4   preparation: 5 minutes   cooking time: 5 minutes
per serving: 220 cals; 11g fat; 32g carbohydrate

Sticky Plum Tart

125g (4oz) plain flour, plus extra to dust	1 egg yolk
1tsp ground cinnamon	450g (1lb) plums, halved, stoned and sliced
salt	2tbsp golden caster sugar
75g (3oz) butter	3tbsp apricot jam or redcurrant jelly

1 Sift the flour into a food processor, add the cinnamon, a pinch of salt, the butter and egg yolk and whiz for 30 seconds or until evenly combined. Add 1tbsp chilled water and whiz for 30 seconds. Knead together lightly, then roll out on a lightly floured surface to a 25.5cm (10 inch) diameter circle. Put on a baking sheet and chill for 10–15 minutes.
2 Preheat the oven to 200°C (180°C fan oven) mark 6. Prick the pastry all over with a fork. Bake for 20–25 minutes or until golden brown, then remove from the oven.
3 Arrange the plums over the cooked pastry and sprinkle with the sugar. Put back in the oven and cook for 45–50 minutes or until the plums are tender.
4 Melt the jam or jelly with 2tbsp water, bring to the boil and bubble for 1 minute. Brush or spoon over the warm tart. Serve warm.

Serves 6   preparation: 5 minutes, plus chilling   cooking time: 1 hour 5 minutes–1¼ hours
per serving: 240 cals; 12g fat; 33g carbohydrate

14

Hot puddings

Rhubarb and Apple Cobbler

900g (2lb) rhubarb, cut into 2.5cm (1 inch)
  lengths
450g (1lb) Bramley or other cooking apples,
  peeled, quartered, cored and sliced
135g (4½oz) golden caster sugar
200g (7oz) plain flour
1tbsp cornflour
½tsp ground ginger

65g (2½oz) butter, diced, plus a knob
grated zest of 1 orange
2tsp baking powder
pinch of salt
125ml (4fl oz) buttermilk (or full-fat milk
  plus a squeeze of lemon juice)
2tbsp double cream
1tsp demerara sugar

1 Preheat the oven to 220°C (200°C fan oven) mark 7. Put the fruit, 75g (3oz) sugar, 50g (2oz) flour, the cornflour, ginger, knob of butter and orange zest in a 25.5cm (10 inch) shallow ovenproof dish, toss to mix and put to one side.

2 To make the cobbler dough, sift the remaining flour, the baking powder and salt together into a bowl. Rub in the diced butter until the mixture resembles fine breadcrumbs. Stir in the remaining sugar, then add the milk and mix with a knife to a soft dough.

3 Spoon the dough on to the fruit in clumps, making sure it doesn't completely cover it. Mix the cream with the demerara sugar and drizzle over the top.

4 Stand the dish on a baking tray and bake for 10 minutes. Reduce the oven temperature to 190°C (170°C fan oven) mark 5 and bake for 20–30 minutes or until the cobbler is puffed and brown and the fruit is just soft.

5 Remove from the oven and leave the pudding to stand for 10 minutes. Serve with pouring cream or custard.

Serves 6 preparation: 20 minutes plus standing cooking time: 30–40 minutes
per serving: 370 cals; 13g fat; 63g carbohydrate

Impress-your-friends Apple Tart

375g pack ready-rolled puff pastry
500g (1lb 2oz) Cox's apples

juice of 1 lemon
golden icing sugar, to dust

1   Preheat the oven to 200°C (180°C fan oven) mark 6. Put the pastry on a 28 x 38cm (11 x15 inch) baking sheet and roll over it lightly with a rolling pin to smooth down the pastry. Score lightly around the edge, to create a 3cm (1¼ inch) border.
2   Core and thinly slice the apples (don't peel them), then toss them in the lemon juice.
3   Carefully arrange the apple slices on top of the pastry, within the border. Turn the edge of the pastry halfway over, so that it reaches the edge of the apples, then press down and use your fingers to crimp the edge. Dust heavily with icing sugar.
4   Bake for 20–25 minutes until the pastry is cooked and the sugar has caramelised. Serve warm, dusted with more icing sugar.

Serves 8   preparation: 15 minutes   cooking time: 20–25 minutes
per serving: 210cals; 11g fat; 25g carbohydrate

Caramelised Apple Tarts

40g (1½oz) butter, plus extra to grease
1 sheet pastry from a 375g pack all-butter
   puff pastry
plain flour, to dust
125g (4oz) white marzipan, chilled and
   coarsely grated

4 Braeburn apples, quartered, cored and
   sliced
juice of 1 large lemon
25g (1oz) demerara sugar
½tsp ground mixed spice

1   Grease the bases of six 7.5cm (3 inch) individual tartlet tins. Roll out the pastry sheet on a lightly floured surface a little more thinly. Using a saucer as a guide, stamp out six 12.5cm (5 inch) rounds of pastry. Line the tins and prick the bases twice with a fork. Chill for 10 minutes. Preheat the oven to 200°C (180°C fan oven) mark 6.
2   Line the pastry with greaseproof paper and baking beans. Bake for 10 minutes, then remove the paper and beans and cook for a further 10 minutes. Remove from the oven and sprinkle in the marzipan, then return to the oven and cook for 5 minutes or until the marzipan melts and the pastry is cooked.
3   Heat the butter in a large non-stick frying pan. Add the apples, lemon juice, sugar and spice and cook over a high heat for 5 minutes, turning as needed until most of the lemon juice has evaporated and the apples are just tender. Pile into the warm pastry cases, then put back in the oven for 2–3 minutes. Serve with crème fraîche.

Serves 6   preparation: 5 minutes, plus chilling   cooking time: 25 minutes
per serving: 400 cals; 23g fat; 44g carbohydrate

14

Hot puddings

Rhubarb and Orange Crumble Tart

250g (9oz) plain flour, plus extra to dust
150g (5oz) butter, cut into small pieces
75g (3oz) golden caster sugar
575g (1¼lb) rhubarb, cut into 2.5cm
  (1 inch) pieces
grated zest of 1 orange, plus juice of
  ½ orange

25g (1oz) ground almonds
50g (2oz) light muscovado sugar
284ml carton double cream
1tsp golden icing sugar
1tbsp elderflower cordial

1 To make the pastry, put 200g (7oz) flour, 125g (4oz) butter and 75g (3oz) caster sugar into a food processor and whiz briefly until it resembles breadcrumbs. Add 2tbsp cold water and whiz briefly again to form a soft pastry. Wrap the pastry in clingfilm and put in the fridge to chill for at least 30 minutes.

2 Unwrap the pastry and turn out on to a lightly floured surface. Roll out and use to line a 10 x 35.5cm (4 x 14 inch) loose-based tranche tin, or a 23cm (9 inch) round fluted loose-based tin. Put the pastry case in the fridge to chill for 30 minutes.

3 Preheat the oven to 200°C (180°C fan oven) mark 6. Line the chilled pastry case with greaseproof paper and weigh down with baking beans. Bake for 10–12 minutes, then remove the beans and the paper and put back in the oven for a further 10 minutes until the pastry is lightly golden. Take out of the oven and put to one side.

4 Meanwhile, make the filling: put the rhubarb, remaining caster sugar, the orange zest and juice in a pan and bring to the boil. Cook gently for 6–8 minutes until the rhubarb has just softened. Leave to cool.

5 To make the crumble topping, put the remaining flour, the almonds, muscovado sugar and remaining butter into the food processor and whiz briefly until it resembles breadcrumbs.

6 Spoon the rhubarb filling into the pastry case and level out. Top with an even layer of the crumble mixture, return to the oven and bake for 20 minutes until pale golden. Remove from the oven and leave to cool slightly before serving.

7 To make the elderflower cream, put the cream, icing sugar and elderflower cordial into a bowl and whisk with an electric hand whisk until soft peaks form. Serve with the warm tart.

Serves 8   preparation: 25 minutes, plus chilling   cooking time: 45 minutes
per serving: 502 cals; 34g fat; 46g carbohydrate

Walnut and Apple Tart

225g (8oz) plain flour, plus extra to dust
2tbsp golden icing sugar
125g (4oz) butter, chilled and diced
4 eggs
200g (7oz) runny honey
125g (4oz) unsalted butter, softened

125g (4oz) light muscovado sugar
zest and juice of 1 lemon
125g (4oz) walnuts, roughly chopped
125g (4oz) ready-to-eat dried apples and
    pears, roughly chopped, plus 3 dried pear
    slices, to garnish

1   To make the pastry, put the flour and icing sugar into the bowl of a food processor. Add the 125g (4oz)
    chilled butter and whiz until the mixture resembles fine breadcrumbs. Beat one egg in a bowl and add
    to the mixture with 1tbsp cold water and pulse until the mixture just starts to come together. Tip the
    pastry on to a lightly floured surface and knead it briefly to form a ball. Wrap in clingfilm and chill for
    30 minutes.

2   Warm 175g (6oz) honey in a small pan over a low heat. Put the 125g (4oz) unsalted butter in a large
    bowl with the muscovado sugar. Using an electric hand whisk, mix until light and fluffy. Beat the
    remaining eggs and add to the bowl with the lemon zest and juice, walnuts, apples, pears and warm
    honey. Stir well and put to one side.

3   Put the pastry between two sheets of greaseproof paper and roll out thinly. Peel off and discard the
    top sheet, then flip over and put the pastry into a 23cm (9 inch) loose-based tart tin. Peel off the
    paper and put to one side. Ease the pastry into the tin, trim the edge, then prick the pastry base with
    a fork. Cover with clingfilm and chill for 30 minutes.

4   Preheat the oven to 180°C (160°C fan oven) mark 4. Line the pastry case with greaseproof paper, fill
    with baking beans and bake for 10–15 minutes. Remove the paper and beans and bake the pastry
    for a further 5 minutes until golden. Take out of the oven and pour the walnut and apple filling on to
    the pastry and arrange the pear slices on top. Brush with the remaining honey.

5   Put the tart on a baking sheet, cover with foil and bake for 20 minutes. Remove the foil and bake for
    a further 25 minutes until the tart is golden brown and slightly risen. Remove from the oven and cool
    in the tin, then remove, put on a plate and serve with crème fraîche.

Serves 8   preparation: 25 minutes, plus chilling   cooking time: 1 hour 5 minutes
per serving: 620 cals; 37g fat; 66g carbohydrate

Rhubarb Crumble

450g (1lb) rhubarb, chopped
2 balls stem ginger in syrup, drained and
  roughly chopped

125g (4oz) light muscovado sugar
75g (3oz) butter
125g (4oz) plain flour

1 Preheat the oven to 180°C (160°C fan oven) mark 4. Put the rhubarb in a 1.1 litre (2 pint) pie dish. Mix in the stem ginger and sprinkle half the sugar over the rhubarb.
2 Put the butter and flour in a food processor and whiz briefly until it resembles breadcrumbs. Add the remaining sugar and pulse once or twice to mix everything.
3 Spoon the topping over the fruit and bake the crumble for 50 minutes–1 hour or until it is golden brown and bubbling. Serve warm or cool, with cream or custard.

Serves 6 preparation: 15 minutes cooking time: 50 minutes–1 hour
per serving: 250 cals; 10g fat; 39g carbohydrate

Macadamia and Maple Tart

225g (8oz) macadamia nuts, halved
350g (12oz) shortcrust pastry (page 13)
plain flour, to dust
3 eggs, beaten
75g (3oz) butter, softened
75g (3oz) dark muscovado sugar
1tsp cornflour

50ml (2fl oz) maple syrup, plus extra to
  drizzle
250ml (8fl oz) golden syrup
grated zest of 1 lemon, plus 2tbsp
  lemon juice
1tsp vanilla extract

1 Preheat the grill to high. Put the macadamia nuts on a baking sheet and toast under the grill until golden brown. Leave to cool.
2 Roll out the pastry on a lightly floured surface and line a 23 x 4cm (9 x 1½ inch) deep fluted loose-bottomed tart tin, leaving the pastry hanging over the edges to prevent shrinkage. Prick the pastry base well with a fork, then freeze for 30 minutes.
3 Preheat the oven to 200°C (180°C fan oven) mark 6. Line the pastry case with greaseproof paper, fill with baking beans and bake for 15 minutes. Remove the paper and beans and bake for 10–15 minutes until golden. Brush the base and sides of the pastry case with a little beaten egg and return to the oven for 3–4 minutes. Remove from the oven and, using a sharp knife, trim the overhanging pastry to a neat edge.
4 Beat the butter with the sugar until pale and creamy, then slowly add the beaten egg and cornflour. Stir in all the remaining ingredients. The mix will look curdled but don't panic. Stir in the toasted nuts and pour into the cooked pastry case.
5 Bake the tart for 35–40 minutes or until the filling is just set. Remove from the oven and leave to cool for 10 minutes. Serve with crème fraîche.

Serves 8 preparation: 15 minutes, plus freezing cooking time: 40 minutes
per serving: 620 cals; 42g fat; 55g carbohydrate

14

Hot puddings

Cinnamon Pancakes with Rhubarb Compôte

150ml (¼ pint) fresh orange juice
175g (6oz) golden caster sugar
700g (1½lb) fresh rhubarb, chopped
2tbsp stem ginger syrup, plus 1tbsp finely
  chopped stem ginger
175g (6oz) plain flour
2tbsp light muscovado sugar
1tsp baking powder
½tsp bicarbonate of soda

¼tsp salt
2tsp ground cinnamon
284ml carton buttermilk
2 large eggs, beaten
50g (2oz) butter, melted
vegetable oil
crème fraîche
ground cinnamon, to dust

1 To make the compôte, put the orange juice and caster sugar in a pan with 75ml (3fl oz) water and heat gently until the sugar has dissolved. Add the rhubarb, bring to the boil, reduce the heat and simmer gently for 5–10 minutes or until tender. Lift out the rhubarb and put to one side. Add the ginger syrup and bubble for 5 minutes or until syrupy. Remove from the heat. Add the chopped ginger to the rhubarb.

2 To make the pancakes, put the flour, muscovado sugar, baking powder, bicarbonate of soda, salt and cinnamon in a bowl, mix thoroughly and make a well in the centre. Whisk together the buttermilk and eggs and pour into the well, stirring until smooth. Stir in the melted butter.

3 Heat a little oil in a non-stick frying pan. Ladle the batter into the pan to form a 10cm (4 inch) diameter pancake. Cook until small bubbles form and the edges begin to turn brown, then flip over and cook for 1 minute or until cooked through. Transfer to kitchen paper and keep warm, covered with foil. Repeat with the remaining batter, adding more oil as required.

4 Sandwich two pancakes together with the warm rhubarb compôte. Top with compôte and a spoonful of crème fraîche and dust with cinnamon to serve.

Serves 6   preparation: 30 minutes   cooking time: 15–20 minutes
per serving: 370 cals; 10g fat; 66g carbohydrate

Illustrated on page 564.

Mincemeat and Ricotta Tart

175g (6oz) plain flour, plus extra to dust
125g (4oz) chilled butter, cut into cubes
25g (1oz) ground almonds
25g (1oz) golden caster sugar
3 large egg yolks
250g tub ricotta cheese
25g (1oz) icing sugar

3tbsp double cream
700g (1½lb) good-quality mincemeat
grated zest of 1 lemon
1tbsp brandy or lemon juice
25g (1oz) glacé cherries, sliced
2tbsp flaked almonds
icing sugar, to dust

1 To make the pastry, whiz the flour and the butter in a food processor until the mixture resembles fine breadcrumbs. Add the ground almonds, caster sugar and 1 egg yolk with 1tbsp cold water. Pulse until the mixture just comes together, then turn out on to a floured surface, knead lightly, wrap and chill for at least 30 minutes. Alternatively, sift the flour into a large bowl, rub in the butter to form fine breadcrumbs and stir in the remaining pastry ingredients. Continue as above.

2 Roll out the pastry on a lightly floured surface to a 15 x 38cm (6 x 15 inch) rectangle. Line a 10 x 33cm (4 x 13 inch) loose-based tin with the pastry, prick the pastry base well with a fork and chill for 30 minutes.

3 Preheat the oven to 190°C (170°C fan oven) mark 5. Line the pastry case with greaseproof paper, fill with baking beans and bake for 15 minutes. Remove the paper and beans and cook for 10–15 minutes or until the pastry is just cooked in the centre. Remove from the oven and cool for 15 minutes. Reduce the oven temperature to 180°C (160°C fan oven) mark 4.

4 Beat the ricotta with the icing sugar, remaining egg yolks and the cream until combined. Spread over the pastry base and cook for 20–25 minutes or until lightly set.

5 Mix the mincemeat with the lemon zest and brandy or lemon juice and spoon over the tart. Scatter the cherries and almonds on top and bake for 20 minutes. Remove from the oven, leave to cool a little, then dust with icing sugar to serve.

Serves 8 preparation: 45 minutes, plus chilling and cooling cooking time: 1¼ hours
per serving: 600 cals; 29g fat; 83g carbohydrate

14

Hot puddings

Bakewell Tart

Sweet Tart Pastry (page 14), made with
175g (6oz) flour
flour, to dust
4tbsp strawberry or raspberry jam
125g (4oz) ground almonds

125g (4oz) golden caster sugar
50g (2oz) butter, softened
3 eggs, beaten
¼tsp almond extract
icing sugar, to dust

1 Preheat the oven to 200°C (180°C fan oven) mark 6. Roll out the pastry on a lightly floured surface and use to line a 23cm (9 inch) shallow pie plate.
2 Knock up the edge of the pastry with the back of a knife and mark the rim with the prongs of a fork. Spread the jam evenly over the base. Chill while you make the filling.
3 To make the filling, beat the almonds, sugar, butter, eggs and almond extract together in a bowl. Pour the filling over the jam in the pastry case and spread evenly.
4 Bake for 10 minutes. Reduce the oven temperature to 190°C (170°C fan oven) mark 5 and bake for 20 minutes or until the filling is set.
5 Remove from the oven, dust with icing sugar and serve warm or cold, with cream or custard.

Serves 6   preparation: 15 minutes, plus pastry   cooking time: 30 minutes
per serving: 610 cals; 40g fat; 55g carbohydrate

Rustic Blackberry and Apple Pie

200g (7oz) plain flour
125g (4oz) chilled unsalted butter, diced,
  plus extra to grease
1 egg, beaten
75g (3oz) golden caster sugar, plus 3tbsp
salt

500g (1lb 2oz) eating apples, quartered,
  cored and cut into chunky wedges
300g (11oz) blackberries
¼tsp ground cinnamon
juice of 1 small lemon

1 Put the flour and butter into a processor and pulse until it resembles coarse crumbs. Add the egg, 2tbsp sugar and a pinch of salt and pulse again to combine. Wrap in clingfilm and chill for at least 15 minutes.
2 Preheat the oven to 200°C (180°C fan oven) mark 6. Put the apples, blackberries, the 75g (3oz) sugar, the cinnamon and lemon juice in a bowl and toss together, making sure the sugar dissolves in the juice.
3 Grease a 25.5cm (10 inch) enamel or metal pie dish. Using a lightly floured rolling pin, roll out the pastry on a large sheet of baking parchment to a 30.5cm (12 inch) circle. Lift up the paper, upturn the pastry on to the pie dish and peel away the paper.
4 Put the prepared fruit in the centre of the pie dish and fold the pastry edges up and over the fruit. Sprinkle with the remaining 1tbsp sugar and bake for 40 minutes until the fruit is tender and the pastry golden. Remove from the oven and cool slightly before serving.

Serves 6   preparation: 25 minutes, plus chilling   cooking time: 40 minutes
per serving: 407 cals; 19g fat; 58g carbohydrate

Rhubarb and Cinnamon Pie

175g (6oz) plain flour, plus extra to dust
125g (4oz) butter
150g (5oz) golden caster sugar
700g (1½lb) rhubarb, cut into bite-sized
  chunks

2tbsp cornflour
½tsp cinnamon
a little milk and sugar, to glaze

1 Put the flour, butter and 25g (1oz) sugar in a processor and whiz until the pastry comes together to form a ball. If it is slightly sticky, roll it in some flour and chill for 20 minutes or until it is firm enough to handle. Meanwhile, grease a 23cm (9 inch) round ovenproof dish with sides at least 5cm (2 inches) deep.
2 Roll out the pastry on a lightly floured surface to a large circle, making sure you leave the edges ragged and uneven. It should be large enough to line the dish and to allow the edges of the pastry to drape over the sides.
3 Preheat the oven to 200°C (180°C fan oven) mark 6. Toss the rhubarb in the remaining sugar, the cornflour and cinnamon and spoon into the dish. Bring the pastry edges up and over the fruit, leaving a gap in the centre to reveal the filling. Glaze with milk and sprinkle with sugar.
4 Put on a baking sheet and bake for about 50 minutes or until the pastry is golden brown and the juice is bubbling up around the pastry. Serve hot with ice cream.

Serves 4 preparation: 15 minutes cooking time: 50 minutes
per serving: 570 cals; 26g fat; 83g carbohydrate

Pear Tarte Tatin

100g (3½oz) golden caster sugar
50g (2oz) butter
1 cinnamon stick, broken in half
2 ripe pears, peeled, quartered and cored

½ vanilla pod, split lengthways
200g (7oz) ready-rolled puff pastry
plain flour, to dust

1 Preheat the oven to 200°C (180°C fan oven) mark 6. Put the sugar and butter in a pan and gently heat until the sugar dissolves (don't stir as the sugar may crystallise). Increase the heat, bubble until the mixture is a deep caramel colour, then pour into a 20cm (8 inch) diameter round cake tin.
2 Add the cinnamon pieces to the tin, then arrange the pears over the caramel. Scrape out the seeds from the vanilla pod and spread over the pears. Leave the caramel to cool until it sets.
3 Meanwhile, roll out the pastry on a lightly floured surface to a 23cm (9 inch) circle. Cover the pears with the pastry, tucking the edges inside the tin. Make six slashes in the pastry to let the steam out.
4 Bake for 30–35 minutes or until golden. Remove from the oven and leave the tart to stand for 10 minutes before carefully inverting it on to a deep plate. Serve with cream.

Serves 4 preparation: 15 minutes, plus cooling and standing cooking time: 45 minutes
per serving: 430 cals; 22g fat; 58g carbohydrate

Maple Pecan Pie

250g (9oz) plain flour, plus extra to dust
pinch of salt
225g (8oz) unsalted butter
100g (3½oz) light muscovado sugar
125g (4oz) dates, pitted and roughly
  chopped

grated zest and juice of ½ lemon
100ml (3½fl oz) maple syrup, plus 4tbsp
  extra to glaze
1tsp vanilla extract
4 eggs
300g (11oz) pecan nut halves

1 To make the pastry, put the flour and salt into a food processor. Dice 125g (4oz) butter, add to the flour and whiz until the mixture resembles fine breadcrumbs, then add 2tbsp cold water and whiz briefly until the dough just comes together. Wrap in clingfilm and chill for 30 minutes. Soften the remaining butter.

2 Roll out the pastry on a lightly floured surface and use to line a 25.5cm (10 inch) fluted loose-based tart tin, about 4cm (1½ inches) deep. Chill for 30 minutes.

3 Preheat the oven to 200°C (180°C fan oven) mark 6. Prick the pastry base, line with greaseproof paper and fill with baking beans. Bake for 15 minutes, remove the beans and paper and bake for a further 5 minutes, then take out of the oven.

4 Meanwhile, make the filling. Put the softened butter, sugar and dates into the food processor and whiz to cream together. Add the lemon zest and juice, maple syrup, vanilla extract, eggs and 200g (7oz) nuts. Whiz until the nuts are finely chopped – the mixture will look curdled but don't worry. Pour into the pastry case and top with the rest of the nuts.

5 Return the case to the oven and bake for 40–45 minutes until almost set in the middle, covering with greaseproof paper for the last 10 minutes if the nuts turn very dark. Leave in the tin for 5 minutes, then remove and brush with maple syrup to glaze. Serve warm, with cream or ice cream.

Serves 10–12 preparation: 40 minutes, plus chilling cooking time: about 1 hour
per serving: 600–500 cals; 43–35g fat; 50–41g carbohydrate

14

Hot puddings

Plum and Cardamom Pie

250g (9oz) ready-rolled sweet shortcrust
  pastry
plain flour, to dust
900g (2lb) mixed yellow and red plums,
  halved, stoned and quartered

2–3 green cardamom pods, split open,
  seeds removed and crushed or chopped
50–75g (2–3oz) golden caster sugar, plus
  extra to dust
beaten egg or milk, to glaze

1 Heat a flat baking sheet in the oven at 220°C (200°C fan oven) mark 7.
2 Roll out the pastry on a lightly floured surface a little thinner into a rough circle about 30cm (12 inches) in diameter. Put it on a floured baking sheet, preferably without a lip.
3 Pile the fruit in the centre of the pastry and sprinkle with the crushed cardamom seeds and sugar (if the plums are tart you'll need all of it, if ripe and sweet use a little less). Fold in the pastry edges and pleat together around the plums.
4 Brush the pastry with beaten egg or milk and sprinkle with sugar. Put on the preheated sheet and bake for 30 minutes or until the pastry is golden brown and the plums just tender. The juices will begin to bubble a little from the pie as it cooks.
5 Remove from the oven and leave the pie to cool for 10 minutes. Carefully loosen the pastry around the edges and cool for another 20 minutes. Transfer very carefully to a serving plate. Sprinkle the pie with a little extra sugar and serve warm with cream or vanilla ice cream.

Serves 6 preparation: 15 minutes, plus cooling cooking time: 30 minutes
per serving: 280 cals; 12g fat; 44g carbohydrate

14

Hot puddings

Sugar-crusted Fruit Pie

350g (12oz) cherries, pitted
75g (3oz) golden caster sugar, plus 2tbsp
75g (3oz) hazelnuts, toasted and cooled

175g (6oz) plain flour, plus extra to dust
125g (4oz) butter, softened
275g (10oz) cooking apples

1 Put the cherries in a bowl with 25g (1oz) sugar, cover and put to one side. To make the hazelnut pastry, put 50g (2oz) hazelnuts in a food processor with the flour and pulse to a powder. Remove and set aside. Put the butter and 50g (2oz) sugar in the food processor and whiz until blended. Add the flour mixture and pulse until it forms a dough. Turn out on to a lightly floured surface and knead lightly, then wrap and chill for 30 minutes. If the pastry cracks, just work it together.

2 Preheat the oven to 180°C (160°C fan oven) mark 4. Peel, quarter and core the apples. Cut into small chunks and put in a 900ml (1½ pint) oval ovenproof pie dish. Spoon the cherries on top. Roll out the pastry on a lightly floured surface to a thickness of about 5mm (¼ inch). Cut into 1cm (½ inch) strips. Dampen the edge of the pie dish with a little water and press a few of the strips on to the rim to cover it, using the knife to help lift the pastry into position. Dampen the pastry rim. Arrange the remaining pastry strips over the cherries to create a lattice pattern.

3 Brush the pastry with water and sprinkle with the 2tbsp sugar. Bake for 30–35 minutes or until the pastry is golden. Remove from the oven and leave to cool for 15 minutes.

4 Chop the remaining toasted hazelnuts and sprinkle over the tart. Serve with whipped double cream.

Serves 4   preparation: 30 minutes, plus chilling and cooling   cooking time: 35 minutes
per serving: 580 cals; 33g fat; 70g carbohydrate

American-style Plum Cobbler

900g (2lb) plums, halved and stoned
175g (6oz) golden caster sugar, plus 3tbsp
1tbsp cornflour
250g (9oz) self-raising flour

100g (3½oz) chilled unsalted butter, diced
175ml (6fl oz) buttermilk or whole natural
  yogurt

1 Preheat the oven to 200°C (180°C fan oven) mark 6. Cut the plums into chunky wedges. Tip into a 25.5 x 18 x 7.5cm (10 x 7 x 3 inch) ovenproof dish and toss together with the 3tbsp sugar and the cornflour.

2 Put the flour into a processor, add the butter and 100g (3½oz) sugar and whiz until the mixture forms fine crumbs. Add the buttermilk or yogurt and whiz for a few seconds until just combined.

3 Scatter clumps of the squidgy dough over the plums, leaving some of the fruit exposed. Sprinkle the cobbler with the remaining sugar and bake for 40 minutes until the fruit is tender and the topping is pale golden.

Serves 6   preparation: 25 minutes   cooking time: 40 minutes
per serving: 467 cals; 14g fat; 48g carbohydrate

14

Hot puddings

Oven-baked Mini Christmas Puddings

150g (5oz) each currants, raisins and
  sultanas
150g (5oz) each dates and prunes, chopped
100ml (3½fl oz) each Grand Marnier and
  Guinness
finely grated zest and juice of 1 orange
175g (6oz) butter, plus extra to grease
175g (6oz) molasses sugar

3 eggs, beaten
75g (3oz) self-raising flour, sifted
1tbsp ground mixed spice
1 carrot, about 75g (3oz), peeled and grated
150g (5oz) fresh white breadcrumbs
75g (3oz) blanched almonds, toasted and
  chopped
50g (2oz) pecans, toasted and chopped

1   Put the dried fruit in a large bowl with the alcohol, orange zest and juice and leave to macerate.
2   Grease twelve 150ml (¼ pint) ovenproof cups or individual pudding moulds and line each with a
    25.5cm (10 inch) square piece of muslin, or line the bases with baking parchment. (Don't worry if you
    only have six moulds – you can bake the puds in two batches, and the uncooked mixture will happily
    sit overnight.)
3   Put the butter and sugar in a large bowl and, using an electric hand mixer, whisk for 5 minutes until
    pale and fluffy. Beat in the eggs, one at a time, adding a little flour if the mixture looks as if it might
    curdle. Using a large metal spoon, carefully fold in the remaining flour, the mixed spice, carrot,
    breadcrumbs, nuts, soaked fruit and alcohol until just combined.
4   Divide the mixture among the cups or moulds. Smooth the surfaces, gather the muslin up and over
    each pudding, then twist and secure with string.
5   Preheat the oven to 180°C (160°C fan oven) mark 4. Wrap each pudding in foil, put in a roasting tin
    and pour in enough boiling water to come two-thirds of the way up the cups. Cover the whole tin with
    foil and bake for 2½ hours. Remove from the oven and cool, then remove the puddings from the
    cups and wrap in foil. Store in a cool dark place.
6   To serve, preheat the oven to 180°C (160°C fan oven) mark 4. Take the puddings out of their clingfilm
    and foil wrappers and put the muslin-covered puddings back in their basins. Wrap completely in new
    foil. Put in a roasting tin and pour in enough boiling water to come two-thirds of the way up their
    sides. Cover the roasting tin with foil and reheat in the oven for 1 hour. When ready to serve, have an
    ovenproof glove to hand and a sharp pair of scissors to snip the puds out of their wrappings.

Makes 12 x 150ml (¼ pint) individual puddings   preparation: 30 minutes   cooking time: 2½ hours
per serving: 470 cals; 20g fat; 65g carbohydrate

14

Hot puddings

Warm Ginger and Ricotta Cheesecake

225g (8oz) digestive biscuits
75g (3oz) butter, melted
200g (7oz) full-fat soft cheese
225g (8oz) ricotta cheese
4tbsp double cream
3 eggs, separated
1tbsp cornflour

1 ball stem ginger in syrup, drained and
   finely chopped, plus stem ginger syrup
   from the jar
125g (4oz) golden icing sugar, sifted
300ml (½ pint) single cream
2tsp whisky

1 Preheat the oven to 200°C (180°C fan oven) mark 6. To make the base, put the biscuits into a food processor and whiz to fine crumbs. Add the melted butter and mix until well combined.
2 Line the base of a 20.5cm (8 inch) spring-release cake tin with baking parchment and cover the base with two-thirds of the crumb mixture, then put to one side.
3 For the filling, put the cheeses, double cream, egg yolks, cornflour, ginger and 1tbsp ginger syrup in the cleaned processor bowl and whiz briefly until the mixture is evenly blended and the ginger is roughly chopped through it. Transfer to a large bowl.
4 Whisk the egg whites in a clean grease-free bowl until soft peaks form. Gradually whisk in the sugar, keeping the meringue very stiff and shiny. Fold into the ginger mixture and spoon into the tin. Sprinkle over the remaining biscuit crumbs.
5 Bake the cheesecake for 30 minutes. Cover loosely with foil, reduce the oven temperature to 180°C (160°C fan oven) mark 4 and bake for 45 minutes or until the filling feels just set in the centre. Remove from the oven and leave to cool on a wire rack for 15 minutes; the cheesecake will sink slightly.
6 To make the sauce, put the single cream, 2tsp ginger syrup and the whisky in a pan and heat, but do not boil.
7 Unmould the cheesecake and serve warm with the ginger and whisky sauce.

Serves 6–8   preparation: 25 minutes   cooking time: 1¼ hours, plus cooling
per serving: 760–570 cals; 56–42g fat; 55–41g carbohydrate

14

Hot puddings

Bermuda Banana Pudding

40g (1½oz) butter, at room temperature,
plus extra to grease
5tbsp light muscovado sugar
6 large bananas – 5 mashed, 1 sliced

3tbsp plain flour, sifted
3tbsp milk
few drops of vanilla extract

1   Preheat the oven to 190°C (170°C fan oven) mark 5. Grease a 16.5cm (6½ inch) diameter shallow cake tin and line the base with non-stick baking parchment. Beat the butter with the sugar until combined. Add the mashed bananas, flour, milk and vanilla extract and mix well. Fold in the sliced banana.
2   Pour the mixture into the tin and bake for 45–50 minutes or until firm to the touch.
3   Remove from the oven and turn out, then remove the paper. Cut into eight, arrange two wedges on each plate and serve with vanilla ice cream (page 545).

Serves 4   preparation: 15 minutes, plus cooling   cooking time: 50 minutes
per serving: 310 cals; 9g fat; 58g carbohydrate

Glazed Berry Pudding

butter to grease
1 vanilla pod or 1tsp vanilla extract
4 large eggs, separated
50g (2oz) golden caster sugar
25g (1oz) plain flour
142ml carton double cream

150ml (¼ pint) full-fat milk
225g (8oz) icing sugar, plus extra to dust
450g (1lb) mixed red fruits, frozen compôte
or conserve
blueberries and raspberries, to decorate

1   Lightly grease eight 150ml (¼ pint) ramekins and put in the freezer to chill. Split the vanilla pod lengthways and scrape the seeds into the bowl with the egg yolks. Combine the yolks and caster sugar and beat until pale, then stir in the flour.
2   Bring the cream and milk to the boil in a small pan then pour over the yolks, stirring. Return the mixture to the pan and cook over a gentle heat for 2 minutes, stirring all the time, or until thick and smooth. Turn into a clean bowl, add the vanilla extract, if using, cover and cool.
3   Put the egg whites and icing sugar in a large heatproof bowl set over a pan of simmering water and whisk for 10 minutes until thick. Remove from the heat and whisk until cool.
4   Put 2tbsp of the fruits in the base of each ramekin. Fold the meringue into the custard and pile on top of the fruits, then put back in the freezer for at least 7 hours or until firm.
5   Preheat the oven to 220°C (200°C fan oven) mark 7. Remove the ramekins from the freezer, put on a baking sheet and dust thickly with icing sugar. Bake for 20 minutes, decorate with the berries and serve immediately.

Serves 8   preparation: 20 minutes, plus freezing   cooking time: 25 minutes
per serving: 300 cals; 12g fat; 45g carbohydrate

Sticky Marmalade Pudding

175g (6oz) butter
175g (6oz) light muscovado sugar
about 300g (11oz) Seville orange
   marmalade
2 seedless oranges, peeled, all pith
   removed and sliced thinly into rounds

2 large eggs, beaten
175g (6oz) self-raising flour
1½tsp ground ginger
40g (1½oz) stem ginger in syrup, drained
   and finely chopped

1 Preheat the oven to 180°C (160°C fan oven) mark 4. Line the base of a round 23cm (9 inch) wide, minimum 5cm (2 inch) deep tin with non-stick baking parchment. Warm 50g (2oz) each of the butter and sugar with half the marmalade. Spoon into the tin and arrange the orange slices over.

2 Beat together the remaining butter and sugar. Gradually beat in the eggs. Sift the flour and ground ginger and fold into the mixture with the remaining marmalade and the stem ginger. Spread over the oranges.

3 Stand the tin on a baking sheet and bake for 1 hour 10 minutes or until just firm to the touch. If necessary, cover with foil.

4 Remove from the oven and loosen around the edges of the tin, then invert the pudding on to an edged serving plate. Serve warm with custard.

Serves 8 preparation: 20 minutes   cooking time: 1 hour
per serving: 370 cals; 20g fat; 45g carbohydrate

Sweet Carrot Pudding

450g (1lb) carrots, peeled and coarsely
   grated
750ml (1¼ pints) full-fat milk
150ml (¼ pint) single cream
75g (3oz) sugar
1tbsp treacle

3tbsp melted butter
125g (4oz) ground almonds
seeds of 6 green cardamoms, crushed
25g (1oz) sultanas
chopped pistachios, to decorate

1 Put the carrots in a large heavy-based pan. Pour in the milk and cream and bring to the boil, stirring constantly. Reduce the heat and simmer very gently, stirring occasionally to prevent sticking, for at least 2 hours until the milk has evaporated and the mixture is greatly reduced.

2 Stir in the sugar and treacle, then simmer for 30 minutes, stirring occasionally to prevent sticking.

3 Add the melted butter, almonds, cardamom seeds and sultanas. Cook, stirring, for 5–10 minutes until the mixture begins to look oily on the surface. Transfer to a serving dish and decorate with the pistachios. Serve hot or cold.

Serves 4–6 preparation: 5 minutes   cooking time: 2¾ hours
per serving: 630–420 cals; 44–30g fat; 46–31g carbohydrate

Saucy Hot Lemon Puddings

50g (2oz) butter, plus extra to grease
125g (4oz) golden caster sugar
finely grated zest and juice of 2 lemons

2 eggs, separated
50g (2oz) self-raising flour
300ml (½ pint) semi-skimmed milk

1 Preheat the oven to 190°C (170°C fan oven) mark 5. Lightly grease four 200ml (7fl oz) ovenproof cups. Cream together the butter, sugar and lemon zest in a bowl until pale and fluffy. Beat in the egg yolks, then the flour until combined. Stir in the milk and lemon juice – the mixture will curdle but don't panic. Whisk the egg whites in a clean grease-free bowl until they stand in soft peaks, then fold into the lemon mixture. (The mixture will still look curdled – don't worry.) Divide the mixture among the four cups and stand them in a roasting tin.
2 Pour in enough boiling water to come at least halfway up their sides and bake the puddings for 35–40 minutes or until spongy and light golden. If you prefer softer tops, cover the entire tin with foil. When cooked, the puddings will have separated into a tangy lemon custard layer on the bottom, with a light sponge on top.

Serves 4   preparation: 10 minutes   cooking time: 35–40 minutes
per serving: 340 cals; 15g fat; 46g carbohydrate

Easy Jam Sponge Pudding

125g (4oz) butter, softened, plus extra to
  grease
4tbsp raspberry jam
grated zest of ½ orange, plus about 8tbsp
  juice

50g (2oz) golden caster sugar
1 large egg, lightly beaten
125g (4oz) self-raising flour, sifted

1 Grease the inside of four 175ml (6fl oz) pudding basins with butter. Put 1tbsp jam in the base of each and put to one side. Preheat the oven to 200°C (180°C fan oven) mark 6.
2 Whisk together the butter and orange zest with a small electric whisk until smooth. Whisk in the sugar until thoroughly combined – about 10 minutes – then gradually whisk in the egg. Fold in the flour, then sufficient orange juice to give a soft dropping consistency. Spoon on top of the jam and smooth the surfaces.
3 Grease four discs of foil, measuring about 12.5cm (5 inches) across, and cover the puddings with them, folding under the rim to secure. Put the basins in a large roasting tin. Pour in enough boiling water to come at least halfway up their sides. Cook for 45 minutes or until the puddings are risen, cooked to the centre and golden brown on top. Lift out of the roasting tin, unmould when ready and serve with pouring cream or custard.

Serves 4   preparation: 20 minutes   cooking time: 45 minutes
per serving: 460 cals; 28g fat; 50g carbohydrate

14

Hot puddings

Queen of Puddings

600ml (1 pint) full-fat milk
25g (1oz) butter
grated zest of 1 large lemon
3 large eggs, separated

175g (6oz) golden caster sugar
100g (3½oz) fine fresh breadcrumbs
4tbsp lemon curd

1 Put the milk, butter and lemon zest in a pan and heat gently until the butter melts. Put to one side until lukewarm. Mix the egg yolks with 25g (1oz) sugar in a bowl until thoroughly combined, then blend in the warm milk. Add the breadcrumbs and pour into a 1.1 litre (2 pint) ovenproof dish. Leave to stand for 20 minutes. Preheat the oven to 180°C (160°C fan oven) mark 4.

2 Put the dish in a roasting tin and pour in enough boiling water to come halfway up the side of the dish. Bake for 25–30 minutes or until just set to the centre. Remove from the oven and leave to cool for about 20 minutes. Spread the lemon curd over the top. Reduce the oven temperature to 170°C (150°C fan oven) mark 3.

3 Whisk the egg whites in a clean grease-free bowl until stiff peaks form, then whisk in 3tbsp sugar, 1tbsp at a time, until stiff and glossy. Carefully fold in the rest of the sugar with a large spoon. Spoon the meringue on top of the lemon curd and bake for 10–15 minutes or until golden and crisp. Serve warm or at room temperature.

Serves 6 preparation: 10 minutes, plus standing and cooling   cooking time: 50 minutes
per serving: 330 cals; 12g fat; 48g carbohydrate

14

Hot puddings

Date and Walnut Pudding with Chocolate Sauce

125g (4oz) butter, softened, plus extra
  to grease
125g (4oz) golden caster sugar
3 eggs, beaten
175g (6oz) self-raising flour
3tbsp milk
75g (3oz) walnuts, toasted and
  roughly chopped

175g (6oz) pitted dates, roughly chopped
50g (2oz) unsalted butter
50g (2oz) light muscovado sugar
50g (2oz) good-quality plain dark chocolate
  (with minimum 50% cocoa solids),
  in pieces
100ml (3½fl oz) double cream

I Half-fill a steamer or large pan with water and put it on to boil. Grease a 1.1 litre (2 pint) pudding basin.
2 Put the 125g (4oz) butter, the caster sugar, eggs, flour and milk in a bowl and beat with an electric beater until smooth. Fold in the nuts and dates.
3 Spoon the mixture into the prepared pudding basin and smooth the surface. Cover with greased and pleated greaseproof paper and foil, and secure under the rim with string.
4 Steam the pudding for 2 hours, checking the water level from time to time and topping up with boiling water as necessary. Lift the pudding out of the pan and leave to rest for 15 minutes.
5 Meanwhile, make the chocolate fudge sauce. Put the unsalted butter, muscovado sugar and chocolate into a pan and heat gently until the chocolate has melted. Add the cream, bring to a simmer and let bubble for 3 minutes until thickened.
6 To serve, unmould the pudding on to a warmed plate. Cut into wedges and serve with the chocolate fudge sauce poured over.

Serves 8 preparation: 20 minutes, plus standing   cooking time: 2 hours
per serving: 550 cals; 33g fat; 59g carbohydrate

14

Hot puddings

Baked Egg Custard

butter, to grease
600ml (1 pint) full-fat milk
3 large eggs

2tbsp golden caster sugar
freshly grated nutmeg, to taste

1 Preheat the oven to 170°C (150°C fan oven) mark 3. Grease a 900ml (1½ pint) ovenproof dish. Warm the milk in a pan, but do not boil. Whisk the eggs and sugar together lightly in a bowl, then pour on the hot milk, stirring.
2 Strain the mixture into the prepared dish. Grate the nutmeg on top and bake in the middle of the oven for about 45 minutes until set and firm to the touch. Serve hot or cold.

Serves 4 preparation: 5 minutes cooking time: 45 minutes
per serving: 210 cals; 13g fat; 15g carbohydrate

Rhubarb and Pear Crumble Pudding

450g (1lb) rhubarb, cut into 2.5cm (1 inch)
  pieces
2 ripe pears, peeled, cored and roughly
  chopped
75g (3oz) demerara sugar
1tsp ground cinnamon

50g (2oz) chilled butter
75g (3oz) self-raising flour
2 shortbread fingers
50g (2oz) whole hazelnuts
500g tub Greek-style yogurt

1 Preheat the oven to 180°C (160°C fan oven) mark 4. Put the fruit into a small shallow baking dish, sprinkle over 25g (1oz) sugar and the cinnamon and mix well.
2 To make the crumble, put the butter in a food processor, add the flour and remaining sugar and whiz until it resembles rough breadcrumbs.
3 Break the shortbread fingers into pieces and add to the processor with the hazelnuts. Whiz again for 4–5 seconds until the crumble is blended but still looks rough. Sprinkle the crumble over the fruit, spreading it up to the edges and pressing down with the back of a wooden spoon.
4 Bake for 40–45 minutes or until the topping is golden brown and crisp. Remove from the oven and leave to cool.
5 Divide half the cooled crumble among eight 200ml (7fl oz) serving dishes or glasses. Spoon the yogurt on top, then finish with the remaining crumble. Using a knife or skewer, make a figure of eight to swirl the crumble roughly into the yogurt. Serve warm or chilled.

Serves 8 preparation: 25 minutes cooking time: 40–45 minutes
per serving: 300 cals; 18g fat; 28g carbohydrate

Summer Gratin

3 ripe peaches, halved, stoned and sliced
225g (8oz) wild strawberries or raspberries
3tbsp Kirsch or Eau de Vie de Mirabelle
4 large egg yolks
50g (2oz) sugar

1   Put the peach slices in a bowl with the strawberries or raspberries and 2tbsp Kirsch or Eau de Vie.
2   Put the egg yolks, sugar, remaining Kirsch and 2tbsp water in a heatproof bowl set over a pan of barely simmering water. Whisk for 5–10 minutes or until the mixture leaves a trail and is warm in the centre. Remove from the heat. Preheat the grill.
3   Arrange the fruit in four shallow heatproof dishes and spoon the sauce over. Cook under the grill for 1–2 minutes until light golden. Serve immediately.

Serves 4   preparation: 15 minutes   cooking time: 15 minutes
per serving: 180 cals; 6g fat; 22g carbohydrate

Almond, Apple and Pineapple Puddings

50g (2oz) chilled butter, diced, plus extra to
    grease
50g (2oz) plain flour, plus extra to dust
1 apple, cut vertically into six slices
75g (3oz) golden caster sugar, plus extra to
    dust
1tsp baking powder
pinch of salt

50g (2oz) ground almonds
100g (3½oz) each cooking apple and
    pineapple, peeled, cored and diced
1 large egg, lightly beaten
¼tsp almond essence
crystalised violets, mint sprigs and crushed
    cardamom seeds, to decorate

1   Preheat the oven to 180°C (160°C fan oven) mark 4. Grease six 150ml (¼ pint) pudding basin moulds or ramekins, line the bases with greaseproof paper and dust the sides with flour. Using a pastry cutter the same size as the base of the moulds, stamp out circles from the apple slices. Dust the slices with sugar and fry in a hot non-stick frying pan until caramelised on both sides. Place a slice in the base of each mould.
2   Sift the flour, baking powder and salt into a bowl, then add the sugar, almonds and diced butter. Rub in until the mixture resembles fine crumbs. (Alternatively, you can whiz the mixture in a food processor.) Stir in the cooking apple, pineapple, egg and almond essence.
3   Spoon the mixture into the moulds until they're half full. Bake for 35–40 minutes or until golden and firm in the centre. Remove from the oven and leave the puddings in the moulds for 15 minutes, then carefully run a knife inside the mould to loosen the puddings. Turn out and decorate with crystalised violets, mint sprigs and crushed cardamom seeds.

Serves 6   preparation: 20 minutes   cooking time: 45 minutes, plus standing
per serving: 230 cals; 13g fat; 26g carbohydrate

14

Hot puddings

Pear and Cranberry Strudel

75g (3oz) butter, melted
zest and juice of 1 lemon
25g (1oz) golden caster sugar
1tbsp fresh white breadcrumbs
1tsp ground cinnamon
125g (4oz) fresh cranberries

550g (1¼lb) William or Comice pears, cored
 and sliced
50g (2oz) Brazil nuts, chopped and toasted
7 sheets filo pastry
icing sugar, to dust

1 Preheat the oven to 190°C (170°C fan oven) mark 5. Grease a large baking sheet. Mix the lemon zest with 1tbsp caster sugar, the breadcrumbs and cinnamon and put to one side.
2 Put 6 cranberries on one side, then toss the rest with the pears, lemon juice and nuts. Mix in the breadcrumb mixture.
3 Lay a clean tea-towel on a board and put three sheets of filo pastry on it, each overlapping the other by 12.5cm (5 inches) to make a rectangle measuring 56 x 48cm (22 x 19 inches). Brush with melted butter, then put three more sheets on top and brush again.
4 Spoon the pear mixture along the nearest, longest length and roll up. Trim the edges, then carefully lift on to the baking sheet so the seam is underneath.
5 Brush the remaining sheet of filo pastry with butter, fold in half and cut out six holly leaves. Arrange three together on one half of the log and the remaining three on the other half and brush with melted butter.
6 Sprinkle the strudel with the remaining caster sugar and bake for 40–45 minutes, covering with foil if the top browns too quickly.
7 Remove from the oven and arrange the reserved cranberries on the holly leaves, then dust the strudel heavily with icing sugar. Serve at once with a dollop of thick cream.

Serves 8   preparation: 20 minutes   cooking time: 40–45 minutes
per serving: 210 cals; 12g fat; 24g carbohydrate

Mincemeat Streusel

340g pack sweet dessert pastry
75g (3oz) self-raising flour
finely grated zest of ½ lemon
50g (2oz) unsalted butter, chilled and cut
   into cubes, plus extra to grease

50g (2oz) light muscovado sugar
25g (1oz) ground almonds
350g jar mincemeat

1 Preheat the oven to 180°C (160°C fan oven) mark 4. Grease a 33 x 10cm (13 x 4 inch) fluted rectangular tin and line the base with greaseproof paper.
2 Roll out the pastry on a lightly floured surface to fit the tin, line the tin and prick the pastry with a fork. Line the pastry case with baking parchment, fill with baking beans and bake for 15 minutes. Remove the parchment and beans and bake for a further 15 minutes, then leave to cool for 5 minutes.
3 To make the streusel topping, put the flour and lemon zest in a bowl and rub in the butter, until the mixture becomes crumbly. Stir in the sugar and almonds.
4 Spread the mincemeat evenly over the pastry and sprinkle the streusel on top. Bake for 15 minutes until the topping is golden. Remove from the oven and leave to cool for 30 minutes. Remove from the tin, cut into slices and serve warm.

Serves 8   preparation: 15 minutes   cooking time: 45 minutes
per serving: 430 cals; 20g fat; 52g carbohydrate

Exotic Boozy Pancakes

2 x 500g packs frozen tropical fruit
6tbsp rum
50g (2oz) butter
2tbsp golden caster sugar

6 ready-made pancakes
200ml carton crème fraîche
freshly grated nutmeg, to serve

1 Put the fruit into a large frying pan. Add the rum, butter and sugar and cook over a low heat for 7–10 minutes or until the fruit has thawed but isn't too soft. Remove the fruit with a slotted spoon, cover and set aside. Bring the juice in the pan to the boil, then cook for 7–10 minutes or until reduced to a syrupy consistency.
2 Meanwhile, heat the pancakes in microwave on High for 1 minute 50 seconds (based on a 900W oven), or according to the packet instructions. Alternatively, wrap the pancakes in foil and steam over a pan of boiling water for 5 minutes until heated through.
3 Serve each pancake topped with fruit and drizzled with the syrup. Add a generous dollop of crème fraîche, then sprinkle a little nutmeg over the top.

Serves 6   preparation: 5 minutes   cooking time: 20 minutes
per serving: 500 cals; 29g fat; 49g carbohydrate

Chocoholics

The title of this chapter says it all – you know if you're one or not. No half measures. So, you'll be in heaven here with spectacular chocolate cakes, gateaux and roulades; custards, creams and terrines – smooth and rich; and intensely flavoured puddings – lusciously gooey chocolate centres encased in rich chocolate sponge.

Then there are soft, melting meringues enveloped in chocolate – Chocolate-dipped Brown Sugar Meringues, and Chocolate and Hazelnut Meringues, topped with cream, fruit and chocolate curls; not to mention a chocolate version of Baked Alaska and a chocolate Strawberry Pavlova.

And what goes perfectly with a cup of tea, coffee or, even hot chocolate? Chocolate cookies and brownies – try the White and Dark Cookies for a tempting treat.

If you're baking someone a special cake, make them one to remember – the Wicked Chocolate Cake is a rich chocolate and marzipan cake drizzled with chocolate ganache and decorated with sugared almonds. Or, simply The Best Chocolate Cake in the World – rich, delicious and perfect for any occasion.

Easy Chocolate Curls

200g (7oz) good-quality white or dark chocolate

knob of butter

1 Melt the chocolate and butter in a heatproof bowl set over a pan of barely simmering water, stirring until smooth. Pour into a small rectangular container (a 250g margarine tub is ideal) and leave to cool and harden.
2 Before shaping the curls, leave the chocolate at warm room temperature to soften slightly, then turn the chocolate out on to a marble slab or clean surface.
3 Hold the chocolate in a piece of kitchen paper and use a swivelled vegetable peeler to shave off curls along the length of the block.
4 Store the curls, interleaved with greaseproof paper, in an airtight container in a cool place for up to one week.

preparation: 15 minutes, plus cooling   cooking time: 10 minutes
1050 cals; 58g fat; 130g carbohydrate

Baked Chocolate and Coffee Custards

284ml carton semi-skimmed milk
142ml carton double cream
200g (7oz) good-quality plain chocolate, semi-sweet such as Bournville, broken into small pieces
4 large egg yolks

1tbsp golden caster sugar
3tbsp very strong cold black coffee
125g (4oz) mascarpone
1tsp icing sugar
grated zest and juice of ½ orange, plus extra zest to decorate (optional)

1 Preheat the oven to 170°C (150°C fan oven) mark 3. Put the milk, cream and chocolate in a heavy-based pan over a very gentle heat until melted. Stir until smooth.
2 Mix the egg yolks, caster sugar and coffee in a bowl, then pour on the warm chocolate milk. Mix briefly, then strain through a sieve into a jug. Pour the mixture into six 150ml (¼ pint) ovenproof custard cups or ramekins.
3 Stand the dishes in a large roasting tin and pour enough boiling water into the tin to come halfway up their sides. Bake for 20–25 minutes or until just set and still a little wobbly in the middle – they'll firm up as they cool. Carefully lift the dishes out of the roasting tin and leave to cool, then stand them on a small tray and chill for at least 3 hours.
4 To make the topping, beat the mascarpone, icing sugar, orange zest and juice together until smooth. Cover and chill for 1–2 hours.
5 To serve, put a spoonful of the mascarpone mixture on top of each custard and decorate with grated orange zest, if using. Serve with thin shortbread biscuits.

Serves 6 preparation: 15 minutes, plus chilling   cooking time: 20–25 minutes
per serving: 460 cals; 36g fat; 31g carbohydrate

Chocolate Terrine with Vanilla Bean Sauce

350g (12oz) good-quality plain dark
   chocolate (with 70% cocoa solids), broken
   into small pieces
40g (1½oz) cocoa powder
oil, to grease
6 large eggs, beaten, plus 4 large egg yolks
125g (4oz) light muscovado sugar
284ml carton double cream

5tbsp brandy (optional)
568ml carton single cream
1 vanilla pod, split, seeds removed
   and reserved
75g (3oz) golden caster sugar
½tsp cornflour
cocoa powder, to dust

1 Put the chocolate and cocoa in a heatproof bowl set over a pan of barely simmering water and stir occasionally until melted and glossy. Leave to cool.

2 Preheat the oven to 150°C (130°C fan oven) mark 2. Grease a 900g (2lb) loaf tin and line the base with greaseproof paper. Whisk together the 6 beaten eggs and the muscovado sugar, then whisk the double cream until soft peaks form. Gradually combine the egg mixture, chocolate and cream. Add the brandy, if using. Pour the mixture into the loaf tin and tap on a work surface to level.

3 Stand the loaf tin in a roasting tin and pour enough boiling water into the tin to come halfway up the sides of the loaf tin, then cover with non-stick baking parchment. Bake for 1¾ hours or until just set at the centre. Remove from the oven and leave in tin for 30 minutes, then lift out and chill overnight.

4 To make the sauce, gently heat the single cream and vanilla seeds in a heavy-based pan until the cream just comes to the boil. Put to one side to cool for 15 minutes.

5 Whisk the egg yolks with the caster sugar and cornflour, add a little of the cooled cream and whisk until smooth. Add the remaining cream and stir well. Pour back into the cleaned pan and stir over a medium heat for 5 minutes or until thickened (it should coat the back of a spoon). Strain, cool, cover and chill.

6 Serve the terrine in slices with the vanilla bean sauce poured around, dusted with cocoa powder.

Serves 12   preparation: 45 minutes, plus cooling and chilling   cooking time: 1¾ hours
per serving: 480 cals; 36g fat; 28g carbohydrate

Cheat's Chocolate Pots

500g carton fresh custard

200g (7oz) good-quality plain dark
   chocolate (with minimum 50% cocoa
   solids), broken into pieces

1 Put the custard in a small pan with the chocolate pieces. Heat gently, stirring all the time, until the chocolate has melted.

2 Pour the mixture into four small coffee cups, put on to saucers and serve immediately, or leave the mixture to cool slightly and serve as a chocolate sauce with vanilla ice cream.

Serves 4   preparation: 5 minutes   cooking time: 5 minutes
per serving: 380 cals; 17g fat; 53g carbohydrate

White Chocolate Mousse

100ml (3½fl oz) milk
1 cinnamon stick
250g (9oz) good-quality white chocolate, broken into pieces
284ml carton double cream
3 large egg whites

50g (2oz) good-quality plain dark chocolate (with minimum 50% cocoa solids), in one piece
a little cocoa powder and ground cinnamon, to decorate

1 Put the milk and cinnamon stick in a small pan and warm over a medium heat until the milk is almost boiling. Take the pan off the heat and put to one side.
2 Meanwhile, bring a small pan of water to a gentle simmer. Put the white chocolate in a small heatproof bowl and put it over the pan. Turn the heat off and leave the bowl over the hot water for 15 minutes or until the chocolate has melted. Take the bowl off the pan and leave to cool a little.
3 Strain the warm milk on to the melted chocolate and stir until completely smooth. Leave to cool for 10 minutes.
4 Whip the cream in a bowl until it just begins to hold its shape – it should still be a bit floppy. Whisk the egg whites in a clean grease-free bowl until soft peaks form.
5 Using a large metal spoon, fold the whipped cream into the chocolate mixture, then carefully fold in the egg whites. Spoon the mixture into six 150ml (¼ pint) small bowls or glasses and chill for up to 4 hours or overnight.
6 Pull a vegetable peeler across the edge of the plain chocolate to make rough curls and sprinkle them over the mousse. Dust with cocoa powder and a pinch of cinnamon to serve.

Serves 6 preparation: 15 minutes, plus chilling   cooking time: 15 minutes
per serving: 180 cals; 15g fat; 3g carbohydrate

Chocolate Mousse

350g (12oz) good-quality plain chocolate, semi-sweet such as Bournville, broken into pieces

6 tbsp rum, brandy or cold black coffee
6 large eggs, separated

1 Put the chocolate, rum, brandy or black coffee in a heatproof bowl set over a pan of barely simmering water. Leave to melt, stirring occasionally. Remove from the heat and cool slightly for 3–4 minutes, stirring frequently.
2 Beat the egg yolks with 2tbsp water, then beat into the chocolate mixture until evenly blended.
3 Whisk the egg whites with the salt in a clean grease-free bowl until stiff peaks form, then fold into the chocolate mixture.
4 Pour the mixture into a 1.4–1.7 litre (2½–3 pint) soufflé dish or divide among six to eight 150ml (¼ pint) ramekins. Chill for at least 4 hours, or overnight, until set.

Serves 6–8 preparation: 20 minutes, plus chilling
per serving: 440–330 cals; 24–18g fat; 38–28g carbohydrate

Chocolate-dipped Brown Sugar Meringues

3 large egg whites
50g (2oz) golden caster sugar
125g (4oz) light muscovado sugar

200g (7oz) good-quality plain dark
   chocolate (with minimum 50% cocoa
   solids)

1 Line three baking sheets with baking parchment and preheat the oven to 130°C (110°C fan oven) mark ½.
2 Whisk the egg whites in a clean grease-free bowl until stiff peaks form. Mix both sugars together, then add to the whites, 1tbsp at a time, and whisk in until the meringue is stiff and shiny.
3 Secure the parchment to each baking sheet with a little meringue, then shape the mixture into quenelles as follows: using two dessertspoons and working quickly, take a scoop of the meringue with one spoon and scrape from one to the other three times to form a smooth oval. Carefully transfer each meringue to the parchment, spacing them well apart.
4 Bake for 1½ hours or until the meringues lift off the baking parchment easily. Remove from the oven now for a gooey centre or leave in a cooling oven for a further 2 hours to dry out completely.
5 Melt the chocolate in a heatproof bowl (deep enough to dip the meringues up to halfway) set over a pan of barely simmering water, stirring occasionally. Dip the meringues to half-coat them in chocolate, then leave to set on parchment. When cool, arrange on a plate and serve with whipped cream.

Makes about 20   preparation: 30 minutes   cooking time: 1½–3½ hours, to taste
per meringue: 90 cals; 3g fat; 16g carbohydrate

Chocolate Orange Pots

2 x 100g bars dark chocolate, roughly
  broken

500g carton fromage frais

1 Melt the chocolate in a heatproof bowl set over a pan of simmering water, stirring occasionally.
2 Put the fromage frais in a heatproof bowl set over a pan of simmering water and warm for just 4 minutes.
3 Pour the fromage frais into the chocolate and mix. Spoon into four coffee cups and chill for 15 minutes–2 hours before serving.

Serves 4   preparation: 5 minutes   cooking time: 5 minutes, plus chilling
per serving: 390 cals; 28g fat; 19g carbohydrate

Chocolate and Hazelnut Meringues

125g (4oz) hazelnuts, toasted
125g (4oz) golden caster sugar
75g (3oz) good-quality plain dark chocolate
  (with 70% cocoa solids), in pieces
2 large egg whites

284ml carton double cream
strawberries and redcurrants, to decorate
chocolate curls (page 608, optional)

1 Preheat the oven to 110°C (100°C fan oven) mark ¼. Line two baking sheets with non-stick baking parchment. Put the hazelnuts in a food processor with 3tbsp sugar and whiz to a fine powder. Add the chocolate and pulse until roughly chopped.
2 Whisk the egg whites in a clean grease-free bowl until stiff peaks form. Gradually whisk in the remaining sugar, 1tbsp at a time, until the meringue is stiff and shiny. Fold in the nut mixture.
3 Put spoonfuls of the meringue in rough mounds, about 9cm (3 inches) in diameter, on the baking sheets. Bake for about 45 minutes or until the meringues have dried out just enough to peel off the parchment.
4 Gently push in the base of each meringue to form a deep hollow and return to the oven for 1¼ hours or until crisp and dry. Transfer to a wire rack and leave to cool.
5 Whip the cream until it just holds its shape, then spoon three-quarters on to the meringues. Leave in the fridge to soften for up to 2 hours.
6 To serve, put a meringue on each serving plate and top with the remaining cream, the fruit and chocolate curls, if using. Serve immediately.

Serves 6   preparation: 25 minutes, plus softening   cooking time: 2 hours
per serving: 440 cals; 35g fat; 29g carbohydrate

Chocoholics

Baked Alaska

50g (2oz) butter, plus extra to grease
200g (7oz) plain chocolate digestive
    biscuits, finely crushed
600ml (1 pint) good-quality chocolate
    ice cream
2 chocolate flake bars, roughly chopped

4 large egg whites
225g (8oz) golden caster sugar
50g (2oz) desiccated coconut
cocoa powder, to dust
toasted coconut shavings (optional)

1 Lightly grease a baking sheet. Melt the butter and while it is still hot stir in the biscuits. Using a 6cm (2½ inch) pastry cutter as a template, press the mixture into six circles on the baking sheet and freeze for 30 minutes.
2 Beat the ice cream to soften it slightly and pile into mounds on the biscuit bases. Make a shallow hollow in the centre of each ice cream mound and fill with the chocolate flakes. Return to the freezer for at least 1 hour until firm.
3 Put the egg whites and sugar in a large bowl set over a pan of barely simmering water. Using an electric whisk, beat for 10 minutes or until the mixture is thick and glossy. Fold in the desiccated coconut. Leave to cool for 5 minutes.
4 Cover the ice cream mounds completely with a thick layer of meringue. Return to the freezer for at least 4 hours or overnight.
5 To serve, preheat the oven to 220°C (200°C fan oven) mark 7. Bake the puddings for 5 minutes or until golden. Dust with cocoa powder, top with toasted coconut, if using, and serve immediately.

Serves 6   preparation: 20 minutes, plus freezing   cooking time: 5 minutes
per serving: 630 cals; 30g fat; 84g carbohydrate

Chocolate and Ginger Truffles

142ml carton double cream
125g (4oz) good-quality plain chocolate,
    roughly chopped
15 ready-to-eat ginger slices

1 Pour the cream into a small pan and bring to the boil. Turn off the heat, add the chocolate and stir to mix. Pour into a bowl, leave to cool, then chill for 2 hours.
2 Put a 1cm (½ inch) nozzle into a piping bag and spoon in the chocolate ganache. Arrange 12 ginger slices on a tray and pipe a blob of ganache on to each. Put to one side. (You can freeze any leftover ganache and use to make more truffles.)
3 Thinly slice the three remaining pieces of ginger and use to decorate the top of each chocolate truffle. Chill overnight. Remove from the fridge 10–15 minutes before serving.

Makes 12   preparation: 10 minutes, plus chilling   cooking time: 3 minutes
per truffle: 120 cals; 9g fat; 12g carbohydrate

Chocolate Peanut Butter Chunks

butter, to grease
400g (14oz) good-quality white chocolate,
  broken into pieces

400g (14oz) good-quality plain chocolate,
  broken into pieces
150g (5oz) crunchy peanut butter

1   Grease a shallow 30.5 x 20.5cm (12 x 8 inch) tin and line with baking parchment.
2   Melt the white chocolate in a heatproof bowl set over a pan of barely simmering water. Stir until smooth, then remove the bowl from the pan. Melt the plain chocolate in the same way and remove from the heat.
3   Add the peanut butter to the white chocolate and stir well until smooth.
4   Drop alternate spoonfuls of each chocolate into the prepared tin, then tap the tin to level the mixture. Drag a skewer through both mixtures to create a marbled effect. Tap the tin again to level the mixture, then chill for 2–3 hours until firm.
5   Turn out on to a board and cut into 10 fingers, then cut each finger into 8 chunks. Pack into boxes or an airtight container, separating the layers with baking parchment. Store in the fridge for up to one month.

Makes 80   preparation: 30 minutes, plus chilling   cooking time: 10–15 minutes
per chunk: 70 cals; 4g fat; 6g carbohydrate

Nutty Chocolate Truffles

100g (3½oz) hazelnuts
200g (7oz) good-quality plain dark
  chocolate (with minimum 50% cocoa
  solids), broken into pieces

25g (1oz) butter
142ml carton double cream
3tbsp each cocoa powder and golden
  icing sugar

1   Put the hazelnuts in a dry frying pan and heat gently for 3–4 minutes, shaking the pan occasionally, to toast all over. Put 30 whole nuts into a bowl and leave to cool. Whiz the remaining nuts in a processor until finely chopped, then put into a shallow dish and put to one side.
2   Melt the chocolate in a heatproof bowl set over a pan of barely simmering water, stirring occasionally. Put the butter and cream in a separate pan and heat gently until the butter has melted, then bring just to the boil and remove from the heat. Carefully stir into the chocolate and whisk until cool and thick, then chill for 1–2 hours.
3   Sift the cocoa and icing sugar into separate shallow dishes. Scoop up 1tsp of truffle mix and push a whole hazelnut into the centre. Working quickly, shape into a ball, then roll in the cocoa powder, icing sugar or chopped nuts. Repeat with the remaining mixture, then chill. Store in an airtight container in the fridge for up to two weeks.

Makes about 30   preparation: 15–20 minutes   cooking time: 12 minutes, plus chilling
per truffle: 80 cals; 6g fat; 6g carbohydrate

Chocolate Orange Tart

150g (5oz) plain flour, plus extra to dust
pinch of salt
75g (3oz) unsalted butter, chilled and cut
  into cubes
25g (1oz) golden icing sugar, plus extra
  to dust
grated zest of 1 orange

2 large egg yolks, plus 2 whole
  medium eggs
175g (6oz) good-quality plain dark
  chocolate (with minimum 50% cocoa
  solids), in pieces
175ml (6fl oz) double cream
75g (3oz) light muscovado sugar
1tbsp Grand Marnier or Cointreau

1 To make the pastry, put the flour, salt and butter into a processor and pulse until the mixture resembles breadcrumbs. Add the icing sugar and orange zest, pulse again to mix, then add the egg yolks and pulse until the mixture just comes together to form a soft dough.
2 Turn the dough out on to a lightly floured surface and knead gently to form into a ball. Flatten slightly, then wrap in clingfilm and chill for at least 30 minutes.
3 Roll out the pastry on a lightly floured surface, then use to fill a 20.5cm (8 inch) loose-based tart tin. Prick the base all over with a fork, put the tin on a baking sheet and chill for 30 minutes. Preheat the oven to 190°C (170°C fan oven) mark 5.
4 Line the tart with greaseproof paper and fill with baking beans. Bake for 15 minutes, then remove the paper and beans and bake for a further 5–10 minutes until the pastry is dry to the touch. Remove from the oven and put to one side.
5 Reduce the oven temperature to 170°C (150°C fan oven) mark 3. To make the filling, melt the chocolate in a heatproof bowl set over a pan of barely simmering water, stirring occasionally, then cool for 10 minutes.
6 Put the cream, muscovado sugar, whole eggs and liqueur into a bowl and stir, using a wooden spoon to mix thoroughly. Slowly add the chocolate and stir in, then pour the mix into the pastry case and bake for 30 minutes until just set.
7 Serve warm or cold: cut it into slices, dust liberally with icing sugar and serve with crème fraîche.

Serves 8 preparation: 30 minutes, plus chilling   cooking time: 1 hour, plus cooling
per serving: 430 cals; 30g fat; 33g carbohydrate

15

Chocoholics

Chocolate Strawberry Pavlova

4 egg whites
225g (8oz) golden caster sugar
1tbsp cornflour
2tsp distilled malt vinegar
½tsp vanilla extract

450g (1lb) strawberries
284ml carton double cream
1tbsp icing sugar, plus extra to dust
chocolate-coated strawberries and mint
    leaves, to decorate

1   Preheat the oven to 130°C (110°C fan oven) mark ½. Draw a 23cm (9 inch) circle on a sheet of non-stick baking parchment. Turn the paper over and put on a baking sheet. Put the egg whites in a clean grease-free bowl and whisk until frothy using an electric whisk. Add the caster sugar 1tbsp at a time, whisking thoroughly after each addition, until stiff and shiny (don't hurry this process or the meringue will be floppy and weep). With the machine running slowly, whisk in the cornflour, vinegar and vanilla extract.

2   Spread the meringue on the baking parchment, within the marked circle, leaving a large dip in the centre. Rough up the edges with a palette knife. Bake for 1¼ hours or until crisp around the edges and soft in the centre. Remove from the oven and leave to cool, then peel off the lining paper.

3   Hull and halve the strawberries. Lightly whip the cream, then whisk in 1tbsp icing sugar. About 1 hour before serving, spoon the cream and strawberries into the centre of the pavlova. Top with chocolate-coated strawberries and mint leaves and dust with icing sugar.

Serves 8   preparation: 40 minutes   cooking time: 1¼ hours
per serving: 330 cals; 19g fat; 42g carbohydrate

Chocolate and Chestnut Torte

50g (2oz) butter
200g (7oz) Bourbon or chocolate digestive
  biscuits, very finely crushed
225g (8oz) good-quality milk chocolate
250g (9oz) mascarpone
75g (3oz) unsweetened chestnut purée
4 large eggs, separated

50g (2oz) golden caster sugar
142ml carton extra-thick double cream
175g (6oz) good-quality plain chocolate,
  plus extra to decorate
white chocolate truffles, to decorate
cocoa powder, to dust

1 Melt the butter and while it is still hot stir in the biscuits. Press the crumb mixture into a 20.5cm (8 inch) spring-release cake tin and chill for about 20 minutes or until firm.

2 Meanwhile, melt the milk chocolate in a heatproof bowl set over a pan of barely simmering water. Put the mascarpone and chestnut purée in a large bowl and beat together, then beat in the warm melted chocolate thoroughly.

3 Using an electric whisk, beat the egg yolks with the sugar until pale and thick, then, using a large metal spoon, stir into the chestnut mixture. Next, fold in the cream.

4 Whisk the egg whites in a clean grease-free bowl until soft peaks form, then, using a large metal spoon, stir one large spoonful into the chocolate mixture. Carefully fold in the remainder, pour on to the biscuit base and freeze overnight.

5 To decorate the torte, cut two strips of non-stick baking parchment, each 35.5cm (14 inches) long and 5cm (2 inches) wide. Melt the plain chocolate in a small heatproof bowl set over a pan of barely simmering water and spread it evenly along the parchment strips.

6 Take the torte out of the freezer, run a palette knife around the outside, then unclip and remove the spring-release tin. Carefully wrap the chocolate-covered strips (with the chocolate side facing inwards) around the torte and return the torte to the freezer for about 1 hour.

7 Peel away the parchment strips to leave a thin chocolate 'collar' around the torte, then put in the fridge to thaw overnight. Remove from the fridge, arrange the white chocolate truffles on top around the edge, then dust generously with cocoa powder and grate over some plain chocolate just before serving.

Serves 8–10   preparation: 1 hour, plus chilling and freezing
per serving: 780–620 cals; 55–44g fat; 63–50g carbohydrate

Chocolate Cup Cakes

125g (4oz) unsalted butter, softened
125g (4oz) light muscovado sugar
2 eggs, beaten
15g (½oz) cocoa powder, sifted
100g (3½oz) self-raising flour, sifted

pinch of baking powder
200g (7oz) good-quality plain dark
   chocolate (with 70% cocoa solids)
142ml carton double cream

1 Preheat the oven to 190°C (170°C fan oven) mark 5. Put the butter, sugar, eggs, cocoa powder, flour and baking powder into the large bowl of a freestanding mixer or in a food processor. Mix slowly to start with and then increase the speed slightly until the mixture is well combined.

2 Roughly chop half the chocolate and fold into the creamed mixture.

3 Line muffin tins with 18 muffin cases, and divide the mixture among them. Lightly flatten the surface with the back of a spoon. Bake for 20 minutes or until risen and cooked. Remove from the oven and cool in the cases.

4 To decorate, break up the remaining chocolate and put with the cream into a heavy-based pan and heat until melted together. Leave to cool for 10 minutes and thicken slightly, then pour over the cooled cakes. Leave to set for 30 minutes before serving.

Makes 18   preparation: 15 minutes   cooking time: 20 minutes
per cake: 300 cals; 15g fat; 40g carbohydrate

Chocoholics

Black Forest Roulade

125g (4oz) good-quality plain dark
 chocolate (with 70% cocoa solids),
 in pieces
4 large eggs, separated
125g (4oz) golden caster sugar, plus extra
 to dust

142ml carton whipping cream
1tsp icing sugar, plus extra to dust
75ml (3fl oz) Greek-style yogurt
2 x 425g cans morello cherries, drained,
 pitted and halved
cocoa powder, to dust

1 Preheat the oven to 180°C (160°C fan oven) mark 4. Line a 33 x 23cm (13 x 9 inch) Swiss roll tin with non-stick baking parchment.
2 Melt the chocolate in a heatproof bowl set over a pan of barely simmering water. Stir until smooth, then leave to cool. Whisk the egg yolks and caster sugar together in a large bowl until thick and creamy. Whisk in the melted chocolate.
3 Whisk the egg whites in a clean grease-free bowl until stiff and shiny. Lightly fold into the chocolate mixture. Pour into the prepared tin and smooth the surface, then bake for 20 minutes or until firm to the touch.
4 Turn the roulade out on to a sheet of greaseproof paper dusted with icing sugar and carefully peel off the lining parchment. Cover with a damp cloth and leave to cool for 30 minutes.
5 For the filling, lightly whip the cream with the icing sugar, then fold in the yogurt. Spread the filling over the cold roulade and scatter the cherries on top. Roll up from one of the narrow ends, using the greaseproof paper to help. Chill for 30 minutes.
6 Slice the roulade and serve, dusted with cocoa powder and icing sugar.

Serves 10   preparation: 35 minutes, plus cooling   cooking time: 20 minutes
per serving: 260 cals; 14g fat; 30g carbohydrate

15

Chocoholics

Chocolate Meringue Roulade

5 large egg whites
175g (6oz) golden caster sugar
1tsp cornflour
4tbsp half-fat crème fraîche, plus extra
  to serve

125g (4oz) chocolate spread
50g (2oz) cooked vacuum-packed
  chestnuts, roughly chopped (optional)
icing sugar and cocoa powder, to dust
chocolate curls (page 608), to decorate

1   Preheat the oven to 110°C (90°C fan oven) mark ¼. Line a 20.5 x 30.5cm (8 x 12 inch) Swiss roll tin with non-stick baking parchment.
2   Using an electric whisk, whisk the egg whites in a large grease-free heatproof bowl until frothy, then whisk in the sugar. Stand the bowl over a pan of gently simmering water and whisk at high speed until very thick and shiny, about 4–5 minutes. Take off the heat and whisk in the cornflour.
3   Spoon the mixture into the prepared tin and level the surface, then bake for 1 hour or until just firm on top. Remove from the oven and leave to cool for 1 hour; don't worry if the meringue weeps a little.
4   Beat the crème fraîche into the chocolate spread. Fold in the chopped chestnuts, if using.
5   Turn the meringue out on to a sheet of baking parchment dusted with icing sugar and carefully peel off the lining parchment. Make a shallow cut in the meringue, 2.5cm (1 inch) in from the edge of a short end. Spread the chocolate mixture over the meringue and roll it up, from the cut end.
6   Dust with icing sugar and cocoa and decorate with chocolate curls. Serve with half-fat crème fraîche.

Serves 6–8   preparation: 30 minutes, plus cooling   cooking time: 1 hour
per serving: 370–280 cals; 14–10g fat; 59–44g carbohydrate

15

Chocoholics

Chocolate and Banana Roll

4tbsp cocoa powder, sifted
150ml (¼ pint) milk
4 eggs, separated
125g (4oz) golden caster sugar, plus 2tbsp
   to dust

250g tub mascarpone cheese
1tbsp maple syrup
3tbsp double cream
1 banana
1tsp vanilla extract

1 Preheat the oven to 180°C (160°C fan oven) mark 4. Line a 20.5 x 30.5cm (8 x 12 inch) Swiss roll tin with non-stick baking parchment.

2 Mix the cocoa with 3tbsp milk to form a paste. Heat the remaining milk in a small pan, then slowly pour on to the cocoa paste and stir to combine evenly. Cool for 10 minutes.

3 Whisk the egg yolks with 125g (4oz) sugar in a freestanding mixer until pale, thickened and mousse-like. Gradually whisk in the cooling chocolate milk mixture.

4 Whisk the egg whites in a clean grease-free bowl until stiff peaks form. Using a large metal spoon, gently fold one-third into the chocolate mixture to loosen slightly, then carefully fold in the remainder.

5 Spoon the mixture into the prepared tin and bake for 25 minutes until risen and just firm to the touch. Remove from the oven and leave the sponge in the tin to cool for 2 minutes. Turn the sponge out on to a sheet of baking parchment dusted with the 2tbsp sugar and carefully peel off the lining parchment. Cover with a warm damp tea-towel to prevent the sponge from drying out, then cool for at least 30 minutes (or up to 8 hours).

6 Put the mascarpone in a bowl and stir in the syrup and cream. Peel and slice the banana and put the slices in a small bowl, then pour on the vanilla extract and stir to mix.

7 Remove the tea-towel from the chocolate sponge and, using a palette knife, spread over half the mascarpone mixture. Sprinkle over the banana. Starting at one of the short edges and using the paper underneath to help you, gently roll up the chocolate sponge. Slide on to a serving plate and eat within 3 hours, with dollops of the remaining mascarpone mixture.

Serves 6   preparation: 25 minutes, plus cooling   cooking time: 27 minutes
per serving: 440 cals; 29g fat, 36g carbohydrate

Chocolate and Chestnut Slice

butter, to grease
3 eggs
125g (4oz) golden caster sugar, plus extra
  to sprinkle
40g (1½oz) flour
3tbsp cocoa powder
½tsp baking powder

7tbsp chocolate-flavoured liqueur
284ml carton double cream
230g can sweetened chestnut purée
4tbsp banoffee toffee dulce de leche, plus
  extra to drizzle
25g (1oz) plain chocolate, grated

1 Preheat the oven to 220°C (200°C fan oven) mark 7. Grease a 20.5 x 30.5cm (8 x 12 inch) Swiss roll tin and line with non-stick baking parchment.

2 Using an electric hand mixer, whisk the eggs with the sugar until pale and thickened. Sift the flour, cocoa and baking powder into the bowl, add 3tbsp liqueur and, using a large metal spoon, fold everything together. Spoon the mixture into the prepared tin, smooth the surface and bake for 12 minutes.

3 Remove from the oven and leave the sponge in the tin to cool for 1–2 minutes. Turn the sponge out on to a large sheet of greaseproof paper dusted with sugar.

4 Put the cream in a medium bowl and use an electric hand mixer to whisk until soft peaks form. Put the chestnut purée into a separate bowl, add the banoffee toffee and 1tbsp liqueur and use the mixer (no need to rinse the whisks) to beat together. Using a large metal spoon, fold in the cream gently.

5 Carefully peel the lining parchment away from the sponge. Slice the sponge into three widthways, then sprinkle the top of each slice with 1tbsp liqueur. Spread the chestnut cream over the three pieces, then put them one on top of the other. Scatter over the grated chocolate and squeeze over a little dulce de leche, or pipe it through an icing nozzle for a decorative effect.

Serves 6 preparation: 18 minutes cooking time: 12 minutes
per serving: 540 cals; 29g fat; 59g carbohydrate

15

Chocoholics

The Ultimate Brownie

350g (12oz) good-quality plain chocolate,
   semi-sweet such as Bournville, broken
   into pieces
175g (6oz) butter, plus extra to grease
3 eggs
225g (8oz) golden caster sugar
3tbsp dark rum

1tsp vanilla extract
100g (3½oz) self-raising flour, sifted
1tbsp cocoa powder, sifted
100g (3½oz) Brazil nuts, toasted and
   roughly chopped
icing sugar, to dust

1 Preheat the oven to 190°C (170°C fan oven) mark 5. Grease a 27 x 16cm (10¼ x 6½ inch) baking
   tin and line with greaseproof paper. Put the chocolate and butter in a pan and melt over a low heat.
2 Beat the eggs, caster sugar, rum and vanilla extract in a bowl until thoroughly mixed.
3 Add the flour, cocoa powder, Brazil nuts and melted chocolate mixture and stir to combine. Pour
   into the prepared tin and bake for 30–35 minutes.
4 Remove from the oven and leave to cool in the tin. Dust with icing sugar and cut into 16 pieces. Wrap
   in clingfilm and store for up to one week in an airtight container.

Makes 16   preparation: 25 minutes   cooking time: 30–35 minutes
per brownie: 339 cals; 21g fat; 35g carbohydrate

White and Dark Chocolate Cookies

125g (4oz) unsalted butter, softened, plus
   extra to grease
125g (4oz) golden caster sugar
2 eggs, beaten
2tsp vanilla extract
250g (9oz) self-raising flour, sifted, plus
   extra to dust

finely grated zest of 1 orange
100g (3½oz) good-quality white chocolate,
   roughly chopped
100g (3½oz) good-quality plain dark
   chocolate (with minimum 50% cocoa
   solids), roughly chopped

1 Cream the butter and sugar together in a bowl until pale and creamy. Gradually beat in the eggs and
   vanilla extract.
2 Sift in the flour, add the orange zest, then sprinkle in the white and dark chocolate pieces. Mix the dough
   together with floured hands. Knead lightly, then wrap in clingfilm and chill for at least 30 minutes.
3 Preheat the oven to 180°C (160°C fan oven) mark 4. Grease two or three large baking sheets. Divide
   the dough into 26 pieces, roll each into a ball and flatten slightly to make a disc. Using a palette knife,
   transfer to the baking sheets, spacing the discs well apart. Bake for 10–12 minutes or until golden,
   but still fairly soft.
4 Remove from the oven and leave on the baking sheets for 5 minutes, then transfer to a wire rack to
   cool completely.

Makes 26   preparation: 15 minutes, plus chilling   cooking time: 10–12 minutes
per cookie: 140 cals; 7g fat; 17g carbohydrate

Low-fat Brownies

50ml (2fl oz) sunflower oil, plus extra to
   grease
250g (9oz) good-quality plain dark
   chocolate (with minimum 50% cocoa
   solids), broken into pieces
4 eggs

150g (5oz) light muscovado sugar
1tsp vanilla extract
75g (3oz) plain flour
¼tsp baking powder
1tbsp cocoa powder

1   Preheat the oven to 200°C (180°C fan oven) mark 6. Grease a 20.5cm (8 inch) square tin and line with
    greaseproof paper. Melt the chocolate in a heatproof bowl set over a pan of barely simmering water,
    stirring occasionally. Take the bowl off the pan and put to one side to cool slightly.

2   Put the eggs into a clean bowl, add the oil, sugar and vanilla extract and whisk together until pale and
    thick. Sift the flour, baking powder and cocoa powder into the bowl, then carefully pour in the
    chocolate. Using a large metal spoon, gently fold all the ingredients together – if you fold too roughly
    the chocolate will seize up and become unusable.

3   Carefully pour the brownie mixture into the prepared tin and bake for 20 minutes – when cooked, the
    brownies should still be fudgy inside and the top should be cracked and crispy.

4   Remove from the oven and cut into squares immediately, then leave them to cool in the tin. Transfer
    to a serving plate or wrap the brownies in clingfilm and put in an airtight container. They'll keep for
    up to three days.

Makes 16   preparation: 10 minutes   cooking time: 20 minutes
per square: 180 cals; 11g fat; 17g carbohydrate

15

Chocoholics

White chocolate and Macadamia Nut Brownies

75g (3oz) butter, plus extra to grease
1tsp vanilla extract
500g (1lb 2oz) good-quality white
   chocolate, roughly chopped
3 large eggs

175g (6oz) golden caster sugar
175g (6oz) self-raising flour
pinch of salt
175g (6oz) macadamia nuts, roughly
   chopped

1   Preheat the oven to 190°C (170°C fan oven) mark 5. Grease a 19 x 27cm (7½ x 10½ inch) baking
    tin and line with greaseproof paper. Melt 125g (4oz) white chocolate with the butter in a heatproof bowl
    set over a pan of barely simmering water, stirring occasionally. Take the bowl off the pan and leave
    to cool slightly.
2   Whisk the eggs and sugar together in a large bowl until smooth, then gradually beat in the melted
    chocolate mixture; the consistency will become quite firm. Sift the flour and salt over the mixture, then
    fold in together with the nuts, the remaining chopped chocolate and the vanilla extract.
3   Turn the mixture into the prepared tin and level the surface. Bake for 30–35 minutes until risen and
    golden and the centre is just firm to the touch – the mixture will still be soft under the crust; it firms
    up on cooling. Remove from the oven and leave to cool in the tin. Turn out and cut into squares.
    Store in an airtight container for up to one week.

Makes 12   preparation: 20 minutes, plus cooling   cooking time: 30–35 minutes
per brownie: 490 cals; 20g fat; 29g carbohydrate

Banana and Chocolate Bread Pudding

225g (8oz) crustless white bread
butter, to grease
2 bananas
4 eggs
175g (6oz) golden caster sugar
284ml carton double cream
300ml (½ pint) semi-skimmed milk

2 tsp vanilla extract
½tsp ground cinnamon
150g (5oz) good-quality plain chocolate,
   roughly chopped
50g (2oz) shelled pecan nuts, roughly
   chopped

1   Cut the bread into bite-sized cubes and spread out on a board. Leave to dry out for at least 4 hours.
2   Preheat the oven to 190°C (170°C fan oven) mark 5. Grease a 2 litre (3½ pint) shallow ovenproof dish.
3   Mash the bananas in a bowl using a fork, then beat in the eggs. Stir in the sugar, cream, milk, vanilla
    extract and cinnamon. Fold the chopped chocolate and pecan nuts into the mixture with the bread
    cubes, then pour into the prepared dish.
4   Bake the pudding for 50 minutes or until the top is firm and golden brown. Remove from the oven and
    leave to stand for about 10 minutes to allow the custard to firm up slightly. Spoon into warm serving
    bowls and serve with cream or vanilla ice cream.

Serves 6   preparation time: 15 minutes, plus standing   cooking time: 50 minutes
per serving: 730 cals; 43g fat; 76g carbohydrate

Chocolate Puddings

250g (9oz) unsalted butter, plus extra
   to grease
200g (7oz) good-quality plain dark
   chocolate (minimum 70% cocoa solids),
   broken into small pieces
4tbsp Tia Maria or dark rum

125g (4oz) golden caster sugar
4 large eggs, plus 2 large yolks
1tsp vanilla extract
65g (2½oz) plain flour
1tsp ground cinnamon
icing sugar, to dust

1   Preheat the oven to 200°C (180°C fan oven) mark 6. Lightly grease ten 150ml (¼ pint) ovenproof coffee
   cups or bowls.
2   Melt the butter and chocolate in a heatproof bowl set over a pan of barely simmering water, stirring
   occasionally. Once they have melted, take the pan off the heat, add the Tia Maria or dark rum and
   stir the mixture until it is smooth and glossy.
3   Meanwhile, put the caster sugar, whole eggs, yolks and vanilla extract in a large bowl. Whisk on a high
   speed with an electric hand whisk or in a freestanding food mixer for about 10 minutes, until the
   mixture has doubled in volume. The mixture should look like a mousse and leave a ribbon-like trail
   when the whisk is lifted over it.
4   Pour the melted chocolate into the whisked egg mixture, then sift in the flour and cinnamon. Using
   a large metal spoon, carefully fold everything together. If you are making the puddings in advance,
   cover the bowl and chill at this stage.
5   Divide the mixture among the prepared cups or bowls – you may find it easier to use a ladle here –
   and put them on a baking tray.
6   Bake the puddings for 10–12 minutes until they are just firm round the edges; they will still be a little
   runny in the centre. Remove from the oven, dust them with icing sugar, and serve – the longer they
   stand, the less gooey they'll be.

Serves 10   preparation: 15 minutes   cooking time: 20 minutes
per serving: 420 cals; 32g fat; 23g carbohydrate

15

Chocoholics

Cherry Chocolate Pudding

125g (1oz) butter, plus extra for greasing
425g can pitted black cherries in
  syrup, drained and syrup reserved,
  cherries halved
125g (4oz) golden caster sugar
250g (9oz) good-quality plain chocolate,
  roughly chopped
2 eggs

1tsp vanilla extract
75g (3oz) self-raising flour

1 Preheat the oven to 190°C (170°C fan oven) mark 5. Grease an 18cm (7 inch) square cake tin and line the base with greaseproof paper.
2 Put the reserved cherry syrup in a small pan with 25g (1oz) sugar. Bring to the boil, then reduce the heat and simmer until reduced by half, then leave to cool.
3 Put the butter in a small heatproof bowl with 75g (3oz) chocolate and melt over a pan of barely simmering water, stirring occasionally. Remove from the heat and cool.
4 Put the eggs in a bowl with the remaining sugar and the vanilla extract and beat together until the mixture is thick and pale. Sift in the flour, then fold in the cooled chocolate mixture and the remaining chocolate.
5 Arrange the cherries in the base of the cake tin and pour over the chocolate mixture. Bake for 30 minutes, cover with foil and bake for a further 15 minutes. Remove from the oven and leave to cool in the tin for 5 minutes, then turn out by covering with a large plate or board and carefully inverting it. Peel off the lining paper and pour over the reserved cherry syrup while the cake is still warm. Serve with fresh vanilla custard.

Serves 6 preparation: 15 minutes cooking time: 55 minutes
per serving: 600 cals; 31g fat; 77g carbohydrate

15

Chocoholics

Mini Chocolate, Nut and Cherry Puddings

125g (4oz) unsalted butter, melted and
  cooled, plus extra to grease
75g (3oz) hazelnuts, plus extra to decorate
200g (7oz) good-quality plain chocolate,
  broken into small pieces
4 large eggs
125g (4oz) golden caster sugar
50g (2oz) self-raising flour

1tbsp cocoa powder
75g (3oz) pitted morello cherries in syrup,
  drained and halved, plus extra to decorate
2tbsp Kirsch or brandy, plus extra to drizzle
  (optional)
142ml carton double cream

1 Preheat the oven to 180°C (160°C fan oven) mark 4. Grease eight 150ml (¼ pint) dariole moulds
  and line the bases with greaseproof paper. Preheat the grill, spread the hazelnuts in the grill pan and
  toast until lightly browned. Leave to cool, then chop.
2 Melt 125g (4oz) chocolate in a heatproof bowl set over a pan of barely simmering water, stirring
  occasionally until smooth, then leave to cool.
3 Beat the eggs and sugar together in a bowl until the mixture is pale and light and has doubled
  in volume.
4 Sift the flour and cocoa powder together over the whisked mixture. Pour the melted butter around
  the edge of the bowl, then, using a large metal spoon or spatula, fold to combine. Fold in the melted
  chocolate, chopped hazelnuts and cherries.
5 Spoon the mixture into the prepared moulds and stand them on a baking sheet. Bake for 25–30
  minutes, covering lightly with foil if the tops appear to be browning too quickly.
6 Meanwhile, make the sauce. Put the remaining chocolate, 2tbsp Kirsch and the cream in a small pan
  and heat gently until smooth.
7 Turn out the puddings on to warmed serving plates and spoon 1tsp Kirsch over each one, if using.
  Spoon over the chocolate sauce and top with the extra cherries and hazelnuts. Serve straightaway,
  with a jug of pouring cream.

Serves 8   preparation: 35 minutes   cooking time: 25–30 minutes
per serving: 520 cals; 36g fat; 43g carbohydrate

Chocoholics

Gooey Chocolate Soufflés

125g (4oz) golden caster sugar
50g (2oz) cocoa powder
9 egg whites, at room temperature
pinch of cream of tartar
15g (½oz) good-quality plain dark chocolate
  (with 60–70% cocoa solids), coarsely

grated or finely chopped
2tsp dark rum
1tsp vanilla extract

1 Preheat the oven to 180°C (160°C fan oven) mark 4. Sift 100g (3½oz) sugar with the cocoa powder and put to one side.
2 Put the egg whites and the cream of tartar in a clean grease-free bowl and, using an electric whisk, beat until foamy. Continue whisking at high speed, gradually adding the remaining sugar 1tbsp at a time, until the meringue holds stiff peaks.
3 Using a large metal spoon, carefully fold the sugar and cocoa mixture into the meringue with the chocolate, rum and vanilla extract. The mixture should be evenly combined but still stiff.
4 Spoon the mixture into eight 175ml (6fl oz) ovenproof tea or coffee cups. Stand the cups in a large roasting tin and pour enough boiling water into the tin to come at least halfway up their sides. Bake for 12–15 minutes or until the soufflés are puffed and set round the edges but still soft in the centre. Serve at once.

Serves 8   preparation: 10 minutes   cooking time: 12–15 minutes
per serving: 110 cals; 2g fat; 18g carbohydrate

15

Chocoholics

Chocolate, Prune and Orange Soufflés

butter, to grease
5tbsp golden caster sugar
175g (6oz) pitted, ready-to-eat prunes
2tbsp vegetable oil
5tbsp unsweetened orange juice
50g (2oz) good-quality plain chocolate,
  chopped into small pieces

grated zest of 1 orange
5 egg whites
¼tsp cream of tartar
pinch of salt
icing sugar, to dust

1　Preheat the oven to 180°C (160°C fan oven) mark 4. Lightly grease eight 150ml (¼ pint) ramekins and sprinkle with 1tbsp caster sugar.
2　Put the prunes, oil and orange juice in a blender and whiz for 2–3 minutes to form a purée. Transfer to a large bowl and stir in the chocolate, 2tbsp of the remaining caster sugar and the orange zest.
3　Put the egg whites, cream of tartar and salt in a clean grease-free bowl and whisk until stiff but not dry. Add the remaining 2tbsp caster sugar and continue to whisk until the mixture is very stiff and shiny.
4　Using a large metal spoon, stir a quarter of the egg whites into the prune mixture, then gently fold in the remainder.
5　Spoon the mixture into the ramekins. Stand them in a large roasting tin and pour enough boiling water into the tin to come halfway up their sides. Bake for 15–20 minutes or until the soufflés are just set. Remove from the oven, dust with icing sugar and serve immediately.

Makes 8　preparation: 20 minutes　cooking time: 15–20 minutes
per serving: 150 cals; 5g fat; 26g carbohydrate

Zuppe Inglese

175g (6oz) golden icing sugar
25g (1oz) plain flour
4 large egg yolks
1tbsp vanilla extract
750ml (1¼ pints) full-fat milk
142ml carton whipping cream
175g (6oz) good-quality plain chocolate,
   chopped

3tsp cocoa powder
350g (12oz) Madeira cake, thinly sliced
   lengthways
2tbsp each brandy and rum
grated chocolate or chocolate curls (page
   608), to decorate

1   Sift the sugar and flour into a large bowl. Make a well in the centre, add the egg yolks and vanilla extract
    and stir until mixed.
2   Heat the milk and cream to scalding point. Add to the egg mixture, stirring all the time. Return to the
    pan and cook over a medium heat, stirring, for 5–6 minutes, until it forms a thin coating consistency.
    Remove half the custard and put to one side.
3   Add the chocolate to the remaining custard in the pan and stir in until melted. Spoon half the chocolate
    custard into the base of a glass serving dish. Dust with 1tsp cocoa powder and cover with a third of
    the Madeira slices. Drizzle with 4tsp of the mixed brandy and rum.
4   Spoon over half the reserved vanilla custard and dust with 1tsp cocoa powder. Cover the vanilla
    custard with half the remaining cake slices, and drizzle with more of the alcohol.
5   Spoon the remaining chocolate custard on top and dust with the remaining cocoa powder. Add a final
    layer of cake, drizzle with the remaining alcohol and spoon over the remaining vanilla custard.
6   Cover the bowl with clingfilm and chill for 3 hours or overnight. Decorate with grated chocolate or
    chocolate curls before serving.

Serves 6   preparation: 10 minutes   cooking time: 10 minutes, plus chilling
per serving: 780 cals; 38g fat; 96g carbohydrate

Chocoholics

White Chocolate and Red Fruit Trifle

3 x 500g bags frozen mixed berries
125g (4oz) golden caster sugar, plus 1tsp
250g (9oz) biscotti or cantuccini biscuits
5tbsp dessert wine or fruit juice, such as
  cranberry and orange
450ml (¾ pint) double cream

200g (7oz) good-quality white chocolate,
  broken into pieces
500g carton fresh custard, at room
  temperature
500ml carton crème fraîche

1 Make this a day ahead so the flavours have time to develop. Put the mixed berries in a large pan with 125g (4oz) sugar, and heat gently for about 5 minutes until the sugar has dissolved and the berries have thawed. Tip the berry mixture into a sieve over a bowl to catch the juices. Return the juices to the pan, then tip the berries into the bowl. Bring the juices to the boil, then reduce the heat and simmer for 10 minutes or until reduced to about 150ml (¼ pint). Pour over the berries and leave to cool.

2 Lay the biscuits over the base of a 3 litre (5¼ pint) trifle dish, or individual glass dishes, and sprinkle with the wine or fruit juice. Scatter the cooled berries over the top.

3 For the topping, lightly whip the cream. Transfer half of it to another bowl, cover and put in the fridge; leave the remainder at room temperature. Melt the white chocolate in a heatproof bowl set over a pan of barely simmering water, stirring occasionally.

4 Pour the melted chocolate into a cold bowl, at the same time gradually folding in the custard. Fold in the whipped cream at room temperature. (Doing it in this order stops the chocolate separating.) Pour the white chocolate custard over the fruit to cover it evenly.

5 Beat the crème fraîche until smooth, fold in the reserved chilled whipped cream and the 1tsp sugar, then spoon over the custard. Chill for 2 hours. Remove the trifle from the fridge 20 minutes before serving.

Serves 8–10   preparation: 45 minutes, plus chilling   cooking time: 15 minutes
per serving: 930–740 cals; 64–51g fat; 79–63g carbohydrate

15

Chocoholics

Vanilla Tiramisu

200g (7oz) mascarpone
1 vanilla pod
450ml (¾ pint) strong warm black coffee
4 egg yolks
75g (3oz) golden caster sugar

284ml carton double cream
100ml (4fl oz) grappa
200g packet Savoiardi or sponge fingers
1tbsp cocoa powder, to dust

1 Put the mascarpone into a bowl. Split the vanilla pod in half lengthways, scrape out the seeds and add them to the mascarpone.
2 Pour the coffee into a shallow dish, add the vanilla pod and put to one side to allow the flavours to mingle.
3 Whisk the egg yolks and sugar together in a large bowl until pale and thick, then whisk in the mascarpone until smooth.
4 Whip the cream in another bowl until soft peaks form, then fold into the mascarpone mixture with the grappa.
5 Take half the sponge fingers and dip each in turn into the coffee mixture, then arrange over the base of a 2.4 litre (4¼ pint) shallow dish. Spread a layer of mascarpone mixture over the sponge fingers, then dip the remaining sponge fingers into the coffee and arrange on top. Finish with a final layer of mascarpone. Cover and chill for at least 2 hours. It improves in flavour if you make it a day in advance.
6 To serve, dust with cocoa powder and, using a sharp knife, cut into individual portions. Use a spatula to lift the tiramisu portions neatly on to individual plates.

Serves 10   preparation time: 20 minutes, plus chilling
per serving: 380 cals; 27g fat; 27g carbohydrate

15

Chocoholics

The Best Chocolate Cake in the World

150g (5oz) butter, plus extra to grease
300g (11oz) good-quality plain chocolate,
   broken into pieces
8 eggs, separated

200g (7oz) golden caster sugar
75ml (3fl oz) double cream
chocolate curls (page 608), to decorate

1 Preheat the oven to 180°C (160°C fan oven) mark 4. Grease a 23cm (9 inch) spring-release cake tin and line with baking parchment.

2 Melt 200g (7oz) chocolate with 125g (4oz) butter in a heatproof bowl set over a pan of barely simmering water, stirring occasionally. Remove from the heat and leave to cool for a few minutes.

3 Put the egg yolks and sugar in a food mixer or large bowl and whisk until pale, thick and mousse-like, then whisk in the chocolate mixture.

4 Whisk the egg whites in a clean grease-free bowl until soft peaks form. Using a large metal spoon, add one-third of the whites to the chocolate mixture and fold in lightly, then carefully fold in the remaining egg whites.

5 Immediately pour the mixture into the prepared tin and bake for 1¼ hours. Turn off the oven. Cover the cake with a damp tea-towel and leave to cool in the oven; it will sink in the centre as it cools.

6 To make the chocolate ganache coating, melt the remaining chocolate with the butter and cream in a heatproof bowl set over a pan of barely simmering water.

7 Take the cake out of the tin and peel off the lining paper. Put on a serving plate and ladle the ganache over the cake, so it covers the top and drizzles down the sides. Leave until just set. Using a palette knife, scatter the chocolate curls on top of the cake to serve. (Alternatively, for a simple finish, omit the chocolate curls and dust the top of the cake liberally with 2tbsp each cocoa powder and icing sugar.)

Cuts into 16 slices preparation: 20 minutes cooking time: 1¼ hours
per slice: 310 cals; 20g fat; 29g carbohydrate

15

Chocoholics

Decadent Chocolate Cake

225g (8oz) unsalted butter, softened, plus
  extra to grease
525g (1lb 3oz) good-quality dark chocolate,
  broken into pieces
225g (8oz) golden caster sugar
225g (8oz) ground almonds

8 large eggs, separated
125g (4oz) fresh brown breadcrumbs
4tbsp apricot jam (optional)
75g (3oz) butter, softened
4tbsp double cream

1 Preheat the oven to 180°C (160°C fan oven) mark 4. Grease a 23cm (9 inch) spring-release cake tin and line with greaseproof paper.

2 Melt 300g (11oz) chocolate in a heatproof bowl set over a pan of barely simmering water, stirring occasionally. Remove from the heat.

3 Put the unsalted butter and sugar into a large bowl and beat together until light and creamy. Add the almonds, egg yolks and breadcrumbs and beat well until thoroughly mixed. Slowly add the chocolate and carefully stir it in, taking care not to over-mix as the chocolate may seize up.

4 Whisk the egg whites in a clean grease-free bowl until stiff peaks form. Using a large metal spoon, add half the whites to the chocolate mixture, fold in lightly, then carefully fold in the remaining egg whites.

5 Pour the mixture into the prepared tin and smooth the surface. Bake for 1 hour 20 minutes or until the cake is firm to the touch and a skewer inserted into the centre comes out clean. Remove from the oven and cool in the tin for 5 minutes, then transfer to a rack for 2–3 hours to cool completely. Peel off the greaseproof paper.

6 If using, put the jam into a pan and melt over a low heat. Brush the jam over the top and sides of the cooled cake.

7 To make the chocolate ganache coating, put the remaining chocolate, the butter and cream into a bowl and rest it over a pan of hot water as in step 2. When it has melted, stir the mixture just once until smooth – too much stirring at this stage will over-thicken it. To ice the cake, either raise it off the worktop on the upturned tin or put it (still on the rack) on to a tray to catch the drips. Pour the ganache over the centre and tip the cake to let it run down the sides evenly or spread it with a palette knife. Leave to set.

Cuts into 12 slices   preparation: 30 minutes   cooking time: 1½ hours, plus cooling
per slice: 690 cals; 49g fat; 54g carbohydrate

Ultra-Dark Chocolate Cake with Raspberries

200g (7oz) butter, preferably unsalted, plus
   extra to grease
5tbsp plain white flour
1tsp baking powder
500g (1lb 2oz) plain dark chocolate (with
   70% cocoa solids), broken into pieces

5 large eggs
225g (8oz) golden caster sugar
125g (4oz) golden syrup
125–175g (4–6oz) raspberries
chocolate-coated coffee beans
chocolate curls (page 608), to decorate

1 Preheat the oven to 170°C (150°C fan oven) mark 3. Line the base of a 25.5cm (10 inch) spring-release cake tin with non-stick baking parchment, then lightly grease the sides. Sift together the flour and baking powder. Melt 275g (10oz) chocolate and the butter in a heatproof bowl set over a pan of gently simmering water. Take off the heat, stir until smooth and leave to cool.

2 Put the eggs and sugar in a food mixer or large bowl and whisk until very thick and mousse-like. Carefully fold in the cooled chocolate mix, followed by the flour. Pour immediately into the prepared tin and bake for 1 hour until a crust has formed on the surface. Test by inserting a thin skewer into the centre – it should come out clean.

3 Remove the cake from the oven and leave to cool in the tin for 5 minutes, then cover with a damp cloth and leave to cool completely. Dampen the cloth again, put it on the cake and cover with clingfilm. Leave to stand for up to 12 hours before turning out. (You can serve the cake 2 or 3 hours after baking, rather than leaving it to stand for 12 hours, but the texture will be much more crumbly.)

4 To make the chocolate sauce, put the syrup in a pan with 200ml (7fl oz) water. Add the remaining chocolate and set over a gentle heat until the chocolate has melted, then bring to the boil, reduce the heat and simmer for 5 minutes. Take off the heat and leave to cool (or you can use it warm if preferred).

5 Arrange the raspberries and coffee beans on top of the cake, then drizzle with the sauce. Decorate with chocolate curls and cut into slices to serve.

Cuts into 16 slices   preparation: 15 minutes, plus cooling and standing   cooking time: 1 hour
per slice: 370 cals; 24g fat; 34g carbohydrate

Chocoholics

Chocolate Pancakes

150g (5oz) good-quality plain chocolate,
100g (3½oz) plain flour
1 large egg
pinch of salt
300ml (½ pint) skimmed milk
25g (1oz) butter
1tbsp light muscovado sugar

4 medium bananas
8tbsp brandy
vegetable oil, to brush
icing sugar, to dust
chocolate shavings, to decorate

1 Put 50g (2oz) chocolate in a food processor and chop. Add the flour, egg, salt and milk and whiz until smooth. Cover and chill for 30 minutes.
2 Melt the butter and muscovado sugar in a frying pan. Peel and thickly slice the bananas, add them to the pan and stir-fry over a medium heat for 3 minutes. Add the brandy (take care when doing this as it may ignite in the warm pan) and continue to simmer until the bananas soften and the liquid is syrupy – about 2 minutes. Put to one side.
3 Lightly brush an 18cm (7 inch) non-stick crêpe or small frying pan with oil and heat. Stir the batter and coat the base of the pan thinly with about 4tbsp. Cook the pancake for 2 minutes or until golden brown, then flip over and cook for 1 minute. Transfer to a plate, cover and keep warm. Cook the remaining batter in the same way.
4 Chop the remaining chocolate. Place two spoonfuls of banana filling over one half of each pancake and sprinkle with some of the chocolate. Fold in half, then in half again. Keep warm while filling the remaining pancakes. Dust with icing sugar, decorate with chocolate shavings and serve warm with yogurt.

Makes 8–12 pancakes   preparation: 15 minutes, plus chilling   cooking time: 30–40 minutes
per pancake: 280–180 cals; 9–6g fat; 37–25g carbohydrate

15

Chocoholics

Wicked Chocolate Cake

125g (4oz) white marzipan
175g (6oz) unsalted butter, plus extra
  to grease
225g (8oz) good-quality plain dark
  chocolate (with 70% cocoa solids), broken
  into pieces
175g (6oz) golden caster sugar
5 eggs, lightly beaten
125g (4oz) self-raising flour, sifted

3tbsp cocoa powder, sifted
4tbsp Amaretto liquer
175g (6oz) good-quality plain chocolate,
  broken into pieces
4tbsp double cream
75g (3oz) butter
12 lilac sugar-coated almonds, to decorate

1 Preheat the oven to 190°C (170°C fan oven) mark 5. Freeze the marzipan for 30 minutes to firm up and make grating easier. Grease a 20.5cm (8 inch) spring-release cake tin and line with baking parchment. Melt 225g (8oz) plain dark chocolate in a heatproof bowl set over a pan of barely simmering water, stirring occasionally.

2 Cream together the unsalted butter and sugar in a freestanding electric mixer until pale and fluffy. Gradually beat in 3 eggs – don't worry if the mixture curdles. Sift in 3tbsp flour and all the cocoa powder, then gradually beat in the remaining eggs. Fold in the rest of the flour.

3 Grate the chilled marzipan and crumble into the cake mixture. Pour all the melted chocolate into the mixture, then stir in using a large metal spoon, making sure it's evenly distributed. Add 2tbsp Amaretto and stir thoroughly to combine.

4 Spoon the mixture into the prepared cake tin, spread evenly and bake for 45 minutes. (If the cake is browning too quickly, cover it with foil.) If necessary, continue to cook for an extra 5–10 minutes or until a skewer inserted in the centre comes out clean. Remove from the oven and cool in the tin for 30 minutes. Remove the cake from the tin and cool on a wire rack, then drizzle with the remaining Amaretto.

5 To make the chocolate ganache coating, melt the 175g (6oz) plain chocolate in a heatproof bowl set over a pan of simmering water. Warm the cream over a gentle heat. Add the butter and warm cream to the chocolate and stir everything together until smooth.

6 Position the cake and rack over a tray and ladle the warm ganache coating over the top, letting it trickle down the cake sides. Use a palette knife to spread the ganache evenly over the cake. Decorate with sugar-coated almonds and store in an airtight container. Eat within one week.

Cuts into 16 slices   preparation: 50 minutes, plus cooling   cooking time: 1¼ hours
per slice: 469 cals; 31g fat; 40g carbohydrate

The Easiest-ever Celebration Chocolate Cake

butter, to grease
200g (7oz) good-quality plain chocolate,
  broken into pieces
5 large eggs
125g (4oz) golden caster sugar

100g (3½oz) ground almonds
1tbsp coffee liqueur, such as Tia Maria
cocoa powder, to dust
raspberries, to decorate

1 Grease a 12.5 x 8cm (5 x 3½ inch) deep round cake tin and line with greaseproof paper, making sure the paper comes to about 5–7.5cm (2–3 inches) above the tin.

2 Melt the chocolate in a heatproof bowl set over a pan of barely simmering water, stirring occasionally, then leave to cool. Meanwhile, preheat the oven to 170°C (150°C fan oven) mark 3.

3 Separate all but one of the eggs and put the whites to one side. Put the yolks, the remaining whole egg and the sugar in the bowl of a freestanding mixer. Whisk at high speed for 5 minutes or until the mixture is pale and leaves a ribbon trail.

4 Set the mixer to a very low speed, add the chocolate and then the almonds and mix until evenly combined. Put to one side.

5 Whisk the egg whites in a clean grease-free bowl until soft peaks form. Beat one quarter of the egg whites into the chocolate mixture to loosen, then, using a large metal spoon, carefully fold in the remainder.

6 Pour the mixture into the prepared cake tin and bake for 1 hour 5 minutes–1¼ hours or until a skewer inserted into the centre of the cake for 30 seconds comes out hot with a few crumbs on it. Remove from the oven and make several holes in the cake with the skewer, then pour over the liqueur while still hot. Leave the cake to cool in the tin for 30 minutes, then turn out on to a wire rack to cool completely. Wrap the cake in foil and store in an airtight container for up to five days.

7 To decorate the cake, dust heavily with cocoa powder, then lift on to an 18cm (7 inch) diameter silver cake board. Spoon fresh raspberries on top and tie a silver ribbon around the cake.

Cuts into 16 slices   preparation: 2½ hours, plus cooling   cooking time: about 1¼ hours
per slice: 180 cals; 12g fat; 14g carbohydrate

15

Chocoholics

Sauces
and salsas

A really good savoury sauce will brighten up a simple bowl of pasta, anoint a plainly grilled chop, or complement a perfectly cooked whole fish. Pour some thick, chunky Fresh Tomato Sauce, with garlic, oregano and basil, over cooked penne or other pasta shapes, crumble some cheese on top and put under the grill until it's bubbling. Simple, but guaranteed to cheer anyone up.

Pesto, too, is made in minutes and can be done in advance and kept in the fridge. The Roast Nut and Herb Pesto, with parsley, almonds and garlic, is great with grilled vegetables.

For pan-fries, a Creamy Mushroom and Wine Sauce is ready in the time it takes to cook the meat and its smooth richness works so well with steaks and chicken. Having a barbecue? Try the home-made mayonnaises and dressings. Caper and Lemon Dressing, with its kick of chilli and garlic, is fantastic with fishcakes or grilled salmon, while Smoky Pepper Mayo is great for dunking fat, sticky sausages in.

If you're sharing a big bowl of creamy vanilla ice cream, pour over some Strawberry or Passion-fruit Sauce for a fruity combination, or try the Heavenly Fudge Sauce for pure indulgence.

Special Bread Sauce

1 onion, peeled and quartered
4 cloves
2 bay leaves
450ml (¾ pint) full-fat milk
150g (5oz) fresh white breadcrumbs

½tsp freshly grated nutmeg, or to taste
50g (2oz) butter
200ml carton crème fraîche
salt and pepper

1 Stud each onion quarter with a clove. Put the onion, bay leaves and milk into a pan and heat very gently on the lowest possible heat for 15 minutes.
2 Remove the onions and bay leaves, then add the breadcrumbs, nutmeg and butter and stir to combine. Add the crème fraîche and season to taste. Serve warm with roast turkey.

Serves 8   preparation: 10 minutes   cooking time: 15 minutes
per serving: 210 cals; 16g fat; 13g carbohydrate

Microwave Bread Sauce

1 onion, peeled and quartered
4 cloves
450ml (¾ pint) full-fat milk
150g (5oz) fresh white breadcrumbs

1tbsp green peppercorns
50g (2oz) butter, cut into cubes
200ml carton crème fraîche

1 Stud each onion quarter with a clove. Put the onions into a microwave-proof bowl and cover with the milk. Heat gently on Defrost for 5 minutes (based on a 900W oven) to let the flavours infuse.
2 Remove the onions and cloves, add the breadcrumbs, peppercorns and butter and stir to combine, then add the crème fraîche.
3 Cook on Medium for 5–6 minutes, stirring halfway through, until thickened and evenly heated.

Serves 6   preparation: 10 minutes   cooking time: 10–11 minutes
per serving: 280 cals; 22g fat; 17g carbohydrate

Sauces and salsas

Rosemary Bread Sauce

300ml (½ pint) full-fat milk

1 small onion, peeled and quartered

4 cloves

½ cinnamon stick

pinch of freshly grated nutmeg

2 bay leaves

2 rosemary sprigs, bruised

125g (4oz) fresh breadcrumbs

200ml carton crème fraîche

15g (½oz) butter

salt and pepper

1 Put the milk, onion, cloves, cinnamon, nutmeg, bay leaves and 1 bruised rosemary sprig in a small pan. Bring to the boil, turn off the heat and leave to infuse for 30 minutes.
2 Strain the milk into a clean pan, discard the onion, spices and herbs and add the breadcrumbs, crème fraîche and butter. Season well to taste. Bring to the boil, then reduce the heat and cook gently, stirring, for 1–2 minutes until the mixture thickens. Serve with the other rosemary sprig.

Serves 8 preparation: 5 minutes, plus infusing   cooking time: 3 minutes
per serving: 160 cals; 12g fat; 18g carbohydrate

Cheese and Grainy Mustard Sauce

50g (2oz) butter

450ml (¾ pint) full-fat milk

50g (2oz) plain flour

75g (3oz) mature Cheddar cheese, grated

1tsp grainy mustard

salt and pepper

1 Put the butter and milk in a pan, heat to melt the butter, then bring to a good rolling boil.
2 Put the flour in a food processor and, with the machine running at full speed, pour in the still bubbling milk. Whiz for 30 seconds, scrape down the sides of the bowl with a spatula and add the Cheddar, mustard and seasoning. Whiz for a further 30 seconds, then use, or cool quickly, cover and refrigerate for up to two days. To use, bring slowly to the boil and simmer for 2–3 minutes. Use as a topping for cooked vegetables or grilled chicken and brown under the grill.

Serves 4–6   preparation: 5 minutes   cooking time: 5 minutes
per serving: 290–190 cals; 21–14g fat; 15–10g carbohydrate

16

Sauces and salsas

Microwave Cheese Sauce

25g (1oz) butter, cut into cubes
25g (1oz) plain flour
300ml (½ pint) full-fat milk
50g (2oz) finely grated Gruyère or Cheddar
   cheese

generous pinch of mustard powder
salt and pepper

1 Put the butter, flour and milk into a microwave-proof bowl and whisk together.
2 Cook in the microwave on High for 4 minutes (based on a 900W oven) or until the sauce has boiled and thickened, whisking every minute.
3 Stir in the cheese until it melts. Stir in the mustard powder and season to taste. Use the sauce over cauliflower cheese or in lasagne.

Makes 300ml (½ pint) preparation: 5 minutes cooking time: 4 minutes
per serving: 610 cals; 42g fat; 34g carbohydrate

Fresh Tomato Sauce

900g (2lb) vine-ripened tomatoes, roughly
   chopped
2tbsp extra-virgin olive oil
2 garlic cloves, peeled and crushed
grated zest of 1 lemon

1tsp dried oregano
2tbsp chopped basil
salt and pepper
pinch of sugar, or to taste (optional)

1 Put the tomatoes in a pan with the olive oil, garlic, lemon zest and oregano. Bring to the boil, cover the pan, reduce the heat and simmer gently for 20 minutes.
2 Add the basil, seasoning to taste and a little sugar, if required. Simmer, uncovered, for a further 10 minutes or until the sauce is slightly thickened. If a smooth sauce is preferred, pass through a sieve and reheat before serving. This is a good sauce for pasta.

Serves 4 preparation: 10 minutes cooking time: about 30 minutes
per serving: 100 cals; 7g fat; 8g carbohydrate

Rich Tomato Sauce

50g (2oz) butter
1 onion, peeled and finely chopped
2 garlic cloves, peeled and finely chopped
2 x 400g cans plum tomatoes with
    their juice

3tbsp sun-dried tomato paste
2 oregano sprigs, or 1tsp dried
salt and pepper

1 Melt the butter in a pan, add the onion and garlic and cook gently for about 10 minutes until softened.
2 Add the tomatoes with the tomato paste and oregano and cook, uncovered, over a low heat for
   25–30 minutes, stirring occasionally, until the sauce is thick and pulpy.
3 Discard the oregano and season to taste.

Serves 4–6   preparation: 10 minutes   cooking time: about 40 minutes
per serving: 150–100 cals; 11–7g fat; 11–7g carbohydrate

Tomato and Basil Sauce

1tbsp extra-virgin olive oil
3 garlic cloves, peeled and crushed
500g carton creamed tomatoes or passata
1 bay leaf and 1 thyme sprig

salt and pepper
golden caster sugar
3tbsp chopped basil

1 Heat the oil in a pan, add the garlic and fry for 30 seconds only – cook it very briefly; if it browns it will
   taste bitter.
2 Immediately add the tomatoes or passata, bay leaf and thyme. Season to taste and add a large pinch
   of sugar. Bring to the boil, then reduce the heat and simmer, uncovered, for 5–10 minutes.
3 Remove the bay leaf and thyme, add the basil and use immediately. This is good with pasta, or
   cooked meats such as lamb, pork or chicken.

Serves 4   preparation: 5 minutes   cooking time: 15 minutes
per serving: 60 cals; 3g fat; 6g carbohydrate

16

Sauces and salsas

Curried Coconut Sauce

2tbsp extra-virgin olive oil
175g (6oz) onions, peeled and
   finely chopped
2 garlic cloves, peeled and crushed
2.5cm (1 inch) piece fresh root ginger,
   peeled and grated

3–4tbsp mild curry paste
3tbsp coconut milk powder
salt

1   Heat the oil in a pan, add the onions with 1tbsp water and cook gently for 10 minutes or until softened and golden brown.
2   Add the garlic, ginger and curry paste and cook for 1–2 minutes.
3   Mix the coconut milk powder with 450ml (³/₄ pint) warm water, stir into the curried mixture and bring to the boil. Let it bubble for 5–10 minutes. Season with salt to taste. This curried sauce is particularly good with fish and shellfish.

Serves 6   preparation: 5 minutes   cooking time: 20 minutes
per serving: 80 cals; 7g fat; 3g carbohydrate

Creamy Mushroom and Wine Sauce

2tbsp oil
2 shallots or 1 onion, peeled and
   finely diced
175g (6oz) button or cup mushrooms, sliced
150g (5oz) mixed wild mushrooms, sliced

2 garlic cloves, peeled and crushed
150ml (¼ pint) white wine
200ml (7fl oz) crème fraîche
salt and pepper
2tsp chopped thyme

1   Heat the oil in a pan, add the shallots and cook gently for 10 minutes. Add all the mushrooms and garlic and cook over a high heat for 4–5 minutes until tender and all the moisture has been driven off. Pour in the wine, bring to the boil and let bubble until reduced by half.
2   Add the crème fraîche, 100ml (3½fl oz) water and seasoning. Bring to the boil and bubble for 5 minutes or until the liquid is slightly thickened and syrupy.
3   Add the thyme, adjust the seasoning and serve immediately. This sauce is great with pan-fried steak or chicken.

Serves 6   preparation: 10 minutes   cooking time: 20 minutes
per serving: 190 cals; 18g fat; 3g carbohydrate

Wild Mushroom Sauce

25g (1oz) butter
2 shallots, blanched in boiling water,
   drained, peeled and finely chopped
100g (3½oz) button mushrooms, sliced
100g (3½oz) wild mushrooms, sliced

50ml (2fl oz) brandy
200ml (7fl oz) red wine
2tsp plain flour
600ml (1 pint) hot chicken stock
salt and pepper

1 Melt the butter in a large frying pan, add the shallots and fry for 1 minute. Add all the mushrooms and cook for 2 minutes, then pour in the brandy.
2 Bring to the boil and bubble to reduce by half. Add the wine, return to the boil and reduce until syrupy.
3 Stir in the flour, mix until smooth, then add the hot stock. Bring to the boil and bubble for 15–20 minutes until syrupy. Adjust the seasoning to taste. Cover and refrigerate for up to two days; bring slowly to the boil to use. Good with grilled steaks.

Serves 8 preparation: 10 minutes cooking time: 30 minutes
per serving: 60 cals; 3g fat; 2g carbohydrate

Shallot and Mushroom Sauce

400g (14oz) shallots, blanched in boiling
   water, drained and peeled
1tbsp olive oil
300ml (½ pint) red wine
225g (8oz) button mushrooms, quartered
1 celery stalk, cut in half

4 thyme sprigs
40g (1½oz) butter
350g (12oz) shallots, blanched in boiling
   water, drained and peeled
1tsp golden caster sugar
15g (½oz) plain flour

1 To make the sauce, finely chop 2 shallots. Heat the olive oil in a pan and cook the chopped shallots until golden brown. Add the wine, bring to the boil and bubble until reduced to about 2tbsp.
2 Add the mushrooms and cook for 3–4 minutes. Add 600ml (1 pint) water, the celery and thyme, bring to the boil, then reduce the heat and simmer for 20 minutes.
3 Meanwhile, heat 25g (1oz) butter in a frying pan and add the remaining whole shallots and the sugar. Cover and cook over a low heat for 20–25 minutes.
4 Remove the thyme and celery from the sauce and pour over the shallots. Bring to the boil and bubble, uncovered, until reduced by half. To thicken the sauce, soften the remaining butter and combine with the flour, then whisk into the sauce. Simmer for 1–2 minutes, then season and serve. A good sauce for pan-fried steak or chicken.

Serves 4–6 preparation: 10 minutes cooking time: 1 hour 20 minutes
per serving: 170–110 cals;12–8g fat; 12–8g carbohydrate

16

Sauces and salsas

Onion Sauce

125g (4oz) unsalted butter
5 onions, peeled and sliced
1.1 litres (2 pints) semi-skimmed milk
2 cloves

125g (4oz) plain flour
½tsp freshly grated nutmeg
142ml carton double cream
salt and pepper

1 Put 50g (2oz) butter in a pan and melt over a low heat. Add the onions and cook for 25 minutes until soft but not coloured. Stir to make sure they don't stick. Take off the heat and mash.
2 Meanwhile, pour the milk into a pan and add the cloves. Bring to the boil, then turn off the heat and leave to infuse.
3 Melt the remaining butter in a pan. Add the flour and nutmeg and stir with a wooden spoon for 2–3 minutes until the mixture browns.
4 Add one-third of the milk, stirring all the time to remove any lumps. As the sauce starts to thicken, stir in the remaining milk, leaving the cloves behind in the pan. Bring to the boil, then reduce the heat and simmer for 1 minute.
5 Stir in the cream, then add the cooked mashed onions. Season and continue to cook over a low heat for 30 minutes, stirring every now and then. Spoon into a warm bowl and serve with roast goose.

Serves 8   preparation: 10 minutes   cooking time: 55 minutes
per serving: 360 cals; 24g fat; 29g carbohydrate

Caramelised Onion Sauce

scant 60g (2½oz) butter
250g (9oz) onions, peeled and finely sliced
4tsp golden caster sugar
4tsp balsamic vinegar
200ml (7fl oz) white wine

450ml (¾ pint) fresh chicken or
   vegetable stock
salt and pepper
20g (¾ oz) plain flour

1 Melt 40g (1½oz) butter in a pan, add the onions and cook gently for 5–10 minutes or until soft.
2 Add the sugar and vinegar, bring to the boil and bubble until almost all the liquid has evaporated and the onions are dark brown.
3 Add the wine and bring to the boil, then bubble to reduce by half. Add the stock, bring to the boil and bubble for 5 minutes; season to taste.
4 To thicken the sauce, soften the remaining butter and combine with the flour. Whisk into the bubbling sauce, a little at a time, and simmer for 3–4 minutes. Check the seasoning and serve, or cover and chill for up to 24 hours, then reheat the sauce in a pan. This goes well with roast pork.

Serves 4–6   preparation: 10 minutes   cooking time: 45–50 minutes
per serving: 190–120 cals; 12–8g fat; 14–9g carbohydrate

16

Sauces and salsas

Sweet Onion and Mustard Sauce

75g (3oz) butter
350g (12oz) onions, peeled and finely sliced
200ml (7fl oz) hot brown stock, such as beef
  or chicken

1tbsp Dijon mustard
1tsp sugar
salt and pepper

1 Melt the butter in a heavy-based pan, add the onions, cover and cook over a low heat for 20–25 minutes. Cook, uncovered, for a further 5 minutes or until all the liquid has evaporated and the onions have turned golden brown.
2 Add the hot stock, mustard and sugar and season well. Bubble for about 10 minutes or until reduced and syrupy. This sauce goes well with bubble and squeak.

Serves 4–6   preparation: 5 minutes   cooking time: 40 minutes
per serving: 180–120 cals; 15–10g fat; 8–5g carbohydrate

Mustard and Caper Sauce

2 hard-boiled eggs
2tsp smooth Dijon mustard
2tbsp white wine vinegar
8tbsp olive oil

2tbsp chopped capers
1tbsp chopped shallot
pinch of sugar
salt and pepper

1 Mash the egg yolks with the mustard. Add the vinegar and slowly whisk in the olive oil.
2 Add the capers, shallot and a pinch of sugar. Season well and serve with grilled fish, beef, pork or sausages.

Serves 4–6   preparation: 15 minutes
per serving: 280–190 cals; 29–19g fat; 1–1g carbohydrate

Parsley Sauce

300ml (½ pint) full-fat milk
15g (½oz) each butter and plain flour

2tbsp chopped flat-leafed parsley
salt and pepper

1 Put the milk, butter and flour in a pan. Heat gently, whisking all the time, and bring to the boil. Simmer for 3–5 minutes, then add the parsley and season well. Use at once – it goes well with roasted cod.

Serves 4–6   preparation: 5 minutes   cooking time: 3–5 minutes
per serving: 90–60 cals; 6–4g fat; 7–4g carbohydrate

Sauces and salsas

Red Onion and Thyme Confit

3tbsp olive oil
450g (1lb) red onions, peeled and
  finely chopped
1tsp chopped thyme

200ml (7fl oz) dry white wine
3tbsp wine vinegar
2tbsp dark muscovado sugar
salt and pepper

1 Heat the olive oil in a small pan, then add the onions and thyme. Cook, stirring, for 10 minutes or until the onions are soft.

2 Add the wine, vinegar and sugar to the pan. Bring to the boil, then reduce the heat and simmer gently for 40 minutes or until the onions are very soft and almost all the liquid has evaporated. Season well and serve warm.

Serves 4   preparation: 15 minutes   cooking time: 55 minutes
per tbsp: 20 cals; 1g fat; 2g carbohydrate

Hot Harissa Paste

25g (1oz) dried red chillies
1 garlic clove, skinned and chopped
1 level tsp caraway seeds
1 level tsp cumin seeds

1 level tsp coriander seeds
pinch of salt
olive oil

1 Soak the chillies in hot water for 1 hour. Drain well, then put in a pestle and mortar or electric mill with the garlic clove and spices, and grind to a paste.

2 Put into a small jar, cover with olive oil and seal. Harissa will keep in the fridge for up to 2 months. The oil can be used in salad dressings.

Serves 4   preparation: 10 minutes, plus standing
per serving 15 cals; 3g fat; 0g carbohydrate

16

Sauces and salsas

Apple Sauce

2 large **Bramley cooking apples**, peeled,
  cored and roughly chopped
juice of 1 orange and 1 lemon
50g (2oz) light muscovado sugar

25g (1oz) butter
good pinch of freshly grated nutmeg
salt and pepper

1 Put the apples in a pan and add the orange and lemon juice and 125ml (4fl oz) water. Cook gently for 5–10 minutes until the apples are soft.
2 Take off the heat and mash the apples, then add the sugar, butter and grated nutmeg. Season, then return to the hob and bring to the boil. Reduce the heat and simmer for 1 minute. Traditionally served with roast pork, but also great with goose.

Serves 8 preparation: 5 minutes cooking time: 6–11 minutes
per serving: 70 cals; 3g fat; 13g carbohydrates

Sauces and salsas

Cranberry Sauce

350g (12oz) cranberries
125g (4oz) golden caster sugar
grated rind and juice of 1 orange

1–2tbsp port
8 juniper berries, crushed

1 Put all the ingredients in a pan, bring to the boil, then reduce the heat and simmer until the cranberries pop and the sauce thickens. Serve at Christmas with the turkey.

Serves 8   preparation: 5 minutes   cooking time: 5 minutes
per serving: 70 cals; 0g fat; 18g carbohydrate

Cranberry, Honey and Ginger Sauce

zest of 1 and juice of 2 large oranges
350g (12oz) fresh or thawed frozen
   cranberries
4tbsp runny honey

150ml (¼ pint) port or red wine
2.5cm (1 inch) piece fresh root ginger,
   peeled and finely grated

1 Put all the ingredients into a pan and bring to the boil, then reduce the heat and simmer gently, uncovered, for about 25 minutes.
2 Using a slotted spoon, remove about half the cranberries and put them into a blender. Whiz until smooth, then return the purée to the pan and mix in well.
3 Taste the sauce and add extra honey if necessary. Cool, put into an airtight container and freeze for up to one month.

Serves 8   preparation: 10 minutes   cooking time: 25–30 minutes
per serving: 60 calories, 0g fat, 11g carbohydrate

Cranberry and Red Onion Marmalade

2tbsp olive oil
500g (1lb 2oz) red onions, peeled and sliced
juice of 1 orange
1tbsp pickling spice

150g (5oz) dark muscovado sugar
150ml (¼ pint) ruby port
450g (1lb) fresh cranberries

1 Heat the olive oil in a pan and fry the onions gently for 5 minutes. Add the orange juice, spice, sugar and port and simmer gently for 40 minutes.
2 Add the cranberries and cook over a medium heat for 20 minutes. Cool and chill for up to two days. Serve at room temperature.

Serves 12   preparation: 10 minutes, plus chilling   cooking time: 1 hour 5 minutes
per serving: 110 cals; 2g fat; 20g carbohydrate

Cranberry, Orange and Port Sauce

450g (1lb) cranberries
2 large oranges, zest grated and flesh cut
    into segments

125g (4oz) golden caster sugar
150ml (¼ pint) port

1 Cook the cranberries and the orange zest in a heavy-based pan over a low heat for 5 minutes or until the cranberry skins begin to split. Using a draining spoon, remove the cranberries from the pan and put in a bowl.
2 Add the sugar and port to the pan. When the sugar has dissolved, bring to the boil and bubble until reduced by half, then pour over the cranberries. Allow to cool, then add the orange segments. Cool, cover and chill for up to four days.

Serves 8–10   preparation: 15 minutes   cooking time: 20 minutes
per serving: 100–80 cals;   0g fat; 23–18g carbohydrate

Tarragon and Grape Sauce

125ml (4fl oz) sweet wine, such as Muscat
    Beaume de Venise
1 bunch of tarragon or 5 thyme sprigs
600ml (1 pint) chicken stock

25g (1oz) butter
225g (8oz) white seedless grapes, halved
salt and pepper

1 Put the wine in a pan with the tarragon or thyme, bring to the boil and bubble for 5 minutes or until reduced by half.
2 Add the stock, bring back to the boil and bubble the sauce for 10 minutes or until reduced by half.
3 Discard the herbs, reduce the heat and whisk in the butter, then add the grapes and bubble for 1 minute. Season to taste and serve immediately. This recipe relies on good-quality stock, if you don't have time to make your own, buy fresh stock from a supermarket. Serve the sauce with roast chicken.

Serves 4   preparation: 5 minutes   cooking time: 26 minutes
per tbsp: 10 cals; 1g fat; 1g carbohydrate

16

Sauces and salsas

Warm Olive Oil Sauce

3 shallots or 1 small onion, peeled and
  finely chopped
125ml (4fl oz) dry white wine
2 large eggs
salt and pepper

cayenne pepper
300ml (½ pint) extra-virgin olive oil
1 lemon
3tbsp chopped flat-leafed parsley
1tbsp chopped dill

1 Put the shallots or onion in a pan with the wine, bring to the boil and bubble the liquid to reduce to 2tbsp.

2 Meanwhile, put the eggs in a food processor with salt, pepper and a small pinch of cayenne and whiz until the mixture is well blended, fluffy and light in colour. Add the reduced wine and shallot mixture and whiz for 1 minute.

3 Warm the oil until hot and, with the processor running at full speed, pour the hot oil in a thin, steady stream on to the eggs. Leave the machine running for 2–3 minutes – the sauce should be thick and creamy. Add 1–2tbsp lemon juice and the herbs and adjust the seasoning. Serve warm spooned over grilled or steamed fish or to accompany steamed vegetables.

Serves 4   preparation: 15 minutes   cooking time: 7 minutes
per serving: 650 cals; 69g fat; 3g carbohydrate

16

Sauces and salsas

The Ultimate Barbecue Sauce

3tbsp olive oil
3 garlic cloves, peeled and finely chopped
3tbsp balsamic vinegar
4tbsp dry sherry
3tbsp sun-dried tomato paste or
   tomato purée

3tbsp sweet chilli sauce
300ml (½ pint) passata
5tbsp runny honey

1 Put the olive oil, garlic, vinegar, sherry, tomato paste or purée and chilli sauce in a bowl and mix.
2 Pour into a pan and add the passata and honey. Bring to the boil, then reduce the heat and simmer for 10–15 minutes until thick and glossy.

Makes 300ml (½ pint)   preparation: 5 minutes   cooking time: 10–15 minutes
per tbsp: 30 cals; 2g fat; 4g carbohydrate

16

Sauces and salsas

Pesto Sauce

75g (3oz) basil
50g (2oz) Parmesan cheese
25g (1oz) pine nuts

1 small garlic clove, peeled and crushed
50–75ml (2–3fl oz) extra-virgin olive oil
salt and pepper

1　Put the basil, Parmesan, pine nuts and garlic in a food processor and whiz. With the motor running, slowly add the olive oil to make a paste. Season well and chill for up to three days until needed. Pesto makes a great pasta sauce and is good in soups.

Serves 4　preparation: 5 minutes
per 1tbsp: 90 cals; 9g fat; Trace carbohydrate

Roast Nut and Herb Pesto

50g (2oz) flat-leafed parsley
1 thick slice stale bread, crusts removed
2tbsp lemon juice

1–2 garlic cloves, peeled
50g (2oz) toasted almonds
200ml (7fl oz) olive oil

1　Put the parsley, bread, lemon juice and one or two garlic cloves in a processor and whiz to combine. Add the almonds and olive oil and whiz to a smooth sauce. Use with pasta and grilled chicken or vegetables.

Serves 4　preparation: 5 minutes
per tbsp: 120 cals; 12g fat; 1g carbohydrate

Parsley and Almond Pesto

50g (2oz) blanched almonds
4 x 20g packs flat-leafed parsley or
　1 large bunch
4 x 20g packs basil or 1 large basil plant
3 garlic cloves, peeled and chopped

2tsp sea salt
100g (3½oz) each freshly grated Parmesan
　and Cheddar cheese
350ml (12fl oz) extra-virgin olive oil, plus
　extra to seal

1　Heat a dry frying pan over a medium heat and toast the nuts lightly for 2–3 minutes. Put to one side.
2　Put the parsley into a food processor, add the basil, almonds, garlic, sea salt, cheeses and olive oil and whiz to a smooth green sauce. You may have to make the pesto in two batches.
3　Spoon into two 450g (1lb) sterilised jars, pour in a little olive oil – just enough to cover the top in a thin layer – then seal and store in the fridge for up to two weeks.

Makes about three 300g (11oz) jars　preparation: 10 minutes
per 1tbsp serving: 110 cals; 11g fat; Trace carbohydrate

Quick Salsa

½ ripe avocado, peeled and
   roughly chopped
4 tomatoes, roughly chopped

1tsp olive oil
juice of ½ lime

1 Put all the ingredients in a bowl and stir well. Serve at once with grilled fish or chicken.

Serves 4   preparation: 5 minutes
per tbsp: 15 cals; 1g fat; 1g carbohydrate

Roasted Red Pepper Salsa

1 large red pepper
4tbsp olive oil

2tsp balsamic vinegar
salt and pepper

1 Preheat the oven to 220°C (200°C fan oven) mark 7. Put the red pepper on a roasting tray and drizzle
   1tbsp olive oil over. Roast the pepper for 30–40 minutes or until it is slightly charred. Put them in a
   bowl, cover with clingfilm and leave to cool, then remove the skin, core and seeds.
2 Cut the pepper into strips or dice, then mix with the remaining olive oil, the vinegar and seasoning.
   Keep the salsa covered in the fridge for up to three days. Great with grilled chicken.

Serves 4   preparation: 10 minutes, plus cooling   cooking time: 30 minutes
per tbsp: 60 cals; 6g fat; 1g carbohydrate

Herb and Lemon Salad Dressing

3tbsp apple juice
grated zest of ½ lemon, plus 1tbsp
   lemon juice

4tbsp grapeseed oil
2tsp chopped thyme
black pepper, to taste

1 Put all the ingredients in a small bowl and whisk to combine. This is a good low-salt dressing.

Serves 4   preparation: 5 minutes
per tbsp: 50 cals; 6g fat; 1g carbohydrate

Caper and Lemon Dressing

1 red chilli, deseeded and finely chopped
8tbsp capers
1 garlic clove, peeled and crushed
4tbsp each chopped dill and chives

8tbsp lemon juice (about 3 lemons)
300ml (½ pint) olive oil
salt and pepper

1   Put the chilli, capers and garlic in a bowl with the dill and chives. Add the lemon juice, then whisk in the olive oil and season to taste. Good with fish cakes or grilled salmon.

Serves 12   preparation: 15 minutes
per serving: 220 cals; 22g fat; trace carbohydrate

Caesar Dressing

2 eggs
2 garlic cloves, peeled
juice of 1 lemon
4tsp Dijon mustard

2tsp balsamic vinegar
300ml (½ pint) sunflower oil
salt and pepper

1   Put the eggs, garlic, lemon juice, mustard and vinegar in a food processor and whiz until smooth then, with the motor running, gradually add the oil and whiz until smooth.
2   Season, cover and chill for up to three days. Serve as a salad dressing or over cold chicken.

Serves 30   preparation: 5 minutes
per serving: 80 cals; 9g fat; 0g carbohydrate

Mango Mayo

1 large mango, peeled and stoned
2tsp chopped coriander
1tsp peeled and grated fresh root ginger

juice of 1 lime
salt and pepper
200ml (7fl oz) sunflower oil

1   Mash the flesh of the mango in a bowl and add the coriander, ginger and lime juice. Season well.
2   Slowly whisk in the oil until the mayonnaise is thick. Great with barbecued chicken or gammon.

Serves 2   preparation: 5 minutes
per serving: 800 cals; 33g fat; 97g carbohydrate

Smoky Pepper Mayo

1 grilled red pepper, peeled and chopped
1 garlic clove, peeled
250ml (8fl oz) mayonnaise

2tsp chilli oil
2tbsp lemon juice

Put the red pepper, garlic and mayonnaise in a processor and whiz to combine, then stir in the chilli oil and lemon juice. Serve with barbecued pork or sausages.

Serves 4   preparation: 5 minutes
per tbsp: 110 cals; 11g fat; trace carbohydrate

Mustard and Beer Marinade

4tbsp grainy mustard

150ml (¼ pint) beer

1   Mix the mustard with the beer and use for marinating beef steaks or pork.

Serves 4   preparation: 5 minutes
per tbsp: 5 cals; trace fat; trace carbohydrate

Pineapple and Coconut Marinade

½ lime
¼ pineapple, peeled and chopped

200ml carton coconut milk
1tsp Tabasco sauce

1   Scoop the flesh out of the lime and put in a processor with the pineapple. Whiz until smooth.
2   Stir in the coconut milk and Tabasco and use for marinating chicken or pork.

Serves 4   preparation: 10 minutes
per tbsp: 10 cals; 1g fat; 1g carbohydrate

16

Sauces and salsas

Sticky Kumquat Compôte

450g (1lb) kumquats, halved lengthways
200g (7oz) golden caster sugar
1 cinnamon stick, crumbled

2 cloves
freshly grated nutmeg
50g (2oz) chopped unsalted pistachio nuts

1 Put the kumquats in a pan of cold water, bring to the boil and cook for 10–15 minutes or until soft.
2 Drain, then return the kumquats to the pan with the sugar, 450ml (¾ pint) water, the cinnamon stick, cloves and a generous grating of nutmeg. Gently bring to the boil and bubble for 20 minutes or until the liquid is reduced by half and syrupy.
3 Add the pistachios and serve warm.

Serves 8–10   preparation: 5 minutes
per serving: 160–130 cals; 4–3g fat; 32–26g carbohydrate

Fresh Vanilla Custard

600ml (1 pint) full-fat milk
284ml carton single cream
4tsp vanilla bean paste or 4tsp
   vanilla extract

2 strips of lemon zest
6 large egg yolks
3tbsp golden caster sugar
4tsp cornflour

1 Pour the milk and cream into a pan and add the vanilla and lemon zest. Bring to the boil, then turn off the heat immediately and leave to cool for 15 minutes.
2 Put the egg yolks in a heatproof bowl and whisk in the sugar and cornflour. Gradually whisk in the cooled milk mixture, then put the bowl over a pan of simmering water, making sure the base of the bowl doesn't touch the water.
3 Heat gently for 10 minutes, stirring constantly until the mixture thickens and coats the back of a spoon easily. Pour into a jug and cover the surface with a circle of greaseproof paper, then cover the jug with clingfilm and chill for up to one day.

Serves 8   preparation: 5 minutes, plus cooling   cooking time: 10 minutes
per serving: 200 cals; 14g fat; 13g carbohydrate

Passion-fruit Sauce

8 ripe passion fruit, halved

6tbsp icing sugar, plus extra if needed

1 Scoop out the passion fruit pulp into a food processor, add the sugar and whiz well to combine.
2 Sieve the sauce and taste – you may need to add more sugar if the fruit is underripe. Serve.

Serves 4   preparation: 10 minutes
per tbsp: 30 cals; 0g fat; 7g carbohydrate

Strawberry Sauce

225g (8oz) strawberries, hulled   **2–3 tbsp icing sugar**

1   Put the strawberries and sugar in a food processor and whiz well to combine.
2   Sieve the sauce and serve.

Serves 8   preparation: 10 minutes
per tbsp: 20 cals; 0g fat; 5g carbohydrate

Microwave Chocolate Sauce

200g (7oz) good-quality plain dark   **284ml carton double cream**
chocolate (with minimum 50% cocoa   **25g (1oz) butter, cut into cubes**
solids), roughly chopped

1   Put the chocolate, cream and butter in a microwave-proof bowl and melt on Medium for 1–2 minutes
(based on a 900W oven). Stir until smooth. If the sauce is not being eaten immediately, add 2tbsp runny
honey, which will help to keep it smooth and will stop the sauce becoming grainy as it cools. Serve
this sauce over profiteroles, meringues, ice cream or crêpes.

Makes 450ml (¾ pint)   preparation: 5 minutes   cooking time: 2 minutes
per serving: 2500 cals; 215g fat; 137g carbohydrate

Heavenly Fudge Sauce

75g (3oz) unsalted butter   **2tbsp full-fat milk**
50g (2oz) light muscovado sugar   **225g (8oz) condensed milk**

1   Put the butter and sugar in a small pan. Heat very gently, stirring occasionally until the sugar has
completely dissolved. Bring to the boil and bubble for 1 minute only.
2   Take the pan off the heat and whisk in the milk and condensed milk. Bring back to the boil, whisking
to get rid of any lumps, and bubble for 2 minutes or until the mixture turns golden and thickens to the
consistency of extra-thick cream. Pour into a sterilised glass or ceramic jar, then cool and chill. Great
over ice cream or with bananas.

Makes one 300ml (½ pint) jar, enough for 8 servings
per serving: 170 cals; 8g fat; 23g carbohydrate

Preserves

Stuck for ideas for an unusual present? Why not give a jar of Spiced Clementines and Kumquats in Brandy, or Spiced Pickled Peaches? Tart up the jar with a fancy label and some raffia and it will look very special indeed.

The same goes for chutnies – friends will love your homemade Mango and Ginger; Pumpkin, Apricot and Almond; or Spiced Pepper, and they're so easy to make.

Pickles are great served with cold meats, Ploughman's, salads, fish and chips, black pudding – you name it. Summer Pickle is packed with vegetables, mushrooms and tomatoes and is perfect for serving when you're having a barbecue. While Pickled Onions and Pickled Red Cabbage are great Christmas favourites.

And talking of Christmas, the Almond Whisky Mincemeat; Kumquat; Spicy Carrot; or Mixed Fruit and Nut mincemeats will really get your mince pies talked about. Packed with fruit, spices, nuts and alcohol, they can be made ahead and kept for months.

Jam – rich and dark, light and lemony, or sweet and sharp, smeared onto buttery toast or crumbly scones, it's what teatime is all about. And don't forget the marmalade – try Ginger and Grapefruit Jelly, with the citrus tang of grapefruit and the spicy zing of fresh and preserved ginger.

Get preserving!

Ingredients

Always try to use unwaxed fruit. If you can't get unwaxed, rub the fruit with a tiny drop of washing-up liquid, rinse well and dry.

Pectin is naturally present in fruit, and reacts with sugar and acid to set jams, jellies, marmalades and conserves. Some fruits, such as cooking apples, lemons, Seville oranges, gooseberries and damsons, are high in natural pectin and acid. Eating apples, raspberries, blackberries, apricots and plums have a medium pectin and acid content, while cherries, grapes, peaches, rhubarb and strawberries score low on both counts.

Fruits with a low or medium pectin content should be cooked together with a fruit that is high in pectin to achieve a satisfactory set. Lemon juice is most commonly used since it is rich in both pectin and acid; 2tbsp lemon juice to 1.8kg (4lb) fruit should be enough. Alternatively, use 'sugar with pectin' (see below) or commercially produced bottled pectin to ensure a good set.

Sugar acts as a preservative as well as helping to achieve a set, so it is important to use the amount stated in the recipe. Granulated sugar is fine for jams and most preserves, though preserving sugar will give a clearer finish and is the best choice for jellies. Caster sugar or muscovado sugar can also be used. Muscovado sugar lends a distinctive flavour and darker colour and is more suited to chutneys and pickles. 'Sugar with pectin' or 'jam sugar' is granulated sugar with added pectin and citric acid, and is used for jams made with fruit that is low in pectin. Preserves made with this should reach setting point in just 4 minutes.

Vinegar acts as a preservative in pickles and some chutneys. Virtually any vinegar is suitable – red, white or flavoured vinegar – providing that the acetic acid content is 5 per cent or more, as is generally the case.

Testing for a set

Jams, jellies, marmalades and conserves are cooked sufficiently when setting point is reached. It is important to test regularly for a set; if boiled for too long preserves darken and caramelise. Note that if using a saucepan rather than a preserving pan the preserve will take much longer to reach the setting point owing to the reduced surface area.

There are various tests to determine setting point. Remove the pan from the heat while you are testing, to prevent overcooking.

Temperature test The preserve is ready when it registers 105°C on a sugar thermometer.

Chutneys and pickles There is no accurate test for chutneys and pickles, as they are not cooked to a setting point. Instead, be guided by the consistency and cooking time specified. Chutneys and pickles are ready when no excess liquid remains and the mixture is very thick

Saucer test For this, you will need one or two chilled saucers. Spoon a little of the jam or marmalade on to a cold saucer. Push a finger across the preserve: if the surface wrinkles and it is beginning to set, it has reached 'setting point'. If not, boil for another 5 minutes and repeat the test.

Flake test Using a wooden spoon, lift a little of the preserve out of the pan. Let it cool slightly, then tip the spoon so that the preserve drops back into the pan. If the drips run together and fall from the spoon in a 'flake' rather than as drips, it is ready.

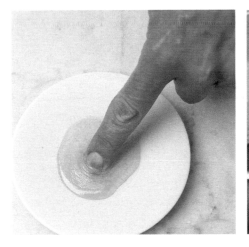 

Potting preserves

All preserves must be potted in scrupulously clean, sterilised containers. Wash the jars or bottles in very hot soapy water, rinse thoroughly, then put upturned on a baking sheet in the oven at 140°C (120°C fan oven) mark 1 for 10–15 minutes until completely dry. Stand the jars upside down on a clean tea-towel until the preserve is ready.

Once setting point is reached, leave the hot jam or marmalade to stand for 15 minutes. Pour into the jars while they are still warm, to reduce the chances of the glass cracking, and fill them almost to the top. If potting jam, marmalade or conserve, immediately cover with a waxed disc, wax side down, while the preserve is warm. Leave to go cold, then cover the jar with a dampened cellophane disc and secure with an elastic band. If you seal while the preserve is warm, mould will grow on the surface.

Chutneys and pickles are covered in the same way. For long-term storage, cover the jar with a screw top as well.

Spiced Pickled Peaches

about 30 cloves

900g (2lb) peaches, skinned, stoned
and halved

450g (1lb) sugar

300ml (½ pint) white wine vinegar

thinly pared rind of ½ lemon

1 small cinnamon stick

1 Push two cloves into each peach half. Put the sugar, vinegar, lemon rind and cinnamon in a pan and heat gently, stirring, for about 5 minutes or until the sugar has dissolved. Add the peach halves to the pan and simmer the fruit in the sweetened vinegar until soft.

2 Drain the fruit and pack into jars. Continue boiling the vinegar until it is slightly reduced and beginning to thicken. Strain the vinegar syrup and pour sufficient over the fruit to cover.

3 Cover and seal with vinegar-proofs tops. Label the jars and store for 2–3 months before use.

Serves 6　preparation: 15 minutes, plus maturing　cooking time: about 15 minutes
per serving: 350 cals; 0g fat; 91g carbohydrate

Spiced Vinegar

1.1 litres (2 pints) vinegar

2tbsp blades of mace

1tbsp each allspice berries and
whole cloves

18cm (7 inch) cinnamon stick

6 peppercorns

4 dried red chillies

1 small bay leaf

1 Put the vinegar, spices and bay leaf in a medium pan, bring to the boil and pour into a bowl. Cover and leave to marinate for 2 hours.

2 Strain the vinegar through muslin, pour into sterilised bottles and seal with airtight and vinegar-proof tops. Label the bottles.

Makes 1.1 litres (2 pints)　preparation: 10 minutes, plus standing　cooking time: 5 minutes
per 1tbsp serving: 0 cals; 0g fat; 0g carbohydrate

17

Preserves

Prunes in Brandy

225g (8oz) pitted, ready-to-eat prunes   **200ml (7fl oz) brandy**

1 Put the prunes in a jar or bowl and cover with the brandy. Cover the jar with a lid or clingfilm and
   leave for 2–3 days before using.

Serves 8   preparation: 10 minutes, plus 2–3 days soaking and maturing
per serving: 100 cals, 0g fat; 11g carbohydrate

Kumquats in Brandy Syrup

1kg (2¼lb) kumquats, destalked   **200ml (7fl oz) brandy**
1kg pack golden granulated sugar

1 Wash the kumquats, prick them all over with a skewer and put in a large heavy-based pan. Add the
   sugar and brandy and heat gently to dissolve the sugar – this may take up to 10 minutes.
2 When all the sugar has dissolved, increase the heat and bring to the boil. Bubble for 10–15 minutes
   or until syrupy, then leave to cool.
3 Spoon the kumquats into sterilised jars and cover. Label the jars and store in a cool dark place for
   up to 2 months.

Makes about 5 x 300g (11oz) jars   preparation: 15 minutes plus cooling   cooking time: 35 minutes
per jar: 946 cals; 0g fat; 227g carbohydrate

17

Preserves

Spiced Clementines and Kumquats in Brandy

350g (12oz) golden castor sugar
14 kumquats, halved lengthways, seeds removed
5cm (2 inch) piece fresh root ginger, peeled and finely sliced

1tsp allspice berries
8 clementines, peel and pith removed
6 bay leaves
225ml (8fl oz) brandy

1 Put 175g (6oz) sugar with 300ml (½ pint) water in a wide pan and heat gently to dissolve the sugar. Add the kumquats, ginger and allspice berries and, bring to a simmer, then cover the pan and poach for 8 minutes until softened.
2 Lift the kumquats and spices out of the pan with a slotted spoon and put to one side. Add the remaining sugar and dissolve, stirring, over a low heat. Increase the heat and boil uncovered for about 5 minutes or until the liquid measures about 250ml (9fl oz). Cool slightly.
3 Pierce the clementines all over with a skewer and arrange in the jars with the kumquats, spices and bay leaves. Add the brandy to the syrup and pour over the fruit, making sure it's submerged. Cover and seal, Label the jars and store in a cool, dark place.

Makes 2 x 500ml (17fl oz) jars   preparation: 25 minutes   cooking time: 13 minutes
per jar: 1040 cals; 0g fat; 210g carbohydrate

Green Tomato Chutney

450g (1lb) Bramley or other cooking apples, peeled, quartered and cored
2 onions, peeled and grated
1.4kg (3lb) underripe green tomatoes, thinly sliced
225g (8oz) sultanas

225g (8oz) demerara sugar
2tsp salt
450ml (pint) malt vinegar
4 small pieces dried root ginger
½tsp cayenne pepper
1tsp mustard powder

1 Grate the apples finely. Put into a large preserving pan together with all the remaining ingredients. Bring the mixture slowly to the boil, stirring occasionally to make sure the sugar has dissolved.
2 Reduce the heat and simmer the chutney gently for about 2 hours, stirring occasionally, until the mixture is reduced to a thick consistency, and no excess liquid remains. Discard the ginger.
3 Spoon the chutney into warmed sterilised jars and leave to cool. Cover and seal with vinegar proof tops.
4 Label the jars and store in a cool, dark place for 2–3 months before eating. Once opened, store in the fridge and use within 1 month.

Makes 1.4kg (3lb)   preparation: 20 minutes, plus maturing   cooking time: about 2 hours
per 1tbsp serving: 20 cals; trace fat; 5g carbohydrate

17

Preserves

Spiced Tomato Chutney

1kg (2¼lb) ripe tomatoes, chopped
2 onions, peeled and finely chopped
3 garlic cloves, peeled and crushed
2 red peppers, cored, deseeded and finely chopped
1 red chilli, deseeded and diced
450ml (¾ pint) distilled malt vinegar or white wine vinegar

350g (12oz) light muscovado sugar
100g (3½oz) raisins
1tsp black mustard seeds
1tsp salt
2tsp smoked paprika
1 cinnamon stick
¼tsp ground cloves

1 Put the tomatoes into a large preserving pan, add all the remaining ingredients and stir together. Bring slowly to the boil, stirring from time to time to make sure the sugar has dissolved.
2 Reduce the heat and cook the chutney at a medium simmer for 1–1½ hours, stirring occasionally, until it is reduced to a thick, jammy consistency, and no excess liquid remains. It's ready when a wooden spoon drawn through the chutney leaves a clear channel with just a little juice.
3 Spoon the chutney into warmed sterilised jars and allow to cool. Cover and seal with vinegar-proof tops. Label the jars and store in a cool, dark place for at least 1 month, or up to 3 months, before using. Once opened, store the chutney in the fridge and use within 1 month.

Makes about 1.2kg (2¾lb)   preparation: 15 minutes, plus maturing   cooking time: about 2 hours
per 1tbsp serving: 25 cals; trace fat; 6g carbohydrate

Tomato and Apple Chutney

700g (1½lb) tomatoes, peeled, deseeded and chopped
1 apple, peeled, cored and roughly chopped
50g (2oz) onion, peeled and finely chopped
1 garlic clove, peeled and crushed
125g (4oz) light muscovado sugar

1tsp finely chopped peeled fresh root ginger
½tsp ground turmeric
125g (4oz) sultanas
50ml (2fl oz) white wine vinegar

1 Mix all the ingredients in a large pan, then bring to the boil, reduce the heat and simmer for 30 minutes or until reduced and thick. Cool.
2 Spoon the chutney into warmed sterilised jars and allow to cool. Cover and seal with vinegar-proof tops. Label the jars and store in a cool, dark place for at least 1 month, or up to 3 months, before using. Once opened, store in the fridge and use within 1 month.

Makes about 1.2kg (2¾lb)   preparation: 20 minutes, plus standing   cooking time: 35 minutes
per 1tbsp serving: 30 cals; trace fat; 7g carbohydrate

17

Preserves

Mango and Ginger Chutney

4 firm mangoes, about 1.4kg (3lb)
    total weight
350g (12oz) light muscovado sugar
large pinch of cumin seeds
4 cardamom pods, split open
1tsp ground turmeric

1 whole clove
5cm (2 inch) piece fresh of root ginger,
    peeled and finely grated
400ml (14fl oz) distilled malt vinegar
3 large garlic cloves, peeled
1 large onion, peeled and finely chopped

1 Peel the mangoes with a vegetable peeler. Cut all the flesh away from the stone, then chop into bite-sized chunks and put into a large bowl. Stir in the sugar, cover and leave to marinate overnight.
2 Put the mixture into a large pan, then add the remaining ingredients. Bring to the boil, reduce the heat and simmer gently for about 1½ hours, stirring occasionally, until the mango is translucent and most of the excess liquid has evaporated.
3 Remove the pan from the heat and leave the chutney to cool for 10 minutes. Ladle it into sterilised jars, cover and seal while hot, then label. Once opened, store in the fridge and use within 1 month.

Makes about two 2 x 350g (12oz) jars   preparation: 20 minutes, plus marinating   cooking time: 1½ hours
per 1tbsp serving: 45 cals; trace of fat; 11g carbohydrate

Rhubarb, Ginger and Allspice Chutney

1kg (2¼ lb) thick rhubarb stems, trimmed
    and cut into 5 cm (2 inch) pieces
4tsp salt
225g (8oz) red onions, peeled and cut into
    thick slices
700g (1½ lb) dark muscovado sugar

450ml (¾ pint) white wine vinegar
25g (1oz) piece fresh root ginger, peeled
    and coarsely grated
¼tsp ground allspice
125g (4oz) raisins

1 Put the rhubarb in a non-metallic bowl, mix with 1tsp salt, then cover and leave in a cool place for 12 hours.
2 Drain and rinse the rhubarb, then put into a preserving pan with all the remaining ingredients except the raisins. Cook over a gentle heat until the sugar has dissolved, then increase the heat and bubble for 45 minutes–1 hour or until well reduced and pulpy.
3 Add the raisins and bubble for 5 minutes. Pot hot or cool (not warm), then cover and seal and label the jars.

Makes about 1.6kg (3½lb)   preparation: 15 minutes, plus standing   cooking time: 1¼ hours
per 1tbsp serving: 40 cals; trace of fat; 10g carbohydrate

Pumpkin, Apricot and Almond Chutney

450g (1lb) wedge of pumpkin
600ml (1 pint) cider vinegar
450g (1lb) light muscovado sugar
225g (8oz) sultanas
2 large onions, peeled and sliced
225g (8oz) ready-to-eat dried apricots, cut
  into chunks

finely grated zest and juice of 1 orange
2tbsp salt
½tsp ground turmeric
2 cardamom pods, crushed
1tsp mild chilli seasoning
2tsp coriander seeds
125g (4oz) blanched almonds

1 Remove any seeds from the pumpkin and cut off the skin. Cut the flesh into 2.5cm (1 inch) cubes.
2 Put the vinegar and sugar into a large heavy-based pan and heat gently, stirring until the sugar has dissolved. Bring slowly to the boil.
3 Add the pumpkin, together with all the remaining ingredients, except the almonds. Stir well and bring to the boil. Reduce the heat and cook gently for about 1 hour until soft and thick, stirring occasionally while the mixture is still runny, but more frequently as the chutney thickens; do not let it catch and burn. To test, draw a wooden spoon through the mixture – it should leave a clear trail at the bottom of the pan, which fills up slowly.
4 Stir in the almonds and pack the chutney into warmed sterilised jars, then leave to cool. Cover and seal with vinegar-proof tops. Label the jars and store in a cool dark place for at least 1 month before using. Once opened, store in the fridge and use within 1 month.

Makes 1.8kg (4lb)   preparation: 30 minutes, plus maturing   cooking time: 1–1¼ hours
per 1 tbsp serving: 40 cals; 1g fat; 8g carbohydrate

Spiced Pepper Chutney

3 red peppers and 3 green peppers,
  deseeded and finely chopped
450g (1lb) onions, peeled and sliced
450g (1lb) tomatoes, peeled and chopped
450g (1lb) apples, peeled, cored
  and chopped

250g (8oz) demerara sugar
1tsp ground allspice
450ml (¾ pint) malt vinegar
1tsp each peppercorns and mustard seeds

1 Put the chopped peppers in a preserving pan with the onions, tomatoes, apples, sugar, allspice and vinegar. Tie the peppercorns and mustard seeds in a piece of muslin and add to the pan.
2 Bring to the boil, then reduce the heat and simmer over a medium heat for about 1½ hours until soft, pulpy and well reduced.
3 Remove the muslin bag and, spoon the chutney into warmed sterilised jars. Seal and cover at once. Label the jars and store and use within 1 month.

Makes about 1.6kg (3½lb)   preparation: 20 minutes   cooking time: 1¾ hours
per 1tbsp serving: 15 cals, 0g fat; 4g carbohydrate

17

Preserves

Fresh Coriander Chutney

125g (4oz) fresh coriander, washed
 and dried
1 medium onion, peeled and
 roughly chopped
2 green chillies, deseeded

2.5cm (1 inch) piece fresh root
 ginger, peeled
1tsp salt
2tbsp lemon or lime juice
1tbsp desiccated coconut

1 Put all the ingredients in a blender or food processor and blend until smooth.
2 Transfer to a glass or plastic bowl, cover and chill in the refrigerator. It will keep for up to 1 week.

Makes 275g (10oz) preparation: 10 minutes
per 1tbsp serving: 15 cals; 1g fat; 2g carbohydrate

Fresh Coconut and Tamarind Chutney

125g (4oz) sweetened, tenderised,
 shredded coconut
1 garlic clove, peeled and crushed
1 small onion, peeled and very finely
 chopped or grated
1tbsp tamarind paste or 1tbsp
 chopped mint

2tbsp natural yogurt
1tsp white wine vinegar
1tbsp olive oil
½tsp salt
¼tsp pepper

1 Combine all the ingredients, cover and chill – ideally for a few hours to allow the flavours to develop.

Makes 275g (10oz) preparation: 5 minutes, plus chilling
per 1tbsp serving: 32 cals; 3g fat; 1g carbohydrate

Fresh Pineapple Chutney

250g (9oz) fresh pineapple cubes in natural
 juice, chopped, plus 2 tbsp juice
2 shallots, blanched in boiling water,
 drained, peeled and finely chopped

5mm (¼inch) piece fresh root ginger, peeled
 and grated

1 Combine all the ingredients, cover and chill – ideally for a few hours to allow the flavours to develop.

Makes 275g (10oz) preparation: 20 minutes, plus chilling
per 1tbsp serving: 10 cals; trace fat; 2g carbohydrate

Cranberry and Apple Chutney

1 cinnamon stick
1tsp allspice berries, crushed
1tsp cumin seeds
1kg (2¼lb) cranberries

1kg (2¼lb) Granny Smith apples, peeled,
  cored and diced
450g (1lb) onions, peeled and chopped
500g (1lb 2oz) light muscovado sugar
300ml (½ pint) distilled malt vinegar

1 Put the cinnamon, allspice and cumin seeds in a piece of muslin, tie with string and put in a preserving pan.
2 Add the cranberries, apples, onions, sugar and vinegar and bring to the boil. Reduce the heat and simmer very slowly, uncovered, stirring occasionally, for around 1½ hours or until the mixture is thick and pulpy. There should be hardly any liquid left when you draw a wooden spoon through the bottom of the pan. Take off the heat and remove the bag of spices.
3 Pot, and cover and seal with vinegar-proof tops. Label the jars and store for up to 3 months.

Makes about 5 x 300g (11oz) jars   preparation: 30 minutes   cooking time: 1¾ hours 45 minutes
per 1tbsp serving: 25 cals; trace fat; 7g carbohydrate

Pickled Pears

900g (2lb) ripe but firm William pears
300ml (½ pint) each distilled malt vinegar,
  plus a dash, and white wine vinegar
450g (1lb) golden granulated sugar
2.5cm (1 inch) piece fresh root ginger,
  peeled and thinly sliced

finely pared zest of 1 lemon
1tbsp allspice berries
1tbsp cloves
1 cinnamon stick or a few pieces
  cassia bark

1 Carefully peel the pears. Halve or quarter them, then remove the cores. Put into a bowl of water with a dash of vinegar added to prevent discoloration.
2 Put the vinegars and sugar into a pan and dissolve over a gentle heat. Add the ginger, lemon zest, spices and drained pears. Slowly bring to the boil, then reduce the heat and simmer gently for about 20 minutes or until the pears are just tender, but still whole.
3 Lift out the pears with a slotted spoon and pack into sterilised jars, with an even distribution of the cooked spices.
4 Bring the syrup to the boil and boil for 10 minutes or until syrupy. Pour over the pears, making sure they are all covered. Cover and seal with vinegar-proof lids. Label the jars and store in a cool dark place for at least 2 weeks before using. Use within 6 months.

Makes 900g (2lb)   preparation: 20 minutes, plus maturing   cooking time: about 30 minutes
per 25g (1oz): 60 cals; 0g fat; 16g carbohydrate

Pickled Onions

1.8kg (4lb) pickling onions, unpeeled
450g (1lb) salt

1.1 litres (2 pints) Spiced Vinegar (page 682)

1 Put the unpeeled onions in a large bowl. Dissolve half the salt in 2.3 litres (4 pints) water, then pour this brine over the onions and leave to marinate for 12 hours.
2 Drain and peel the onions and put into a clean bowl. Dissolve the remaining salt in 2.3 litres (4 pints) water. Pour this fresh brine over the onions and leave for 24–36 hours.
3 Drain the onions, rinse well and pack into jars. Pour over enough Spiced Vinegar to cover them completely. Cover and seal the jars with vinegar-proof tops. Label the jars and leave for 3 months before using.

Makes 1.8kg (4lb)   preparation: 25 minutes, plus standing and maturing
per serving: 10 cals; trace fat; 2g carbohydrate

Summer Pickle

225g (8oz) each celery, carrots, cucumber,
  red peppers and red onions
100g125g (4oz) each green beans, baby
  sweetcorn and button mushrooms
600ml (1 pint) distilled malt vinegar
6 whole allspice
6 black peppercorns

1 blade of mace and 1 bay leaf
2 cloves
pinch of saffron or ground turmeric
2tbsp light muscovado sugar
100g125g (4oz) cherry tomatoes
6tbsp walnut oil
salt and pepper

1 Trim and thinly slice the celery. Trim and scrape the carrots, thinly slice lengthways and cut into triangles. Halve the cucumber lengthways and thickly slice. Deseed the red pepper and cut into similar-sized pieces. Trim the onions, leaving the root intact, and cut each into eight wedges. Top and tail the green beans and sweetcorn; trim and wipe the mushrooms.
2 Combine all the ingredients, except the cherry tomatoes and walnut oil, in a preserving pan or large pan and season. Bring to the boil, then reduce the heat and simmer, stirring gently, for 5 minutes.
3 Stir in the cherry tomatoes and walnut oil, then transfer to a non-metallic bowl. Cool, cover with a plate and leave to marinate overnight.
4 Pack the pickle into jars, then cover and seal with vinegar-proof tops. Label the jars and store in a cool dark place for at least 1 month before using.

preparation: 20 minutes, plus maturing   cooking time: ten minutes, plus marinating
per 25g (1oz): 15 cals; 1g fat; 1g carbohydrate

17

Preserves

Pickled Red Cabbage

about 1.4kg (3lb) firm, red cabbage,
finely shredded
2 large onions, peeled and sliced

4tbsp salt
2.3 litres (4 pints) Spiced Vinegar (page 682)
1tbsp dark muscovado sugar

1 Layer the cabbage and onions in a large bowl, sprinkling each layer with salt, then cover and leave to stand overnight.
2 Drain the cabbage and onions, rinse off the salt and drain thoroughly. Pack the cabbage mixture into jars.
3 Pour the Spiced Vinegar into a pan and heat gently. Add the sugar and stir until dissolved. Leave to cool.
4 Pour the cooled vinegar over the cabbage and onion, cover and seal with vinegar-proof tops. Label the jars and use within 2–3 weeks – any longer and the cabbage tends to lose its crispness.

Makes 1.4kg (3lb)   preparation: 20 minutes, plus standing   cooking time: 5 minutes
per 25g (1oz): 5 cals; trace fat; 1g carbohydrate

Bread and Butter Pickle

3 large ridged or smooth-skinned
cucumbers, thinly sliced
4 large onions, peeled and sliced
3tbsp salt

450ml (¾ pint) distilled white vinegar
150g (5oz) sugar
1tsp celery seeds
1tsp black mustard seeds

1 Layer the cucumber and onion slices in a large bowl, sprinkling each layer with salt. Leave for 1 hour, then drain and rinse well.
2 Put the vinegar, sugar and celery and mustard seeds in a pan and heat gently, stirring, until the sugar has dissolved. Bring to the boil and boil for 3 minutes.
3 Pack the vegetable slices into preheated jars and add enough hot vinegar mixture to cover. Cover and seal with vinegar-proof tops. Label the jars and store in a dark place (or the cucumber will lose its colour) for 2 months to mature before eating.

preparation: 15 minutes, plus marinating and maturing   cooking time: 15 minutes
per 25g (1oz): 10 cals; trace fat; 2g carbohydrate

Pickled Cucumbers

cucumbers   Spiced Vinegar (page 682)
salt

1 Split the cucumbers from end to end and cut into 5cm (2 inch) pieces. Put in a large bowl, cover with salt and leave for 24 hours.
2 Drain the liquid from the cucumbers, rinse and drain again. Pack into sterilised jars and fill up with the cold Spiced Vinegar. Cover and seal with vinegar-proof tops. Label the jars and leave to mature for about 3 months before opening.

preparation: cucumber preparation, plus maturing
per 25g (1oz): 5 cals; 0g fat; 1g carbohydrate

Mixed Dill Pickle

1 cauliflower, about 550g (1¼lb), divided   225g (8oz) coarse salt
  into small florets   1.1–1.3 litres (2–2¼ pints) white
175g (6oz) courgettes, sliced into 5mm   wine vinegar
  (¼ inch) diagonal pieces   2tbsp pickling spice
1 green pepper, about 225g (8oz), deseeded   1tbsp salt
  and cut into 5mm (¼ inch) strips   125g (4oz) sugar
175g (6oz) fine green beans, halved   2 garlic cloves, peeled
125g (4oz) pickling or button onions, peeled   2 large dill stalks
  with roots left intact   1tsp dried dill
1 cucumber, halved lengthways and   2 tarragon stalks
  thickly sliced

1 Put all the prepared vegetables in a large bowl and cover with the coarse salt. Mix, cover and leave in a cold place for 24 hours.
2 Put the remaining ingredients in a preserving pan. Heat gently to simmering point. Remove from the heat and leave to cool completely.
3 Drain the vegetables, rinse well and drain again. Bring two large pans of water to the boil. Add the vegetables and bring back to the boil. Drain the vegetables and refresh under cold water to stop the cooking process and preserve the colour. Allow to drain well.
4 Pack the vegetables into preheated jars. Leave to stand for 1 hour, then drain off the excess liquid. Pour over the cooled pickling vinegar to cover completely. Cover and seal with vinegar-proof tops and label the jars. The pickle will darken a little on storing but it will remain clear if stored in the refrigerator.

Makes 2.3 litres (4 pints)   preparation: 30 minutes, plus standing   cooking time: 15 minutes
per 1tbsp without liquid: 14 cals; trace fat; 1g carbohydrate

Piccalilli

1.4kg (3lb) mixed marrow, cucumber, beans, small onions and cauliflower (prepared weight – see method)
175g (6oz) salt
140g (4½oz) sugar
1½tsp English mustard powder
1tsp ground ginger
1 garlic clove, peeled and crushed
600ml (1 pint) distilled vinegar
25g (1oz) plain flour
1tbsp ground turmeric

1 Deseed the marrow. Finely dice the marrow and cucumber. Top, tail and slice the beans, peel and halve the onions and break the cauliflower into small florets. Layer the vegetables in a large bowl, sprinkling each layer with salt. Add 1.7 litres (3 pints) water, cover and leave for 24 hours in a cool place.
2 The next day, remove the vegetables and rinse and drain them well. Blend the sugar, mustard, ginger and garlic with 450ml (¾ pint) of the vinegar in a large pan. Heat to dissolve the sugar.
3 Add the vegetables, bring to the boil and simmer for 20 minutes or until the vegetables are cooked but still crisp.
4 Blend the flour and turmeric with the remaining vinegar and stir into the cooked vegetables. Bring to the boil and cook for 2 minutes.
5 Spoon the pickle into jars, then cover and seal with vinegar-proof tops. Label the jars and store in a cool dark place for 1 month before using.

Makes 1.5kg (3¼lb)   preparation: 30 minutes, plus standing and maturing   cooking time: 25 minutes
per 1tbsp: 15 cals; trace fat; 3g carbohydrate

Beet Relish

900g (2lb) cooked fresh beetroot, skinned and diced
450g (1lb) white cabbage, finely shredded
75g (3oz) fresh horseradish, grated
1tbsp English mustard powder
600ml (1 pint) malt vinegar
225g (8oz) sugar
pinch of cayenne pepper

1 Combine all the ingredients in a large pan and bring slowly to the boil, then reduce the heat and simmer for 30 minutes, stirring occasionally.
2 Spoon into preheated jars, and cover at once and seal with airtight, vinegar-proof tops.
3 Store in a cool, dry, dark place for 2–3 months before using.

Makes about 700g (1½lb)   preparation: 1 hour 30 minutes, plus maturing
cooking time: about 45 minutes
per 1tbsp: 40cals, trace fat; 9g carbohydrate

17

Preserves

Mixed Fruit and Nut Mincemeat

1.6kg (3½lb) dried mixed fruit
225g (8oz) cooking apples, peeled, cored
   and grated (use a firm hard type of apple,
   such as Wellington; a juicy apple, such
   as a Bramley, may make the mixture
   too moist)
125g (4oz) blanched almonds, chopped

450g (1lb) dark muscovado sugar
175g (6oz) shredded suet
1tsp each freshly grated nutmeg and
   ground cinnamon
grated zest, rind and juice of 1 lemon and
   1 orange
300ml (½ pint) brandy or sherry

1 Put the dried fruits, apples and almonds in a large bowl. Add the sugar, suet, spices, lemon and orange zest and juice and brandy or sherry, then mix all the ingredients thoroughly. Cover the mincemeat and leave to stand for 2 days.
2 Stir well, pack into jars and cover as for jam. Label the jars and leave to mature for at least 2 weeks before using.

Makes about 2.5kg (5½lb)   preparation: 10 minutes, plus standing and maturing
per 1tbsp: 50 cals; 1.5g fat; 9.5g carbohydrate

Quick Mincemeat

225g (8oz) cooking apples, peeled, cored
   and roughly chopped
450g (1lb) seedless raisins and currants,
   mixed, or 450g (1lb) sultanas
125g (4oz) chopped mixed peel
125g (4oz) demerara sugar

225g (8oz) seedless green grapes, skinned
   and chopped
grated zest of 1 orange and 1 lemon
1tbsp lemon juice
1tsp ground cinnamon or mixed spice
pinch of salt

1 Mix the apples, dried fruit and peel in a large bowl. Add the sugar and mix well.
2 Add the remaining ingredients, mix well, pot and cover as for jam. Label the jars and store in a cool place for no more than 1 week. This is a quick, fruity mincemeat, not suitable for long keeping, but popular with those who do not like suet.

Makes 900g (2lb)   preparation: 15 minutes
per 1tbsp serving: 70 cals; 2g fat; 12g carbohydrate

Almond Whisky Mincemeat

125g (4oz) each blanched almonds and no-
  soak dried apricots, finely chopped
50g (2oz) each dried figs and dried dates,
  finely chopped
350g (12oz) cooking apples, peeled, cored
  and finely chopped
225g (8oz) sultanas
150g (5oz) seedless raisins
175g (6oz) shredded suet

1tsp each ground cinnamon and freshly
  grated nutmeg
pinch of ground allspice
125g (4oz) dark brown soft
  muscovado sugar
300ml (½ pint) whisky
finely grated zest and strained juice of
  2 oranges and 1 small lemon

1 Put all the ingredients except the citrus zest and juice in a non-metallic bowl.
2 Stir in the citrus zest and juice, cover and leave to stand overnight.
3 Stir the mixture well, pack tightly into jars and cover as for jam. Label the jars and store in a cool, dry place for about 6 weeks before using. Use within a further 3 months.

Makes about 1.1kg (2½lb)   preparation: 20 minutes, plus standing and maturing
per 1tbsp serving: 100 cals; 5g fat; 11g carbohydrate

Kumquat Mincemeat

225g (8oz) kumquats
150ml (¼ pint) Grand Marnier
225g (8oz) Bramley apples, cored
  and chopped
350g (12oz) each raisins, sultanas
  and currants

175g (6oz) each light and dark muscovado
  sugar
1tbsp ground mixed spice
pinch of ground nutmeg
grated zest and juice of 2 medium oranges

1 Put the kumquats into a pan with the Grand Marnier and 150ml (¼ pint) water. Bring to the boil, then reduce the heat and simmer for 15 minutes or until tender. Remove the kumquats with a slotted spoon and leave the liquid to cool.
2 Cut the apples in half, discarding the pips, roughly chop and put into a large bowl. Add the kumquats, cooled liquid and remaining ingredients and stir thoroughly.
3 Pack tightly into jars and cover as for jam. Label the jars and store in a cool, dark place for up to 3 months.

Makes about 1.6kg (3½lb)   preparation: 15 minutes, plus cooling   cooking time: 15 minutes
per 1tbsp serving: 70 cals; 0g fat; 17g carbohydrate

Spicy Carrot Mincemeat

225g (8oz) cooking apples, peeled, cored
  and finely grated
100g125g (4oz) carrots, peeled and
  finely grated
450g (1lb) sultanas
225g (8oz) currants
grated zest and juice of 1 orange

125g (4oz) shredded suet
pinch of salt
125g (4oz) demerara sugar
60ml (4tbsp) sherry
1tsp each freshly grated nutmeg,
  ground cloves, ground cinnamon
  and ground allspice

1 Put the apples and carrots in a large bowl, add all the remaining ingredients and mix well.
3 Pot into jars and cover as for jam. Label the jars and store in a cool dark place for 2 weeks before using.

Makes 1.1kg (2½lb) preparation: 15 minutes, plus maturing
per 1tbsp serving: 65 cals; 2g fat; 12g carbohydrate

Blackcurrant Jam

900g (2lb) blackcurrants

1.4kg (3lb) sugar

1 If you have time, gently prick each currant and place in a bowl with the sugar. Cover and leave overnight.
2 Transfer the fruit and sugar to a pan, bring slowly to the boil and boil for 3 minutes or until setting point is reached.
3 Remove the pan from the heat and leave for about 30 minutes, until a skin begins to form. Stir gently to distribute the fruit, then pot and cover and label the jars.

Makes 2.3kg (5lb) preparation: 10 minutes, plus standing   cooking time: 10 minutes
per 1tbsp serving: 65 cals; 0g fat; 17g carbohydrate

17

Preserves

Blackberry and Apple Jam

900g (2lb) Bramley or other cooking apples,
  peeled, cored and diced
juice of 1 large lemon
900g (2lb) blackberries

1.2kg (2¾lb) granulated sugar
5tbsp crème de mûre (blackberry liqueur)
15g (½oz) butter

1 Put the apples and 300ml (½ pint) water into a preserving pan and bring to the boil. Reduce the heat and cook gently for 10–12 minutes or until soft.
2 Add the lemon juice and blackberries and return to the boil, then reduce the heat and simmer for 12–15 minutes or until the blackberries begin to break up.
3 Add the sugar to the pan and heat slowly until it has dissolved, stirring occasionally. Increase the heat and cook at a rolling boil for 10–12 minutes. Add the liqueur and test for a set.
4 Once setting point is reached, stir in the butter and leave to settle. Take off the heat, remove the scum with a slotted spoon and leave to stand for 15 minutes, then pot and cover and label the jars.

Makes 2.7kg (6lb)   preparation: 10 minutes, plus standing   cooking time: 50 minutes
per 1tbsp serving: 30 cals; trace fat; 9g carbohydrate

Strawberry Jam

900g (2lb) strawberries, hulled
1kg (2¼lb) sugar with pectin

juice of ½ lemon

1 Put the strawberries in a preserving pan with the sugar and lemon juice. Heat gently until the sugar has dissolved, stirring frequently.
2 Bring to the boil and boil steadily for about 4 minutes or until setting point is reached.
3 Take off the heat, remove any scum with a slotted spoon and leave to stand for 15–20 minutes.
4 Stir the jam gently, then pot and cover and label the jars.

Makes 1.8kg (4lb)   preparation: 10 minutes, plus standing   cooking time: 10 minutes
per 1tbsp serving: 60 cals; 0g fat; 15g carbohydrate

17

Preserves

Strawberry and Redcurrant Jam

700g (1½lb) granulated or preserving sugar
1kg (2¼lb) strawberries, hulled and halved
   if large

225g (8oz) redcurrants, stripped from
   their stalks
juice of 1 lemon

1 Preheat the oven to 180°C (160°C fan oven) mark 4. Put the sugar in a roasting tin and warm in the oven for 10 minutes. Put half the strawberries and all the redcurrants in a preserving pan over a low heat and cook until soft and the juice runs.
2 Add the remaining strawberries to the pan and bring to the boil. Add the lemon juice and warmed sugar to the pan, bring to the boil, then reduce the heat and simmer until the sugar dissolves. Bubble for 25 minutes or until setting point is reached.
3 Stir the jam gently, then leave to cool. Pot and cover, and and label the jars.

Makes about 1.4kg (3lb)   preparation: 20 minutes   cooking time: 30 minutes
per 1tbsp serving: 30 cals; 0g fat; 9g carbohydrate

Raspberry and Cinnamon Jam

900g (2 lb) granulated or preserving sugar
900g (2 lb) raspberries
juice of 1 lemon

1 cinnamon stick, crushed and tied
   in muslin

1 Preheat the oven to 180°C (160°C fan oven) mark 4. Put the sugar in a roasting tin and warm in the oven for 10 minutes. Put the raspberries in a preserving pan and cook over a low heat for 5 minutes or until the juices run. Add the sugar, lemon juice and cinnamon stick.
2 Bring to the boil, then reduce the heat and simmer until the sugar has dissolved. Bubble for 15 minutes or until setting point is reached; remove the cinnamon stick. Pot hot or cool (not warm), then cover and seal and label the jars.

Makes about 1kg (2¼ lb)   preparation: 10 minutes   cooking time: 20 minutes
per 1tbsp serving: 50 cals; 0g fat; 14g carbohydrate

Summer Jam

900g (2lb) summer fruit
900g (2lb) granulated or preserving sugar

juice of 2 large lemons, strained
salt

1 Prepare the fruit, then layer, without stirring or bruising, in a non-metallic bowl with the sugar. Drizzle the lemon juice over the fruit and sugar; cover and leave for at least 8 hours or until the sugar has dissolved.
2 Put the fruit and juices in a preserving pan and bring slowly to the boil, then boil as rapidly as possible without letting the jam boil over, until setting point has been is reached. Add a pinch of salt.
3 Cool slightly, then pot and seal. Label the jars and store in a cool, dark place for up to 2 years.

Makes 3.2kg (7lb)   preparation: 15 minutes, plus standing   cooking time: 1¼ hours
per 1tbsp serving: 55 cals; 0g fat; 15g carbohydrate

Uncooked Freezer Jam

1.4kg (3lb) raspberries or
  strawberries, hulled
1.8kg (4lb) golden caster sugar

4tbsp lemon juice
227ml bottle commercial pectin

1 Put the fruit in a large bowl and very lightly crush with a fork. Stir in the sugar and lemon juice and leave at room temperature, stirring occasionally, for about 1 hour until the sugar has dissolved.
2 Gently stir in the pectin and continue stirring for 2 minutes.
3 Pour the jam into small freezerproof containers, leaving a little space at the top to allow for expansion. Cover and leave at room temperature for 24 hours.
4 Label and freeze. To serve, thaw at room temperature for about 1 hour.

Makes about 3.2kg (7lb)   preparation: 15 minutes, plus macerating and standing
per 1tsp serving: 55 cals, 0g fat; 14g carbohydrate

17

Preserves

Plum Jam

2.7kg (6lb) cooking plums
2.7kg (6lb) sugar

knob of butter

1 Put the plums and 900ml (1½ pints) water in a preserving pan and simmer gently for about 30 minutes, until the fruit is very soft and the contents of the pan are well reduced.
2 Take the pan off the heat, add the sugar and stir until dissolved, then add the butter. Bring to the boil and boil rapidly for 10–15 minutes, stirring frequently or until the setting point is reached.
3 Take the pan off the heat. Using a slotted spoon, remove the plum stones and skim off any scum from the surface of the jam. Pot and cover, then label the jars.

Makes about 4.5kg (10lb)   preparation: 15 minutes   cooking time: 45 minutes
per 1tbsp serving: 40 cals; trace fat; 10g carbohydrate

Apricot Jam

1.8kg (4lb) apricots, halved and stoned,
  stones reserved
juice of 1 lemon

1.8kg (4lb) sugar
knob of butter

1 Crack a few of the apricot stones with a nutcracker, take out the kernels and blanch them in boiling water for 1 minute, then drain.
2 Put the apricots, lemon juice, apricot kernels and 450ml (¾ pint) water in a preserving pan and simmer for about 15 minutes or until well reduced and the fruit is soft.
3 Take off the heat and add the sugar, then stir until dissolved. Add the butter and boil rapidly for 15 minutes or until the setting point is reached.
4 Take off the heat and remove any scum with a slotted spoon, then pot and cover and label the jars.

Makes about 3kg (6½lb)   preparation: 20 minutes   cooking time: about 40 minutes
per 1tbsp serving: 40 cals; trace fat; 10g carbohydrate

17

Mixed Fruit Marmalade

**2 each Seville oranges, yellow grapefruit
and limes
4 large lemons**

3kg (6½lb) preserving or granulated sugar

1 Weigh the fruit – you need around 1.6kg (3½lb) in total – then cut all in half. Squeeze by hand or with an electric juicer to extract as much juice as possible, then pour into a jug through a sieve to catch any pips. Put the pips to one side.
2 Cut the halves into quarters. Cut away the membrane and add to the pips, then cut away a thin layer of pith and add to the pips. Chop the peel into thin strips and tip into a preserving pan. Cut out a 35.5cm (14 inch) square of muslin, pile the pips, membrane and pith in the middle, gather up and tie with a 45.5cm (18 inch) piece of string.
3 Tie the muslin bag to the pan handle, so it hangs near the bottom of the pan. Add the juice and 3 litres (5¼ pints) cold water. Bring to the boil, then reduce the heat and simmer, uncovered, for 2 hours or until the peel is very, very tender and the liquid has reduced. Skim off any scum during cooking and discard.
4 Preheat the oven to 110°C (100°C fan oven) mark ¼. Warm the sugar in a large roasting tin for 20 minutes. Add to the pan and stir until dissolved. Rest a warmed sugar thermometer in the liquid, bring to the boil, then reduce the heat and bubble until the temperature registers 104°C 'jam stage'. Cook at this temperature for about 10 minutes or until setting point is reached. Use the saucer method.
5 Take the pan off the heat and remove any scum with a slotted spoon. Leave to stand for 15 minutes, then stir to distribute the peel. Pot and cover. Label the jars and store in a cool, dark place for up to 1 year.

Makes 4kg (9lb)   preparation: 2 hours, plus standing   cooking time: about 2¼ hours
per 1tbsp serving: 40 cals, 0g fat; 11g carbohydrate

Lemon Marmalade

450g (1lb) ripe, juicy lemons, washed   **700g (1½lb) sugar**

1   Halve the lemons and squeeze out the juice and pips. Cut each 'cap' of peel in half and, with a sharp knife, remove the membrane and some of the pith from the peel. Tie the membrane, pith and pips in a piece of muslin.
2   Slice the peel to the desired thickness and put it in a preserving pan with the juice, muslin bag and 1.1 litres (2 pints) water. Bring to the boil, then reduce the heat and simmer gently for about 1¼ hours or until the peel is soft and the contents of the pan reduced by half.
3   Remove the muslin bag, squeezing it well and letting the juice run back into the pan.
4   Add the sugar and heat gently, stirring until dissolved, then bring to the boil and boil rapidly for about 15 minutes or until setting point is reached. Take off the heat and remove any scum with a slotted spoon, leave the marmalade to stand for about 15 minutes, then stir to distribute the peel. Pot and cover, then and label the jars.

Makes 1.4kg (3lb)   preparation: 40 minutes, plus standing   cooking time: 1 hour
per 1tbsp serving: 65 cals; 0g fat; 17g carbohydrate

Seville Orange Marmalade

450g (1lb) Seville oranges   **900g (2lb) sugar**
juice of 1 lemon

1   Halve the oranges and squeeze out the juice and pips. Tie the pips, and any extra membrane that has come away during squeezing, in a piece of muslin.
2   Slice the orange peel thinly or thickly, as preferred, and put in a preserving pan with the fruit juices, muslin bag and 1.1 litres (2 pints) water. Simmer gently for about 2 hours or until the peel is really soft and the liquid reduced by about half.
3   Remove the muslin bag, squeezing it well and letting the juice to run back into the pan.
4   Add the sugar and heat gently, stirring until the sugar has dissolved, then bring to the boil and boil rapidly for about 15 minutes or until setting point is reached. Take off the heat and remove any scum with a slotted spoon, then pot and cover and label the jars.

Makes 1.4kg (3lb)   preparation: 25 minutes   cooking time: 2 hours 25 minutes
per 1tbsp serving: 60 cals; 0g fat; 17g carbohydrate

Preserves

Ginger and Grapefruit Jelly Marmalade

5 large grapefruit, about 1.8kg (4lb), cut
  into quarters
2.5cm (1 inch) piece fresh root ginger,
  peeled and thinly sliced

granulated sugar
preserved stem ginger in syrup, drained

1   Chop the grapefruit finely, using a sharp knife or the slicing blade of a food processor.
2   Put the grapefruit and root ginger in a preserving pan and add 2.8 litres (5 pints) water. Bring to the boil, half cover the pan and boil gently for about 1 hour or until the fruit is very soft and the contents of the pan reduced to a thick pulp (there should be little free liquid).
3   Spoon the contents of the pan into a jelly bag or cloth attached to the legs of an upturned stool, and leave to strain into a large bowl for at least 12 hours.
4   Discard the pulp remaining in the jelly bag. Measure the extract (there should be about 1.7 litres/3 pints) and return to the preserving pan.
5   Add 450g (1lb) sugar and 25g (1oz) finely shredded stem ginger for each 600ml (1 pint) extract. Heat gently, stirring, until the sugar has dissolved.
6   Bring to the boil and boil rapidly for about 10 minutes or until setting point is reached. Take off the heat and remove any scum with a slotted spoon, then leave the marmalade to stand for 10–15 minutes to allow the jelly to thicken sufficiently to suspend the ginger. Pot and cover, then label the jars.

Makes 1.8kg (4lb)   preparation: 30 minutes, plus standing   cooking time: 1 hour 20 minutes
  per 1tbsp serving: 75 cals; 0g fat; 20g carbohydrate

17

Preserves

Microwave Orange Marmalade

900g (2lb) Seville oranges
juice of 2 lemons

900g (2lb) sugar
knob of butter

1 Pare the rind from the oranges, avoiding the white pith. Shred or chop the rind and put to one side. Put the fruit pith, flesh and pips in a food processor and chop until the pips are broken.
2 Put the chopped mixture and lemon juice in a large heatproof bowl and add 900ml (1½ pints) boiling water. Microwave on High for 15 minutes (based on a 900W oven).
3 Strain the mixture through a sieve into another large bowl and press the cooked pulp until all the juice is squeezed out. Discard the pulp. Stir the shredded rind into the hot juice and microwave on High for 15 minutes or until the rind is tender, stirring occasionally. Stir in the sugar until dissolved.
4 Microwave on High for about 10 minutes, stirring once during cooking, until setting point is reached. Stir in the butter, then remove any scum with a slotted spoon. Leave to cool for 15 minutes, then pot and cover and label the jars.

Makes about 1.1kg (2½lb) preparation: 25 minutes, plus standing cooking time: about 40 minutes
per 1tbsp serving: 90 cals; trace amounts of fat; 23g carbohydrate

17

Preserves

Fresh Orange Curd

grated zest and juice of 2 large oranges
juice of ½ lemon
225g (8oz) golden caster sugar

125g (4oz) unsalted butter
3 egg yolks, beaten

1   Put all the ingredients into a double boiler or a large heatproof bowl set over a pan of simmering water. Stir the mixture until the sugar has dissolved. Continue to heat gently, stirring frequently, for 20 minutes or until the curd is thick enough to coat the back of a spoon – don't allow it to boil or it will curdle.
2   Strain the curd through a fine sieve, then pot and cover and leave to cool. Label the jars, store in the fridge and use within 1 week.

Makes about 2 x 250g (9oz) jars   preparation: 20 minutes   cooking time: 20 minutes
per 1tbsp serving: 110 cals; 6g fat; 13g carbohydrate

Fresh Lemon Curd

grated zest and juice of 4 medium ripe,
   juicy lemons
4 medium eggs, beaten

125g (4oz) butter, cut into small pieces
350g (12oz) golden caster sugar

1   Put all the ingredients into a double boiler or a large heatproof bowl set over a pan of simmering water. Stir the mixture until the sugar has dissolved. Continue to heat gently, stirring frequently, for about 20 minutes until thick enough to coat the back of the spoon; do not allow to boil or it will curdle.
2   Strain the lemon curd through a fine sieve, then pot and cover and leave to cool. Label the jars, and store in the fridge and use within 2 weeks.

Makes about 700g (1½lb)   preparation: 20 minutes   cooking time: about 25 minutes
per 1tbsp serving: 60 cals; 3g fat; 8g carbohydrate

17

Preserves

Baking

What better smell than the enticing aroma coming out of your kitchen of home-baked bread, a moist, fragrant cake, or a big tray of cookies? Small bakes, cakes, sweet and savoury breads, tray bakes, biscuits and sponges are all here – easy to make and just the thing with a cup of tea or when friends pop round.

Whip up a tray of Caramelised Hazelnut Shortbread, some Macaroons, or Sultana and Pecan Cookies just before friends arrive and fill the house with the tempting smell of baking.

Enjoy the simple pleasure of a slice of home-baked Quick Zucchini, Lemon and Parmesan Bread spread with Sun-dried Tomato Butter – a fantastic combination.

Finally, Christmas Cake. The Classic or Light and Easy, filled with fruit and nuts, drenched in alcohol and finished with smooth white icing are truly festive favourites. And don't forget the Freeze-ahead Mince Pies, with banana, marmalade and whisky. Scrumptious.

Lemon and Saffron Cake

175g (6oz) unsalted butter, softened, plus
   extra to grease
grated zest of 1½ lemons, plus 225ml
   (8fl oz) lemon juice
625g (1lb 7oz) golden caster sugar
5 large eggs, separated

3tbsp ground almonds
275g (10oz) self-raising flour, sifted
large pinch of saffron (optional)
lemon slices and rose petals, to decorate
  (optional)

1 Preheat the oven to 170°C (150°C fan oven) mark 3. Grease a 23cm (9 inch) spring-release cake tin and line the base with greaseproof paper. Beat together the butter, lemon zest and 275g (10oz) caster sugar in a large mixing bowl until thoroughly combined, then mix in 75ml (3fl oz) lemon juice, 1tbsp at a time. Beat in the egg yolks and ground almonds, then fold in the flour.

2 Whisk the egg whites in a large clean grease-free bowl until soft peaks form. Using a large metal spoon, stir a quarter of the egg whites into the butter mixture, then gently fold in the remainder with 2tbsp cold water.

3 Pour the mixture into the prepared cake tin and smooth the top. Bake for 50–60 minutes or until a skewer inserted in the centre comes out clean. Remove from the oven and leave the cake in the tin to cool for 30 minutes.

4 Meanwhile, make the syrup. Put the remaining lemon juice and caster sugar, the saffron and 300ml (½ pint) water in a heavy-based pan. Dissolve the sugar over a low heat, then bring to the boil. Put to one side until the cake is cool.

5 Leaving the cake in the tin, put the tin on a baking tray with a lip. Drizzle the lemon syrup over the cake and leave to soak in for 30 minutes.

6 Unmould the cake, slice and, if you like, decorate with lemon slices and rose petals. Serve with crème fraîche or mascarpone.

Serves 8–10   preparation: 30 minutes, plus cooling and soaking   cooking time: 1 hour
per serving: 670–540 cals; 26–21g fat; 108–87g carbohydrate

18

Baking

Lemon Syrup Cake

250g pack unsalted butter, softened, plus
    extra to grease
5 unwaxed lemons, plus juice of 2 lemons
525g (1lb 3oz) golden caster sugar
5 eggs, beaten
175g (6oz) self-raising flour, sifted

75g (3oz) semolina
100g (3½oz) ground almonds, sifted
150ml (¼ pint) brandy
3tbsp runny honey
50g (2oz) blanched almonds

1　Grease a 23cm (9 inch) spring-release cake tin and line the base with greaseproof paper.
2　To make the cake, put 3 lemons in a pan, cover with cold water and bring to the boil. Boil for 45 minutes or until tender. Lift out of the pan and cool. When cold, cut in half, remove the pips and roughly chop the flesh. Put in a food processor and whiz for 2 minutes to a purée.
3　Preheat the oven to 180°C (160°C fan oven) mark 4. Cream the butter and 225g (8oz) sugar with an electric whisk until light and fluffy. Gradually add the eggs, stirring in a little flour if the mixture looks as if it may curdle.
4　Using a large metal spoon, fold in the remaining flour, the semolina, ground almonds and lemon purée. Spoon into the prepared cake tin and bake for 40–50 minutes or until a skewer inserted comes out clean. Remove from the oven and leave the cake in the tin to cool for 20 minutes.
5　Meanwhile, make the syrup. Cut each of the remaining 2 lemons into 12 wedges. Put the remaining sugar, the brandy, lemon juice and honey in a pan. Add 150ml (¼ pint) water and heat gently to dissolve the sugar. Increase the heat and boil for 3 minutes. Add the lemon wedges and cook for 5 minutes or until soft. Add the blanched almonds to the pan.
6　Put the cake on a serving plate, pierce it several times with a skewer and spoon the lemon pieces and almonds on top. Pour the syrup over and serve with yogurt.

Cuts into 16 slices　preparation: 25 minutes, plus cooling　cooking time: 1 hour 50 minutes
per slice: 420 cals; 20g fat; 52g carbohydrate

Baking

Raspberry and Peach Cake

200g (7oz) unsalted butter, melted, plus
  extra to grease
250g (9oz) self-raising flour, sifted
100g (3½oz) golden caster sugar
4 eggs, beaten

small punnet, about 125g (4oz), raspberries
2 large almost-ripe peaches or nectarines,
  halved, stoned and sliced
4tbsp apricot jam
juice of ½ lemon

1 Preheat the oven to 190°C (170°C fan oven) mark 5. Grease a 20.5cm (8 inch) spring-release cake tin and line the base with baking parchment.
2 Put the flour and sugar into a large bowl. Make a well in the centre, add the melted butter and the eggs and mix well.
3 Spread half the mixture over the base of the cake tin and add half the raspberries and sliced peaches or nectarines. Spoon on the remaining cake mixture, smooth over, then add the remaining raspberries and peaches, pressing them down into the mixture slightly.
4 Bake for 1–1¼ hours or until risen and golden and a skewer inserted into the centre comes out clean. Remove from the oven and leave in the tin to cool for 10 minutes.
5 Warm the jam and the lemon juice together and brush over the top of the cake to glaze.

Serves 8 preparation: 15 minutes plus cooling cooking time: 1–1¼ hours
per serving: 410 cals; 24g fat; 45g carbohydrate

Orange and Almond Cake

butter, to grease
60g (2oz) fine breadcrumbs, plus extra to
  line the tin
juice of 3 oranges, plus grated zest of
  1 orange
125g (4oz) ground almonds

1tbsp orange-flower water (if available)
4 eggs, separated
125g (4oz) golden caster sugar
½tsp salt
150ml (¼ pint) whipping cream

1 Preheat the oven to 180°C (160°C fan oven) mark 4. Grease a square cake tin, line with baking parchment and grease again, then sprinkle with breadcrumbs. Mix the breadcrumbs, orange juice and zest, then add the almonds and the orange-flower water, if using.
2 Beat the egg yolks with the sugar and salt until almost white. Add to the first mixture. Beat the egg whites in a clean grease-free bowl until stiff peaks form, then fold in. Pour into the prepared cake tin and bake for about 40 minutes.
3 Remove from the oven and leave in the tin until cold. When cold, turn the cake out and cover the top with whipped cream. For a special occasion, sprinkle the cream-smothered cake with silver balls and surround it with a silver ribbon to decorate.

Serves 10 preparation: 20 minutes plus cooling cooking time: 40 minutes
per serving: 180 cals; 9g fat; 18g carbohydrate

18

Baking

Marshmallow Meringue Cake

225g (8oz) golden caster sugar
125g (4oz) light muscovado sugar
6 large eggs, separated
1tsp cornflour
½tsp vinegar
50g (2oz) flaked almonds, toasted (optional)
450ml (¾ pint) full-fat milk
1tsp vanilla extract

200g (7oz) small white marshmallows
284ml carton double cream, lightly whipped
125g (4oz) good-quality plain chocolate,
   semi-sweet such as Bournville,
   roughly chopped
4 bananas, about 450g (1lb)
chocolate shavings and icing sugar, to dust

1 Preheat the oven to 130°C (110°C fan oven) mark ½. Line two baking sheets with non-stick baking parchment. Using a felt-tip pen, mark out two 23cm (9 inch) diameter circles, then turn the paper over.

2 To make the meringue, sift the caster and muscovado sugars together. Whisk the egg whites in a clean grease-free bowl until they're stiff and dry. Whisk in the sugars, 1tbsp at a time, until the mixture is glossy and very stiff – about 5 minutes; then whisk in the cornflour and vinegar.

3 Spoon just over half the meringue on to one of the baking sheets in a garland shape and sprinkle with half the almonds, if using. Spread the remaining mixture evenly over the other circle to cover it completely. Sprinkle with the remaining almonds and bake for 2–2½ hours, then turn off the oven and leave the meringues inside to cool for 30 minutes.

4 To make the ice cream, bring the milk to scalding point in a small pan, add the vanilla extract, then pour over the egg yolks, whisking. Pour back into the clean pan and cook over a low heat, stirring until the liquid coats the back of a spoon. Place the marshmallows in a bowl, pour the strained warm custard over and stir until they've almost melted.

5 Cook quickly, then cover and chill for 30 minutes. Fold the cream into the custard. Pour into a freezerproof container and freeze for 3–4 hours or until just firm. (Alternatively, if you have an ice cream machine, churn the custard until just firm to give a smoother texutre.) Stir in the chocolate and freeze until you're ready to assemble the cake.

6 About 30 minutes before serving, remove the ice cream from the freezer to soften. Place the meringue circle on a serving plate. Slice the bananas and scatter evenly over the base, reserving a few to stir into the softened ice cream.

7 Using a spoon or ice cream scoop, spoon the ice cream mixture over the bananas and place the meringue garland on top, pressing down gently. Decorate with chocolate shavings and a dusting of icing sugar then serve immediately.

Serves 10–12 preparation: 45 minutes, plus chilling, freezing and softening
cooking time: 2½ hours, plus cooling
per serving: 570–470 cals; 27–22g fat; 76–64g carbohydrate

18

Walnut and Coffee Layer Cake

300g (10oz) unsalted butter at room
   temperature, plus extra to grease
250g (9oz) walnuts, plus extra to decorate
100g (3½oz) plain flour
9 large eggs

250g (9oz) golden caster sugar
3tbsp instant coffee granules
450g (1lb) golden icing sugar, sifted
gold almond dragées, to decorate (optional)

1 Preheat the oven to 170°C (150°C fan oven) mark 3. Grease a 23cm (9 inch) spring-release cake tin and line the base with non-stick baking parchment. Whiz the walnuts in a food processor until roughly chopped. Add the flour and whiz to a fine powder. Put to one side.

2 Separate the eggs, then put the yolks in the bowl of a food mixer and 5 egg whites in a large mixing bowl. (Freeze the remaining whites for use later.) Add the caster sugar to the yolks and beat until pale and very thick.

3 Using a metal spoon, fold the walnut and flour powder into the yolk mixture. Whisk the egg whites in a clean grease-free bowl until soft peaks form. Add one-third of the egg white to the yolk mixture, then carefully fold in the rest. Pour the mixture into the prepared tin.

4 Bake for 55–60 minutes or until a skewer inserted in the centre for 30 seconds comes out clean. Remove from the oven and leave in the tin to cool for 15 minutes, then turn out on to a cooling rack.

5 To make the filling, dissolve the coffee in 3tbsp boiling water and put to one side. Put the butter in a bowl and beat until very soft and creamy. Gradually beat in 300g (10oz) icing sugar and 4tsp of the dissolved coffee (reserve the rest) until well combined and fluffy.

6 Cut the cake horizontally into three layers. Put the bottom layer on a serving plate and spread half the filling over it. Gently press the second layer into position and spread with the remaining filling. Lift the top of the cake into position and press down gently. The cake can be frozen at this stage.

7 For the icing, put the remaining icing sugar into a bowl, add ½–1tsp of the reserved coffee and 2–3tbsp boiling water and combine thoroughly. Pour the icing on to the cake, then, using a round-bladed palette knife, quickly spread in an even layer to the edge. Scatter the extra walnuts and the gold dragées, if using, around the edge. Allow the icing to set (about 2 hours) before serving. The cake will keep well for about 5 days.

Serves 12   preparation: 1 hour, plus cooling and setting   cooking time: 55–60 minutes
per serving: 670 cals; 41g fat; 69g carbohydrate

18

Sticky Ginger Ring

100g (3½oz) butter, cut into cubes, plus
  extra to grease
100g (3½oz) dark muscovado sugar
3tbsp black treacle
100ml (3½fl oz) full-fat milk
2tbsp brandy
1 large egg, beaten
150g (5oz) plain flour

2tsp each ground ginger and
  ground cinnamon
1tsp bicarbonate of soda
75g (3oz) ready-to-eat pitted prunes,
  coarsely chopped
225g (8oz) golden icing sugar, sifted
2 balls stem ginger in syrup, drained and
  cut into thin strips

1 Preheat the oven to 150°C (130°C fan oven) mark 2. Using your hands, generously grease a 600ml (1 pint) capacity, 22cm (8½ inch) round ring mould with butter. (If you don't have a ring mould, cook the mixture in a 450g (1lb) loaf tin for 1 hour 5 minutes–1 hour 10 minutes, or use a 16cm (6½ inch) square, 4cm (1½ inch) deep, tin and bake for 55 minutes.)

2 Put the butter, sugar and treacle in a pan and heat gently until melted, stirring all the time. Add the milk and brandy and, when cool, beat in the egg.

3 Sift the flour, spices and bicarbonate of soda into a large mixing bowl, make a well in the centre, pour in the treacle mixture and stir together until all the flour has been combined. It should have a soft dropping consistency. Stir in the prunes.

4 Pour the mixture into the prepared mould and bake for 1 hour, or until the cake is firm to the touch and a skewer inserted in the centre comes out clean. Remove from the oven and leave in the tin to cool for 10 minutes, then loosen the sides of the cake and turn out on to a wire rack. At this stage you can wrap the cake in greaseproof paper and keep in an airtight container for 1 week.

5 To make the icing, mix the icing sugar with about 2tbsp hot water to create a coating consistency. Pour over the cake, allowing it to drizzle down the sides, then decorate with the stem ginger. Leave to set.

Serves 8   preparation: 15 minutes   cooking time: 1 hour
per serving: 420 cals; 13g fat; 75g carbohydrate

18

Baking

Carrot Cake

250ml (8fl oz) sunflower oil, plus extra
  to grease
225g (8oz) light muscovado sugar
3 large eggs
225g (8oz) self-raising flour
large pinch of salt
½tsp each ground mixed spice, ground
  nutmeg and ground cinnamon

250g (9oz) carrots, peeled and
  coarsely grated
50g (2oz) butter, preferably unsalted, at
  room temperature
225g pack Philadelphia cream cheese
25g (1oz) golden icing sugar
½tsp vanilla extract
8 pecan halves, roughly chopped

1 Preheat the oven to 180°C (160°C fan oven) mark 4. Grease two 18cm (7 inch) sandwich tins and
   line the bases with greaseproof paper.
2 Using a hand-held electric whisk, whisk the oil and muscovado sugar together to combine, then
   whisk in the eggs, one at a time.
3 Sift the flour, salt and spices together over the mixture, then gently fold in, using a large metal spoon.
   Tip the carrots into the bowl and fold in.
4 Divide the cake mixture between the prepared tins and bake for 30–40 minutes or until golden and
   a skewer inserted into the centre comes out clean. Remove from the oven and leave in the tins for
   10 minutes, then turn out on to a wire rack to cool.
5 To make the frosting, beat the butter and cream cheese together in a bowl until light and fluffy. Sift in
   the icing sugar, add the vanilla extract and beat well until smooth.
6 Spread one third of the frosting over one cake and sandwich together with the other cake. Spread
   the remaining frosting on top and sprinkle with the pecans. Store the cake in an airtight container and
   eat within 2 days. Alternatively, the cake will keep for up to 1 week in an airtight tin if it is stored before
   the frosting is applied.

Cuts into 12 slices   preparation: 15 minutes   cooking time: 40 minutes, plus cooling
per slice: 450 cals; 32g fat; 38g carbohydrate

18

Baking

Coffee Genoese Sponge

50g (2oz) butter
4 large eggs
125g (4oz) golden caster sugar
125g (4oz) plain flour

2tbsp instant espresso granules
250g tub mascarpone
125g (4oz) golden icing sugar, sifted, plus
  extra to dust

1 Preheat the oven to 190°C (170°C fan oven) mark 5. Grease two 18cm (7 inch) sandwich tins and line the bases with non-stick baking parchment.
2 Put the butter in a bowl and melt in the microwave on High for 30 seconds (based on a 900W oven).
3 Put the eggs and caster sugar into the bowl of a freestanding electric mixer and whisk until pale and creamy. Lift the whisk – the mixture should be thick enough to leave a trail. Using a large metal spoon, fold half the flour into the mixture.
4 Dissolve 1tbsp espresso granules in 2tsp boiling water, mix into the butter and pour half around the edge of mixture. Add the remaining flour, then the rest of the coffee and butter. Gradually fold in.
5 Divide the mixture between the prepared tins and bake for 25 minutes until risen, firm to the touch and shrinking away from the sides of the tin. Remove from the oven and upturn on to wire racks and cool.
6 Dissolve the remaining espresso granules in 1tbsp boiling water, then mix with the mascarpone and icing sugar and use to sandwich the cake together. Dust with icing sugar.

Serves 8   preparation: 15 minutes   cooking time: 25 minutes, plus cooling
per serving: 410 cals; 23g fat; 46g carbohydrate

Sour Cherry Cakes

175g (6oz) butter, at room temperature
175g (6oz) golden caster sugar
3 eggs
175g (6oz) self-raising flour, sifted
pinch of baking powder

75g pack dried sour cherries
2tbsp milk
225g (8oz) golden icing sugar, sifted
3tbsp lemon juice, strained

1 Preheat the oven to 190°C (170°C fan oven) mark 5. Line a muffin tin with 12 muffin cases.
2 Put the butter, sugar, eggs, flour and baking powder in the large bowl of a freestanding electric mixer or in a food processor. Mix slowly to start with, then increase the speed slightly until the mixture is well combined.
3 Reserve 12 dried sour cherries, then fold in the remainder and mix everything together.
4 Spoon the mixture into the cases and bake for 15–20 minutes, until pale golden, risen and springy to the touch. Remove from the oven and cool on a wire rack.
5 To make the icing, put the icing sugar in a bowl and mix with the lemon juice to make a smooth dropping consistency. Spoon the icing on to the cakes and decorate each with a reserved sour cherry. Leave to set before serving.

Makes 12   preparation: 30 minutes   cooking time: 15–20 minutes
per cake: 330 cals; 14g fat; 50g carbohydrate

Lemon and Coconut Sponge

250g (9oz) unsalted butter, softened, plus
   extra to grease
500g (1lb 2oz) golden caster sugar
6 eggs
375g (13oz) self-raising flour, sifted

1tsp vanilla extract
142ml carton soured cream
zest of 2 lemons, plus juice of 2½ lemons
150g (4½oz) sweetened, tenderised
   coconut

1 Preheat the oven to 180°C (160°C fan oven) mark 4. Grease a deep 20.5cm (8 inch) cake tin and line with greaseproof paper.
2 Cream the butter and 375g (13oz) sugar in a large bowl until light and fluffy. Add the eggs one at a time and beat in. If the mixture looks likely to curdle, add 1tbsp flour.
3 Add the remaining flour, the vanilla extract, cream, lemon zest, juice of 2 lemons and 100g (3½oz) coconut, then fold together. Pour into the prepared tin and bake for 1¼ hours until well risen, golden and a skewer inserted into the centre comes out clean. Remove the cake from the oven.
4 To make the topping, put the remaining sugar in a pan and add the juice of ½ lemon. Heat gently to dissolve the sugar, then bring to the boil and simmer for 1–2 minutes to make a syrup. Pierce the top of the cake all over with a thin skewer. Pour the syrup over, allowing it to sink into the cake and drip down the sides, then sprinkle with the remaining coconut.

Serves 12   preparation: 20 minutes   cooking time: 1 hour 20 minutes
per serving: 560 cals; 30g fat; 71g carbohydrate

18

Baking

Victoria Jam Sandwich with Mascarpone

175g (6oz) butter, at room temperature, plus
  extra to grease
175g (6oz) golden caster sugar
3 eggs, beaten
175g (6oz) self-raising flour, sifted

150g (5oz) mascarpone
1tsp milk (optional)
1tsp icing sugar (optional), plus extra
  to dust
4tbsp raspberry conserve

1   Preheat the oven to 180°C (160°C fan oven) mark 4. Grease two 18cm (7 inch) sandwich cake tins and line the bases with greaseproof paper.
2   Put the butter and castor sugar into a large bowl and cream together with a hand-held electric beater (or a freestanding electric mixer) until light and fluffy.
3   Gradually beat in the eggs until the mixture is smooth, then, using a large metal spoon or spatula, gently fold in the flour.
4   Divide the mixture between the prepared tins and gently level the surface with a palette knife. Bake for about 25 minutes until golden, firm to the touch and beginning to shrink away from the sides of the tin.
5   Remove from the oven and leave the cakes in the tins to cool for 5 minutes, then turn out each layer on to a wire rack and leave to cool completely.
6   To make the filling, beat the mascarpone to loosen, adding the milk if it is too thick to spread. Sweeten with icing sugar, if you like.
7   Spread the mascarpone on top of one cake layer, then cover with the raspberry conserve. Put the other layer on top and lightly press the two together. Using a fine sieve, dust the top liberally with icing sugar.

Cuts into 6–8 slices   preparation: 20 minutes   cooking time: 25 minutes, plus cooling
per slice: 610–460 cals; 39–30g fat; 61–46g carbohydrate

Variations
Basic Victoria sandwich: Omit the mascarpone and simply sandwich the cake layers together with raspberry or strawberry conserve. Dredge the top with caster sugar.
Chocolate sandwich cake: Replace 3tbsp flour with cocoa powder. Sandwich the cakes with vanilla or chocolate buttercream (page 730).
Coffee sandwich cake: Blend 2tsp instant coffee granules with 1tbsp boiling water. Cool and add to the creamed mixture with the eggs. Sandwich the cakes with vanilla or coffee buttercream (page 730).
Citrus sandwich cake: Add the finely grated zest of 1 orange, lime or lemon to the mixture. Sandwich the cakes together with orange, lime or lemon buttercream (page 730).

18

Baking

Buttercream

75g (3oz) unsalted butter, softened
175g (6oz) icing sugar, sifted

few drops of vanilla extract
1–2tbsp milk or water

1   Put the butter into a bowl and beat with a wooden spoon until it is light and fluffy.
2   Gradually stir in the icing sugar, vanilla extract and milk or water. Beat well until light and smooth.

Makes 250g (9oz)   preparation: 5 minutes
per 25g (1oz): 130 cals; 6g fat; 18g carbohydrate

Note: This quantity is sufficient to cover the top of a 20.5cm (8 inch) cake. To make enough to cover the top and sides, increase the quantities by one-third.

Variations
orange, lime or lemon buttercream: Replace the vanilla extract with a little finely grated orange, lime or lemon zest. Add 1–2 tbsp juice from the fruit instead of the milk, beating well to avoid curdling the mixture. If the mixture is to be piped, omit the zest.
chocolate buttercream: Blend 1tbsp cocoa powder with 2tbsp boiling water and cool before adding to the mixture.
coffee buttercream: Replace the vanilla extract with 2tsp instant coffee granules dissolved in 1tbsp boiling water; cool before adding to the mixture.

18

Baking

Classic Christmas Cake

150g (5oz) each organic currants, organic sultanas and organic raisins
100g (3½oz) natural glacé cherries, halved
50g (2oz) preserved stem ginger in syrup, drained and chopped
grated zest and juice of 1 unwaxed lemon
juice of ½ lemon
1tsp vanilla extract
75ml (2½fl oz) each ginger wine and Cognac, plus extra Cognac to drizzle
175g (6oz) butter, at room temperature, plus extra to grease
175g (6oz) dark muscovado sugar

2 eggs, beaten
175g (6oz) self-raising flour
1tsp ground mixed spice
½tsp each ground cinnamon and ground ginger
50g (2oz) mixed nuts, such as almonds, walnuts and brazils, roughly chopped
50g (2oz) carrots, peeled and coarsely grated
700g (1½lb) almond paste (page 734)
800g (1¾lb) royal icing (page 734)
green and red food colourings
edible glitter flakes (optional)

1 Put the dried fruit, glacé cherries, stem ginger, lemon zest and juice and the vanilla extract into a bowl. Pour the ginger wine and Cognac over, stir, then cover and leave to macerate in a cool place for 1–5 days.

2 Preheat the oven to 170°C (150°C fan oven) mark 3. Grease a 20.5cm (8 inch) round, 7.5cm (3 inch) deep cake tin and line with baking parchment. Wrap a double layer of brown paper, 2.5cm (1 inch) deeper than the tin, around the outside of the tin and secure with string. This will prevent the outside of the cake from overcooking.

3 Cream the butter and sugar together in a large bowl, using a freestanding mixer if you have one, for 5 minutes until light and fluffy. Add the eggs, one at a time, mixing well between each addition. If the mixture looks like curdling, add 2tbsp flour with the second egg.

4 Sift the remaining flour and spices together, then fold half into the creamed mixture.

5 Put half the soaked fruit mixture into a food processor with some of the soaking liquid and whiz to a purée. Fold this into the cake mixture together with the remaining soaked fruit and liquor, the nuts, carrots and the remaining flour.

6 Turn the mixture into the prepared cake tin and spread evenly, then make a dip in the middle. Bake for 2 hours or until a skewer inserted into the centre for 30 seconds comes out clean. Remove from the oven and leave the cake in the tin to cool for 20 minutes, then turn out on to a wire rack and drizzle with 2tsp Cognac. Leave to cool completely.

7 Wrap the cake in greaseproof paper and foil and store in an airtight tin for up to 1 month.

8 About 5 days before Christmas, unwrap the cake and put it on a 25.5cm (10 inch) board. Cut off a quarter of the almond paste and wrap in clingfilm. Use the rest of the almond paste to cover the top and sides of the cake, adding the trimmings to the wrapped portion. Leave the cake to dry for a day or two before applying the royal icing.

9 Spread half the royal icing over the top and sides of the cake with a palette knife. Either pipe the rest of the icing in wavy lines on top of the cake or apply with the palette knife and flick up to create peaks, resembling snow.

Cuts into 16 slices   preparation: 45 minutes, plus macerating   cooking time: 2 hours, plus cooling
per slice: 240 cals; 12g fat; 30g carbohydrate

Light and Easy Christmas Cake

375g (13oz) raisins
150ml (¼ pint) dark rum
175g (6oz) butter, softened, plus extra
  to grease
175g (6oz) golden caster sugar, plus extra
  for the physalis
3 eggs, beaten
150g (5oz) ground almonds

175g (6oz) self-raising flour
zest of 1 small orange
3tbsp apricot jam
500g pack fondant icing
a little icing sugar and Gold Edible Lustre
  Dust
6 physalis (cape gooseberries), unwashed

1 Preheat the oven to 170°C (150°C fan oven) mark 3. Grease a 20.5cm (8 inch) loose-based cake tin and line with greaseproof paper. Soak the raisins in a bowl with the rum and put to one side.

2 Put 175g (6oz) butter into a bowl. Using an electric hand whisk, beat in the caster sugar, one large spoonful at a time, until light and fluffy. Beat in the eggs, a little at a time, then add the almonds and mix well. Stir in the soaked raisins. If the mixture looks curdled, leave for 5 minutes to allow the almonds to swell, then stir again.

3 Using a large metal spoon, fold in the flour and orange zest. Spoon the mixture into the prepared tin and smooth the top. Bake for 50 minutes–1 hour or until a metal skewer inserted into the centre comes out clean. Remove from the oven and leave the cake in the tin to cool for 10 minutes, then turn out on to a wire rack to cool completely.

4 Carefully turn the cake upside down, put on a serving plate and remove the greaseproof paper.

5 To decorate the cake, heat the jam in a pan for 2–3 minutes, sieve into a bowl, then brush over the top and sides of the cake. Roll out the icing to a 35.5cm (14 inch) circle, lift it on to the cake and smooth over the top and sides. Cut away any extra icing.

6 Before serving, sift 2tbsp icing sugar into a bowl and mix in a knifepoint of gold lustre, then tip into a fine sieve or tea strainer and dust over the top of the cake.

7 Pull the leaves back from the physalis to reveal the fruit. Put the caster sugar in a bowl and dip in the physalis – the sugar will cling to the sticky surface. Arrange on top of the cake. Finish by tying a gold ribbon around the cake.

Makes 1 x 20.5cm (8 inch) cake, cuts into 12 slices preparation: 20 minutes
cooking time: 50 minutes–1 hour
per serving: 550 cals; 20g fat; 85g carbohydrate

Almond Paste

225g (8oz) ground almonds
125g (4oz) golden caster sugar
125g (4oz) golden icing sugar
1 large egg (see note)

1tsp lemon juice
1tsp sherry
1–2 drops of vanilla extract

1   Put the almonds, caster sugar and icing sugar into a bowl and mix. In a separate bowl, whisk the egg
    with the remaining ingredients and add to the dry mixture.
2   Stir well to mix, pounding gently to release some of the oil from the almonds. Knead with your hands
    until smooth. Cover until ready to use.

Makes 450g (1lb)   preparation: 10 minutes
per 25g (1oz): 130 cals; 7g fat; 15g carbohydrate

Note: If you wish to avoid using raw egg to bind the almond paste,
mix the other liquid ingredients with a little water instead.

Royal Icing

2 large egg whites, or 1 tbsp egg albumen
  powder

2tsp liquid glycerine (optional)
450g (1lb) icing sugar, sifted

1   If using the egg whites and the glycerine, put them in a bowl and stir just enough to break up the egg
    whites. If using albumen powder, mix according to the instructions on the packet.
2   Add a little icing sugar and mix gently with a wooden spoon to incorporate as little air as possible.
3   Add a little more icing sugar as the mixture becomes lighter. Continue to add the icing sugar, stirring
    gently but thoroughly until the mixture is stiff and stands in soft peaks. For coating it should form soft
    peaks; for piping it should be a little stiffer.

Makes 450g (1lb)   preparation: 20 minutes
per 25g (1oz): 100 cals; 0g fat; 26g carbohydrate

Sweet Pumpkin Cake with Toffee Sauce

Butter to grease
250ml (9fl oz) sunflower oil
275g (10oz) light muscovado sugar
3 large eggs
225g (8oz) self-raising flour
1 level tsp bicarbonate of soda
2 level tsp ground ginger
1tsp each of ground cinnamon and nutmeg

A pinch each of ground cloves and ground
 allspice
For the toffee sauce
300g (11oz) light muscovado sugar
284ml carton double cream
50g (2oz) unsalted butter

1   Preheat the oven to 200°C (180°C fan oven) mark 6. Put the pumpkin on a baking sheet and roast
    for 40 minutes until tender.
2   Grease a 23cm (9in) Kugelhopf tin generously with butter and dust with flour.
3   Remove pumpkin from oven and allow to cool for 15 minutes. Reduce oven temperature to 180°C
    (160°C fan oven) mark 4. Spoon out 250g (9oz) pumpkin flesh, put in a mini processor and whiz to
    a purée.
4   Put the oil and sugar in a freestanding mixer and whisk for 2 minutes, then whisk in the eggs one at
    a time.
5   Add flour, bicarbonate of soda, ginger, cinnamon, nutmeg, cloves and allspice and fold in. Add the
    purée and stir in gently.
6   Pour into the prepared tin. Bake for 40–45 minutes until the cake is risen, springy and shrinking from
    the edges. Leave to cool in the tin for 10 minutes then use a palette knife to ease the cake away from
    the edges. Turn out and cool on a wire rack.
7   For the sauce, put the sugar, cream and butter in a small heavy-based pan. Heat gently to dissolve
    sugar, then simmer and stir for 3 minutes to thicken slightly. Pour into a jug.
8   Drizzle the toffee sauce over the cake and serve.

Serves 16   preparation time: 25 min; cooking time: 1 hour 30 minutes
per slice: 440cals; 26g fat; 49g carbohydrate

Mango and Lime Swiss Roll

A little vegetable oil to grease
125g (4oz) golden caster sugar, plus
  extra to dust and dredge
125g (4oz) plain flour, plus extra to dust
3 medium eggs
Zest of 1 lime

For the filling:
200g tub low-fat crème fraiche, drained of
  any liquid
1tsp lime juice
1 medium mango, peeled, stoned and sliced

1 Preheat the oven to 200°C (180°C fan oven) mark 6. Grease and line a 33 x 23 cm (13 x 9 in) Swiss roll tin with baking parchment, then grease the paper. Dust with caster sugar and flour.

2 Put the eggs and sugar in a bowl, place over a pan of hot water and whisk with an electric hand whisk for 5min until pale, creamy and thick enough to leave a trail on the surface when the whisk is lifted.

3 Remove the bowl from the heat and whisk until cool. Sift half the flour over the egg and sugar mixture and use a metal spoon to fold in lightly. Sift and fold in the remaining flour, then lightly stir in 1tbsp hot water and the lime zest.

4 Pour the mixture into the tin and tilt it backwards and forwards to spread in an even layer. It may look very thin, but don't worry – it will rise. Bake in the oven for 10–12 minutes until golden, well risen and firm to the touch.

5 Meanwhile, put a large sheet of baking parchment paper on top of a damp tea-towel and dredge the paper thickly with caster sugar. Quickly turn out the sponge on to the paper, then peel the baking parchment off the sponge. Trim the crusty edges, then leave to cool.

7 To make the filling, put the crème fraiche in a bowl, add the lime juice and mix together. Spread over the sponge, then top with the mango slices.

8 Starting at a short edge, use the paper to roll up the sponge. Make the first turn firmly so it rolls evenly and has a good shape, but roll more lightly after this. Place seam-side down on a serving plate and dredge with sugar. Eat within a few hours.

Serves 8   preparation time: 20 minutes; cooking time: 15–17 minutes
per serving; 210cals, 6g fat, 33g carbs

18

Baking

Kugelhopf

200g (7oz) raisins, preferably black
   seedless
3tbsp light rum
2tsp easy-blend yeast
300g (11oz) plain flour, plus extra to dust
4 large eggs
100ml (4fl oz) full-fat milk
225g (8oz) unsalted butter, softened, plus
   extra to grease

75g (3oz) golden caster sugar
generous pinch of salt
finely grated zest of 1 lemon
100g (3½oz) split blanched almonds
icing sugar, to dust
whole glacé fruits, nuts and dragées,
   to decorate

1   Put the raisins in a small bowl, pour the rum over, cover and leave in a cool place overnight.
2   Put the yeast in a food mixer with the flour. Whisk the eggs and milk together lightly. With the machine running on a slow speed, pour in the egg mixture and mix for about 10 minutes or until the dough is very smooth, shiny and elastic.
3   Meanwhile, put the butter in a bowl and beat in the caster sugar, salt and the lemon zest. With the machine running, add the butter and sugar mixture to the dough, spoonful by spoonful, until evenly incorporated. Turn the mixture into a large, lightly floured bowl, then cover with clingfilm and refrigerate overnight.
4   Lightly toast the almonds. Heavily butter a 2 litre (3½ pint) Kugelhopf ring mould. Take a third of the almonds and press on to the sides of the mould; refrigerate. Roughly chop the remaining almonds and mix by hand into the chilled dough, along with the raisins and rum. Carefully place the dough in the prepared mould, then cover and leave in a warm, draught-free place until the dough feels spongy and has risen to within 2cm (¾in) of the top of the mould.
5   Bake the Kugelhopf at 200°C (180°C fan oven) mark 6 on a shelf below the centre of the oven for 10 minutes, then cover with greaseproof paper and turn the oven down to 190°C (375°F) mark 5 for 40–45 minutes or until the Kugelhopf sounds hollow when you tap the mould.
6   Allow the Kugelhopf to cool in the tin for 15 minutes, then turn on to a cooling rack to cool completely. Serve the cake dusted with icing sugar and decorated with a mixture of glacé fruits, nuts and dragées.

Serves 12–14   preparation: 45 minutes, plus chilling and rising
cooking time: 50 minutes   per serving: 410–350 cals; 21–21g fat; 40–35g carbohydrate

18

Baking

Hot Cross Buns

100ml (3½fl oz) warm milk, plus extra
  to glaze
15g (½oz) fresh yeast or 7g sachet (2tsp)
  dried yeast
50g (2oz) golden caster sugar, plus extra
  to glaze
350g (12oz) strong plain white flour, sifted,
  plus extra to dust
pinch each of salt, ground cinnamon and
  freshly grated nutmeg

25g (1oz) chopped mixed candied peel
125g (4oz) mixed raisins, sultanas
  and currants
25g (1oz) butter, melted and cooled
  until tepid
1 egg, beaten
vegetable oil, to grease

1   Mix the warm milk with an equal quantity of warm water. Put the yeast in a small bowl with 1tbsp of the warm liquid and 1tsp sugar and put to one side for 5 minutes.

2   Put 225g (8oz) flour and the salt into a large bowl, make a well in the middle and pour in the yeast mixture. Cover with a clean tea-towel and leave in a warm place for 20 minutes to 'sponge'.

3   Mix the remaining flour and sugar together with the spices, peel and dried fruit. Add to the yeast mixture with the melted butter and egg. Mix thoroughly to form a soft dough, adding a little more liquid if needed.

4   Put the dough in a lightly oiled bowl, cover and leave to rise in a warm place for 1–1½ hours or until doubled in size. Grease a large baking sheet.

5   Knock back the dough and knead lightly on a lightly floured surface for 1–2 minutes. Divide the dough into 15 equal-sized pieces and shape into buns. Put well apart on the baking sheet. Make a deep cross on the top of each one with a sharp knife, then cover with a tea-towel and leave in a warm place for about 30 minutes until doubled in size.

6   Preheat the oven to 220°C (200°C fan oven) mark 7. Brush each bun with milk and sprinkle with sugar, then bake for 15–18 minutes or until the buns sound hollow when tapped underneath. Remove from the oven and transfer to a wire rack to cool. Serve warm.

Makes 15 buns   preparation: 30 minutes, plus sponging and rising
cooking time: 15–18 minutes, plus cooling
per bun: 120 cals; 2g fat; 22g carbohydrate

18

Baking

Plain Scones

225g (8oz) self-raising flour, plus extra
  to dust
salt
75g (3oz) butter, cut into cubes, at room
  temperature

40g (1½oz) golden caster sugar
1 large egg
2–5tbsp buttermilk or milk, plus extra
  to glaze

1 Preheat the oven to 220°C (200°C fan oven) mark 7. Sift the flour into a bowl, add a pinch of salt and mix. Add the butter and lightly rub in with fingertips until the mixture looks like breadcrumbs. Add the sugar and stir in.

2 Put the egg into a jug, add 2tbsp buttermilk or milk and beat together. Make a well in the centre of the crumble and add the egg mixture. Using a round-bladed knife, mix the egg gradually into the crumble. As the dough forms, bring it together with your hands – it should be soft but not sticky. If it feels dry, add extra buttermilk or milk, 1tsp at a time. Shape the dough into a rough ball, then pat into a round.

3 With a floured rolling pin, gently roll out the dough on a lightly floured surface into a round at least 2.5cm (1 inch) thick. Dip a 5cm (2 inch) cutter in flour. Cut out each scone by placing the cutter on the dough and giving it a quick push downwards. Don't twist the cutter; just lift it and ease the dough out. You'll get five or six scones out of the round. Gather the trimmings into a round and re-roll to the same thickness and cut more, repeating until you have a total of eight.

4 Dust a large baking tray with flour and arrange the scones on it. Lightly brush each one with buttermilk or milk, then dust with a little more flour.

5 Bake on the top shelf of the oven for 10–12 minutes, or until well risen and golden. Remove from the oven and transfer the scones to a wire rack to cool for 5 minutes or until just warm. Slice them in half and serve with unsalted butter or with clotted cream and strawberry jam.

Makes 8   preparation: 15 minutes   cooking time: 10–12 minutes
per scone: 200 cals; 9g fat; 27g carbohydrate

Variations

Wholemeal scones: Replace half of the white flour with wholemeal flour.
Fruit scones: Add 50g (2oz) currants, sultanas, raisins or chopped dates (or a mixture) to the dry ingredients.
Cheese and herb scones: Sift 1tsp mustard powder with the dry ingredients. Stir 50g (2oz) finely grated Cheddar cheese into the mixture before adding the milk. After glazing, sprinkle the tops with a little cheese.

Apple and Cherry Scones

1 quantity plain scone dough (page 739)
1tsp baking powder
1 small cooking apple, about 175g (6oz), peeled, cored and diced

50g (2oz) dried cherries
¼tsp ground cinnamon
1tbsp demerara sugar
2tbsp flaked almonds

1　Preheat the oven to 200°C (180°C fan oven) mark 6. Make the plain scone dough as above then stir in the baking powder, apple and cherries.

2　With a floured rolling pin, gently roll out the dough on a lightly floured surface into a round at least 2.5cm (1 inch) thick. Dip a 7.5cm (3 inch) cutter in flour. Cut out each scone by placing the cutter on the dough and giving it a quick push downwards. Don't twist the cutter; just lift it and ease the dough out. Gather the trimmings into a round and gently re-roll and cut the dough until you have six scones. Any leftover trimmings can be made into a couple of smaller ones.

3　Dust a large baking tray with flour and put the scones on it in two rows of three, arranged so that they're just touching. Brush the tops with milk. Mix together the cinnamon, sugar and almonds, then sprinkle over the top.

4　Bake for 25–30 minutes or until risen and golden. Remove from the oven and cool on the tray for 10 minutes, then turn on to a wire rack. Separate the scones, then serve warm or toasted with unsalted butter and raspberry jam.

Makes 6　preparation: 15 minutes　cooking time: 25–30 minutes
per scone: 320 cals; 15g fat; 43g carbohydrate

Streusel Blueberry and Pecan Muffins

40g (1½oz) demerara sugar
285g (10½oz) plain flour, sifted
1¼tsp ground cinnamon
20g (¾oz) butter, melted
175g (6oz) light muscovado sugar
3½tsp baking powder

¼tsp salt
2 eggs, beaten
175ml (6fl oz) full-fat milk
100ml (4fl oz) sunflower oil
100g (3½oz) frozen blueberries
100g (3½oz) pecans, roughly chopped

1 To make the topping, put the demerara sugar, 40g (1½oz) flour and ¼tsp cinnamon in a bowl. Pour in the butter and stir with a fork until crumbly.
2 Preheat the oven to 200°C (180°C fan oven) mark 6. Line a 12-cup muffin tray with 150ml (¼ pint) muffin cases. Put the remaining flour, the muscovado sugar, baking powder, salt and remaining cinnamon in a bowl, mix well and make a well in the centre. Whisk the eggs, milk and oil together and pour into the well. Whisk until smooth.
3 Add the blueberries and pecans to the mixture and, using a large metal spoon, carefully and quickly fold through. Fill each muffin cup with the mixture and sprinkle with a little topping.
4 Bake for 20–25 minutes or until golden and firm to the touch. Remove from the oven, take the muffins out of the tray and transfer to a wire rack. Leave to cool for 10 minutes. Serve warm.

Makes 12   preparation: 30 minutes   cooking time: 20–25 minutes
per muffin: 300 cals; 15g fat; 40g carbohydrate

18

Baking

Wholemeal Banana Muffins

butter, to grease (optional)
50g (2oz) raisins
grated zest and juice of 1 orange
125g (4oz) wholemeal flour
25g (1oz) wheatgerm
0tbsp golden caster sugar
2tsp baking powder
pinch of salt

1 large egg, beaten
50ml (2fl oz) full-fat milk
50ml (2fl oz) sunflower oil
2 medium-sized ripe bananas, about
   225g (8oz) when peeled, roughly mashed
5tbsp orange marmalade
50g (2oz) banana chips
50g (2oz) roughly chopped walnuts

1 Line six muffin tins with paper muffin cases or grease the tins well. Place the raisins in a bowl, pour the orange juice over and leave to soak for 1 hour.

2 Preheat the oven to 200°C (180°C fan oven) mark 6. Put the orange zest in a bowl with the next five ingredients and mix together. Make a well in the centre.

3 In a separate bowl, mix the egg, milk and oil, then pour into the flour mixture and stir until just blended. Peel the bananas and roughly mash. Drain the raisins, reserving 1tbsp juice, and stir into the mixture with the bananas. Don't over-mix.

4 Fill each muffin case two-thirds full. Bake for 20–25 minutes or until a skewer inserted into the centre comes out clean. Remove from the oven and transfer the muffins to a wire rack to cool slightly.

5 For the topping, gently heat the marmalade with the reserved orange juice until melted. Simmer for 1 minute, then add the banana chips and walnuts and spoon on top of the muffins. Serve while still warm.

Makes 6   preparation: 15 minutes, plus soaking   cooking time: 20–25 minutes
per muffin: 370 cals; 16g fat; 52g carbohydrate

Dainty Cup Cakes

175g (6oz) butter, softened
175g (6oz) golden caster sugar, plus extra
  to dust
3 eggs, plus 1 egg white
175g (6oz) self-raising flour, sifted
zest and juice of 1 lemon, plus 2–3tbsp

lemon juice, strained
6 edible flowers, such as violas, pansies,
  nasturtiums or marigolds
225g (8oz) icing sugar, sifted
1 drop violet food colouring

1 Preheat the oven to 190°C (170°C fan oven) mark 5. Line a muffin tin with 12 muffin cases. Put the butter and caster sugar in a bowl and cream together until pale, light and fluffy.
2 Add the whole eggs, one at a time, and beat together, folding in a little flour if the mixture looks as if it's going to curdle.
3 Using a large metal spoon, fold in the remaining flour, the zest and juice of 1 lemon and mix well.
4 Spoon the mixture into the cases and bake for 15–20 minutes until pale golden, risen and springy to touch. Remove from the oven and cool on a wire rack.
5 To make the frosted flowers, whisk the egg white in a clean grease-free bowl for 30 seconds until frothy. Brush the white over the flower petals and put on a wire rack resting on top of a piece of greaseproof paper. Dust heavily with caster sugar, then leave the flowers to dry.
6 To make the icing, put the icing sugar in a bowl with the violet food colouring. Mix in the remaining lemon juice to create a smooth dropping consistency. Spoon the icing on to the cakes, decorate with the frosted flowers and leave to set. Serve when the icing is completely set.

Makes 12   preparation: 15 minutes   cooking time: 15–20 minutes
per cake: 320 cals; 14g fat; 48g carbohydrate

18

Baking

Vanilla and White Chocolate Cup Cakes

125g (4oz) butter, at room temperature
125g (4oz) golden caster sugar, plus extra
  to dust
1 vanilla pod
2 eggs, plus 1 egg white

125g (4oz) self-raising flour, sifted
1tbsp vanilla extract
6 edible violets
200g (7oz) good-quality white chocolate
  flavoured with vanilla, in small pieces

1 Preheat the oven to 190°C (170°C fan oven) mark 5. Line a 12-hole muffin tin with paper muffin cases.
2 Put the butter and sugar in a bowl. Split the vanilla pod lengthways, scrape out the seeds and add them to the bowl. Add the eggs, flour and vanilla extract and beat thoroughly, using an electric whisk, until smooth and creamy. (Use a freestanding mixer if you have one.)
3 Spoon the mixture into the muffin cases and bake for 15–20 minutes until pale golden, risen and springy to the touch. Remove from the oven and leave in the tin for 2–3 minutes, then transfer to a wire rack to cool.
4 To make the decoration, whisk the egg white in a clean grease-free bowl for 30 seconds until frothy. Brush over the violet petals and put on a wire rack. Lightly dust with caster sugar and leave to dry.
5 Put the chocolate in a heatproof bowl set over a bowl of barely simmering water and leave until melted. Alternatively, microwave on Medium for 2 minutes (based on a 900W oven) or until just melted. Stir the chocolate until smooth and let cool slightly.
6 Spoon the chocolate on to the cakes. Top each with a sugared flower and leave to set before serving.

Makes 12   preparation: 25 minutes, plus cooling   cooking time: 15–20 minutes
per cake: 270 cals; 15g fat; 30g carbohydrate

Lemon Angel Cakes

vegetable cooking spray, to grease
50g (2oz) plain flour
1tbsp cornflour
100g (3½oz) golden caster sugar
5 large egg whites
¼tsp salt

½tsp cream of tartar
½tsp each vanilla extract and rosewater
seeds from 3 large cardamom pods, finely
  crushed
grated zest of 1 lemon

1 Preheat the oven to 170°C (150°C fan oven) mark 3. Grease an 18cm (7 inch) square cake tin and line the base with non-stick baking parchment. Sift the flour, cornflour and 50g (2oz) sugar into a bowl and put to one side.
2 Whisk the egg whites in a clean grease-free bowl with the salt, cream of tartar, vanilla extract, rosewater and 1tbsp cold water until stiff peaks form. Gradually whisk in the remaining sugar and continue to whisk until stiff and glossy. Sift the flour mixture over the egg whites and carefully fold in the cardamom seeds and lemon zest. Spoon into the prepared tin and level the surface.
3 Bake for 35 minutes or until firm to the touch and the cake has shrunk from the sides of the tin. Remove from the oven and loosen round the sides with a palette knife, then flip the tin upside down on to a cooling rack and leave the cake in the tin to cool.
4 Remove the cake from the tin and cut into 9 squares, then halve to make 18 triangles. Serve plain or with fromage frais, berries and pineapple, dusted with icing sugar.

Makes 18 triangles   preparation: 20 minutes, plus cooling   cooking time: 35 minutes
per triangle: 40 cals; trace fat; 9g carbohydrate

Pastel Meringues

4 large egg whites
250g (9oz) icing sugar, sifted

1tsp vanilla extract
red food colouring

1 Preheat the oven to 130°C (110°C fan oven) mark ½. Line three baking trays with baking parchment.
2 Put the egg whites in a clean grease-free bowl of a freestanding mixer and whisk until stiff. Add the sugar 1tbsp at a time, whisking well between additions for a stiff, shiny meringue. The mixture shouldn't move around in the bowl. Whisk in the vanilla extract.
3 Divide the mixture into two. Add 1–2 drops of red food colouring, one drop at a time, to one bowl to make a pale pink and add 2–3 drops to the other bowl for a darker pink. Mix each well.
4 For oval shapes, take two dessertspoons. Take a spoonful of mixture and use the other spoon to scrape the meringue away from you on to the parchment. For hearts, fit a piping bag with a 1cm (½ inch) plain nozzle and pipe heart shapes on to the parchment.
5 Bake for 1 hour, turn off the heat and leave in the oven for 1–1 ½ hours to dry out. Remove from the oven and cool on a wire rack. Store in an airtight container for up to 2 weeks.

Serves 10   preparation: 30 minutes, plus drying out   cooking time: 1 hour
per serving: 100 cals; 0g fat; 26g carbohydrate

Freeze-ahead Mince Pies

75g (3oz) each unsalted butter and white vegetable fat, softened
40g (1½oz) icing sugar, sifted, plus extra to dust
350g (12oz) plain flour, plus extra to dust
1 egg
1 banana
500g (1lb 2oz) mixed dried fruit

3tbsp fine-shred marmalade
75g (3oz) dark muscovado sugar
a few gratings of nutmeg
1tsp ground cinnamon and ½tsp mixed spice
zest of 2 oranges, plus juice of ½ orange
3tbsp whisky
golden caster sugar, to sprinkle

1 First, make the pastry. Put the butter in a large bowl, add the vegetable fat and icing sugar and mix with a fork until just combined.
2 Add the flour and mix well until the mixture resembles fine breadcrumbs. Break up any lumps of fat with the back of the fork.
3 Put the egg in a bowl or jug and add 6tbsp cold water. Whisk together lightly, then add the egg to the dry ingredients. Still using the fork, bring the ingredients together to form a ball of pastry. If the mixture doesn't come together, add another 1tbsp water.
4 Lightly flour the work surface and knead the pastry gently. Shape the dough into a ball, wrap in clingfilm and chill for at least 30 minutes.
5 Meanwhile, make the mincemeat. Peel and chop the banana and put in a bowl. Add the dried fruit, marmalade, muscovado sugar, spices, orange zest and juice and the whisky, then mix well. Put half in a food processor, whiz to chop roughly, then return to the bowl. Cover and chill.
6 Roll out the pastry on a lightly floured surface to measure 51 x 51cm (20 x 20 inches). Using a 7.5cm (3 inch) cutter, cut out 24 circles and use to line two 12-hole patty tins. Prick the base of each circle a couple of times with a fork. Spoon 1 heaped tbsp mincemeat into the centre of each pie.
7 Re-roll the pastry trimmings and cut out 24 star, tree or holly-leaf shapes. Put the pastry shapes on top of the mincemeat, brush with a little water and sprinkle with caster sugar. (You can freeze the pies at this stage: don't brush with water or sprinkle with sugar. Leave the pies in the tins, cover with clingfilm and freeze for up to 1 month. Cook from frozen for 20–25 minutes until golden.)
8 Chill the mince pies for 15 minutes. Meanwhile, preheat the oven to 220°C (200°C fan oven) mark 7. Bake the pies for 15 minutes or until golden and crisp. Remove from the oven and dust with icing sugar to serve. To reheat the pies, preheat the oven to 200°C (180°C fan oven) mark 6. Warm the pies on a baking sheet for 8–10 minutes.

Makes 24 pies   preparation: 20 minutes, plus chilling   cooking time: 15 minutes
per pie: 190 cals; 6g fat; 32g carbohydrate

18

Baking

Millionaire's Shortbread

260g (9½oz) butter
250g (9oz) plain flour
75g (3oz) golden caster sugar
2 x 397g cans sweetened condensed milk

100g (3½oz) light muscovado sugar
250g (9oz) good-quality plain chocolate

1 Preheat the oven to 180°C (160°C fan oven) mark 4. Grease a 30.5 x 20.5cm (12 x 8 inch) Swiss roll tin and line with greaseproof paper. Cut 175g (6oz) butter into cubes and bring to room temperature.
2 Put the flour, caster sugar and cubed butter in a food processor and whiz until the mixture forms crumbs, then pulse a little more until it forms a ball.
3 Turn the dough out on to a lightly floured surface and knead to combine. Press into the prepared tin and bake for 20 minutes until firm to the touch and very pale brown. Remove from the oven and put to one side.
4 Put the condensed milk, muscovado sugar and remaining butter in a bowl and microwave on High for 7–8 minutes (based on a 900W oven), beating thoroughly with a balloon whisk every 2–3 minutes until the mixture is thick and fudgey. Pour on to the shortbread and smooth over.
5 Melt the chocolate in the microwave on Medium for 2 minutes and pour it over the caramel. Leave to set at room temperature, then cut into 20 squares to serve.

Serves 20   preparation: 20 minutes   cooking time: 30 minutes
per serving/square: 350 cals; 15g fat; 50g carbohydrate

Shortbread Biscuits

175g (6oz) unsalted butter, softened
75g (3oz) golden caster sugar
200g (7oz) plain flour, sifted, plus extra
   to dust

50g (2oz) cornflour
white caster sugar, to sprinkle

1 Whiz the butter and golden caster sugar together in a food processor for 1 minute until pale and fluffy. Add the flour and cornflour and whiz briefly until the mixture just comes together. Wrap in clingfilm and chill for 30 minutes.
2 Preheat the oven to 190°C (170°C fan oven) mark 5. Line a baking sheet with baking parchment. Roll out the dough on a lightly floured surface to a 1cm (½ inch) thickness. Using a 7cm (2¾ inch) fluted cutter, cut out 12 rounds and put on the baking sheet. Gently press a 4cm (1½ inch) plain cutter into the centre of each to mark a circle and, using a fork, prick the dough within the circle.
3 Bake for about 15 minutes until pale golden. Remove from the oven and sprinkle with white caster sugar, then transfer to a wire rack to cool. Store in an airtight tin for up to 5 days.

Makes 12   preparation: 15 minutes, plus chilling   cooking time: 15 minutes, plus cooling
per biscuit: 200 cals; 12g fat; 23g carbohydrate

Caramelised Hazelnut Shortbread

225g (8oz) unsalted butter
175g (6oz) light muscovado sugar
200g (7oz) toasted chopped hazelnuts
225g (8oz) plain flour, sifted
125g (4oz) semolina
8tbsp lemon curd
12 nectarines, stoned and cut into bite-
   sized pieces

golden caster sugar, to dust
568ml carton double cream
1tsp orange-flower water or vanilla extract
175g (6oz) raspberries
icing sugar, to dust

1 Line two baking sheets with non-stick baking parchment. Put the butter and 125g (4oz) muscovado sugar in a bowl and beat until light. Mix 125g (4oz) hazelnuts with the flour and semolina, then mix into the butter mixture. Divide the mixture into two and shape into two 25.5cm (10 inch) circles on the baking sheets. Score each into six wedges and chill for 30 minutes.
2 Preheat the oven to 150°C (130°C fan oven) mark 2. Bake for 25–30 minutes, or until just beginning to colour at the edges. Remove from the oven and leave to cool on the baking sheets.
3 Put the remaining muscovado sugar and hazelnuts and the lemon curd into a frying pan. Heat gently until the sugar dissolves and caramelises. Spoon over the top of each round of shortbread. Leave to cool and set, then cut into wedges.
4 Dust the nectarines with caster sugar. Whip the cream and orange-flower water until soft peaks form. Divide the nectarines and raspberries between plates, top with the cream and shortbread and dust with icing sugar to serve.

Serves 6   preparation: 25 minutes, plus chilling   cooking time: 35 minutes, plus cooling
per serving: 640 cals; 46g fat; 53g carbohydrate

Frosted Holly Biscuits

175g (6oz) unsalted butter, softened
200g (7oz) golden caster sugar
1 egg

2tsp vanilla extract
300g (11oz) plain flour, plus extra to dust
25g (1oz) icing sugar, to dust

1 Cream the butter and caster sugar together in a food processor. Add the egg, vanilla extract and flour and pulse until the mixture comes together. Wrap and chill for 1–2 hours.
2 Preheat the oven to 190°C (170°C fan oven) mark 5. Line two baking trays with baking parchment.
3 Roll out the pastry thinly on a lightly floured surface. Using a 9 x 5cm (3½ x 2 inch) holly cutter, press out leaf shapes. Divide between the baking trays and bake for 10 minutes or until lightly coloured at the edges.
4 Remove from the oven, dust heavily with icing sugar and leave to cool for 5 minutes, then transfer with the parchment on to a rack to cool. Store in an airtight container for up to 5 days.

Makes 24   preparation: 25 minutes, plus hours chilling   cooking time: 10 minutes
per biscuit: 130 cals; 6g fat; 18g carbohydrate

Figgy Fruit Slice

2 x 250g packs ready-to-eat dried figs, hard
  stalks removed
50g (2oz) candied orange peel,
  finely chopped
75g (3oz) hazelnuts, toasted
50g (2oz) shelled pistachio nuts

50g (2oz) good-quality plain chocolate
50g (2oz) ready-to-eat pitted dates
¼tsp ground cinnamon
pinch of ground nutmeg
4tbsp brandy, plus extra to drizzle

1 Put the figs and candied orange peel in a food processor and whiz for 1 minute to mince the fruit finely. Tip into a large bowl.
2 Put the hazelnuts, pistachios, chocolate and dates in the food processor with the spices and 4tbsp brandy and pulse to chop roughly. Add to the fig mixture and mix, using your hands.
3 Put a sheet of rice paper on a baking tray. Spoon the fig mixture evenly on top, then press down with the back of a wet spoon to form an even layer. Put another sheet of rice paper on top and press down well. Chill for 1 hour.
4 Cut the slice into four rectangles to serve. If not serving straightaway, wrap in non-stick baking parchment and tie up with string. Store in the fridge for up to 4 weeks, unwrapping and drizzling with 1tsp brandy every week.

Makes 4 preparation: 30 minutes, plus chilling   cooking time: 10 minutes
per slice: 560 cals; 17g fat; 89g carbohydrate

Crumbly Cheese Biscuits

125g (4oz) unsalted butter
125g (4oz) Stilton cheese, without the
  rind, crumbled
50g (2oz) whole blanched almonds,
  finely chopped

125g (4oz) plain white flour, plus extra
  to dust
a few drops of Tabasco sauce
1 beaten egg, to glaze, and poppy seeds
  to sprinkle

1 Put the butter into a large bowl, add the cheese and beat together until soft and creamy.
2 Add the almonds, flour and Tabasco and beat well until thoroughly mixed.
3 With floured hands, shape the dough into a 3cm (1¼ inch) diameter log. Wrap in clingfilm and chill for 1 hour.
4 Preheat the oven to 180°C (160°C fan oven) mark 4. Lightly grease three baking sheets. Unwrap the dough and use a sharp knife to cut thin slices from the log. Lay them on the baking sheets, spaced well apart, and brush with a little beaten egg. Sprinkle with poppy seeds and bake for about 15 minutes or until crisp and golden. Remove from the oven and cool the biscuits on a wire rack, then store in an airtight container.

Makes 60 biscuits   preparation: 10 minutes, plus chilling   cooking time: 15 minutes
per biscuit: 40 cals; 3g fat; 2g carbohydrate

Carrot Tray Bake

100g (3½oz) butter, chopped, plus extra to grease
125g (4oz) carrots, peeled and grated
100g (3½oz) each sultanas and chopped dried dates
50g (2oz) tenderised coconut
1tsp ground cinnamon
½tsp freshly grated nutmeg
330g bottle maple syrup
150ml (¼ pint) apple juice

zest and juice of 2 oranges, plus pared zest from ½–1 orange
225g (8oz) wholemeal self-raising flour, sifted
2tsp bicarbonate of soda
125g (4oz) walnut pieces
200g (7oz) cream cheese
200ml carton crème fraîche
2tbsp icing sugar
1tsp vanilla extract

1 Preheat the oven to 190°C (170°C fan oven) mark 5. Grease a 23 x 23cm (9 x 9 inch) cake tin and line with greaseproof paper.

2 Put the carrots, butter, sultanas, dates, coconut, spices, maple syrup, apple juice and the orange zest and juice of 2 oranges in a large pan. Cover and bring to the boil, then cook for 5 minutes. Tip into a bowl and leave to cool.

3 Put the flour, bicarbonate of soda and walnuts in a large bowl and stir together. Add the cooled carrot mixture and stir well.

4 Spoon the mixture into the prepared tin and bake for 45 minutes–1 hour until firm. Remove from the oven and leave in the tin for 10 minutes, then turn out on to a wire rack and leave to cool.

5 To make the topping, finely slice the orange zest from the remaining orange. Put the cream cheese, crème fraîche, sugar and vanilla extract in a bowl and stir with a spatula. Spread over the cake and top with the zest.

Serves 15   preparation: 30 minutes   cooking time: 50 minutes–1 hour 5 minutes
per serving: 370 cals; 24g fat; 38g carbohydrate

18

Baking

Chocolate and Pistachio Biscotti

300g (11oz) plain flour
75g (3oz) cocoa powder
1tsp baking powder
150g (5oz) plain chocolate chips
150g (5oz) shelled pistachio nuts

1tsp salt
75g (3oz) unsalted butter, softened
225g (8oz) granulated sugar
2 large eggs, beaten
1tbsp icing sugar

1   Preheat the oven to 180°C (160°C fan oven) mark 4. Line a large baking sheet with non-stick baking parchment.
2   Mix the flour with the cocoa powder, baking powder, chocolate chips, pistachios and salt.
3   Using an electric whisk, beat together the butter and sugar until light and fluffy. Gradually whisk in the eggs.
4   Stir the dry ingredients into the mixture until it forms a stiff dough. With floured hands, shape the dough into two slightly flattened logs, each about 30.5 x 5cm (12 x 2 inches). Sprinkle with icing sugar. Put the logs on the baking sheet and bake for 40–45 minutes or until they are slightly firm to the touch.
5   Remove from the oven and cool the logs on the baking sheet for 10 minutes, then cut diagonally into 2cm (¾ inch) thick slices. Arrange them, cut side down, on the baking sheet and bake again for 15 minutes or until crisp. Cool on a wire rack. Keep the biscotti in an airtight container for up to 1 week or freeze them for up to 1 month.

Makes 30 biscuits   preparation: 15 minutes   cooking time: 1 hour 10 minutes
per biscuit: 160 cals; 7g fat (of which 3g saturates); 20g carbohydrate

Macaroons

2 egg whites
225g (8oz) golden caster sugar
125g (4oz) ground almonds

¼tsp almond extract
25 blanched almonds

1   Preheat the oven to 180°C (fan oven 160°C) mark 4. Line several baking trays with baking parchment. Whisk the egg whites in a clean grease-free bowl until stiff peaks form. Using a large metal spoon, gradually fold in the sugar, then gently stir in the ground almonds and almond extract to make a firm paste.
2   Spoon teaspoonfuls of the mixture on to the baking trays, spacing them slightly apart. Press a blanched almond into the centre of each one and bake for 12–15 minutes until just golden and firm to the touch.
3   Remove from the oven and leave on the baking sheets for 10 minutes, then transfer to wire racks to cool completely. On cooling, these biscuits have a soft, chewy centre and harden up after a few days. Once made, eat within 1 week. Store in airtight containers or wrap in cellophane for a gift.

Makes 25   preparation: 10 minutes   cooking time: 12–15 minutes, plus cooling
per biscuit: 80 cals; 4g fat; 10g carbohydrate

Spiced Star Biscuits

2tbsp runny honey
25g (1oz) unsalted butter
50g (2oz) light muscovado sugar
finely grated zest of ½ lemon and ½ orange
225g (8oz) self-raising flour
1tsp each ground cinnamon and
  ground ginger
½tsp freshly grated nutmeg

pinch each of ground cloves and salt
1tbsp finely chopped candied peel
50g (2oz) ground almonds
1 large egg, beaten
1½tbsp milk
150g (5oz) icing sugar
silver sugar balls

1 Put the honey, butter, sugar and citrus zests into a small pan and stir over a low heat until the butter has melted and the ingredients are well combined.
2 Sift the flour, spices and salt together into a bowl, then add the candied peel and almonds. Add the melted mixture, egg and milk and mix until the dough comes together. Knead the dough briefly until smooth, then wrap in clingfilm and chill for at least 4 hours, or overnight.
3 Preheat the oven to 180°C (160°C fan oven) mark 4. Roll out the dough on a lightly floured surface to a 5mm (¼ inch) thickness. Using a 5cm (2 inch) cutter, stamp out stars and put on baking sheets.
4 Bake for 15–20 minutes or until just beginning to brown at the edges. Remove from the oven and transfer the biscuits to a wire rack to cool. Store in an airtight tin for up to 1 week.
5 To decorate, mix the icing sugar with 1½tbsp warm water to make a smooth icing. Coat some of the biscuits with icing and finish with a piped edging if you like, then decorate each point or across the middle with silver balls. Pipe dots of icing on the points of the plain biscuits and attach silver balls. Allow the icing to set, then store the biscuits in an airtight container for up to 1 week.

Makes about 35   preparation: 15 minutes, plus chilling   cooking time: 15–20 minutes, plus cooling
per biscuit: 50 cals; 2g fat; 7g carbohydrate

Orange Tuile Biscuits

3 large egg whites
100g (3½oz) icing sugar, sifted
100g (3½oz) plain flour

grated zest of 1 orange
75g (3oz) melted, unsalted butter

1 Lightly whisk the egg whites with the sugar. Stir in the flour, orange zest and melted butter, then cover and chill for 30 minutes.
2 Preheat the oven to 200°C (180°C fan oven) mark 6. Line a baking sheet with non-stick baking parchment. Place 3 teaspoonfuls of the mixture well apart on the baking sheet and spread out to 9cm (3½ inch) circles. Bake for 12 minutes or until just brown around the edges.
3 Remove from the oven and while still warm, shape each biscuit over a rolling pin to curl. Repeat with the remaining mixture.

Makes about 24   preparation: 10 minutes, plus chilling   cooking time: 1 hour 36 minutes
per biscuit: 60 cals; 3g fat; 8g carbohydrate

Cranberry Biscuits

125g (4oz) chilled butter
50g (2oz) golden caster sugar
25g (1oz) dried cranberries

125g (4oz) plain flour, plus extra to dust
75g (3oz) ground rice

1 Put the butter and sugar in a food processor and whiz to combine. Add the cranberries, flour and ground rice and pulse until the mixture comes together. Turn out on to a lightly floured surface and shape into an oblong about 12.5 x 7.5cm (5 x 3 inches) and 2cm (¾ inch) thick. Wrap in clingfilm and chill for 30 minutes.
2 Preheat the oven to 200°C (180°C fan oven) mark 6. Cut the dough into 3mm (⅛inch) slices and put on a non-stick baking sheet. Bake for 8–10 minutes or until golden. Remove from the oven and cool before removing from the sheet.

Makes 24 biscuits   preparation: 15 minutes, plus chilling   cooking time: 8–10 minutes plus cooling
per biscuit: 80 cals; 4g fat; 9g carbohydrate

Sultana and Pecan Cookies

225g (8oz) butter, at room temperature, plus
  extra to grease
175g (6oz) light muscovado sugar
2 eggs, lightly beaten
225g (8oz) pecan halves

300g (11oz) self-raising flour, sifted
¼tsp baking powder
125g (4oz) sultanas
2tbsp maple syrup

1 Preheat the oven to 190°C (170°C fan oven) mark 5. Grease four baking sheets.
2 Put the butter and sugar in the bowl of a freestanding mixer and cream together with the K beater attachment until mixture is pale and fluffy. Or, beat together with a wooden spoon. Gradually beat in the eggs until thoroughly combined.
3 Put 10 pecan nut halves to one side, breaking each in two, then roughly chop the rest and fold into the mixture with the flour, baking powder, sultanas and maple syrup.
4 Roll the mixture into 20 balls and position them, spaced well apart, on the baking sheets. Flatten the cookies with a dampened palette knife and top each with a piece of pecan nut. Bake for 12–15 minutes until pale golden. Alternatively, to serve freshly baked biscuits at another time, freeze one tray of unbaked cookies and cook from frozen for 18–20 minutes.
5 Remove from the oven and leave the cookies to cool on the baking sheet for 5 minutes, then cool completely on a wire rack.

Makes 20   preparation: 15 minutes   cooking time: 12–15 minutes, plus cooling
per cookie: 274 cals; 18g fat; 27g carbohydrate

18

Baking

Spiced Sultana and Lemon Cookies

225g (8oz) butter, at room temperature, plus
  extra to grease
175g (6oz) golden caster sugar
2 eggs, lightly beaten
350g (12oz) self-raising flour, sifted

¼tsp baking powder
pinch of bicarbonate of soda
1tsp ground mixed spice
150g (5oz) sultanas
finely grated zest of 2 lemons

1 Preheat the oven to 190°C (170°C fan oven) mark 5. Grease a baking sheet.
2 Put the butter and sugar in a bowl and use a hand whisk to cream together until pale and fluffy.
   Add the eggs, one at a time, beating well to make sure the mixture is thoroughly combined.
3 Add the flour, baking powder, bicarbonate of soda, mixed spice, sultanas and lemon zest to the bowl
   and fold everything together.
4 Take a dessertspoon of the mixture and roll into a ball. Put on the baking sheet and repeat to make
   five more balls. Dip a palette knife in water, then use to flatten the rounds slightly. Bake for 15 minutes.
5 Remove from the oven and cool the cookies on a wire rack and repeat the process until all the mixture
   is used up. Store the biscuits in an airtight tin and eat within 2 days.

Makes 20   preparation: 15 minutes   cooking time: about 1 hour
per cookie: 200 cals; 10g fat; 27g carbohydrate

Brown Loaf

300g (11oz) strong plain white flour, sifted,
  plus extra to dust
200g (7oz) strong plain wholemeal flour

15g (½oz) fresh yeast, or 1tsp dried yeast
2tsp salt
vegetable oil, to grease

1 Put both flours into a large bowl, make a well in the middle and pour in 325ml (11fl oz) tepid water.
   Crumble the fresh yeast into the water (if using dried yeast, just sprinkle it over). Draw a little of the
   flour into the water and yeast, and mix to form a batter. Sprinkle the salt over the remaining dry flour,
   so that it doesn't come into contact with the yeast. Cover with a clean tea-towel and leave to 'sponge'
   for 20 minutes. This process adds a fermentation stage, which gives a slightly lighter loaf.
2 Combine the flour and salt with the batter to make a soft dough and knead for at least 10 minutes
   until the dough feels smooth and elastic. Shape into a ball, put into an oiled bowl, cover with the tea-
   towel and leave to rise at warm room temperature until doubled in size, about 2–3 hours.
3 Knock back the dough, knead briefly and shape into a round on a lightly floured baking sheet. Slash
   the top with a sharp knife and dust with flour. Cover and leave to rise for 45 minutes–1½ hours or until
   doubled in size and spongy.
4 Preheat the oven to 200°C (180°C fan oven) mark 6. Bake the loaf for 45–50 minutes or until it sounds
   hollow when tapped underneath. Transfer to a wire rack and leave to cool.

Cuts into 16 slices   preparation: 25 minutes, plus sponging and rising
cooking time: 45–50 minutes, plus cooling
per slice: 100 cals; 1g fat; 22g carbohydrate

Cornbread with Cherry and Thyme Stuffing

50g (2oz) butter, melted, plus extra
  to grease
6 sage leaves
225g (8oz) good-quality sausages such as
  Lincolnshire, skinned
25g (1oz) dried cherries
1tbsp chopped thyme
salt and pepper
175g (6oz) cornmeal

75g (3oz) plain flour
25g (1oz) freshly grated Parmesan cheese
1tbsp baking powder
50ml (2fl oz) full-fat milk, plus a little extra
100g (3½oz) Greek-style yogurt
2 eggs, lightly beaten
340g can sweetcorn, drained and whizzed
  in a processor for 2 minutes

1 Grease a 900g (2lb) loaf tin and line the base with greaseproof paper. Arrange the sage leaves along the bottom. Put the sausage meat in a large bowl along with the cherries and thyme, then season well and mix thoroughly.
2 Preheat the oven to 200°C (180°C fan oven) mark 6. Put the cornmeal, flour, Parmesan, baking powder and ½tsp salt in a large bowl and mix. Add the milk, yogurt, eggs, butter and sweetcorn, season well with pepper and mix to form a wet dough. You may need to add a little more milk.
3 Put half the cornmeal mixture into the prepared tin and smooth the surface. Spread the stuffing over and top with the remaining cornmeal mixture. Smooth over and bake for 40–45 minutes or until golden brown and a skewer inserted into the centre comes out piping hot. Cover with foil if the top browns too quickly.
4 Remove from the oven and cool slightly before turning out of the tin, then peel off the greaseproof paper and cut into eight slices.

Serves 8 preparation: 30 minutes cooking time: 45 minutes
per serving: 300 cals; 15g fat; 33g carbohydrate

18

Baking

Chilli Cornbread

1 large egg
200g (7oz) Greek-style yogurt
25g (1oz) butter, melted
150g (5oz) fine cornmeal
25g (1oz) potato flour
1tbsp wheat/gluten-free baking powder
1tsp salt

pinch of cayenne pepper
1 large red chilli, deseeded and
  finely chopped
75g (3oz) spring onions, finely sliced
125g (4oz) sweetcorn
50g (2oz) freshly grated Parmesan cheese

1 Preheat the oven to 180°C (160°C fan oven) mark 4. Line the base of a 450g (1lb) non-stick loaf tin with non-stick baking parchment. Whisk the egg in a large bowl until frothy, then stir in the yogurt and melted butter.
2 Stir in the cornmeal, flour, baking powder, salt and cayenne pepper, then add all the remaining ingredients and mix until thoroughly combined.
3 Turn the mixture into the prepared tin and bake for 45 minutes or until a skewer inserted into the centre comes out clean.
4 Remove from the oven and leave the cornbread in the tin to cool for 10 minutes, then turn out on to a cooling rack. When completely cold, cut into slices and serve.

Cuts into 10 slices preparation: 20 minutes cooking time: 45 minutes, plus cooling
per slice: 150 cals; 7g fat; 16g carbohydrate

18

Baking

Walnut Bread

500g (1lb 2oz) strong white flour with
   kibbled grains of rye and wheat, sifted,
   plus extra to dust
7g pack fast-action dried yeast
2tsp salt

2tbsp malt extract
50g (2oz) butter, softened
3 garlic cloves, peeled and crushed
100g pack walnut pieces
1tbsp milk

1 Lightly grease a 20.5cm (8 inch) spring-release tin. Put the flour, yeast and salt in the bowl of a freestanding mixer with dough hook attachment. Add 300ml (½ pint) lukewarm water and 1tbsp malt extract, then mix to a pliable dough. Increase the speed and machine-knead for 5 minutes.

2 Turn out the dough on a lightly dusted surface and roll into a rectangle measuring about 40.5 x 28cm (16 x 11 inches). Mix the butter with the garlic and spread over the dough. Scatter the walnuts over and, starting at the long edge, roll up into a sausage. Cut into eight slices and put into the prepared tin. Cover with lightly oiled clingfilm and leave to rise in a warm place for 45 minutes or until doubled in size.

3 Preheat the oven to 220°C (200°C fan oven) mark 7 and put a baking sheet in to heat. Remove the clingfilm from the dough, cover the dough with foil, put on the hot baking sheet and bake for 20 minutes.

4 Reduce the oven temperature to 200°C (180°C fan oven) mark 6 and bake for 40 minutes. Remove from the oven and leave in the tin to cool. Freeze for up to 1 month.

5 To cook from frozen, cover, put on a hot baking sheet and bake at 220°C (200°C fan oven) mark 7, for 45 minutes. Mix the milk with the remaining malt extract and brush the glaze over the bread. Bake, uncovered, for 5 minutes or until golden brown. Leave in the tin to cool slightly, then turn out and serve warm.

Serves 8   preparation: 20 minutes, plus rising and freezing   cooking time: 1 hour 50 minutes
per serving: 330 cals; 12g fat; 48g carbohydrate

Quick Zucchini, Lemon and Parmesan Bread

butter, to grease
175g (6oz) plain flour, sifted, plus extra
  to dust
175g (6oz) courgettes, coarsely grated
75g (3oz) wholemeal flour
1tbsp each golden caster sugar and baking
  powder
½tsp salt

finely grated zest of 1 lemon
75g (3oz) freshly grated Parmesan cheese,
  plus extra to sprinkle
black pepper
200ml (7fl oz) full-fat milk
75ml (3fl oz) olive oil
2 eggs, beaten
flavoured butter (see below), to serve

1 Preheat the oven to 190°C (170°C fan oven) mark 5. Grease a 900g (2lb) non-stick loaf tin, line the base with greaseproof paper and dust with flour. Put the zucchini (courgettes) on kitchen paper and dry well.

2 Put the plain and wholemeal flours, sugar, baking powder, salt and lemon zest in a bowl and mix well. Add the courgettes to the dry ingredients with the Parmesan and pepper and mix lightly with a fork. Make a well in the centre. Whisk together the milk, olive oil and eggs and pour into the well, stirring until smooth.

3 Pour into the prepared tin and level the surface with a knife. Bake for about 50 minutes or until a skewer inserted into the centre of the loaf comes out clean. Remove from the oven and leave in the tin to cool for 10 minutes before turning out on to a wire rack. Leave to cool, then sprinkle grated Parmesan on top. Serve with a flavoured butter (see below).

Cuts into 12 slices preparation: 25 minutes, plus 10 minutes cooling cooking time: 50 minutes
per slice: 180 cals; 10g fat; 18g carhohydrate

Sun-dried Tomato Butter

1 Mix 125g (4oz) softened unsalted butter with 3tbsp sun-dried tomato paste, 2tbsp chopped basil and ½tsp salt.

Serves 6 preparation: 5 minutes
per serving: 160 cals; 17g fat; 1g carbohydrate

Caper Mustard Butter

1 Mix 125g (4oz) softened unsalted butter with 2tbsp chopped, well-drained capers, 2tbsp Dijon mustard and season with salt and pepper.

Serves 6 preparation: 5 minutes
per serving: 150 cals; 17g fat; trace carbohydrate

Sweet Mocha Bread

425g (15oz) strong plain white flour, plus
  extra to dust
1tsp salt
7g sachet fast-action dried yeast
150g (6oz) golden caster sugar
3 large eggs
150ml (¼ pint) double cream

50g (2oz) butter, melted
oil, to grease
4tbsp instant coffee granules
200g (7oz) good-quality plain chocolate,
  semi-sweet such as Bournville, chopped
50g (2oz) pecan nuts

1 Sift the flour and salt into a bowl. Stir in the yeast and 75g (3oz) sugar. In a separate bowl, lightly beat the eggs, cream and butter. Make a well in the centre of the flour mixture, then pour in the egg mixture and mix to a soft dough.

2 Turn the dough out on to a lightly floured surface and knead for 5–10 minutes until smooth and elastic. Transfer to a lightly oiled bowl, cover with clingfilm and leave in a warm place to rise until doubled in size.

3 For the filling, put 50g (2oz) sugar in a small pan with 5tbsp water and heat gently until the sugar dissolves. Stir in the coffee granules and bring to the boil. Simmer for 1 minute, then leave to cool.

4 Grease and line a 20.5cm (8 inch) spring-release cake tin. Turn the dough out on to a lightly floured surface and divide into four pieces. Roll out one piece to a 25.5cm (10 inch) round and press into the base of the tin so the edges come slightly up the sides. Scatter over 50g (2oz) chocolate, then spoon over about a third of the coffee syrup.

5 Roll out another piece of dough to a 25.5cm (10 inch) round and lay over the first, letting the excess dough come up the sides of the tin and pinching the edges firmly into the first layer of dough. Repeat the layering, finishing with a round of dough. Brush the top lightly with water and scatter with the pecan nuts.

6 Cover the tin with lightly oiled clingfilm and leave to rise in a warm place until the dough nearly reaches the top of the tin.

7 Preheat the oven to 220°C (200°C fan oven) mark 7. Bake the bread for 15 minutes, then reduce the oven temperature to 170°C (150°C fan oven) mark 3. Cover the tin with foil and bake for 30 minutes. Remove from the oven and transfer the bread to a wire rack.

8 Put the remaining sugar in a small pan with 4tbsp water and heat gently until the sugar dissolves. Bring to the boil and boil for 1 minute. Remove from the heat and stir in the remaining chocolate. Drizzle the bread with the chocolate sauce and leave to cool.

Cuts into 10 slices   preparation: 25 minutes, plus rising   cooking time: 45 minutes
per slice: 480 cals; 23g fat; 61g carbohydrate

18

Baking

Sweet Cherry Bread

oil, to grease
350g (12oz) strong plain white flour, plus
  extra to dust
½tsp salt
2tsp ground mixed spice
1tbsp cinnamon
25g (1oz) golden caster sugar
75g (3oz) unsalted butter, diced

25g (1oz) fresh yeast or 15g (½oz)
  dried yeast
200ml (7fl oz) full-fat milk, warmed
125g (4oz) white almond paste, roughly
  chopped
125g (4oz) glacé cherries
3tbsp honey, warmed
75g (3oz) icing sugar, sieved

1 Grease a 20.5cm (8 inch) deep cake tin and line the base with greaseproof paper. Sift the flour, salt, spices and caster sugar into a bowl (add the easy-blend yeast at this point, if using) and rub in the butter. Dissolve the fresh yeast in the milk, then add to the flour to make a dough (if you find the dough is too dry, add a little more milk).

2 Turn the dough out on to a lightly floured surface and knead for 10 minutes. Don't be afraid of being rough with the dough. For speed, place the dough in a food processor that has a dough hook and process for 2–3 minutes. Place the dough in a lightly oiled bowl, cover and leave in a warm place for 2 hours or until doubled in size.

3 Turn the dough out on to a lightly floured surface and knead lightly. Shape into a 60cm (24 inch) long oval. Scatter the almond paste and cherries over the surface and roll the dough up lengthways, then form a tight coil. Put in the prepared tin, cover and leave in a warm place for 30 minutes or until doubled in size and spongy to the touch. Preheat the oven to 180°C (160°C fan oven) mark 4.

4 Bake the bread for 40 minutes or until golden and the bread sounds hollow when tapped underneath. Remove from the oven and transfer to a cooling rack. When cool, glaze with honey.

5 To make the icing, mix the icing sugar with a few drops of water to form a paste, then drizzle over the bread. Leave to set before serving.

Serves 8   preparation: 40 minutes, plus rising   cooking time: 40 minutes
per serving: 400 cals; 13g fat; 68g carbohydrate

18

Baking

Blackberry and Cinnamon Loaf

125ml (4fl oz) sunflower oil, plus extra
  to grease
175g (6oz) plain flour
1½tsp each baking powder and
  ground cinnamon
200g (7oz) frozen blackberries

125g (4oz) golden caster sugar
grated zest and juice of 1 lemon
125g (4oz) Greek-style yogurt
3 eggs
golden icing sugar, to dust

1 Preheat the oven to 170°C (150°C fan oven) mark 3. Grease a 900g (2lb) loaf tin and line the base with greaseproof paper.
2 Sift the flour, baking powder and cinnamon into a bowl, add the frozen blackberries and turn to coat. Make a well in the centre.
3 In another bowl, whisk together the caster sugar, oil, lemon zest and juice, yogurt and eggs. Pour into the well in the flour mixture and stir to combine.
4 Spoon the mixture into the prepared loaf tin and level the surface. Bake for 55 minutes, covering the top with foil if it begins to brown too quickly. To test, insert a skewer into the centre of the loaf – it should come out clean.
5 Remove from the oven and leave in the tin for 10 minutes, then turn out on to a wire rack to cool completely.
6 When cool, dust the loaf with icing sugar. Cut into slices to serve.

Cuts into 8 slices   preparation: 15 minutes   cooking time: 55 minutes, plus cooling
per slice: 320 cals; 18g fat; 35g carbohydrate

18

Baking

Extra-moist fruit Tea Bread

1 Darjeeling tea bag

75g (3oz) each ready-to-eat dried figs and
   ready-to eat dried pears, roughly chopped

225g (8oz) sultanas

grated zest and juice of 1 orange

125g (4oz) butter, softened, plus extra
   to grease

175g (6oz) dark muscovado sugar

2 eggs, beaten

225g (8oz) self-raising flour, sifted

1tsp ground mixed spice

demerara sugar, to sprinkle

1 Put the tea bag in a jug, add 150ml (¼ pint) boiling water and leave for 3 minutes. Remove and discard the tea bag.
2 Put the figs, pears, sultanas, orange zest and juice in a bowl, then add the tea. Cover and leave to soak for 6 hours or overnight. (If you don't have time to soak the fruit, microwave the mixture on Defrost for 5 minutes, based on a 900W oven.)
3 Preheat the oven to 180°C (160°C fan oven) mark 4. Grease and line a 900g (2lb) loaf tin. Put the butter and muscovado sugar in a large bowl and cream together with an electric hand-held whisk. Add the eggs and beat well, then add the flour, mixed spice and soaked fruit and mix well until thoroughly combined.
4 Put the mixture into the prepared tin and bake in the middle of the oven for 50 minutes. Remove from the oven, sprinkle with demerara sugar, cover with foil and return to the oven for 55 minutes or until a skewer inserted in the centre comes out clean.
5 Cool, then wrap in clingfilm and store in an airtight container for up to 2 weeks. Cut into slices to serve.

Serves 12   preparation: 30 minutes, plus soaking   cooking time: 1¾ hours
per serving: 290 cals; 10g fat; 49g carbohydrate

Coconut and Cherry Loaf

150g (5oz) unsalted butter, softened, plus
   extra to grease
75g (3oz) golden caster sugar
3 eggs, separated
150g (5oz) desiccated coconut

125g (4oz) self-raising flour, sifted
200g (7oz) natural glacé cherries,
   roughly chopped
75g (3oz) strawberry jam, warmed
   and sieved

1 Preheat the oven to 170°C (150°C fan oven) mark 3. Grease a 900g (2lb) loaf tin and line the base
  with greaseproof paper.
2 Using an electric whisk, cream the butter and sugar together in a bowl until light and fluffy. Add the
  egg yolks slowly, beating well between each addition. Fold in 75g (3oz) desiccated coconut, the flour
  and 125g (4oz) glacé cherries.
3 Whisk the egg whites in a clean grease-free bowl until soft peaks form and beat one spoonful into the
  cake mixture to lighten it. Using a large metal spoon, lightly fold in the rest.
4 Pour the mixture into the prepared loaf tin and bake for 45–50 minutes, covering the top with foil if it
  begins to brown too quickly. To test, insert a skewer into the centre of the loaf – it should come out
  clean. Remove from the oven and leave the loaf in the tin to cool completely – this will take about 3 hours.
5 For the topping, brush the top of the loaf with the jam to glaze, then top with the remaining glacé cherries
  and sprinkle with the remaining coconut. Leave to cool and set. Cut into slices to serve.

Makes 8 slices   preparation: 20 minutes   cooking time: 50 minutes, plus cooling
per slice: 440 cals; 28g fat; 43g carbohydrate

18

Baking

American Banana Loaf

225g (8oz) plain flour
1tsp bicarbonate of soda
½tsp cream of tartar
100g (3½oz) butter, plus extra to grease
175g (6oz) golden caster sugar
1tsp lemon juice

3tbsp milk
2 bananas, about 300g (11oz), peeled
finely grated zest of 1 lemon
2 eggs, beaten
½tsp vanilla extract
golden granulated sugar, to dredge

1 Preheat the oven to 180°C (160°C fan oven) mark 4. Put the flour, bicarbonate of soda and cream of tartar into a food processor and pulse to mix. Add the butter and whiz until the mixture resembles breadcrumbs. Add the caster sugar and whiz briefly.
2 Mix the lemon juice and milk together in a jug and leave to stand for 1 minute. Grease a 900g (2lb) loaf tin and line the base with greaseproof paper.
3 Mash the bananas in a bowl, then stir in the lemon zest, eggs, milk mixture and vanilla extract. Add to the food processor and whiz until combined.
4 Put the mixture into the loaf tin, dredge with granulated sugar and bake for 1¼ hours or until risen and golden and a skewer inserted into the centre comes out clean.
5 Remove from the oven and leave in the tin for 5 minutes, then turn out on to a wire rack to cool completely. Cut into slices to serve.

Cuts into 10 slices   preparation: 20 minutes   cooking time: 1¼ hours, plus cooling
per slice: 280 cals; 11g fat; 43g carbohydrate

Lime Drizzle Loaf

175g (6oz) self-raising flour, sifted with a
   pinch of salt
175g (6oz) butter, diced
175g (6oz) golden caster sugar
3 eggs, beaten

50g (2oz) sweetened and tenderised
   coconut, plus 1tbsp to decorate
zest and juice of 2 limes, plus 1 whole lime
1tsp baking powder
125g (4oz) golden icing sugar, sifted

1 Preheat the oven to 180°C (160°C fan oven) mark 4. Line a 900g (2lb) loaf tin with a greaseproof loaf liner.
2 Put the flour, salt, butter, caster sugar, eggs, 50g (2oz) coconut, the lime zest and juice and baking powder in the bowl of a freestanding mixer, fitted with a beater. Mix slowly, gradually increasing the speed and mixing for 2 minutes.
3 Pour the mixture (it will be quite runny) into the prepared tin and bake for 45–55 minutes or until golden, well risen and cooked through – a skewer inserted into the centre should come out clean. Remove from the oven and leave to cool for 10 minutes, then lift out the cake, keeping it in the liner.
4 To make the icing, finely grate the zest from the remaining lime and cut away the white pith. Chop the lime flesh, then put in a mini processor with the zest and whiz for 1–2 minutes until finely chopped. Add the icing sugar and blend until smooth. Pour over the cake then sprinkle the coconut on top to decorate. Leave to set before serving.

Serves 12   preparation: 15 minutes   cooking time: 45–55 minutes
per serving: 310 cals; 17g fat; 38g carbohydrate

Index

Index